C000090440

THE CRICKETERS'
WHO'S WHO
1990

THE
CRICKETERS'
WHO'S WHO
1990

**compiled and edited by
IAIN SPROAT**

WILLOW BOOKS
Collins

Willow Books
William Collins Sons & Co. Ltd
London · Glasgow · Sydney · Auckland
Toronto · Johannesburg

First published in Great Britain in 1990 by
William Collins Sons & Co. Ltd, 8 Grafton Street,
London W1X 3LA in association with The
Cricketers' Who's Who Limited
© Iain Sproat 1990

A CIP catalogue record for this book is available from the British Library.
ISBN 0-00-218352-8 hardback
ISBN 0-00-218353-6 paperback

Cover photographs of
Angus Fraser and Nasser Hussain
by Graham Morris

Portraits by Bill Smith

Typeset by Rowland Phototypesetting Ltd
Bury St Edmunds, Suffolk
Printed and bound in Great Britain by
William Collins Sons & Co. Ltd, Glasgow

PREFACE

THE CRICKETERS listed in this volume include those who played for their county at least once last season, either in the County Championship, Refuge Assurance League, Benson & Hedges or NatWest matches. The statistics are accurate up to the end of the last English season – with one exception: it has proved impossible to guarantee the accuracy of the statistics of certain matches, classified as first-class, in India and Pakistan. However, Test match figures in those countries have been included. Figures about 1000 runs in a season refer to matches in England only. First-class figures do not include figures for Test matches which are listed separately. One-day 50s and 100s are for English domestic competitions plus all Internationals, home and abroad. The RAL figures do not include the Refuge Assurance Cup knock-out games.

The following abbreviations apply: * means not out; RAL means Refuge Assurance League; and B & H means Benson & Hedges. The figures for batting and bowling averages refer to the full first-class English list for 1989, followed in brackets by the 1988 figures. Inclusion in the batting averages depends on a minimum of eight innings, and an average of at least 10 runs; a bowler has had to have taken at least 10 wickets in at least 10 innings. The same qualification has been used for compiling the bowlers' strike rate.

Readers will notice certain occasional differences in the way the same kind of information is presented. This is because I have usually tried to follow the way in which the cricketers themselves have provided the relevant information.

Each year in *The Cricketers' Who's Who*, in addition to

those cricketers who are playing during the current season, I also include the biographical and career details of those who played in the previous season but retired at the end of it. The purpose of this is to have, on the record, the full and final first-class cricketing achievements of every player when his career has ended.

A book of this complexity and detail has to be prepared several months in advance of the cricket season, and occasionally there are recent changes in a player's circumstances which cannot be included in time. Many examples of facts and statistics which can quickly become outdated in the period between the actual compilation of the book and its publication, months later, will spring to the reader's mind, and I ask him or her to make the necessary commonsense allowance and adjustments.

I am indebted to Mr Les Hatton for his splendidly professional work in the collection of statistics, and to Mr Bill Smith, FRPS, who personally took most of the photographs. I should also like to thank Mr James Vyvyan, Miss Helma van Ekeren, and Miss Angela Krassowski for their help in the production of this book. Above all I am grateful to the cricketers themselves without whose support this book could not have been compiled.

Iain Sproat
January 1990

FOREWORD

V. G. RAMSDEN
Chairman, Refuge Assurance p.l.c.

IN MOST SPORTS there are books that are essential reading for a true enjoyment of the game . . . and *The Cricketers' Who's Who* is most definitely one of these.

It's a fascinating read for all cricket lovers, who will not be able to put it down once they have dipped into it. It's packed full of useful statistics, the lifeblood of this great game. And it presents the human face of cricket: where else could you read about a player nicknamed 'Fergie', another who plays the tuba, and a third who won't eat curry before a match!?

The 1989 season gave us a change of Sunday champions. Lancashire kept us on tenterhooks before winning their first League title since 1970; and Essex, in a thrilling last over, just pipped Nottinghamshire at the post to take the Refuge Assurance Cup at Edgbaston.

Now we can look forward to 1990, with this new edition of *The Cricketers' Who's Who* to add an extra sparkle.

ADAMS, C. J.   Derbyshire

Full Name: Christopher John
Adams
Role: Right-hand bat, off-break
bowler
Born: 6 May 1970, Whitwell,
Derbyshire
Height: 6′
County debut: 1988
1st-Class 50s scored: 1
Place in batting averages: 131st av.
26.10
1st-Class catches 1989: 10 (career 11)
Family links with cricket: Brother
David played 2nd XI cricket for
Derbyshire and Somerset
Education: Repton School
Best batting performance: 79
Derbyshire v Lancashire,
Chesterfield 1989

LAST SEASON: BATTING

	I.	N.O.	R.	H.S.	AV.
TEST					
1ST-CLASS	11	1	261	79	26.10
INT					
RAL	3	1	47	46*	23.50
NAT.W.					
B & H					

CAREER: BATTING

	I.	N.O.	R.	H.S.	AV.
TEST					
1ST-CLASS	12	1	282	79	25.63
INT					
RAL	3	1	47	46*	23.50
NAT.W.					
B & H					

---

1. Who won the Nehru Cup in 1989?
2. Who was the losing finalist in the Nehru Cup in 1989?
3. Who was captain of England in the West Indies, 1990?

AFFORD, J. A.   Nottinghamshire

Full Name: John Andrew Afford
Role: 'Occasional right-hand batsman', slow left-arm bowler and 'far-flung fielder!'
Born: 12 May 1964, Crowland, Nr Peterborough
Height: 6′ 2½″ **Weight:** 13st
Nickname: Aff
County debut: 1984
50 wickets in a season: 1
1st-Class 5 w. in innings: 7
1st-Class 10 w. in match: 1
Place in bowling averages: 71st av. 30.54
Strike rate 1989: 61.75 (career 63.85)
1st-Class catches 1989: 4 (career 14)
Parents: Jill
Wife and date of marriage: Lynn, 1 October 1988
Family links with cricket: 'Uncle played for school 2nd XI!'
Education: Spalding Grammar School; Stamford College for Further Education
Qualifications: 5 O-levels, NCA Coaching Certificate
Off-season 1989–90: Touring Zimbabwe with England 'A'; working in Nottingham
Cricketing superstitions or habits: 'Always like to have a confident lbw shout against me in the first two balls. Wore the same boots all last season.'
Overseas teams played for: Upper Hutt CC, New Zealand 1985–87
Overseas tours: England 'A' to Zimbabwe 1989–90
Cricketers particularly learnt from: 'David Johnson at Bourne CC and everyone at Nottinghamshire, especially Eddie Hemmings. Everyone seems to know more than I do.'
Cricketers particularly admired: Richard Hadlee, Bishan Bedi, Derek Underwood
Other sports followed: 'Will give anything a whirl, but nothing too serious. Able to watch most things – just can't fathom out people's fascination for horse racing. Follow Peterborough United FC through thick and thin – mainly thin!'
Relaxations: 'Hanging about at home, undercoating woodwork, and non-stop wall-papering!'
Opinions on cricket: 'Sixteen four-day games seems generally to have much support among the players – though as a game it seems only to come into its

own when time is lost due to bad weather. Generally, the wickets, and indeed the match, tend not to last four whole days' play.'
Best batting performance: 22* Nottinghamshire v Leicestershire, Trent Bridge 1989
Best bowling performance: 6-81 Nottinghamshire v Kent, Trent Bridge 1986

LAST SEASON: BATTING

	I.	N.O.	R.	H.S.	AV.
TEST					
1ST-CLASS	16	7	60	22*	6.66
INT					
RAL	2	1	0	0*	0.00
NAT.W.	1	1	0	0*	–
B & H	1	1	1	1*	–

CAREER: BATTING

	I.	N.O.	R.	H.S.	AV.
TEST					
1ST-CLASS	47	23	108	22*	4.50
INT					
RAL	2	1	0	0*	0.00
NAT.W.	1	1	0	0*	–
B & H	1	1	1	1*	–

LAST SEASON: BOWLING

	O.	M.	R.	W.	AV.
TEST					
1ST-CLASS	545.3	145	1619	53	30.54
INT					
RAL	29	3	142	2	71.00
NAT.W.	24	5	60	4	15.00
B & H	33	3	120	6	20.00

CAREER: BOWLING

	O.	M.	R.	W.	AV.
TEST					
1ST-CLASS	1511.2	420	4406	142	31.02
INT					
RAL	37	4	169	3	56.33
NAT.W.	24	5	60	4	15.00
B & H	41	3	175	6	29.16

AGNEW, J. P.   Leicestershire

Full Name: Jonathan Philip Agnew
Role: Right-hand bat, right-arm fast bowler, outfielder
Born: 4 April 1960, Macclesfield, Cheshire
Height: 6′ 4″ **Weight:** 12st 6lbs
Nickname: Spiro (after former US Vice-President Spiro Agnew), Rambo, Aggie
County debut: 1978
County cap: 1984
Test debut: 1984
No. of Tests: 3
No. of One-Day Internationals: 3
50 wickets in a season: 6
1st-Class 50s scored: 2
1st-Class 5 w. in innings: 32
1st-Class 10 w. in match: 6
Place in batting averages: 245th av. 12.13 (1988 242nd av. 12.90)
Place in bowling averages: 85th av. 33.17 (1988 50th av. 25.45)

Strike rate 1989: 62.78 (career 52.28)
1st-Class catches 1989: 3 (career 34)
Parents: Philip and Margaret
Wife and date of marriage: Beverley, 8 October 1983
Children: Jennifer, 31 October 1985; Rebecca, 18 September 1988
Family links with cricket: First cousin, Mary Duggan, Captain of England's Women's XI in 1960s. Father very keen cricketer
Education: Taverham Hall Prep School; Uppingham School
Qualifications: 9 O-levels, 2 A-levels in German and English
Jobs outside cricket: Cricket Coach. Spent 1981–82 off-season coaching at Sindia High School, Zimbabwe. Production control at T. L. Bennett's Windows Ltd. Sports producer at BBC Radio Leicester
Off-season 1989–90: Leicestershire's Cricket Development Officer, selling cricket to children and particularly teachers
Cricketing superstitions or habits: 'I never use a bowling marker so am never popular with groundsmen! Don't whiten boots.'
Overseas tours: Young England to Australia 1978–79; Leicestershire CCC to Zimbabwe 1981; England to India and Australia 1984–85; England B to Sri Lanka 1986
Overseas teams played for: Whitbread scholarship, playing for Essendon CC, Melbourne 1978, 1980; Alexandra CC, Harare, Zimbabwe 1981–82; Central Cumberland District Cricket Club, Sydney 1982–83
Cricketers particularly learnt from: Ken Higgs, Frank Tyson, Peter Willey, Ken Shuttleworth
Cricketers particularly admired: Imran Khan, Wayne Larkins
Other sports played: Hockey, golf
Relaxations: Music (all kinds). Playing piano and tuba. Coaching cricket. 'I became very interested in game viewing in Zimbabwe. I spent days driving around to study and photograph – particularly elephants. Watching "Only Fools and Horses", "Minder", and "Blackadder".'
Extras: Played for Surrey 2nd XI 1976–77. Leicestershire CCC Player of the

LAST SEASON: BATTING

	I.	N.O.	R.	H.S.	AV.
TEST					
1ST-CLASS	31	8	279	39	12.13
INT					
RAL	9	2	53	17	7.57
NAT.W.	1	0	6	6	6.00
B & H	–	–	–	–	–

LAST SEASON: BOWLING

	O.	M.	R.	W.	AV.
TEST					
1ST-CLASS	732.3	132	2322	70	33.17
INT					
RAL	107.1	16	384	16	24.00
NAT.W.	24	4	79	2	39.50
B & H	38	8	99	4	24.75

CAREER: BATTING

	I.	N.O.	R.	H.S.	AV.
TEST	4	3	10	5	10.00
1ST-CLASS	202	41	1851	90	11.49
INT	1	1	2	2*	–
RAL	33	15	198	23*	11.00
NAT.W.	7	4	34	8*	11.33
B & H	12	3	64	23*	7.11

CAREER: BOWLING

	O.	M.	R.	W.	AV.
TEST	92	22	373	4	93.25
1ST-CLASS	5197.2	1000	16916	603	28.05
INT	21	0	120	3	40.00
RAL	478.4	33	2115	73	28.97
NAT.W.	156	25	560	17	32.94
B & H	269.2	42	984	38	25.89

Year 1987. One of *Wisden*'s Five Cricketers of the Year 1987. Writes weekly column in *Today*. Author of *Eight Days a Week* published in 1988
Opinions on cricket: 'Now we have had a taster, let's have a 16 four-day match championship.'
Best batting performance: 90 Leicestershire v Yorkshire, Scarborough 1987
Best bowling performance: 9-70 Leicestershire v Kent, Leicester 1985

ALIKHAN, R. K.   Surrey

Full Name: Rehan Kebal Alikhan
Role: Right-hand bat
Born: 28 December 1962, London
Height: 6' 2" **Weight:** 'Varies between 13st and 14st.'
Nickname: Prince, Old Boy, Munch
County debut: 1986 (Sussex), 1989 (Surrey)
1st-Class 50s scored: 18
One-Day 50s: 2
Place in batting averages: 150th av. 23.40 (1988 161st av 22.57)
1st-Class catches 1989: 7 (career 41)
Parents: Akbar and Farida
Marital status: Single
Family links with cricket: Father played at university and at club level
Education: King's College School, Wimbledon

Qualifications: 2 A-levels, 8 O-levels
Jobs outside cricket: Insurance Broker
Off-season 1989–90: Playing cricket in Perth, Western Australia
Cricketing superstitions or habits: 'I never bat with a cap on.'
Overseas tours: King's College School, Wimbledon to Holland 1978 and 1980; Surrey Schools U-19 to Australia 1979–80; Club Cricket Conference to Kenya 1986
Overseas teams played for: Mosman Middle Harbour District CC 1982–84; P.I.A. (Pakistan) 1986–87; Claremont CC, Perth 1987–90
Cricketers particularly learnt from: Imran Khan, Geoff Arnold, Chris Waller
Cricketers particularly admired: Zaheer Abbas, Imran Khan, Sunil Gavaskar, Majid Khan, Graham Thorpe, Tony Pigott, Alec Stewart
Other sports played: Squash, tennis, golf
Other sports followed: Rugby, soccer
Relaxations: 'Spending time with Neene.'

12

Extras: Released by Sussex at end of 1988 season. Surrey 2nd XI Player of the Year 1989
Opinions on cricket: 'Four-day cricket and truer wickets would be a much better preparation for Test cricket.'
Best batting performance: 98 Sussex v Somerset, Bath 1988
Best bowling performance: 2-19 Sussex v West Indians, Hove 1988

LAST SEASON: BATTING

	I.	N.O.	R.	H.S.	AV.
TEST					
1ST-CLASS	17	2	351	84*	23.40
INT					
RAL					
NAT.W.					
B & H					

LAST SEASON: BOWLING

	O.	M.	R.	W.	AV.
TEST					
1ST-CLASS	5.1	0	24	1	24.00
INT					
RAL					
NAT.W.					
B & H					

CAREER: BATTING

	I.	N.O.	R.	H.S.	AV.
TEST					
1ST-CLASS	120	10	2701	98	24.55
INT					
RAL	8	2	72	23	12.00
NAT.W.	8	1	125	41	17.85
B & H	3	0	137	71	45.66

CAREER: BOWLING

	O.	M.	R.	W.	AV.
TEST					
1ST-CLASS	32.5	1	148	4	37.00
INT					
RAL	9	0	47	0	–
NAT.W.					
B & H					

ALLEYNE, H. L. Kent

Full Name: Hartley Leroy Alleyne
Role: Right-hand bat; right-arm fast bowler
Born: 28 February 1957, Barbados
Height: 6′ **Weight:** 12st 3lbs
County debut: 1980 (Worcestershire), 1988 (Kent)
County cap: 1981 (Worcestershire)
50 wickets in a season: 1
1st-Class 50s scored: 1
1st-Class 5 w. in innings: 9
1st-Class 10 w. in match: 2
1st-Class catches 1989: 0 (career 17)
Parents: Ruth and Norman
Marital status: Single
Family links with cricket: Brother played club cricket in Barbados
Off-season 1989–90: 'On the beach watching the sun set.'
Cricketing superstitions or habits: 'Joking with spectators.'

Overseas tours: West Indies to Zimbabwe 1981–82, 1983–84
Overseas teams played for: Barbados 1978–83; club cricket in Victoria for St Kilda 1981–82, 1982–83; Natal 1986–89
Cricketers particularly learnt from: Joel Garner, Norman Gifford
Cricketers particularly admired: Vivian Richards, Malcolm Marshall, Graham Gooch 'and lots more'
Other sports played: Golf
Other sports followed: Football, tennis, athletics
Relaxations: Music, swimming and beach cricket
Extras: Banned from playing for West Indies because of playing in South Africa. Recommended to Kent by Mike Procter. Released by Kent at end of 1989 season
Best batting performance: 72 Worcestershire v Lancashire, Stourport-on-Severn 1980
Best bowling performance: 8-43 Worcestershire v Middlesex, Lords 1981

LAST SEASON: BATTING

	I.	N.O.	R.	H.S.	AV.
TEST					
1ST-CLASS	8	3	48	28	9.60
INT					
RAL	5	2	8	3	2.66
NAT.W.					
B & H	–	–	–	–	–

LAST SEASON: BOWLING

	O.	M.	R.	W.	AV.
TEST					
1ST-CLASS	117.4	12	434	9	48.22
INT					
RAL	50.4	4	239	10	23.90
NAT.W.					
B & H	9.3	0	23	3	7.66

CAREER: BATTING

	I.	N.O.	R.	H.S.	AV.
TEST					
1ST-CLASS	95	25	709	72	10.12
INT					
RAL	22	5	185	32	10.88
NAT.W.	4	1	27	19	9.00
B & H	7	2	30	10	6.00

CAREER: BOWLING

	O.	M.	R.	W.	AV.
TEST					
1ST-CLASS	2204.4	398	7013	254	27.61
INT					
RAL	261	16	1070	48	22.29
NAT.W.	42	7	134	7	19.14
B & H	151.4	22	542	16	33.87

4. Who was vice-captain of England in the West Indies, 1990?

5. What is the minimum pay for a senior, capped county player in 1990: £8,500, £10,250, or £20,250?

6. Which West Indian Test cricketer was nicknamed 'Electric Heels'?

ALLEYNE, M. W.   Gloucestershire

Full Name: Mark Wayne Alleyne
Role: Right-hand bat, medium pace
bowler, cover fielder, occasional
wicket-keeper
Born: 23 May 1968, Tottenham
Height: 5′ 10½″ **Weight:** 12st 10lbs
Nickname: Boo-Boo
County debut: 1986
1st-Class 50s scored: 12
1st-Class 100s scored: 2
Place in batting averages: 99th
av. 30.04 (1988 229th av. 15.00)
1st-Class catches 1989: 30
(career 45 + 1 stumping)
Parents: Euclid Clevis and
Hyacinth Cordeilla
Marital status: Single
Family links with cricket: Brother
played for Gloucestershire 2nd XI

and Middlesex YCs. Father played club cricket in Barbados and England
Education: Harrison College, Barbados and Cardinal Pole School, E London
Qualifications: 6 O-levels, NCA senior coaching award, and volleyball coaching certificate
Jobs outside cricket: Accounts clerk, office junior with ANZ Bank
Off-season 1989–90: In Barbados and London with Deluxe Coachlines
Overseas tours: South of England YC to Bermuda; England YC to Sri Lanka 1987; Gloucestershire CC to Sri Lanka 1987; England YC to Australia 1988
Overseas teams played for: Preston CC, Melbourne 1987–88

LAST SEASON: BATTING

	I.	N.O.	R.	H.S.	AV.
TEST					
1ST-CLASS	28	4	721	111	30.04
INT					
RAL	15	3	196	41*	16.33
NAT.W.	1	0	0	0	0.00
B & H	3	2	47	23*	47.00

LAST SEASON: BOWLING

	O.	M.	R.	W.	AV.
TEST					
1ST-CLASS	45.5	7	187	4	46.75
INT					
RAL	60	3	294	8	36.75
NAT.W.	10	2	43	1	43.00
B & H	22	1	103	6	17.16

CAREER: BATTING

	I.	N.O.	R.	H.S.	AV.
TEST					
1ST-CLASS	97	17	2042	116*	25.52
INT					
RAL	40	15	604	49*	24.16
NAT.W.	7	3	11	9	2.75
B & H	9	2	111	36	15.85

CAREER: BOWLING

	O.	M.	R.	W.	AV.
TEST					
1ST-CLASS	289.3	55	1138	21	54.19
INT					
RAL	202	7	988	37	26.70
NAT.W.	34	4	144	2	72.00
B & H	67.1	4	272	16	17.00

Cricketers particularly learnt from: Seymour Nurse (former coach)
Cricketers particularly admired: Gordon Greenidge, Viv Richards
Other sports played: Basketball
Other sports followed: Football, volleyball, athletics
Relaxations: Watching films and sport; listening to music
Extras: Youngest player to score a century for Gloucestershire. Kept wicket for the first time in first-class game v Hampshire
Best batting performance: 116* Gloucestershire v Sussex, Bristol 1986
Best bowling performance: 4-48 Gloucestershire v Glamorgan, Bristol 1988

ALLOTT, P. J. W. Lancashire

Full Name: Paul John Walter Allott
Role: Right-hand bat, right-arm fast-medium bowler
Born: 14 September 1956, Altrincham, Cheshire
Height: 6′ 4″ **Weight:** 14st
Nickname: Walt
County debut: 1978
County cap: 1981
Benefit: 1990
Test debut: 1981
No. of Tests: 13
No. of One-Day Internationals: 13
50 wickets in a season: 5
1st-Class 50s scored: 9
1st-Class 5 w. in innings: 30
Place in batting averages: 247th av. 11.94 (1988 244th av. 12.83)
Place in bowling averages: 36th av. 25.65 (1988 15th av. 20.56)
Strike rate 1989: 64.78 (career 58.35)
1st-Class catches 1989: 25 (career 120)
Parents: John Norman and Lillian Patricia
Wife and date of marriage: Helen, 27 October 1979
Family links with cricket: Father was dedicated club cricketer for 20 years with Ashley CC and is now active with Bowdon CC (Cheshire County League) as a selector, administrator and junior organiser
Education: Altrincham Grammar School; Bede College, Durham
Qualifications: Qualified teacher; cricket coach
Jobs outside cricket: Teacher; cricket coach for Manchester Education Committee; coach in Tasmania for Tasmanian Cricket Association

Off-season 1989–90: Working as director of Blackspur Advertising and Marketing Ltd
Overseas tours: With England to India 1981–82; India and Australia 1984–85; International XI to Jamaica 1982–83
Cricketers particularly learnt from: Dennis Lillee, Steve Murrills
Other sports played: Golf, football, squash, rugby, tennis
Relaxations: Playing golf, watching all sports, listening to music, eating out, photography
Extras: Played as goalkeeper for Cheshire schoolboys. Took part in 10th wicket record partnership for England with Bob Willis, 70 v India, at Lord's, June 1982. Wears contact lenses
Best batting performance: 88 Lancashire v Hampshire, Southampton 1987
Best bowling performance: 8-48 Lancashire v Northamptonshire, Northampton 1981

LAST SEASON: BATTING

	I.	N.O.	R.	H.S.	AV.
TEST					
1ST-CLASS	23	5	215	28	11.94
INT					
RAL	5	3	30	12*	15.00
NAT.W.	2	2	11	11*	–
B & H	2	0	23	22	11.50

LAST SEASON: BOWLING

	O.	M.	R.	W.	AV.
TEST					
1ST-CLASS	442.4	115	1052	41	25.65
INT					
RAL	101	15	317	17	18.64
NAT.W.	35.2	12	90	7	12.85
B & H	41.1	7	115	3	38.33

CAREER: BATTING

	I.	N.O.	R.	H.S.	AV.
TEST	18	3	213	52*	14.20
1ST-CLASS	230	57	2970	88	17.16
INT	6	1	15	8	3.00
RAL	57	26	495	43	15.96
NAT.W.	12	5	65	19*	9.28
B & H	22	7	153	23*	10.20

CAREER: BOWLING

	O.	M.	R.	W.	AV.
TEST	370.5	75	1084	26	41.69
1ST-CLASS	5658.5	1565	14335	594	24.13
INT	136.3	19	552	15	36.80
RAL	857	80	3323	128	25.96
NAT.W.	232	51	670	43	15.58
B & H	399.2	70	1260	54	23.33

7. Which county won the 2nd XI Championship in 1989?

8. Which former Test cricketer captained the 2nd XI champions in 1989?

AMBROSE, C. E. L.   Northamptonshire

Full Name: Curtly Elconn Lynwall
Ambrose
Role: Left-hand bat, right-arm fast
bowler
Born: 21 September 1963, Antigua
Height: 6′ 7″ **Weight:** 14st 4lbs
Nickname: Ambie
County debut: 1989
Test debut: 1987–88
No. of Tests: 17
No. of One-Day Internationals: 24
1st-Class 50s scored: 1
1st-Class 5 w. in innings: 6
1st-Class 10 w. in match: 1
Place in batting averages: 228th
av. 14.11
Place in bowling averages: 59th
av. 28.39
Strike rate 1989: 60.21
(career 54.06)

1st-Class catches 1989: 2 (career 10)
Parents: Jasper (deceased) and Hillie
Marital status: Single
Family links with cricket: Brother used to play club cricket and got trials for
Antigua but gave it up and is now living in America. Cousin Rolston Otto
plays for Antigua and Leeward Islands
Education: Swetes Primary School; All Saints Secondary School
Qualifications: 3 O-levels, 3 A-levels
Jobs outside cricket: 'Used to be a carpenter, but none at the moment, haven't
got time. Help out a very good friend of mine around his garage in the little
time I have.'
Off-season 1989–90: 'Well, at the end of the season I'll go back home for two
weeks then I'll be off to India with the West Indies team.'
Cricketing superstitions or habits: 'I never put my pads on until the batsman
I'm going in after is on his way out to the middle. If I do it before, I believe
we'll lose quick wickets.'
Overseas tours: West Indies to England 1988; West Indies to Australia 1988–
89
Overseas teams played for: Boughton Hall, Chester 1986; Heywood, Central
Lancashire League 1987
Cricketers particularly learnt from: 'No-one in my struggle to the top. Now
I'm at the top I learn from everyone and am still learning.'

Cricketers particularly admired: 'David Gower, Ian Botham, Allan Lamb, Richard Hadlee, and of course my West Indian colleagues.'
Other sports played: Basketball, soccer
Other sports followed: Lawn tennis, athletics
Relaxations: Listening to music, relaxing on the beach, going to the cinema
Extras: Only began playing cricket seriously at age 17. Took a wicket with his first and last ball on Championship debut for Northamptonshire against Glamorgan
Opinions on cricket: 'It's a hard game. But with hard work and dedication along with consistency and a good head you can stay at the top for a long time. Don't forget fitness.'
Best batting performance: 59 West Indies v Sussex, Hove 1988
Best bowling performance: 7-61 Leeward Islands v Guyana, St John's 1987–88

LAST SEASON: BATTING

	I.	N.O.	R.	H.S.	AV.
TEST					
1ST-CLASS	14	5	127	23*	14.11
INT					
RAL	6	1	23	13*	4.60
NAT.W.	–	–	–	–	–
B & H	1	1	17	17*	–

LAST SEASON: BOWLING

	O.	M.	R.	W.	AV.
TEST					
1ST-CLASS	281	70	795	28	28.39
INT					
RAL	77.3	12	254	10	25.40
NAT.W.	33.5	5	91	6	15.16
B & H	11	0	66	1	66.00

CAREER: BATTING

	I.	N.O.	R.	H.S.	AV.
TEST	25	6	282	44	14.84
1ST-CLASS	35	8	482	59	17.85
INT	12	7	87	23	17.40
RAL	6	1	23	13*	4.60
NAT.W.	–	–	–	–	–
B & H	1	1	17	17*	–

CAREER: BOWLING

	O.	M.	R.	W.	AV.
TEST	611.1	132	1641	60	27.35
1ST-CLASS	722.3	158	1980	88	22.50
INT	214.5	28	787	47	16.74
RAL	77.3	12	254	10	25.40
NAT.W.	33.5	5	91	6	15.16
B & H	11	0	66	1	66.00

9. True or false: in 1989 Worcestershire were top of the County Championship and bottom of the 2nd XI Championship?

10. Who was captain of the England A team to Zimbabwe, 1989–90?

ANDREW, S. J. W.   Hampshire

Full Name: Stephen Jon Walter Andrew
Role: Right-hand bat, right-arm medium bowler
Born: 27 January 1966, London
Height: 6′ 3″ **Weight:** 13st
Nickname: Rip
County debut: 1984
1st-Class 5 w. in innings: 4
Place in batting averages: —
(1988 187th av. 20.50)
Place in bowling averages: 101st av. 40.23 (1988 47th av. 24.67)
Strike rate 1989: 78.84
(career 54.83)
1st-Class catches 1989: 4 (career 15)
Parents: Jon Trevor and Victoria Julia Maud
Marital status: Single
Education: Hordle House Prep. School; Milton Abbey Public School
Qualifications: 3 O-levels
Overseas teams played for: Pirates CC, Durban, South Africa 1983–84; South African Police CC 1984
Overseas tours: Young England to West Indies 1985
Cricketers particularly learnt from: Peter Sainsbury, Malcolm Marshall
Cricketers particularly admired: Dennis Lillee, Malcolm Marshall
Other sports played: Squash, golf
Other sports followed: Interested in most sports

LAST SEASON: BATTING

	I.	N.O.	R.	H.S.	AV.
TEST					
1ST-CLASS	5	0	21	14	4.20
INT					
RAL	–	–	–	–	–
NAT.W.					
B & H					

LAST SEASON: BOWLING

	O.	M.	R.	W.	AV.
TEST					
1ST-CLASS	170.5	29	523	13	40.23
INT					
RAL	6	0	35	0	–
NAT.W.					
B & H					

CAREER: BATTING

	I.	N.O.	R.	H.S.	AV.
TEST					
1ST-CLASS	32	18	105	14	7.50
INT					
RAL	1	1	1	1*	–
NAT.W.	1	1	0	0*	–
B & H	3	3	5	4*	

CAREER: BOWLING

	O.	M.	R.	W.	AV.
TEST					
1ST-CLASS	1343.3	286	4251	147	28.91
INT					
RAL	127.3	1	635	12	52.91
NAT.W.	50	5	185	5	37.00
B & H	109	11	363	20	18.15

Relaxations: Listening to music
Extras: Youngest bowler to have opened bowling for Hampshire
Best batting performance: 14 Hampshire v Surrey, The Oval 1989
Best bowling performance: 7-92 Hampshire v Gloucestershire, Southampton 1987

ARNOLD, G. G.   Surrey

Full Name: Geoffrey Graham Arnold
Role: Right-hand bat, right-arm fast medium bowler
Born: 3 September 1944, Balham
Height: 6′ 1″ **Weight:** 13st 7lbs
Nickname: Horse
County debut: 1963 (Surrey), 1978 (Sussex), 1989 (Surrey)
County cap: 1967 (Surrey), 1979 (Sussex)
Benefit: 1976 (£15,000)
Test debut: 1967
No. of Tests: 34
No. of One-Day Internationals: 14
50 wickets in a season: 10
1st-Class 5 w. in innings: 46
1st-Class 10 w. in match: 3
Parents: Arthur Wilfred and Amelia May Blanche
Wife and date of marriage: Jacqueline, 4 October 1969

LAST SEASON: BATTING

	I.	N.O.	R.	H.S.	AV.
TEST					
1ST-CLASS					
INT					
RAL	1	1	4	4*	–
NAT.W.					
B & H					

LAST SEASON: BOWLING

	O.	M.	R.	W.	AV.
TEST					
1ST-CLASS					
INT					
RAL	6	3	7	1	7.00
NAT.W.					
B & H					

CAREER: BATTING

	I.	N.O.	R.	H.S.	AV.
TEST	46	11	421	59	12.03
1ST-CLASS	333	79	3531	73	13.90
INT	6	3	48	18*	16.00
RAL	78	29	442	24*	9.02
NAT.W.	23	8	113	18*	7.53
B & H	20	7	73	12*	5.61

CAREER: BOWLING

	O.	M.	R.	W.	AV.
TEST	192.1 1018.5	33 251	3254	115	28.30
1ST-CLASS	139.4 8711.1	18 2275	21507	1015	21.18
INT	115.4	19	339	19	17.84
RAL	1070.1	132	3677	174	21.13
NAT.W.	457.5	92	1203	81	14.85
B & H	389	88	1098	52	21.11

Children: Matthew Paul, 20 March 1972; Joanna Claire, 28 May 1975
Education: Elliott Comprehensive, Putney Heath
Jobs outside cricket: George Wimpey & Co, Hammersmith, as a draughtsman; Cannon Davies Associates, Woking, as a sales executive
Family links with cricket: Father played club cricket
Overseas tours: England to Pakistan 1966–67; India, Pakistan and Sri Lanka 1972–73; West Indies 1973–74; Australia, New Zealand 1974–75
Overseas teams played for: Orange Free State 1966–67 and 1976–77
Cricketers particularly learnt from: Peter Loader, Fred Trueman
Other sports played: Soccer (for Corinthian Casuals), golf, squash
Extras: Retired from Sussex 1982. Joined Surrey as coach
Best batting performance: 73 MCC U-25 XI v Central Zone, Sahiwal 1966–67
Best bowling performance: 8-41 Surrey v Gloucestershire, The Oval 1967

ASIF DIN, M. Warwickshire

Full Name: Mohamed Asif Din
Role: Right-hand bat, leg-break bowler
Born: 21 September 1960, Kampala, Uganda
Height: 5′ 9″ **Weight:** 10st 7lbs
Nickname: Gunga 'and many others'
County debut: 1981
County cap: 1987
1000 runs in a season: 2
1st-Class 50s scored: 32
1st-Class 100s scored: 5
1st-Class 5 w. in innings: 1
One-Day 50s: 11
One-Day 100s: 2
Place in batting averages: 101st av. 29.92 (1988 42nd av. 38.51)
1st-Class catches 1989: 8 (career 88)
Parents: Jamiz and Mumtaz
Wife and date of marriage: Ahmevin, 27 September 1987
Family links with cricket: Brothers Khalid and Abid play in the leagues in Birmingham
Education: Ladywood Comprehensive School, Birmingham
Qualifications: CSEs and O-levels
Jobs outside cricket: Argos Distributors Limited

Off-season 1989–90: Working in Birmingham
Cricketing superstitions or habits: 'Mixing my batting gloves around every time.'
Overseas tours: MCC to East Africa 1981; MCC to Bangladesh 1980–81; Dennis Amiss XI to Barbados 1985
Overseas teams played for: Rugby Union CC, Bathurst, New South Wales 1984–85; Blayney CC, Blayney, New South Wales 1985–86
Cricketers particularly admired: Zaheer Abbas, Majid Khan
Other sports played: Squash, badminton, golf, snooker
Other sports followed: American football, basketball
Injuries 1989: Broke little finger in right hand, and bruised other fingers at the same time – out for two games
Relaxations: Staying in
Opinions on cricket: 'Too much cricket. Would like to see 16 four-day matches.'
Best batting performance: 158* Warwickshire v Cambridge University, Cambridge 1988
Best bowling performance: 5-100 Warwickshire v Glamorgan, Edgbaston 1982

LAST SEASON: BATTING

	I.	N.O.	R.	H.S.	AV.
TEST					
1ST-CLASS	28	3	748	82*	29.92
INT					
RAL	11	2	257	89	28.55
NAT.W.	4	3	186	94*	186.00
B & H	3	0	37	27	12.33

LAST SEASON: BOWLING

	O.	M.	R.	W.	AV.
TEST					
1ST-CLASS	94.3	4	422	8	52.75
INT					
RAL	11	0	75	1	75.00
NAT.W.					
B & H					

CAREER: BATTING

	I.	N.O.	R.	H.S.	AV.
TEST					
1ST-CLASS	255	38	6585	158*	30.34
INT					
RAL	100	17	2138	108*	25.75
NAT.W.	19	7	460	94*	38.33
B & H	26	4	635	107	28.86

CAREER: BOWLING

	O.	M.	R.	W.	AV.
TEST					
1ST-CLASS	813.2	129	3321	58	57.25
INT					
RAL	26.3	1	165	4	41.25
NAT.W.	9.1	1	24	2	12.00
B & H	11	0	62	1	62.00

11. Who was vice-captain of the England A team to Zimbabwe, 1989–90?

12. Who was top of England's Test batting averages v Australia, 1989?

ATHERTON, M. A.　　　　Lancashire

Full Name: Michael Andrew Atherton
Role: Right-hand bat, leg-break bowler, slip fielder
Born: 23 March 1968, Manchester
Height: 6' **Weight:** 12st 7lbs
Nickname: Athers
County debut: 1987
Test debut: 1989
1000 runs in a season: 3
1st-Class 50s scored: 11
1st-Class 100s scored: 7
One-Day 50s: 2
Place in batting averages: 92nd av. 31.36 (1988 14th av. 48.73)
Place in bowling averages: 103rd av. 40.60 (1988 135th av. 75.18)
Strike rate 1989: 86.92 (career 104.70)
1st-Class catches 1989: 16 (career 38)
Parents: Alan and Wendy
Marital status: Single
Family links with cricket: Father plays club cricket with Widhowes CC in Lancashire and Cheshire League
Education: The Manchester Grammar School; Downing College, Cambridge
Qualifications: 10 O-levels, 3 A-levels; BA Cantab.
Off-season 1989–90: Touring Zimbabwe as vice-captain of England A. Toured Barbados as captain of British Universities team September 1989

LAST SEASON: BATTING

	I.	N.O.	R.	H.S.	AV.
TEST	4	0	73	47	18.25
1ST-CLASS	29	3	868	115*	33.38
INT					
RAL					
NAT.W.	1	0	35	35	35.00
B & H	5	0	160	66	32.00

LAST SEASON: BOWLING

	O.	M.	R.	W.	AV.
TEST	8	0	34	0	–
1ST-CLASS	397.4	89	1103	28	39.39
INT					
RAL					
NAT.W.	2	0	12	0	–
B & H	16	0	86	4	21.50

CAREER: BATTING

	I.	N.O.	R.	H.S.	AV.
TEST	4	0	73	47	18.25
1ST-CLASS	91	11	3182	152*	39.77
INT					
RAL	3	0	25	22	8.33
NAT.W.	1	0	35	35	35.00
B & H	12	0	331	66	27.58

CAREER: BOWLING

	O.	M.	R.	W.	AV.
TEST	8	0	34	0	–
1ST-CLASS	829.4	147	2454	48	51.12
INT					
RAL					
NAT.W.	2	0	12	0	–
B & H	19	0	116	4	29.00

Cricketing superstitions or habits: 'Always put left pad on first; won't eat curry before a match.'
Overseas tours: NCA to Bermuda 1985; Young England to Sri Lanka 1986; Young England to Australia 1987; England A to Zimbabwe 1989–90
Cricketers particularly learnt from: Father, Graham Saville (Cambridge coach), Gehan Mendis
Cricketers particularly admired: Gehan Mendis
Other sports played: Golf, squash
Other sports followed: Most sports except horse racing, wrestling and boxing
Opinions on cricket: 'Over-rate fines should be abolished. Four-day cricket is extremely boring. County cricket too often takes the brunt for failures in the Test arena (e.g. the substitute rule in 1988).'
Best batting performance: 152* Lancashire v Sussex, Hove 1988
Best bowling performance: 3-32 Lancashire v Middlesex, Old Trafford 1988

ATHEY, C. W. J.   Gloucestershire

Full Name: Charles William Jeffrey Athey
Role: Right-hand bat, right-arm medium bowler
Born: 27 September 1957, Middlesbrough
Height: 5' 10" **Weight:** 12st 3lbs
Nickname: Bumper, Wingnut, Ath
County debut: 1976 (Yorkshire), 1984 (Gloucestershire)
County cap: 1980 (Yorkshire), 1985 (Gloucestershire)
Benefit: 1990
Test debut: 1980
No. of Tests: 23
No. of One-Day Internationals: 31
1000 runs in a season: 7
1st-Class 50s scored: 76
1st-Class 100s scored: 32
One-Day 50s: 58
One-Day 100s: 6
Place in batting averages: 118th av. 27.88 (1988 4th av. 66.50)
1st-Class catches 1989: 31 (career 312 + 2 stumpings)
Parents: Peter and Maree
Wife and date of marriage: Janet Linda, 9 October 1982

Family links with cricket: 'Father played league cricket in North Yorkshire and South Durham League for 29 years, 25 of them with Middlesbrough. President of Middlesbrough CC since 1975. Brother-in-law Colin Cook played for Middlesex, other brother-in-law (Martin) plays in Thames Valley League. Father-in-law deeply involved in Middlesex Youth cricket.'

Education: Linthorpe Junior School; Stainsby Secondary School; Acklam Hall High School

Qualifications: 4 O-levels, some CSEs, National Cricket Association Coaching Certificate

Jobs outside cricket: Barman, building labourer, sports shop assistant

Off-season 1989–90: Touring South Africa with unofficial English team. Working for financial planning company

Overseas tours: Derrick Robins' XI to Canada 1976; South America 1979; Australasia 1980; England U-19 to West Indies 1976; England to West Indies 1981; Barbican XI to Gulf States 1983; England B to Sri Lanka 1985–86; England to Australia 1986–87; World Cup, Pakistan, Australia and New Zealand 1987–88

Overseas teams played for: Manly Warringah, Sydney, Australia 1977–78, 1978–79, 1979–80; Balmain, Sydney 1980–81; Schoeman Park, Bloemfontein, South Africa 1981–82; Papatoetoe, Auckland, New Zealand 1983–84

Cricketers particularly learnt from: Doug Padgett

Cricketers particularly admired: Gordon Greenidge, Malcolm Marshall, Chris Smith

Other sports played: Squash, tennis, soccer

Other sports followed: Most sports

Injuries 1989: Off for two weeks with broken thumb

Relaxations: Music, good films, good food

Extras: Played for Teesside County Schools U-16s at age 12. Made debut in 1972 North Yorkshire and South Durham League. Played for Yorkshire Colts 1974. Played for North of England Young Cricketers XI v West Indies Young Cricketers at Old Trafford in 1974. Played football for Middlesbrough

LAST SEASON: BATTING

	I.	N.O.	R.	H.S.	AV.
TEST					
1ST-CLASS	36	2	948	108	27.88
INT					
RAL	15	0	269	65	17.93
NAT.W.	2	1	81	56*	81.00
B & H	5	0	144	54	28.80

LAST SEASON: BOWLING

	O.	M.	R.	W.	AV.
TEST					
1ST-CLASS	38.4	13	112	2	56.00
INT					
RAL	8	0	36	1	36.00
NAT.W.					
B & H					

CAREER: BATTING

	I.	N.O.	R.	H.S.	AV.
TEST	41	1	919	123	22.97
1ST-CLASS	485	48	15007	184	34.34
INT	30	3	848	142*	31.40
RAL	163	13	5055	121*	33.70
NAT.W.	30	5	980	115	39.20
B & H	52	7	1539	95	34.20

CAREER: BOWLING

	O.	M.	R.	W.	AV.
TEST					
1ST-CLASS	541.4	101	1818	39	46.61
INT	1	0	10	0	–
RAL	103.4	1	581	22	26.40
NAT.W.	19.1	1	106	1	106.00
B & H	56.4	4	242	12	20.16

Schools U-16 XI 1972–74. Played for Middlesbrough Juniors 1974–75. Offered but declined apprenticeship terms with Middlesbrough FC. Captained North Riding U-19 XI 1975–76. Has Union Jack tattoo on left shoulder. Resigned as captain of Gloucestershire at end of 1989 season
Opinions on cricket: 'Should play four-day cricket, playing each county once. Over-rate fines are not realistic.'
Best batting performance: 184 England B v Sri Lanka XI, Galle 1985–86
Best bowling performance: 3-3 Gloucestershire v Hampshire, Bristol 1985

ATKINS, P. D. Surrey

Full Name: Paul David Atkins
Role: Right-hand bat, right-arm bowler
Born: 11 June 1966, Aylesbury
Height: 6′ 1″ **Weight:** 13st 7lbs
Nickname: Ripper
County debut: 1988
1st-Class 50s scored: 1
1st-Class 100s scored: 1
One-Day 50s: 1
Place in batting averages: —
(1988 55th av. 35.70)
1st-Class catches 1989: 3 (career 3)
Parents: Brian Alan Arthur and Thelma
Marital status: Single
Family links with cricket: Father plays club cricket for Dinton CC
Education: Aylesbury Grammar School
Qualifications: 7 O-levels, 3 A-levels
Jobs outside cricket: Carpet fitter
Off-season 1989–90: Playing for Perth CC, Western Australia
Cricketing superstitions or habits: Always bats with cap or helmet
Overseas tours: NAYC U-19 to Bermuda 1985; Surrey CCC to United Arab Emirates 1988 and 1989
Overseas teams played for: Pietermaritzburg University 1985–86; Alexandrians, South Africa 1986–88; Perth CC, Australia 1988–89, 1989–90
Cricketers particularly learnt from: Roy Wills, Chris Waller, Geoff Arnold
Cricketers particularly admired: Gordon Greenidge
Other sports played: Golf, football

Other sports followed: Supports Portsmouth FC
Injuries 1989: Chipped shin bone – off for four weeks
Relaxations: Listening to music
Extras: Played for Buckinghamshire CCC 1985–87. Won Wilfred Rhodes Trophy for Top Minor Counties batsman 1986. Won Gold Award on Nat West debut. Seventh Surrey player to score hundred on debut. Scored 99 on County Championship debut.
Opinions on cricket: 'Avoid politics and play cricket with all races and anywhere in the world.'
Best batting performance: 114* Surrey v Cambridge University, Cambridge 1988

LAST SEASON: BATTING

	I.	N.O.	R.	H.S.	AV.
TEST					
1ST-CLASS	5	1	91	30*	22.75
INT					
RAL					
NAT.W.					
B & H	3	1	15	9	7.50

CAREER: BATTING

	I.	N.O.	R.	H.S.	AV.
TEST					
1ST-CLASS	16	2	448	114*	32.00
INT					
RAL	1	0	2	2	2.00
NAT.W.	2	0	82	82	41.00
B & H	3	1	15	9	7.50

ATKINSON, J. C. M. Somerset

Full Name: Jonathan Colin Mark Atkinson
Role: Right-hand bat, right-arm medium bowler
Born: 10 July 1968, Butleigh
Height: 6' 4" **Weight:** 14st 7lbs
Nickname: Ako, Atki, Pike
County debut: 1985
1st-Class 50s scored: 5
One-Day 50s: 1
Place in batting averages: 160th av. 22.35 (1988 177th av. 21.41)
1st-Class catches 1989: 8 (career 12)
Parents: Colin (C. R. M.) and Shirley
Marital status: Single
Family links with cricket: Father captain of Somerset CCC 1965–67. On TCCB
Education: Millfield School; Cambridge University
Qualifications: 13 O-levels, 3 A-levels, 1 S-level

28

Off-season 1989–90: At Cambridge University
Overseas tours: Millfield School to Barbados 1986; with Combined Universities to Barbados 1989
Cricketers particularly learnt from: Father, Gerry Wilson (Millfield pro.), Martin Crowe, Peter Robinson (Somerset CC coach)
Cricketers particularly admired: 'Vivian Richards and Ian Botham for their competitive natures, Imran Khan, Dennis Lillee, Richard Hadlee and Paul Veness.'
Other sports played: Rugby, hockey, basketball, golf
Injuries 1989: Injured ligaments in right shoulder
Relaxations: 'Socialising and vodka.'
Extras: Hit highest score of 79 v Northamptonshire on his first-class debut 1985
Opinions on cricket: 'I think it's upsetting that politics should interfere with cricket re South Africa with so much talent in that country. I found the politics of a cricket dressing-room sometimes volatile and juvenile, but most of all interesting. Things are finally going right at Somerset CCC.'
Best batting performance: 79 Somerset v Northamptonshire, Weston 1985
Best bowling performance: 2-80 Somerset v India, Taunton 1986

LAST SEASON: BATTING

	I.	N.O.	R.	H.S.	AV.
TEST					
1ST-CLASS	20	0	447	57	22.35
INT					
RAL	2	0	75	69	37.50
NAT.W.					
B & H	4	0	25	16	6.25

LAST SEASON: BOWLING

	O.	M.	R.	W.	AV.
TEST					
1ST-CLASS	15	3	70	0	–
INT					
RAL					
NAT.W.					
B & H					

CAREER: BATTING

	I.	N.O.	R.	H.S.	AV.
TEST					
1ST-CLASS	43	3	942	79	23.55
INT					
RAL	4	0	77	69	19.25
NAT.W.	–	–	–	–	–
B & H	7	0	60	24	8.57

CAREER: BOWLING

	O.	M.	R.	W.	AV.
TEST					
1ST-CLASS	131	20	538	5	107.60
INT					
RAL					
NAT.W.	6	2	16	1	16.00
B & H	7	0	46	0	–

13. Who was top of Australia's Test batting averages v England, 1989?

14. Who was top of England's bowling averages v Australia, 1989?

AUSTIN, I. D. — Lancashire

Full Name: Ian David Austin
Role: Left-hand bat, right-arm medium bowler
Born: 30 May 1966, Haslingden, Lancashire
Height: 5′ 10″ **Weight:** 14st 7lbs
Nickname: Oscar, Bully
County debut: 1986
1st-Class 50s scored: 2
1st-Class 5 w. in innings: 1
One-Day 50s: 1
Place in batting averages: 210th av. 17.10 (1988 84th av. 30.85)
Place in bowling averages: 28th av. 22.52 (1988 35th av. 23.13)
Strike rate 1989: 53.66 (career 53.83)
1st-Class catches 1989: 2 (career 3)
Parents: Jack and Ursula
Wife and date of marriage: Gina, 24 September 1988
Family links with cricket: Father opened batting for Haslingden CC
Education: Haslingden High School
Qualifications: 3 O-levels; NCA coaching award
Jobs outside cricket: Carpet fitter and cabinet maker
Off-season 1989–90: Labouring
Overseas tours: NCA North U-19 to Bermuda 1985; Lancashire CCC to Jamaica 1987 and 1988; Lancashire CCC to Zimbabwe 1989
Overseas teams played for: Morochydore, Queensland 1987

LAST SEASON: BATTING

	I.	N.O.	R.	H.S.	AV.
TEST					
1ST-CLASS	13	3	171	38	17.10
INT					
RAL	6	3	57	19*	19.00
NAT.W.					
B & H					

LAST SEASON: BOWLING

	O.	M.	R.	W.	AV.
TEST					
1ST-CLASS	187.5	46	473	21	22.52
INT					
RAL	79.5	2	287	15	19.13
NAT.W.					
B & H					

CAREER: BATTING

	I.	N.O.	R.	H.S.	AV.
TEST					
1ST-CLASS	25	5	428	64	21.40
INT					
RAL	20	8	193	41	16.08
NAT.W.					
B & H	4	0	111	80	27.75

CAREER: BOWLING

	O.	M.	R.	W.	AV.
TEST					
1ST-CLASS	376.5	104	948	42	22.57
INT					
RAL	205.5	6	899	31	29.00
NAT.W.					
B & H	50	6	197	3	65.66

Cricketers particularly learnt from: Hartley Alleyne, Robby Bentley
Cricketers particularly admired: Ian Botham, Clive Lloyd
Other sports played: Squash, golf
Other sports followed: Football, rugby, golf
Relaxations: Listening to music, playing golf, reading
Extras: Holds amateur Lancashire League record for highest individual score for amateur since limited overs (149*)
Opinions on cricket: 'A good idea to introduce first-class umpires to 2nd XI cricket, and an even better one to make a 2nd XI championship. This should encourage some counties to play positive cricket from an earlier stage.'
Best batting performance: 64 Lancashire v Derbyshire, Old Trafford 1988
Best bowling performance: 5-79 Lancashire v Surrey, The Oval 1988

AYMES, A. N. Hampshire

Full Name: Adrian Nigel Aymes
Role: Wicket-keeper
Born: 4 June 1964, Southampton
Height: 6' **Weight:** 13st
Nickname: Adi
County debut: 1987
1st-Class 50s scored: 1
Parents: Michael and Barbara
Marital status: Single
Education: Shirley Middle; Bellemoor Secondary; Hill College
Qualifications: 3 O-levels, 1 A-level
Jobs outside cricket: Sports shop salesman, labourer
Cricketing superstitions or habits: Tap four corners of the batting crease
Cricketers particularly learnt from: Andy Brassington, David Evans (umpire)
Cricketers particularly admired: Bob Taylor, Malcolm Marshall, Gordon Greenidge, David Turner
Other sports played: Football, tennis
Other sports followed: American football, Australian rules football, golf
Injuries 1989: Cyst formed on cartilage on right leg – off for last 3 weeks of season (September). Operation to remove cartilage in September 1989

Relaxations: 'Watching films; working on my car; DIY in my flat.'
Extras: Half century on debut v Surrey
Best batting performance: 58 Hampshire v Surrey, Southampton 1987

LAST SEASON: BATTING

	I.	N.O.	R.	H.S.	AV.
TEST					
1ST-CLASS	1	1	24	24*	–
INT					
RAL					
NAT.W.					
B & H					

LAST SEASON: WICKET KEEPING

	C.	ST.			
TEST					
1ST-CLASS	10	–			
INT					
RAL					
NAT.W.					
B & H					

CAREER: BATTING

	I.	N.O.	R.	H.S.	AV.
TEST					
1ST-CLASS	2	1	82	58	82.00
INT					
RAL	–	–	–	–	–
NAT.W.					
B & H					

CAREER: WICKET KEEPING

	C.	ST.			
TEST					
1ST-CLASS	14	–			
INT					
RAL	2	1			
NAT.W.					
B & H					

BABINGTON, A. M.   Sussex

Full Name: Andrew Mark
Babington
Role: Left-hand bat, right-arm
fast-medium bowler
Born: 22 July 1963, London
Height: 6′ 2″ **Weight:** 13st 7lbs
Nickname: Hagar, Vinny Jones,
Turbo
County debut: 1986
1st-Class 5 w. in innings: 2
Place in bowling averages: 82nd
av. 32.78 (1988 102nd av. 33.22)
Strike rate 1989: 65.31 (career
65.11)
1st-Class catches 1989: 4 (career 19)
Parents: Roy and Maureen
Wife and date of marriage: Lisa,
30 September 1989
Family links with cricket: 'Father

played good club cricket. Brother plays club cricket. Mother used to wash my
whites.'
Education: Reigate Grammar School; Borough Road PE College

Qualifications: 5 O-levels, 2 A-levels; Member of Institute of Legal Executives

Jobs outside cricket: Work for father's and other firms of solicitors as legal executive. Worked on building sites. Associate with Abbey Life Assurance Company

Off-season 1989–90: Working for Kevin Gibbs Enterprises Ltd

Cricketing superstitions or habits: 'Always put my kit on in the same order.'

Overseas tours: Surrey Schools Cricket Association to Australia 1980

Cricketers particularly learnt from: Bob Cottam, Kevin Gibbs, John Snow, Norman Gifford, John Goodey and staff at Sussex CCC

Cricketers particularly admired: Dennis Lillee, John Snow, Andy Roberts, Michael Holding, Kevin Gibbs, John Goodey

Other sports played: Football, squash, golf, snooker

Other sports followed: Motor racing, boxing

Injuries 1989: Leg infection, after cutting knee by sliding into a metal boundary board at Edgbaston – off for one week

Relaxations: 'Driving, eating, drinking, visiting friends, spending time at home with my wife.'

Extras: Took hat-trick v Gloucestershire in 1986, with second, third and fourth balls in Championship cricket

Opinions on cricket: 'We should play 16 four-day games. Cricketers should be free to play anywhere in the world without political repercussions. After all Indian and Pakistani players play in our game alongside South Africans and their governments do not complain then. Overseas players should be limited to one per county, that is, one registered and only one eligible.'

Best batting performance: 18* Sussex v Hampshire, Southampton 1989

Best bowling performance: 5-37 Sussex v Lancashire, Liverpool 1989

LAST SEASON: BATTING

	I.	N.O.	R.	H.S.	AV.
TEST					
1ST-CLASS	15	9	50	18*	8.33
INT					
RAL	4	2	1	1*	0.50
NAT.W.	–	–	–	–	–
B & H	2	1	10	9	10.00

LAST SEASON: BOWLING

	O.	M.	R.	W.	AV.
TEST					
1ST-CLASS	511.4	97	1541	47	32.78
INT					
RAL	108	3	475	18	26.38
NAT.W.	23	1	85	4	21.25
B & H	43.2	10	150	6	25.00

CAREER: BATTING

	I.	N.O.	R.	H.S.	AV.
TEST					
1ST-CLASS	59	26	196	18*	5.93
INT					
RAL	8	3	2	1*	0.40
NAT.W.	2	2	4	4*	–
B & H	4	2	15	9	7.50

CAREER: BOWLING

	O.	M.	R.	W.	AV.
TEST					
1ST-CLASS	1432.3	268	4415	132	33.44
INT					
RAL	268	10	1254	34	36.88
NAT.W.	64	1	280	11	25.45
B & H	105.2	13	423	19	22.26

BAILEY, R. J.　　　　Northamptonshire

Full Name: Robert John Bailey
Role: Right-hand bat, off-break bowler
Born: 28 October 1963, Biddulph, Stoke-on-Trent
Height: 6′ 3″ **Weight:** 14st
Nickname: Bailers, Nose Bag ('I eat a lot!')
County debut: 1982
County cap: 1985
Test debut: 1988
No. of Tests: 1
No. of One-Day Internationals: 3
1000 runs in a season: 6
1st-Class 50s scored: 43
1st-Class 100s scored: 17
1st-Class 200s scored: 2
One-Day 50s: 24
One-Day 100s: 5
Place in batting averages: 76th av. 33.42 (1988 48th av. 36.20)
Place in bowling averages: 121st av. 55.20
Strike rate: 83.50 (career 72.04)
1st-Class catches 1989: 25 (career 115)
Parents: John and Marie
Wife and date of marriage: Rachel, 11 April 1987
Family links with cricket: Father played in North Staffordshire League for 30 years for Knypersley and Minor Counties cricket for Staffordshire as wicket-keeper. Second cousin to Phil Bainbridge of Gloucestershire
Education: Biddulph High School
Qualifications: 6 CSEs, 1 O-level
Jobs outside cricket: Worked for three winters in electrical trade
Off-season 1989–90: Touring with England in West Indies
Overseas tours: England to Sharjah 1985 and 1987 for Rothmans One-Day International tournament; West Indies 1989–90
Overseas teams played for: Rhodes University, Grahamstown 1982–83; Witenhage CC, South Africa 1983–84, 1984–85; Fitzroy CC, Melbourne 1985–86; Gosnells CC, Perth 1987–88
Cricketers particularly learnt from: 'My father, Stan Crump, Dennis Lillee (since his arrival at Northampton).'
Other sports played: Badminton, football, golf
Other sports followed: 'Like to see Port Vale and Stoke City doing well.'
Relaxations: Listening to music

Extras: Played for Young England v Young Australia, 1983. Scored two hundreds in match v Middlesex 2nd XI 1984. The only Northants batsman to score 1000 championship runs in 1988. Was picked for cancelled tour of India 1988–89

Best batting performance: 224* Northamptonshire v Glamorgan, Swansea 1986

Best bowling performance: 3-27 Northamptonshire v Glamorgan, Wellingborough 1988

LAST SEASON: BATTING

	I.	N.O.	R.	H.S.	AV.
TEST					
1ST-CLASS	44	4	1337	134	33.42
INT					
RAL	15	3	546	106*	45.50
NAT.W.	3	1	116	86*	58.00
B & H	5	1	151	69*	37.75

LAST SEASON: BOWLING

	O.	M.	R.	W.	AV.
TEST					
1ST-CLASS	139.1	19	552	10	55.20
INT					
RAL	3.1	0	26	0	–
NAT.W.	2	0	6	0	–
B & H					

CAREER: BATTING

	I.	N.O.	R.	H.S.	AV.
TEST	2	0	46	43	23.00
1ST-CLASS	260	39	8637	224*	39.08
INT	3	2	95	43*	95.00
RAL	85	12	2665	125*	36.50
NAT.W.	17	5	430	86*	35.83
B & H	27	2	1084	134	43.36

CAREER: BOWLING

	O.	M.	R.	W.	AV.
TEST					
1ST-CLASS	288.1	54	1014	24	42.25
INT	6	0	25	0	–
RAL	13.1	0	108	3	36.00
NAT.W.	4	0	22	1	22.00
B & H	10	3	29	1	29.00

15. Who was top of Australia's bowling averages v England, 1989?

16. Which two cricketers played in a Test for England before playing for a first-class county?

17. Who was the manager of Australia in England in 1989?

BAINBRIDGE, P. Gloucestershire

Full Name: Philip Bainbridge
Role: Right-hand bat, right-arm
medium bowler
Born: 16 April 1958, Stoke-on-
Trent
Height: 5' 9½" **Weight:** 12st 7lbs
Nickname: Bains, Robbo
County debut: 1977
County cap: 1981
Benefit: 1989
1000 runs in a season: 7
1st-Class 50s scored: 64
1st-Class 100s scored: 20
1st-Class 5 w. in innings: 7
One-Day 50s: 18
One-Day 100s: 1
Place in batting averages: 89th
av. 31.83 (1988 51st av. 36.05)
Place in bowling averages: 70th
av. 30.48 (1988 133rd av. 62.00)

Strike rate 1989: 67.00 (career 72.20)
1st-Class catches 1989: 4 (career 106)
Parents: Leonard George and Lilian Rose
Wife and date of marriage: Barbara, 22 September 1979
Children: Neil, 11 January 1984; Laura, 15 January 1985
Family links with cricket: Cousin, Stephen Wilkinson, played for Somerset
1969–72. Second cousin to Rob Bailey of Northamptonshire
Education: Hanley High School; Stoke-on-Trent Sixth Form College;
Borough Road College of Education
Qualifications: 9 O-levels, 2 A-levels, BEd, MCC Coaching Certificate
Jobs outside cricket: PE Lecturer, Marketing Executive with Gloucestershire
CCC until 1988, sales representative
Overseas tours: Holland with NCA North of England Youth team 1976;
Barbados, Trinidad and Tobago with British Colleges 1978; Barbados with
Gloucestershire CCC 1980; Pakistan for two Zaheer Abbas benefit matches
1983; Zimbabwe with English Counties XI 1985; Barbados with David
Graveney Benefit Tour 1986; Sri Lanka with Gloucestershire 1987; Zim-
babwe with Gloucestershire CCC 1988; Sri Lanka with Gloucestershire 1989
Cricketers particularly learnt from: All senior players at Gloucestershire –
and county coach
Cricketers particularly admired: Mike Procter
Other sports played: Football, rugby, squash, golf

36

Other sports followed: All sports

Relaxations: Photography, wine-making, beer-making, listening to music. 'Walking in the country with my Golden Retriever dog and my wife, entertaining my children.'

Extras: Played for four 2nd XIs in 1976 – Gloucestershire, Derbyshire, Northamptonshire and Warwickshire. Played for Young England v Australia 1977. Won Commercial Union U-23 Batsman of the Year 1981. Scored first century for Stoke-on-Trent aged 14. One of *Wisden*'s Five Cricketers of the Year, 1985. Stood down from vice captaincy of the county to concentrate on Benefit in 1989

Opinions on cricket: 'I think the authorities should consider 16 four-day games in future. Coloured clothes as well as ball should be introduced for Refuge knock-out competition to increase interest.'

Best batting performance: 169 Gloucestershire v Yorkshire, Cheltenham 1988
Best bowling performance: 8-53 Gloucestershire v Somerset, Bristol 1986

LAST SEASON: BATTING

	I.	N.O.	R.	H.S.	AV.
TEST					
1ST-CLASS	33	3	955	128	31.83
INT					
RAL	14	0	308	72	22.00
NAT.W.	1	0	13	13	13.00
B & H	5	0	147	53	29.40

LAST SEASON: BOWLING

	O.	M.	R.	W.	AV.
TEST					
1ST-CLASS	279.1	63	762	25	30.48
INT					
RAL	73.2	6	396	13	30.46
NAT.W.	17	0	64	3	21.33
B & H	38	6	95	4	23.75

CAREER: BATTING

	I.	N.O.	R.	H.S.	AV.
TEST					
1ST-CLASS	396	57	11246	169	33.17
INT					
RAL	132	23	2299	106*	21.09
NAT.W.	19	2	541	89	31.82
B & H	39	8	904	96	29.16

CAREER: BOWLING

	O.	M.	R.	W.	AV.
TEST					
1ST-CLASS	3152.5	716	9470	262	36.14
INT					
RAL	850.4	31	4311	148	29.12
NAT.W.	221	26	754	27	27.92
B & H	331.3	37	1157	36	32.13

---

18. How many times did W. G. Grace score 1000 runs in a season: 28, 18, or 8?

19. Who scored 1000 runs in a season most often: G. Boycott, D. L. Amiss or M. C. Cowdrey?

BAIRSTOW, D. L.   Yorkshire

Full Name: David Leslie Bairstow
Role: Right-hand bat, wicket-keeper, occasional medium pacer
Born: 1 September 1951, Bradford
Height: 5' 10" **Weight:** 14st 7lbs
Nickname: Bluey
County debut: 1970
County cap: 1973
Benefit: 1982 (£56,913)
Testimonial: 1990
Test debut: 1979
No. of Tests: 4
No. of One-Day Internationals: 21
1000 runs in a season: 3
1st-Class 50s scored: 72
1st-Class 100s scored: 10
One-Day 50s: 19
One-Day 100s: 1
Place in batting averages: 151st
av. 23.35 (1988 182nd av. 20.80)
Wife and date of marriage: Janet, 14 October 1988
Children: Andrew David
Family links with cricket: Father, Leslie, played cricket for Laisterdyke
Education: Hanson Grammar School, Bradford
Qualifications: O and A-levels
Jobs outside cricket: Runs his own office automation company
Off-season 1989–90: Working for his own company
Cricketing superstitions or habits: 'I will pat the ground three times or fiddle with my gloves three times. It is ridiculous but I do not want to stop it. I was in a pub a couple of days before the Leeds Test, and a lad I had never seen before gave me a medallion, and told me to keep it in my pocket for luck. Many people would have forgotten completely, but that medallion went into the pocket of my flannels, and stayed there for the whole match.'
Overseas tours: England to Australia 1978–79 and 1979–80; West Indies 1981
Overseas teams played for: Griqualand West 1966–67 and 1977–78
Cricketers particularly learnt from: Laurie Bennett (maths and sports master at school), Mike Fearnley
Other sports played: Golf
Injuries 1989: Missed half the season with broken thumb
Relaxations: Gardening
Extras: Turned down an offer to play for Bradford City FC. Played for MCC Schools at Lord's in 1970. First Yorkshire wicket-keeper to get 1000 runs in a

season (1982) since Arthur Wood in 1935. Set Yorkshire record of seven catches v Derbyshire at Scarborough, 1982. 133 consecutive John Player League matches. His 145 for Yorkshire v Middlesex is the highest score by a Yorkshire wicket-keeper. Allowed to take an A-level at 6 am at school in order to make Yorkshire debut. Published *A Yorkshire Diary – a year of crisis* 1984. Captain 1984–86. Completed his 1000 dismissals for Yorkshire in last match of 1988 season
Best batting performance: 145 Yorkshire v Middlesex, Scarborough 1980
Best bowling performance: 3-25 Yorkshire v MCC, Scarborough 1987

LAST SEASON: BATTING

	I.	N.O.	R.	H.S.	AV.
TEST					
1ST-CLASS	17	3	327	101*	23.35
INT					
RAL	8	1	189	65*	27.00
NAT.W.	–	–	–	–	–
B & H	4	3	132	51*	132.00

LAST SEASON: BOWLING

	O.	M.	R.	W.	AV.
TEST					
1ST-CLASS					
INT					
RAL					
NAT.W.					
B & H					

CAREER: BATTING

	I.	N.O.	R.	H.S.	AV.
TEST	7	1	125	59	20.83
1ST-CLASS	634	118	13657	145	26.46
INT	20	6	206	23*	14.71
RAL	221	48	3605	83*	20.83
NAT.W.	27	5	492	92	22.36
B & H	57	13	935	103*	21.25

CAREER: BOWLING

	O.	M.	R.	W.	AV.
TEST					
1ST-CLASS	97	19	308	9	34.22
INT					
RAL					
NAT.W.					
B & H	3	0	17	0	–

LAST SEASON: WICKET KEEPING

	C.	ST.		
TEST				
1ST-CLASS	22	1		
INT				
RAL	7	2		
NAT.W.	–	–		
B & H	3	–		

CAREER: WICKET KEEPING

	C.	ST.		
TEST	12	1		
1ST-CLASS	936	137		
INT	17	4		
RAL	229	23		
NAT.W.	38	3		
B & H	116	5		

20. Which three batsmen have scored the most first-class runs in their whole career?

21. Who are the top three batsmen in terms of career averages and what were these averages?

BAKKER, P.-J.   Hampshire

Full Name: Paul-Jan Bakker
Role: Right-hand bat, right-arm medium pace bowler
Born: 19 August 1957, Vlaardingen, Holland
Height: 6' 1" **Weight:** 14st
Nickname: Nip, Peech, Dutchie
County debut: 1986
No. of One-Day Internationals: 17 (for Holland)
50 wickets in a season: 1
1st-Class 5 w. in innings: 6
Place in batting averages: —
(1988 213th av. 16.66)
Place in bowling averages: 27th av. 22.49 (1988 29th av. 22.33)
Strike rate 1989: 49.06 (career 51.98)
1st-Class catches 1989: 3 (career 4)
Parents: Hubertus Antonius Bakker and Wilhelmina Hendrika Bakker-Goos
Marital status: Single
Family links with cricket: 'Father is the scorer for the first team of my club in The Hague, and has been scorer of Hague CC for 15 years.'
Education: Ie VCL and Hugo de Groot College, The Hague, Holland
Qualifications: 'We have a different school system but finished my HAVO schooling.' Ski-instructor
Jobs outside cricket: Ski-instructor, public relations officer
Off-season 1989–90: 'Holiday in Aruba; tour to Zimbabwe with Unibind Cricket School, The Hague; skiing; tour to Argentina with the MCC – I hope! –; and finally, Barbados with Hampshire CCC.'
Cricketing superstitions or habits: 'I need coffee before a game and cigarettes at tea when my side is fielding. I always wear a T-shirt and short-sleeved sweater.'
Overseas tours: South Africa 1978 with Klaas Vervelde XI; several tours to England with Dutch clubs
Overseas teams played for: Green Point CC, Cape Town 1981–86; Flamingo Touring Club, Kent and Essex 1983; with Holland to Gloucester, Essex and MCC 1984 and ICC trophy 1986
Cricketers particularly learnt from: Laddy Outschoorn, Hylton Ackerman
Cricketers particularly admired: Malcolm Marshall ('he has the ball on a string'), Michael Holding ('he has the most beautiful run up ever')
Other sports played: 'I ski, play a bit of golf and like to drive fast.'

Other sports followed: Formula One motor racing, tennis, football, golf and most other sports

Injuries 1989: 'One game off because of tiredness.'

Relaxations: Social visits to pubs, bars and restaurants; films and newspapers

Extras: First ever Dutch player to play professional cricket

Opinions on cricket: 'I think this South African issue has been blown out of all proportion. It must be my right as a professional cricketer, living in a "free" world to travel when and where I want to, and to make a living out of cricket as I please. After a whole season of playing first-class cricket, I believe there is too much of it. Players tend to get too tired to give 100 per cent. Cricket becomes a routine, and it therefore does not produce the kind of players Test countries are looking for and need.'

Best batting performance: 22 Hampshire v Yorkshire, Southampton 1989

Best bowling performance: 7-31 Hampshire v Kent, Bournemouth 1987

LAST SEASON: BATTING

	I.	N.O.	R.	H.S.	AV.
TEST					
1ST-CLASS	18	3	96	22	6.40
INT					
RAL	5	5	5	2*	–
NAT.W.	–	–	–	–	–
B & H	–	–	–	–	–

CAREER: BATTING

	I.	N.O.	R.	H.S.	AV.
TEST					
1ST-CLASS	32	12	152	22	7.60
INT					
RAL	6	6	11	6*	–
NAT.W.	1	0	2	2	2.00
B & H	–	–	–	–	–

LAST SEASON: BOWLING

	O.	M.	R.	W.	AV.
TEST					
1ST-CLASS	629.4	157	1732	77	22.49
INT					
RAL	87	8	299	18	16.61
NAT.W.	44	10	129	3	43.00
B & H	44	8	146	3	48.66

CAREER: BOWLING

	O.	M.	R.	W.	AV.
TEST					
1ST-CLASS	1083	286	2871	125	22.96
INT					
RAL	157.1	10	610	37	16.48
NAT.W.	67.4	13	199	8	24.87
B & H	55	13	165	5	33.00

22. Who has the top career average of English cricketers?

23. What is Allan Border's nickname?

24. Who was in the final of the NatWest Trophy last season and who won?

BALL, M. C. J.   Gloucestershire

Full Name: Martyn Charles John Ball
Role: Right-hand bat, off-break
bowler
Born: 26 April 1970, Bristol
Height: 5′ 9″ **Weight:** 11st 4lbs
Nickname: Benny (after Benny the
Ball in the cartoon, Top Cat)
County debut: 1988
Place in bowling averages: 54th
av. 28.00
Strike rate 1989: 51.66 (career 56.70)
1st-Class catches 1989: 5 (career 5)
Parents: Kenneth Charles and
Pamela Wendy
Marital status: Single
Education: King Edmund Secondary
School, Yate; Bath College of
Further Education

Qualifications: 6 O-levels, 3 A-O-levels
Off-season 1989–90: 'Doing odd jobs in the Bristol area, and a five-week hike
around Europe.'
Cricketing superstitions or habits: When bowling in long sleeve shirt always
has right cuff undone
Overseas teams played for: Preston CC, Melbourne 1988; N. Melbourne CC
1988–89
Cricketers particularly learnt from: Graham Wiltshire, John Shepherd,
Simon Packer (school PE Teacher who played for Young England and
Gloucestershire), David Graveney

LAST SEASON: BATTING

	I.	N.O.	R.	H.S.	AV.
TEST					
1ST-CLASS	8	3	31	17*	16.20
INT					
RAL	1	0	4	4	4.00
NAT.W.	–	–	–	–	–
B & H					

CAREER: BATTING

	I.	N.O.	R.	H.S.	AV.
TEST					
1ST-CLASS	9	3	33	17*	5.50
INT					
RAL	1	0	4	4	4.00
NAT.W.	–	–	–	–	–
B & H					

LAST SEASON: BOWLING

	O.	M.	R.	W.	AV.
TEST					
1ST-CLASS	155	26	504	18	28.00
INT					
RAL	8	0	49	0	–
NAT.W.	12	1	42	3	14.00
B & H					

CAREER: BOWLING

	O.	M.	R.	W.	AV.
TEST					
1ST-CLASS	189	34	594	20	29.70
INT					
RAL	8	0	49	0	–
NAT.W.	12	1	42	3	14.00
B & H					

Cricketers particularly admired: Ian Botham, John Emburey, Vic Marks, David Graveney

Other sports played: 'I enjoy all sports, and have represented the County in rugby and football.'

Other sports followed: 'I love watching all sports except synchronised swimming and show jumping.'

Relaxations: Following Manchester City FC and listening to music

Extras: Represented County at rugby and football. Represented Young England in the One-Day and Test Series v New Zealand 1989

Opinions on cricket: 'I hold the popular opinion that four-day cricket on good pitches is a must to improve the form of our national side.'

Best batting performance: 17* Gloucestershire v Hampshire, Portsmouth 1989

Best bowling performance: 4-53 Gloucestershire v Kent, Maidstone 1989

BANKS, D. A.　　　　Warwickshire

Full Name: David Andrew Banks
Role: Right-hand bat, occasional seamer 'but trying to develop "offies"'
Born: 11 January 1961, Pensnett
Height: 6′ 3″ **Weight:** 15st
Nickname: Banksy, Old Dog
County debut: 1983 (Worcestershire), 1988 (Warwickshire)
1st-Class 50s scored: 5
1st-Class 100s scored: 1
One-Day 50s: 2
Place in batting averages: —
(1988 145th av. 24.37)
1st-Class catches 1989: 1 (career 15)
Parents: William and Betty
Marital status: Single
Family links with cricket: Father and brother both played for same club – Brierley Hill Athletic Club

Education: Biros Meadow Infants (Pensnett); St Marks Primary (Pensnett); The Pensnett School and Dudley Technical College

Qualifications: 4 O-levels, 4 CSEs (City and Guilds Fabrication, Mechanical and Electrical Engineering); NCA Coaching Certificate

Jobs outside cricket: Engineering apprenticeship (4 years) with Gibbons Bros; Groundsman (2 years) with Stourbridge Cricket Club

Cricketing superstitions or habits: Left pad on first
Overseas tours: Tour to Barbados 1981
Overseas teams played for: North Perth CC (Western Australia) 1982–83; Melville CC (Western Australia) 1983–84 and 1984–85; Collingwood Park CC (Albany, Western Australia) 1986–88
Cricketers particularly learnt from: Gordon Smith (Stourbridge CC), 'the best bowler outside first-class cricket and still playing at 53.'
Cricketers particularly admired: Graeme Hick, Gordon Greenidge (consistency on all wickets at the highest level), Dennis Lillee, Michael Holding
Other sports played: Soccer, golf, tennis
Other sports followed: Aussie rules
Relaxations: 'Music (mainly soul). Read the occasional book.'
Extras: Left Worcestershire to join Warwickshire in 1988. Left Warwickshire at end of 1989 season
Opinions on cricket: 'A cricketer should be allowed to earn his living anywhere (without complications) as in other professions. The game is bigger than any person/s.'
Best batting performance: 100 Worcestershire v Oxford University, Oxford 1983 (on debut)

LAST SEASON: BATTING

	I.	N.O.	R.	H.S.	AV.
TEST					
1ST-CLASS	7	3	148	60*	37.00
INT					
RAL	2	0	2	1	1.00
NAT.W.					
B & H					

LAST SEASON: BOWLING

	O.	M.	R.	W.	AV.
TEST					
1ST-CLASS	5	1	13	0	–
INT					
RAL					
NAT.W.					
B & H					

CAREER: BATTING

	I.	N.O.	R.	H.S.	AV.
TEST					
1ST-CLASS	45	7	1034	100	27.21
INT					
RAL	18	2	221	51*	13.81
NAT.W.	4	2	128	62*	64.00
B & H					

CAREER: BOWLING

	O.	M.	R.	W.	AV.
TEST					
1ST-CLASS	10	2	30	0	–
INT					
RAL					
NAT.W.	8	0	49	2	24.50
B & H					

25. Who was in the final of the Refuge Assurance Cup last season, and who won?

BARNETT, K. J. Derbyshire

Full Name: Kim John Barnett
Role: Right-hand bat, leg-break or seam bowler, cover fielder
Born: 17 July 1960, Stoke-on-Trent
Height: 6′ 1″ **Weight:** 13st 7lbs
Nickname: Wristy
County debut: 1979
County cap: 1982
Test debut: 1988
No. of Tests: 4
No. of One-Day Internationals: 1
1000 runs in a season: 7
1st-Class 50s scored: 76
1st-Class 100s scored: 26
1st-Class 200s scored: 1
1st-Class 5 w. in innings: 1
One-Day 50s: 34
One-Day 100s: 6
Place in batting averages: 65th
av. 35.54 (1988 9th av. 57.96)
Place in bowling averages: 79th av. 31.30 (1988 79th av. 29.57)
Strike rate 1989: 68 (career 82.42)
1st-Class catches 1989: 16 (career 169)
Parents: Derek and Doreen
Marital status: Separated
Children: Rebecca, 13 September 1986
Education: Leek High School, Staffs
Qualifications: 7 O-levels
Off-season 1989–90: Touring South Africa with unofficial English team
Jobs outside cricket: Bank clerk, National Westminster Bank 1978
Overseas tours: With England Schools to India 1977; Young England to Australia 1978–79; Derrick Robins' XI to New Zealand and Australia 1979–80; England B to Sri Lanka 1986 (vice-captain)
Overseas teams played for: Boland, South Africa, 1982–83, 1984–85, 1987–88
Cricketers particularly learnt from: Eddie Barlow
Cricketers particularly admired: Gordon Greenidge, Richard Hadlee
Other sports played: Football (has played soccer semi-professionally for Cheshire League side, Leek Town FC), tennis, squash
Other sports followed: Horse racing, football
Relaxations: Watching racing on TV, reading, eating
Extras: Played for Northants 2nd XI when aged 15. Played one Minor County match for Staffordshire; also for Warwickshire 2nd XI. Became youngest

captain of a first-class county when appointed in 1983. Chris Cowdrey of Kent and England was best man at his wedding

Opinions on cricket: 'I would still like to see the introduction of 16 four-day games to promote more attacking cricket with better wickets. I would also like to see a more general acceptance of wickets which have a fair balance between bat and ball, and produce results. Wickets should not be "up and down" in bounce, but neither should they be so fast that batsmen completely dominate the game resulting in boredom for spectators.'

Best batting performance: 239* Derbyshire v Leicestershire, Leicester 1988
Best bowling performance: 6-115 Derbyshire v Yorkshire, Bradford 1985

LAST SEASON: BATTING

	I.	N.O.	R.	H.S.	AV.
TEST	5	0	141	80	28.20
1ST-CLASS	31	1	1103	118	36.76
INT					
RAL	12	1	317	100*	28.81
NAT.W.	2	0	71	55	35.50
B & H	4	0	226	101	56.50

LAST SEASON: BOWLING

	O.	M.	R.	W.	AV.
TEST	6	0	32	0	–
1ST-CLASS	107.2	24	281	11	25.54
INT					
RAL	14.2	1	48	2	24.00
NAT.W.					
B & H					

CAREER: BATTING

	I.	N.O.	R.	H.S.	AV.
TEST	7	0	207	80	29.57
1ST-CLASS	413	34	13887	239*	36.64
INT	1	0	84	84	84.00
RAL	146	23	4104	131*	33.36
NAT.W.	23	2	738	88	35.14
B & H	42	2	1294	115	32.35

CAREER: BOWLING

	O.	M.	R.	W.	AV.
TEST	6	0	32	0	–
1ST-CLASS	1161.4	241	3648	86	42.41
INT					
RAL	60.5	3	348	9	38.66
NAT.W.	29.4	5	107	11	9.72
B & H	9	2	33	2	16.50

26. What did Richard Hutton, John Jameson, Roger Knight and Bill Merry have in common last season?

27. Which country scored the lowest ever in a Test match, and how much?

BARTLETT, R. J. Somerset

Full Name: Richard James
Bartlett
Role: Right-hand bat
Born: 8 October 1966, Ash
Priors, Somerset
Height: 5′ 9″ **Weight:** 12st
Nickname: Pumpy
County debut: 1986
1st-Class 50s scored: 4
1st-Class 100s scored: 2
One-Day 50s: 5
Place in batting averages: 245th
av. 12.00 (1988 133rd av. 25.25)
1st-Class catches 1989: 10 (career 27)
Parents: Richard and Barbara
Family links with cricket: Father
plays for local club side. Both
parents are members of Somerset
CCC
Education: Taunton School
Jobs outside cricket: Worked for British Van Heusen and British Gas as an
office clerk. Worked at Bingo Club for five months. Indoor cricket umpire,
coach, and bar worker in Australia
Overseas tours: Taunton School Under-15s to Sri Lanka 1982; England South
to Bermuda 1985
Overseas teams played for: Manly CC, Sydney 1986–87, 1987–88
Cricketers particularly learnt from: Andrew Kennedy, Martin Crowe, Steve
Waugh

LAST SEASON: BATTING

	I.	N.O.	R.	H.S.	AV.
TEST					
1ST-CLASS	19	0	228	54	12.00
INT					
RAL	10	0	234	47	23.40
NAT.W.					
B & H	5	1	76	36	19.00

CAREER: BATTING

	I.	N.O.	R.	H.S.	AV.
TEST					
1ST-CLASS	60	5	1242	117*	22.58
INT					
RAL	23	1	576	55	26.18
NAT.W.	3	1	147	85	73.50
B & H	7	1	80	36	13.33

LAST SEASON: BOWLING

	O.	M.	R.	W.	AV.
TEST					
1ST-CLASS					
INT					
RAL					
NAT.W.					
B & H					

CAREER: BOWLING

	O.	M.	R.	W.	AV.
TEST					
1ST-CLASS	30	4	145	4	36.25
INT					
RAL					
NAT.W.					
B & H					

Cricketers particularly admired: Dennis Breakwell, Trevor Gard, Colin Dredge, Steve Waugh
Other sports played: Represented Somerset at U-21 hockey. Golf
Relaxations: Watching TV, music, socialising
Extras: First Somerset player to score a century on first-class debut since Harold Gimblett. Won Gray-Nicholls Trophy 1985 as most improved schools cricketer. Represented England Schools and England Young Cricketers
Opinions on cricket: 'The county cricketer should have a larger say in the running of the game, i.e. the Players Association should be a bigger voice in cricket. Sides should only have *one* registered overseas player attached to the club. All committee members should get to know the names of *all* the players on their staff.'
Best batting performance: 117* Somerset v Oxford University, Oxford 1986
Best bowling performance: 1-9 Somerset v Glamorgan, Taunton 1988

BARWICK, S. R.   Glamorgan

Full Name: Stephen Royston Barwick
Role: Right-hand bat, right-arm medium bowler
Born: 6 September 1960, Neath
Height: 6′ 2″ **Weight:** 13st 2lbs
Nickname: Baz
County debut: 1981
County cap: 1987
50 wickets in a season: 2
1st-Class 5 w. in innings: 9
1st-Class 10 w. in match: 1
Place in bowling averages: 69th av. 30.43 (1988 104th av. 33.25)
Strike rate 1989: 73.25 (career 69.99)
1st-Class catches 1989: 6 (career 30)
Parents: Margaret and Roy
Wife and date of marriage: Margaret, 12 December 1987

Family links with cricket: 'My Uncle David played for Glamorgan 2nd XI.'
Education: Cwrt Sart Comprehensive School; Dwr-y-Felin Comprehensive School
Qualifications: 'Commerce, human biology, mathematics, English.'
Jobs outside cricket: Ex-steel worker
Other sports played: Badminton, squash, table tennis, football

Other sports followed: Watching Swansea City FC
Opinions on cricket: 'I think there should be more four-day cricket played.'
Best batting performance: 30 Glamorgan v Hampshire, Bournemouth 1988
Best bowling performance: 8-42 Glamorgan v Worcestershire, Worcester 1983

LAST SEASON: BATTING

	I.	N.O.	R.	H.S.	AV.
TEST					
1ST-CLASS	27	13	65	23	4.64
INT					
RAL	6	4	70	48*	35.00
NAT.W.	–	–	–	–	–
B & H	3	0	4	4	1.33

CAREER: BATTING

	I.	N.O.	R.	H.S.	AV.
TEST					
1ST-CLASS	135	55	647	30	8.08
INT					
RAL	28	18	156	48*	15.60
NAT.W.	6	3	18	6	6.00
B & H	17	9	56	18	7.00

LAST SEASON: BOWLING

	O.	M.	R.	W.	AV.
TEST					
1ST-CLASS	781.2	232	1948	64	30.43
INT					
RAL	83.5	6	376	15	25.06
NAT.W.	8	1	28	1	28.00
B & H	35.2	4	140	3	46.66

CAREER: BOWLING

	O.	M.	R.	W.	AV.
TEST					
1ST-CLASS	3558.1	881	10096	305	33.10
INT					
RAL	546	35	2441	82	29.76
NAT.W.	104.4	26	279	18	15.50
B & H	242.3	38	874	32	27.31

BASE, S. J. Derbyshire

Full Name: Simon John Base
Role: Right-hand bat, right-arm medium bowler
Born: 2 January 1960, Maidstone
Height: 6′ 3″ **Weight:** 13st 9lbs
Nickname: Basey, Herman
County debut: 1986 (Glamorgan), 1988 (Derbyshire)
50 wickets in a season: 1
1st-Class 5 w. in innings: 6
1st-Class 10 w. in match: 1
Place in bowling averages: 34th av. 24.18 (1988 105th av. 33.40)
Strike rate 1989: 41.06 (career 46.95)
1st-Class catches 1989: 7 (career 20)
Parents: Christine and Peter
Family links with cricket: Grandfather used to play
Education: Fish Hoek Primary School, Fish Hoek High School, Cape Town, South Africa

Qualifications: High School, School Certificate Matriculation. Refrigeration and air conditioning technician

Jobs outside cricket: Hall-Thermotank in South Africa as a technician and S.A. Sea Products, G.S.P.K. Electronics in North Yorkshire, England

Off-season 1989–90: Playing for Border CC, South Africa

Overseas teams played for: Western Province B 1982–83; Boland 1986–89

Cricketers particularly learnt from: Stuart Leary, Graham Gooch, Kevin Lyons, Alan Jones, James Crawford-Porter

Cricketers particularly admired: Eddie Barlow, Graham Gooch, Graeme Pollock

Other sports played: Football, golf, windsurfing

Other sports followed: Golf, tennis, snooker, all sports

Relaxations: Windsurfing, golf, reading science fiction, watching films, music

Extras: Suspended from first-class cricket for ten weeks during 1988 season for a supposed breach of contract, joining Derbyshire when he was still said to be contracted to Glamorgan. The TCCB fined Derbyshire £2000

Opinions on cricket: 'I feel that politics should not interfere with international sport at any level.'

Best batting performance: 38 Glamorgan v Gloucestershire, Swansea 1987

Best bowling performance: 7-60 Derbyshire v Yorkshire, Chesterfield 1989

LAST SEASON: BATTING

	I.	N.O.	R.	H.S.	AV.
TEST					
1ST-CLASS	25	6	181	32*	9.52
INT					
RAL	4	1	10	6*	3.33
NAT.W.					
B & H	2	1	10	6*	10.00

CAREER: BATTING

	I.	N.O.	R.	H.S.	AV.
TEST					
1ST-CLASS	78	22	558	38	9.96
INT					
RAL	13	2	51	19	4.63
NAT.W.					
B & H	5	2	30	12	10.00

LAST SEASON: BOWLING

	O.	M.	R.	W.	AV.
TEST					
1ST-CLASS	417.2	73	1451	60	24.18
INT					
RAL	104.4	2	409	21	19.47
NAT.W.					
B & H	41	4	172	2	86.00

CAREER: BOWLING

	O.	M.	R.	W.	AV.
TEST					
1ST-CLASS	1447.3	212	4625	184	25.13
INT					
RAL	200.4	5	846	36	23.50
NAT.W.					
B & H	69	5	319	5	63.80

28. What was the longest Test match, and how many days?

BASTIEN, S.   Glamorgan

Full Name: Steven Bastien
Role: Right-hand bat, right-arm
fast-medium bowler, 'outstanding'
fielder
Born: 13 March 1963, Stepney
Height: 6′ 1″ **Weight:** 12st 7lbs
Nickname: Bassie
County debut: 1988
1st-Class 5 w. in innings: 1
1st-Class catches 1989: 0 (career 1)
Parents: Francisca and Anthony
Marital status: Single
Education: St Mary's Academy
School, Dominica, West Indies;
St Bonaventure School, London E7
Qualifications: 3 CSEs;
NCA Coaching Course; Carpentry;
CCPR Course
Jobs outside cricket: Salesman,
labourer, carpenter
Cricketing superstitions or habits: 'I don't believe in any luck.'
Overseas tours: Haringey Cricket College to Barbados, Trinidad and Tobago
1986–87 and Jamaica 1988–89; Glamorgan CCC to Barbados 1989
Cricketers particularly learnt from: 'My cousin G. Thomas.'
Cricketers particularly admired: Viv Richards, David Gower, Ian Botham,
Michael Holding, Joel Garner, Clive Lloyd, Andy Roberts
Other sports followed: Football, boxing, athletics
Relaxations: Watching movies, listening to reggae, soul and calypso music

LAST SEASON: BATTING

	I.	N.O.	R.	H.S.	AV.
TEST					
1ST-CLASS	2	2	1	1*	–
INT					
RAL	1	0	1	1	1.00
NAT.W.					
B & H	1	0	7	7	7.00

CAREER: BATTING

	I.	N.O.	R.	H.S.	AV.
TEST					
1ST-CLASS	8	4	58	36*	14.50
INT					
RAL	1	0	1	1	1.00
NAT.W.					
B & H	1	0	7	7	7.00

LAST SEASON: BOWLING

	O.	M.	R.	W.	AV.
TEST					
1ST-CLASS	59	12	202	4	50.50
INT					
RAL	15	0	65	0	–
NAT.W.					
B & H	11	1	64	0	–

CAREER: BOWLING

	O.	M.	R.	W.	AV.
TEST					
1ST-CLASS	178.1	47	491	12	40.91
INT					
RAL	15	0	65	0	–
NAT.W.					
B & H	11	1	64	0	–

Extras: Took five wickets on debut 1988
Opinions on cricket: 'There is still too much three-day cricket. I think we should have more four-day games instead, because there is a better chance of getting a result.'
Best batting performance: 36* Glamorgan v Warwickshire, Edgbaston 1988
Best bowling performance: 5-90 Glamorgan v Leicester, Neath 1988

BATTY, J. D. Yorkshire

Full Name: Jeremy David Batty
Role: Right-hand bat, right-arm off-spin bowler, outfielder
Born: 15 May 1971, Bradford
Height: 6' 1" **Weight:** 12½st
Nickname: Nora, Wally
County debut: 1989
1st-Class 5 w. in innings: 1
Parents: David and Rosemary
Marital status: Single
Family links with cricket: 'Father is YCA U-16 manager, coach and also good league cricketer.'
Education: Parkside Middle School; Bingley Grammar School
Qualifications: 5 O-levels; BTEC National Leisure Studies; Coaching Certificate
Jobs outside cricket: Assisting in parents' sports shop

LAST SEASON: BATTING

	I.	N.O.	R.	H.S.	AV.
TEST					
1ST-CLASS	2	1	4	4*	4.00
INT					
RAL					
NAT.W.					
B & H					

CAREER: BATTING

	I.	N.O.	R.	H.S.	AV.
TEST					
1ST-CLASS	2	1	4	4*	4.00
INT					
RAL					
NAT.W.					
B & H					

LAST SEASON: BOWLING

	O.	M.	R.	W.	AV.
TEST					
1ST-CLASS	64.1	17	193	8	24.12
INT					
RAL					
NAT.W.					
B & H					

CAREER: BOWLING

	O.	M.	R.	W.	AV.
TEST					
1ST-CLASS	64.1	17	193	8	24.12
INT					
RAL					
NAT.W.					
B & H					

Off-season 1989–90: Playing club cricket and coaching in Zimbabwe. England Young Cricketers Tour to Australia 1990
Cricketing superstitions or habits: 'Always put left pad on first.'
Overseas tours: England Young Cricketers to Australia 1989–90
Cricketers particularly learnt from: David Batty, Neil Hartley, Steve Oldham
Cricketers particularly admired: Allan Lamb, Viv Richards
Other sports played: Golf
Other sports followed: Leeds Rugby League FC
Relaxations: Watching any sport, going out socialising
Best batting performance: 4* Yorkshire v Lancashire, Scarborough 1989
Best bowling performance: 5-118 Yorkshire v Lancashire, Scarborough 1989

BENJAMIN, J. E. — Warwickshire

Full Name: Joseph Emmanuel Benjamin
Role: Right-hand bat, right-arm fast-medium bowler
Born: 2 February 1961, St Kitts, West Indies
Height: 6′ 1″ **Weight:** 12st 10lbs
Nickname: Boggy, Strop
County debut: 1988
Place in batting averages: 93rd av. 36.07
1st-Class catches 1989: 2 (career 2)
Parents: Henry and Judith
Marital status: Single
Education: Cayon High School, St Kitts; Mount Pleasant, Highgate, Birmingham
Qualifications: 4 O-levels
Jobs outside cricket: Trainee manager, landscape gardener, labourer
Off-season 1989–90: 'Working for Top Man.'
Cricketing superstitions or habits: 'Always put left pad, boot and glove on first.'
Cricketers particularly learnt from: Bob Cottam, Gordon Smith, Ron Headley
Cricketers particularly admired: Imran Khan, Michael Holding, Dean Jones
Other sports played: Football, squash, basketball
Other sports followed: American football, tennis
Relaxations: Music, reading, going to the cinema

Opinions on cricket: 'I think with cricket being so commercial, it could help a lot of players whose careers have been cut short through injury. I also think they should dig Fenners up and build a council estate. It's the worst wicket I have ever played on.'

Best batting performance: 8* Warwickshire v Australians, Edgbaston 1989
Best bowling performance: 3-55 Warwickshire v Somerset, Edgbaston 1989

LAST SEASON: BATTING

	I.	N.O.	R.	H.S.	AV.
TEST					
1ST-CLASS	4	1	25	8*	8.33
INT					
RAL	1	1	9	9*	–
NAT.W.					
B & H					

CAREER: BATTING

	I.	N.O.	R.	H.S.	AV.
TEST					
1ST-CLASS	4	1	25	8*	8.33
INT					
RAL	1	1	9	9*	–
NAT.W.	2	0	24	19	12.00
B & H					

LAST SEASON: BOWLING

	O.	M.	R.	W.	AV.
TEST					
1ST-CLASS	177	44	505	14	36.07
INT					
RAL	16	0	57	0	–
NAT.W.					
B & H					

CAREER: BOWLING

	O.	M.	R.	W.	AV.
TEST					
1ST-CLASS	194	50	558	14	39.85
INT					
RAL	16	0	57	0	–
NAT.W.	23	4	102	3	34.00
B & H					

29. Who was the youngest Test player, and how old was he?

30. Who was the youngest player to play Test cricket for Australia?

31. Who was the oldest player for England on his debut?

BENJAMIN, W. K. M.   Leicestershire

Full Name: Winston Keithroy Matthew Benjamin
Role: Right-hand bat, right-arm fast bowler
Born: 31 December 1964, All Saints, Antigua
County debut: 1986
Test debut: 1987–88
No. of Tests: 8
No. of One-Day Internationals: 38
50 wickets in a season: 1
1st-Class 50s scored: 6
1st-Class 5 w. in innings: 15
1st-Class 10 w. in match: 2
Place in batting averages: 214th av. 16.05 (1988 209th av. 17.00)
Place in bowling averages: 6th av. 17.94 (1988 3rd av. 14.15)
Strike rate 1989: 42.10 (career 49.16)
1st-Class catches 1989: 7 (career 39)
Education: All Saints School, Antigua
Off-season 1989–90: Touring with the West Indies
Overseas teams played for: Leeward Islands since 1985
Extras: Played Minor Counties cricket for Cheshire since 1985. Appeared for Rest of the World XI v D. B. Close's XI at Scarborough 1985
Best batting performance: 95* Leicestershire v India, Leicester 1986
Best bowling performance: 7-54 Leicestershire v Australians, Leicester 1989

LAST SEASON: BATTING

	I.	N.O.	R.	H.S.	AV.
TEST					
1ST-CLASS	19	2	273	41	16.05
INT					
RAL	7	2	86	41*	17.20
NAT.W.	1	0	17	17	17.00
B & H	–	–	–	–	–

CAREER: BATTING

	I.	N.O.	R.	H.S.	AV.
TEST	10	1	125	41*	13.88
1ST-CLASS	91	25	1485	95*	22.50
INT	22	3	92	31	4.84
RAL	22	6	211	41*	13.18
NAT.W.	3	1	24	17	12.00
B & H	6	2	60	21	15.00

LAST SEASON: BOWLING

	O.	M.	R.	W.	AV.
TEST					
1ST-CLASS	484.1	145	1238	69	17.94
INT					
RAL	74.1	8	265	9	29.44
NAT.W.	24	7	78	2	39.00
B & H	20	5	57	3	19.00

CAREER: BOWLING

	O.	M.	R.	W.	AV.
TEST	208	38	564	26	21.69
1ST-CLASS	1857	439	5529	226	24.46
INT	340.1	25	1382	37	37.35
RAL	196.2	13	802	28	28.64
NAT.W.	69	13	209	9	23.22
B & H	98.4	16	328	22	14.90

BENSON, J. D. R.   Leicestershire

Full Name: Justin David Ramsay Benson
Role: Right-hand bat, wicket-keeper
Born: 1 March 1967, Dublin
Height: 6′ 3″ **Weight:** 14st
Nickname: Rambo, Lager Monster, Garibaldi
County debut: 1988
One-Day 50s: 1
1st-Class catches 1989: 1 (career 1)
Parents: Malcolm and Elizabeth
Marital status: Single
Family links with cricket: Father is a qualified first-class umpire
Education: St Faith, The Leys, Cambridge; Cambridge College of Further Education
Qualifications: 10 O-levels
Jobs outside cricket: Coach and social organiser
Off-season 1989–90: Playing in South Africa
Overseas teams played for: Cotton Ground, Nevis, West Indies 1987–88; Durbanville, Cape Town, South Africa 1988–89
Cricketers particularly learnt from: Phil Redfern, Nigel Gadsby, Gordon Parsons
Cricketers particularly admired: Derek Parry, Gordon Parsons, Richard Edmunds
Other sports played: Rugby, hockey, darts, skittles, pool, dominoes, spoof

LAST SEASON: BATTING

	I.	N.O.	R.	H.S.	AV.
TEST					
1ST-CLASS	8	0	110	45	13.75
INT					
RAL	5	1	90	41	22.50
NAT.W.					
B & H					

LAST SEASON: BOWLING

	O.	M.	R.	W.	AV.
TEST					
1ST-CLASS	9.3	0	44	1	44.00
INT					
RAL					
NAT.W.					
B & H					

CAREER: BATTING

	I.	N.O.	R.	H.S.	AV.
TEST					
1ST-CLASS	9	0	113	45	12.55
INT					
RAL	10	2	209	42*	26.12
NAT.W.	1	0	85	85	85.00
B & H	1	1	37	37*	–

CAREER: BOWLING

	O.	M.	R.	W.	AV.
TEST					
1ST-CLASS	9.3	0	44	1	44.00
INT					
RAL					
NAT.W.	2.1	0	13	0	–
B & H					

Other sports followed: Athletics, golf, any sport on TV
Relaxations: Reggae music, drinking, socialising, talking about cricket
Extras: Scored 85 and won the Man of the Match Award for Cambridgeshire on his NatWest Trophy debut v Yorkshire at Headingley in 1986
Opinions on cricket: 'Overseas players should be restricted to one or none per county and a player should be able to play anywhere in the world he so chooses!'
Best batting performance: 45 Leicestershire v Kent, Leicester 1989
Best bowling performance: 1-44 Leicestershire v Hampshire, Bournemouth 1989

BENSON, M. R.   Kent

Full Name: Mark Richard Benson
Role: Left-hand bat, off-break bowler
Born: 6 July 1958, Shoreham, Sussex
Height: 5' 9½" **Weight:** 12st 7lbs
Nickname: Benny
County debut: 1980
County cap: 1981
Test debut: 1986
No. of Tests: 1
No. of One-Day Internationals: 1
1000 runs in a season: 8
1st-Class 50s scored: 71
1st-Class 100s scored: 29
One-Day 50s: 30
One-Day 100s: 3
Place in batting averages: 12th av. 54.12 (1988 64th av. 34.08)
1st-Class catches 1989: 1 (career 91)
Parents: Frank and Judy
Wife and date of marriage: Sarah, 20 September 1986
Children: Laurence Mark Edward, 16 October 1987
Family links with cricket: Father played for Ghana
Education: Sutton Valence School
Qualifications: O- and A-levels and 1 S-level. Qualified tennis coach
Jobs outside cricket: Marketing assistant with Shell UK Oil; Financial adviser
Cricketing superstitions or habits: Left pad on first. 'Never shave during a game unless I score a hundred in the first innings!'
Overseas teams played for: Balfour Guild CC 1979–80; Johannesburg

Municipals 1980–81; Port Adelaide CC 1981–82; Avendale CC, Cape Town 1983–84

Cricketers particularly learnt from: Chris Tavaré, Colin Cowdrey

Cricketers particularly admired: Malcolm Marshall, Jimmy Cook, Chris Tavaré

Other sports played: Golf, bowls, tennis

Other sports followed: Football, horse racing

Injuries 1989: Broken thumb – out for three weeks; cracked rib – out for three weeks

Relaxations: Windsurfing

Extras: Scored 1000 runs in first full season. Record for most runs in career and season at Sutton Valence School

Opinions on cricket: 'Four-day cricket, with each county playing against each other once.'

Best batting performance: 162 Kent v Hampshire, Southampton 1985

Best bowling performance: 2-55 Kent v Surrey, Dartford 1986

LAST SEASON: BATTING

	I.	N.O.	R.	H.S.	AV.
TEST					
1ST-CLASS	29	5	1299	157	54.12
INT					
RAL	6	0	115	45	19.16
NAT.W.	1	0	64	64	64.00
B & H	6	0	237	65	39.50

LAST SEASON: BOWLING

	O.	M.	R.	W.	AV.
TEST					
1ST-CLASS	8	0	66	0	–
INT					
RAL					
NAT.W.					
B & H					

CAREER: BATTING

	I.	N.O.	R.	H.S.	AV.
TEST	2	0	51	30	25.50
1ST-CLASS	327	26	12002	162	39.87
INT	1	0	24	24	24.00
RAL	96	1	2640	97	27.78
NAT.W.	23	1	832	113*	37.81
B & H	42	6	1304	113	36.22

CAREER: BOWLING

	O.	M.	R.	W.	AV.
TEST					
1ST-CLASS	53.5	1	378	3	126.00
INT					
RAL					
NAT.W.					
B & H					

32. In what year was the MCC founded: 1787, 1837, or 1907?

BENT, P.   Worcestershire

Full Name: Paul Bent
Role: Right-hand bat, off-break
bowler
Born: 1 May 1965, Worcester
Height: 6′ **Weight:** 12st 7lbs
Nickname: Benty, Bodell
County debut: 1985
1st-Class 50s scored: 3
1st-Class 100s scored: 1
Place in batting averages: 144th
av. 24.09
1st-Class catches 1989: 1 (career 1)
Parents: Emily and Roy
Family links with cricket: Brother
plays local club cricket
Education: Worcester Royal
Grammar School
Qualifications: 7 O-levels, 2 A-
levels; Senior award coach
Jobs outside cricket: Coaching abroad
Off-season 1989–90: 'Hopefully, buying a house and working in England.'
Cricketing superstitions or habits: Always wears headgear whilst batting, i.e.
helmet, cap, etc. Uses various pieces of lucky kit
Overseas teams played for: Birkenhead City CC, Auckland, New Zealand
1985–88; SAP, Pretoria, South Africa 1988–89
Cricketers particularly learnt from: County team mates, particularly Mark
Scott; John Bracewell (of New Zealand)
Cricketers particularly admired: Graeme Hick, Ian Botham, Richard Stemp
('one of the best leg-spinners to play for Barns Green CC')
Other sports played: Soccer, golf
Other sports followed: Supports West Bromwich Albion
Relaxations: Sleeping-in, dining out, listening to music
Extras: Hat-trick v Leicestershire 2nd XI, 1988. Fielded as 12th man for
England v India at Lord's while still on Lord's ground staff

LAST SEASON: BATTING

	I.	N.O.	R.	H.S.	AV.
TEST					
1ST-CLASS	22	0	530	144	24.09
INT					
RAL	1	0	2	2	2.00
NAT.W.					
B & H					

CAREER: BATTING

	I.	N.O.	R.	H.S.	AV.
TEST					
1ST-CLASS	29	1	655	144	23.39
INT					
RAL	3	0	51	36	17.00
NAT.W.					
B & H					

BEVINS, S. R. Worcestershire

Full Name: Stuart Roy Bevins
Role: Right-hand bat,
wicket-keeper
Born: 8 March 1967, Solihull,
West Midlands
Height: 5' 6½" **Weight:** 11st
Nickname: Budgie, Tot
County debut: 1989
Parents: Roy and Gwen
Marital status: Single
Family links with cricket: 'Grandad
and father played club cricket.
Brother Martyn plays for
Warwickshire Schools, Midlands
and English Public Schools. Other
brother Dave plays Subbuteo
cricket!'
Education: Solihull School; Solihull
College of Technology
Qualifications: 3 O-levels; Diploma in Business Studies
Jobs outside cricket: Worked at Cadbury's; sales assistant in sports shop;
groundsman work
Off-season 1989–90: 'Working in sports shop, plus hockey and cricket coaching.'
Cricketing superstitions or habits: 'Never retake guard when batting; use
same pair of keeping gloves for as long as possible.'
Overseas teams played for: Old Hararians, Zimbabwe 1984–85; Alexandria,
Zimbabwe 1985–86
Cricketers particularly learnt from: Alan Knott, Dave Houghton, Steve
Rhodes
Cricketers particularly admired: Rodney Marsh, Richard Hadlee, Ian
Botham
Other sports played: Hockey, Warwickshire U-21, football, golf
Other sports followed: 'I enjoy watching rugby internationals and American
football.'
Relaxations: Watching videos, listening to music, eating and drinking

Opinions on cricket: 'Second team venues and umpiring need to improve to give better breeding for first-class cricket.'

LAST SEASON: BATTING

	I.	N.O.	R.	H.S.	AV.
TEST					
1ST-CLASS	2	1	11	6*	11.00
INT					
RAL	–	–	–	–	–
NAT.W.					
B & H					

LAST SEASON: WICKET KEEPING

	C.	ST.			
TEST					
1ST-CLASS	7	–			
INT					
RAL	1	–			
NAT.W.					
B & H					

CAREER: BATTING

	I.	N.O.	R.	H.S.	AV.
TEST					
1ST-CLASS	2	1	11	6*	11.00
INT					
RAL	–	–	–	–	–
NAT.W.					
B & H					

CAREER: WICKET KEEPING

	C.	ST.			
TEST					
1ST-CLASS	7	–			
INT					
RAL	1	–			
NAT.W.					
B & H					

BICKNELL, D. J. Surrey

Full Name: Darren John Bicknell
Role: Left-hand opening bat, close fielder
Born: 24 June 1967, Guildford
Height: 6′ 5″ **Weight:** 13½st
Nickname: Denzil
County debut: 1987
1000 runs in a season: 1
1st-Class 50s scored: 12
1st-Class 100s scored: 5
One-Day 50s: 1
One-Day 100s: 1
Place in batting averages: 61st av. 35.69 (1988 199th av. 19.05)
1st-Class catches 1989: 15 (career 23)
Parents: Vic and Valerie
Marital status: Single
Family links with cricket: Brother Martin plays for Surrey, father is a qualified umpire; little brother Stuart plays for Guildford CC
Education: Robert Haining County Secondary, Mytchett, Hampshire
Qualifications: 2 O-levels, 5 CSEs, City and Guilds qualification in Recreation Administration and Sports Studies

Jobs outside cricket: Sports centre lifeguard; sales rep for Notts. Sport (artificial cricket pitches, etc.)

Off-season 1989–90: Working with Notts. Sport, and then touring Zimbabwe with England A

Cricketing superstitions or habits: 'Always try to keep same routine if it has been successful previously.'

Overseas tours: Surrey CCC to Sharjah 1988 and 1989; England A to Zimbabwe 1990

Overseas teams played for: Coburg CC, Melbourne 1987–88

Cricketers particularly learnt from: David Smith, Geoff Arnold, Graham Clinton

Cricketers particularly admired: Graham Gooch, Graham Clinton, Allan Border, Gordon Greenidge

Other sports played: 'Football for Mytchett FC and The Bowne FC, and any others that I can.'

Other sports followed: Aldershot FC and West Ham

Relaxations: Listening to good music, and eating out at good restaurants

Extras: Supporters Young Player of the Year 1987. 'Paul Atkins and myself were both out for 99, lbw on the same day, Paul at Southport on his first-class debut and I at Chelmsford in a 2nd XI game.'

Opinions on cricket: 'All second team games should be played on county grounds, and all groundsmen should endeavour to produce the best possible pitches at all times.'

Best batting performance: 119 Surrey v Yorkshire, The Oval 1989

Best bowling performance: 1-73 Surrey v Kent, Canterbury 1989

LAST SEASON: BATTING

	I.	N.O.	R.	H.S.	AV.
TEST					
1ST-CLASS	45	6	1392	119	35.69
INT					
RAL	7	1	151	56	25.16
NAT.W.	3	1	183	135*	91.50
B & H	3	0	32	13	10.66

LAST SEASON: BOWLING

	O.	M.	R.	W.	AV.
TEST					
1ST-CLASS	16.4	1	74	1	74.00
INT					
RAL					
NAT.W.					
B & H					

CAREER: BATTING

	I.	N.O.	R.	H.S.	AV.
TEST					
1ST-CLASS	84	10	2335	119	31.55
INT					
RAL	8	1	182	56	26.00
NAT.W.	3	1	183	135*	91.50
B & H	4	0	49	17	12.25

CAREER: BOWLING

	O.	M.	R.	W.	AV.
TEST					
1ST-CLASS	18.4	1	93	1	93.00
INT					
RAL					
NAT.W.					
B & H					

BICKNELL, M. P. — Surrey

Full Name: Martin Paul Bicknell
Role: Right-hand bat, right-arm
fast medium bowler
Born: 14 January 1969, Guildford
Height: 6′ 5″ **Weight:** 14st
Nickname: Bickers, Spandau
County debut: 1986
50 wickets in a season: 2
1st-Class 5 w. in innings: 7
Place in batting averages: 241st
av. 13.00
Place in bowling averages: 41st
av. 26.41 (1988 84th av. 30.22)
Strike rate 1989: 57.46 (career 55.37)
1st-Class catches 1989: 5 (career 17)
Parents: Vic and Valerie
Marital status: Single
Family links with cricket: Brother
Darren 'plays a bit'. Father is
qualified umpire. Younger brother Stuart played for Guildford Colts
Education: Robert Haining County Secondary, Mytchett, Hampshire
Qualifications: 2 O-levels, 5 CSEs
Jobs outside cricket: Coach
Off-season 1989–90: Touring Zimbabwe with England A
Cricketing superstitions or habits: 'Left pad on first, not that it helps!'
Overseas tours: Surrey Young Cricketers to Australia 1985–86; Young
England to Sri Lanka 1987; England YC to Australia 1988; England A to
Zimbabwe 1989–90
Overseas teams played for: Suburbs, New Zealand 1987–88
Cricketers particularly learnt from: Geoff Arnold, Mickey Stewart, Graham
Saville, Tim Lamb, Bob Cottam
Cricketers particularly admired: Richard Hadlee, Dennis Lillee, Sylvester
Clarke
Other sports played: Football, snooker
Other sports followed: 'Football. Anything except horse racing.'
Injuries 1989: Damaged left knee tendon – out for two weeks
Relaxations: Reading, music
Extras: Youngest player to play for Surrey since David Smith. On County
debut first two overs were maidens. Scored four successive ducks in June.
1986 won Supporters Young Player of the Year, also George Brittain Young
Player of the Year. Best bowling figures for Surrey for 30 years, 9 for 45.
Surrey Bowler of the Year 1989 (with A. J. Murphy)

63

Opinions on cricket: 'Championship should be 16 four-day games. Too many boring captains; there is nothing to lose by going for a result. The better team will always come out on top. Less cricket: the amount we play breeds mediocrity.'
Best batting performance: 40* Surrey v Gloucestershire, The Oval 1989
Best bowling performance: 9-45 Surrey v Cambridge University, Cambridge 1988

LAST SEASON: BATTING

	I.	N.O.	R.	H.S.	AV.
TEST					
1ST-CLASS	24	6	234	40*	13.00
INT					
RAL	4	1	13	7	4.33
NAT.W.	–	–	–	–	–
B & H	4	1	28	11*	9.33

CAREER: BATTING

	I.	N.O.	R.	H.S.	AV.
TEST					
1ST-CLASS	61	18	456	40*	10.60
INT					
RAL	13	6	54	13	7.71
NAT.W.	6	3	7	2*	2.33
B & H	6	2	29	11*	7.25

LAST SEASON: BOWLING

	O.	M.	R.	W.	AV.
TEST					
1ST-CLASS	622.3	136	1717	65	26.41
INT					
RAL	91	6	388	14	27.71
NAT.W.	33	5	105	8	13.12
B & H	41	6	155	5	31.00

CAREER: BOWLING

	O.	M.	R.	W.	AV.
TEST					
1ST-CLASS	1698.1	409	4825	184	26.22
INT					
RAL	297	14	1190	35	34.00
NAT.W.	125	17	405	15	27.00
B & H	77	11	273	14	19.50

BISHOP, I. R. Derbyshire

Full Name: Ian Raphael Bishop
Role: Right-hand bat, right-arm fast bowler
Born: 24 October 1967, Port of Spain, Trinidad, West Indies
Height: 6′ 5½″ **Weight:** 15st 10lbs
Nickname: Bish
County debut: 1989
Test debut: 1988–89
No. of Tests: 4
No. of One-Day Internationals: 17
1st-Class 5 w. in innings: 6
Place in batting averages: 262nd av. 10.00
Place in bowling averages: 26th av. 22.43
Strike rate 1989: 49.31 (career 47.61)
1st-Class catches 1989: 2 (career 10)
Parents: Randolph and Recalda

Marital status: Single
Family links with cricket: Uncle played for Young West Indies against England U-20 in the Caribbean 1984–85
Education: Belmont Primary and Belmont Secondary Schools
Qualifications: 2 O-levels
Off-season 1989–90: Touring with West Indies
Overseas tours: Trinidad school team to India 1984; West Indies to England 1988; West Indies to Australia 1988–89; West Indies to Sharjah 1988
Overseas teams played for: Tynedale CC, Northumberland 1987
Cricketers particularly learnt from: Malcolm Marshall
Cricketers particularly admired: Michael Holding, Gordon Greenidge
Other sports played: Basketball
Other sports followed: Athletics, soccer, basketball
Relaxations: Watching television, reading sports magazines and theological books
Extras: 'I am a born-again Christian.'
Opinions on cricket: 'I think that more preparation should go into the wickets at County level, thereby encouraging bowlers and batters to learn their trade more thoroughly. The present fining for slow over rates is ridiculous.'
Best batting performance: 30* West Indies v India, Port of Spain, Trinidad 1988–89
Best bowling performance: 6-39 West Indies v Kent, Canterbury 1988

LAST SEASON: BATTING

	I.	N.O.	R.	H.S.	AV.
TEST					
1ST-CLASS	20	2	180	28*	10.00
INT					
RAL	1	1	16	16*	–
NAT.W.					
B & H					

CAREER: BATTING

	I.	N.O.	R.	H.S.	AV.
TEST	5	3	55	30*	27.50
1ST-CLASS	50	17	387	28*	11.72
INT	6	5	43	33*	43.00
RAL	1	1	16	16*	–
NAT.W.					
B & H					

LAST SEASON: BOWLING

	O.	M.	R.	W.	AV.
TEST					
1ST-CLASS	337	66	920	41	22.43
INT					
RAL	8	0	51	1	51.00
NAT.W.					
B & H					

CAREER: BOWLING

	O.	M.	R.	W.	AV.
TEST	137	38	371	16	23.18
1ST-CLASS	926.2	156	2801	118	23.73
INT	152.1	7	581	29	20.03
RAL	8	0	51	1	51.00
NAT.W.					
B & H					

BLAKEY, R. J.   Yorkshire

Full Name: Richard John Blakey
Role: Right-hand bat, occasional
wicket-keeper, right-arm medium
bowler
Born: 15 January 1967, Huddersfield
Height: 5′ 10″ **Weight:** 11st 6lbs
Nickname: Dick, Mutley, Warren
County debut: 1985
County cap: 1987
1000 runs in a season: 2
1st-Class 50s scored: 19
1st-Class 100s scored: 3
1st-Class 200s scored: 1
One-Day 50s: 9
Place in batting averages: 85th
av. 32.19 (1988 164th av. 22.30)
1st-Class catches 1989: 43 (career 114
+ 4 stumpings)
Parents: Brian and Pauline
Marital status: Single
Family links with cricket: Father played local cricket
Education: Woodhouse Primary; Rastrick Grammar School
Qualifications: 4 O-levels, NCA Coaching Certificate
Off-season 1989–90: Touring Zimbabwe with England A. Also playing and
coaching in Zimbabwe
Overseas tours: Young England to West Indies 1985; Yorkshire CCC to Saint
Lucia 1987; England A to Zimbabwe 1989–90
Overseas teams played for: Waverley CC, Melbourne 1985–86, 1986–87

LAST SEASON: BATTING

	I.	N.O.	R.	H.S.	AV.
TEST					
1ST-CLASS	39	3	1159	97	32.19
INT					
RAL	16	3	655	94*	50.38
NAT.W.	2	0	39	22	19.50
B & H	4	0	81	39	20.25

CAREER: BATTING

	I.	N.O.	R.	H.S.	AV.
TEST					
1ST-CLASS	132	14	3722	204*	31.54
INT					
RAL	22	6	750	94*	46.87
NAT.W.	5	1	57	22	14.25
B & H	11	2	245	58	27.22

LAST SEASON: WICKET KEEPING

	C.	ST.			
TEST					
1ST-CLASS	33	2			
INT					
RAL	3	–			
NAT.W.					
B & H					

CAREER: WICKET KEEPING

	C.	ST.			
TEST					
1ST-CLASS	65	4			
INT					
RAL	7	–			
NAT.W.					
B & H					

Cricketers particularly learnt from: My father Brian, Doug Padgett, Steve Oldham, Martyn Moxon and all Yorkshire's capped players
Cricketers particularly admired: Arnie Sidebottom, Geoff Boycott
Other sports played: Squash, snooker
Other sports followed: 'Football, most other sports but not ice skating.'
Relaxations: Music and watching Leeds United FC. Keeps rabbits and guinea pigs
Extras: Established himself in Huddersfield League. Made record 2nd XI score – 273* v Northamptonshire 1986. Played as wicket-keeper when Bairstow was injured in 1989. Yorkshire's Young Player of the Year 1989
Opinions on cricket: 'Too much cricket is played. I would like to see 16 four-day games, which would make for a much more fair Championship.'
Best batting performance: 204* Yorkshire v Gloucestershire, Leeds 1987
Best bowling performance: 1-68 Yorkshire v Nottinghamshire, Sheffield 1986

BODEN, D. J. P.   Middlesex

Full Name: David Jonathan Peter Boden
Role: Right-hand bat, right-arm fast-medium bowler
Born: 26 November 1970, Eccleshall, Stafford
Height: 6' 3" **Weight:** 13st 5lbs
Nickname: Boders
County debut: 1989
1st-Class catches 1989: 1 (career 1)
Parents: Peter and Mary
Marital status: Single
Family links with cricket: Uncle played in local league; two other uncles played for Shropshire Gents
Education: Eccleshall Primary and Middle School; Alleynes High School, Stone, Staffs

Qualifications: 4 O-levels, 3 CSEs, B.TEC Diploma in Business Studies
Jobs outside cricket: Work in restaurant and bar
Off-season 1989–90: Playing cricket in New Zealand
Cricketing superstitions or habits: Always puts left sock, boot and pad on before right ones
Cricketers particularly learnt from: Don Wilson, Brian Reynolds, Martin Robinson, Alan Hill

Cricketers particularly admired: Ian Botham, Richard Hadlee, Neil Foster

Other sports played: Squash, rugby, pool

Other sports followed: Rugby, tennis

Relaxations: 'I enjoy watching TV comedy, swimming and listening to music – pop and rock.'

Extras: Played for village team Eccleshall CC and then Stone CC. Played tennis and table tennis for Staffordshire U-13

Opinions on cricket: 'More cricket is played at professional level now which is probably a good thing but I feel more time to train and tone yourself up would be welcome. A lot more four-day cricket should be played in England which would give more time for a batsman to build an innings, and a bowler should learn to bowl in more test match conditions. Wickets in these matches should be top quality; that is, with an even pace and bounce, and quick enough to carry to the keeper. This would give both batsmen and bowlers an equal chance of showing their skills.'

Best bowling performance: 4-11 Middlesex v Oxford University, Oxford 1989

LAST SEASON: BOWLING

	O.	M.	R.	W.	AV.
TEST					
1ST-CLASS	14.5	7	26	4	6.50
INT					
RAL					
NAT.W.					
B & H					

CAREER: BOWLING

	O.	M.	R.	W.	AV.
TEST					
1ST-CLASS	14.5	7	26	4	6.50
INT					
RAL					
NAT.W.					
B & H					

33. What's the highest score made at Lord's, and by whom?

34. What is the longest ever recorded hit?

BOILING, J. Surrey

Full Name: James Boiling
Role: Right-hand bat, off-break
bowler, gully fielder
Born: 8 April 1968, New Delhi,
India
Height: 6' 2½" **Weight:** 12st 11lbs
Nickname: Boilers
County debut: 1988
1st-Class catches 1989: 1 (career 1)
Parents: Graham and Geraldine
Marital status: Single
Family links with cricket: 'Both
grandfathers played club cricket.
Father played school 2nd XI cricket.
Brother turns out for club 4th XI.
Mother played rounders!'
Education: Rutlish School, Merton;
Durham University
Qualifications: 10 O-levels, 3
A-levels; studying for a BA Hons Degree in History
Jobs outside cricket: Stacking shelves in Sainsbury's, clerical assistant in
passport office 'and valet to Ray Alikhan!'
Off-season 1989–90: At university
Cricketing superstitions or habits: 'Don't like bowling in a long-sleeved shirt.'
Overseas tours: Surrey Schools U-19 to Australia 1985–86; Young England to
Australia, Youth World Cup 1988
Cricketers particularly learnt from: Jim Laker, Chris Waller, Mickey
Stewart, Bob Cottam
Cricketers particularly admired: Jim Laker, Nasser Hussain, Mike Gatting
('the best destroyer of spin bowling in English cricket') and Graham Thorpe
('the most exciting young batsman in English cricket')
Other sports played: Rowing, swimming
Relaxations: 'Cinema, a wide variety of music, keeping members of the
Surrey dressing-room amused, practising various impersonations, discussing
aspects of the county circuit with Graham Thorpe.'
Extras: Surrey Young Cricketer of the Year 1985 and 1987. *Daily Telegraph*
Bowler of the Year (U-19) 1986. Member of the 1989 successful Combined
Universities team. Playing for Combined Universities against own county,
Surrey, in B & H, 1989, took 3 for 9 in 8 overs, winning Gold Award
Opinions on cricket: 'This season has merely reinforced Oxbridge's lack of
credibility at first-class level. The sooner Oxford and Cambridge lose their
first-class status, the better, as their admissions policies are not relaxing with

69

regard to sportsmen and particularly cricketers. Don't agree with those who argue that by allowing overseas cricketers to play in the County Championship, we teach them how to beat us at our own game – look at players like Mark Taylor, Dean Jones and Geoff Lawson who have played a major part in Australia winning the Ashes in 1989 but have never experienced county cricket before. The amount of travelling we do in a season must be reduced, or coaches must be provided to take players to *all* away games: otherwise I can see cricketers being killed in car crashes on the M1. Despite the all-pervasive influence of sponsorship, increasing commercialism, and an ever critical media presence in the game, cricketers should not lose sight of the fact that we are privileged to be paid for playing the greatest game in the world.'

Best batting performance: 15 Surrey v Glamorgan, The Oval 1989
Best bowling performance: 3-40 Surrey v Lancashire, Old Trafford 1989

LAST SEASON: BATTING

	I.	N.O.	R.	H.S.	AV.
TEST					
1ST-CLASS	4	2	29	15	14.50
INT					
RAL					
NAT.W.					
B & H	3	3	4	2*	–

LAST SEASON: BOWLING

	O.	M.	R.	W.	AV.
TEST					
1ST-CLASS	66.4	26	162	5	32.40
INT					
RAL					
NAT.W.					
B & H	49.3	7	189	5	37.80

CAREER: BATTING

	I.	N.O.	R.	H.S.	AV.
TEST					
1ST-CLASS	6	3	38	15	12.66
INT					
RAL					
NAT.W.					
B & H	7	6	20	9*	20.00

CAREER: BOWLING

	O.	M.	R.	W.	AV.
TEST					
1ST-CLASS	81.4	29	202	5	40.40
INT					
RAL					
NAT.W.					
B & H	88.4	7	359	10	35.90

35. Who holds the record for the most consecutive county appearances?

36. What was the significance of F. Wasserman in the French National side v MCC last season?

BOON, T. J.   Leicestershire

Full Name: Timothy James Boon
Role: Right-hand bat, right-arm
medium bowler
Born: 1 November 1961,
Doncaster, South Yorkshire
Height: 5′ 11½″ **Weight:** 12st 3lbs
Nickname: Ted Moon, Cod
County debut: 1980
County cap: 1986
1000 runs in a season: 4
1st-Class 50s scored: 32
1st-Class 100s scored: 6
One-Day 50s: 3
Place in batting averages: 93rd
av. 30.73 (1988 158th av. 22.95)
1st-Class catches 1989: 13 (career
67)
Parents: Jeffrey and Elizabeth
Marital status: Single
Family links with cricket: Father
played club cricket
Education: Mill Lane Primary; Edlington Comprehensive. Three months at
Doncaster Art School
Qualifications: 1 A-level, 6 O-levels. Coaching qualifications
Jobs outside cricket: Worked with Leicester Dyers, 1986–1987
Cricketing superstitions or habits: 'Constantly changing.'
Overseas tours: Toured the Caribbean with England Young Cricketers 1980,
as captain; Leicestershire CCC to Zimbabwe 1981

LAST SEASON: BATTING

	I.	N.O.	R.	H.S.	AV.
TEST					
1ST-CLASS	39	5	1045	80*	30.73
INT					
RAL	5	1	69	39*	17.25
NAT.W.	1	0	24	24	24.00
B & H	4	1	67	40	22.33

CAREER: BATTING

	I.	N.O.	R.	H.S.	AV.
TEST					
1ST-CLASS	224	30	5945	144	30.64
INT					
RAL	58	10	925	61	19.27
NAT.W.	7	3	96	24	24.00
B & H	15	5	318	58*	31.80

LAST SEASON: BOWLING

	O.	M.	R.	W.	AV.
TEST					
1ST-CLASS	7.5	0	41	1	41.00
INT					
RAL					
NAT.W.					
B & H					

CAREER: BOWLING

	O.	M.	R.	W.	AV.
TEST					
1ST-CLASS	57.2	7	290	6	48.33
INT					
RAL	2	0	14	0	–
NAT.W.	1	0	2	0	–
B & H					

Overseas teams played for: Old Hararians, Zimbabwe 1980–81; Ceylon CC, Colombo 1981–82; Pirates CC, Durban 1982–83, 1984–85
Cricketers particularly learnt from: The late Mike Fearnley, Ken Higgs, Chris Balderstone, Peter Willey
Cricketers particularly admired: 'Those who make the most of their ability.'
Other sports played: 'Enjoy playing and watching all sports.'
Relaxations: Sleeping, barbecue in garden, dining out
Extras: Captain England Young Cricketers Tour West Indies 1980; Captain England Young Cricketers v Indian Young Cricketers 1981; Most Promising Schoolboy Cricketer 1979. Missed 1985 season due to broken leg sustained in a car crash in South Africa the previous winter
Best batting performance: 144 Leicestershire v Gloucestershire, Leicester 1984
Best bowling performance: 3-40 Leicestershire v Yorkshire, Leicester 1986

BOOTH, P. A. Warwickshire

Full Name: Paul Antony Booth
Role: Left-hand bat, left-arm spin bowler
Born: 5 September 1965, Huddersfield
Height: 6′ **Weight:** 11st 7lbs
Nickname: Boot, Spike
County debut: 1982 (Yorkshire)
1st-Class 5 w. in innings: 1
Place in batting averages: — (1988 220th av. 16.00)
Place in bowling averages: — (1988 99th av. 32.81)
1st-Class catches 1989: 2 (career 7)
Parents: Colin and Margaret
Marital status: Single
Family links with cricket: Father played local cricket for over 30 years
Education: Meltham Church of England; Honley High School
Qualifications: Mathematics, Woodwork
Jobs outside cricket: Joiner, postman

Off-season 1989–90: Working as a postman. Training and getting fit for the new season
Overseas tours: Young England to the West Indies 1985

Cricketers particularly learnt from: Doug Padgett, Phil Carrick
Cricketers particularly admired: Derek Underwood
Other sports played: Football, golf
Other sports followed: Football – Leeds United
Relaxations: Listening to tapes and records; round of golf
Extras: Made debut when 17 years 3 days. First wicket was Allan Lamb. Released by Yorkshire at end of 1989 season, and joined Warwickshire
Opinions on cricket: 'Bring back uncovered pitches and uncovered run-ups, which would bring spinners back into the game. Sport should be left out of politics.'
Best batting performance: 33* Yorkshire v Lancashire, Old Trafford 1988
Best bowling performance: 5-98 Yorkshire v Lancashire, Old Trafford 1988

LAST SEASON: BATTING

	I.	N.O.	R.	H.S.	AV.
TEST					
1ST-CLASS	3	3	15	8*	–
INT					
RAL	–	–	–	–	–
NAT.W.					
B & H	–	–	–	–	–

LAST SEASON: BOWLING

	O.	M.	R.	W.	AV.
TEST					
1ST-CLASS	26	11	47	1	47.00
INT					
RAL	3	0	10	0	–
NAT.W.					
B & H	4	0	19	0	–

CAREER: BATTING

	I.	N.O.	R.	H.S.	AV.
TEST					
1ST-CLASS	29	9	193	33*	9.65
INT					
RAL	–	–	–	–	–
NAT.W.	1	1	6	6*	–
B & H	1	0	1	1	1.00

CAREER: BOWLING

	O.	M.	R.	W.	AV.
TEST					
1ST-CLASS	652.5	216	1517	35	43.34
INT					
RAL	11	0	67	1	67.00
NAT.W.	11	2	33	0	–
B & H	12	0	47	2	23.50

---

37. Who never missed a match for Yorkshire from debut to final appearance?

38. Who made the most appearances ever for any first-class county?

BOTHAM, I. T. Worcestershire

Full Name: Ian Terrence Botham
Role: Right-hand bat, right-arm
fast-medium bowler, slip fielder
Born: 24 November 1955, Heswall,
Cheshire
Height: 6′ 2″ **Weight:** 15st 5lbs
Nickname: Guy, Both, Beefy
County debut: 1974 (Somerset), 1987
(Worcestershire)
County cap: 1976 (Somerset), 1987
(Worcestershire)
Benefit: 1984 (£90,822)
Test debut: 1977
No. of Tests: 97
No. of One-Day Internationals: 98
1000 runs in a season: 4
50 wickets in a season: 7
1st-Class 50s scored: 82
1st-Class 100s scored: 31
1st-Class 200s scored: 2
1st-Class 5 w. in innings: 56
1st-Class 10 w. in match: 8
One-Day 50s: 33
One-Day 100s: 6
Place in batting averages: 198th av. 18.21
Place in bowling averages: 42nd av. 25.30
Strike rate 1989: 53.21 (career 67.53)
1st-Class catches 1989: 14 (career 317)
Parents: Les and Marie
Wife and date of marriage: Kathryn, 31 January 1976
Children: Liam James, 26 August 1977; Sarah Lianne, 3 February 1979;
Rebecca Kate, 13 November 1985
Family links with cricket: Father played for Navy and Fleet Air Arm; mother
played for VAD nursing staff
Education: Millford Junior School; Buckler's Mead Secondary School,
Yeovil
Overseas tours: England to Pakistan and New Zealand 1977–78; Australia
1978–79; Australia and India 1979–80; West Indies 1981 as captain; India
1981–82; Australia and New Zealand 1982–83; West Indies 1986
Cricketers particularly learnt from: Brian Close
Cricketers particularly admired: Viv Richards, David Gower, Allan Border,
Andy Roberts ('the fastest bowler I ever faced')

Off-season 1989–90: Touring UK with own one-man talk-show. Captain of the celebrity team in the BBC quiz show, 'A Question of Sport'

Other sports played: Captained school soccer team, and has played for Scunthorpe United, making debut as striker v Bournemouth in March 1980. Offered terms by Crystal Palace. Now plays for Yeovil Town. U-16 Somerset champion, badminton doubles

Other sports followed: Rugby, football, American sports, 'virtually anything'

Injuries 1989: Had to withdraw from First Test v Australia after having top-edged a ball from Steve Barwick of Glamorgan into his face, fracturing his cheek bone – out for three weeks. Dislocated and fractured finger on right hand – out for two weeks

Relaxations: Golf, shooting, fishing (salmon and trout), flying

Extras: Captain of England 1980–81. Took five Australian wickets in his first day of Test Match cricket aged 21. Played for County 2nd XI 1971. On MCC staff 1972–73. One of *Wisden*'s Five Cricketers of the Year, 1977. Subject of 'This is Your Life' television programme in November 1981. Was Best Man at Viv Richards' wedding in March 1981 in Antigua. Voted BBC TV Sportsview Sporting Personality of 1981. Having a go at baseball in Los Angeles in September 1981 easily exceeded the striking rate of established American baseball stars: he complained that Americans could not pitch the ball fast enough. Scored fastest 100 of 1982 and 1985 seasons. Scored 200 in 272 minutes for England v India at The Oval, 9 July 1982, third fastest Test double century by an Englishman, after Walter Hammond (240 mins v New Zealand in 1932) and Denis Compton (245 mins v Pakistan in 1954). Crashed two £12,000 sports cars at 100 mph in same afternoon in May 1982. Published books include *High, Wide and Handsome*, an account of his record-breaking 1985 season and *It Sort of Clicks*, in collaboration with his former Somerset colleague Peter Roebuck, and *Cricket My Way* with Jack Bannister. First cricketer since W. G. Grace to have painting commissioned by National Portrait Gallery. Captain of Somerset 1984–85. Holds record for having scored 1000 runs and taken 100 wickets in fewest Test matches. First player to score a century and take 8 wickets in an innings in a Test Match, v Pakistan at Lord's in 1978. Most sixes in a first-class season 1985. Left Somerset at the beginning of 1987 to join Worcestershire after Somerset had decided not to renew the contracts of Richards and Garner. Missed nearly all 1988 season with back injury. Captains his own team on BBC's *A Question of Sport*. Appeared on Desert Island Discs in November 1989, when his choice of music ranged from Elton John and the Beatles, to Beethoven and 'Land of Hope and Glory'. The one book he wanted was an encyclopedia of fishes, and his luxury was a fishing rod.

Opinions of cricket: 'The Comprehensive (school) system is a disgrace. How can we bring our youngsters on when there are 3000 kids in one school, and no facilities for cricket. When I was a lad we would stay on after school, being taught how to play by an experienced cricket master. Now the kids are just not being given the chance.'

Best batting performance: 228 Somerset v Gloucestershire, Taunton 1980
Best bowling performance: 8-34 England v Pakistan, Lord's 1978

LAST SEASON: BATTING

	I.	N.O.	R.	H.S.	AV.
TEST	4	0	62	46	15.50
1ST-CLASS	20	1	357	73	18.78
INT	3	1	37	25*	18.50
RAL	8	0	230	70	28.75
NAT.W.	1	0	53	53	53.00
B & H	4	0	78	37	19.50

LAST SEASON: BOWLING

	O.	M.	R.	W.	AV.
TEST	80	15	241	3	80.33
1ST-CLASS	416.4	94	1176	53	22.18
INT	32.1	1	113	2	56.50
RAL	58	3	282	12	23.50
NAT.W.	35	3	157	11	14.27
B & H	31	2	127	9	14.11

CAREER: BATTING

	I.	N.O.	R.	H.S.	AV.
TEST	154	5	5119	208	34.35
1ST-CLASS	379	33	11722	228	33.87
INT	89	12	1730	72	22.46
RAL	147	22	4073	175*	32.58
NAT.W.	31	6	979	101	39.16
B & H	59	7	1199	126*	23.05

CAREER: BOWLING

	O.	M.	R.	W.	AV.
TEST	259.4 3200.5	42 720	10633	376	28.27
1ST-CLASS	190.3 8141.4	43 1876	17764	685	25.93
INT	38.7 826.5	2 94	3511	118	29.75
RAL	1055.2	64	4698	207	22.69
NAT.W.	388.3	59	1348	53	25.43
B & H	661.4	122	2265	112	20.22

BOWLER, P. D. Derbyshire

Full Name: Peter Duncan Bowler
Role: Right-hand opening bat, off-spinner
Born: 30 July 1963, Plymouth; Australia
Height: 6′ 2″ **Weight:** 13st
Nickname: Skippy
County debut: 1986 (Leicestershire), 1988 (Derbyshire)
1000 runs in a season: 2
1st-Class 50s scored: 20
1st-Class 100s scored: 7
One-Day 50s: 8
Place in batting averages: 103rd av. 29.71 (1988 21st av. 46.62)
1st-Class catches 1989: 22 (career 37 + 1 stumping)
Parents: Peter and Etta
Marital status: Single
Education: Daramalan College, Canberra, Australia
Qualifications: Australian Yr 12 Certificate

Overseas teams played for: Manly CC 1982; Westbury CC 1983–87
Cricketers particularly learnt from: Rob Jeffery, Bill Carracher, Gus Valence
Cricketers particularly admired: Greg Chappell, Richard Hadlee, Dennis Lillee
Other sports played: Rugby union
Relaxations: Music, reading, newspapers. Playing sports other than cricket. Relaxing with family
Extras: First Leicestershire player to score a first-class hundred on debut (100 not out v Hampshire 1986). Moved to Derbyshire at end of 1987 season and then scored a century for Derbyshire on his debut for them v Cambridge University
Best batting performance: 159* Derbyshire v Essex, Chesterfield 1988
Best bowling performance: 2-1 Derbyshire v Leicestershire, Derby 1989

LAST SEASON: BATTING

	I.	N.O.	R.	H.S.	AV.
TEST					
1ST-CLASS	46	1	1337	157	29.71
INT					
RAL	15	2	468	71	36.00
NAT.W.	2	0	17	9	8.50
B & H	4	0	42	17	10.50

LAST SEASON: BOWLING

	O.	M.	R.	W.	AV.
TEST					
1ST-CLASS	32	5	138	3	46.00
INT					
RAL					
NAT.W.					
B & H					

CAREER: BATTING

	I.	N.O.	R.	H.S.	AV.
TEST					
1ST-CLASS	102	7	3326	159*	35.01
INT					
RAL	40	3	931	71	25.16
NAT.W.	5	0	82	46	16.40
B & H	10	0	233	64	23.30

CAREER: BOWLING

	O.	M.	R.	W.	AV.
TEST					
1ST-CLASS	232.3	43	812	10	81.20
INT					
RAL	32	1	185	4	46.25
NAT.W.	3	0	14	0	–
B & H	41	7	125	4	31.25

39. Who has captained a Test side most often, and how often?
40. What is the highest first-class score and by whom?

Full Name: Nigel Edwin Briers
Role: Right-hand bat, right-arm medium bowler, cover fielder
Born: 15 January 1955, Leicester
Height: 6' **Weight:** 12st 5lbs
Nickname: Kudu
County debut: 1971 (aged 16 yrs 104 days)
County cap: 1981
1000 runs in a season: 6
1st-Class 50s scored: 57
1st-Class 100s scored: 13
1st-Class 200s scored: 1
One-Day 50s: 29
One-Day 100s: 3
Place in batting averages: 132nd av. 25.87 (1988 63rd av. 34.23)
1st-Class catches 1989: 6 (career 106)
Parents: Leonard Arthur Roger and Eveline
Wife and date of marriage: Suzanne Mary Tudor, 3 September 1977
Children: Michael Edward Tudor, 25 March 1983; Andrew James Tudor, 30 June 1986
Family links with cricket: Father was captain and wicket-keeper of Narborough and Littlethorpe CC, first division of Leicestershire League, for 15 years. Mother was scorer for team. Father was Captain of South Leicestershire Representative XI and played for the Royal Marines in the same team as Trevor Bailey. Cousin, Norman Briers, played for Leicestershire once in 1967
Education: Lutterworth Grammar School; Borough Road College
Qualifications: Qualified teacher (Certificate of Education), BEd Hons, MCC Advanced Coach
Jobs outside cricket: Lecturer in Physical Education at Leicester Polytechnic
Off-season 1989–90: Teaching PE and history at Ludgrove School
Overseas tours: Derrick Robins' XI to South America 1979; MCC to Far East 1981; Leicestershire CCC to Zimbabwe 1981
Cricketers particularly learnt from: 'My father, Maurice Hallam, Jack Birkenshaw, Ray Illingworth.'
Extras: Captained Leicestershire in David Gower's absence in 1988. Vice-captain of Leicestershire 1988, 1989. Captain in 1990

Best batting performance: 201* Leicestershire v Warwickshire, Edgbaston 1983
Best bowling performance: 4-29 Leicestershire v Derbyshire, Leicester 1985

LAST SEASON: BATTING

	I.	N.O.	R.	H.S.	AV.
TEST					
1ST-CLASS	44	3	1061	73	25.87
INT					
RAL	15	1	241	45	17.21
NAT.W.	2	0	23	15	11.50
B & H	4	0	80	71	20.00

CAREER: BATTING

	I.	N.O.	R.	H.S.	AV.
TEST					
1ST-CLASS	418	40	11124	201*	29.42
INT					
RAL	151	22	4213	119*	32.65
NAT.W.	25	2	433	59	18.82
B & H	36	2	566	71*	16.64

LAST SEASON: BOWLING

	O.	M.	R.	W.	AV.
TEST					
1ST-CLASS					
INT					
RAL					
NAT.W.					
B & H					

CAREER: BOWLING

	O.	M.	R.	W.	AV.
TEST					
1ST-CLASS	341.2	70	988	32	30.87
INT					
RAL	80.2	5	384	10	38.40
NAT.W.	14	0	75	6	12.50
B & H	55	3	266	3	88.66

BROAD, B. C.   Nottinghamshire

Full Name: Brian Christopher Broad
Role: Left-hand bat, right-arm medium bowler
Born: 29 September 1957, Bristol
Height: 6′ 4″ **Weight:** 14st 7lbs
Nickname: Walter, Broadie
County debut: 1979 (Gloucestershire), 1984 (Nottinghamshire)
County cap: 1981 (Gloucestershire), 1984 (Nottinghamshire)
Test debut: 1984
No. of Tests: 25
No. of One-Day Internationals: 34
1000 runs in a season: 7
1st-Class 50s scored: 84
1st-Class 100s scored: 28
One-Day 50s: 50
One-Day 100s: 5

Place in batting averages: 44th av. 38.76 (1988 132nd av. 25.64)
1st-Class catches 1989: 24 (career 149)

Parents: Nancy and Kenneth
Wife and date of marriage: Carole Ann, 14 July 1979
Children: Gemma Joanne, 14 January 1984; Stuart Christopher John, 24 June 1986
Family links with cricket: Father and grandfather both played local cricket. Father member of Gloucestershire Committee until retired
Education: Colston's School, Bristol; St Paul's College, Cheltenham
Qualifications: 5 O-levels, NCA advanced coach
Jobs outside cricket: Runs his own furniture import business
Off-season 1989–90: Touring South Africa with unofficial English team
Cricketing superstitions or habits: Puts left pad on first
Overseas tours: Gloucestershire CCC to Malawi 1978 and Barbados 1980; British Colleges to Trinidad and Barbados 1979; English Counties to Zimbabwe 1985; International XI to Jamaica 1985; England to West Indies 1986; World Cup, Pakistan, New Zealand and Australia 1987–88
Overseas teams played for: Somerville CC, Melbourne 1979–80, Takapuna CC, Auckland 1982–83, 1983–84, Orange Free State 1985–86 (captain)
Cricketers particularly learnt from: Reg Sinfield, Sadiq Mohammed, John Sullivan
Cricketers particularly admired: Graham Gooch, Richard Hadlee, Clive Rice
Other sports played: Played Rugby for English Colleges, Bristol United, St Paul's College, and Clifton
Relaxations: 'Playing any sport, spending time with my family.'
Extras: Struck down by osteomyelitis at age 15. First played adult cricket for Downend CC, where W. G. Grace learnt to play; then Long Ashton CC; Gloucestershire U-19s; Gloucestershire Young Cricketers'; NAYC v MCC Schools. Played with Allan Border in Gloucestershire 2nd XI. Played with Tim Robinson in 1977 for NAYC v Young Australians. Published autobiography *Home Thoughts from Abroad* in 1987. Hit three centuries in a row in Test series v Australia, 1986–87. Uses a bat weighing 3lbs

LAST SEASON: BATTING

	I.	N.O.	R.	H.S.	AV.
TEST	4	0	82	37	20.50
1ST-CLASS	37	2	1430	144	40.85
INT					
RAL	9	0	267	71	29.66
NAT.W.	2	0	67	63	33.50
B & H	7	0	344	106	49.14

LAST SEASON: BOWLING

	O.	M.	R.	W.	AV.
TEST					
1ST-CLASS					
INT					
RAL					
NAT.W.					
B & H	7.2	0	26	1	26.00

CAREER: BATTING

	I.	N.O.	R.	H.S.	AV.
TEST	44	2	1661	162	39.54
1ST-CLASS	397	28	13195	171	35.75
INT	34	0	1361	106	40.02
RAL	118	6	3630	104*	32.14
NAT.W.	25	0	887	98	35.48
B & H	46	2	1379	122	31.34

CAREER: BOWLING

	O.	M.	R.	W.	AV.
TEST	1	0	4	0	–
1ST-CLASS	269.5	60	1032	16	64.50
INT	1	0	6	0	–
RAL	111.3	4	602	19	31.68
NAT.W.					
B & H	58	2	308	6	51.33

Opinions on cricket: 'I would have loved playing as an amateur. I am an unashamed traditionalist.'
Best batting performance: 171 Nottinghamshire v Derbyshire, Derby 1985
Best bowling performance: 2-14 Gloucestershire v West Indies, Bristol 1980

BROWN, A. M.   Derbyshire

Full Name: Andrew Mark Brown
Role: Left-hand bat, right-arm medium bowler
Born: 6 November 1964, Heanor, Derbyshire
Height: 5' 9" **Weight:** 10½st
Nickname: Brownie
County debut: 1985
1st-Class 50s scored: 1
1st-Class catches 1989: 1 (career 2)
Parents: John and Marion
Marital status: Single
Family links with cricket: 'Father, John, County Coaching Organiser for Derbyshire; brother Stephen played in County Junior teams.'
Education: Langley Mill Junior School; Aldercar Comprehensive School; South-East Derbyshire College of PE
Qualifications: 8 O-levels, 1 A-level; Coaching Certificate
Off-season 1989–90: 'Playing and coaching in Palmerston North, New Zealand.'
Cricketing superstitions or habits: 'Left pad on first.'
Overseas teams played for: Counties CC, New Zealand 1983–84; Metro CC, Pukekohe, New Zealand 1983–84; Old Boys Hastings, Hastings, New Zealand 1984–85, 1985–86; Hawkes Bay, New Zealand 1984–86; Manawatu, New Zealand 1988–89; Kia Toa University, Palmerston North, New Zealand 1988–89
Cricketers particularly learnt from: John Wright, John Wiltshire, Neil Weightman
Cricketers particularly admired: John Wright, Bob Taylor
Other sports played: 'Don't have time!'
Other sports followed: Football: season ticket at Nottingham Forest
Injuries 1989: Twisted ankle – off for 2 weeks in July

Relaxations: 'Lying on beaches and attempting to surf.'
Extras: 'Had opening partnership of 240-0 dec with Neil Weightman for Langley Mill; neither of us scored a hundred.'
Opinions on cricket: 'Players should have right to go to South Africa as individuals, and coach without any penalty.'
Best batting performance: 65 Derbyshire v Nottinghamshire, Derby 1989

LAST SEASON: BATTING

	I.	N.O.	R.	H.S.	AV.
TEST					
1ST-CLASS	4	0	109	65	27.25
INT					
RAL					
NAT.W.					
B & H					

CAREER: BATTING

	I.	N.O.	R.	H.S.	AV.
TEST					
1ST-CLASS	7	1	162	65	27.00
INT					
RAL	1	1	2	2*	–
NAT.W.					
B & H					

BROWN, K. R.   Middlesex

Full Name: Keith Robert Brown
Role: Right-hand bat, wicket-keeper
Born: 18 March 1963, Edmonton
Height: 5′ 11″ **Weight:** 13st 7lbs
Nickname: Browny, Gloves, Scarface
County debut: 1984
1st-Class 50s scored: 14
1st-Class 100s scored: 3
One-Day 50s: 1
One-Day 100s: 1
Place in batting averages: 5th av. 58.00 (1988 110th av. 28.34)
1st-Class catches 1989: 11 (career 75)
Parents: Kenneth William and Margaret Sonia
Wife and date of marriage: Marie, 3 November 1984
Children: Zachary, 24 February 1987
Family links with cricket: Brother Gary was on Middlesex staff for 3 years and now plays for Durham. Father is qualified umpire and played club cricket
Education: Chace Boys' School, Enfield
Qualifications: French O-level; Junior and Senior Cricket Coach
Jobs outside cricket: Plasterer, light engineering, painter, decorator

Off-season 1989–90: Plastering. Playing rugby. Spending as much time as possible with wife and family

Cricketing superstitions or habits: Nelson 111. Puts left pad on first

Overseas tours: NCA to Denmark 1981. Pre-season trips with Middlesex to La Manga 1985 and 1986

Overseas teams played for: Sydney University 1988–89

Cricketers particularly learnt from: Father, Clive Radley

Cricketers particularly admired: Clive Radley

Other sports played: Rugby, tennis, snooker. 'I'll have a go at most sports.'

Other sports followed: All of them except motor racing, especially boxing, football and rugby

Relaxations: 'Playing with young son, Zachary; taking family dogs for long walks, ending up with a pint or two at the local!'

Extras: Had promising boxing career but gave it up in order to concentrate on cricket. Picked to play rugby for Essex

Opinions on cricket: 'While four-day cricket provides better preparation for Test matches, I think that it makes batsmen get into a more negative state of mind.'

Best batting performance: 131* Middlesex v Nottinghamshire, Lord's 1988

Best bowling performance: 2-7 Middlesex v Gloucestershire, Bristol 1987

LAST SEASON: BATTING

	I.	N.O.	R.	H.S.	AV.
TEST					
1ST-CLASS	12	3	522	91	58.00
INT					
RAL	6	1	59	20*	11.80
NAT.W.					
B & H	1	0	12	12	12.00

LAST SEASON: BOWLING

	O.	M.	R.	W.	AV.
TEST					
1ST-CLASS					
INT					
RAL	0.2	0	6	0	–
NAT.W.					
B & H					

CAREER: BATTING

	I.	N.O.	R.	H.S.	AV.
TEST					
1ST-CLASS	98	15	2594	131*	31.25
INT					
RAL	30	6	550	102	22.91
NAT.W.	4	1	92	37*	30.66
B & H	5	1	85	32*	21.25

CAREER: BOWLING

	O.	M.	R.	W.	AV.
TEST					
1ST-CLASS	16.4	4	64	3	21.33
INT					
RAL	1.2	0	7	0	–
NAT.W.					
B & H	1	1	0	0	–

LAST SEASON: WICKET KEEPING

	C.	ST.			
TEST					
1ST-CLASS	5	–			
INT					
RAL					
NAT.W.					
B & H					

CAREER: WICKET KEEPING

	C.	ST.			
TEST					
1ST-CLASS	21	–			
INT					
RAL	6	1			
NAT.W.					
B & H					

BROWN, S. J.   Northamptonshire

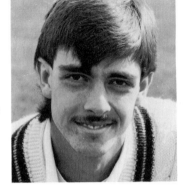

Full Name: Simon John Brown
Role: Right-hand bat, left-arm medium pace bowler, gully fielder
Born: 29 June 1969, Cleadon Village, Sunderland
Height: 6′ 3″ **Weight:** 13st
Nickname: Chubby, Biffa
County debut: 1987
1st-Class catches 1989: 0 (career 3)
Parents: Ernie and Doreen
Marital status: Single
Education: Boldon Comprehensive, Tyne & Wear
Qualifications: 5 O-levels, 5 CSEs
Jobs outside cricket: Sales assistant, part-time groundsman, furniture van driver, security guard, shop assistant, electrician's mate
Off-season 1989–90: Working as electrician's mate and training
Overseas tours: England YC to Sri Lanka 1987; to Australia for Youth World Cup 1988
Cricketers particularly learnt from: Alec Coxon, Dennis Lillee, Bob Carter
Cricketers particularly admired: John Lever, Dennis Lillee, Richard Hadlee, Ian Botham
Other sports played: Basketball, football, tennis, golf, swimming, squash
Other sports followed: Basketball
Relaxations: Listening to U2, renovating old cars

LAST SEASON: BATTING

	I.	N.O.	R.	H.S.	AV.
TEST					
1ST-CLASS	1	1	5	5*	–
INT					
RAL					
NAT.W.					
B & H					

LAST SEASON: BOWLING

	O.	M.	R.	W.	AV.
TEST					
1ST-CLASS	31	6	127	1	127.00
INT					
RAL					
NAT.W.					
B & H					

CAREER: BATTING

	I.	N.O.	R.	H.S.	AV.
TEST					
1ST-CLASS	12	5	64	25*	9.14
INT					
RAL	1	0	1	1	1.00
NAT.W.					
B & H	–	–	–	–	–

CAREER: BOWLING

	O.	M.	R.	W.	AV.
TEST					
1ST-CLASS	215	63	564	19	29.68
INT					
RAL	44.3	1	241	8	30.12
NAT.W.					
B & H	7	0	33	0	

Extras: Offered basketball scholarship in America. Also professional terms with Sunderland FC. Took wicket with first ball in Sunday League
Opinions on cricket: 'Too much cricket is played during the season. Players should be rested more often.'
Best batting performance: 25* Northamptonshire v Gloucestershire, Northampton 1988
Best bowling performance: 3-20 Northamptonshire v Oxford University, Oxford 1988

BULLEN, C. K.   Surrey

Full Name: Christopher Keith Bullen
Role: Right-hand bat, off-break bowler, slip/gully fielder, backward point on Sunday afternoon
Born: 5 November 1962, Clapham
Height: 6′ 5½″ **Weight:** 14st 7lbs
Nickname: CB, Jasper, Bullo, Donkey
County debut: 1982
1st-Class 50s scored: 4
1st-Class 5 w. in innings: 1
Place in batting averages: —
(1988 171st av. 21.75)
Place in bowling averages: —
(1988 70th av. 28.72)
1st-Class catches 1989: 2 (career 26)

Parents: Keith Thomas and Joan
Marital status: Single
Family links with cricket: 'Parents are enthusiastic cricket watchers. Father claims he played cricket at a high standard, but there's no evidence! Cousin David is an up-and-coming Under 12 with Cornwall Schools.'
Education: Glenbrook Primary; Chaucer Middle; Rutlish School
Qualifications: 6 O-levels
Jobs outside cricket: Labourer, car washer, packer, sales rep
Off-season 1989–90: Working for Notts Sport selling artificial cricket pitches; playing rugby, football and golf
Cricketing superstitions or habits: 'Always put left things on first, i.e. socks, shoes, batting gloves. Always brush hair before going out to field.'
Overseas tours: Surrey Schools U-19 to Australia 1980–81
Overseas teams played for: Claremont Cottesloe, Perth 1984–85, 1985–86

Cricketers particularly learnt from: Mickey Stewart, Geoff Arnold, Chris Waller, Roy Miles
Cricketers particularly admired: Jim Laker, Chris Brown, John Gerard, Brian Richardson
Other sports played: Golf, rugby
Other sports followed: American football
Injuries 1989: Bad back for first two months of season; frustration for whole of the season
Relaxations: 'Cinema, leisurely walk after a golf ball, my girlfriend.'
Extras: Spends free time playing club cricket for Wimbledon and Old Rutlishians. Captain of Surrey U-25 side which won Warwick Trophy in 1986. Once a night-watchman in B & H semi-final. Member of Surrey 2nd XI which won 2nd XI Championship in 1988
Opinions on cricket: 'Four-day county games should be played on good wickets. English registration is given too freely. 2nd XI matches should be played under same conditions as first-class games. More should be done by clubs to look after their players during the winter, especially those staying in this country.'
Best batting performance: 65 Surrey v Pakistanis, The Oval 1987
Best bowling performance: 6-119 Surrey v Middlesex, Lord's 1987

LAST SEASON: BATTING

	I.	N.O.	R.	H.S.	AV.
TEST					
1ST-CLASS	3	1	53	31	26.50
INT					
RAL	9	6	64	28*	21.33
NAT.W.	1	0	8	8	8.00
B & H	4	3	67	35*	67.00

CAREER: BATTING

	I.	N.O.	R.	H.S.	AV.
TEST					
1ST-CLASS	34	6	626	65	22.35
INT					
RAL	29	13	240	28*	15.00
NAT.W.	6	2	41	22	10.25
B & H	7	4	125	35*	41.66

LAST SEASON: BOWLING

	O.	M.	R.	W.	AV.
TEST					
1ST-CLASS	12	1	46	0	–
INT					
RAL	99.5	6	457	19	24.05
NAT.W.	36	1	114	1	114.00
B & H	30	5	97	4	24.25

CAREER: BOWLING

	O.	M.	R.	W.	AV.
TEST					
1ST-CLASS	381.5	108	1030	34	30.29
INT					
RAL	315.2	17	1480	56	26.42
NAT.W.	104	9	332	7	47.42
B & H	119.5	11	459	11	41.72

41. What is the highest first-class score by an Englishman?
42. Who has captained Australia most often?

BUNTING, R. A. Sussex

Full Name: Rodney Alan Bunting
Role: Right-hand bat, right-arm
fast-medium bowler
Born: 25 April 1965, King's Lynn
Height: 6' 5" **Weight:** 13st 9lbs
Nickname: Herman, Tiddler
County debut: 1988
1st-Class 5 w. in innings: 3
Place in bowling averages: —
(1988 96th av. 32.19)
1st-Class catches 1989: 0 (career 2)
Parents: Geoffrey Thomas and
Frances
Wife and date of marriage: Christine
Antoinette, 7 March 1986
Children: Jonathan Charles,
16 September 1986

Family links with cricket: Two elder
brothers played county schools
cricket. Parents very interested in cricket
Education: King Edward VII Grammar School
Qualifications: 6 O-levels
Jobs outside cricket: Farm work
Cricketing superstitions or habits: Tapping bat twice on the floor before going
out to bat
Overseas teams played for: Uitenhage, South Africa 1983–84; Humansdorp,
South Africa 1984–85, 1985–86
Cricketers particularly admired: Bob Willis, Mike Hendrick

LAST SEASON: BATTING

	I.	N.O.	R.	H.S.	AV.
TEST					
1ST-CLASS	2	1	79	73	79.00
INT					
RAL					
NAT.W.					
B & H					

LAST SEASON: BOWLING

	O.	M.	R.	W.	AV.
TEST					
1ST-CLASS	36	6	153	5	30.60
INT					
RAL					
NAT.W.					
B & H					

CAREER: BATTING

	I.	N.O.	R.	H.S.	AV.
TEST					
1ST-CLASS	23	6	175	73	10.29
INT					
RAL	1	1	5	5*	–
NAT.W.					
B & H	2	1	0	0*	0.00

CAREER: BOWLING

	O.	M.	R.	W.	AV.
TEST					
1ST-CLASS	436	75	1473	46	32.02
INT					
RAL	8	0	49	2	24.50
NAT.W.					
B & H	22	0	88	3	29.33

Other sports played: Occasional golf, soccer
Other sports followed: Soccer, American football
Relaxations: Easy crosswords, playing with young son, drinking when allowed
Opinions on cricket: 'Disagree with politics interfering with sport.'
Best batting performance: 73 Sussex v Warwickshire, Hove 1989
Best bowling performance: 5-44 Sussex v Warwickshire, Hove 1988

BURNS, N. D.   Somerset

Full Name: Neil David Burns
Role: Left-hand bat,
wicket-keeper
Born: 19 September 1965,
Chelmsford
Height: 5' 10" **Weight:** 11½st
Nickname: Burnsie, Ernie, George
County debut: 1986 (Essex),
1987 (Somerset)
County cap: 1987 (Somerset)
1st-Class 50s scored: 11
1st-Class 100s scored: 2
One-Day 50s: 1
Place in batting averages: 98th
av. 30.29 (1988 127th av. 26.22)
Parents: Roy and Marie
Wife and date of marriage: Susan,
26 September 1987
Family links with cricket: Father
Roy played club cricket for Finchley CC; brother Ian captained Essex U-19
and plays for Woodford Wells CC and MCC
Education: Mildmay Junior and Moulsham High School
Qualifications: 5 O-levels, Advanced Cricket Coach
Jobs outside cricket: Director of NBC Ltd, a sports promotion and manage-
ment company; cricket coach
Off-season 1989–90: Working for NBC Ltd; assisting Peter Roebuck with his
benefit year; playing in Australia in 1990
Cricketing superstitions or habits: Must go through a particular warm-up and
practice before every day's play. Always keep wicket in county cap and long-
sleeved shirt
Overseas tours: Young England to West Indies 1985; Essex CCC to Barbados
1986
Overseas teams played for: Northerns-Goodwood CC (Cape Town) 1984–85,
1985–86; Western Province B in S.A.B. Castle Bowl 1985–86

Cricketers particularly learnt from: Ray East, Graham Saville, Alan Knott, Robin Jackman, Martin Crowe, Allan Border

Cricketers particularly admired: Alan Knott, Bob Taylor, Rod Marsh, Graham Gooch, Martin Crowe, John Lever, Steve Waugh, Peter Roebuck

Other sports played: Soccer, squash, tennis, golf

Other sports followed: Most sports particularly soccer ('I'm an ardent fan of West Ham United.')

Injuries 1989: Fractured cheek-bone under right eye – off for one week in June, missing Bath Festival

Relaxations: Relaxing at home with my wife, music, theatre, watching and playing sport, TV, dining at home, training in off-season

Extras: Former schoolboy footballer with Tottenham Hotspur FC and Orient FC. Joined Somerset in 1987 on two-year contract to further career after spending four years at Essex. Signed further four-year contract in 1989. Once took 8 stumpings in match v Kent 2nd XI at Dartford 1984. Essex Young Player of Year 1984. Trained with West Ham United FC, when an Essex player. Has twice stumped a batsman off wides. Once took a hat-trick of stumpings off Nasser Hussain's leg-breaks for Essex U-11s v Berkshire U-11s. Scored maiden 1st-class century against old county at Chelmsford

Opinions on cricket: 'There should be a regular overseas tour by England 2nd XI, or U-25s. Better pitches for county cricket plus quality practice pitches at all county grounds. Championship should be 16 four-day games. Minimum over-rate requirement should comply with close of play. Sunday cricket should be more commercially exploited to attract more revenue: for example, coloured clothing, white balls, etc. Test Match fees should be abolished, and there should be expenses only. Counties should pay players their true value subsidised by a TCCB share-out, which would take financial pressure away from Test players, relieving them of insecurity, and allowing them to play with the natural freedom and expression which had them selected on their county form. More support from the media for the nation's sports teams!'

Best batting performance: 133* Somerset v Sussex, Hove 1988

LAST SEASON: BATTING

	I.	N.O.	R.	H.S.	AV.
TEST					
1ST-CLASS	33	6	818	90	30.29
INT					
RAL	13	6	184	38*	26.28
NAT.W.	1	0	3	3	3.00
B & H	4	1	19	8	6.33

CAREER: BATTING

	I.	N.O.	R.	H.S.	AV.
TEST					
1ST-CLASS	110	20	2339	133*	25.98
INT					
RAL	36	10	407	38*	15.65
NAT.W.	4	1	39	18	13.00
B & H	10	4	171	51	28.50

LAST SEASON: WICKET KEEPING

	C.	ST.			
TEST					
1ST-CLASS	45	6			
INT					
RAL	19	4			
NAT.W.	2	1			
B & H	8	2			

CAREER: WICKET KEEPING

	C.	ST.			
TEST					
1ST-CLASS	156	16			
INT					
RAL	48	9			
NAT.W.	4	3			
B & H	18	3			

BUTCHER, A. R.   Glamorgan

Full Name: Alan Raymond Butcher
Role: Left-hand bat, slow left-arm or medium pace bowler
Born: 7 January 1954, Croydon
Height: 5′ 8″ **Weight:** 11st 7lbs
Nickname: Butch, Budgie
County debut: 1972 (Surrey), 1987 (Glamorgan)
County cap: 1975 (Surrey), 1987 (Glamorgan)
Benefit: 1985 (Surrey)
Test debut: 1979
No. of Tests: 1
No. of One-Day Internationals: 1
1000 runs in a season: 10
1st-Class 50s scored: 93
1st-Class 100s scored: 35
1st-Class 200s scored: 1
1st-Class 5 w. in innings: 1
One-Day 50s: 45
One-Day 100s: 4
Place in batting averages: 18th av. 46.62 (1988 68th av. 33.73)
1st-Class catches 1989: 11 (career 161)
Parents: Raymond and Jackie
Wife and date of marriage: Elaine, 27 September 1972
Children: Mark, Gary, Lisa

LAST SEASON: BATTING

	I.	N.O.	R.	H.S.	AV.
TEST					
1ST-CLASS	40	5	1632	171*	46.62
INT					
RAL	15	1	335	76*	23.92
NAT.W.	2	0	53	42	32.50
B & H	4	0	92	41	23.00

CAREER: BATTING

	I.	N.O.	R.	H.S.	AV.
TEST	2	0	34	20	17.00
1ST-CLASS	595	52	18623	216*	34.29
INT	1	0	14	14	14.00
RAL	197	23	4804	113*	27.60
NAT.W.	30	3	821	86*	30.40
B & H	65	4	1518	80	24.88

LAST SEASON: BOWLING

	O.	M.	R.	W.	AV.
TEST					
1ST-CLASS	41.1	6	177	4	44.25
INT					
RAL	8	0	55	1	55.00
NAT.W.					
B & H	9	0	61	3	20.33

CAREER: BOWLING

	O.	M.	R.	W.	AV.
TEST	2	0	9	0	—
1ST-CLASS	1631.3	333	5226	138	37.86
INT					
RAL	336.2	22	1500	37	40.54
NAT.W.	67.2	10	249	5	49.80
B & H	184.3	32	587	27	21.74

Family links with cricket: Brother Martin played for MCC Young Professionals. Brother Ian plays for Gloucestershire CC. Son Mark made his Surrey 2nd XI debut in 1989
Education: Heath Clark Grammar School
Qualifications: 5 O-levels, 1 A-level
Jobs outside cricket: Football coach, PE master
Other sports played: Football
Relaxations: Most sport, rock music, reading
Extras: Scored a century before lunch v Glamorgan at The Oval, 1980. Released by Surrey at end of 1986 season. Joined Glamorgan in 1987. First Englishman to score 1000 runs in 1989 season. Appointed Captain of Glamorgan during 1989 after Hugh Morris resigned in mid-season
Best batting performance: 216* Surrey v Cambridge University, Cambridge 1980
Best bowling performance: 6-48 Surrey v Hampshire, Guildford 1972

BUTCHER, I. P.   Gloucestershire

Full Name: Ian Paul Butcher
Role: Right-hand bat, slip fielder
Born: 1 July 1962, Farnborough, Kent
Height: 6′ **Weight:** 14st
Nickname: Butch-Dog, Buster
County debut: 1980 (Leicestershire), 1988 (Gloucestershire)
County cap: 1984 (Leicestershire)
1000 runs in a season: 2
1st-Class 50s scored: 22
1st-Class 100s scored: 10
One-Day 50s: 8
One-Day 100s: 2
Place in batting averages: 165th av. 21.85
1st-Class catches 1989: 4 (career 83)

Parents: Raymond and Jackie
Wife and date of marriage: Marie, 12 March 1983
Family links with cricket: Brother Alan captains Glamorgan CCC. Brother Martin on MCC ground-staff and captains club side
Education: John Ruskin High School
Qualifications: Preliminary Coaching Certificate

Jobs outside cricket: Football coach, Cumnor House School, South Croydon. Asst Sports Director, Leicester University

Cricketing superstitions or habits: 'I have many . . . If I score runs I like to do everything (if possible) the same, the following day. I always wear a sweatband on left wrist while batting.'

Overseas tours: England Young Cricketers to West Indies 1980

Overseas teams played for: Johannesburg Municipals 1981–82

Cricketers particularly learnt from: Brian Davison, Graham Gooch, Chris Balderstone, Paddy Clift, David Gower

Other sports played: Football, golf. 'I'll try my hand at anything!'

Relaxations: Sleeping, good beer, good food, music, TV

Extras: Made his debut for Leicestershire CCC in the John Player League v Surrey 1979. Scored century on championship debut at Grace Road. Moved to Gloucestershire for 1988, but missed most of season through injury

Opinions on cricket: 'I feel that counties should be limited to one overseas player registered at any one time. It would make counties select their players more wisely, i.e. as regards possible fitness problems having no back-up overseas players and any gambles can be left to home-grown players. Let's get back to playing on decent surfaces.'

Best batting performance: 139 Leicestershire v Nottinghamshire, Leicester 1983

Best bowling performance: 1-2 Leicestershire v Essex, Chelmsford 1983

LAST SEASON: BATTING

	I.	N.O.	R.	H.S.	AV.
TEST					
1ST-CLASS	23	3	437	105*	21.85
INT					
RAL	4	0	43	26	10.75
NAT.W.	2	0	73	71	35.50
B & H					

LAST SEASON: BOWLING

	O.	M.	R.	W.	AV.
TEST					
1ST-CLASS	4	1	15	0	–
INT					
RAL					
NAT.W.					
B & H					

CAREER: BATTING

	I.	N.O.	R.	H.S.	AV.
TEST					
1ST-CLASS	182	12	4967	139	29.21
INT					
RAL	54	3	971	71	19.03
NAT.W.	9	0	245	81	27.22
B & H	18	1	647	103*	38.05

CAREER: BOWLING

	O.	M.	R.	W.	AV.
TEST					
1ST-CLASS	14	3	43	1	43.00
INT					
RAL	1	0	4	0	–
NAT.W.	0.3	0	6	1	6.00
B & H					

BUTCHER, R. O. Middlesex

Full Name: Roland Orlando Butcher
Role: Right-hand bat, right-arm medium bowler
Born: 14 October 1953, East Point, St Philip, Barbados
Height: 5' 7" **Weight:** 12st
Nickname: Butch, Bland (in West Indies)
County debut: 1974
Benefit: 1989
County cap: 1979
Test debut: 1980–81
No. of Tests: 3
No. of One-Day Internationals: 3
1000 runs in a season: 4
1st-Class 50s scored: 65
1st-Class 100s scored: 17
One-Day 50s: 26
One-Day 100s: 1

Place in batting averages: 110th av. 28.33 (1988 88th av. 30.61)
1st-Class catches 1989: 13 (career 287 + 1 stumping)
Parents: Robert and Doreen
Wife: Cheryl Denise
Children: Paul Nicholas Roland, 2 January 1979; Michelle Denise, 11 November 1982
Family links with cricket: Cousin is Basil Butcher, of Guyana and West Indies
Education: St Catherine's School, St Philip, Barbados; Shephalbury Secondary; Hitchin College
Qualifications: Advanced Cricket Coaching Certificate, Football Association Preliminary Coaching Certificate
Jobs outside cricket: Football coach, insurance salesman
Off-season 1989–90: Resting for new season
Overseas tours: England to West Indies 1981
Overseas teams played for: Barbados in 1974–75 Shell Shield Competition; Tasmania 1982; Takapuna CC, Auckland 1984–85; Hawkesbury CC, Australia 1986–87
Cricketers particularly admired: Sunil Gavaskar, Viv Richards, Ian Chappell, John Inverarity, Colin Bland
Other sports played: Football
Injuries 1989: Compound dislocation of little finger on left hand
Relaxations: 'My family.'

Extras: Arrived in England aged 13. First black man to play Test cricket for England, 14 March 1981, at Kensington Oval, Barbados. Played semi-professional soccer for Biggleswade and Stevenage. Played for Gloucestershire Second XI 1969. On MCC staff, 1970. Played for Middlesex 2nd XI 1972 and 1973. ('When I joined the MCC staff, I was a leg-spinner who could bat a bit.') Does work for Inter-Action Group in deprived areas of London. A devout member of the Anglican church. Authorised biography *Rising to the Challenge* published 1989. Has captained Middlesex in absence of Gatting. Originally agreed to join the unofficial England tour to South Africa in 1989–90 but withdrew under pressure

Best batting performance: 197 Middlesex v Yorkshire, Lord's 1982

Best bowling performance: 2-37 Middlesex v Gloucestershire, Cheltenham 1986

LAST SEASON: BATTING

	I.	N.O.	R.	H.S.	AV.
TEST					
1ST-CLASS	20	2	519	126	28.83
INT					
RAL	10	0	266	67	26.60
NAT.W.	1	0	3	3	3.00
B & H	4	0	52	25	13.00

LAST SEASON: BOWLING

	O.	M.	R.	W.	AV.
TEST					
1ST-CLASS					
INT					
RAL					
NAT.W.					
B & H					

CAREER: BATTING

	I.	N.O.	R.	H.S.	AV.
TEST	5	0	71	32	14.20
1ST-CLASS	419	41	11867	197	31.39
INT	3	0	58	52	19.33
RAL	155	15	3172	100	22.65
NAT.W.	27	5	504	65	22.90
B & H	35	3	749	85	23.40

CAREER: BOWLING

	O.	M.	R.	W.	AV.
TEST					
1ST-CLASS	49.1	10	180	4	45.00
INT					
RAL	1.2	0	5	0	–
NAT.W.	2	0	18	1	18.00
B & H					

43. What have D. R. Shepherd, M. Moxon, and M. Maynard got in common?

44. Who has made two centuries in the same match most often?

BUTLER, K. A.   Essex

Full Name: Keith Andrew Butler
Role: Right-hand bat, right-arm medium bowler, all round
Born: 20 January 1971, Camden Town
Height: 5′ 8″ **Weight:** 11st 5lbs
Nickname: Billy
County debut: 1989
Parents: John and Kath
Marital status: Single
Family links with cricket: Dad played for local club side
Education: William Ford Primary, Dagenham Priory Comprehensive
Qualifications: 2 O-levels, Coaching Exam
Jobs outside cricket: Worked as air freight clerk
Off-season 1989–90: Playing for East Torrens in Adelaide
Cricketing superstitions or habits: 'Don't like having throw downs before game.'
Overseas tours: Touring this winter with Young England in Australia
Cricketers particularly learnt from: Ray East, Keith Fletcher, Nick King (Coach)
Cricketers particularly admired: Graham Gooch, Viv Richards, Ian Botham
Other sports played: Snooker, golf
Other sports followed: Football, fan of West Ham United
Relaxations: Enjoys watching videos and listening to music
Best batting performance: 10* Essex v Cambridge University, Cambridge 1989

LAST SEASON: BATTING

	I.	N.O.	R.	H.S.	AV.
TEST					
1ST-CLASS	1	1	10	10*	–
INT					
RAL	–	–	–	–	–
NAT.W.					
B & H					

CAREER: BATTING

	I.	N.O.	R.	H.S.	AV.
TEST					
1ST-CLASS	1	1	10	10*	–
INT					
RAL	–	–	–	–	–
NAT.W.					
B & H					

BYAS, D.   Yorkshire

Full Name: David Byas
Role: Left-hand bat, right-arm
medium bowler, slip/cover fielder
Born: 26 August 1964, Driffield,
East Yorkshire
Height: 6′ 4″ **Weight:** 14st 7lbs
Nickname: Bingo
County debut: 1986
1st-Class 50s scored: 9
1st-Class 100s scored: 2
One-Day 50s: 2
Place in batting averages: 123rd
av. 26.90 (1988 139th av. 24.66)
1st-Class catches 1989: 14 (career
27)
Parents: Richard and Anne
Marital status: Single
Family links with cricket: Father
played in local league
Education: Scarborough College
Qualifications: 1 O-level (Engineering)
Jobs outside cricket: Working on family farm
Cricketing superstitions or habits: Left boot and pad on before right. Always
wears same clothing during an innings
Overseas teams played for: Auckland, New Zealand 1988–89
Cricketers particularly learnt from: Doug Padgett
Cricketers particularly admired: David Gower, Viv Richards, Ian Botham
Other sports played: Hockey, squash

LAST SEASON: BATTING

	I.	N.O.	R.	H.S.	AV.
TEST					
1ST-CLASS	33	2	844	117	27.22
INT					
RAL	16	2	260	47*	18.57
NAT.W.	2	0	71	54	35.50
B & H	4	1	54	27*	18.00

CAREER: BATTING

	I.	N.O.	R.	H.S.	AV.
TEST					
1ST-CLASS	59	3	1436	117	25.64
INT					
RAL	28	5	551	69*	23.95
NAT.W.	2	0	71	54	35.50
B & H	5	1	56	27*	14.00

LAST SEASON: BOWLING

	O.	M.	R.	W.	AV.
TEST					
1ST-CLASS	41.4	10	176	6	29.33
INT					
RAL	51.1	1	262	11	23.81
NAT.W.					
B & H	34.1	4	105	4	26.25

CAREER: BOWLING

	O.	M.	R.	W.	AV.
TEST					
1ST-CLASS	53	10	240	6	40.00
INT					
RAL	51.1	1	262	11	23.81
NAT.W.					
B & H	34.1	4	105	4	26.25

Relaxations: Game shooting, rallying, eating out
Best batting performance: 117 Yorkshire v Kent, Scarborough 1989
Best bowling performance: 2-25 Yorkshire v Worcestershire, Sheffield 1989

CAIRNS, C. L.   Nottinghamshire

Full Name: Christopher Lance Cairns
Role: Right-hand bat, right-arm fast medium bowler
Born: 13 June 1970, Picton, New Zealand
Height: 6' 2" **Weight:** 14st
Nickname: Sheep
County debut: 1988
1st-Class 100s scored: 1
Place in batting averages: 95th av. 30.71 (1988 —)
Place in bowling averages: — (1988 53rd av. 25.60)
1st-Class catches 1989: 1 (career 7)

Parents: Lance and Sue
Marital status: Single
Family links with cricket: Father played Test cricket, uncle played first-class cricket in New Zealand
Education: Christchurch Boys' High School, New Zealand
Qualifications: 5th and 6th form certificates
Jobs outside cricket: Labourer
Off-season 1989–90: Touring with New Zealand
Cricketing superstitions or habits: Putting right pad on first
Overseas tours: New Zealand Youth XI to Australia for Youth World Cup 1988
Cricketers particularly learnt from: Father, Billy Ibadullah, Dennis Lillee, Bob Carter
Cricketers particularly admired: Mick Newell, Richard Hadlee, Dennis Lillee
Other sports played: Rugby
Other sports followed: Most sports
Relaxations: 'Sleeping and ignoring Mick Newell!'
Opinions on cricket: 'Great game.'

Best batting performance: 110 Northern Districts v Auckland, Hamilton 1988–89
Best bowling performance: 4-70 Nottinghamshire v Kent, Dartford 1988

LAST SEASON: BATTING

	I.	N.O.	R.	H.S.	AV.
TEST					
1ST-CLASS	8	1	215	58	30.71
INT					
RAL	1	0	4	4	4.00
NAT.W.					
B & H					

LAST SEASON: BOWLING

	O.	M.	R.	W.	AV.
TEST					
1ST-CLASS	101.2	19	433	13	33.30
INT					
RAL	8	0	38	2	19.00
NAT.W.					
B & H					

CAREER: BATTING

	I.	N.O.	R.	H.S.	AV.
TEST					
1ST-CLASS	24	5	477	110	25.10
INT					
RAL	2	0	8	4	4.00
NAT.W.					
B & H					

CAREER: BOWLING

	O.	M.	R.	W.	AV.
TEST					
1ST-CLASS	448.3	68	1631	49	33.28
INT					
RAL	13	1	68	2	34.00
NAT.W.					
B & H					

CANN, M. J.   Glamorgan

Full Name: Michael James Cann
Role: Left-hand bat, off-break bowler
Born: 4 July 1965, Cardiff
Height: 5′ 9″ **Weight:** 11½st
Nickname: Tin, Canny, The Big Fella, BJ, Beetlejuice
County debut: 1986
1st-Class 50s scored: 5
1st-Class 100s scored: 1
Place in batting averages: 116th av. 27.97
1st-Class catches 1989: 6 (career 12)
Parents: Leslie and Catherine
Marital status: Single
Education: St Illtyds College, Cardiff; Swansea University
Qualifications: 10 O-levels, 3 A-levels, Degree in Biochemistry, Senior NCA coach

Cricketing superstitions or habits: 'I don't have any. I don't consider cricket to be a game of luck!'

Overseas tours: Glamorgan CCC to Barbados 1987
Cricketers particularly learnt from: Tom Cartwright, Alan Jones, Tony Cordle
Cricketers particularly admired: Barry Lloyd
Other sports played: Squash, cards, snooker
Other sports followed: Football (Cardiff City)
Relaxations: Contract bridge, general socialising, going out for meals, reading cricket books
Extras: Represented Combined Universities in B & H Cup 1987
Opinions on cricket: 'Registration rules are a farce. People should learn a few facts about South Africa before they pass comments. Four-day cricket is a must. It is good to see the game being increasingly better marketed. The introduction of 12-month contracts, I believe, would increase the professionalism of the game.'
Best batting performance: 109 Glamorgan v Somerset, Cardiff 1989
Best bowling performance: 3-30 Glamorgan v Middlesex, Abergavenny 1989

LAST SEASON: BATTING

	I.	N.O.	R.	H.S.	AV.
TEST					
1ST-CLASS	34	2	895	109	27.97
INT					
RAL	3	0	6	5	2.00
NAT.W.	2	1	4	2*	4.00
B & H	3	1	37	15	18.50

LAST SEASON: BOWLING

	O.	M.	R.	W.	AV.
TEST					
1ST-CLASS	74	14	297	7	42.42
INT					
RAL					
NAT.W.	11	2	40	3	13.33
B & H					

CAREER: BATTING

	I.	N.O.	R.	H.S.	AV.
TEST					
1ST-CLASS	44	5	1013	109	25.97
INT					
RAL	3	0	6	5	2.00
NAT.W.	2	1	4	2*	4.00
B & H	6	2	97	46	24.25

CAREER: BOWLING

	O.	M.	R.	W.	AV.
TEST					
1ST-CLASS	112.5	20	470	12	39.16
INT					
RAL					
NAT.W.	11	2	40	3	13.33
B & H	27	0	127	2	63.50

45. Who has captained England most often, and how often?

CAPEL, D. J.   Northamptonshire

Full Name: David John Capel
Role: Right-hand bat, right-arm
fast medium bowler, all-rounder
Born: 6 July 1963, Northampton
Height: 6′ **Weight:** 12st 6lbs
Nickname: Capes, Fiery
County debut: 1981
County cap: 1986
Test debut: 1987
No. of Tests: 11
No. of One-Day Internationals: 11
50 wickets in a season: 3
1000 runs in a season: 2
1st-Class 50s scored: 41
1st-Class 100s scored: 7
1st-Class 5 w. in innings: 10
One-Day 50s: 13
Place in batting averages: 56th
av. 36.41 (1988 69th av. 33.54)
Place in bowling averages: 65th
av. 29.70 (1988 112th av. 35.39)
Strike rate 1989: 54.45 (career 60.52)
1st-Class catches 1989: 7 (career 79)
Parents: John and Angela Janet
Wife and date of marriage: Debbie, 21 September 1985
Children: Jenny, 21 October 1987
Family links with cricket: Father played in local league and brother Andrew in County League
Education: Roade Primary and Roade Comprehensive School
Qualifications: 3 O-levels, 4 CSEs, NCA Coaching Certificate
Jobs outside cricket: Hand-made surgical shoemaker (when 16–17)
Off-season 1989–90: Touring India and West Indies with England
Cricketing superstitions or habits: 'I try to change in same place at different grounds around the circuit.'
Overseas tours: Dubai with *The Cricketer* XI 1983; England to Sharjah 1986; England to Pakistan, New Zealand and Australia 1987–88; England to India 1989; England to West Indies 1990
Overseas teams played for: Latrobe, Tasmania 1982–83; Westview CC, Port Elizabeth 1983–84–85; Grey School and Eastern Province 1985–86–87; Scarborough CC, Western Australia 1988–89
Cricketers particularly learnt from: Brian Reynolds (coach), Wayne Larkins, Geoff Cook, Dennis Lillee

Cricketers particularly admired: Barry Richards, Richard Hadlee, Ian Botham, Clive Rice, Kepler Wessels

Other sports played: Golf

Other sports followed: 'I follow the results of Northampton Town FC.'

Relaxations: 'I enjoy swimming, watching TV – particularly good comedy programmes, and listening to most kinds of music.'

Extras: Played for his village team, Roade, and swam for Northamptonshire, both at age 11. Played for Young England v West Indies 1982. Only second Northampton-born man to play for England

Opinions on cricket: 'There should definitely be 16 four-day games, one against each county. The other, one-day competitions should be limited to two, with the one-day games being played at the weekend, and the four-day games mid-week.'

Best batting performance: 134 Eastern Province v Western Province, Port Elizabeth 1986–87

Best bowling performance: 7-46 Northamptonshire v Yorkshire, Northampton 1987

LAST SEASON: BATTING

	I.	N.O.	R.	H.S.	AV.
TEST	2	0	21	17	10.50
1ST-CLASS	37	3	1290	126	37.94
INT					
RAL	13	3	346	63	34.60
NAT.W.	3	1	177	92*	88.50
B & H	4	1	44	21	14.66

CAREER: BATTING

	I.	N.O.	R.	H.S.	AV.
TEST	18	0	293	98	16.27
1ST-CLASS	265	43	6754	134	30.42
INT	11	2	221	50*	24.55
RAL	84	19	1793	83	27.58
NAT.W.	17	7	470	92*	47.00
B & H	26	5	464	97	22.09

LAST SEASON: BOWLING

	O.	M.	R.	W.	AV.
TEST	24	2	101	2	50.50
1ST-CLASS	493.2	90	1592	55	28.94
INT					
RAL	94.3	2	421	16	26.31
NAT.W.	34.4	2	148	6	24.66
B & H	40	0	144	8	18.00

CAREER: BOWLING

	O.	M.	R.	W.	AV.
TEST	209.2	33	628	12	52.33
1ST-CLASS	3059.1	573	9937	312	31.84
INT	97	6	433	11	39.36
RAL	449.4	15	2063	67	30.79
NAT.W.	124.1	17	457	16	28.56
B & H	235	26	838	37	22.64

46. Who won the County Championship in 1989?

CARR, J. D. Middlesex

Full Name: John Donald Carr
Role: Right-hand bat, off-break
bowler, slip fielder
Born: 15 June 1963, St John's
Wood, London
Height: 6′ **Weight:** 12st
Nickname: Carsy
County debut: 1983
County cap: 1987
1000 runs in a season: 2
1st-Class 50s scored: 26
1st-Class 100s scored: 10
1st-Class 5 w. in innings: 3
One-Day 50s: 8
Place in batting averages: 139th
av. 24.70 (1988 59th av. 35.05)
1st-Class catches 1989: 20 (career 82)
Parents: Donald and Stella
Marital status: Single
Family links with cricket: Father, D. B. Carr, was secretary of TCCB and
played for Oxford University, Derbyshire and England, captaining all three
at some stage
Education: The Hall School, Repton School and Oxford University (Worcester College)
Qualifications: BA Hons (Philosophy, Politics and Economics)
Jobs outside cricket: Taught one term at St George's School, Windsor.
Worked briefly at DHSS in Oxford
Overseas tours: Australia with Repton Pilgrims 1982–83; La Manga with
Hertfordshire 1983; Australia and Hong Kong with Oxbridge 1985–86;
Troubadours tour to Argentina and Brazil 1989
Overseas teams played for: Sydney University 1986; Western Creek,
Canberra 1986–87
Cricketers particularly learnt from: Eric Marsh, Walter Hadlee, Kevin
Hayes, Don Bennett, Donald Carr
Cricketers particularly admired: Viv Richards, Ian Botham, Michael Holding, Graeme Hick, Richard Hadlee, Imran Khan, Malcolm Marshall
Other sports played: Eton fives, golf, squash, soccer
Other sports followed: 'I like watching any sport played well.'
Relaxations: 'Music, films, good food; thinking about what career I want to
pursue "next year"; trying to get our bowlers to bowl at me in the nets.'
Extras: Played for Oxford in Varsity Match 1984. Secretary of University in
1984. Came on as substitute fielder for Middlesex in the 1983 Benson &

Hedges Cup Final, holding a vital catch to help his side defeat Essex. Received special clearance to play in the match having previously appeared for Combined Universities in the same competition. Announced his retirement from first-class cricket on last day of 1989 season: 'I have very much enjoyed my seven years playing for Oxford University and Middlesex, but I am disappointed not to have made more progress since gaining my county cap in 1987.'

Opinions on cricket: 'There should be some small reward for drawing as opposed to losing a Championship game. Perhaps two points. The difference between "win" bonus points and "draw" bonus points would still be great enough to encourage positive and adventurous cricket.'

Best batting performance: 156 Middlesex v Essex, Lord's 1987

Best bowling performance: 6-61 Middlesex v Gloucestershire, Lord's 1985

LAST SEASON: BATTING

	I.	N.O.	R.	H.S.	AV.
TEST					
1ST-CLASS	34	3	766	153*	24.70
INT					
RAL	15	1	350	86	25.00
NAT.W.	4	0	147	83	36.75
B & H	4	0	114	43	28.50

LAST SEASON: BOWLING

	O.	M.	R.	W.	AV.
TEST					
1ST-CLASS	74	20	154	3	51.33
INT					
RAL	71	4	291	11	26.45
NAT.W.	6	0	19	1	19.00
B & H	14	1	36	1	36.00

CAREER: BATTING

	I.	N.O.	R.	H.S.	AV.
TEST					
1ST-CLASS	184	21	5395	156	33.09
INT					
RAL	48	6	1012	84	24.09
NAT.W.	11	0	248	83	22.54
B & H	19	1	514	67	28.55

CAREER: BOWLING

	O.	M.	R.	W.	AV.
TEST					
1ST-CLASS	1050.4	274	2742	59	46.47
INT					
RAL	105.2	5	470	17	27.64
NAT.W.	21	1	67	4	16.75
B & H	95.2	10	363	8	45.37

47. Who was runner-up in the County Championship in 1989?

48. Who was vice-captain of Australia in the 1989 Ashes series?

CARRICK, P. Yorkshire

Full Name: Phillip Carrick
Role: Right-hand bat, slow left-arm
bowler, slip fielder
Born: 16 July 1952, Leeds
Height: 6′ **Weight:** 14st
Nickname: Fergie
County debut: 1970
County cap: 1976
Benefit: 1985
50 wickets in a season: 10
1st-Class 50s scored: 34
1st-Class 100s scored: 3
1st-Class 5 w. in innings: 40
1st-Class 10 w. in match: 5
One-Day 50s: 2
Place in batting averages: 207th
av. 17.25 (1988 90th av. 30.18)
Place in bowling averages: 57th
av. 28.12 (1988 88th av. 31.02)

Strike rate 1989: 73.38 (career 71.91)
1st-Class catches 1989: 5 (career 179)
Parents: Arthur (deceased) and Ivy
Wife and date of marriage: Elspeth, 2 April 1977
Children: Emma Elizabeth, 6 May 1980; Philippa Louise, 11 January
1982
Family links with cricket: Father and brother useful league players
Education: Bramley CS, Intake CS, Park Lane College of Further Education
Qualifications: 2 O-levels, 8 CSEs, NCA Coaching Certificate
Jobs outside cricket: Company Director in own promotional business. Cricket
coach
Off-season 1989–90: 'Running my own business.'
Cricketing superstitions or habits: Left pad on first
Overseas tours: Derrick Robins' XI to South Africa 1975–76; Far East 1977;
West Indies with Yorkshire 1987
Overseas teams played for: Eastern Province in 1976–77 Currie Cup Compe-
tition; Northern Transvaal 1982–83
Cricketers particularly learnt from: Geoff Boycott, Ray Illingworth, Mike
Fearnley
Cricketers particularly admired: Graeme Pollock
Other sports played: Golf
Other sports followed: Bradford City FC, rugby league
Relaxations: 'My family.'

Extras: Appointed Yorkshire captain for 1987. Led them to victory in the B & H Cup in first season as captain

Opinions on cricket: 'Before we decide which format of cricket we should play – three-day or four-day – let us please sort the wickets out first!'

Best batting performance: 131* Yorkshire v Northamptonshire 1980

Best bowling performance: 8-33 Yorkshire v Cambridge University, Cambridge 1973

LAST SEASON: BATTING

	I.	N.O.	R.	H.S.	AV.
TEST					
1ST-CLASS	31	3	483	65*	17.25
INT					
RAL	13	2	143	48*	13.00
NAT.W.	2	1	50	33*	50.00
B & H	3	1	20	18*	10.00

CAREER: BATTING

	I.	N.O.	R.	H.S.	AV.
TEST					
1ST-CLASS	487	86	8810	131*	21.97
INT					
RAL	121	34	1260	48*	14.48
NAT.W.	20	3	294	54	17.29
B & H	30	5	286	58	11.44

LAST SEASON: BOWLING

	O.	M.	R.	W.	AV.
TEST					
1ST-CLASS	697.1	242	1603	57	28.12
INT					
RAL	100	9	448	11	40.72
NAT.W.	24	2	77	1	77.00
B & H	44	5	141	3	47.00

CAREER: BOWLING

	O.	M.	R.	W.	AV.
TEST					
1ST-CLASS	10991.1	3535	27308	917	29.77
INT					
RAL	861	40	3903	120	32.52
NAT.W.	216.5	46	590	16	36.87
B & H	398.3	54	1301	34	38.26

CHILDS, J. H. — Essex

Full Name: John Henry Childs
Role: Left-hand bat, slow left-arm orthodox bowler
Born: 15 August 1951, Plymouth
Height: 6' **Weight:** 12st 6lbs
Nickname: Charlie
County debut: 1975 (Gloucestershire), 1985 (Essex)
County cap: 1977 (Gloucestershire), 1986 (Essex)
Testimonial: 1985
Test debut: 1988
No. of Tests: 2
50 wickets in a season: 5
1st-Class 5 w. in innings: 38
1st-Class 10 w. in match: 8
Place in batting averages: —
(1988 261st av. 10.42)

Place in bowling averages: 29th av. 22.70 (1988 49th av. 25.12)
Strike rate 1989: 60.88 (career 67.11)
1st-Class catches 1989: 5 (career 85)
Parents: Sydney and Barbara (both deceased)
Wife and date of marriage: Jane Anne, 11 November 1978
Children: Lee Robert, 28 November 1980; Scott Alexander, 21 August 1984
Education: Audley Park Secondary Modern, Torquay
Qualifications: Advanced Cricket Coach
Jobs outside cricket: Signwriter
Overseas tours: Zambia 1977; Barbados 1983
Cricketers particularly admired: Gary Sobers, Mike Procter
Other sports played: Most ball games
Relaxations: 'Watching rugby, decorating at home, walking on moors and beaches, enjoying my family.'
Extras: Played for Devon 1973–74. Released by Gloucestershire at end of 1984 and joined Essex. One of *Wisden*'s Five Cricketers of the Year, 1986
Opinions on cricket: 'Everything I had aimed for in cricket came about in three seasons (1986, 1987, 1988) – winning the County Championship, getting an England cap and then being selected for an overseas tour.'
Best batting performance: 34* Gloucestershire v Nottinghamshire, Cheltenham 1982
Best bowling performance: 9-56 Gloucestershire v Somerset, Bristol 1981

LAST SEASON: BATTING

	I.	N.O.	R.	H.S.	AV.
TEST					
1ST-CLASS	23	11	86	24	7.16
INT					
RAL	–	–	–	–	–
NAT.W.					
B & H	–	–	–	–	–

LAST SEASON: BOWLING

	O.	M.	R.	W.	AV.
TEST					
1ST-CLASS	679.5	265	1521	67	22.70
INT					
RAL	20	0	73	2	36.50
NAT.W.					
B & H	11	0	46	2	23.00

CAREER: BATTING

	I.	N.O.	R.	H.S.	AV.
TEST	4	4	2	2*	–
1ST-CLASS	238	112	1036	34*	8.22
INT					
RAL	22	12	88	16*	8.80
NAT.W.	4	3	22	14*	22.00
B & H	7	5	25	10	12.50

CAREER: BOWLING

	O.	M.	R.	W.	AV.
TEST	86	29	183	3	61.00
1ST-CLASS	7532	2299	19776	678	29.16
INT					
RAL	365.1	19	1637	45	36.37
NAT.W.	60	12	180	7	25.71
B & H	167	35	512	16	32.00

CLARKE, A. R.　　　　　Sussex

Full Name: Andrew Russell Clarke
Role: Right-hand bat, leg spin bowler
Born: 23 December 1961, Brighton
Height: 5′ 9″ **Weight:** 12st
Nickname: Nobby, Charles
County debut: 1988
1st-Class 50s scored: 1
1st-Class 5 w. in innings: 2
Place in batting averages: —
(1988 235th av. 14.04)
Place in bowling averages: —
(1988 120th av. 37.50)
1st-Class catches 1989: 0 (career 7)
Parents: Ken and Gwen
Wife and date of marriage: Jennifer, 12 September 1987
Family links with cricket: Father played club cricket, as did his two brothers
Education: Longhill High School
Qualifications: 2 O-levels, 7 CSEs; NCA cricket coach. Qualified financial consultant
Jobs outside cricket: Accounts clerk for Legal and General
Off-season 1989–90: Coaching at a school in Cape Town, South Africa
Cricketing superstitions or habits: 'Have a habit of dropping catches, and letting the ball through my legs!'
Cricketers particularly learnt from: Nick Falkner, Chris Waller

LAST SEASON: BATTING

	I.	N.O.	R.	H.S.	AV.
TEST					
1ST-CLASS	5	1	69	36*	17.25
INT					
RAL	5	1	13	9*	3.25
NAT.W.	2	1	5	3	5.00
B & H	2	0	1	1	0.50

LAST SEASON: BOWLING

	O.	M.	R.	W.	AV.
TEST					
1ST-CLASS	81	22	222	9	24.66
INT					
RAL	97	8	431	15	28.73
NAT.W.	36	6	147	3	49.00
B & H	43	5	155	4	38.75

CAREER: BATTING

	I.	N.O.	R.	H.S.	AV.
TEST					
1ST-CLASS	37	9	406	68	14.50
INT					
RAL	7	1	20	9*	3.33
NAT.W.	3	1	29	24	14.50
B & H	2	0	1	1	0.50

CAREER: BOWLING

	O.	M.	R.	W.	AV.
TEST					
1ST-CLASS	699	179	1872	53	35.32
INT					
RAL	161.4	15	698	32	21.81
NAT.W.	36	6	147	3	49.00
B & H	43	5	155	4	38.75

Cricketers particularly admired: Meyrick Pringle, James Hall
Other sports played: Football, golf, snooker, pool
Other sports followed: Football, golf, snooker
Relaxations: Gambling, reading, watching video films, eating and drinking
Extras: 'From the age of 15 to 26 I didn't have any coaching so I had to teach myself.' The only specialist leg spinner playing county cricket in 1988. Played for Preston Nomads in Brighton Club Cricket. Played for South of England Schools. Played four matches for Sussex 2nd XI in 1987. Became Sussex's regular night-watchman in 1988
Opinions on cricket: 'I am in favour of four-day cricket, if the pitches are good enough. Batsmen should be given out lbw to a ball pitching outside the leg stump if the ball would have hit the wicket.'
Best batting performance: 68 Sussex v Hampshire, Eastbourne 1988
Best bowling performance: 5-60 Sussex v Hampshire, Eastbourne 1988

CLARKE, S. T. Surrey

Full Name: Sylvester Theophilus Clarke
Role: Right-hand bat, right-arm fast bowler, gully fielder
Born: 11 December 1955, Lead Vale, Christchurch, Barbados
Height: 6′ 2″ Weight: 15st
Nickname: Silvers
County debut: 1979
County cap: 1980
Benefit: 1987
Test debut: 1977–78
No. of Tests: 11
No. of One-Day Internationals: 10
50 wickets in a season: 5
1st-Class 50s scored: 6
1st-Class 100s scored: 1
1st-Class 5 w. in innings: 58
1st-Class 10 w. in match: 10
Place in batting averages: — (1988 225th av. 15.66)
Place in bowling averages: — (1988 4th av. 14.49)
1st-Class catches 1989: 0 (career 142)
Parents: Marjorie and Ashton
Children: Desiree, 8 December 1974; Dawn, 18 August 1976; Shelly, 2 July 1978

108

Family links with cricket: Half-brother Damien is professional at Todmorden CC
Education: St Bartholomew Boys' School
Jobs outside cricket: Carpenter
Overseas tours: West Indies to India and Sri Lanka 1978–79, Pakistan 1980–81, Australia 1981–82; Rebel West Indian XI to South Africa 1982–83 and 1983–84
Overseas teams played for: Local club in Barbados Cricket League; Barbados 1977–82; Transvaal 1983–86; Orange Free State 1987–88; Northern Transvaal 1988–89
Cricketers particularly learnt from: Vanburn Holder
Other sports played: Football
Other sports followed: Tennis
Relaxations: 'Music and parties.'
Extras: Made fastest century of the 1981 season in 62 mins v Glamorgan. Took Championship hat-trick in 1980 season v Nottinghamshire. Released by Surrey in mid-1989
Best batting performance: 100* Surrey v Glamorgan, Swansea 1981
Best bowling performance: 8-62 Surrey v Northamptonshire, The Oval 1987

LAST SEASON: BATTING

	I.	N.O.	R.	H.S.	AV.
TEST					
1ST-CLASS					
INT					
RAL					
NAT.W.					
B & H	1	1	2	2*	–

LAST SEASON: BOWLING

	O.	M.	R.	W.	AV.
TEST					
1ST-CLASS					
INT					
RAL					
NAT.W.					
B & H	11	2	29	1	29.00

CAREER: BATTING

	I.	N.O.	R.	H.S.	AV.
TEST	16	5	172	35*	15.63
1ST-CLASS	242	38	3031	100*	14.85
INT	8	2	60	20	10.00
RAL	53	16	479	34*	12.94
NAT.W.	14	4	168	45*	16.80
B & H	27	5	211	39	9.59

CAREER: BOWLING

	O.	M.	R.	W.	AV.
TEST	412.5	79	1170	42	27.85
1ST-CLASS	6423.1	1741	1755	880	19.94
INT	87.2	13	245	13	18.84
RAL	603.1	48	2446	95	25.74
NAT.W.	258.2	56	634	40	15.85
B & H	435.4	91	1211	70	17.30

49. Who was England's Man of the Series, v Australia, 1989?

CLEAL, M. W.   Somerset

Full Name: Matthew William Cleal
Role: Right-hand bat, right-arm medium bowler, 'boundary fielder'
Born: 23 July 1969, Yeovil
Height: 6′ 3″ **Weight:** 13½st
Nickname: Hogg, Beaker
County debut: 1988
Place in bowling averages: —
(1988 72nd av. 29.10)
1st-Class catches 1989: 2 (career 4)
Parents: Michael Gordon and Diana Alma
Marital status: Single
Family links with cricket: 'Dad played for Somerset U-15 and U-16, and Yeovil Town.'
Education: Parcroft Junior School, Yeovil; Preston Comprehensive, Yeovil
Qualifications: 6 CSEs
Jobs outside cricket: Apprentice painter and decorator
Off-season 1989–90: Playing football for Westland FC; working on the groundstaff at the county ground
Cricketing superstitions or habits: 'Always carry a set of old cricket bails in my cricket coffin, never taken out all season.'
Overseas teams played for: Wanganui, New Zealand 1988–89
Cricketers particularly learnt from: Father, Peter Robinson (coach at Somerset), Nigel Felton, Adrian Jones, Neil Mallender, Trevor Gard
Cricketers particularly admired: Dennis Lillee, Steve Waugh ('very hard, but very fair competitor'), Colin Dredge, Malcolm Marshall, Trevor Gard
Other sports played: Football, golf, tennis, badminton
Other sports followed: Football, Yeovil Town FC
Injuries 1989: Strained lateral hamstring – out for two weeks in June
Relaxations: 'Spending time with my girlfriend. Going to the Electric Studios night-club, Yeovil.'
Extras: Bowler of tournament in 7 Nations International Youth Festival in Ireland 1987. Somerset Young Player of Year 1988. Sponsored by local newspaper. Joined Somerset on a YTS scheme. Made first-class debut v West Indies, at 18 years old
Opinions on cricket: 'I think more time should be spent practising in group nets, rather than playing 2nd XI cricket on bad club ground pitches. Second team pitches must be improved.'

110

Best batting performance: 30 Somerset v Leicestershire, Taunton 1989
Best bowling performance: 4-41 Somerset v West Indians, Taunton 1988

LAST SEASON: BATTING

	I.	N.O.	R.	H.S.	AV.
TEST					
1ST-CLASS	7	0	68	30	9.71
INT					
RAL	2	1	23	15	23.00
NAT.W.	2	1	28	25	28.00
B & H					

LAST SEASON: BOWLING

	O.	M.	R.	W.	AV.
TEST					
1ST-CLASS	95.4	19	327	6	54.50
INT					
RAL	26	2	120	0	–
NAT.W.	20	0	86	2	43.00
B & H					

CAREER: BATTING

	I.	N.O.	R.	H.S.	AV.
TEST					
1ST-CLASS	19	1	165	30	9.16
INT					
RAL	3	1	24	15	12.00
NAT.W.	2	1	28	25	28.00
B & H					

CAREER: BOWLING

	O.	M.	R.	W.	AV.
TEST					
1ST-CLASS	263.4	44	909	26	34.96
INT					
RAL	36	2	187	0	–
NAT.W.	20	0	86	2	43.00
B & H					

CLINTON, G. S.   Surrey

Full Name: Grahame Selvey Clinton
Role: Left-hand bat, right-arm
medium bowler
Born: 5 May 1953, Sidcup
Height: 5′ 6″
Nickname: Clint, Grimbo (at Kent)
County debut: 1974 (Kent),
1979 (Surrey)
County cap: 1980 (Surrey)
Benefit: 1989
1000 runs in a season: 6
1st-Class 50s scored: 65
1st-Class 100s scored: 19
One-Day 50s: 29
One-Day 100s: 4
Place in batting averages: 148th
av. 23.51 (1988 25th av. 43.91)
1st-Class catches 1989: 7 (career 90)
Wife: Cathy
Children: Three boys
Family links with cricket: Father captained Kemnal Manor CC. Younger
brothers Neil and Tony regular members of Blackheath CC
Education: Chislehurst and Sidcup Grammar School

Jobs outside cricket: PE, rugby and cricket teacher at Dartford Grammar School

Overseas tours: East Africa with London Schools 1969; India with England Schoolboys 1970; England Young Cricketers to West Indies 1972; Barbados for own benefit tour 1989

Cricketers particularly learnt from: George Pope of Kent Schools team; Fred Ingram from London Schools; George Fowler of Kent U-19

Other sports played: Alleged by Steve Davis to have a highest snooker break of 14

Extras: Formerly played for Kent, where he made his debut 1974. Left after 1978 season to join Surrey. Renowned as a dressing-room wit and as being one of the most injury-prone cricketers. Claims to have seen the inside of the casualty departments in 15 out of 17 counties. Scored his first first-class century for Surrey in his first match against his old county, Kent. Top scorer for Surrey, with 6, when they were dismissed for 14 by Essex at Chelmsford in 1983. At age 11, he played for Kemnal Manor, Kent. Later played club cricket for Sidcup and for Blackheath. Played for London Colts in 1968 with Emburey and Gooch and topped the batting averages

Best batting performance: 192 Surrey v Yorkshire, The Oval 1984

Best bowling performance: 2-8 Kent v Pakistan, Canterbury 1978

LAST SEASON: BATTING

	I.	N.O.	R.	H.S.	AV.
TEST					
1ST-CLASS	40	3	870	90*	23.51
INT					
RAL	16	0	585	78	36.56
NAT.W.	3	1	42	40	21.00
B & H	4	0	143	74	35.75

LAST SEASON: BOWLING

	O.	M.	R.	W.	AV.
TEST					
1ST-CLASS					
INT					
RAL					
NAT.W.					
B & H					

CAREER: BATTING

	I.	N.O.	R.	H.S.	AV.
TEST					
1ST-CLASS	418	49	11826	192	32.04
INT					
RAL	85	9	2543	105*	33.46
NAT.W.	26	2	697	146	29.04
B & H	45	2	1493	121*	34.72

CAREER: BOWLING

	O.	M.	R.	W.	AV.
TEST					
1ST-CLASS	26.4	2	201	4	50.25
INT					
RAL					
NAT.W.	4	2	2	0	—
B & H	1.2	0	10	0	—

50. Who was Australia's Man of the Series, v England, 1989?

COBB, R. A. Leicestershire

Full Name: Russell Alan Cobb
Role: Right-hand opening bat, slow left-arm bowler, close fielder '–sometimes too close, i.e. short leg or silly point.'
Born: 18 May 1961, Leicester
Height: 5′ 11″ **Weight:** 12st '– or just over!'
Nickname: Cobby
County debut: 1980
County cap: 1986
1000 runs in a season: 1
1st-Class 50s scored: 23
One-Day 50s: 1
Place in batting averages: 205th av. 17.44 (1988 148th av. 24.00)
1st-Class catches 1989: 5 (career 72)
Parents: Alan and Betty
Wife and date of marriage: Sharon, 30 March 1985
Family links with cricket: Father a club cricketer, a wicket-keeper. God-father, Maurice Hallam, former Leicestershire captain
Education: Dovelands Junior School; Woodbank School, Leicester; Trent College, Nottingham
Qualifications: 7 O-levels, NCA Advanced Coaching Certificate; private pilot's licence
Jobs outside cricket: Costing clerk for British Shoe Corporation, Leicester. Worked on promotion for Leicestershire CCC. Worked for shoe company in Australia
Cricketing superstitions or habits: 'Always put my left pad on first. Must wear some sort of headgear.'
Off-season 1989–90: Playing and coaching in South Africa; coaching in townships, and running coaching courses for black school-teachers; playing on Saturdays for a Teachers' Training College. Captain of Northern Transvaal B
Overseas tours: Young England to Australia 1979; Derrick Robins' XI to New Zealand 1979–80; Young England to West Indies 1980; Leicestershire to Zimbabwe 1981; Leicestershire to Holland 1988
Overseas teams played for: Glenelg, Adelaide, South Australia 1980–81; Teachers Training College, Pretoria 1983–84, 1984–85, 1985–86, 1986–87, 1987–88; Natal B 1988–89

Cricketers particularly learnt from: Jack Birkenshaw, Ken Higgs, Chris Balderstone '– and of course all my team-mates.'
Cricketers particularly admired: 'All who have played top class cricket for a number of years.'
Other sports played: Squash, badminton
Other sports followed: Most sports, particularly rugby
Relaxations: 'A little gardening, walking, eating out, and socialising with good friends.'
Opinions on cricket: 'Fine idea that a first-class umpire stands in second XI cricket. The non-first-class umpires can only benefit from this. I find some of the views in the media and elsewhere about South Africa very hypocritical.'
Best batting performance: 91 Leicestershire v Northamptonshire, Leicester 1986

LAST SEASON: BATTING

	I.	N.O.	R.	H.S.	AV.
TEST					
1ST-CLASS	9	0	157	47	17.44
INT					
RAL					
NAT.W.					
B & H					

CAREER: BATTING

	I.	N.O.	R.	H.S.	AV.
TEST					
1ST-CLASS	195	15	4388	91	24.37
INT					
RAL	6	4	60	24	30.00
NAT.W.	8	1	182	66*	26.00
B & H	2	0	26	22	13.00

CONNOR, C. A. — Hampshire

Full Name: Cardigan Adolphus Connor
Role: Right-hand bat, right-arm fast-medium bowler
Born: 24 March 1961, West End, Anguilla
Height: 5′ 10″ **Weight:** 11st 6lbs
Nickname: 'Christy, Cardy and many more.'
County debut: 1984
County cap: 1988
50 wickets in a season: 3
1st-Class 5 w. in innings: 8
1st-Class 10 w. in match: 1
Place in batting averages: 256th av. 10.75
Place in bowling averages: 17th av. 21.27 (1988 64th av. 27.21)
Strike rate 1989: 45.08 (career 61.38)

1st-Class catches 1989: 0 (career 29)
Parents: Ethleen Snagg
Marital status: Single
Education: Valley Secondary School, Anguilla; Langley College
Qualifications: Engineer
Jobs outside cricket: Timko Engineering, Slough Trading Estate
Cricketing superstitions or habits: Never change before the end of play
Overseas tours: Hampshire CCC tour of Hong Kong, Singapore, New Zealand and Australia 1983
Overseas teams played for: Merriweather CC, Newcastle, Australia 1983–84 and 1984–85; West End CC, Anguilla 1973–76
Cricketers particularly learnt from: Tim Tremlett
Cricketers particularly admired: Viv Richards, Andy Roberts, Richard Hadlee
Other sports played: Most other sports
Other sports followed: Football, boxing, tennis
Relaxations: Music, wine bars, meeting people
Extras: Played for Buckinghamshire in Minor Counties before joining Hampshire. First Anguillan-born player to appear in the County Championship
Best batting performance: 36 Hampshire v Northamptonshire, Northampton 1985
Best bowling performance: 7-31 Hampshire v Gloucestershire, Portsmouth 1989

LAST SEASON: BATTING

	I.	N.O.	R.	H.S.	AV.
TEST					
1ST-CLASS	14	2	129	24	10.75
INT					
RAL	7	1	58	19	9.66
NAT.W.	–	–	–	–	–
B & H	1	1	4	4*	–

CAREER: BATTING

	I.	N.O.	R.	H.S.	AV.
TEST					
1ST-CLASS	90	29	466	36	7.63
INT					
RAL	18	10	81	19	10.12
NAT.W.	2	1	8	5	8.00
B & H	5	4	13	5*	13.00

LAST SEASON: BOWLING

	O.	M.	R.	W.	AV.
TEST					
1ST-CLASS	443.2	99	1255	59	21.27
INT					
RAL	115	15	459	23	19.95
NAT.W.	47.4	7	204	10	20.40
B & H	34.1	4	155	7	22.14

CAREER: BOWLING

	O.	M.	R.	W.	AV.
TEST					
1ST-CLASS	2987.3	647	8845	292	30.29
INT					
RAL	606	45	2610	108	24.16
NAT.W.	141.3	21	497	19	26.15
B & H	217.4	27	818	36	22.72

COOK, G.   Northamptonshire

Full Name: Geoffrey Cook
Role: Right-hand bat, slow left-arm
bowler, occasional wicket-keeper
Born: 9 October 1951,
Middlesbrough, Yorkshire
Height: 6' **Weight:** 12st 10lbs
Nickname: Geoff
County debut: 1971
County cap: 1975
Benefit: 1985
Test debut: 1981–82
No. of Tests: 7
No. of One-Day Internationals: 6
1000 runs in a season: 12
1st-Class 50s scored: 111
1st-Class 100s scored: 36
1st-Class 200s scored: 1
One-Day 50s: 51
One-Day 100s: 4

Place in batting averages: 63rd av. 35.57 (1988 99th av. 29.31)
1st-Class catches 1989: 7 (career 417 + 3 stumpings)
Parents: Harry and Helen
Wife and date of marriage: Judith, 22 November 1975
Children: Anna, 21 May 1980
Family links with cricket: Father and brother David very keen club cricketers.
'Father was virtually "Mr Cricket" in Middlesbrough cricket in the 1960s
being secretary, president and chairman of various leagues at one time or
another.'
Education: Middlesbrough High School
Qualifications: 6 O-levels, 1 A-level
Jobs outside cricket: Has taught at Spratton Hall Prep. School
Overseas tours: England to India and Sri Lanka 1981–82, Australia 1982–83
Overseas teams played for: Eastern Province 1978–81
Cricketers particularly learnt from: Wayne Larkins
Cricketers particularly admired: Clive Rice
Other sports played: 'All sports when given opportunity.' Football with
Wellingborough in the Southern League
Relaxations: Walking, reading, crosswords
Extras: 'Great believer in organised recreation for young people. Would
enjoy time and scope to carry my beliefs through.' Captain from 1981 to 1988.
Voluntarily stepped down from captaincy at the end of the 1988 season.
Chairman of the Cricketers' Association

Opinions on cricket: Following his departure as captain, Cook said 'It is not only a team that needs motivating. The captain needs a certain amount of motivating as well.'

Best batting performance: 203 Northamptonshire v Yorkshire, Scarborough 1988

Best bowling performance: 3-47 England XI v South Australia, Adelaide 1982–83

LAST SEASON: BATTING

	I.	N.O.	R.	H.S.	AV.
TEST					
1ST-CLASS	36	3	1174	138	35.57
INT					
RAL	8	1	249	77	35.57
NAT.W.	3	0	53	45	17.66
B & H	5	1	266	72*	66.50

CAREER: BATTING

	I.	N.O.	R.	H.S.	AV.
TEST	13	0	203	66	15.61
1ST-CLASS	768	64	22787	203	32.36
INT	6	0	106	32	17.66
RAL	220	20	4767	98	23.83
NAT.W.	42	2	1520	130	38.00
B & H	68	6	1875	108	30.24

LAST SEASON: BOWLING

	O.	M.	R.	W.	AV.
TEST					
1ST-CLASS	2	0	15	0	–
INT					
RAL					
NAT.W.					
B & H					

CAREER: BOWLING

	O.	M.	R.	W.	AV.
TEST	7	3	27	0	–
1ST-CLASS	199.2	40	779	15	51.93
INT					
RAL	2	0	10	0	–
NAT.W.					
B & H					

COOK, N. G. B.   Northamptonshire

Full Name: Nicholas Grant Billson Cook
Role: Right-hand bat, slow left-arm bowler, backward short-leg fielder
Born: 17 June 1956, Leicester
Height: 6' **Weight:** 12st 8lbs
Nickname: Beast, Rag'ead
County debut: 1978 (Leicestershire), 1986 (Northamptonshire)
County cap: 1982 (Leicestershire), 1987 (Northamptonshire)
Test debut: 1983
No. of Tests: 15
No. of One-Day Internationals: 2
50 wickets in a season: 8
1st-Class 50s scored: 4
1st-Class 5 w. in innings: 28

1st-Class 10 w. in match: 3
Place in bowling averages: 21st av. 21.77 (1988 42nd av. 24.04)
Strike rate 1989: 57.73 (career 72.88)
1st-Class catches 1989: 19 (career 169)
Parents: Peter and Cynthia
Marital status: Divorced
Family links with cricket: Father played club cricket
Education: Stokes Croft Junior; Lutterworth High; Lutterworth Upper
Qualifications: 7 O-levels, 1 A-level, Advanced Cricket Coach
Jobs outside cricket: Has worked for Leicestershire CCC on promotions, organising lotteries, sponsored walks, general fund-raising projects
Off-season 1989–90: To India with England for Nehru Trophy
Overseas tours: Whitbread Scholarship to Perth, Australia 1980–81; Far East tour with MCC to Bangkok, Singapore, Hong Kong 1981; Australia and New Zealand with Derrick Robins' XI 1980; Zimbabwe with Leicestershire CCC 1981; Dubai with Barbican XI 1982; America with MCC 1982–83; Kuwait with MCC 1983; New Zealand and Pakistan with England 1983–84; to Zimbabwe with English Counties XI 1984–85; to Zimbabwe with England B 1985–86; Sri Lanka with England B 1986; Pakistan with England 1987; MCC to Bermuda 1987; with England to India for Nehru Trophy 1989
Overseas teams played for: Claremont-Cottesloe CC, Perth 1980–81
Cricketers particularly learnt from: Jack Birkenshaw, Roger Tolchard
Other sports followed: Soccer, rugby, horse racing
Relaxations: Crosswords, watching horse racing and football (especially Leicester City), reading (especially Wilbur Smith), good comedy programmes, good food
Extras: Played for ESCA 1975. Played for Young England v Young West Indies 1975. Played for MCC v Middlesex at start of 1981 season. Played for England B Team v Pakistan, August 1982. Left Leicestershire to join Northamptonshire for 1986 season
Opinions on cricket: 'After the demise of England against the Australians last

LAST SEASON: BATTING

	I.	N.O.	R.	H.S.	AV.
TEST	5	3	45	31	22.50
1ST-CLASS	27	6	143	21	6.80
INT					
RAL	4	2	28	13*	14.00
NAT.W.	1	1	0	0*	–
B & H	2	1	21	14	21.00

CAREER: BATTING

	I.	N.O.	R.	H.S.	AV.
TEST	25	4	179	31	8.52
1ST-CLASS	274	71	2435	75	11.99
INT	–	–	–	–	–
RAL	32	15	171	13*	10.05
NAT.W.	4	1	26	13	8.66
B & H	13	5	127	23	15.87

LAST SEASON: BOWLING

	O.	M.	R.	W.	AV.
TEST	103.5	29	282	5	56.40
1ST-CLASS	483.1	177	1046	56	18.67
INT					
RAL	81	6	288	15	19.20
NAT.W.	35	4	131	1	131.00
B & H	24.1	3	66	5	13.20

CAREER: BOWLING

	O.	M.	R.	W.	AV.
TEST	695.4	226	1689	52	32.48
1ST-CLASS	8387.2	2469	19394	696	27.86
INT	14	1	52	3	17.33
RAL	520.5	36	2213	77	28.74
NAT.W.	142	24	482	14	34.42
B & H	247.1	29	887	20	44.35

summer, the surfaces on which we play county cricket must change. We need 16 four-day games on good, hard surfaces. Groundsmen are put under too much pressure from captains and managers to produce result wickets. One solution would be that groundsmen should be employed by the TCCB, with the directive that they should produce the best wickets they can. Then bowlers have little margin for error, the batsmen will not be faced with the ball seaming about all over the place, and the uneven bounce should be eradicated, because of the better wickets. Confidence will therefore return, and the best batsmen and bowlers will flourish; we will not see Mickey-Mouse fourth seamers top of the averages. Also, the ball needs a flatter seam.'

Best batting performance: 75 Leicestershire v Somerset, Taunton 1980
Best bowling performance: 7-63 Leicestershire v Somerset, Taunton 1982

COOK, S. J. Somerset

Full Name: Stephen James Cook
Role: Right-hand bat
Born: 31 July 1953, Johannesburg
Height: 6′ 3″ **Weight:** 14st
Nickname: Mutley
County debut: 1989
County cap: 1989
1000 runs in a season: 1
1st-Class 50s scored: 56
1st-Class 100s scored: 32
1st-Class 200s scored: 1
One-Day 50s: 4
One-Day 100s: 3
Place in batting averages: 3rd
av. 60.56
1st-Class catches 1989: 13 (career 98)
Parents: Denzil Chesney and Nancy
Harding
Wife and date of marriage: Linsey,
11 April 1981
Children: Stephen Craig, 29 November 1982; Ryan Lyall, 2 October 1985
Family links with cricket: Father played local club cricket
Education: Rosebank Primary and Hyde Park High Schools; Wits University; Johannesburg College of Education
Qualifications: Matric Pass; TTHD from Johannesburg College of Education
Jobs outside cricket: School teacher; Manager of Cricket Affairs at Rand Afrikaans University
Off-season 1989–90: Playing for Transvaal in the South African season

Cricketing superstitions or habits: 'Left boot and bat first; mark the crease each time I face at a new end.'

Overseas tours: Played in all unofficial Tests and 1-day matches against England, West Indies, Sri Lanka and Australia

Overseas teams played for: Transvaal 1972–1989; South Africa 1982–1989

Cricketers particularly learnt from: Clive Rice, Graeme Pollock, Kevin McKenzie

Cricketers particularly admired: Barry Richards, Clive Rice, Vince Van Der Bijl, Graeme Pollock, Kevin McKenzie, Henry Fotheringham

Other sports played: Football (Pro. with Wits University 1976–84), golf

Other sports followed: Golf, football, rugby, tennis, athletics

Relaxations: Quiet meal and a glass of wine with family and friends

Extras: 'Scored 114 against England on my debut in unofficial Tests.' Highest run aggregate (556) for a Sunday League debut season. Wombwell Cricket-Lovers Society Cricketer of the Year 1989. Came to England as manager of South African Schools side in 1983, 1988

Opinions on cricket: 'Would like to see fewer matches of the 3-day variety and more 4-day games. The over rate of 18.5 is too much – 17–17.5 is more realistic. Players should be able to play against whoever they wish without government interference.'

Best batting performance: 201* Transvaal v Eastern Province, Port Elizabeth 1982–83

Best bowling performance: 1-15 Transvaal v Natal, Durban 1975–76

LAST SEASON: BATTING

	I.	N.O.	R.	H.S.	AV.
TEST					
1ST-CLASS	41	4	2241	156	60.56
INT					
RAL	16	1	556	124*	37.06
NAT.W.	2	0	34	33	17.00
B & H	6	0	312	79	52.00

LAST SEASON: BOWLING

	O.	M.	R.	W.	AV.
TEST					
1ST-CLASS					
INT					
RAL					
NAT.W.					
B & H					

CAREER: BATTING

	I.	N.O.	R.	H.S.	AV.
TEST					
1ST-CLASS	302	32	12220	201*	45.25
INT					
RAL	16	1	556	124*	37.06
NAT.W.	2	0	34	33	17.00
B & H	6	0	312	79	52.00

CAREER: BOWLING

	O.	M.	R.	W.	AV.
TEST					
1ST-CLASS	10	1	34	1	34.00
INT					
RAL					
NAT.W.					
B & H					

COOPER, K. E.   Nottinghamshire

Full Name: Kevin Edwin Cooper
Role: Left-hand bat, right-arm
fast-medium bowler
Born: 27 December 1957,
Sutton-in-Ashfield
Height: 6′ **Weight:** 12st 4lbs
Nickname: Henry
County debut: 1976
County cap: 1980
50 wickets in a season: 7
1st-Class 5 w. in innings: 22
1st-Class 10 w. in match: 1
Place in batting averages: 246th av.
11.95 (1988 257th av. 11.28)
Place in bowling averages: 40th
av. 26.36 (1988 21st av. 21.57)
Strike rate 1989: 61.93 (career 59.11)
1st-Class catches 1989: 7 (career 76)
Parents: Gerald Edwin and Margaret
Wife and date of marriage: Linda Carol, 14 February 1981
Children: Kelly Louise, 8 April 1982; Tara Amy, 22 November 1984
Family links with cricket: Father played local cricket
Jobs outside cricket: Warehouseman and maintenance man, public relations
officer in free trade department of local brewery
Off-season 1989–90: Working for Marketing Department at Trent Bridge
Overseas tours: Australasia with Derrick Robins' U-23 XI 1979–80
Overseas teams played for: Nedlands CC, Perth, Western Australia 1978–79
Cricketers particularly admired: John Snow

LAST SEASON: BATTING

	I.	N.O.	R.	H.S.	AV.
TEST					
1ST-CLASS	27	6	251	33*	11.95
INT					
RAL	7	2	79	28*	15.80
NAT.W.	1	0	6	6	6.00
B & H	2	1	18	17*	18.00

CAREER: BATTING

	I.	N.O.	R.	H.S.	AV.
TEST					
1ST-CLASS	253	61	1912	46	9.95
INT					
RAL	46	15	199	31	6.41
NAT.W.	6	1	35	11	7.00
B & H	19	11	99	25*	12.37

LAST SEASON: BOWLING

	O.	M.	R.	W.	AV.
TEST					
1ST-CLASS	609	177	1553	59	26.32
INT					
RAL	107.4	5	418	13	32.15
NAT.W.	24	5	54	2	27.00
B & H	72.1	13	192	11	17.45

CAREER: BOWLING

	O.	M.	R.	W.	AV.
TEST					
1ST-CLASS	6407	1776	17012	650	26.17
INT					
RAL	935.4	61	4082	124	32.91
NAT.W.	241.2	55	652	30	21.73
B & H	515.5	98	1733	62	27.95

Relaxations: Golf, clay pigeon shooting
Extras: In 1974, playing for Hucknall Ramblers CC, took 10 wickets for 6 runs in one innings against Sutton College in the Mansfield and District League. First bowler to take 50 first-class wickets in 1988 season
Best batting performance: 46 Nottinghamshire v Middlesex, Trent Bridge 1985
Best bowling performance: 8-44 Nottinghamshire v Middlesex, Lord's 1984

COTTEY, P. A.   Glamorgan

Full Name: Phillip Anthony Cottey
Role: Right-hand opening bat, cover point fielder
Born: 2 June 1966, Swansea
Height: 5′ 5″ **Weight:** 9st 10lbs
County debut: 1986
Nickname: Cotts
1st-Class 50s scored: 5
One-Day 50s: 1
Place in batting averages: —
(1988 91st av. 30.15)
1st-Class catches 1989: 2 (career 10)
Parents: Bernard John and Ruth
Marital status: Engaged
Family links with cricket: Father played for Swansea CC
Education: Bishopston Comprehensive School, Swansea
Qualifications: 9 O-levels
Jobs outside cricket: Played professional soccer for Swansea City until 1985
Off-season 1989–90: Working for an employment agency linked to Glamorgan CCC. Also playing soccer for Llanelli AFC
Overseas tours: Glamorgan to La Manga 1988; and to Barbados 1989
Overseas teams played for: Penrith DCC 1986–87; Benoni CC, Johannesburg 1988–89
Cricketers particularly learnt from: Alan Jones, Tom Cartwright, John Hopkins, A. L. Jones, John Steele
Cricketers particularly admired: Alan Jones, Ian Botham, Viv Richards, Geoff Boycott
Other sports played: Soccer, golf, squash, weight training
Relaxations: Anything revolving around sport. Watching videos, listening to music. 'Working on my new house – or rather trying to turn it into a new house!'

122

Extras: Left school at 16 to play for Swansea City FC for three years as a professional. Captained Welsh Youth Soccer XI (3 caps). Played in Football League

Opinions on cricket: 'I think that 16 four-day games would make for a fairer county championship. Wickets around the country are still of a generally poor standard. I think there should be an incentive for groundsmen to produce good pitches, i.e. "Groundsman of the Year", which would be judged by a panel of ex-players, ex-groundsmen and umpires and would involve a worthwhile cash prize. I do not think that sport and politics should mix. It baffles me that young cricketers are encouraged not to go to South Africa, and yet in the county championships all nationalities play with South Africans. South African-born players even play for England. There is a double standard somewhere.'

Best batting performance: 92 Glamorgan v Cambridge University, Cambridge 1988

LAST SEASON: BATTING

	I.	N.O.	R.	H.S.	AV.
TEST					
1ST-CLASS	6	0	56	24	9.33
INT					
RAL	3	1	65	34*	32.50
NAT.W.					
B & H	4	0	76	68	19.00

CAREER: BATTING

	I.	N.O.	R.	H.S.	AV.
TEST					
1ST-CLASS	44	5	844	92	21.64
INT					
RAL	10	1	86	34*	9.55
NAT.W.					
B & H	6	0	105	68	17.50

51. Who was Australia's wicket-keeper in the 1989 Ashes series?

52. Who was the first Englishman to score 1000 runs last season?

53. Who was the first batsman to reach 1000 runs last season?

COWANS, N. G.   Middlesex

Full Name: Norman George Cowans
Role: Right-hand bat, right-arm
fast bowler
Born: 17 April 1961, Enfield St
Mary, Jamaica
Height: 6′ 3″ **Weight:** 14st 7lbs
Nickname: Flash, George, Seed
County debut: 1980
County cap: 1984
Test debut: 1982–83
No. of Tests: 19
No. of One-Day Internationals: 23
50 wickets in a season: 6
1st-Class 50s scored: 1
1st-Class 5 w. in innings: 22
1st-Class 10 w. in match: 1
Place in bowling averages: 18th
av. 21.30 (1988 7th av. 18.16)
Strike rate 1989: 47.66 (career 45.40)
1st-Class catches 1989: 2 (career 51)

Parents: Gloria and Ivan
Children: Kimberley, 27 December 1983
Education: Park High Secondary, Stanmore, Middlesex
Qualifications: Qualified coach
Jobs outside cricket: Squash and real tennis professional. Glassblower with
Whitefriars hand-made glass
Off-season 1989–90: Setting up business ventures
Overseas tours: Young England to Australia 1979; Middlesex to Zimbabwe
1980; *The Cricketer* to Dubai 1981; England to Australia and New Zealand
1982–83 and New Zealand and Pakistan 1983–84; International tour to
Jamaica 1983; India and Australia with England 1984–85; England B to Sri
Lanka 1986
Overseas teams played for: Claremont-Cottesloe CC, Perth, Australia
Cricketers particularly learnt from: Dennis Lillee, Wayne Daniel, Michael
Holding. 'The aggression of Lillee, the power of Daniel, and the smoothness
of Holding.'
Cricketers particularly admired: Viv Richards, Malcolm Marshall
Other sports played: Basketball, squash, table tennis, real tennis
Other sports followed: Football (Arsenal FC), athletics, boxing
Injuries 1989: Strained side muscle – missed two games
Relaxations: Fishing, photography, travelling, being with friends, listening to
reggae and soul music

Extras: Two Young England Tests, one One-Day Youth International. Has won athletics championships in sprinting and javelin throwing. Played 13 Tests for England before being awarded Middlesex cap

Opinions on cricket: 'The county programme is far too intense, and I think that 16 four-day games would be a much better system for producing quality players.'

Best batting performance: 66 Middlesex v Surrey, Lord's 1984

Best bowling performance: 6-31 Middlesex v Leicestershire, Leicester 1985

LAST SEASON: BATTING

	I.	N.O.	R.	H.S.	AV.
TEST					
1ST-CLASS	24	7	127	21*	7.47
INT					
RAL	4	1	5	4	1.66
NAT.W.	–	–	–	–	–
B & H	2	0	1	1	0.50

CAREER: BATTING

	I.	N.O.	R.	H.S.	AV.
TEST	29	7	175	36	7.95
1ST-CLASS	153	36	1043	66	8.91
INT	8	3	13	4*	2.60
RAL	22	8	96	20	6.85
NAT.W.	10	2	33	12*	4.12
B & H	10	4	22	6	3.66

LAST SEASON: BOWLING

	O.	M.	R.	W.	AV.
TEST					
1ST-CLASS	492.3	117	1321	62	21.30
INT					
RAL	99	28	275	14	19.64
NAT.W.	55.4	10	173	5	34.60
B & H	34	8	101	6	16.83

CAREER: BOWLING

	O.	M.	R.	W.	AV.
TEST	575.2	113	2003	51	39.27
1ST-CLASS	3488.5	750	10482	486	21.56
INT	213.4	17	913	23	39.70
RAL	470.2	51	1783	70	25.47
NAT.W.	247.4	42	799	36	22.19
B & H	231.1	34	717	38	18.86

54. Who was Sid Hobbins?

55. Which book, published in 1989, has parodies of cricket writing by Proust, P. G. Wodehouse, Anthony Powell, Conan Doyle and Ian Fleming?

COWDREY, C. S.   Kent

Full Name: Christopher Stuart
Cowdrey
Role: Right-hand bat, right-arm
medium bowler
Born: 20 October 1957,
Farnborough, Kent
Height: 6' **Weight:** 14st
Nickname: Cow, Woody
County debut: 1977
County cap: 1979
Benefit: 1989
Test debut: 1984–85
No. of Tests: 6
No. of One-Day Internationals: 3
1000 runs in a season: 4
1st-Class 50s scored: 54
1st-Class 100s scored: 18
1st-Class 5 w. in innings: 2
One-Day 50s: 38
One-Day 100s: 2
Place in batting averages: 43rd av. 38.96 (1988 103rd av. 29.06)
Place in bowling averages: 124th av. 66.50 (1988 75th av. 29.25)
Strike rate 1989: 113.75 (career 72.32)
1st-Class catches 1989: 19 (career 278)
Parents: Michael Colin and Penelope Susan
Wife and date of marriage: Christel, 1 January 1989
Family links with cricket: Grandfather, Stuart Chiesman, on Kent Com-
mittee, 12 years as Chairman. Pavilion on Kent's ground at Canterbury
named after him. Father played for Kent and England, brother made Kent
debut 1984
Education: Wellesley House, Broadstairs; Tonbridge School
Jobs outside cricket: Director of Ten Tenths Travel. Consultant to Stuart
Canvas Products
Off-season 1989–90: Touring South Africa with unofficial English team
Overseas tours: Captained Young England to West Indies 1976; with Derrick
Robins' XI to Sri Lanka 1977–78, and Far East, South America and
Australasia 1979–80; India and Australia with England 1984–85
Overseas teams played for: Avendale CC, Cape Town 1983–84; Cumberland
CC, Sydney 1978–79 and 1982–83
Cricketers particularly learnt from: Asif Iqbal, Allan Lamb, Clive Radley,
John Inverarity
Cricketers particularly admired: David Gower

126

Other sports played: Golf, tennis, backgammon

Other sports followed: All sports

Relaxations: Dining at Silks Restaurant with Richard Scott and taking Blaise Craven's money at backgammon

Extras: Played for Kent 2nd XI at age 15. Vice-captain 1984. Captain 1985. Captain of England for one Test v West Indies, 1988. Injury kept him out of next Test; then astonishingly not picked for next Test. Best man at wedding of Kim Barnett of Derbyshire and England. David Gower was his best man. Is credited with the following joke: Scene, Third Test at Calcutta, 1984 v India. Gower, England's captain is discussing field placing, and in particular Gatting at first slip, with the bowler, Cowdrey. Gower: 'Do you want Gatt a foot wider?' Cowdrey: 'No, he would burst.' Published autobiography, *Good Enough?*, 1986

Opinions on cricket: 'None that can be quoted!'

Best batting performance: 159 Kent v Surrey, Canterbury 1985

Best bowling performance: 5-46 Kent v Hampshire, Canterbury 1986

LAST SEASON: BATTING

	I.	N.O.	R.	H.S.	AV.
TEST					
1ST-CLASS	34	4	1169	146*	38.96
INT					
RAL	16	3	406	78	31.23
NAT.W.	2	1	121	69*	121.00
B & H	6	0	25	9	4.16

LAST SEASON: BOWLING

	O.	M.	R.	W.	AV.
TEST					
1ST-CLASS	227.3	32	798	12	66.50
INT					
RAL	65.1	1	389	10	38.90
NAT.W.	2	0	15	0	–
B & H	56	5	203	6	33.83

CAREER: BATTING

	I.	N.O.	R.	H.S.	AV.
TEST	8	1	101	38	14.42
1ST-CLASS	413	60	11195	159	31.71
INT	3	1	51	46*	25.50
RAL	165	26	3672	95	26.41
NAT.W.	28	6	830	122*	37.72
B & H	54	8	1305	114	28.36

CAREER: BOWLING

	O.	M.	R.	W.	AV.
TEST	66.3	2	309	4	77.25
1ST-CLASS	2272.1	437	7379	190	38.83
INT	8.4	0	55	2	27.50
RAL	618.2	9	3011	105	28.67
NAT.W.	166	17	599	22	27.22
B & H	320.4	17	1373	37	37.10

56. What official honour was conferred by the Australian Prime Minister on Allan Border following his team's Ashes victory in 1989?

COWDREY, G. R.   Kent

Full Name: Graham Robert Cowdrey
Role: Right-hand bat, right-arm medium bowler, cover fielder
Born: 27 June 1964, Farnborough, Kent
Height: 5′ 10″ **Weight:** 13st 7lbs
Nickname: Van, Cow
County debut: 1984
County cap: 1988
1st-Class 50s scored: 13
1st-Class 100s scored: 2
One-Day 50s: 6
One-Day 100s: 1
Place in batting averages: 122nd av. 27.11 (1988 108th av. 28.62)
1st-Class catches 1989: 4 (career 34)
Parents: Michael Colin and Penelope Susan
Marital status: Single
Family links with cricket: 'Father had a couple of knocks with England, and brother likewise.'
Education: Wellesley House, Broadstairs; Tonbridge School; Durham University
Qualifications: 8 O-levels, 3 A-levels, University entrance
Cricketing superstitions or habits: 'Say a prayer at the top of the steps before batting. Have to run every day. Unless the conditions are arctic, do not wear a sweater.'
Overseas tours: Australia with Tonbridge School 1980; Christians in Sport India tour 1985–86; Barbados with Fred Rumsey XI 1988
Overseas teams played for: Avendale CC, Cape Town 1983–84; Mosman CC, Sydney 1985–86; Randwick CC, Sydney 1986–87
Cricketers particularly learnt from: 'My father. I have found it best to listen to any cricketers. It is up to the individual to work out what is best for him. All at Kent CCC.'
Cricketers particularly admired: Mark Benson, Terry Alderman, Robin Smith, Murray Nissan
Other sports played: Squash, cross-country running, golf, tennis
Other sports followed: Rugby union
Injuries 1989: Ankle ligaments – four weeks off, missing B & H semi-final – 'a great disappointment.'
Relaxations: Reading, theatre, and music. 'I have seen the Irish musician Van Morrison 70 times in concert. A wonderful musician – truly a genius.'

128

Extras: Played for Young England and Australia. 1000 runs for Kent 2nd XI first season on staff, captain of Kent 2nd XI in 1984. Very interested in psychology of cricket. Broke 2nd XI record with 1300 runs in 26 innings in 1985. Wears contact lenses – 'Might try to do without them next year – it might help!'

Opinions on cricket: 'Less cricket must enhance the quality. Four days a week would allow more time for quality practice, and for better fitness. Four-day cricket is an improvement for the players, but I do not think necessarily for the crowd.'

Best batting performance: 145 Kent v Essex, Chelmsford 1988

Best bowling performance: 1-5 Kent v Warwickshire, Edgbaston 1988

LAST SEASON: BATTING

	I.	N.O.	R.	H.S.	AV.
TEST					
1ST-CLASS	12	3	244	108*	27.11
INT					
RAL	10	3	251	102*	35.85
NAT.W.	1	1	34	34*	–
B & H	3	1	50	37	25.00

CAREER: BATTING

	I.	N.O.	R.	H.S.	AV.
TEST					
1ST-CLASS	89	11	1967	145	25.21
INT					
RAL	45	9	857	102*	23.80
NAT.W.	5	2	108	34*	36.00
B & H	16	2	462	69	33.00

LAST SEASON: BOWLING

	O.	M.	R.	W.	AV.
TEST					
1ST-CLASS	6	0	29	1	29.00
INT					
RAL	9	0	47	0	–
NAT.W.					
B & H	7.4	2	22	1	22.00

CAREER: BOWLING

	O.	M.	R.	W.	AV.
TEST					
1ST-CLASS	124.4	23	486	9	54.00
INT					
RAL	96	3	441	21	21.00
NAT.W.	38	11	94	5	18.80
B & H	17.4	4	57	2	28.50

57. Which current England Test cricketer is also a distinguished artist?

58. What is David Gower's nickname?

COWLEY, N. G.

Glamorgan

Full Name: Nigel Geoffrey Cowley
Role: Right-hand bat, off-break bowler
Born: 1 March 1953, Shaftesbury, Dorset
Height: 5' 7" **Weight:** 12st 5lbs
Nickname: Dougal
County debut: 1974 (Hampshire), 1990 (Glamorgan)
County cap: 1978 (Hampshire)
Benefit: 1988 (£88,274)
1000 runs in a season: 1
50 wickets in a season: 2
1st-Class 50s scored: 30
1st-Class 100s scored: 2
1st-Class 5 w. in innings: 5
One-Day 50s: 5
Place in bowling averages: — (1988 86th av. 30.36)
1st-Class catches 1989: 0 (career 96)
Parents: Geoffrey and Betty
Wife: Susan
Children: Mark and Darren
Family links with cricket: Father played good club cricket; son Mark played for Hampshire Schools U-16, and son Darren captained Hampshire Schools U-12
Education: Mere Dutchy Manor, Mere, Wiltshire

LAST SEASON: BATTING

	I.	N.O.	R.	H.S.	AV.
TEST					
1ST-CLASS	2	0	68	42	34.00
INT					
RAL	6	0	27	9	4.50
NAT.W.	1	1	8	8*	—
B & H	2	1	10	6	10.00

CAREER: BATTING

	I.	N.O.	R.	H.S.	AV.
TEST					
1ST-CLASS	358	58	6773	109*	22.57
INT					
RAL	144	31	2049	74	18.13
NAT.W.	25	6	342	63*	18.00
B & H	43	5	522	59	13.73

LAST SEASON: BOWLING

	O.	M.	R.	W.	AV.
TEST					
1ST-CLASS	27	1	102	2	51.00
INT					
RAL	84.2	4	385	14	27.50
NAT.W.	21	0	101	1	101.00
B & H	31	2	119	1	119.00

CAREER: BOWLING

	O.	M.	R.	W.	AV.
TEST					
1ST-CLASS	5127.1	1338	13979	425	32.89
INT					
RAL	1048	53	5019	169	29.69
NAT.W.	293.1	37	906	29	31.24
B & H	449.3	66	1422	31	45.87

Off-season 1989–90: Playing in Durban, South Africa
Overseas tours: England to Sri Lanka 1977; West Indies 1980
Overseas teams played for: Paarl CC, Cape Town 1981–83; Amanzimoti, Durban 1983–85
Cricketers particularly learnt from: Peter Sainsbury
Other sports played: Golf (9 handicap), football
Injuries 1989: Lower stomach strain – out for two and a half months, off and on
Extras: At Hampshire, was in charge of pre-season and match day training. Left Hampshire at end of 1989 season and signed two-year contract with Glamorgan
Best batting performance: 109* Hampshire v Somerset, Taunton 1977
Best bowling performance: 6-48 Hampshire v Leicestershire, Southampton 1982

CROFT, R. D. B. Glamorgan

Full Name: Robert Damien Bale Croft
Role: Off-spin bowler, right-hand bat, all rounder
Born: 25 May 1970, Swansea
Height: 5′ 11″ **Weight:** 11st 5lbs
Nickname: Crofty
County debut: 1989
Place in batting averages: 168th av. 21.50
1st-Class catches 1989: 1 (career 1)
Parents: Malcolm and Susan
Family links with cricket: Father played local league
Education: St John Lloyd Comprehensive, West Glamorgan Institute of Higher Education
Qualifications: 9 O-levels; OND Business Studies; Final Year HND Business Studies; NCA Senior Coaching Certificate; Senior Coaching Award
Off-season 1989–90: Completing Final Year HND Business Studies
Cricketing superstitions or habits: Left pad on first
Overseas tours: WCA U-17s Tour to Barbados (captain); WSCA U-18s Tour to Australia
Cricketers particularly learnt from: Tom Cartwright, Alan Jones, Don Shepherd

Other sports played: Rugby, squash, badminton, golf
Other sports followed: Rugby, soccer
Relaxations: Shooting, fishing
Extras: Captained England South to victory in International Youth Tournament 1989; also voted Player of Tournament
Best batting performance: 45 Glamorgan v Worcestershire, Pontypridd 1989
Best bowling performance: 1-35 Glamorgan v Surrey, The Oval 1989

LAST SEASON: BATTING

	I.	N.O.	R.	H.S.	AV.
TEST					
1ST-CLASS	8	2	129	45	21.50
INT					
RAL	1	1	3	3*	–
NAT.W.					
B & H					

LAST SEASON: BOWLING

	O.	M.	R.	W.	AV.
TEST					
1ST-CLASS	94	21	312	1	312.00
INT					
RAL	5	0	28	0	–
NAT.W.					
B & H					

CAREER: BATTING

	I.	N.O.	R.	H.S.	AV.
TEST					
1ST-CLASS	8	2	129	45	21.50
INT					
RAL	1	1	3	3*	–
NAT.W.					
B & H					

CAREER: BOWLING

	O.	M.	R.	W.	AV.
TEST					
1ST-CLASS	94	21	312	1	312.00
INT					
RAL	5	0	28	0	–
NAT.W.					
B & H					

59. What is Ian Gould's nickname?
60. What is Chris Smith's nickname?
61. Who has taken the most wickets in a first-class county game?

CURRAN, K. M. Gloucestershire

Full Name: Kevin Malcolm Curran
Role: Right-hand bat, right-arm
fast-medium bowler
Born: 7 September 1959,
Rusape, Rhodesia
Height: 6' 2" **Weight:** 13st 8lbs
Nickname: KC
County debut: 1985
County cap: 1985
No. of One-Day Internationals: 11
1000 runs in a season: 4
50 wickets in a season: 2
1st-Class 50s scored: 28
1st-Class 100s scored: 13
1st-Class 5 w. in innings: 8
1st-Class 10 w. in match: 3
One-Day 50s: 15
Place in batting averages: 67th
av. 35.31 (1988 46th av. 37.22)
Place in bowling averages: 46th av. 26.76 (1988 19th av. 21.30)
Strike rate 1989: 52.97 (career 46.31)
1st-Class catches 1989: 8 (career 78)
Parents: Kevin Patrick and Sylvia
Marital status: Single
Family links with cricket: Father played for Rhodesia 1947–54. Cousin
Patrick Curran played for Rhodesia 1975
Education: Marandellas High School, Zimbabwe
Qualifications: 6 O-levels, 2 M-levels
Jobs outside cricket: Tobacco buyer/farmer
Off-season 1989–90: Playing for Natal
Cricketing superstitions or habits: 'Always change them when they fail –
which is very often!'
Overseas tours: With Zimbabwe to Sri Lanka 1982 and 1984; to England 1982;
World Cup 1983 with Zimbabwe; World XI to West Indies 1985; World Cup
1987
Overseas teams played for: Harare SC, Zimbabwe 1981–85; Natal 1988–89,
1989–90
Cricketers particularly learnt from: Brian Davison, Duncan Fletcher, Mike
Procter, John Traicos
Other sports played: 'Golf, tennis, squash. I play most sports depending on
what country I'm in at the time.'
Other sports followed: Rugby union

Injuries 1989: Shoulder injury; torn muscle – prevented bowling for a month

Relaxations: 'Game fishing, especially along the North Natal coast, the Mozambique coast, and Magaruque Island.'

Extras: First player to take a Sunday League hat-trick, and score a 50 (in fact 54) in the same match, Gloucestershire v Warwickshire, Edgbaston 1989

Opinions on cricket: 'Too much cricket is played in an English County season. Players need time to prepare themselves and rest minor injuries, to obtain better results. Games need to be made more of a spectacle than an everyday occurrence. Marketing of the game in England is below par. More money needs to be injected into the game, as well as the players' back pockets. What game in the world do you play 24 first-class matches, a total of 68 days' cricket (including four-day cricket) to win £35,000 in prize money? Divided amongst 17 players, this is £2000 each! It is ludicrous – seems a long time to earn peanuts. Players' wages need to be reviewed. Capped players' minimum wage should be £20,000. This would secure those county players who cannot obtain winter employment. And your above-average player should earn up to £40,000. This would ensure a comfortable living, after our short careers are over. County clubs may need to speculate more to accumulate. More professional businessmen are required to run County Cricket Clubs. Public Companies may be the answer.'

Best batting performance: 142 Gloucestershire v Middlesex, Lord's 1988

Best bowling performance: 7-54 Gloucestershire v Leicestershire, Gloucester 1988

LAST SEASON: BATTING

	I.	N.O.	R.	H.S.	AV.
TEST					
1ST-CLASS	39	4	1236	128	35.31
INT					
RAL	14	0	287	54	20.50
NAT.W.	2	1	92	47	92.00
B & H	5	2	85	36	28.33

CAREER: BATTING

	I.	N.O.	R.	H.S.	AV.
TEST					
1ST-CLASS	226	37	6616	142	35.00
INT	11	0	287	73	26.09
RAL	69	13	1671	71*	29.83
NAT.W.	13	2	367	58*	33.36
B & H	19	6	472	57	36.30

LAST SEASON: BOWLING

	O.	M.	R.	W.	AV.
TEST					
1ST-CLASS	415.5	85	1258	47	26.76
INT					
RAL	72.5	2	366	14	26.14
NAT.W.	12	2	41	1	41.00
B & H	47	7	138	9	15.33

CAREER: BOWLING

	O.	M.	R.	W.	AV.
TEST					
1ST-CLASS	1909.2	403	6048	247	24.48
INT	114.2	3	398	9	44.22
RAL	288.1	13	1377	66	20.86
NAT.W.	96.5	18	301	12	25.08
B & H	177.1	21	636	28	22.71

CURTIS, T. S.   Worcestershire

Full Name: Timothy Stephen Curtis
Role: Right-hand bat, leg-break bowler
Born: 15 January 1960, Chislehurst, Kent
Height: 5′ 11″ **Weight:** 12st 5lbs
Nickname: TC, Duracell, Professor
County debut: 1979
County cap: 1984
Test debut: 1988
No. of Tests: 5
1000 runs in a season: 6
1st-Class 50s scored: 58
1st-Class 100s: 16
One-Day 50s: 35
One-Day 100s: 2
Place in batting averages: 27th av. 43.33 (1988 37th av. 39.32)
1st-Class catches 1989: 13 (career 96)
Parents: Bruce and Betty
Wife and date of marriage: Philippa, 21 September 1985
Family links with cricket: Father played good club cricket in Bristol and Stafford
Education: The Royal Grammar School, Worcester; Durham University; Cambridge University
Qualifications: 12 O-levels, 4 A-levels, BA (Hons) English, postgraduate certificate in Education in English and Games
Jobs outside cricket: Schoolmaster

LAST SEASON: BATTING

	I.	N.O.	R.	H.S.	AV.
TEST	5	0	71	41	14.20
1ST-CLASS	30	2	1359	156	48.53
INT					
RAL	12	0	437	79	36.41
NAT.W.	4	1	155	91*	51.66
B & H	4	0	79	38	19.75

CAREER: BATTING

	I.	N.O.	R.	H.S.	AV.
TEST	9	0	140	41	15.55
1ST-CLASS	293	38	9900	156	38.82
INT					
RAL	85	13	2755	102	38.26
NAT.W.	22	3	966	120	50.84
B & H	27	2	716	78	28.64

LAST SEASON: BOWLING

	O.	M.	R.	W.	AV.
TEST	3	0	7	0	–
1ST-CLASS	5.3	0	12	0	–
INT					
RAL					
NAT.W.					
B & H					

CAREER: BOWLING

	O.	M.	R.	W.	AV.
TEST	3	0	7	0	–
1ST-CLASS	94.5	12	374	7	53.42
INT					
RAL					
NAT.W.	4	1	15	2	7.50
B & H	0.2	0	4	0	–

Off-season 1989–90: Teaching at Royal Grammar School, Worcester
Overseas tours: NCA U-19 tour of Canada 1979
Cricketers particularly learnt from: Glenn Turner
Other sports played: Rugby, tennis, squash, golf
Extras: Captained Durham University to a UAU Championship. Made highly favourable Test debut v West Indies 1988
Opinions on cricket: '16 four-day matches would seem to be the best combination for championship cricket, with one-day competitions taking place at the weekends. This would reduce the amount of cricket played and place a greater emphasis on the quality of the cricket.'
Best batting performance: 156 Worcestershire v Essex, Colchester 1989
Best bowling performance: 2-58 Cambridge University v Nottinghamshire, Cambridge 1983

DALE, A. Glamorgan

Full Name: Adrian Dale
Role: Right-hand bat, right-arm medium bowler, all-rounder
Born: 24 October 1968
Height: 6' **Weight:** 11st 6lbs
Nickname: Arthur, Gilbert, Emma
County debut: 1989
One-Day 50s: 1
Place in batting averages: 190th av. 19.14
Parents: John and Maureen
Marital status: Single
Family links with cricket: Father played for Glamorgan 2nd XI and Chepstow Cricket Club
Education: Pembroke Primary, Chepstow Comprehensive and Swansea University
Qualifications: 9 O-levels, 3 A-levels
Jobs outside cricket: Paper boy, stock taker, labourer
Off-season 1989–90: Studying for a degree in Economics at Swansea University
Overseas tours: Welsh Schools tour to Australia 1986–87; Combined Universities to Barbados 1989
Cricketers particularly learnt from: Alan Jones, John Steele, Tom Cartwright, Charles Toole
Cricketers particularly admired: Ian Botham, Michael Holding

Other sports played: Football, squash, swimming
Other sports followed: Arsenal FC
Relaxations: 'Eating out and most other sports. Making my own compilation music tapes.'
Extras: Played in successful Combined Universities side of 1989
Opinions on cricket: 'Too much cricket, together with the travelling, makes it difficult to prepare mentally and physically for each game. Therefore, sixteen four-day matches seems reasonable. Better practice facilities along with video cameras help players to see their own faults and work on them.'
Best batting performance: 44 Glamorgan v Gloucestershire, Bristol 1989
Best bowling performance: 1-41 Glamorgan v Hampshire, Cardiff 1989

LAST SEASON: BATTING

	I.	N.O.	R.	H.S.	AV.
TEST					
1ST-CLASS	8	1	134	44	19.14
INT					
RAL	7	2	139	67*	27.80
NAT.W.	1	0	10	10	10.00
B & H	4	1	45	21*	15.00

CAREER: BATTING

	I.	N.O.	R.	H.S.	AV.
TEST					
1ST-CLASS	8	1	134	44	19.14
INT					
RAL	7	2	139	67*	27.80
NAT.W.	1	0	10	10	10.00
B & H	4	1	45	21*	15.00

LAST SEASON: BOWLING

	O.	M.	R.	W.	AV.
TEST					
1ST-CLASS	39	10	129	2	64.50
INT					
RAL	49	1	299	6	49.83
NAT.W.	19.4	1	70	3	23.33
B & H	47	4	168	8	21.00

CAREER: BOWLING

	O.	M.	R.	W.	AV.
TEST					
1ST-CLASS	39	10	129	2	64.50
INT					
RAL	49	1	299	6	49.83
NAT.W.	19.4	1	70	3	23.33
B & H	47	4	168	8	21.00

62. Who has taken the most wickets ever in a Test match?
63. What record is held by R. J. Crisp of Western Province, South Africa?

DAVIS, R. P. Kent

Full Name: Richard Peter Davis
Role: Slow left-arm bowler
Born: 18 March 1966, Westgate
Height: 6′ 5″ **Weight:** 15st
Nickname: Dickie, Doughnut
County debut: 1986
1st-Class 50s scored: 1
1st-Class 5 w. in innings: 1
Place in batting averages: 219th
av. 15.47
Place in bowling averages: 117th
av. 48.16 (1988 118th av. 37.07)
Strike rate 1989: 102.38 (career
93.28)
1st-Class catches 1989: 15 (career 33)
Parents: Brian and Silvia
Marital status: Single
Family links with cricket: Father
played league cricket in Yorkshire

and local cricket in Kent and is an NCA coach
Education: King Ethelberts School, Birchington; Thanet Technical College,
Broadstairs
Qualifications: 8 CSEs
Jobs outside cricket: Carpenter, builder, roofing with D. Sabine 1988–89
Off-season 1989–90: Labouring, carpentry
Overseas tours: Kent Schools CA U-17s Canadian tour 1983
Overseas teams played for: Hutt District CC, New Zealand 1986–87, 1987–88
Cricketers particularly learnt from: Derek Underwood, Eldine Baptiste,
Colin Page, John Inverarity, Graham Newdick (Wellington, New Zealand),
'my father'
Cricketers particularly admired: Derek Underwood, Chris Tavaré
Other sports played: Golf, football, badminton, tennis
Other sports followed: American football, rugby
Injuries 1989: Fractured right thumb – off 2 days in July
Relaxations: Reading, sport, TV, a drink down the local
Extras: Played for Kent Schools, 1983; Kent Colts, 1983. Was offered
a contract in 1984 by Derbyshire, but preferred to stay in his native
county
Opinions on cricket: 'I would like to see the Championship consist of 16 four-
day games, but it would only work if the wickets were produced to last four
days. The wickets should be hard and brown so that it encourages quick
bowling, and on the third and fourth day the spin bowlers would get a chance

to bowl long spells on wickets that would probably assist. This would encourage better Test Match standards.'

Best batting performance: 67 Kent v Hampshire, Southampton 1989
Best bowling performance: 5-132 Kent v Essex, Chelmsford 1988

LAST SEASON: BATTING

	I.	N.O.	R.	H.S.	AV.
TEST					
1ST-CLASS	23	6	263	67	15.47
INT					
RAL	5	0	28	16	5.60
NAT.W.	1	1	1	1*	–
B & H	–	–	–	–	–

LAST SEASON: BOWLING

	O.	M.	R.	W.	AV.
TEST					
1ST-CLASS	716.4	199	2023	42	48.16
INT					
RAL	65	1	307	12	25.58
NAT.W.	24	7	64	2	32.00
B & H	5	0	21	1	21.00

CAREER: BATTING

	I.	N.O.	R.	H.S.	AV.
TEST					
1ST-CLASS	54	19	421	67	12.02
INT					
RAL	10	2	42	16	5.25
NAT.W.	2	1	1	1*	1.00
B & H	1	1	0	0*	–

CAREER: BOWLING

	O.	M.	R.	W.	AV.
TEST					
1ST-CLASS	1492.3	333	4026	96	41.93
INT					
RAL	199.2	10	899	35	25.68
NAT.W.	42.3	10	127	6	21.16
B & H	44.1	2	200	3	66.66

DAVIS, W. W.   Northamptonshire

Full Name: Winston Walter Davis
Role: Right-hand bat, right-arm fast bowler
Born: 18 September 1958, St Vincent, Windward Islands
Height: 6′ 2″ **Weight:** 12st
Nickname: Davo
County debut: 1982 (Glamorgan), 1987 (Northamptonshire)
County cap: 1987 (Northamptonshire)
Test debut: 1982–83
No. of Tests: 15
No. of One-Day Internationals: 35
50 wickets in a season: 5
1st-Class 50s scored: 4
1st-Class 5 w. in innings: 27
1st-Class 10 w. in match: 7
Place in batting averages: 254th av. 11.06 (1988 87th av. 20.40)
Place in bowling averages: 52nd av. 27.76 (1988 25th av. 22.10)

Strike rate 1989: 50.76 (career 48.46)
1st-Class catches 1989: 4 (career 54)
Jobs outside cricket: Clerk
Overseas tours: Young West Indies to Zimbabwe 1981–82; West Indies to India 1983–84, 1987–88; Australia 1983–84, 1984–85; England 1984
Overseas teams played for: Windward Islands, Combined Islands, Campbelltown DCC in Australia; Tasmania 1985–86
Cricketers particularly learnt from: Andy Roberts, Joel Garner
Cricketers particularly admired: 'I like watching Viv Richards bat and Malcolm Marshall bowl.'
Other sports played: Table tennis
Other sports followed: Soccer, athletics, lawn tennis
Relaxations: 'Reading, watching television, playing with my children.'
Opinions on cricket: 'I should like to see the leg-bye rule changed for all one-day matches. No runs should be allowed for a ball coming off the batsman's pads. Cricket is a game very true to life, and because of that I believe it helps those who play it to understand and to cope with life's ups and downs better.'
Best batting performance: 77 West Indies v England, Old Trafford 1984
Best bowling performance: 7-52 Northamptonshire v Sussex, Northampton 1988

LAST SEASON: BATTING

	I.	N.O.	R.	H.S.	AV.
TEST					
1ST-CLASS	19	4	166	40*	11.06
INT					
RAL	1	0	2	2	2.00
NAT.W.					
B & H	–	–	–	–	–

LAST SEASON: BOWLING

	O.	M.	R.	W.	AV.
TEST					
1ST-CLASS	440	68	1444	52	27.76
INT					
RAL	31	0	108	8	13.50
NAT.W.					
B & H	33	3	129	1	129.00

CAREER: BATTING

	I.	N.O.	R.	H.S.	AV.
TEST	17	4	202	77	15.53
1ST-CLASS	183	52	1755	60	13.39
INT	15	3	28	10	2.33
RAL	12	4	91	34	11.37
NAT.W.	6	3	24	14*	8.00
B & H	9	3	64	15*	10.66

CAREER: BOWLING

	O.	M.	R.	W.	AV.
TEST	462.1	53	1472	45	32.71
1ST-CLASS	4352.2	843	13974	551	25.36
INT	320.3	31	1302	39	33.28
RAL	253.4	19	1062	45	23.60
NAT.W.	91.5	13	306	10	30.60
B & H	163.2	16	644	22	29.27

64. Who is the only man ever to take two first-class hat tricks in the same innings?

DEFREITAS, P. A. J. Lancashire

Full Name: Phillip Anthony Jason
DeFreitas
Role: Right-hand bat, right-arm
fast-medium bowler, cover fielder
Born: 18 February 1966, Dominica
Height: 5′ 11″ **Weight:** 12st 7lbs
Nickname: Daffy
County debut: 1985 (Leicestershire),
1989 (Lancashire)
County cap: 1986 (Leicestershire)
Test debut: 1986–87
No. of Tests: 13

No. of One-Day Internationals: 41
50 wickets in a season: 4
1st-Class 50s scored: 13
1st-Class 100s scored: 2
1st-Class 5 w. in innings: 21
1st-Class 10 w. in match: 2
One-Day 50s: 2
Place in batting averages: 161st
av. 22.30 (1988 175th av. 21.54)
Place in bowling averages: 45th av. 26.73 (1988 44th av. 24.29)
Strike rate 1989: 54.25 (career 53.33)
1st-Class catches 1989: 4 (career 33)
Parents: Sybil and Martin
Marital status: Single
Family links with cricket: Father played in the Windward Islands. All six
brothers play
Education: Willesden High School
Qualifications: 2 CSEs
Off-season 1989–90: Touring with England in India and West Indies
Overseas tours: Young England to West Indies 1985; England to Australia
1986–87; World Cup, Pakistan, Australia and New Zealand 1987–88; Lancashire to Zimbabwe 1988–89; England to India and West Indies 1989–90
Overseas teams played for: Port Adelaide CC 1985–86
Cricketers particularly learnt from: Ian Botham, Mike Gatting
Cricketers particularly admired: Viv Richards, Malcolm Marshall
Other sports played: Football, golf
Other sports followed: Rugby union – Leicester Tigers
Extras: Left Leicestershire and joined Lancashire at end of 1988 season.
Originally picked for unofficial England tour of South Africa 1989–90, but
withdrew under pressure

Opinions on cricket: 'Fines on over rates to be abolished. 2nd XI wickets ought to be much better.'
Best batting performance: 113 Leicestershire v Nottinghamshire, Worksop 1988
Best bowling performance: 7-21 Leicestershire v Middlesex, Lord's 1989

LAST SEASON: BATTING

	I.	N.O.	R.	H.S.	AV.
TEST	2	0	22	21	11.00
1ST-CLASS	26	2	558	78	23.25
INT	2	1	17	17*	17.00
RAL	9	1	75	25	9.37
NAT.W.	2	0	25	25	12.50
B & H	2	1	59	30	59.00

CAREER: BATTING

	I.	N.O.	R.	H.S.	AV.
TEST	19	1	204	40	11.33
1ST-CLASS	122	11	2349	113	21.16
INT	28	11	306	33	18.00
RAL	41	6	381	37	10.88
NAT.W.	8	1	166	69	23.71
B & H	11	3	170	59	21.25

LAST SEASON: BOWLING

	O.	M.	R.	W.	AV.
TEST	63.3	10	216	3	72.00
1ST-CLASS	551.2	115	1602	65	24.64
INT	30	2	117	3	39.00
RAL	84	4	327	14	23.35
NAT.W.	32.5	7	70	7	10.00
B & H	54.1	10	188	9	20.88

CAREER: BOWLING

	O.	M.	R.	W.	AV.
TEST	453.1	97	1296	26	49.84
1ST-CLASS	2675.4	545	7818	326	23.98
INT	386.2	53	1397	50	27.94
RAL	352.2	17	1608	64	25.12
NAT.W.	114.2	22	333	19	17.52
B & H	169.5	24	539	24	22.45

DENNIS, S. J. Glamorgan

Full Name: Simon John Dennis
Role: Right-hand bat, left-arm fast-medium bowler
Born: 18 October 1960, Scarborough
Height: 6' 1" **Weight:** 13st
Nickname: Donkey
County debut: 1980 (Yorkshire), 1989 (Glamorgan)
County cap: 1983 (Yorkshire)
50 wickets in a season: 1
1st-Class 50s scored: 1
1st-Class 5 w. in innings: 6
Place in batting averages: 259th av. 10.38
Place in bowling averages: 88th av. 34.17
Strike rate 1989: 71.74 (career 60.69)
1st-Class catches 1989: 3 (career 23)
Parents: Margaret and Geoff
Marital status: Single
Family links with cricket: Father captained Scarborough for many years.

Uncle, Frank Dennis, played for Yorkshire 1928–33. Uncle, Sir Leonard Hutton, played for Yorkshire and England
Education: Northstead County Primary School; Scarborough College
Qualifications: 7 O-levels, 1 A-level, City and Guilds Computer Literacy
Jobs outside cricket: Assistant groundsman at Scarborough CC. Furniture salesman. Worked for a Scarborough printing firm. Worked for G. A. Pinder & Sons Ltd in sales department
Off-season 1989–90: Working for Kelter Recruitment on Glamorgan's winter employment scheme
Cricketing superstitions or habits: 'If I have a good day I try to do everything the same the next day before the game.'
Overseas tours: ESCA to India 1978–79; Young England to Australia 1980; MCC to East and Central Africa 1981; MCC to America 1982; Sheffield Cricket Lovers to Gibraltar 1983; Yorkshire to Barbados 1987; Yorkshire to La Manga 1988
Overseas teams played for: Orange Free State 1982–83; Durban Collegians 1985–86
Cricketers particularly learnt from: Doug Padgett, Don Wilson, Ray Illingworth
Cricketers particularly admired: Dennis Lillee, John Lever
Injuries 1989: Groin strain – off for ten days in June
Relaxations: Car maintenance, wine- and beer-making. Photography and real ale. Home computer, video games. 'Also terrible snooker player.'
Extras: On debut for Yorkshire v Somerset, at Weston 1980, got Gavaskar as his first wicket. Released by Yorkshire at end of 1988 season. Joined Glamorgan for 1989
Opinions on cricket: 'Glamorgan's winter employment scheme is a great step forward, and should be looked at by other counties.'
Best batting performance: 53* Yorkshire v Nottinghamshire, Trent Bridge 1984
Best bowling performance: 5-35 Yorkshire v Somerset, Sheffield 1981

LAST SEASON: BATTING

	I.	N.O.	R.	H.S.	AV.
TEST					
1ST-CLASS	19	1	187	38	10.38
INT					
RAL	7	2	24	8	4.80
NAT.W.	1	0	1	1	1.00
B & H	3	0	1	1	0.33

CAREER: BATTING

	I.	N.O.	R.	H.S.	AV.
TEST					
1ST-CLASS	90	28	643	53*	10.37
INT					
RAL	26	13	111	16*	8.53
NAT.W.	3	0	15	14	5.00
B & H	5	0	11	10	2.20

LAST SEASON: BOWLING

	O.	M.	R.	W.	AV.
TEST					
1ST-CLASS	418.3	110	1196	35	34.17
INT					
RAL	90.1	3	459	11	41.72
NAT.W.	18	6	56	0	–
B & H	36	5	104	2	52.00

CAREER: BOWLING

	O.	M.	R.	W.	AV.
TEST					
1ST-CLASS	2316.3	486	7257	229	31.68
INT					
RAL	351.1	17	1647	38	43.34
NAT.W.	70.2	14	258	6	43.00
B & H	123	20	431	9	47.88

DERRICK, J. Glamorgan

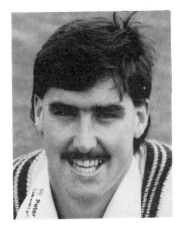

Full Name: John Derrick
Role: Right-hand bat, right-arm medium bowler
Born: 15 January 1963, Aberdare, South Wales
Height: 6′ 1″ **Weight:** 14st 5lbs
Nickname: JD, Bo
County debut: 1983
County cap: 1988
1st-Class 50s scored: 11
1st-Class 5 w. in innings: 2
Place in batting averages: —
(1988 260th av. 10.40)
Place in bowling averages: —
(1988 95th av. 32.14)
1st-Class catches 1989: 7 (career 40)
Parents: John Raymond and Megan Irene
Wife and date of marriage: Anne Irene, 20 April 1985
Children: Liam Kyle, 3 April 1987
Family links with cricket: Father and brother play club cricket for Aberdare
Education: Glynhafod and Blaengwawr Primary Schools; Blaengwawr Comprehensive School
Qualifications: School Certificate
Jobs outside cricket: Coaching cricket; working for Ryan International
Off-season 1989–90: Working for Ryan International
Overseas tours: Barbados 1989 with Glamorgan CCC
Overseas teams played for: Toombul CC, Brisbane 1982–85; Te Puke CC & Bay of Plenty Red Team New Zealand 1985–86; Northern Districts 1986–87
Cricketers particularly learnt from: Tom Cartwright, Don Wilson, Andy Wagner, John Steele and senior Glamorgan players, Lance Cairns and Andy Roberts in New Zealand
Cricketers particularly admired: Geoff Boycott, John Snow, Dennis Lillee, Graeme Hick
Other sports played: Soccer, squash, golf – 'give anything a try'
Other sports followed: Rugby, Chelsea FC
Injuries 1989: Torn intercostal muscle – out for six weeks
Relaxations: 'Days off when I can take my little boy for walks. TV and video.'
Extras: Spent three years on MCC groundstaff 1980–82. Coached at Lord's in winter of 1981. Captained Welsh Schools U-11s on tour to Lancashire and

144

Cheshire. Took 9 for 9 off 9 overs v Lancashire and 6 for 6 off 6 overs v Cheshire

Opinions on cricket: 'During a Test series, our Test players should be playing a limited number of county games and not every day.'

Best batting performance: 78* Glamorgan v Derbyshire, Abergavenny 1986
Best bowling performance: 6-54 Glamorgan v Leicestershire, Leicester 1988

LAST SEASON: BATTING

	I.	N.O.	R.	H.S.	AV.
TEST					
1ST-CLASS	7	1	182	67	30.33
INT					
RAL	4	1	26	15	8.66
NAT.W.					
B & H	1	0	0	0	0.00

CAREER: BATTING

	I.	N.O.	R.	H.S.	AV.
TEST					
1ST-CLASS	121	34	1941	78*	22.31
INT					
RAL	44	13	356	26	11.48
NAT.W.	3	1	10	4	5.00
B & H	9	2	87	42	12.42

LAST SEASON: BOWLING

	O.	M.	R.	W.	AV.
TEST					
1ST-CLASS	155.5	42	439	11	39.90
INT					
RAL	37	1	184	4	46.00
NAT.W.					
B & H	9	2	14	1	14.00

CAREER: BOWLING

	O.	M.	R.	W.	AV.
TEST					
1ST-CLASS	1650.5	368	5089	136	37.41
INT					
RAL	385.3	7	1957	57	34.33
NAT.W.	58.3	10	178	12	14.83
B & H	126	19	428	19	22.52

DILLEY, G. R. Worcestershire

Full Name: Graham Roy Dilley
Role: Left-hand bat, right-arm fast bowler
Born: 18 May 1959, Dartford
Height: 6′ 4″ **Weight:** 15st
Nickname: Picca
County debut: 1977 (Kent), 1987 (Worcestershire)
County cap: 1980 (Kent), 1987 (Worcestershire)
Test debut: 1979–80
No. of Tests: 41
No. of One-Day Internationals: 36
50 wickets in a season: 3
1st-Class 50s scored: 4
1st-Class 5 w. in innings: 31
1st-Class 10 w. in match: 3
Place in batting averages: 167th av. 21.66 (1988 256th av. 11.30)

Place in bowling averages: 36th av. 23.96 (1988 30th av. 22.40)
Strike rate 1989: 42.23 (career 52.82)
1st-Class catches 1989: 2 (career 70)
Parents: Geoff and Jean
Wife and date of marriage: Helen, 6 November 1980
Children: Paul and Christopher
Family links with cricket: Father and grandfather both played local cricket. Wife is sister of former Kent colleague Graham Johnson
Education: Dartford West Secondary School
Qualifications: 3 O-levels
Jobs outside cricket: Diamond setter. Spent two winters carrying sheets of plaster-board for uncle's office partitioning company. Doing cricket commentary for Radio Medway
Off-season 1989–90: Touring South Africa with unofficial English team
Overseas tours: With England to Australia 1979–80; India 1980; West Indies 1981; India and Sri Lanka 1981–82; New Zealand and Pakistan 1983–4; Australia 1986–87; World Cup, Pakistan, New Zealand and Australia 1987–88
Overseas teams played for: Natal 1985–86
Cricketers particularly learnt from: Dennis Lillee, John Snow
Other sports played: Golf, squash, badminton
Injuries 1989: Missed all One-Day Internationals and First Test v Australia through knee injury
Relaxations: Music
Extras: Got sacked from his first job with a Hatton Garden diamond firm after taking time off to play for Kent 2nd XI. Suffered from glandular fever at end of 1980 season, causing him to miss Centenary Test. Voted Young Cricketer of the Year 1980 by Cricket Writers' Club. Missed 1984 season after suffering back injury on 1983–84 tour. Joined Worcestershire in 1987. Autobiography *Swings and Roundabouts*, 1988

LAST SEASON: BATTING

	I.	N.O.	R.	H.S.	AV.
TEST	3	1	42	24	21.00
1ST-CLASS	14	10	88	31	22.00
INT					
RAL	–	–	–	–	–
NAT.W.	–	–	–	–	–
B & H	1	1	0	0*	–

LAST SEASON: BOWLING

	O.	M.	R.	W.	AV.
TEST	85	12	318	5	63.60
1ST-CLASS	337.2	64	1120	55	20.36
INT					
RAL	21	0	86	3	28.66
NAT.W.	22	7	85	1	85.00
B & H	27	2	91	6	15.16

CAREER: BATTING

	I.	N.O.	R.	H.S.	AV.
TEST	58	19	521	56	13.35
1ST-CLASS	171	63	1535	81	14.21
INT	18	8	114	31*	11.40
RAL	27	8	252	33	13.26
NAT.W.	13	4	105	25	11.66
B & H	26	8	154	37*	8.55

CAREER: BOWLING

	O.	M.	R.	W.	AV.
TEST	1365.2	281	4107	138	29.76
1ST-CLASS	3802.2	794	11560	449	25.74
INT	340.3	33	1291	48	26.89
RAL	486.2	35	1988	77	25.81
NAT.W.	214.4	40	669	35	19.11
B & H	403.2	53	1322	66	20.03

Opinions on cricket: 'For years counties have held almost a feudal grip on their players. While I accept that some clubs have not been able to pay their players more than the basic minimum agreed by the Professional Cricketers' Association, they have always had a hold over their unhappy employees who have been forced to show a false sense of loyalty with the hope of a lucrative benefit. The system had one merit in that a player around the age of 30 to 35 was given the chance to make enough money in a year to make himself financially secure for life. But it failed to take into account others less fortunate who might have been forced out of the game at a younger age without any lump sum, no formal training in any other profession than cricket, and with little hope for the future.'

Best batting performance: 81 Kent v Northamptonshire, Northampton 1979
Best bowling performance: 7-63 Natal v Transvaal, Johannesburg 1985–86

DOBSON, M. C. Kent

Full Name: Mark Christopher Dobson
Role: Right-hand opening bat, slow left-arm spin bowler
Born: 24 October 1967, Canterbury
Height: 5' 10" **Weight:** 12st 7lbs
Nickname: Dobbo
County debut: 1989
1st-Class 50s scored: 1
Place in batting averages: 221st av. 15.22
Parents: Bryan and Yvonne
Marital status: Single
Family links with cricket: Father was good local club cricketer
Education: Simon Langton Grammar School for Boys, Canterbury
Qualifications: 8 O-levels, 2 A-levels
Jobs outside cricket: Accounts clerk at Lloyds Bank, Herne Bay, labourer

Off-season 1989–90: Working in Canterbury area
Overseas tours: Kent Schools CA Canadian Tour 1983
Overseas teams played for: Glenwood Old Boys, Durban, South Africa 1988–89
Cricketers particularly learnt from: Hartley Alleyne, Roy Pienaar, Colin Page, Alan Ealham

Cricketers particularly admired: Richard Davis, Mark Benson
Other sports played: Football
Other sports followed: Keen Chelsea fan. Also follows QPR. Grandfather played for them in 1930s
Injuries 1989: Knee injury in late August – missed one week's cricket
Relaxations: Listening to music, socialising with friends
Opinions on cricket: 'All 2nd team grounds should have proper practice facilities.'
Best batting performance: 52 Kent v Glamorgan, Canterbury 1989
Best bowling performance: 2-20 Kent v Glamorgan, Canterbury 1989

LAST SEASON: BATTING

	I.	N.O.	R.	H.S.	AV.
TEST					
1ST-CLASS	10	1	137	52	15.22
INT					
RAL	1	0	21	21	21.00
NAT.W.					
B & H					

LAST SEASON: BOWLING

	O.	M.	R.	W.	AV.
TEST					
1ST-CLASS	118.3	22	417	8	52.12
INT					
RAL					
NAT.W.					
B & H					

CAREER: BATTING

	I.	N.O.	R.	H.S.	AV.
TEST					
1ST-CLASS	10	1	137	52	15.22
INT					
RAL	1	0	21	21	21.00
NAT.W.					
B & H					

CAREER: BOWLING

	O.	M.	R.	W.	AV.
TEST					
1ST-CLASS	118.3	22	417	8	52.12
INT					
RAL					
NAT.W.					
B & H					

65. Who has taken the most first-class hat-tricks?

66. Who is the only man to have taken over 300 wickets in a season?

DODEMAIDE, A. I. C. Sussex

Full Name: Anthony Ian Christopher Dodemaide
Role: Right-hand bat, right-arm fast-medium bowler, all-rounder
Born: 5 October 1963, Williamstown, Victoria, Australia
Height: 6′ 2″ **Weight:** 13½st
Nickname: Dodders
County debut: 1989
Test debut: 1987–88
No. of Tests: 8
No. of One-Day Internationals: 12
50 wickets in a season: 1
1st-Class 50s scored: 15
1st-Class 5 w. in innings: 7
Place in batting averages: 82nd av. 32.52
Place in bowling averages: 67th av. 30.32
Strike rate 1989: 62.05 (career 70.58)
1st-Class catches 1989: 11 (career 48)
Parents: Ian and Irene
Wife and date of marriage: Danielle, 7 April 1989
Family links with cricket: 'Brother Alan plays district cricket in Melbourne. Brother Warren and several uncles were keen club cricketers around home town Footscray.'
Education: St Johns & Chisholm College, Braybrook, Footscray; Chisholm Institute of Technology, Melbourne
Qualifications: Higher School Certificate, Bachelor of Applied Science (Physics)
Off-season 1989–90: 'Continuing my first-class career in Australia!'
Cricketing superstitions or habits: 'Seem to be the last one onto the ground on most occasions.'
Overseas tours: Australia U-19 to England 1983; Australia U-25 to Zimbabwe 1985; Australia to Pakistan 1988
Overseas teams played for: Lowerhouse CC, Lancashire League 1986; Nostell CC, Leeds League 1988
Cricketers particularly learnt from: Ken Eastwood, Ian Redpath, Graham McKenzie, Norman Gifford
Cricketers particularly admired: Sunil Gavaskar, Imran Khan, Richard Hadlee, Terry Alderman
Other sports played: Australian Rules football, social tennis, squash, golf

Other sports followed: 'Will watch most sports.'

Injuries 1989: Side muscle strain – missed a couple of games at end of season

Relaxations: Watching movies (particularly old ones), reading, listening to music

Extras: Played for Sussex 2nd XI on Esso Scholarship Scheme in 1985

Opinions on cricket: 'There seems to be a lot of emphasis in the English season on the various forms of the one-day game (e.g. 40, 55, 60 overs) as compared to Championship cricket. This could have an effect on the skill and temperament development of the younger players.'

Best batting performance: 81* Victoria v Western Australia, Perth 1986–87

Best bowling performance: 6-58 Australia v New Zealand, Melbourne 1987–88 on his Test debut

LAST SEASON: BATTING

	I.	N.O.	R.	H.S.	AV.
TEST					
1ST-CLASS	30	9	683	80	32.52
INT					
RAL	12	5	196	40*	28.00
NAT.W.	2	0	8	7	4.00
B & H	4	1	107	38	35.66

CAREER: BATTING

	I.	N.O.	R.	H.S.	AV.
TEST	12	3	171	50	19.00
1ST-CLASS	116	30	2560	81*	29.76
INT	8	5	84	30	28.00
RAL	12	5	196	40*	28.00
NAT.W.	2	0	8	7	4.00
B & H	4	1	107	38	35.66

LAST SEASON: BOWLING

	O.	M.	R.	W.	AV.
TEST					
1ST-CLASS	672.1	133	1971	65	30.32
INT					
RAL	104.4	7	413	16	25.81
NAT.W.	34.4	5	102	4	25.50
B & H	42	6	123	7	17.57

CAREER: BOWLING

	O.	M.	R.	W.	AV.
TEST	310.2	77	803	28	28.67
1ST-CLASS	2477.5	528	7086	209	33.90
INT	109.2	11	360	20	18.00
RAL	104.4	7	413	16	25.81
NAT.W.	34.4	5	102	4	25.50
B & H	46	6	123	7	17.57

67. Who took the most first-class wickets ever?

68. True or false: as well as his legendary Tests as a batsman, W. G. Grace took 2876 first-class wickets, the sixth most of all time?

D'OLIVEIRA, D. B.   Worcestershire

Full Name: Damian Basil D'Oliveira
Role: Right-hand bat, off-break bowler, slip or boundary fielder
Born: 19 October 1960, Cape Town, South Africa
Height: 5' 8" **Weight:** 11st 10lbs
Nickname: Dolly
County debut: 1982
County cap: 1985
1000 runs in a season: 3
1st-Class 50s scored: 30
1st-Class 100s scored: 6
One-Day 50s: 11
One-Day 100s: 1
Place in batting averages: 169th av. 21.27 (1988 239th av. 13.20)
1st-Class catches 1989: 21 (career 120)
Parents: Basil and Naomi
Wife and date of marriage: Tracey Michele, 26 September 1983
Children: Marcus Damian, 27 April 1986; Dominic James, 29 April 1988
Family links with cricket: Father played for Worcestershire and England
Education: St George's RC Primary School; Blessed Edward Oldcorne Secondary School
Qualifications: 3 O-levels, 5 CSEs
Jobs outside cricket: Salesman for Carphone Group p.l.c., and Sexton's In-Car Stereo

LAST SEASON: BATTING

	I.	N.O.	R.	H.S.	AV.
TEST					
1ST-CLASS	37	1	766	63	21.27
INT					
RAL	15	2	470	91*	36.15
NAT.W.	2	0	33	32	16.50
B & H	4	0	62	28	15.50

CAREER: BATTING

	I.	N.O.	R.	H.S.	AV.
TEST					
1ST-CLASS	252	17	6202	146*	26.39
INT					
RAL	95	9	2020	103	23.48
NAT.W.	16	1	359	99	23.93
B & H	28	3	593	66	23.72

LAST SEASON: BOWLING

	O.	M.	R.	W.	AV.
TEST					
1ST-CLASS					
INT					
RAL					
NAT.W.					
B & H					

CAREER: BOWLING

	O.	M.	R.	W.	AV.
TEST					
1ST-CLASS	257.1	49	923	23	40.13
INT					
RAL	39	2	232	7	33.14
NAT.W.	38	5	134	6	22.33
B & H	38	4	148	5	29.60

Off-season 1989–90: Working for the Carphone Group
Overseas tours: English Counties XI to Zimbabwe 1985
Overseas teams played for: West Perth CC, Western Australia 1979–80; Christchurch Shirley 1982–83 and 1983–84 on a Whitbread scholarship
Cricketers particularly admired: Greg Chappell, Viv Richards, Dennis Lillee, Malcolm Marshall, Richard Hadlee
Other sports played: Football
Other sports followed: 'Most others, but not horse racing.'
Injuries 1989: 'Two stitches in right palm caused by catching a fielding helmet from R. K. Illingworth. Missed NatWest quarter-final v Lancashire.'
Relaxations: 'Watching films, TV, eating out, and playing with the kids.'
Best batting performance: 146* Worcestershire v Gloucestershire, Cheltenham 1986
Best bowling performance: 2-17 Worcestershire v Gloucestershire, Cheltenham 1986

DONALD, A. A. Warwickshire

Full Name: Allan Anthony Donald
Role: Right-hand bat, right-arm fast-medium bowler
Born: 20 October 1966, Bloemfontein, South Africa
Height: 6' 3" **Weight:** 13½st
County debut: 1987
County cap: 1989
50 wickets in a season: 1
1st-Class 5 w. in innings: 14
1st-Class 10 w. in match: 1
Place in batting averages: 234th av. 13.43 (1988 259th av. 10.57)
Place in bowling averages: 2nd av. 16.25 (1988 14th av. 20.53)
Strike rate 1989: 37.47 (career 45.80)
1st-Class catches 1989: 3 (career 18)
Parents: Stuart and Francina
Marital status: Single
Education: Grey College High School and Technical High School, Bloemfontein
Qualifications: Matriculation
Off-season 1989–90: Playing cricket in South Africa
Cricketing superstitions or habits: 'Love bowling to left-handers.'

152

Overseas teams played for: Orange Free State, South Africa 1985–90
Cricketers particularly learnt from: Chris Broad, Vanburn Holder, Alvin Kallicharran
Cricketers particularly admired: Ian Botham, Imran Khan
Other sports played: Rugby
Other sports followed: Rugby, football
Injuries 1989: Bruised hip in August
Relaxations: Playing tennis, listening to music
Extras: Played for a South Africa XI v an Australian XI in one 5-day Test and three One-Day Internationals, 1986–87
Opinions on cricket: 'There should not be politics in world sport.'
Best batting performance: 40 Warwickshire v Yorkshire, Edgbaston 1989
Best bowling performance: 8-37 Orange Free State v Transvaal, Johannesburg 1986–87

LAST SEASON: BATTING

	I.	N.O.	R.	H.S.	AV.
TEST					
1ST-CLASS	22	6	215	40	13.43
INT					
RAL	7	2	63	17*	12.60
NAT.W.	1	0	0	0	0.00
B & H	3	3	30	23*	–

CAREER: BATTING

	I.	N.O.	R.	H.S.	AV.
TEST					
1ST-CLASS	89	34	637	40	11.58
INT					
RAL	14	6	111	18*	13.87
NAT.W.	1	0	0	0	0.00
B & H	4	3	30	23*	30.00

LAST SEASON: BOWLING

	O.	M.	R.	W.	AV.
TEST					
1ST-CLASS	537.1	122	1398	86	16.25
INT					
RAL	87	7	342	14	24.42
NAT.W.	47.4	5	137	14	9.78
B & H	42.5	6	158	2	79.00

CAREER: BOWLING

	O.	M.	R.	W.	AV.
TEST					
1ST-CLASS	2076.3	396	6134	272	22.55
INT					
RAL	155	14	638	26	24.53
NAT.W.	77	9	225	24	9.37
B & H	66.1	9	249	9	27.66

69. What was Mike Procter of Gloucestershire and South Africa the only man to do twice?

DONELAN, B. T. P. — Sussex

Full Name: Bradleigh Thomas Peter Donelan
Role: Right-hand bat, right-arm off-spin bowler, cover, gully fielder
Born: 3 January 1968, Middlesex
Height: 6′ 2″ **Weight:** 12½st
Nickname: Rooster, Freddie, Claw
County debut: 1989
Place in bowling averages: 111th av. 45.21
Strike rate 1989: 82.71 (career 82.71)
1st-Class catches 1989: 4 (career 4)
Parents: Terry and Patricia
Marital status: Single
Education: Our Lady of Grace Junior School, Finchley Catholic High School
Qualifications: 8 CSEs
Jobs outside cricket: Playing and coaching overseas
Off-season 1989–90: Playing and coaching in Otago, New Zealand
Cricketing superstitions or habits: Pre-match practice by having a bowl to the wicket-keeper out on the middle before each game to get accustomed to surroundings
Overseas teams played for: Northcote, Melbourne, Australia 1987; Otago B team, New Zealand 1988; Southland 1988
Cricketers particularly learnt from: Don Wilson, Norman Gifford, John Barclay, Martin Robinson

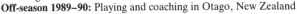

LAST SEASON: BATTING

	I.	N.O.	R.	H.S.	AV.
TEST					
1ST-CLASS	9	3	41	10*	6.83
INT					
RAL	–	–	–	–	–
NAT.W.					
B & H					

CAREER: BATTING

	I.	N.O.	R.	H.S.	AV.
TEST					
1ST-CLASS	9	3	41	10*	6.83
INT					
RAL	–	–	–	–	–
NAT.W.					
B & H					

LAST SEASON: BOWLING

	O.	M.	R.	W.	AV.
TEST					
1ST-CLASS	193	42	633	14	45.21
INT					
RAL	1	0	14	0	–
NAT.W.					
B & H					

CAREER: BOWLING

	O.	M.	R.	W.	AV.
TEST					
1ST-CLASS	193	42	633	14	45.21
INT					
RAL	1	0	14	0	–
NAT.W.					
B & H					

Cricketers particularly admired: Martin Crowe, Paul Parker for their dedication to the game
Other sports played: Darts, snooker, football, table tennis, golf
Other sports followed: Football, golf
Relaxations: Listening to music, sleeping
Extras: Was a late starter at the age of 13; was a product of the MCC ground staff
Opinions on cricket: 'Would like to see 16 four-day games which gives you a day off a week. Improvements needed to prepare better pitches, which will produce better players, and make taking wickets not so easy.'
Best batting performance: 10* Sussex v Worcestershire, Hove 1989
Best bowling performance: 3-51 Sussex v Worcestershire, Hove 1989

DOWNTON, P. R.   Middlesex

Full Name: Paul Rupert Downton
Role: Right-hand bat, wicket-keeper
Born: 4 April 1957, Farnborough, Kent
Height: 5′ 10″ **Weight:** 12st 4lbs
Nickname: Nobby
County debut: 1977 (Kent), 1980 (Middlesex)
County cap: 1979 (Kent), 1981 (Middlesex)
Benefit: 1990
Test debut: 1980–81
No. of Tests: 30
No. of One-Day Internationals: 28
1000 runs in a season: 1
1st-Class 50s scored: 38
1st-Class 100s scored: 6
One-Day 50s: 8
Place in batting averages: 198th av. 18.45 (1988 77th av. 32.31)

Parents: George Charles and Jill Elizabeth
Wife and date of marriage: Alison, 19 October 1985
Children: Phoebe Alice, 16 December 1987, Jonathan George, 20 September 1989
Family links with cricket: Father kept wicket for Kent 1948–49
Education: Sevenoaks School; Exeter University
Qualifications: 9 O-levels, 3 A-levels; Law degree (LLB); NCA Coaching Certificate

Jobs outside cricket: Stockbroker
Off-season 1989–90: Working for James Capel (stockbrokers); organizing benefit
Overseas tours: England Young Cricketers to West Indies 1976; England to Pakistan and New Zealand 1977–78; West Indies 1980–81 and 1986; India, Sri Lanka and Australia 1984–85; Middlesex to Zimbabwe 1980–81
Overseas teams played for: Sandgate, Redcliffe 1981–82; Stellenbosch University 1983–84
Cricketers particularly learnt from: Father, Alan Knott, Clive Radley
Cricketers particularly admired: Alan Knott, Rod Marsh
Other sports played: Rugby (played in England U-19 squad 1975 and Exeter University 1st XV), golf, tennis
Other sports followed: American football
Relaxations: Reading
Extras: Made debut for Kent CCC in 1977, gaining cap in 1979. Played for Kent 2nd XI at age 16. Joined Middlesex in 1980
Opinions on cricket: 'We play too much cricket which inevitably leads to a dilution in quality. Each game should be a big game, but the system rarely allows that.'
Best batting performance: 126* Middlesex v Oxford University, Oxford 1986

LAST SEASON: BATTING

	I.	N.O.	R.	H.S.	AV.
TEST					
1ST-CLASS	34	3	572	100	18.45
INT					
RAL	14	5	137	31*	15.22
NAT.W.	4	2	143	69	71.50
B & H	3	0	47	34	15.66

LAST SEASON: WICKET KEEPING

	C.	ST.		
TEST				
1ST-CLASS	63	6		
INT				
RAL	17	6		
NAT.W.	10	1		
B & H	7	–		

CAREER: BATTING

	I.	N.O.	R.	H.S.	AV.
TEST	48	8	785	74	19.62
1ST-CLASS	327	64	6709	126*	25.50
INT	20	5	242	44*	16.13
RAL	103	31	1507	70	20.93
NAT.W.	27	6	552	69	26.28
B & H	35	12	551	80*	23.95

CAREER: WICKET KEEPING

	C.	ST.		
TEST	70	5		
1ST-CLASS	569	80		
INT	26	3		
RAL	130	36		
NAT.W.	52	7		
B & H	46	9		

EALHAM, M. A.   Kent

Full Name: Mark Alan Ealham
Role: Right-hand bat, right-arm medium bowler, outfielder
Born: 27 August 1969, Ashford
Height: 5′ 10″ **Weight:** 13st 7lbs
Nickname: Ealy, Burger
County debut: 1989
Parents: Alan George Ernest and Sue
Marital status: Single
Family links with cricket: 'My father played county cricket for Kent.'
Education: Stour Valley Secondary School
Qualifications: 8 CSEs
Jobs outside cricket: 'Worked in garage.'
Off-season 1989–90: Helping in family business
Cricketers particularly learnt from: Alan Ealham, Colin Page
Cricketers particularly admired: Ian Botham, Viv Richards, Malcolm Marshall, Robin Smith
Other sports played: Golf, hockey, snooker, darts
Other sports followed: Football
Relaxations: TV, comedy films, various types of music, e.g. U2, INXS, Madonna
Extras: 'Enjoyed playing for Ashford CC since the age of 11.'
Opinions on cricket: 'The whole Championship should be four-day cricket,

LAST SEASON: BATTING

	I.	N.O.	R.	H.S.	AV.
TEST					
1ST-CLASS	3	1	56	45	28.00
INT					
RAL	7	3	45	24	11.25
NAT.W.					
B & H					

LAST SEASON: BOWLING

	O.	M.	R.	W.	AV.
TEST					
1ST-CLASS	29	5	118	1	118.00
INT					
RAL	50	4	222	11	20.18
NAT.W.					
B & H					

CAREER: BATTING

	I.	N.O.	R.	H.S.	AV.
TEST					
1ST-CLASS	3	1	56	45	28.00
INT					
RAL	7	3	45	24	11.25
NAT.W.					
B & H					

CAREER: BOWLING

	O.	M.	R.	W.	AV.
TEST					
1ST-CLASS	29	5	118	1	118.00
INT					
RAL	50	4	222	11	20.18
NAT.W.					
B & H					

each county playing each other once, leaving one-day competitions for the weekend.'
Best batting performance: 45 Kent v Lancashire, Old Trafford 1989
Best bowling performance: 1-92 Kent v Australians, Canterbury 1989

EAST, D. E. Essex

Full Name: David Edward East
Role: Right-hand bat, wicket-keeper
Born: 27 July 1959, Clapton
Height: 5′ 10″ **Weight:** 13st
Nickname: 'Various insults, but Ethel seems popular and Easty.'
County debut: 1981
County cap: 1982
1st-Class 50s scored: 17
1st-Class 100s scored: 4
Place in batting averages: — (1988 149th av. 23.89)
Parents: Edward William and Joan Lillian
Wife and date of marriage: Jeanette Anne, 14 September 1984
Children: Matthew David Leonard, 8 November 1986
Family links with cricket: Father played club cricket for Hadley CC, an Essex touring side
Education: Millfields Primary; Hackney Downs School; University of East Anglia
Qualifications: BSc Hons in Biological Sciences. Advanced Cricket Coach
Jobs outside cricket: Has worked for shipping, insurance and finance brokers, cricket coaching and now cricket administration. Cricket consultant to Pony Sports (UK) Ltd
Off-season 1989–90: Appointed marketing manager to Edington Credit Ltd, London, the finance house of Edington plc, merchant bankers
Overseas teams played for: Avendale CC, Cape Town 1984–85
Cricketing superstitions or habits: 'The number 111. When the side are on 111, I join in the usual foot in the air business. Never take wicket-keeping pads off between sessions unless raining hard!'
Cricketers particularly learnt from: 'Keith Fletcher, "the sage of Essex", has always been very helpful.'
Cricketers particularly admired: 'Alan Knott, simply the best as far as I am concerned.'

158

Injuries 1989: 'I received a serious fracture to my right index finger on 29 April 1989, which prevented me taking any further part in the cricket season.'

Other sports played: Hockey, 'poor squash'

Other sports followed: Interested in most but loathes horse and dog racing. 'I have a passing interest in most other sports.'

Relaxations: Playing the piano, listening to various types of music, video, spending time at home; cooking (especially curry and Chinese); home-made wine and beer. 'I went clay pigeon shooting for the first time in 1988 and think I have got the bug for it.'

Extras: Spent 1980 season with Northamptonshire 2nd XI. Played for Essex 2nd XI at 16. Gordon's Gin Wicket-keeper of the Year 1983. World record holder for most catches in an innings in first-class cricket, 8, on his birthday in 1985

Opinions on cricket: 'The deduction of 25 points for a sub-standard wicket is a very unfair way of penalising a club for such an offence. A fine system should be introduced if it is felt necessary to take action.'

Best batting performance: 134 Essex v Gloucestershire, Ilford 1988

LAST SEASON: BATTING

	I.	N.O.	R.	H.S.	AV.
TEST					
1ST-CLASS	2	0	2	2	1.00
INT					
RAL					
NAT.W.					
B & H	1	1	1	1*	–

CAREER: BATTING

	I.	N.O.	R.	H.S.	AV.
TEST					
1ST-CLASS	254	32	4553	134	20.50
INT					
RAL	58	19	508	43	13.02
NAT.W.	16	5	142	28	12.90
B & H	22	5	235	33	13.82

LAST SEASON: WICKET KEEPING

	C.	ST.			
TEST					
1ST-CLASS	2	–			
INT					
RAL					
NAT.W.					
B & H	3	–			

CAREER: WICKET KEEPING

	C.	ST.			
TEST					
1ST-CLASS	480	53			
INT					
RAL	88	15			
NAT.W.	29	3			
B & H	54	1			

70. Which England-qualified batsman hit the most first-class sixes in 1989?

EDMUNDS, R. H.   Leicestershire

Full Name: Richard Harold Edmunds
Role: Right-hand bat, left-arm
fast-medium bowler
Born: 27 May 1970, Oakham
Height: 6′ 4″ **Weight:** 14st 4lbs
Nickname: Big Dick, Herman,
Milburn, and many others
County debut: 1989
Parents: Alan and Elizabeth
Marital status: Single
Family links with cricket: Father
once played for the Cottesmore
Hunt
Education: Vale of Catmose,
Oakham, Rutland Sixth Form
Qualifications: 2 O-levels
Jobs outside cricket: Labourer
Overseas tours: Rutland Tourists
Jersey 1985, 1986, 1987, and South
Africa 1989
Cricketers particularly learnt from: Len Ellis (Oakham CC), Ken Higgs, and
everyone at Leicester
Cricketers particularly admired: John Lever, Richard Hadlee, Ian Botham
Other sports played: Rugby, snooker, golf
Other sports followed: All sports
Injuries 1989: Chickenpox – off 2 weeks in May; back problem – off three
weeks in August
Relaxations: Drinking, eating, sleeping, reading a good book

LAST SEASON: BATTING

	I.	N.O.	R.	H.S.	AV.
TEST					
1ST-CLASS	3	0	17	17	5.66
INT					
RAL	3	1	14	9	7.00
NAT.W.					
B & H					

CAREER: BATTING

	I.	N.O.	R.	H.S.	AV.
TEST					
1ST-CLASS	3	0	17	17	5.66
INT					
RAL	3	1	14	9	7.00
NAT.W.					
B & H					

LAST SEASON: BOWLING

	O.	M.	R.	W.	AV.
TEST					
1ST-CLASS	37	5	113	3	37.66
INT					
RAL	22	3	118	2	59.00
NAT.W.					
B & H					

CAREER: BOWLING

	O.	M.	R.	W.	AV.
TEST					
1ST-CLASS	37	5	113	3	37.66
INT					
RAL	22	3	118	2	59.00
NAT.W.					
B & H					

160

Extras: Played for Young England v New Zealand 1989. Tragically died in December 1989 following a car accident
Opinions on cricket: 'Counties should give more help to players as regards winter employment. Cricketers should be allowed to play wherever they wish without fear of a ban. More gimmicks are required in the one-day games to bring some much needed money into cricket.'
Best batting performance: 17 Leicestershire v Gloucestershire, Leicester 1989
Best bowling performance: 2-38 Leicestershire v Gloucestershire, Leicester 1989

ELLCOCK, R. M. Middlesex

Full Name: Ricardo McDonald Ellcock
Role: Right-hand bat, right-arm fast-medium bowler
Born: 17 June 1965, Barbados
Height: 5′ 11″ **Weight:** 13st
Nickname: Ricky
County debut: 1982 (Worcestershire), 1989 (Middlesex)
1st-Class 5 w. in innings: 1
Place in bowling averages: 10th av. 19.21
Strike rate 1989: 34.15 (career 48.44)
1st-Class catches 1989: 3 (career 8)
Parents: Everson McDonald (deceased) and Ione Marian
Marital status: Single
Family links with cricket: Brother has played for Barbados

Education: Welches Mixed School, Combermere, Barbados; Malvern College, England
Qualifications: 6 O-levels
Off-season 1989–90: Touring West Indies with England, and 'recovering!'
Overseas tours: Around West Indies with Barbados; England to West Indies 1990
Overseas teams played for: Combined Schools, Barbados 1980; Carlton and Barbados 1983–84
Cricketers particularly learnt from: Victor Sandiford, a personal friend; watching Malcolm Marshall and Michael Holding; and last season, Desmond Haynes and Mike Gatting

Cricketers particularly admired: Alvin Kallicharran, Michael Holding, Malcolm Marshall

Other sports played: Football, basketball

Other sports followed: Motor racing, horse racing

Injuries 1989: 'Bad back caused me to miss two months.' Had to do 15 minutes of exercises every day before even trying to pick up his morning newspaper

Relaxations: Flying

Extras: Selected to tour West Indies with England in 1990, after playing 42 first-class matches in eight seasons, and having missed the first half of 1989 season because of a back injury. Made debut for Worcestershire at age 17

Opinions on cricket: On his selection to tour the West Indies with England: 'In all honesty I'd never thought about playing for England until I received a letter in August asking if I was available. It's a huge jump, and I don't for one moment think it's going to be easy, but the great thing about bowling is that you have to prove yourself all the time, and this is a great opportunity for me to prove something more about myself. I will listen to everything people tell me; I will work hard, and just try to bowl fast. That's all I've ever done.'

Best batting performance: 45* Worcestershire v Essex, Worcester 1984

Best bowling performance: 5-35 Middlesex v Yorkshire, Leeds 1989

LAST SEASON: BATTING

	I.	N.O.	R.	H.S.	AV.
TEST					
1ST-CLASS	6	1	27	9	5.40
INT					
RAL	2	0	18	13	9.00
NAT.W.	1	1	0	0*	–
B & H					

CAREER: BATTING

	I.	N.O.	R.	H.S.	AV.
TEST					
1ST-CLASS	46	12	398	45*	11.70
INT					
RAL	7	2	24	13	4.80
NAT.W.	2	1	6	6	6.00
B & H	2	1	16	12	16.00

LAST SEASON: BOWLING

	O.	M.	R.	W.	AV.
TEST					
1ST-CLASS	182.1	36	615	32	19.21
INT					
RAL	46	4	184	8	23.00
NAT.W.	44	6	188	8	23.50
B & H					

CAREER: BOWLING

	O.	M.	R.	W.	AV.
TEST					
1ST-CLASS	880	128	3190	109	29.26
INT					
RAL	107.3	8	419	21	19.95
NAT.W.	54	8	237	11	21.54
B & H	25	4	98	3	32.66

ELLISON, R. M.

Full Name: Richard Mark Ellison
Role: Left-hand bat, right-arm medium bowler
Born: 21 September 1959, Ashford, Kent
Height: 6′ 3″ **Weight:** 14st 7lbs
Nickname: Elly
County debut: 1981
County cap: 1983
Test debut: 1984
No. of Tests: 11
No. of One-Day Internationals: 14
50 wickets in a season: 4
1st-Class 50s scored: 13
1st-Class 100s scored: 1
1st-Class 5 w. in innings: 14
1st-Class 10 w. in match: 2

One-Day 50s: 4
Place in batting averages: 192nd av. 18.85 (1988 215th av. 16.47)
Place in bowling averages: 38th av. 25.93 (1988 41st av. 23.90)
Strike rate 1989: 60.44 (career 59.55)
1st-Class catches 1989: 4 (career 56)
Parents: Peter Richard Maxwell (deceased) and Bridget Mary
Wife and date of marriage: Fiona, 28 September 1985
Family links with cricket: Brother Charles Christopher blue at Cambridge University 1981–86. Grandfather played with Grace brothers and was secretary of Derby CCC in about 1915
Education: Friars Preparatory School, Great Chart, Ashford; Tonbridge School; St Lukes College; Exeter University
Qualifications: 8 O-levels, 2 A-levels; Degree B.Ed.; Teacher
Jobs outside cricket: Three months teaching winter 1985. Salesman for Panasonic winter 1987
Off-season 1989–90: Touring with unofficial English team in South Africa. Training for the 1990 season
Overseas tours: With England to India and Australia 1984–85; England to Sharjah 1985; England to West Indies 1986
Overseas teams played for: University of Witwatersrand 1982–83, 1983–84; Tasmania 1986–87; Clarence Cricket Club, Hobart 1986–87
Cricketers particularly learnt from: Ray Dovey, Bob Woolmer, John Inverarity, Geoff Arnold

Cricketers particularly admired: Malcolm Marshall, Richard Hadlee, Chris Tavaré, Terry Alderman

Other sports played: Used to play a lot of hockey; golf, snooker

Other sports followed: Anything but horse racing and greyhounds

Relaxations: Social drinking, good food, music: Chris Rea, Dire Straits, New Order

Extras: Did not play at all in 1987 due to back injury. One of *Wisden*'s Five Cricketers of the Year, 1985. Debut for Canterbury Amateur Operatic Society in April 1989, in 'Fiddler on the Roof'

Opinions on cricket: 'We should not be dictated to in the way in which we select the England teams. Manner in which people qualify for English registration is a joke. One overseas player only. Why should we be prevented going to South Africa? A fair few players, whose governments want players who have been there to be banned, allow their individual Test players to come and play against and with the majority of English pros who have at some stage been to South Africa. If they feel that strongly about it, they could ban their own players from coming over here.'

Best batting performance: 108 Kent v Oxford University, Oxford 1984

Best bowling performance: 7-87 Kent v Northamptonshire, Maidstone 1985

LAST SEASON: BATTING

	I.	N.O.	R.	H.S.	AV.
TEST					
1ST-CLASS	16	2	264	39*	18.85
INT					
RAL	5	2	21	9*	7.00
NAT.W.	1	0	14	14	14.00
B & H	4	2	70	29	35.00

CAREER: BATTING

	I.	N.O.	R.	H.S.	AV.
TEST	16	1	202	41	13.46
1ST-CLASS	192	46	3491	108	23.91
INT	12	4	86	24	10.75
RAL	58	25	898	84	27.21
NAT.W.	15	6	275	49*	30.55
B & H	23	6	398	72	23.41

LAST SEASON: BOWLING

	O.	M.	R.	W.	AV.
TEST					
1ST-CLASS	292.1	71	752	29	25.93
INT					
RAL	29.1	2	132	4	33.00
NAT.W.	14	1	60	2	30.00
B & H	36	3	130	7	18.57

CAREER: BOWLING

	O.	M.	R.	W.	AV.
TEST	377.2	90	1048	35	29.94
1ST-CLASS	3295.3	858	8722	335	26.03
INT	116	9	510	12	42.50
RAL	484	28	2167	82	26.42
NAT.W.	188.3	33	602	28	21.50
B & H	275.1	46	916	40	22.90

EMBUREY, J. E.   Middlesex

Full Name: John Ernest Emburey
Role: Right-hand bat, off-break bowler, slip or gully fielder
Born: 20 August 1952, Peckham
Height: 6′ 2″ **Weight:** 14st
Nickname: Embers, Ernie
County debut: 1973
County cap: 1977
Benefit: 1986
Test debut: 1978
No. of Tests: 60
No. of One-Day Internationals: 58
50 wickets in a season: 11
1st-Class 50s scored: 36
1st-Class 100s scored: 3
1st-Class 5 w. in innings: 56
1st-Class 10 w. in match: 9
One-Day 50s: 2
Place in batting averages: 197th av. 18.56 (1988 101st av. 29.26)
Place in bowling averages: 66th av. 30.14 (1988 59th av. 26.60)
Strike rate 1989: 85.87 (career 64.86)
1st-Class catches 1989: 14 (career 320)
Parents: John and Rose
Wife and date of marriage: Susie, 20 September 1980
Children: Clare, 1 March 1983; Chloe, 31 October 1985
Family links with cricket: Brother, Stephen, represented London Schools Colts in 1977
Education: Peckham Manor Secondary School
Qualifications: O-levels, Advanced Cricket Coaching Certificate
Jobs outside cricket: 'No other jobs. Have been abroad coaching most years.'
Off-season 1989–90: Touring with unofficial English team in South Africa
Overseas tours: With England to Australia 1978–79 and 1979–80 (following injury to Geoff Miller), West Indies 1981 and 1986, India 1979–80, 1981–82; World Cup, Pakistan, Australia and New Zealand 1987–88; Derrick Robins' XI to Sri Lanka 1977–78; Middlesex to Zimbabwe 1980; unofficial England tour to South Africa 1981–82
Overseas teams played for: St Kilda CC, Melbourne 1979–80, 1984–85; Prahran, Melbourne 1977–78; Western Province 1982–83, 1983–84
Cricketers particularly learnt from: F. Titmus
Cricketers particularly admired: Ken Barrington, Graham Gooch, Paul Downton

Other sports played: Golf

Relaxations: Reading, gardening, going to the theatre

Extras: Played for Surrey Young Cricketers 1969–70. Whitbread scholarship to Australia, 1977–78. P. H. Edmonds of Middlesex and England was the best man at his wedding. Middlesex vice-captain since 1983. One of *Wisden*'s Five Cricketers of the Year, 1983. Banned from Test cricket for three years after playing for England Rebels in South Africa. Hit 6 sixes in 7 balls for Western Province v Eastern Province 1983–84 (52* in 22 balls). Captain of England v West Indies 1988. Published autobiography *Emburey* in 1988

Opinions on cricket: 'I don't believe that anybody who plays cricket for a living should have his livelihood jeopardised or restricted (by bans on going to South Africa) . . . It can't be right to discriminate against a youngster who is prepared to pay his own fare to coach or play abroad to supplement his income or widen his experience. In fact, it wouldn't be a bad idea if county clubs gave such players a little bit of assistance with their travel costs.'

Best batting performance: 133 Middlesex v Essex, Chelmsford 1983

Best bowling performance: 7-27 Middlesex v Gloucestershire, Cheltenham 1989

LAST SEASON: BATTING

	I.	N.O.	R.	H.S.	AV.
TEST	5	1	131	64	32.75
1ST-CLASS	25	4	333	77*	15.85
INT	1	0	10	10	10.00
RAL	10	2	74	17	9.25
NAT.W.	4	2	77	36	38.50
B & H	3	0	27	18	9.00

CAREER: BATTING

	I.	N.O.	R.	H.S.	AV.
TEST	89	18	1540	75	21.69
1ST-CLASS	376	77	6798	133	22.73
INT	43	10	471	34	14.27
RAL	125	40	1374	50	16.16
NAT.W.	27	9	430	36*	23.88
B & H	40	12	513	50	18.32

LAST SEASON: BOWLING

	O.	M.	R.	W.	AV.
TEST	152	37	342	8	42.75
1ST-CLASS	635.1	229	1316	47	28.00
INT	33	0	139	6	23.16
RAL	93	3	449	18	24.94
NAT.W.	58	16	149	6	24.83
B & H	28	7	85	5	17.00

CAREER: BOWLING

	O.	M.	R.	W.	AV.
TEST	144.4 2178.3	49 686	5105	138	36.99
1ST-CLASS	155.1 9821.5	39 3276	24104	1009	23.88
INT	546.5	38	2226	75	29.68
RAL	1230.5	99	5253	240	21.88
NAT.W.	478.3	92	1267	45	28.15
B & H	485.4	83	1415	50	28.30

71. What do Rob Bailey, John Childs and Phil Neale all have in common?

EVANS, K. P.   Nottinghamshire

Full Name: Kevin Paul Evans
Role: Right-hand bat, right-arm medium bowler, slip fielder
Born: 10 September 1963, Calverton, Nottingham
Height: 6′ 2″ **Weight:** 13st
Nickname: Ghost
County debut: 1984
1st-Class 50s scored: 4
Place in batting averages: 129th av. 26.33 (1988 188th av. 20.30)
Place in bowling averages: 47th av. 26.93 (1988 121st av. 37.68)
Strike rate 1989: 53.55 (career 67.65)
1st-Class catches 1989: 13 (career 38)
Parents: Eric and Eileen
Wife and date of marriage: Sandra, 19 March 1988
Family links with cricket: Brother Russell plays for Nottinghamshire. Father played local cricket
Education: William Lee Primary; Colonel Frank Seely Comprehensive, Calverton
Qualifications: 10 O-levels, 3 A-levels. Qualified coach
Jobs outside cricket: Bank work. Maintenance work
Cricketing superstitions or habits: Left pad on first
Overseas teams played for: Wainuomata, New Zealand 1986–87, 1988–89
Cricketers particularly learnt from: Bob White, Mike Harris, Clive Rice, Mike Bore and 'most of the Nottinghamshire staff'

LAST SEASON: BATTING

	I.	N.O.	R.	H.S.	AV.
TEST					
1ST-CLASS	21	6	395	58	26.33
INT					
RAL	8	2	56	19*	9.33
NAT.W.	2	1	8	8	8.00
B & H	4	0	42	26	10.50

CAREER: BATTING

	I.	N.O.	R.	H.S.	AV.
TEST					
1ST-CLASS	56	10	909	58	19.76
INT					
RAL	27	9	229	28	12.72
NAT.W.	5	1	27	10	6.75
B & H	9	2	124	31*	17.71

LAST SEASON: BOWLING

	O.	M.	R.	W.	AV.
TEST					
1ST-CLASS	258.5	59	781	29	26.93
INT					
RAL	86	3	343	14	24.50
NAT.W.	24	2	74	1	74.00
B & H	63	5	235	9	26.11

CAREER: BOWLING

	O.	M.	R.	W.	AV.
TEST					
1ST-CLASS	676.3	134	2172	60	36.20
INT					
RAL	263.4	7	1296	43	30.13
NAT.W.	83	13	258	9	28.66
B & H	105.2	7	418	15	27.86

Cricketers particularly admired: Richard Hadlee
Other sports played: Football, tennis, squash
Injuries 1989: Broken bone in right hand – had to miss last five weeks of season
Relaxations: Listening to music, reading, DIY, gardening
Extras: Together with brother Russell, first brothers to bat together for Nottinghamshire CCC in 1st-class cricket for 50 years
Opinions on cricket: 'We should play 16 four-day matches, but change the bonus system. To get full batting points, it should change to 300 in 130 overs, or something similar, so that the batsman can concentrate on hitting the bad ball rather than improvising on the good ones.'
Best batting performance: 58 Nottinghamshire v Lancashire, Worksop 1989
Best bowling performance: 3-20 Nottinghamshire v Yorkshire, Leeds 1989

FAIRBROTHER, N. H. Lancashire

Full Name: Neil Harvey Fairbrother
Role: Left-hand bat, left-arm medium bowler
Born: 9 September 1963, Warrington, Cheshire
Height: 5′ 8″ **Weight:** 11st
Nickname: Harvey
County debut: 1982
County cap: 1985
Test debut: 1987
No. of Tests: 4
No. of One-Day Internationals: 11
1000 runs in a season: 6
1st-Class 50s scored: 51
1st-Class 100s scored: 16
One-Day 50s: 22
One-Day 100s: 5
Place in batting averages: 29th av. 42.88 (1988 86th av. 30.64)

1st-Class catches 1989: 8 (career 91)
Parents: Leslie Robert and Barbara
Wife and date of marriage: Audrey, 23 September 1988
Family links with cricket: Father and two uncles played local league cricket
Education: St Margaret's Church of England School, Oxford; Lymn Grammar School
Qualifications: 5 O-levels

168

Off-season 1989–90: 'Playing golf'

Overseas tours: Denmark 1980 with North of England U-19; England to Sharjah 1987; World Cup, Pakistan, Australia and New Zealand 1987–88

Overseas teams played for: Eastern Suburbs CC, Canberra, Australia 1985–86

Cricketers particularly learnt from: 'All the senior players at Old Trafford have been a great help, particularly Messrs Fowler and Allott.'

Cricketers particularly admired: Clive Lloyd, Allan Border

Other sports played: Rugby, squash

Other sports followed: Football, rugby union, rugby league

Relaxations: Music and playing sport

Extras: 'I was named after the Australian cricketer Neil Harvey, who was my mum's favourite cricketer.' Three Tests and two U-19 one-day internationals v Young Australians 1983. Made full Test debut v Pakistan at Old Trafford 1987

Best batting performance: 164* Lancashire v Hampshire, Liverpool 1985

Best bowling performance: 2-91 Lancashire v Nottinghamshire, Old Trafford 1987

LAST SEASON: BATTING

	I.	N.O.	R.	H.S.	AV.
TEST					
1ST-CLASS	38	4	1458	161	42.88
INT					
RAL	15	4	582	100*	52.90
NAT.W.	3	0	63	31	21.00
B & H	5	2	148	69*	49.33

LAST SEASON: BOWLING

	O.	M.	R.	W.	AV.
TEST					
1ST-CLASS	12	1	71	1	71.00
INT					
RAL					
NAT.W.					
B & H					

CAREER: BATTING

	I.	N.O.	R.	H.S.	AV.
TEST	4	0	5	3	1.25
1ST-CLASS	254	34	8481	164*	38.55
INT	11	2	232	54	25.77
RAL	84	19	2388	116*	36.73
NAT.W.	15	3	597	93*	49.75
B & H	24	7	679	116*	39.94

CAREER: BOWLING

	O.	M.	R.	W.	AV.
TEST					
1ST-CLASS	102.2	22	394	5	78.80
INT					
RAL	2	0	15	0	–
NAT.W.	3	0	16	0	–
B & H					

72. Which company sponsored the Test Series, England v West Indies, 1990?

FALKNER, N. J.   Sussex

Full Name: Nicholas James Falkner
Role: Right-hand bat, right-arm
seamer, cover or mid-wicket
fielder
Born: 30 September 1962, Redhill
Height: 5' 10½" **Weight:** 12st 5lbs
Nickname: Beefy, Captain Cutters,
Falksy
County debut: 1984 (Surrey),
1988 (Sussex)
1st-Class 50s scored: 3
1st-Class 100s scored: 2
One-Day 50s: 2
Place in batting averages: —
(1988 214th av. 16.57)
1st-Class catches 1989: 0 (career 14)

Parents: John and Barbara
Wife and date of marriage:
Jacqueline Patricia, 19 March 1988
Family links with cricket: Father plays club cricket for Chipstead and Coulsdon
Education: Yardley Court; Reigate Grammar School
Qualifications: 5 O-levels
Jobs outside cricket: Assistant buyer for Balfour Beatty Int Construction;
worked in insurance company
Off-season 1989–90: Learning a new trade for National Westminster Bank
Cricketing superstitions or habits: Left pad on first. 'If not captaining, I like to
leave the dressing-room last.'
Overseas tours: Captained Surrey Schools to Australia 1980–81; Brighton
Brunswick to Jersey 1988, 1989
Overseas teams played for: Perth Cricket Club 1982–83, 1985–86; University
Cricket Club, Perth 1986–87
Cricketers particularly learnt from: Les Smithers, Father ('Always gives me
sound advice')
Cricketers particularly admired: Ian Botham, Brian Hart
Other sports played: Squash, golf
Other sports followed: All sports '– especially rugby'
Injuries 1989: 'For the first time in eight years I received no injuries, and
therefore I did not miss one game.'
Relaxations: Reading, playing chess, watching videos, pottering around in the
garden
Extras: Scored a century on first-team debut for Surrey, 101* v Cambridge

170

University. 'I have taken only *one* first-class wicket, namely a Test captain –
Imran Khan!' Left Surrey for Sussex at end of 1987 season. Retired from
county cricket at end of 1989 season to take up banking career
Opinions on cricket: 'Sixteen four-day games would be a much fairer system.
There should be only one overseas player per county.'
Best batting performance: 102 Surrey v Middlesex, Lord's 1986
Best bowling performance: 1-3 Surrey v Sussex, Guildford 1986

LAST SEASON: BATTING

	I.	N.O.	R.	H.S.	AV.
TEST					
1ST-CLASS	4	0	76	48	19.00
INT					
RAL	1	0	1	1	1.00
NAT.W.	–	–	–	–	–
B & H	2	0	5	4	2.50

CAREER: BATTING

	I.	N.O.	R.	H.S.	AV.
TEST					
1ST-CLASS	42	3	1042	102	26.71
INT					
RAL	7	0	164	52	23.42
NAT.W.	2	0	36	36	18.00
B & H	7	1	81	58	13.50

FARBRACE, P. Kent

Full Name: Paul Farbrace
Role: Right-hand bat,
wicket-keeper
Born: 7 July 1967, Ash, nr
Canterbury
Height: 5' 10" **Weight:** 12st
Nickname: Farby, Ugly
County debut: 1987
1st-Class 50s scored: 1
Parents: David and Betty
Wife and date of marriage:
Elizabeth Jane, 27 July 1985
Children: Jemma Elizabeth,
30 March 1985; Eleanor Kate,
3 September 1988
Family links with cricket: 'Father
played village cricket, as do my two
brothers – Ian plays in South Wales
and Colin plays for Ash. Dad and
eldest brother both keep wicket.'

Education: Ash CE Primary School; Geoffrey Chaucer School, Canterbury
Qualifications: 2 O-levels, 6 CSEs, NCA Cricket Coaching Certificate and
NCA Senior Coaching Award
Jobs outside cricket: Customs officer; postman; cricket coach. Cricket and
football radio commentator for BBC Radio Kent

Off-season 1989–90: Working as a postman in the mornings, and as a cricket coach in the evenings. Also BBC Radio Kent football commentator

Cricketing superstitions or habits: 'Always arrive at ground very early, then lay all my kit out. Follow captain onto field, then on to collect ball off the umpire. Fiddle with pads, trousers and then gloves when keeping, in sequence before every ball. Too many to mention when batting.'

Overseas tours: Kent Schools U-17 XI to Canada 1983

Cricketers particularly learnt from: Alan Knott, Derek Underwood, Bob Woolmer, Colin Page, Alan Ealham, Steve Marsh

Cricketers particularly admired: Alan Knott, Derek Underwood

Other sports played: Football, golf, rugby, basketball '– anything and everything'

Other sports followed: All sports except horse racing

Injuries 1989: Twisted knee – out for three days

Relaxations: 'Reading and spending as much time with my wife and daughters as possible.'

Extras: Played County Schools football, had England Schools U-18 trial, attracted attention from Notts County, then had extended trials with Coventry City when seventeen as a goalkeeper. Captained Kent v Essex in a five-a-side cricket game in Dartford Tunnel in February 1989 to raise money for Children in Need

Opinions on cricket: 'Keep politics out of sport. County clubs should do more to encourage families into cricket grounds. Make Sunday League cricket into a batsman's game, with coloured clothes and gimmicks to make it more fun!'

Best batting performance: 75* Kent v Yorkshire, Canterbury 1987

LAST SEASON: BATTING

	I.	N.O.	R.	H.S.	AV.
TEST					
1ST-CLASS	3	0	44	35	14.66
INT					
RAL	1	1	1	1*	–
NAT.W.					
B & H					

CAREER: BATTING

	I.	N.O.	R.	H.S.	AV.
TEST					
1ST-CLASS	12	3	193	75*	21.44
INT					
RAL	1	1	1	1*	–
NAT.W.	1	0	4	4	4.00
B & H					

LAST SEASON: WICKET KEEPING

	C.	ST.			
TEST					
1ST-CLASS	5	2			
INT					
RAL					
NAT.W.					
B & H					

CAREER: WICKET KEEPING

	C.	ST.			
TEST					
1ST-CLASS	18	2			
INT					
RAL					
NAT.W.	3	–			
B & H					

FELTHAM, M. A.　　　　　Surrey

Full Name: Mark Andrew Feltham
Role: Right-hand bat, right-arm
fast-medium bowler
Born: 26 June 1963, London
Height: 6′ 2″ **Weight:** 14st
Nickname: Felts, Felpsy, Boff or
Douglas
County debut: 1983
50 wickets in a season: 1
1st-Class 50s scored: 3
1st-Class 5 w. in innings: 4
Place in batting averages: 191st
av. 19.00 (1988 160th av. 22.93)
Place in bowling averages: 77th
av. 31.22 (1988 82nd av. 29.98)
Strike rate 1989: 64.75 (career 60.28)
1st-Class catches 1989: 8 (career 30)
Parents: Leonard William and
Patricia Louise
Family links with cricket: Mother involved in Ken Barrington Cricket Centre
Appeal; brother plays for Surrey Young Cricketers and League cricket
Education: Roehampton Church School; Tiffin Boys' School
Qualifications: 7 O-levels; Advanced Cricket Coach
Jobs outside cricket: Marketing and sales
Off-season 1989–90: Marketing in London and south-east
Cricketing superstitions or habits: 'Left pad on before right. Have favourite
trousers, shirt etc, to bat in.'
Overseas tours: Australia, 1980, with Surrey Cricket Association U-19s;
Barbados, 1981, with MCC Young Professionals
Overseas teams played for: Glenwood High School Old Boys, Durban
1984–85
Cricketers particularly learnt from: Sylvester Clarke
Cricketers particularly admired: Ian Botham, Sylvester Clarke
Other sports played: Football
Other sports followed: Charlton FC, most sports
Injuries 1989: Pulled muscles, and strained ligaments in right shoulder
Relaxations: Listening to music, crosswords – 'although only in *Sun* and *Star*!'
Extras: Played for England Schools at U-15 and U-19 levels. On the MCC
Young Professionals Staff 1981 and 1982
Opinions on cricket: 'It seems to me that the authorities are trying to get more
and more each year from the modern players. Why we couldn't have gone
straight to 16 four-day games seems strange to me. Players should be allowed

to play and earn a living wherever they wish without being put under pressure by politicians. There is so much hypocrisy on this subject it is disgraceful.'
Best batting performance: 76 Surrey v Gloucestershire, The Oval 1986
Best bowling performance: 5-45 Surrey v Lancashire, The Oval 1988

LAST SEASON: BATTING

	I.	N.O.	R.	H.S.	AV.
TEST					
1ST-CLASS	21	2	361	64	19.00
INT					
RAL	8	0	137	35	17.12
NAT.W.	1	1	19	19*	–
B & H	4	0	58	29	14.50

CAREER: BATTING

	I.	N.O.	R.	H.S.	AV.
TEST					
1ST-CLASS	89	24	1335	76	20.53
INT					
RAL	39	12	391	37	14.48
NAT.W.	8	3	67	19*	13.40
B & H	13	3	133	29	13.30

LAST SEASON: BOWLING

	O.	M.	R.	W.	AV.
TEST					
1ST-CLASS	388.3	81	1124	36	31.22
INT					
RAL	78.5	4	354	15	23.60
NAT.W.	29	2	152	4	38.00
B & H	40	4	151	10	15.10

CAREER: BOWLING

	O.	M.	R.	W.	AV.
TEST					
1ST-CLASS	1929.1	419	5916	192	30.81
INT					
RAL	402.5	13	2101	59	35.61
NAT.W.	109	15	476	11	43.27
B & H	193.2	19	765	30	25.50

FELTON, N. A. Northamptonshire

Full Name: Nigel Alfred Felton
Role: Left-hand bat
Born: 24 October 1960, Guildford
Height: 5' 7" **Weight:** 10st 7lbs
Nickname: Will, Twiglets
County debut: 1982 (Somerset), 1989 (Northamptonshire)
County cap: 1986 (Somerset)
1000 runs in a season: 2
1st-Class 50s scored: 32
1st-Class 100s scored: 8
One-Day 50s: 9
Place in batting averages: 136th av. 25.17 (1988 106th av. 28.80)
1st-Class catches 1989: 11 (career 57)
Parents: Ralph and Enid
Marital status: Single
Family links with cricket: Father

played club cricket
Education: Hawes Down Secondary School, West Wickham, Kent; Millfield School, Street, Somerset; Loughborough University

Qualifications: 6 O-levels, 2 A-levels, BSc(Hons), Cert of Education PE/Sports Sciences, qualified teacher

Jobs outside cricket: Teaching, digging holes, working with Somerset CCC marketing dept

Cricketing superstitions or habits: Always puts right pad on first

Overseas tours: English Schools to India 1976–77; Young England to Australia 1978; Scorpions CC to Sierra Leone 1987

Overseas teams played for: Waneroro CC, Perth, Western Australia 1985–86

Other sports followed: Most ball games

Other sports played: Most winter sports

Relaxations: Music, reading, relaxing at home

Extras: Joined Somerset in July 1981. Played a season for Kent in 1980 after leaving Millfield and before going to Loughborough. Left Kent at pre-season training 1981, due to the size of the staff. Joined Somerset at end of first year at Loughborough. Released by Somerset at end of 1988 season

Opinions on cricket: 'I'm in favour of four-day cricket.'

Best batting performance: 173* Somerset v Kent, Taunton 1983

Best bowling performance: 1-58 Northamptonshire v Somerset, Luton 1989

LAST SEASON: BATTING

	I.	N.O.	R.	H.S.	AV.
TEST					
1ST-CLASS	26	3	579	60*	25.17
INT					
RAL	10	3	180	58*	25.71
NAT.W.	3	0	70	41	23.33
B & H	–	–	–	–	–

CAREER: BATTING

	I.	N.O.	R.	H.S.	AV.
TEST					
1ST-CLASS	206	10	5566	173*	28.39
INT					
RAL	48	8	953	96	23.82
NAT.W.	11	2	373	87	41.44
B & H	11	0	146	50	13.27

73. Who was the Cricket Writers Young Cricketer of the Year, 1989?

74. What did Nick Cook and Gladstone Small have in common in the Oval Test, 1989?

FERRIS, G. J. F.   Leicestershire

Full Name: George John Fitzgerald
Ferris
Role: Right-hand and left-hand bat,
right-arm fast bowler
Born: 18 October 1964, Urlings
Village, Antigua
Height: 6′ 3″ **Weight:** 14st 7lbs
Nickname: Ferro, Slugo
County debut: 1983
County cap: 1988
50 wickets in a season: 3
1st-Class 5 w. in innings: 9
1st-Class 10 w. in match: 1
Place in batting averages: 236th
av. 13.33 (1988 251st av. 11.58)
Place in bowling averages: —
(1988 28th av. 22.25)
1st-Class catches 1989: 2 (career 12)
Parents: Leslie and Verona
Wife and date of marriage: Janet, 25 March 1989
Children: Imran J.
Education: Jenning's Secondary
Jobs outside cricket: Physical education teacher
Off-season 1989–90: Playing for the Leeward Islands in Red Stripe competition
Overseas tours: With Young West Indies to England 1982; West Indies U-25s
to Zimbabwe 1983; Young West Indies to Zimbabwe 1983 and 1986; English
Counties XI to New York 1988

LAST SEASON: BATTING

	I.	N.O.	R.	H.S.	AV.
TEST					
1ST-CLASS	9	3	80	30	13.33
INT					
RAL	3	1	7	6	3.50
NAT.W.					
B & H	–	–	–	–	–

CAREER: BATTING

	I.	N.O.	R.	H.S.	AV.
TEST					
1ST-CLASS	99	44	641	36*	11.65
INT					
RAL	12	7	43	13*	8.60
NAT.W.	3	2	3	2*	3.00
B & H	2	2	1	1*	–

LAST SEASON: BOWLING

	O.	M.	R.	W.	AV.
TEST					
1ST-CLASS	124.1	39	327	17	19.23
INT					
RAL	19	2	75	3	25.00
NAT.W.					
B & H	21	2	68	3	22.66

CAREER: BOWLING

	O.	M.	R.	W.	AV.
TEST					
1ST-CLASS	2117.1	400	6873	274	25.08
INT					
RAL	175.3	9	753	31	24.29
NAT.W.	52	5	238	5	47.60
B & H	82	8	347	15	23.13

Overseas teams played for: Leeward Islands 1982–90; Matabeleland
Cricketers particularly learnt from: Andy Roberts (neighbour in Antigua), Ken Higgs
Cricketers particularly admired: Michael Holding
Other sports played: Basketball, volleyball
Other sports followed: Motor sports, boxing, wrestling, tennis
Injuries 1989: Recurring thigh strain – out for six weeks
Relaxations: Listening to gospel music
Extras: Picked out by Viv Richards as one of two future West Indies stars, in 1983. (Richards' other choice was Jeff Dujon)
Best batting performance: 36* Leicestershire v Hampshire, Leicester 1988
Best bowling performance: 7-42 Leicestershire v Glamorgan, Hinckley 1983

FIELD-BUSS, M.   Nottinghamshire

Full Name: Michael Field-Buss
Role: Right-hand bat, off-break bowler
Born: 23 September 1964, Malta
Height: 5′ 10″ **Weight:** 11st
Nickname: Mouse
County debut: 1987 (Essex), 1989 (Nottinghamshire)
1st-Class catches 1989: 1 (career 1)
Parents: Gwyn and Monica
Marital status: Single
Family links with cricket: Father played local cricket with Ilford RAFA
Education: Wanstead High School
Qualifications: Qualified coach
Jobs outside cricket: Warehouse-man
Off-season 1989–90: Working for local council
Cricketing superstitions or habits: 'Always put left pad on first. Never watch too much of the game before going into bat. Wear same clothes if doing well in the game.'
Overseas teams played for: Werribee Cricket Club, Australia 1986, 1987
Cricketers particularly learnt from: Bill Morris (one time coach at Ilford Cricket School), Ray East and David Acfield at Essex, Eddie Hemmings at Nottinghamshire
Other sports played: Football

Other sports followed: 'Watching Leyton Orient FC (although really support Arsenal).'

Injuries 1989: 'Smashed little finger on left hand, which needed an operation to put a pin in. This meant missing 6 weeks of the season (6-6-89 to 17-7-89).'

Relaxations: Sleeping, listening to music, being with family

Extras: Highest first-class score 34 not out (while with Essex) 1987. Best bowling on debut for Nottinghamshire 1989

Opinions on cricket: 'Every effort should be made to bring Second XI wickets up to the standard of first-class.'

Best batting performance: 34* Essex v Middlesex, Lords 1987

Best bowling performance: 4-33 Nottinghamshire v Somerset, Trent Bridge 1989

LAST SEASON: BATTING

	I.	N.O.	R.	H.S.	AV.
TEST					
1ST-CLASS	3	1	12	6*	6.00
INT					
RAL	2	0	5	5	2.50
NAT.W.					
B & H					

LAST SEASON: BOWLING

	O.	M.	R.	W.	AV.
TEST					
1ST-CLASS	48	15	128	7	18.28
INT					
RAL	9	1	54	0	–
NAT.W.					
B & H					

CAREER: BATTING

	I.	N.O.	R.	H.S.	AV.
TEST					
1ST-CLASS	7	2	68	34*	13.60
INT					
RAL	2	0	5	5	2.50
NAT.W.					
B & H					

CAREER: BOWLING

	O.	M.	R.	W.	AV.
TEST					
1ST-CLASS	48	15	128	7	18.28
INT					
RAL	9	1	54	0	–
NAT.W.					
B & H					

75. Who was the manager of the unofficial England tour party to South Africa, 1989–90?

FITTON, J. D. Lancashire

Full Name: John Dexter Fitton
Role: Left-hand bat, off-break bowler
Born: 24 August 1965, Rochdale
Height: 5′ 10″ **Weight:** 12st 7lbs
Nickname: Ted, Philbert, Fergus, Lord
County debut: 1987
1st-Class 5 w. in innings: 3
Place in batting averages: 201st av. 17.68
Place in bowling averages: 108th av. 42.14
Strike rate 1989: 80.65 (career 74.72)
1st-Class catches 1989: 6 (career 6)
Parents: Derek and Jean
Marital status: Engaged
Family links with cricket: Father dedicated cricketer for 20 years with Littleboro in Central Lancashire League and Robinsons in North Manchester League
Education: Redbrook and Auder Hill Upper School
Qualifications: 3 O-levels, Diploma in Business Studies
Jobs outside cricket: Worked for three years as an Export Administrator at Hanson Springs, the steel springs works. Worked in a body repair shop, a brewery and Jack Simmonds Indoor Cricket Centre
Cricketing superstitions or habits: 'Always clean my teeth prior to the start of a match.'
Off-season 1989–90: 'At home, playing football.'
Overseas tours: With Lancashire CCC to Jamaica; to Zimbabwe
Overseas teams played for: Sydenham CC, Christchurch, New Zealand 1987–88
Cricketers particularly learnt from: Dad, Paul Rocca (Rochdale coach), John Abrahams. 'Present staff at Old Trafford, especially Nick Speak for his perceptions and vision of the game.'
Cricketers particularly admired: David Gower, Clive Lloyd, Neil Fairbrother
Other sports played: Football, golf, tennis
Other sports followed: Manchester City FC, greyhound racing at Oldham
Injuries 1989: Inflamed left knee – off for one week
Relaxations: Listening to music, watching comedy films and shows
Extras: Youngest player to take 50 wickets and score 500 runs for Rochdale in the Central Lancashire League. Scored 1000 runs a season for three seasons

running in the same league. Captained Lancashire U-19s, North of England, and NAYC in 1984

Opinions on cricket: 'All 2nd XI games should be played on county grounds. Tea should be 30 minutes. Water-hogs should be banned. We should play 16 four-day games, on consistent pitches.'

Best batting performance: 44 Lancashire v Australians, Old Trafford 1989

Best bowling performance: 6-59 Lancashire v Yorkshire, Old Trafford 1988

LAST SEASON: BATTING

	I.	N.O.	R.	H.S.	AV.
TEST					
1ST-CLASS	25	6	336	44	17.68
INT					
RAL					
NAT.W.					
B & H					

CAREER: BATTING

	I.	N.O.	R.	H.S.	AV.
TEST					
1ST-CLASS	28	7	386	44	18.38
INT					
RAL	1	0	0	0	0.00
NAT.W.					
B & H					

LAST SEASON: BOWLING

	O.	M.	R.	W.	AV.
TEST					
1ST-CLASS	470.3	103	1475	35	42.14
INT					
RAL					
NAT.W.					
B & H					

CAREER: BOWLING

	O.	M.	R.	W.	AV.
TEST					
1ST-CLASS	535.3	119	1618	43	37.62
INT					
RAL	8	0	25	1	25.00
NAT.W.					
B & H					

FLEMING, M. V. Kent

Full Name: Matthew Valentine Fleming
Role: Right-hand bat, right-arm medium bowler, out fielder or slips
Born: 12 December 1964, Macclesfield
Height: 6′ **Weight:** 12st 4lbs
Nickname: Jazz
County debut: 1988
Place in batting averages: 157th av. 22.66
Place in bowling averages: 126th av. 74.16
Strike rate 1989: 52.50 (career 52.50)
1st-Class catches 1989: 1 (career 1)
Parents: Valentine and Elizabeth
Wife and date of marriage: Caroline, 23 September 1989

Family links with cricket: Great grandfather Mr Leslie played for England and apparently hit an all-run 7 at Lord's
Education: St Aubyns School, Rottingdean; Eton College
Qualifications: 8 O-levels, 3 A-levels
Jobs outside cricket: Stockbroker
Off-season 1989–90: 'Getting used to married life and following Arsenal.'
Overseas tours: Army Tour to Hong Kong 1987–88
Overseas teams played for: Avendale, Cape Town 1984
Cricketers particularly learnt from: Vic Cannings, Ron Bell, John Rice, Colin Page
Cricketers particularly admired: Mark Benson and everyone else who hits the ball as hard as they can as often as they can
Other sports played: Shooting, fishing, football, squash, fives, toboganning
Other sports followed: Synchronised swimming
Injuries 1989: Hole in right hamstring, off 3 weeks – June–July
Relaxations: 'Tai-chi', Arsenal FC
Extras: Ex army officer – Royal Green Jackets. First two scoring shots in Championship cricket were sixes
Opinions on cricket: 'Three-day cricket is a waste of time, more often than not played on unsatisfactory wickets and finishing in a contrived one-day game. Trust House Forte should build a hotel next to every first-class venue and sort out their room service!'
Best batting performance: 45 Kent v Warwickshire, Canterbury 1989
Best bowling performance: 2-34 Kent v Warwickshire, Canterbury 1989

LAST SEASON: BATTING

	I.	N.O.	R.	H.S.	AV.
TEST					
1ST-CLASS	12	3	204	45	22.66
INT					
RAL	11	2	176	37	19.55
NAT.W.	1	0	12	12	12.00
B & H	4	0	79	28	19.75

CAREER: BATTING

	I.	N.O.	R.	H.S.	AV.
TEST					
1ST-CLASS	12	3	204	45	22.66
INT					
RAL	12	3	179	37	19.88
NAT.W.	1	0	12	12	12.00
B & H	4	0	79	28	19.75

LAST SEASON: BOWLING

	O.	M.	R.	W.	AV.
TEST					
1ST-CLASS	140	30	445	16	74.16
INT					
RAL	65	2	322	11	29.27
NAT.W.	12	3	37	1	37.00
B & H	40	5	143	4	35.75

CAREER: BOWLING

	O.	M.	R.	W.	AV.
TEST					
1ST-CLASS	140	30	445	16	74.16
INT					
RAL	70	2	356	12	29.66
NAT.W.	12	3	37	1	37.00
B & H	40	5	143	4	35.75

FLETCHER, S. D. — Yorkshire

Full Name: Stuart David Fletcher
Role: Right-hand bat, right-arm
medium bowler
Born: 8 June 1964, Keighley
Height: 5′ 10″ **Weight:** 12st
Nickname: Fletch, Godber, Norman
Stanley, Dr Death, Ghostie
County debut: 1983
County cap: 1988
50 wickets in a season: 1
1st-Class 5 w. in innings: 3
Place in bowling averages: 118th
av. 51.46 (1988 27th av. 22.16)
Strike rate 1989: 92 (career 61.49)
1st-Class catches 1989: 1 (career 17)
Parents: Brough and Norma Hilda
Family links with cricket: Father
played league cricket
Education: Woodhouse Primary;
Reins Wood Secondary
Qualifications: O-level English and Woodwork; City and Guilds in coach-building
Jobs outside cricket: Coachbuilder at Reliance Commercial Vehicles Ltd.
Worked at Ben Shaw's Pop Merchants
Overseas tours: Holland 1983 with National Cricket Association U-19s
Cricketers particularly learnt from: Father, Phil Carrick, Steve Oldham
Cricketers particularly admired: Ian Botham, Arnie Sidebottom
Other sports played: Snooker, golf, football

LAST SEASON: BATTING

	I.	N.O.	R.	H.S.	AV.
TEST					
1ST-CLASS	11	4	33	13	4.71
INT					
RAL	2	1	2	2*	2.00
NAT.W.	1	1	16	16*	–
B & H					

CAREER: BATTING

	I.	N.O.	R.	H.S.	AV.
TEST					
1ST-CLASS	67	26	327	28*	7.97
INT					
RAL	12	8	25	8	6.25
NAT.W.	5	3	21	16*	10.50
B & H	3	1	2	1	1.00

LAST SEASON: BOWLING

	O.	M.	R.	W.	AV.
TEST					
1ST-CLASS	230	37	772	15	51.46
INT					
RAL	64.5	1	336	14	24.00
NAT.W.	21	1	116	0	–
B & H					

CAREER: BOWLING

	O.	M.	R.	W.	AV.
TEST					
1ST-CLASS	1896	330	6166	185	33.32
INT					
RAL	447.1	13	2293	85	26.97
NAT.W.	123.1	14	452	13	34.76
B & H	142.4	8	604	22	27.45

Other sports followed: Watches Leeds United FC
Relaxations: Watching TV, snooker and golf
Extras: Played in the Yorkshire U-19s who were the first Yorkshire side to win the Cambridge and Oxford Festival, 1983
Best batting performance: 28* Yorkshire v Kent, Tunbridge Wells 1984
Best bowling performance: 8-58 Yorkshire v Essex, Sheffield 1988

FOLLEY, I. Lancashire

Full Name: Ian Folley
Role: Right-hand bat, slow left-arm bowler, 'night-watchman and Mendo's bag packer'
Born: 9 January 1963
Height: 5' 9½" **Weight:** 12st
Nickname: Thatch, Axle, Felix, Foll
County debut: 1982
County cap: 1987
50 wickets in a season: 2
1st-Class 50s scored: 1
1st-Class 5 w. in innings: 10
1st-Class 10 w. in match: 1
Place in batting averages: —
(1988 208th av. 17.00)
Place in bowling averages: —
(1988 80th av. 29.84)
1st-Class catches 1989: 1 (career 58)
Parents: James and Constance
Wife and date of marriage: Julie, 27 September 1986
Education: Mansfield High School, Nelson; Colne College
Qualifications: 5 O-levels, Business Studies diploma
Jobs outside cricket: 'Too numerous to mention.'
Off-season 1989–90: 'Getting fit.'
Cricketing superstitions or habits: 'Pre-match bowling to Mendo. Do it as a pastime.'
Overseas tours: Barbados 1982 with Lancashire; Denmark 1981 with NCA; New York 1985 with Lancashire; Jamaica 1987 and 1988 with Lancashire; to Zimbabwe with Lancashire 1988–89
Overseas teams played for: Glenorchy, Tasmania 1985–86; Brighton, Tasmania 1987–88
Cricketers particularly learnt from: D. Bloodworth

Cricketers particularly admired: Clive Lloyd, Viv Richards, Graeme Hick, Malcolm Marshall
Other sports played: Golf, squash, football, '– and definitely no horses.'
Other sports followed: 'I detest watching.'
Injuries 1989: Ligament damage index finger, left hand – 'season 1989!'
Relaxations: Interested in rallying and saloon car racing, listening to music (detests disco music), eating out
Extras: Represented Lancashire Schools U-15s and U-19s as captain. Represented Lancashire Federation 1979–81. Played for England U-19 v India U-19 in three 'Tests' in 1981. Young England v West Indies (three 'Tests') and two One-Day 'Internationals'. Debut for Lancashire v Cambridge University at Fenners. In 1984 changed from left-arm medium pace to slow left-arm bowler
Opinions on cricket: 'Four-day cricket only lasts four days if better pitches are prepared. Over rate fines should be less severe. The "fixture computer" needs a complete overhaul!'
Best batting performance: 69 Lancashire v Yorkshire, Old Trafford 1985
Best bowling performance: 7-15 Lancashire v Warwickshire, Southport 1987

LAST SEASON: BATTING

	I.	N.O.	R.	H.S.	AV.
TEST					
1ST-CLASS	2	0	35	17	17.50
INT					
RAL					
NAT.W.					
B & H					

LAST SEASON: BOWLING

	O.	M.	R.	W.	AV.
TEST					
1ST-CLASS	28	3	128	2	64.00
INT					
RAL					
NAT.W.					
B & H					

CAREER: BATTING

	I.	N.O.	R.	H.S.	AV.
TEST					
1ST-CLASS	156	48	1413	69	13.08
INT					
RAL	10	6	56	19	14.00
NAT.W.	2	1	4	3*	4.00
B & H	5	5	21	11*	–

CAREER: BOWLING

	O.	M.	R.	W.	AV.
TEST					
1ST-CLASS	3137.4	863	8493	278	30.55
INT					
RAL	144	5	703	14	50.21
NAT.W.	39.3	4	114	7	16.28
B & H	84	17	215	14	15.36

76. Who was captain of the unofficial England team party to South Africa, 1989–90?

FORDHAM, A.   Northamptonshire

Full Name: Alan Fordham
Role: Right-hand bat, occasional
right-arm medium pace bowler
Born: 9 November 1964, Bedford
Height: 6' ½" **Weight:** 13st
Nickname: Forders, Fordi
County debut: 1986
1st-Class 50s scored: 7
1st-Class 100s scored: 2
Place in batting averages: 83rd
av. 32.35 (1988 114th av. 27.69)
1st-Class catches 1989: 8 (career
21)
Parents: Clifford and Ruth
Marital status: Single
Family links with cricket: Brother
John played school and college
cricket
Education: Bedford Modern School,
1973–83; Durham University, 1984–87
Qualifications: 9 O-levels, 3 A-levels, BSc Honours Degree in Chemistry,
NCA Coaching Award
Jobs outside cricket: Groundsman, coach, laboratory technician
Off-season 1989–90: Playing and coaching in Bangladesh
Overseas tours: Barbados, 1983, with Bedford Modern School; Jersey and
Guernsey, 1987, with Gentlemen of Leicestershire Cricket Club
Overseas teams played for: Richmond CC, Melbourne 1983–84; Camberwell
CC, Melbourne, Australia 1987–88; Curtin University CC, Perth, Australia
1988–89
Cricketers particularly learnt from: Andy Curtis, Brian Reynolds, Bob
Carter, 'and many at Northants.'
Cricketers particularly admired: Allan Lamb, Bob Willis, Mike Brearley
Other sports played: Squash, used to play table tennis, 'the odd round of golf'
Other sports followed: Rugby union
Relaxations: Rock music, squash

LAST SEASON: BATTING

	I.	N.O.	R.	H.S.	AV.
TEST					
1ST-CLASS	23	3	647	199	32.35
INT					
RAL	6	0	92	31	15.33
NAT.W.					
B & H	–	–	–	–	–

CAREER: BATTING

	I.	N.O.	R.	H.S.	AV.
TEST					
1ST-CLASS	55	9	1310	199	28.47
INT					
RAL	10	0	159	31	15.90
NAT.W.					
B & H	2	0	33	19	16.50

Extras: Also plays for Bedfordshire in Minor Counties Championship when possible. Played for Combined Universities in B & H 1987
Opinions on cricket: 'Groundsmen should be given a directive to produce the best pitches they can for every match. There is enough variety in the weather in this country to give bowlers their day and batsmen theirs.'
Best batting performance: 199 Northamptonshire v Yorkshire, Sheffield 1989

FOSTER, D. J. Somerset

Full Name: Daren Joseph Foster
Role: Right-hand bat, right-arm fast medium bowler
Born: 14 March 1966, London
Height: 5' 9" **Weight:** 9½st
Nickname: DJ
County debut: 1986
Place in batting averages: —
(1988 119th av. 37.28)
1st-Class catches 1989: 1 (career 4)
Parents: Vivian and Sadie
Children: Marcella and Daren
Education: Somerset School; Southgate Technical College
Qualifications: 2 O-levels, 1 CSE. Pre-vocational Studies pass. Commercial Studies pass and credit
Overseas teams played for: Geelong, Victoria
Cricketers particularly learnt from: Malcolm Marshall, Hallam Moseley

LAST SEASON: BATTING

	I.	N.O.	R.	H.S.	AV.
TEST					
1ST-CLASS	8	1	29	11*	4.14
INT					
RAL	3	2	8	8*	8.00
NAT.W.	1	0	0	0	0.00
B & H	1	0	0	0	0.00

CAREER: BATTING

	I.	N.O.	R.	H.S.	AV.
TEST					
1ST-CLASS	26	11	126	20	8.40
INT					
RAL	6	5	13	8*	13.00
NAT.W.	1	0	0	0	0.00
B & H	1	0	0	0	0.00

LAST SEASON: BOWLING

	O.	M.	R.	W.	AV.
TEST					
1ST-CLASS	179	21	647	8	80.87
INT					
RAL	60.5	5	310	7	44.28
NAT.W.	15	3	32	1	32.00
B & H	59	11	206	5	41.20

CAREER: BOWLING

	O.	M.	R.	W.	AV.
TEST					
1ST-CLASS	595.2	77	2210	49	45.10
INT					
RAL	109.5	7	523	12	43.58
NAT.W.	15	3	32	1	32.00
B & H	70	11	263	6	43.83

Cricketers particularly admired: Malcolm Marshall, Michael Holding, Gary Sobers, Viv Richards, Ian Botham, Clive Lloyd
Other sports played: Basketball, table tennis
Other sports followed: American football, athletics
Relaxations: Music
Extras: Appeared for Middlesex and Surrey 2nd XI's in 1985. Released by Somerset at end of 1989 season
Best batting performance: 20 Somerset v Hampshire, Southampton 1988
Best bowling performance: 4-46 Somerset v Worcestershire, Worcester 1988

FOSTER, N. A. Essex

Full Name: Neil Alan Foster
Role: Right-hand bat, right-arm fast-medium bowler, outfielder
Born: 6 May 1962, Colchester
Height: 6′ 4″ **Weight:** 13st
Nickname: Fozzy, Nibbler
County debut: 1980
County cap: 1983
Test debut: 1983
No. of Tests: 28
No. of One-Day Internationals: 48
50 wickets in a season: 7
1st-Class 50s scored: 6
1st-Class 5 w. in innings: 35
1st-Class 10 w. in match: 6
One-Day 50s: 4
Place in batting averages: 159th av. 22.36 (1988 262nd av. 10.05)
Place in bowling averages: 20th av. 21.60 (1988 32nd av. 22.77)
Strike rate 1989: 50.35 (career 47.22)
1st-Class catches 1989: 14 (career 78)
Parents: Jean and Alan
Wife and date of marriage: Romany, 21 September 1985
Family links with cricket: Father and brother both play local cricket
Education: Broomgrove Infant & Junior Schools; Philip Morant Comprehensive, Colchester
Qualifications: 8 O-levels, 1 A-level, NCA Coaching Award. Has Consumer Credit Licence for Financial Consultancy
Jobs outside cricket: Played semi-pro football for some years. Financial Consultant

Off-season 1989–90: Touring South Africa with unofficial English team
Overseas tours: NCA tour of Canada 1978; Young England XI tour of West Indies 1980; England tour of New Zealand and Pakistan 1983–84, India and Australia 1984–85, West Indies 1986, Australia 1986–87; World Cup, Pakistan, Australia and New Zealand 1987–88; picked for cancelled 1988–89 tour to India
Overseas teams played for: Glenorchy (Tasmania) 1981–82 on Whitbread Scholarship
Cricketers particularly learnt from: John Lever, Keith Fletcher and all Essex players
Cricketers particularly admired: Bud Hill, Graeme Labroy
Other sports played: Nearly any sport. Has had football trials with Colchester and Ipswich. Golf, tennis. 'Nothing horsey.'
Injuries 1989: Blistered bowling finger – one week off
Relaxations: 'My Boxer dog – Bertie; kennel name: Tropical Burlington Bertie. Playing golf. Mowing the lawn.'
Extras: Was summoned from school at short notice to play for Essex v Kent at Ilford to open bowling. First ball went for 4 wides, but he went on to dismiss Woolmer, Tavaré and Ealham for 51 runs in 15 overs. Played for Young England v Young India 1981
Opinions on cricket: 'It's about time our Championship consisted of playing each other only once, whether it be in three- or four-day matches.'
Best batting performance: 74* England v Queensland, Brisbane 1986–87
Best bowling performance: 8-107 England v Pakistan, Leeds 1987

LAST SEASON: BATTING

	I.	N.O.	R.	H.S.	AV.
TEST	6	2	68	39	17.00
1ST-CLASS	15	8	178	50*	25.42
INT	1	1	5	5*	–
RAL	3	1	55	44	27.50
NAT.W.	1	0	7	7	7.00
B & H	1	1	2	2*	–

LAST SEASON: BOWLING

	O.	M.	R.	W.	AV.
TEST	167	42	421	12	35.08
1ST-CLASS	546.2	146	1415	73	19.38
INT	32	5	130	6	21.66
RAL	78.4	8	277	16	17.31
NAT.W.	12	1	50	2	25.00
B & H	74.1	12	271	12	22.58

CAREER: BATTING

	I.	N.O.	R.	H.S.	AV.
TEST	43	7	410	39	11.38
1ST-CLASS	153	43	2251	74*	20.46
INT	25	12	150	24	11.53
RAL	25	8	298	44	17.52
NAT.W.	9	1	119	26	14.87
B & H	13	7	137	37*	22.83

CAREER: BOWLING

	O.	M.	R.	W.	AV.
TEST	1013.3	232	2797	88	31.78
1ST-CLASS	4210.5	978	12979	575	22.57
INT	437.5	28	1836	58	31.65
RAL	372.5	27	1585	72	22.01
NAT.W.	164.2	27	491	30	16.36
B & H	340.4	39	1242	60	20.70

FOWLER, G.   Lancashire

Full Name: Graeme Fowler
Role: Left-hand opening bat,
occasional wicket-keeper, 1st slip,
'slow right-hand declaration bowler'
Born: 20 April 1957, Accrington
Height: 5′ 9″ **Weight:** 'Near 11st'
Nickname: Fow, Fox, Foxy
County debut: 1979
County cap: 1981
Test debut: 1982
No. of Tests: 21
No. of One-Day Internationals: 26
1000 runs in a season: 8
1st-Class 50s scored: 70
1st-Class 100s scored: 28
1st-Class 200s scored: 2
One-Day 50s: 31
One-Day 100s: 5
Place in batting averages: 51st
av. 37.02 (1988 87th av. 30.64)
1st-Class catches 1989: 17 (career 121 + 5 stumpings)
Marital status: Divorced, December 1986
Education: Accrington Grammar School; Bede College, Durham University
Jobs outside cricket: Qualified teacher, swimming teacher, Advanced Cricket
Coach
Overseas tours: England to Australia and New Zealand 1982–83; New
Zealand and Pakistan 1983–84; India and Australia 1984–85; International
XI to West Indies 1982–83; Lancashire to West Indies 1987–88
Overseas teams played for: Scarborough, Perth, Western Australia; Tasmania 1981–82
Cricketers particularly learnt from: David Lloyd
Cricketers particularly admired: 'Grahame Clinton: you have to admire
anyone who gets hit on the head so regularly but still carries on.'
Relaxations: Music, gardening, playing drums
Extras: At 15 he was the youngest opener in the Lancashire League. Scored
two consecutive centuries v Warwickshire in July 1982 with aid of a runner.
Never played cricket until he was 12. Played for Accrington and Rawtenstall
in Lancashire League. In 1975 and 1976 played for ESCA, NAYC, and MCC
Schools and Young England. Published *Fox on the Run*, a cricketing diary
from 1984 to 1986, in 1988. First Englishman to score a double century in
India
Opinions on cricket: 'All players' opinions seem to be irrelevant to others –

we only play the same. The cricketing hierarchy is too bizarre for words.'
Best batting performance: 226 Lancashire v Kent, Maidstone 1984
Best bowling performance: 2-34 Lancashire v Warwickshire, Old Trafford 1986

LAST SEASON: BATTING

	I.	N.O.	R.	H.S.	AV.
TEST					
1ST-CLASS	37	0	1370	130	37.02
INT					
RAL	14	1	460	74	35.38
NAT.W.	3	0	30	22	10.00
B & H	4	0	189	78	47.25

LAST SEASON: BOWLING

	O.	M.	R.	W.	AV.
TEST					
1ST-CLASS	13	1	61	0	–
INT					
RAL					
NAT.W.					
B & H					

CAREER: BATTING

	I.	N.O.	R.	H.S.	AV.
TEST	37	0	1307	201	35.32
1ST-CLASS	339	17	11982	226	37.21
INT	26	2	744	81*	31.00
RAL	121	8	3296	112	29.16
NAT.W.	22	0	633	122	28.77
B & H	43	1	1126	97	26.80

CAREER: BOWLING

	O.	M.	R.	W.	AV.
TEST	3	1	11	0	–
1ST-CLASS	48.4	6	221	7	31.57
INT					
RAL	1	0	1	0	–
NAT.W.					
B & H					

FRASER, A. G. J. Essex

Full Name: Alastair Gregory James Fraser
Role: Right-hand bat, right-arm fast medium bowler
Born: 17 October 1967, Edgware
Height: 6′ 1½″ **Weight:** 13st 2lbs
Nickname: Junior
County debut: 1986 (Middlesex)
Parents: Irene and Don
Marital status: Single
Family links with cricket: Brother Angus plays for Middlesex and England. Dad played club cricket, Mum keen follower
Education: Gayton High School; John Lyon School, Harrow Weald 6th Form College
Qualifications: 4 O-levels; qualified coach
Jobs outside cricket: Michael Waite's chauffeur
Off-season 1989–90: Playing for Western Suburbs CC, Sydney

190

Overseas tours: England Young Cricketers to Sri Lanka 1987; U-19 NCA to South Bermuda 1985
Overseas teams played for: Plimmerton CC, Wellington, New Zealand 1986–87 and 1987–88; Greenpoint CC, South Africa 1988–89
Cricketers particularly learnt from: Don Bennett, Gordon Jenkins, Don Wilson
Cricketers particularly admired: Malcolm Marshall, Ian Botham
Other sports played: Football – Southern Amateur League
Other sports followed: Rugby, football, '– keen follower of Liverpool FC.'
Relaxations: Watching Liverpool FC when possible, a pint at the local
Extras: Joined Essex for 1990 season
Opinions on cricket: 'A great pity about South Africa and its cricket. Having been there, you know the facts. 16 four-day games seems ideal.'
Best batting performance: 19* Middlesex v Warwickshire, Uxbridge 1986
Best bowling performance: 3-46 Middlesex v New Zealand, Lord's 1986

LAST SEASON: BATTING

	I.	N.O.	R.	H.S.	AV.
TEST					
1ST-CLASS					
INT					
RAL	–	–	–	–	–
NAT.W.					
B & H					

LAST SEASON: BOWLING

	O.	M.	R.	W.	AV.
TEST					
1ST-CLASS					
INT					
RAL	13	0	57	3	19.00
NAT.W.					
B & H					

CAREER: BATTING

	I.	N.O.	R.	H.S.	AV.
TEST					
1ST-CLASS	5	3	51	19*	25.50
INT					
RAL	1	1	2	2*	–
NAT.W.					
B & H					

CAREER: BOWLING

	O.	M.	R.	W.	AV.
TEST					
1ST-CLASS	84.4	21	247	9	27.44
INT					
RAL	34	0	137	5	27.40
NAT.W.					
B & H					

77. Where will the World Cup be played in 1992?

FRASER, A. R. C.   Middlesex

Full Name: Angus Robert Charles
Fraser
Role: Right-hand bat, right-arm
fast-medium bowler; outfielder
Born: 8 August 1965, Billinge,
Lancashire
Height: 6′ 6″ **Weight:** 15st 3lbs
Nickname: Gus, Lard
County debut: 1984
County cap: 1988
Test debut: 1989
No. of Tests: 3
50 wickets in a season: 2
1st-Class 5 w. in innings: 10
1st-Class 10 w. in match: 2
Place in batting averages: 244th
av. 12.57 (1988 246th av. 12.38)
Place in bowling averages: 13th
av. 20.22 (1988 11th av. 19.37)
Strike rate 1989: 51.98 (career 58.62)
1st-Class catches 1989: 3 (career 8)
Parents: Don and Irene
Marital status: Single
Family links with cricket: Father played and is now keen follower of cricket;
brother Alastair on Essex staff. 'Mum is a nervous watcher!'
Education: Gayton High School, Harrow; Orange High School, Edgware
Qualifications: 7 O-levels, qualified cricket coach
Jobs outside cricket: Worked at Makro in North Acton 1984–85; Norwest
Holst Construction Ltd 1986–87. Reconciliation officer for National Bank,
New Zealand 1987–88
Off-season 1989–90: Touring India and West Indies with England, and
'buying a house with my brother.'
Cricketing superstitions or habits: 'Change in same place at most grounds year
after year.'
Overseas tours: Barbados with Thames Valley Gentlemen 1985; La Manga
with Middlesex 1985 and 1986; Lords Taverners to Hong Kong 1988; India
with England 1989; West Indies with England 1990
Overseas teams played for: Plimmerton CC, Wellington 1985–86, 1987–88;
Western Suburbs CC, Sydney 1988–89
Cricketers particularly learnt from: Don Bennett, Don Wilson, other coaches
at MCC Indoor School, Peter Edwards, Michael Waite 'for his mental
approach to the game.'

Cricketers particularly admired: Dennis Lillee, Richard Hadlee, Allan Border, Wayne Daniel

Other sports played: Rugby, golf, football, '– anything once! Would like to ski again but too risky.'

Other sports followed: Rugby, Liverpool FC 'when I have the chance.'

Injuries 1989: 'Pulled ligaments in right ankle and knee – out for ten days. Usual niggles and aches of a fastish bowler.'

Relaxations: 'A round of golf, having a pint of Benskins at the Seven Balls . . .' Watching Liverpool FC, driving, talking cricket

Extras: Took 3 wickets in 4 balls v Glamorgan in 1985. Hat-trick in B & H Cup v Sussex, 1988. Nixdorf Computers Middlesex Player of the Year, 1988. Has size 13 boots specially made! Still turns out for Stanmore in Middlesex League when Middlesex or England do not need him. Sponsored by Seven Balls pub at one pint per first-class wicket, and two pints per Test wicket

Opinions on cricket: 'I applaud the fact that cricketers went to South Africa this winter, as nobody should be able to tell a person where he can or cannot work, particularly in sport. Like most cricketers, I am fed up with politicians around the world who do not dissuade companies from trading with South Africa, but try to force cricketers not to go there. However, I am surprised and upset to see cricketers accept a five to seven year ban from Test cricket: surely it should mean more to represent your country! Although it hurts me as a bowler to say it, first-class pitches have got to improve.'

Best batting performance: 43* Middlesex v Glamorgan, Abergavenny 1989

Best bowling performance: 7-77 Middlesex v Kent, Canterbury 1989

LAST SEASON: BATTING

	I.	N.O.	R.	H.S.	AV.
TEST	5	0	47	29	9.40
1ST-CLASS	23	7	217	43*	13.56
INT					
RAL	7	3	65	25	16.25
NAT.W.	3	2	27	19	27.00
B & H	1	1	3	3*	–

CAREER: BATTING

	I.	N.O.	R.	H.S.	AV.
TEST	5	0	47	29	9.40
1ST-CLASS	81	23	684	43*	11.79
INT					
RAL	24	11	146	30*	11.23
NAT.W.	3	2	27	19	27.00
B & H	8	3	36	13*	7.20

LAST SEASON: BOWLING

	O.	M.	R.	W.	AV.
TEST	144.2	30	323	9	35.88
1ST-CLASS	652.5	173	1538	83	18.53
INT					
RAL	86.3	10	302	12	25.16
NAT.W.	59	11	190	8	23.75
B & H	38.1	5	101	6	16.83

CAREER: BOWLING

	O.	M.	R.	W.	AV.
TEST	144.2	30	323	9	35.88
1ST-CLASS	2152	568	5207	226	23.03
INT					
RAL	367.3	30	1416	51	27.76
NAT.W.	129.4	32	358	21	17.04
B & H	152.1	20	517	15	34.46

FRENCH, B. N.   Nottinghamshire

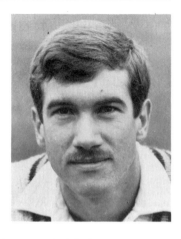

Full Name: Bruce Nicholas French
Role: Right-hand bat, wicket-keeper
Born: 13 August 1959, Warsop, Nottinghamshire
Height: 5′ 8″ **Weight:** 10st
Nickname: Frog
County debut: 1976
County cap: 1980
Test debut: 1986
No. of Tests: 16
No. of One-Day Internationals: 13
1st-Class 50s scored: 20
Parents: Maurice and Betty
Wife and date of marriage:
Ellen Rose, 9 March 1978
Children: Charles Daniel,
31 August 1978; Catherine Ellen,
28 December 1980
Family links with cricket: Brothers,
Neil, David, Charlie, Joe, played for Welbeck CC. Father, Treasurer
Welbeck CC. In 1988 Neil played for Lincolnshire
Education: Meden School, Warsop
Qualifications: O-level and CSE
Off-season 1989–90: Touring South Africa with unofficial English team
Jobs outside cricket: Warehouseman, window cleaner, bricklayer's labourer
Overseas tours: England to India and Sri Lanka 1984–85; West Indies
1985–86; Australia 1986–87; World Cup, Pakistan, Australia and New
Zealand 1987–88
Cricketing superstitions or habits: Right pad on before left when keeping
wicket
Cricketers particularly learnt from: Bob Taylor, Clive Rice
Other sports played: Rock climbing, fell walking and all aspects of mountaineering
Injuries 1989: Missed most of 1988 season following operations in May on
index finger of left hand. 'I broke this index finger two years ago and it gave
me a lot of trouble in pre-season work in the nets. The specialist strongly
advised immediate surgery to fuse the split bone on the top joint of the finger.'
Then, in 1989, broke same finger again, missing end of season.

(French has had a run of extraordinarily bad luck with injuries. In 1986 on
tour with England in the West Indies he was bitten by a dog whilst jogging.
During the Second Test at Lord's in 1986 he had to be carried off the field with
a cut head and concussion, after being struck by a short-pitched delivery from

194

Richard Hadlee. In Australia, 1986–87, he was hit in the chest by a ball and later contracted a chest infection. On the 1987–88 winter tour of Pakistan he needed stitches in a cut eye after being hit by a spectator's throw during a practice session. On the way to hospital a car struck his legs and then after treatment he banged his head on a light fitting. In 1988 he missed the Third Test against Pakistan because of chicken pox.)

Relaxations: Reading, pipe smoking and drinking Theakston's Ale

Extras: Youngest player to play for Nottinghamshire, aged 16 years 10 months. Equalled Nottinghamshire record for dismissals in match with 10 (7ct 3st), and dismissals in innings with 6 catches. New Nottinghamshire record for dismissals in a season with 87 (75ct 12st). Wicket-Keeper of the Year 1984

Best batting performance: 98 Nottinghamshire v Lancashire, Trent Bridge 1984

LAST SEASON: BATTING

	I.	N.O.	R.	H.S.	AV.
TEST					
1ST-CLASS	27	5	537	55*	24.40
INT					
RAL	7	0	63	21	9.00
NAT.W.	1	0	5	5	5.00
B & H	6	4	78	25*	39.00

CAREER: BATTING

	I.	N.O.	R.	H.S.	AV.
TEST	21	4	308	59	18.11
1ST-CLASS	340	66	5252	98	18.96
INT	8	3	34	9*	6.80
RAL	74	22	700	37	13.46
NAT.W.	19	5	296	49	21.14
B & H	35	10	297	48*	11.88

LAST SEASON: WICKET KEEPING

	C.	ST.		
TEST				
1ST-CLASS	26	9		
INT				
RAL	13	1		
NAT.W.	2	–		
B & H	6	–		

CAREER: WICKET KEEPING

	C.	ST.		
TEST	38	1		
1ST-CLASS	584	69		
INT	13	3		
RAL	92	13		
NAT.W.	30	4		
B & H	50	9		

78. When will the World Cup next be played in England?

79. True or false: Japan is now an affiliate member of the ICC?

FROST, M.   Glamorgan

Full Name: Mark Frost
Role: Bowler
Born: 21 October 1962, Barking
Height: 6′ 2″ **Weight:** 14st
Nickname: Harold, Frosty, 'H'
County debut: 1988 (Surrey)
1st-Class 5 w. in innings: 1
Place in bowling averages: 112nd
av. 45.26
Strike rate 1989: 74.13 (career 68.44)
1st-Class catches 1989: 1 (career 2)
Parents: George and Joyce
Marital status: Single
Family links with cricket: All three
brothers play
Education: Alexandra High, Tipton;
St Peters, Wolverhampton;
University of Durham
Qualifications: 10 O-levels, 4 A-
levels, Hons Degree in Geography
Off-season 1989–90: Sales representative for SCS Business Systems
Jobs outside cricket: Senior Buyer, Lucas Electrical
Overseas tours: India 1985, Christians in Sport; Sharjah 1988, Surrey pre-
season tour
Cricketers particularly learnt from: Jack Breakwell, Andy Webster, Mushtaq
Mohammed, Ron Headley, Geoff Arnold
Cricketers particularly admired: Michael Holding, Phil Oliver, Neil Stuart,
Chris Derham, Nick Peters, Graham Stockley

LAST SEASON: BATTING

	I.	N.O.	R.	H.S.	AV.
TEST					
1ST-CLASS	9	1	11	4	1.37
INT					
RAL					
NAT.W.					
B & H					

CAREER: BATTING

	I.	N.O.	R.	H.S.	AV.
TEST					
1ST-CLASS	13	1	22	7	1.83
INT					
RAL					
NAT.W.					
B & H					

LAST SEASON: BOWLING

	O.	M.	R.	W.	AV.
TEST					
1ST-CLASS	185.2	36	679	15	45.26
INT					
RAL					
NAT.W.					
B & H					

CAREER: BOWLING

	O.	M.	R.	W.	AV.
TEST					
1ST-CLASS	285.1	59	1005	25	40.20
INT					
RAL					
NAT.W.					
B & H					

Other sports played: Football, goalkeeper for Tipton Green Juniors
Other sports followed: Soccer, rugby, tennis, athletics
Injuries 1989: Bruised knee – out two weeks in April
Relaxations: Hill walking, climbing, Banks' beer, compact discs
Extras: Member of Christians in Sport. Played for Old Hill CC in Birmingham League 'when we won the National Knockout "Cockspur Cup" in 1987' and for Staffs before joining Surrey. Played for League Cricket Conference against Rest of the World XI 1987. Released by Surrey at end of 1989 season and joined Glamorgan
Opinions on cricket: 'Nationally sponsored youth schemes don't solve the problems of the "dreadful" state of cricket in comprehensive schools.'
Best batting performance: 7 Surrey v Sri Lankans, The Oval 1988
Best bowling performance: 5-40 Surrey v Leicestershire, Leicester 1989

GARD, T. Somerset

Full Name: Trevor Gard
Role: Right-hand bat, wicket-keeper
Born: 2 June 1957, West Lambrook, Somerset
Height: 5' 7" **Weight:** 9st 10lbs
Nickname: Gardy, Rook
County debut: 1976
County cap: 1983
Benefit: 1989 (joint with Dennis Breakwell)
1st-Class 50s scored: 3
Parents: David and Brenda
Wife and date of marriage: Amanda Kay, 29 September 1979
Family links with cricket: Father and brother play local club cricket
Education: Huish Episcopi Secondary Modern
Qualifications: O-level English, O-level Technical Drawing, ONC Aircraft Engineering
Jobs outside cricket: Engineer, farm worker, labourer
Off-season 1989–90: Working for Trak-Ex Plant Sales, heavy plant machinery
Cricketing superstitions or habits: Always wears a county cap when keeping wicket
Overseas tours: Antigua with Somerset 1981, Barbados with Somerset 1985
Cricketers particularly learnt from: D. J. S. Taylor

Cricketers particularly admired: D. J. S. Taylor, Ian Botham, Bob Taylor, Viv Richards
Other sports played: Golf, shooting, bowls
Other sports followed: All sports
Relaxations: Hunting and shooting, reading, gardening
Best batting performance: 51* Somerset v Indians, Taunton 1979

LAST SEASON: BATTING

	I.	N.O.	R.	H.S.	AV.
TEST					
1ST-CLASS	2	0	40	40	20.00
INT					
RAL					
NAT.W.					
B & H					

LAST SEASON: WICKET KEEPING

	C.	ST.			
TEST					
1ST-CLASS	2	–			
INT					
RAL					
NAT.W.					
B & H					

CAREER: BATTING

	I.	N.O.	R.	H.S.	AV.
TEST					
1ST-CLASS	126	25	1389	51*	13.75
INT					
RAL	15	5	88	19	8.80
NAT.W.	5	2	27	17	9.00
B & H	12	5	125	34	17.85

CAREER: WICKET KEEPING

	C.	ST.			
TEST					
1ST-CLASS	178	39			
INT					
RAL	28	7			
NAT.W.	10	4			
B & H	19	2			

GARNHAM, M. A. Essex

Full Name: Michael Anthony Garnham
Role: Right-hand bat, wicket-keeper
Born: 20 August 1960, Johannesburg, South Africa
Height: 5′ 10¾″ **Weight:** 12st
Nickname: Fred
County debut: 1979 (Gloucestershire), 1980 (Leicestershire), 1989 (Essex)
1st-Class 50s scored: 15
1st-Class 100s scored: 1
One-Day 50s: 2
One-Day 100s: 1
Place in batting averages: 97th av. 30.56
Parents: Pauline Anne and Robert Arthur (divorced)
Wife and date of marriage: Lorraine, 15 September 1984

Children: Laura Clare, 3 November 1988

Family links with cricket: Father was a club cricketer in Essex. He lost the sight of an eye keeping wicket

Education: Camberwell Grammar, Melbourne, Australia; Scotch College, Perth, Australia; Park School, Barnstaple, North Devon; North Devon College; University of East Anglia (for one year)

Qualifications: 10 O-levels, 2 A-levels

Overseas tours: England Schools tour of India 1977–78; Young England tour of Australia 1979

Overseas teams played for: Melbourne University & North Sydney 1979–80 (as prize for Young Wicketkeeper of the Year award, 1979); Glenelg, South Australia 1980–81

Cricketers particularly learnt from: Brian Roe (ex-Somerset), Alan Knott

Cricketers particularly admired: Bob Taylor

Off-season 1989–90: 'Working in Essex building an extension on our cottage.'

Other sports played: Squash

Other sports followed: Athletics

Relaxations: Carpentry – 'I make reproduction antique furniture', DIY, music, reading, walking

Extras: Moved to England in 1975 after living in Australia for ten years and in South Africa for four years. Played for Devon in 1976 and 1977 (possibly youngest ever) before joining Gloucestershire. Signed for Leicestershire in 1980 and was banned by the registration committee from competitive first-team cricket for a month for breach of registration regulations. Played for Gloucestershire 2nd XI since 1976, making John Player League debut in 1978 v Warwickshire at Birmingham and Championship debut in 1979. Retired at end of 1985. Returned for five one-day games in 1988 following injury to Phil Whitticase. Signed for Essex in 1989, having been playing Minor Counties Cricket for Cambridgeshire. 'Having run a business making keeping gloves, I wear gloves I have made myself.'

Best batting performance: 100 Leicester v Oxford University, Oxford 1985

LAST SEASON: BATTING

	I.	N.O.	R.	H.S.	AV.
TEST					
1ST-CLASS	32	9	703	91	30.56
INT					
RAL	7	1	41	14	6.83
NAT.W.	1	0	18	18	18.00
B & H	3	1	27	27*	13.50

CAREER: BATTING

	I.	N.O.	R.	H.S.	AV.
TEST					
1ST-CLASS	136	27	2786	100	25.55
INT					
RAL	71	14	934	79*	16.38
NAT.W.	13	3	296	110	29.60
B & H	27	9	402	55	22.33

LAST SEASON: WICKET KEEPING

	C.	ST.
TEST		
1ST-CLASS	48	3
INT		
RAL	11	2
NAT.W.	1	1
B & H	7	0

CAREER: WICKET KEEPING

	C.	ST.
TEST		
1ST-CLASS	210	26
INT		
RAL	88	12
NAT.W.	9	2
B & H	33	3

GATTING, M. W.   Middlesex

Full Name: Michael William
Gatting
Role: Right-hand bat, right-arm
medium bowler, slip fielder
Born: 6 June 1957, Kingsbury,
Middlesex
Height: 5' 10" **Weight:** 14st
Nickname: Gatt
County debut: 1975
County cap: 1977
Benefit: 1988 (£205,000)
Test debut: 1977–78
No. of Tests: 68
No. of One-Day Internationals: 85
1000 runs in a season: 11
1st-Class 50s scored: 117
1st-Class 100s scored: 50
1st-Class 200s scored: 4
1st-Class 5 w. in innings: 2
One-Day 50s: 54
One-Day 100s: 8

Place in batting averages: 9th av. 55.66 (1988 19th av. 47.38)
1st-Class catches 1989: 25 (career 320)
Parents: Bill and Vera
Wife and date of marriage: Elaine, September 1980
Children: Andrew, 21 January 1983; James, 11 July 1986
Family links with cricket: Father used to play club cricket. Brother, Steve,
played for Middlesex 2nd XI
Education: Wykeham Primary School; John Kelly Boys' High School
Qualifications: 4 O-levels
Jobs outside cricket: Part-time plumber
Off-season 1989–90: Captaining unofficial English tour of South Africa
Overseas tours: Whitbread scholarship to Australia with Balmain CC.
England to New Zealand and Pakistan 1977–78; toured West Indies with
England Young Cricketers 1979–80; Middlesex to Zimbabwe 1980–81;
with England in India 1981–82, 1984–85; West Indies 1980–81, 1985–86; New
Zealand and Pakistan 1983–84; Australia 1986–87; World Cup, Pakistan,
Australia and New Zealand 1987–88
Overseas teams played for: Club cricket in Sydney, Australia 1979–80
Cricketers particularly learnt from: Ken Barrington, Mike Brearley
Cricketers particularly admired: Sir Gary Sobers, Sir Leonard Hutton
Other sports played: Football, tennis, swimming, golf, squash

Relaxations: Reading science fiction thrillers, 'hooked on Tolkien' and a great fan of 'Dr Who'; music, including Beethoven, Holst, singing Elton John songs – 'the only music I positively dislike is punk rock and heavy metal.'

Extras: Awarded OBE in Queen's Birthday Honours for services to cricket. Played for England Young Cricketers 1974. Young Cricketer of the Year 1981. Captain of Middlesex since 1983. Captain of England from 1986 to 1988, when he was dropped during the Test series v West Indies. Author of *Limited Overs*, *Triumph in Australia* and autobiography *Leading From the Front*, 1988. Won a bronze medal for ballroom dancing at the Neasden Ritz, as did his brother, Steve. Played football for Edgware FC as a teenager. At school was goalkeeper, but also played centre-half for Brent Schools and then Middlesex Schools. Was wicket-keeper at school, though bowled as well. Played cricket for Middlesex U-15s for two seasons. Played for England Schools v Public Schools and hit a century. Gatting was recommended to West Ham in his 5th year at school, but nothing came of it. Had a junior trial for Queen's Park Rangers. By then Steve had played for Arsenal and Southampton. Mike was offered an apprenticeship by Watford FC. One of *Wisden*'s Five Cricketers of the Year, 1983. Led England on victorious tour of Australia, 1986–87, when England won the Ashes, the Perth Challenge Cup and World Series Cup. Led England to victory against West Indies in Texaco One-Day Trophy, 1988. Was relieved of England captaincy after leading them to draw in First Test against West Indies, 1988, being the first time the West Indies had not beaten England in 14 consecutive matches.

Opinions on cricket: 'There seems to be far too much cricket compressed into our domestic season and with all the travelling involved, it leaves most of us rather jaded by the time September comes.'

Best batting performance: 258 Middlesex v Somerset, Bath 1984

Best bowling performance: 5-34 Middlesex v Glamorgan, Swansea 1982

LAST SEASON: BATTING

	I.	N.O.	R.	H.S.	AV.
TEST	2	0	22	22	11.00
1ST-CLASS	31	6	1481	158*	59.24
INT	3	0	58	37	19.33
RAL	12	3	379	81*	42.11
NAT.W.	5	1	215	132*	53.75
B & H	4	1	198	123*	66.00

LAST SEASON: BOWLING

	O.	M.	R.	W.	AV.
TEST					
1ST-CLASS	26	12	62	0	–
INT					
RAL	12	1	47	5	9.40
NAT.W.					
B & H	2	0	10	0	–

CAREER: BATTING

	I.	N.O.	R.	H.S.	AV.
TEST	117	14	3870	207	37.57
1ST-CLASS	442	68	18693	258	49.98
INT	82	17	2049	115*	31.52
RAL	147	18	3962	109	30.71
NAT.W.	46	11	1539	118*	43.97
B & H	60	17	2133	143*	49.60

CAREER: BOWLING

	O.	M.	R.	W.	AV.
TEST	1 124	0 29	317	4	79.25
1ST-CLASS	19.7 1366.4	13 330	3771	141	26.74
INT	64.2	4	334	10	33.40
RAL	435.5	13	2164	77	28.10
NAT.W.	158.2	23	584	17	34.35
B & H	197.2	16	782	37	21.13

GIDLEY, M. I.   Leicestershire

Full Name: Martyn Ian Gidley
Role: Left-hand bat, right-arm
off-spin bowler
Born: 30 September 1968, Leicester
Height: 6' 1" **Weight:** 11½st
Nickname: Gidders
County debut: 1989
1st-Class catches 1989: 1 (career 1)
Parents: Barry and Susan
Marital status: Single
Family links with cricket: Father was
club cricketer with Loughborough
Town, now chairman
Education: Loughborough Grammar
School 1979–87
Qualifications: 7 O-levels, 3 A-levels
Jobs outside cricket: 'Bank clerk for
6 months when I left school,
factory storeman for Fisons
off-season 1988–89.'

Off-season 1989–90: Playing and coaching in Virginia, Orange Free State,
South Africa
Cricketing superstitions or habits: 'Always bat in long sleeves.'
Overseas teams played for: Harmony Cricket Club, Virginia, South Africa
September 1989–March 1990
Cricketers particularly learnt from: Ray Illingworth, Peter Willey
Cricketers particularly admired: 'David Gower, John Emburey, in particular
– but all first-class players.'

LAST SEASON: BATTING

	I.	N.O.	R.	H.S.	AV.
TEST					
1ST-CLASS	1	0	15	15	15.00
INT					
RAL					
NAT.W.					
B & H					

LAST SEASON: BOWLING

	O.	M.	R.	W.	AV.
TEST					
1ST-CLASS	8	0	23	1	23.00
INT					
RAL					
NAT.W.					
B & H					

CAREER: BATTING

	I.	N.O.	R.	H.S.	AV.
TEST					
1ST-CLASS	1	0	15	15	15.00
INT					
RAL					
NAT.W.					
B & H					

CAREER: BOWLING

	O.	M.	R.	W.	AV.
TEST					
1ST-CLASS	8	0	23	1	23.00
INT					
RAL					
NAT.W.					
B & H					

Other sports played: Most sports, in particular snooker and pool
Other sports followed: Keen football and rugby follower; 'often see Nottingham Forest'
Relaxations: Listen to most types of chart music
Extras: Leicestershire Young Cricketer 1987, England Schools U-19 1987
Opinions on cricket: 'The standard of 2nd XI pitches should be improved. It doesn't help future first-class and Test players to finish three-day games inside two days. Also I am pleased that counties can only have one overseas player from next season as unfortunately they have repeatedly dominated our first-class averages.'
Best batting performance: 15 Leicestershire v Nottinghamshire, Trent Bridge 1989
Best bowling performance: 1-23 Leicestershire v Nottinghamshire, Trent Bridge 1989

GLADWIN, C. Derbyshire

Full Name: Christopher Gladwin
Role: Left-hand bat, right-arm medium bowler
Born: 10 May 1962, East Ham
Height: 6′ 2″ **Weight:** 14st
Nickname: Gladares, Guvnor
County debut: 1982 (Essex), 1989 (Derbyshire)
County cap: 1984 (Essex)
1000 runs in a season: 1
1st-Class 50s scored: 18
1st-Class 100s scored: 1
One-Day 50s: 3
Parents: Ron and Edna
Wife and date of marriage: Julia, 20 September 1986
Family links with cricket: Father and brother played club cricket
Education: Langdon Comprehensive, Newham
Qualifications: 5 CSEs
Overseas tours: Toured West Indies with Young England team 1980
Cricketers particularly learnt from: Graham Gooch, Keith Fletcher, Allan Border
Other sports played: Football, snooker, athletics, table tennis, basketball, golf

Other sports followed: Snooker, football
Best batting performance: 162 Essex v Cambridge University, Cambridge 1984

LAST SEASON: BATTING

	I.	N.O.	R.	H.S.	AV.
TEST					
1ST-CLASS	8	0	127	59	15.87
INT					
RAL	2	0	23	20	11.50
NAT.W.	1	0	8	8	8.00
B & H	–	–	–	–	–

CAREER: BATTING

	I.	N.O.	R.	H.S.	AV.
TEST					
1ST-CLASS	122	7	3080	162	26.78
INT					
RAL	32	1	603	75	19.45
NAT.W.	5	0	34	15	6.80
B & H	11	0	205	41	18.63

GOLDSMITH, S. C. Derbyshire

Full Name: Steven Clive Goldsmith
Role: Right-hand bat, right-arm medium or off-break bowler, cover fielder
Born: 19 December 1964, Ashford, Kent
Height: 5′ 10½″ **Weight:** 12st 7lbs
Nickname: Goldy
County debut: 1987 (Kent), 1988 (Derbyshire)
1000 runs in a season: 1
1st-Class 50s scored: 8
One-Day 50s: 1
Place in batting averages: 193rd av. 18.80 (1988 89th av. 39.60)
1st-Class catches 1989: 5 (career 22)
Parents: Tony and Daphne
Marital status: Engaged
Family links with cricket: Father played for Folkestone, captaining them for a few years
Education: Simon Langton Grammar School, Canterbury
Qualifications: 8 O-levels, NCA Coaching Award
Jobs outside cricket: Bar Steward, waiter, undertaker's assistant
Cricketing superstitions or habits: 'I always buckle my pads on the same way and smoke a fair bit as well as biting my nails down to the elbows.'
Overseas tours: ESCA U-19 to Zimbabwe 1982–83; UK Upsetters to Trinidad and Tobago 1985
Overseas teams played for: Essendon, Melbourne 1984

Cricketers particularly learnt from: Colin Page, Chris Tavaré, Simon Hinks
Cricketers particularly admired: Chris Tavaré, David Gower, Eldine Baptiste
Other sports played: Hockey, golf, snooker – 'and anything else where a ball moves'
Other sports followed: All sports
Relaxations: Golf, serious drinking, comedy on TV, Van Morrison's music, Tony Hancock, Richard Pryor
Injuries 1989: Operation on cyst on knee
Extras: Spent four years on Kent staff. Only wicket in first-class cricket was David Gower's. Released at end of the 1987 season. Joined Derbyshire for 1988
Cricketing opinions: 'With the introduction of uncovered wickets, the bowlers' run-ups should also be uncovered. Four-day cricket would be a good idea but should be confined to say half the matches at the end of the season. All professional cricketers should be made to take an NCA Coaching Award.'
Best batting performance: 89 Derbyshire v Kent, Chesterfield 1988
Best bowling performance: 1-37 Kent v Leicestershire, Canterbury 1987

LAST SEASON: BATTING

	I.	N.O.	R.	H.S.	AV.
TEST					
1ST-CLASS	21	1	376	88	18.80
INT					
RAL	4	1	115	49	38.33
NAT.W.					
B & H	3	1	46	32	23.00

LAST SEASON: BOWLING

	O.	M.	R.	W.	AV.
TEST					
1ST-CLASS					
INT					
RAL					
NAT.W.					
B & H					

CAREER: BATTING

	I.	N.O.	R.	H.S.	AV.
TEST					
1ST-CLASS	64	5	1496	89	25.35
INT					
RAL	21	3	463	61	25.72
NAT.W.					
B & H	8	2	110	32	18.33

CAREER: BOWLING

	O.	M.	R.	W.	AV.
TEST					
1ST-CLASS	49	8	162	1	162.00
INT					
RAL	2	0	23	0	–
NAT.W.					
B & H					

80. What was unusual about Jack Russell's second innings for England v Australia at Old Trafford, 1989?

GOOCH, G. A.   Essex

Full Name: Graham Alan Gooch
Role: Right-hand bat, right-arm
medium bowler
Born: 23 July 1953, Leytonstone
Height: 6′ **Weight:** 13st
Nickname: Zap, Goochie
County debut: 1973
County cap: 1975
Benefit: 1985 (£153,906)
Test debut: 1975
No. of Tests: 73
No. of One-Day Internationals: 70
1000 runs in a season: 13
1st-Class 50s scored: 147
1st-Class 100s scored: 64
1st-Class 200s scored: 5
1st-Class 5 w. in innings: 3
One-Day 50s: 89
One-Day 100s: 27
Place in batting averages: 37th av. 41.86 (1988 5th av. 64.55)
Place in bowling averages: — (1988 122nd av. 40.10)
1st-Class catches 1989: 25 (career 405)
Parents: Alfred and Rose
Wife and date of marriage: Brenda, 23 October 1976
Children: Hannah, Megan, Sally
Family links with cricket: Father played local cricket for East Ham Corinthians. Second cousin, Graham Saville, played for Essex CCC and is now NCA coach for Eastern England
Education: Norlington Junior High School, Leytonstone
Qualifications: Four-year apprenticeship in toolmaking
Jobs outside cricket: Toolmaker
Off-season 1989–90: Captaining England in India and West Indies
Cricketing superstitions or habits: Calls for a fresh right-handed glove when he reaches 50
Overseas tours: West Indies with England Young Cricketers 1972; England to Australia 1978–79 and 1979–80; West Indies 1981 and 1986; India 1979–80, 1981–82; SAB XI to South Africa 1981–82; Sri Lanka 1981–82; World Cup, Pakistan and New Zealand 1987–88; India and West Indies 1989–90
Overseas teams played for: Perth CC, Western Australia; Western Province, South Africa 1982–84
Cricketers particularly admired: Bob Taylor, a model sportsman; Mike Procter for his enthusiasm; Barry Richards for his ability

Other sports played: Squash, soccer, golf. Trains in off-season with West Ham United FC

Relaxations: 'Relaxing at home.'

Extras: One of *Wisden*'s Five Cricketers of the Year, 1979. Published *Batting* in 1980. Wrote a diary of 1981 cricket year. Autobiography *Out of the Wilderness* published by Collins in 1985. Hit a century before lunch v Leicester, 28 June 1981. Kept wicket for England v India in 2nd innings at Madras, 1982. Captained English rebel team in South Africa, 1982 and was banned from Test cricket for three years. Hit a hole in one at Tollygunge Golf Club during England's tour in India, 1981–82. Bowled both right and left handed in a Test match (v India at Calcutta, imitating Dilip Doshi). Shared in second wicket record partnership for county, 321 with K. S. McEwan v Northamptonshire, at Ilford in 1978. Holds record (jointly) for Essex for catches in match (6) and innings (5) v Gloucestershire, 1982. Appointed Essex captain 1986. Resigned captaincy at end of 1987 season. Reappointed captain of Essex for 1989 following retirement of Keith Fletcher. Captain of England for last two Tests against West Indies and Sri Lanka in 1988. Picked to captain England on the cancelled tour of India and in West Indies 1989–90. Keeps four pairs of batting gloves in his cricket bag, marked 'G.A.G. . . . 1 to 4'. When he first joined Essex, he was a batsman who kept wicket: he actually went on a Young England tour to the West Indies as number two wicket-keeper to Andy Stovold of Gloucestershire. Last season had highest ever Sunday League average, of 95.66

Opinions on cricket: Regarding four-day cricket: 'I have changed my views on this. We have had some excellent four-day games, and purely in cricketing terms I believe it is worth trying. The problem at the moment is that Test players do not get enough first-class innings between Tests. Four-day cricket would help if it was scheduled so that Test cricketers were available for almost all the games, which I am assured is possible. It must also be played on good pitches.'

LAST SEASON: BATTING

	I.	N.O.	R.	H.S.	AV.
TEST	9	0	183	68	20.33
1ST-CLASS	22	1	1073	158	57.09
INT	3	0	198	136	66.00
RAL	10	4	574	111*	95.66
NAT.W.	1	0	94	94	94.00
B & H	7	2	264	100*	52.80

LAST SEASON: BOWLING

	O.	M.	R.	W.	AV.
TEST	31	9	72	1	72.00
1ST-CLASS	37	6	173	0	–
INT					
RAL	69	4	267	10	26.70
NAT.W.	11	1	42	1	42.00
B & H	66	7	235	7	33.57

CAREER: BATTING

	I.	N.O.	R.	H.S.	AV.
TEST	132	4	4724	196	36.90
1ST-CLASS	559	49	23277	275	45.64
INT	69	2	2813	142	42.62
RAL	196	19	5938	176	33.54
NAT.W.	36	1	1573	133	44.94
B & H	82	9	3669	198*	50.26

CAREER: BOWLING

	O.	M.	R.	W.	AV.
TEST	6 261.3	1 76	622	14	44.42
1ST-CLASS	1 2363.1	0 589	6491	197	32.94
INT	207.1	13	966	23	42.00
RAL	815.2	41	3667	128	28.64
NAT.W.	247.1	34	741	25	29.64
B & H	509.5	55	1722	58	29.68

Best batting performance: 275 Essex v Kent, Chelmsford 1988
Best bowling performance: 7-14 Essex v Worcestershire, Ilford 1982

GOUGH, D.   Yorkshire

Full Name: Darren Gough
Role: Right-hand bat, right-arm
fast-medium bowler, all-rounder
Born: 18 September 1970, Barnsley
Height: 5′ 11½″ **Weight:** 12st 9lbs
Nickname: Roland, Gazza
County debut: 1989
Parents: Trevor and Christine
Marital status: Single
Family links with cricket: Younger
brother Adrian plays in local league
for Monk Bretton CC
Education: St Helens Primary;
Priory Comprehensive School
Qualifications: 7 CSEs,
B.Tec Leisure Certificate,
NCA Coaching Certificate
Off-season 1989–90: 'Getting fit,
coaching youngsters at the Yorkshire
Cricket School before going to Australia with Young England Cricketers.'
Overseas tours: Australia with Young England Cricketers 1989–90
Cricketers particularly learnt from: Doug Padgett (coach), Steve Oldham
(assistant coach), Ralph Middlebrook (Yorkshire Cricket School)
Cricketers particularly admired: Ian Botham, Richard Hadlee

LAST SEASON: BATTING

	I.	N.O.	R.	H.S.	AV.
TEST					
1ST-CLASS	2	1	11	9	11.00
INT					
RAL					
NAT.W.					
B & H					

LAST SEASON: BOWLING

	O.	M.	R.	W.	AV.
TEST					
1ST-CLASS	65	13	173	6	28.83
INT					
RAL					
NAT.W.					
B & H					

CAREER: BATTING

	I.	N.O.	R.	H.S.	AV.
TEST					
1ST-CLASS	2	1	11	9	11.00
INT					
RAL					
NAT.W.					
B & H					

CAREER: BOWLING

	O.	M.	R.	W.	AV.
TEST					
1ST-CLASS	65	13	173	6	28.83
INT					
RAL					
NAT.W.					
B & H					

Other sports played: Football, swimming, golf
Other sports followed: Football
Injuries 1989: Stress fracture of back – off for three months
Relaxations: 'Like watching television and videos, also listening to music (soul and house music).'
Extras: On first-class debut at Lord's against Middlesex got wicket of Paul Downton with 8th delivery
Best batting performance: 9 Yorkshire v Warwickshire, Leeds 1989
Best bowling performance: 3-44 Yorkshire v Middlesex, Lord's 1989

GOULD, I. J. Sussex

Full Name: Ian James Gould
Role: Left-hand bat, wicket-keeper
Born: 19 August 1957, Taplow, Bucks
Height: 5′ 8″ **Weight:** 12st
Nickname: Gunner
County debut: 1975 (Middlesex), 1981 (Sussex)
County cap: 1977 (Middlesex), 1981 (Sussex)
Benefit: 1990
No. of One-Day Internationals: 18
1st-Class 50s scored: 45
1st-Class 100s scored: 4
One-Day 50s: 17
Place in batting averages: 100th av. 30.00 (1988 76th av. 32.40)
1st-Class catches 1989: 18 (career 528 + 67 stumpings)

Parents: Doreen and George
Wife: Joanne, 25 September 1986
Children: Gemma Louise, 30 June 1984, Michael
Family links with cricket: 'Brothers tried!'
Education: Westgate School
Jobs outside cricket: Barman
Off-season 1989–90: 'Working on my benefit.'
Overseas tours: West Indies with England Young Cricketers 1976; Derrick Robins' XI to Australia, New Zealand and Canada 1978–79; Middlesex to Zimbabwe 1980–81; International XI to Pakistan 1980–81; with England in Australia and New Zealand 1982–83
Overseas teams played for: Auckland 1979–80

Cricketers particularly learnt from: David English
Cricketers particularly admired: Richard Hadlee, David Smith
Other sports played: Amateur footballer for Slough Town FC at full-back; golf, swimming
Other sports followed: Soccer
Relaxations: 'Spending time with the family. Drinking in pubs with the best lager.'
Extras: Made debut for Middlesex in 1975, gaining cap in 1977. Was offered contract for 1981 by Middlesex but chose to join Sussex. Vice-captain in 1985. Took over captaincy during 1986 and officially appointed for 1987. Resigned captaincy at end of 1987 season
Opinions on cricket: 'Wickets need to improve, to help batsmen to play straight and bowlers to bowl straight.'
Best batting performance: 128 Middlesex v Worcestershire, Worcester 1978
Best bowling performance: 3-10 Sussex v Surrey, Oval 1989

LAST SEASON: BATTING

	I.	N.O.	R.	H.S.	AV.
TEST					
1ST-CLASS	33	4	870	125	30.00
INT					
RAL	14	4	385	84*	38.50
NAT.W.	2	0	19	14	9.50
B & H	4	0	19	16	4.75

LAST SEASON: BOWLING

	O.	M.	R.	W.	AV.
TEST					
1ST-CLASS	9	1	41	3	13.66
INT					
RAL					
NAT.W.					
B & H					

CAREER: BATTING

	I.	N.O.	R.	H.S.	AV.
TEST					
1ST-CLASS	387	61	8521	128	26.13
INT	14	2	155	42	12.91
RAL	158	27	2626	84*	20.04
NAT.W.	23	2	417	88	19.85
B & H	50	7	720	72	16.74

CAREER: BOWLING

	O.	M.	R.	W.	AV.
TEST					
1ST-CLASS	74	5	346	7	49.42
INT					
RAL					
NAT.W.					
B & H	0.2	0	0	1	0.00

LAST SEASON: WICKET KEEPING

	C.	ST.			
TEST					
1ST-CLASS	3	–			
INT					
RAL					
NAT.W.					
B & H					

CAREER: WICKET KEEPING

	C.	ST.			
TEST					
1ST-CLASS	528	67			
INT	15	3			
RAL	127	22			
NAT.W.	25	7			
B & H	52	5			

GOVAN, J. W.　　Northamptonshire

Full Name: James Walter Govan
Role: Off-spin bowler, right-hand bat
Born: 6 May 1966, Dunfermline
Height: 5′ 6″ **Weight:** 12st
Nickname: Haggis, Elmur
County debut: 1989
1st-Class 5 w. in innings: 1
1st-Class catches 1989: 2 (career 3)
Parents: James and Robertha
Marital status: Single
Family links with cricket: Dad played club cricket in both Scotland and England
Education: Dunfermline High School, Napier College
Qualifications: 8 O-grades, 4 M-grades, B.Eng Honours Degree
Jobs outside cricket: Vacational jobs and industrial training
Off-season 1989–90: Coaching and playing for Poverty Bay CC in New Zealand
Cricketing superstitions or habits: Left pad on first
Cricketers particularly learnt from: Omar Henry, Richard Swan
Cricketers particularly admired: Omar Henry, Richard Swan, Allan Lamb, Wayne Larkins, Ian Botham
Other sports played: Rugby
Other sports followed: Football, supports Heart of Midlothian

LAST SEASON: BATTING

	I.	N.O.	R.	H.S.	AV.
TEST					
1ST-CLASS	5	0	30	17	6.00
INT					
RAL	1	1	9	9*	–
NAT.W.					
B & H	2	1	54	38*	54.00

LAST SEASON: BOWLING

	O.	M.	R.	W.	AV.
TEST					
1ST-CLASS	97.5	22	269	6	44.83
INT					
RAL	8	2	23	3	7.66
NAT.W.					
B & H	17	3	62	0	–

CAREER: BATTING

	I.	N.O.	R.	H.S.	AV.
TEST					
1ST-CLASS	7	1	39	17	6.50
INT					
RAL	1	1	9	9*	–
NAT.W.	1	0	0	0	0.00
B & H	2	1	54	38*	54.00

CAREER: BOWLING

	O.	M.	R.	W.	AV.
TEST					
1ST-CLASS	195.5	61	472	20	23.60
INT					
RAL	8	2	23	3	7.66
NAT.W.	12	3	29	2	14.50
B & H	17	3	62	0	–

Relaxations: Listening and playing music, reading
Extras: Played for Scottish Colleges and Scottish Students at rugby, Scottish All-rounder of the Year 1988
Best batting performance: 17 Scotland v Ireland, Dublin 1989
Best bowling performance: 5-54 Scotland v Ireland, Dumfries 1988

GOWER, D. I. Hampshire

Full Name: David Ivon Gower
Role: Left-hand bat, off-break bowler
Born: 1 April 1957, Tunbridge Wells
Height: 6' **Weight:** 11st 11lbs
Nickname: Lubo
County debut: 1975 (Leicestershire)
County cap: 1977 (Leicestershire)
Benefit: 1987 (£121,546)
Test debut: 1978
No. of Tests: 106
No. of One-Day Internationals: 105
1000 runs in a season: 9
1st-Class 50s scored: 109
1st-Class 100s scored: 41
1st-Class 200s scored: 2
One-Day 50s: 45
One-Day 100s: 18

Place in batting averages: 47th av. 48.00 (1988 41st av. 38.76)
1st-Class catches 1989: 13 (career 222 + 1 stumping)
Parents: Richard Hallam and Sylvia Mary
Marital status: Single
Family links with cricket: Father was club cricketer
Education: Marlborough House School; King's School, Canterbury; University College, London (did not complete law course)
Qualifications: 8 O-levels, 3 A-levels
Jobs outside cricket: Worked at Bostik Ltd
Cricketing superstitions or habits: 'Any that work: I tried a lot last season!'
Overseas tours: Toured South Africa with English Schools XI 1974–75 and West Indies with England Young Cricketers 1976; Derrick Robins' XI to Canada 1976 and to Far East 1977; with England to Australia 1978–79 and 1979–80, India 1979–80, 1981–82, West Indies 1980–81, Sri Lanka 1981–82, 1984–85; Australia and New Zealand 1982–83, New Zealand 1983–84,

Pakistan 1983–84, India and Australia 1984–85, West Indies 1986, Australia 1986–87
Overseas teams played for: Claremont-Cottesloe, Perth, Australia 1977–78
Cricketers particularly learnt from: 'Ray Illingworth and Jack Birkenshaw, amongst many others whose advice has come my way.'
Cricketers particularly admired: Graeme Pollock and many others
Other sports played: Golf, squash, water and snow skiing. Rode in a British bobsled at Cervinia (Italy) in 1985, diving
Other sports followed: Rugby, bob-sledding
Injuries 1989: Persistent trouble with right shoulder
Relaxations: 'Photography – particularly wild life, good wine, music.'
Extras: Played for King's Canterbury 1st XI for three years. One of *Wisden*'s Five Cricketers of the Year, 1978. Has written *Anyone for Cricket* jointly with Bob Taylor about the 1978–79 Australian tour. Also *With Time to Spare*, an autobiography published in 1980, and *Heroes and Contemporaries* (Collins) 1983, *A Right Ambition* (Collins) 1986. Writes regular column for *Wisden Cricket Monthly*. England and Leicestershire captain 1984–86. Declared himself not available for England tour 1987–88. Reappointed Leicestershire captain for 1988. Reappointed captain of England v Australia in 1989. Sacked as captain and player after losing the Ashes to Alan Border's team. Resigned the Leicestershire captaincy at the end of the season. Surprisingly not selected for England's winter tour of either India or West Indies. Joined Hampshire for 1990
Best batting performance: 215 England v Australia, Edgbaston 1985
Best bowling performance: 3-47 Leicestershire v Essex, Leicester 1977

LAST SEASON: BATTING

	I.	N.O.	R.	H.S.	AV.
TEST	11	0	383	106	34.81
1ST-CLASS	19	1	719	228	39.94
INT	3	0	125	61	41.66
RAL	8	1	225	82	32.14
NAT.W.	2	1	124	101*	124.00
B & H	4	1	68	36	22.66

LAST SEASON: BOWLING

	O.	M.	R.	W.	AV.
TEST					
1ST-CLASS					
INT					
RAL					
NAT.W.					
B & H					

CAREER: BATTING

	I.	N.O.	R.	H.S.	AV.
TEST	183	13	7386	215	43.44
1ST-CLASS	393	38	13608	187	53.36
INT	102	8	3030	158	32.23
RAL	138	21	4249	135*	36.31
NAT.W.	33	5	1516	156	54.14
B & H	52	6	1220	114*	26.52

CAREER: BOWLING

	O.	M.	R.	W.	AV.
TEST	6	1	20	1	20.00
1ST-CLASS	37.1	4	203	3	67.66
INT	0.5	0	14	0	–
RAL					
NAT.W.	2.3	0	16	0	–
B & H					

GRAVENEY, D. A.　　　Gloucestershire

Full Name: David Anthony Graveney
Role: Right-hand bat, slow left-arm
bowler
Born: 2 January 1953, Bristol
Height: 6′ 4″ **Weight:** 14st
Nickname: Gravity, Grav
County debut: 1972
County cap: 1976
Benefit: 1986
50 wickets in a season: 6
1st-Class 50s scored: 15
1st-Class 100s scored: 2
1st-Class 5 w. in innings: 32
1st-Class 10 w. in match: 5
One-Day 50s: 1
Place in batting averages: 251st
av. 11.71 (1988 227th av. 15.40)
Place in bowling averages: 56th
av. 28.07 (1988 51st av. 25.52)
Strike rate 1989: 75.12 (career 67.81)
1st-Class catches 1989: 9 (career 194)
Parents: Ken and Jeanne (deceased)
Wife and date of marriage: Julie, 23 September 1978
Children: Adam, 13 October 1982
Family links with cricket: Son of J. K. Graveney, captain of Gloucestershire,
who took 10 wickets for 66 runs v Derbyshire at Chesterfield in 1949, and
nephew of Tom Graveney of Gloucestershire, Worcestershire and England.
Brother, John, selected for English Public Schools v English Schools at
Lord's
Education: Millfield School, Somerset
Jobs outside cricket: Company director. Accountant
Off-season 1989–90: Touring South Africa with unofficial English team, as
manager
Overseas tours: Gloucestershire CCC to Sri Lanka 1986–87; unofficial Eng-
land tour to South Africa 1989–90
Other sports played: Golf, soccer, squash
Relaxations: 'Playing sport, TV and cinema. Relaxing at a good pub.'
Extras: Treasurer of the County Cricketers' Association. Captain of
Gloucestershire, 1981 to 1988. Dropped as captain at end of 1988 season.
Third member of the Graveney family to be dismissed by Gloucester CCC –
Uncle Tom as captain in 1960 and father Ken as chairman in 1982. Player-
manager of unofficial tour to South Africa 1989–90

Opinions on cricket: 'I must admit I have enjoyed the role of captain, not least the friendships formed with other leaders. Like left-arm spinners, we have our own little "union". Some may think that strange as we spend a fair amount of time trying to do each other out of a job!'

Best batting performance: 119 Gloucestershire v Oxford University, Oxford 1980

Best bowling performance: 8-85 Gloucestershire v Nottinghamshire, Cheltenham 1974

LAST SEASON: BATTING

	I.	N.O.	R.	H.S.	AV.
TEST					
1ST-CLASS	22	8	164	27*	11.71
INT					
RAL	1	0	0	0	0.00
NAT.W.					
B & H	1	1	11	11*	–

CAREER: BATTING

	I.	N.O.	R.	H.S.	AV.
TEST					
1ST-CLASS	473	137	6000	119	17.85
INT					
RAL	130	48	1269	56*	15.47
NAT.W.	25	9	292	44	18.25
B & H	41	14	410	49*	15.18

LAST SEASON: BOWLING

	O.	M.	R.	W.	AV.
TEST					
1ST-CLASS	490.2	164	1095	39	28.07
INT					
RAL	8	0	34	1	34.00
NAT.W.					
B & H	7	1	32	0	–

CAREER: BOWLING

	O.	M.	R.	W.	AV.
TEST					
1ST-CLASS	8907.5	2681	22566	788	28.63
INT					
RAL	931.1	52	4351	129	33.72
NAT.W.	332.5	51	1086	46	23.60
B & H	436.2	42	1577	50	31.54

GREEN, A. M.   Sussex

Full Name: Allan Michael Green
Role: Right-hand bat, off-break bowler, short-leg fielder
Born: 28 May 1960, Pulborough
Height: 5′ 10″ **Weight:** 11st
Nickname: Gilbert, Greenie, Wedgey
County debut: 1980
County cap: 1985
1000 runs in a season: 3
1st-Class 50s scored: 35
1st-Class 100s scored: 9
1st-Class 5 w. in innings: 1
One-Day 50s: 14
One-Day 100s: 1
Place in batting averages: —
(1988 150th av. 23.66)

1st-Class catches 1989: 3 (career 85)
Parents: Sheila Cynthia and Basil Michael
Wife and date of marriage: Kerry Louise, 19 September 1986
Family links with cricket: Father played for Findon CC 'as a fielder'
Education: Knoll School, Hove; Brighton Sixth Form College
Qualifications: 5 O-levels
Jobs outside cricket: Sports shop assistant, labourer
Cricketing superstitions or habits: 'Strap left pad on first and like to bat in same clothes, smell permitting.'
Overseas tours: *The Cricketer* tour to Dubai 1983
Overseas teams played for: Orange Free State, South Africa 1985–87
Cricketers particularly learnt from: Ian Thomson, Chris Waller, Roger Marshall, Tony Buss, Alvin Kallicharran
Other sports played: Golf, snooker, football
Relaxations: 'Sleeping, going to concerts, eating, drinking and watching it rain!'
Extras: Left Sussex at the end of 1989 season by mutual consent
Opinions on cricket: 'Should play 16 four-day championship matches.'
Best batting performance: 179 Sussex v Glamorgan, Cardiff 1986
Best bowling performance: 6-82 Sussex v Hampshire, Southampton 1988

LAST SEASON: BATTING

	I.	N.O.	R.	H.S.	AV.
TEST					
1ST-CLASS	7	0	198	94	28.28
INT					
RAL	3	0	46	28	15.33
NAT.W.	1	0	18	18	18.00
B & H	2	0	9	5	4.50

CAREER: BATTING

	I.	N.O.	R.	H.S.	AV.
TEST					
1ST-CLASS	291	17	7932	179	28.94
INT					
RAL	56	5	1360	83	26.66
NAT.W.	13	0	521	102	24.80
B & H	21	0	436	53	20.76

LAST SEASON: BOWLING

	O.	M.	R.	W.	AV.
TEST					
1ST-CLASS	38	6	111	3	37.00
INT					
RAL					
NAT.W.					
B & H	2	0	8	0	–

CAREER: BOWLING

	O.	M.	R.	W.	AV.
TEST					
1ST-CLASS	672.4	125	2192	49	44.73
INT					
RAL	3.4	1	23	3	7.66
NAT.W.	1.3	0	9	0	–
B & H	8	2	34	1	34.00

GREEN, S. J. Warwickshire

Full Name: Simon James Green
Role: Right-hand bat, left-arm bowler, fields 'anywhere but enjoy slip and gully'
Born: 19 March 1970, Bloxwich, Staffordshire
Height: 6' 2½" **Weight:** 12st 2lbs
Nickname: Charlie, Willie Carson
County debut: 1988
1st-Class catches 1989: 2 (career 2)
Parents: Albert Ernest and Jennifer
Marital status: Single
Education: West House School (Preparatory), Old Swinford Hospital
Qualifications: 3 O-levels, 5 GSEs; 2 years YTS Scheme Coaching Certificate
Off-season 1989–90: In Perth, Western Australia, working and playing cricket for Phoenix Park CC
Cricketing superstitions or habits: 'Always wear inners and wear my St Christopher chain.'
Overseas tours: England (South) U-19 XI to Belfast 1987
Cricketers particularly learnt from: Neil Abberley, Steve Rouse, Norman Gifford, Geoff Humpage, Paul Smith and the rest of Warwickshire 1st XI, David Thomas, Sports Master at Prep School
Cricketers particularly admired: Dennis Lillee, Paul Smith, Joey Benjamin, Simon Myles, Ian Botham
Other sports played: All kind of sports but especially golf
Other sports followed: Derby County FC, and Bath XV
Relaxations: Listening to music
Extras: First 'first-class' innings versus Lancashire was lbw first ball
Opinions on cricket: 'Limit to Sunday cricket. The greatest game known to Mankind and being paid for the privilege of participating.'
Best batting performance: 28 Warwickshire v Lancashire, Nuneaton 1988

LAST SEASON: BATTING

	I.	N.O.	R.	H.S.	AV.
TEST					
1ST-CLASS	3	0	19	11	6.33
INT					
RAL	–	–	–	–	–
NAT.W.					
B & H	1	0	0	0	0.00

CAREER: BATTING

	I.	N.O.	R.	H.S.	AV.
TEST					
1ST-CLASS	5	0	47	28	9.40
INT					
RAL	3	1	11	10*	5.50
NAT.W.					
B & H	1	0	0	0	0.00

GREENE, V. S. Gloucestershire

Full Name: Victor Sylvester Greene
Role: Right-hand bat, right arm
fast-medium bowler
Born: 24 September 1960,
Barbados
Nickname: Vibert
County debut: 1987
County cap: 1989
1st-Class 50s scored: 1
1st-Class 5 w. in innings: 4
1st-Class 10 w. in match: 1
1st-Class catches 1989: 1 (career 11)
Overseas teams played for: Barbados
1985–86
Overseas tours: West Indies B to
Zimbabwe 1986–87
Best batting performance: 62*
Gloucestershire v Leicestershire,
Cheltenham 1987
Best bowling performance: 7-96 Gloucestershire v Nottinghamshire, Trent
Bridge 1987

LAST SEASON: BATTING

	I.	N.O.	R.	H.S.	AV.
TEST					
1ST-CLASS	8	0	30	13	3.75
INT					
RAL	7	3	107	32*	26.75
NAT.W.	–	–	–	–	–
B & H	1	0	1	1	1.00

CAREER: BATTING

	I.	N.O.	R.	H.S.	AV.
TEST					
1ST-CLASS	35	8	332	62*	12.29
INT					
RAL	14	9	170	32*	34.00
NAT.W.	–	–	–	–	–
B & H	1	0	1	1	1.00

LAST SEASON: BOWLING

	O.	M.	R.	W.	AV.
TEST					
1ST-CLASS	145.1	31	485	17	28.53
INT					
RAL	54	7	195	7	27.85
NAT.W.	12	2	43	2	21.50
B & H	18.5	3	42	6	7.00

CAREER: BOWLING

	O.	M.	R.	W.	AV.
TEST					
1ST-CLASS	743.1	144	2273	93	24.44
INT					
RAL	162	12	657	28	23.46
NAT.W.	12	2	43	2	21.50
B & H	18.5	3	42	6	7.00

GREENFIELD, K.   Sussex

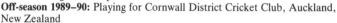

Full name: Keith Greenfield
Role: Right-hand bat, right-arm
medium or off-break bowler,
slip fielder
Born: 6 December 1968, Brighton
Height: 6' **Weight:** 12st 10lbs
Nickname: Grubby
County debut: 1987
Place in batting averages: 211th
av. 16.50
1st-Class catches 1989: 4 (career 6)
Parents: Leslie Ernest and Sheila
Marital status: Single
Education: Coldgan Primary and
Middle Schools, Falmer High
School
Qualifications: O-level Art and
Technical Drawing, B.Tec Leisure
Centre Management Diploma
Off-season 1989–90: Playing for Cornwall District Cricket Club, Auckland,
New Zealand
Cricketing superstitions or habits: 'Always put batting shoes on last when
padding up.'
Overseas teams played for: Cornwall District CC, Auckland 1988–89
Cricketers particularly learnt from: Norman Gifford, Ian Gould
Cricketers particularly admired: Paul Parker, Derek Randall, Ian Botham
Other sports played: Golf, football, tennis, swimming
Other sports followed: Football, golf, rugby
Injuries 1989: Cracked joint on top of right thumb, out one week, then carried
on playing, at beginning of July
Relaxations: Going out with friends, playing music
Opinions on cricket: 'There is too much media abuse of our top English
players which in no way can help them. I support 16 four-day games. People
should support players going to South Africa.'
Best batting performance: 48 Sussex v Cambridge University, Hove 1989

LAST SEASON: BATTING

	I.	N.O.	R.	H.S.	AV.
TEST					
1ST-CLASS	8	0	132	48	16.50
INT					
RAL	3	0	38	22	12.66
NAT.W.					
B & H	1	0	0	0	0.00

CAREER: BATTING

	I.	N.O.	R.	H.S.	AV.
TEST					
1ST-CLASS	12	0	166	48	13.83
INT					
RAL	4	1	46	22	15.33
NAT.W.					
B & H	1	0	0	0	0.00

GREIG, I. A. Surrey

Full Name: Ian Alexander Greig
Role: Right-hand bat, right-arm medium bowler, slip fielder
Born: 8 December 1955, Queenstown, South Africa
Height: 5' 11¾" **Weight:** 12st
Nickname: Wash, Greigy
County debut: 1980 (Sussex), 1987 (Surrey)
County cap: 1981 (Sussex), 1987 (Surrey)
Test debut: 1982
No. of Tests: 2
1000 runs in a season: 1
50 wickets in a season: 3
1st-Class 50s scored: 32
1st-Class 100s scored: 6
1st-Class 5 w. in innings: 10
1st-Class 10 w. in match: 2
One-Day 50s: 5
Place in batting averages: 33rd av. 42.20 (1988 196th av. 19.59)
Place in bowling averages: 120th av. 54.18 (1988 37th av. 23.32)
Strike rate 1989: 98.72 (career 57.36)
1st-Class catches 1989: 7 (career 129)
Parents: Sandy and Joyce
Wife and date of marriage: Cheryl, 8 January 1983
Children: Michelle, 17 December 1984; Andrew, 20 January 1987
Family links with cricket: Brother of Tony, former captain of Sussex and England; brother-in-law Phillip Hodson played for Cambridge University and Yorkshire
Education: Queens College, Queenstown; Downing College, Cambridge
Qualifications: MA Law (Cantab)
Off-season 1989–90: Marketing executive
Cricketing superstitions or habits: Left pad on first
Overseas tours: Captain of Combined Universities to Australia 1979–80; Surrey CCC to Dubai 1988 and 1989
Overseas teams played for: Border, South Africa 1974–75, 1979–80; Griqualand West, South Africa 1975–76
Cricketers particularly learnt from: Geoff Arnold
Cricketers particularly admired: Garth le Roux, Richard Hadlee
Other sports followed: Rugby
Injuries 1989: Damaged shoulder ligaments: could not bowl for four weeks

Relaxations: Relaxing with family, barbecues, fly-fishing '– and still learning'
Opinions on cricket: 'We must move to 16 four-day cricket as soon as possible, played on the best possible surfaces, and reducing the amount of cricket played. A mixture of limited-overs cricket to be carefully restored around the four-day game.'
Best batting performance: 147* Sussex v Oxford University, Oxford 1983
Best bowling performance: 7-43 Sussex v Cambridge University, Cambridge 1981

LAST SEASON: BATTING

	I.	N.O.	R.	H.S.	AV.
TEST					
1ST-CLASS	34	10	1013	107*	42.20
INT					
RAL	16	6	204	61*	20.40
NAT.W.	3	1	113	75	56.50
B & H	4	0	49	33	12.25

LAST SEASON: BOWLING

	O.	M.	R.	W.	AV.
TEST					
1ST-CLASS	181	33	596	11	54.18
INT					
RAL	77.2	2	353	10	35.30
NAT.W.	17	0	83	1	83.00
B & H	37	2	174	4	43.50

CAREER: BATTING

	I.	N.O.	R.	H.S.	AV.
TEST	4	0	26	14	6.50
1ST-CLASS	275	40	6406	147*	27.25
INT					
RAL	97	26	1617	61*	22.77
NAT.W.	17	2	355	82	23.66
B & H	44	3	558	51	13.60

CAREER: BOWLING

	O.	M.	R.	W.	AV.
TEST	31.2	6	114	4	28.50
1ST-CLASS	3754.3	780	11625	392	29.65
INT					
RAL	675	21	3421	119	28.74
NAT.W.	161.4	17	579	22	26.31
B & H	388	38	1428	54	26.44

GRIFFITH, F. A.　　　Derbyshire

Full Name: Frank Alexander Griffith
Role: Right-hand bat, right-arm medium bowler
Born: 15 August 1968, Leyton
Height: 6' **Weight:** 12st
Nickname: Sir Learie
County debut: 1988
Place in batting averages: 261st av. 10.20
1st-Class catches 1989: 4 (career 6)
Parents: Alex and Daisy
Marital status: Single
Family links with cricket: Charlie Griffith played Test cricket for West Indies
Education: William Morris High School, Walthamstow

Qualifications: Food and nutrition and art O-levels; NCA coaching certificate

Jobs outside cricket: Labourer, salesman

Cricketing superstitions or habits: 'I like to be by myself and think about the game.'

Overseas tours: Haringey Cricket College to Barbados, Trinidad and Tobago 1986–87; Jamaica 1988

Cricketers particularly learnt from: 'My brothers Victor and Gline.'

Cricketers particularly admired: Collis King, Franklyn Stephenson

Other sports played: Table tennis, basketball, football

Relaxations: Listening to music

Opinions on cricket: 'We must play more four-day games and get results, instead of playing three-day games and letting the game end in a draw.'

Best batting performance: 37 Derbyshire v Northamptonshire, Northampton 1988

Best bowling performance: 4-47 Derbyshire v Lancashire, Old Trafford 1988

LAST SEASON: BATTING

	I.	N.O.	R.	H.S.	AV.
TEST					
1ST-CLASS	10	0	102	30	10.20
INT					
RAL	4	0	7	5	1.75
NAT.W.					
B & H	1	0	10	10	10.00

CAREER: BATTING

	I.	N.O.	R.	H.S.	AV.
TEST					
1ST-CLASS	17	1	207	37	12.93
INT					
RAL	9	1	36	9	4.50
NAT.W.					
B & H	1	0	10	10	10.00

LAST SEASON: BOWLING

	O.	M.	R.	W.	AV.
TEST					
1ST-CLASS	41	6	152	5	30.40
INT					
RAL	27	2	145	6	24.16
NAT.W.					
B & H					

CAREER: BOWLING

	O.	M.	R.	W.	AV.
TEST					
1ST-CLASS	140.3	26	499	15	33.26
INT					
RAL	55	4	282	9	31.33
NAT.W.					
B & H					

81. Which county batsman scored five centuries in six innings in 1989?

HANSFORD, A. R.　　　　　　　　　Sussex

Full Name: Alan Roderick Hansford
Role: Right-arm medium-fast
bowler, right-hand bat
Born: 1 October 1968, Burgess Hill,
West Sussex
Height: 6′ **Weight:** 13st 7lbs
Nickname: Skater, Sandy, Lumpy,
Olly
County debut: 1989
1st-Class 5 w. in innings: 1
1st-Class catches 1989: 2 (career 2)
Parents: John and Muriel
Marital status: Single
Family links with cricket: Father
played club cricket primarily in
Dorset. Brother Robert played for
ESCA (South) U-15 and in club
and county youth cricket with
other brothers Gerald, Julian and Adrian
Education: Oakmeeds Community School, Burgess Hill; Haywards Heath VI
Form College, Haywards Heath; University of Surrey, Guildford
Qualifications: 10 O-levels, 3 A-levels, presently studying for BSc (Hons)
Degree in Maths and Statistics
Off-season 1989–90: 'Working as an insurance clerk and getting fit!'
Cricketers particularly learnt from: Brian Jefferies (Sussex Colts coach),
Derek Grammer (Brighton & Hove CC), Colin Wells, Peter Moores
Cricketers particularly admired: Ian Botham, Viv Richards, Malcolm Mar-
shall, Sylvester Clarke, Phil Edmonds

LAST SEASON: BATTING

	I.	N.O.	R.	H.S.	AV.
TEST					
1ST-CLASS	4	2	53	18	26.50
INT					
RAL	2	1	3	2*	3.00
NAT.W.	1	1	5	5*	–
B & H	3	2	10	8*	10.00

CAREER: BATTING

	I.	N.O.	R.	H.S.	AV.
TEST					
1ST-CLASS	4	2	53	18	26.50
INT					
RAL	2	1	3	2*	3.00
NAT.W.	1	1	5	5*	–
B & H	3	2	10	8*	10.00

LAST SEASON: BOWLING

	O.	M.	R.	W.	AV.
TEST					
1ST-CLASS	167.2	39	485	20	24.25
INT					
RAL	52	2	220	11	20.00
NAT.W.	12	0	48	2	24.00
B & H	52	12	167	5	33.40

CAREER: BOWLING

	O.	M.	R.	W.	AV.
TEST					
1ST-CLASS	167.2	39	485	20	24.25
INT					
RAL	52	2	220	11	20.00
NAT.W.	12	0	48	2	24.00
B & H	52	12	167	5	33.40

Relaxations: Eating, drinking, sleeping, doing nothing, statistics
Extras: Took wicket with 4th ball in first-class cricket. Was member of historic 1989 Combined Universities side. Has twin brother, Adrian
Opinions on cricket: 'The lunch and tea intervals should be lengthened to one hour and half-an-hour respectively in all games. Coaches should generally become less rigid re unorthodox and individual bowling and batting techniques.'
Best batting performance: 18 Sussex v Gloucestershire, Hove 1989
Best bowling performance: 5-79 Sussex v Hampshire, Hove 1989

HARDEN, R. J. Somerset

Full Name: Richard John Harden
Role: Right-hand bat, left-arm medium bowler
Born: 16 August 1965, Bridgwater
Height: 5' 11" **Weight:** 13st 4lbs
Nickname: Rich
County debut: 1985
1000 runs in a season: 1
1st-Class 50s scored: 15
1st-Class 100s scored: 6
One-Day 50s: 6
Place in batting averages: 71st
av. 34.60 (1988 97th av. 29.50)
1st-Class catches 1989: 10 (career 47)
Parents: Chris and Ann
Marital status: Single
Family links with cricket: Grandfather played club cricket for Bridgwater

Education: Kings College, Taunton
Qualifications: 8 O-levels, 2 A-levels. Coaching award
Jobs outside cricket: Insurance clerk
Cricketing superstitions or habits: Right pad on first
Overseas teams played for: New Plymouth Old Boys 1984–85, 1985–86; Central Districts in New Zealand 1987–88
Cricketers particularly learnt from: Roy Marshall
Cricketers particularly admired: Viv Richards, David Gower, Steve Waugh
Other sports played: Squash, 'struggling golfer'
Relaxations: Listening to music, eating good food, playing snooker or pool, drinking in good wine bars

Opinions on cricket: 'The introduction of four-day cricket is excellent. However, it must be played on decent pitches.'
Best batting performance: 108 Somerset v Sussex, Taunton 1986
Best bowling performance: 2-7 Central Districts v Canterbury, Blenheim 1987–88

LAST SEASON: BATTING

	I.	N.O.	R.	H.S.	AV.
TEST					
1ST-CLASS	34	6	969	115*	34.60
INT					
RAL	15	1	342	61	24.42
NAT.W.	2	0	14	14	7.00
B & H	4	1	81	44	27.00

CAREER: BATTING

	I.	N.O.	R.	H.S.	AV.
TEST					
1ST-CLASS	142	21	3700	108	30.57
INT					
RAL	51	7	1117	73	25.38
NAT.W.	3	0	31	17	10.33
B & H	17	1	279	44	17.43

LAST SEASON: BOWLING

	O.	M.	R.	W.	AV.
TEST					
1ST-CLASS	23.3	4	89	0	–
INT					
RAL					
NAT.W.					
B & H					

CAREER: BOWLING

	O.	M.	R.	W.	AV.
TEST					
1ST-CLASS	139	18	523	10	52.30
INT					
RAL	0.1	0	0	0	–
NAT.W.					
B & H					

HARDIE, B. R. Essex

Full Name: Brian Ross Hardie
Role: Right-hand bat, right-arm medium bowler, bat/pad fielder
Born: 14 January 1950, Stenhousemuir
Height: 5' 10" **Weight:** 12st 7lbs
Nickname: Lager, Bert
County debut: 1973
County cap: 1974
Benefit: 1983 (£48,486)
1000 runs in a season: 11
1st-Class 50s scored: 85
1st-Class 100s scored: 25
One-Day 50s: 47
One-Day 100s: 6
Place in batting averages: 90th av. 31.68 (1988 168th av. 22.17)
1st-Class catches 1989: 25 (career 338)

Parents: James Millar (deceased) and Elspet

Wife and date of marriage: Fiona, 28 October 1977
Family links with cricket: Father and brother, Keith, played for Scotland
Education: Stenhousemuir Primary School; Larbert High School
Qualifications: 7 O-levels, 3 H-levels, NCA Advanced Cricket Coach
Jobs outside cricket: Computer operator, bank clerk, shipping clerk
Off-season 1989–90: Fund-raising at Essex CCC
Overseas teams played for: Two seasons in New Zealand club cricket 1980–81 and 1981–82; Auckland, New Zealand 1988–89
Cricketers particularly learnt from: 'Everyone has something to offer.'
Other sports played: Football, golf
Relaxations: Sport
Extras: Played for Stenhousemuir in East of Scotland League. Debut for Scotland 1970. Scored two centuries for Scotland v MCC at Aberdeen in 1971, but not then regarded as first-class match. Man of the Match in 1985 NatWest Final. Holds the Essex record for the slowest innings: 4 runs in 142 minutes
Best batting performance: 162 Essex v Warwickshire, Edgbaston 1975
162 Essex v Somerset, Southend 1985
Best bowling performance: 2-39 Essex v Glamorgan, Ilford 1979

LAST SEASON: BATTING

	I.	N.O.	R.	H.S.	AV.
TEST					
1ST-CLASS	27	2	792	142*	31.68
INT					
RAL	16	2	480	73*	34.28
NAT.W.	1	0	7	7	7.00
B & H	7	1	175	65	29.16

CAREER: BATTING

	I.	N.O.	R.	H.S.	AV.
TEST					
1ST-CLASS	591	72	17375	162	33.47
INT					
RAL	206	20	5229	109	28.11
NAT.W.	33	1	1112	110	34.75
B & H	76	16	1862	119*	31.03

LAST SEASON: BOWLING

	O.	M.	R.	W.	AV.
TEST					
1ST-CLASS					
INT					
RAL					
NAT.W.					
B & H					

CAREER: BOWLING

	O.	M.	R.	W.	AV.
TEST					
1ST-CLASS	46	3	238	3	79.33
INT					
RAL	4.5	0	24	1	24.00
NAT.W.	8	1	16	1	16.00
B & H					

82. What was unusual about the centuries scored by Mark Nicholas and Robin Smith for Hampshire v Gloucestershire at Cheltenham last season?

HARDY, J. J. E.　　　　　Somerset

Full Name: Jonathan James Ean Hardy
Role: Left-hand bat
Born: 2 October 1960, Nakuru, Kenya
Height: 6′ 3″ **Weight:** 13½st
Nickname: JJ
County debut: 1984 (Hampshire), 1986 (Somerset)
County cap: 1987 (Somerset)
1000 runs in a season: 1
1st-Class 50s scored: 32
1st-Class 100s scored: 2
One-Day 50s: 7
One-Day 100s: 1
Place in batting averages: 154th av. 22.89 (1988 130th av. 25.75)
1st-Class catches 1989: 6 (career 69)
Parents: Ray and Petasue
Wife and date of marriage: Janet, 25 September 1987
Family links with cricket: Father played for Yorkshire Schools; related to Nottinghamshire Gunn's
Education: Pembroke House, Gilgil, Kenya; Canford School, Dorset
Qualifications: 10 O-levels, 3 A-levels (English, Economics, Geography)
Off-season 1989–90: Playing for Cape Town CC; coaching in Cape Town Schools
Overseas teams played for: Pirates, Durban 1981–85; Paarl CC 1985–86; Cape Town CC 1987–89; Western Province 1987–88, 1988–89
Cricketers particularly admired: Graeme Pollock, Greg Chappell, Malcolm Marshall
Other sports played: Hockey (captain Dorset U-19), rugby, squash
Relaxations: Photography, walking
Extras: Suffered from bilharzia, a tropical parasitic disease from 1980 to February 1986. Left Hampshire to join Somerset for 1986 season

LAST SEASON: BATTING

	I.	N.O.	R.	H.S.	AV.
TEST					
1ST-CLASS	23	4	435	65	22.89
INT					
RAL	2	0	1	1	0.50
NAT.W.	1	0	1	1	1.00
B & H	3	0	31	12	10.33

CAREER: BATTING

	I.	N.O.	R.	H.S.	AV.
TEST					
1ST-CLASS	187	19	4917	119	29.26
INT					
RAL	48	7	890	94*	21.70
NAT.W.	8	1	191	100	27.28
B & H	17	1	366	70*	22.87

Opinions on cricket: 'Would like to see an increasing role in championship cricket for spinners and No.6 batsmen and a decreased one for contrived finishes and attempts at under-prepared pitches. Cricket unifies people of different classes and cultures. Politicians should allow it to do so.'
Best batting performance: 119 Somerset v Gloucestershire, Taunton 1987

HARMAN, M. D. Kent

Full Name: Mark David Harman
Role: Right-hand bat, off-break bowler, slip fielder
Born: 30 June 1964, Aylesbury
Height: 5' 11½" **Weight:** 12st 7lbs
Nickname: Harmo
County debut: 1986 (Somerset), 1988 (Kent)
1st-Class 5 w. in innings: 3
Place in batting averages: —
(1988 253rd av. 11.42)
Place in bowling averages: —
(1988 40th av. 23.72)
1st-Class catches 1989: 0 (career 16)
Parents: Michael and Barbara
Wife and date of marriage: Maria, 27 September 1989
Family links with cricket: Father played club cricket

Education: Frome College; Loughborough University
Qualifications: 9 O-levels, 3 A-levels, BSc (First-Class Honours) Degree in Financial Management; cricket coaching awards
Jobs outside cricket: Chartered Accountancy
Off-season 1989–90: Playing and coaching in New Zealand
Cricketing superstitions or habits: 'Like to do a thorough series of stretching exercises before the day's play. Also brush teeth a lot during a day's play!'
Overseas teams played for: Stokes Valley, Lower Hutt 1988–89, 1989–90
Cricketers particularly learnt from: Peter Robinson among many others at Somerset CCC, Roy Pienaar, John Inverarity
Cricketers particularly admired: Vic Marks, Martin Crowe, Steve Waugh, Richard Hadlee, Roger Harper, Chris Tavaré
Other sports played: Soccer, golf, swimming, running
Other sports followed: All sports through TV, media etc
Injuries 1989: Split spinning finger for three weeks; patella tendonitis for latter part of season

Relaxations: 'Reading, sleeping, running.'

Extras: 'Nearly run-out from first delivery in first-class cricket! Left Somerset at the end of 1987 season to join Kent to further my career, as first-team opportunities at Somerset were limited due to presence of Vic Marks in the side.' Released by Kent at end of 1989 season

Opinions on cricket: 'Four-day cricket appears to have worked – and gradual progressions to 16 four-day games would eventually produce a "fairer" championship. The sides which are the strongest in depth and play the more attacking, inventive cricket will ultimately benefit.'

Best batting performance: 41 Somerset v Kent, Bath 1987

Best bowling performance: 5-55 Kent v Oxford University, Oxford 1988

LAST SEASON: BATTING

	I.	N.O.	R.	H.S.	AV.
TEST					
1ST-CLASS	1	1	0	0*	–
INT					
RAL					
NAT.W.					
B & H					

LAST SEASON: BOWLING

	O.	M.	R.	W.	AV.
TEST					
1ST-CLASS	93.4	29	248	10	24.80
INT					
RAL					
NAT.W.					
B & H					

CAREER: BATTING

	I.	N.O.	R.	H.S.	AV.
TEST					
1ST-CLASS	27	11	201	41	12.56
INT					
RAL	2	1	10	8*	10.00
NAT.W.	1	0	0	0	0.00
B & H					

CAREER: BOWLING

	O.	M.	R.	W.	AV.
TEST					
1ST-CLASS	551.5	162	1359	43	31.60
INT					
RAL	14	0	111	2	55.50
NAT.W.	12	1	38	1	38.00
B & H					

83. Which international soccer player played for his country at cricket against the Australians last season?

HARTLEY, P. J.   Yorkshire

Full Name: Peter John Hartley
Role: Right-hand bat, right-arm
fast-medium bowler
Born: 18 April 1960, Keighley
Height: 6′ **Weight:** 13st 4lbs
Nickname: Daisy, Jack
County debut: 1982 (Warwickshire),
1985 (Yorkshire)
County cap: 1987 (Yorkshire)
1st-Class 50s scored: 4
1st-Class 100s scored: 1
1st-Class 5 w. in innings: 4
Place in batting averages: —
(1988 71st av. 33.09)
Place in bowling averages: —
(1988 116th av. 35.85)
1st-Class catches 1989: 0 (career
24)
Parents: Thomas and Molly
Wife and date of marriage: Sharon,
12 March 1988
Family links with cricket: Father played local league cricket
Education: Greenhead Grammar School; Bradford College
Qualifications: City & Guilds in Textiles
Jobs outside cricket: Textile supervisor
Off-season 1989–90: Getting fit for 1990 season
Overseas tours: With Yorkshire CCC to West Indies 1987
Overseas teams played for: Melville CC, Hamilton, New Zealand 1983–84;

LAST SEASON: BATTING

	I.	N.O.	R.	H.S.	AV.
TEST					
1ST-CLASS	–	–	–	–	–
INT					
RAL					
NAT.W.					
B & H					

LAST SEASON: BOWLING

	O.	M.	R.	W.	AV.
TEST					
1ST-CLASS	12	1	51	0	–
INT					
RAL					
NAT.W.					
B & H					

CAREER: BATTING

	I.	N.O.	R.	H.S.	AV.
TEST					
1ST-CLASS	76	21	1354	127*	24.61
INT					
RAL	23	9	148	35	10.57
NAT.W.	4	2	46	23	23.00
B & H	6	3	50	29*	16.66

CAREER: BOWLING

	O.	M.	R.	W.	AV.
TEST					
1ST-CLASS	1532.3	224	5551	156	35.58
INT					
RAL	243.4	7	1177	41	28.70
NAT.W.	59	4	206	14	14.71
B & H	140	12	586	26	22.53

Adelaide CC, Australia 1985–86, 1986–87; Harmony CC, and Orange Free State, South Africa 1988–89

Cricketing superstitions or habits: Puts left pad on first

Cricketers particularly learnt from: Phil Carrick, Steve Oldham, Mike Page, Doug Padgett

Cricketers particularly admired: Dennis Lillee, Richard Hadlee, Gordon Greenidge

Other sports played: Golf

Other sports followed: Bradford City FC

Injuries 1989: Back injury – out for whole season except for one first-class match

Relaxations: Music, golf

Opinions on cricket: 'South Africa should be allowed to play in international cricket.'

Best batting performance: 127* Yorkshire v Lancashire, Old Trafford 1988

Best bowling performance: 6-68 Yorkshire v Nottinghamshire, Sheffield 1986

HARTLEY, S. N.   Yorkshire

Full Name: Stuart Neil Hartley
Role: Right-hand bat, right-arm medium bowler, outfielder
Born: 18 March 1956, Shipley, West Yorkshire
Height: 5′ 11½″ **Weight:** 13st 3lbs
Nickname: Tommy
County debut: 1978
County cap: 1981
1st-Class 50s scored: 25
1st-Class 100s scored: 4
One-Day 50s: 13
1st-Class catches 1989: 0 (career 54)
Parents: Marjorie and Horace
Marital status: Divorced
Family links with cricket: Father played league cricket
Education: Beckfoot Grammar School, Bingley; Cannington High, Perth, Western Australia
Qualifications: 8 O-levels, 3 A-levels; exam passes in insurance

Jobs outside cricket: Trained insurance underwriter; Insurance broker: Windsor Insurance Brokers Ltd
Off-season 1989–90: Working as insurance broker
Overseas tours: Captained North of England NCA team to Holland 1975 and Gibraltar 1981; Yorkshire to West Indies 1987
Overseas teams played for: Orange Free State 1981–82; Durban Collegians
Cricketers particularly learnt from: Doug Padgett, Mike Fearnley, Yorkshire CCC coaching staff
Cricketers particularly admired: Imran Khan, Clive Rice
Other sports played: Golf, rugby union
Injuries 1989: Broke wrist end of season but missed no matches
Extras: 'Started to play cricket in Perth, Western Australia, where I lived for 2½ years, 1967–69. I would like to live in Perth in the future.' Amateur football with Bradford City 1970–75. Rugby Union with Bingley RUFC. Has been acting captain of Yorkshire. Captain of 2nd XI
Opinions on cricket: 'Disappointed at apparent ease with which players are able to qualify as Englishmen, and therefore play "as locals" in county and international cricket.'
Best batting performance: 114 Yorkshire v Gloucestershire, Bradford 1982
Best bowling performance: 4-51 Yorkshire v Surrey, The Oval 1985

LAST SEASON: BATTING

	I.	N.O.	R.	H.S.	AV.
TEST					
1ST-CLASS					
INT					
RAL	6	1	34	13	6.80
NAT.W.	1	0	20	20	20.00
B & H	2	1	52	39	52.00

LAST SEASON: BOWLING

	O.	M.	R.	W.	AV.
TEST					
1ST-CLASS					
INT					
RAL	26.4	0	126	3	42.00
NAT.W.					
B & H	24	3	85	5	17.00

CAREER: BATTING

	I.	N.O.	R.	H.S.	AV.
TEST					
1ST-CLASS	215	28	4667	114	24.95
INT					
RAL	119	25	2087	83*	22.20
NAT.W.	12	0	263	69	21.91
B & H	22	6	460	65*	28.75

CAREER: BOWLING

	O.	M.	R.	W.	AV.
TEST					
1ST-CLASS	597	109	2182	48	45.45
INT					
RAL	281.1	3	1587	48	33.06
NAT.W.	28	2	114	1	114.00
B & H	110	6	421	18	23.38

HAYHURST, A. N.   Somerset

Full Name: Andrew Neil Hayhurst
Role: Right-hand bat, right-arm
medium bowler
Born: 23 November 1962,
Davyhulme, Manchester
Height: 6' **Weight:** 14st
Nickname: Barney, Ritchie
Cunningham
County debut: 1985 (Lancashire)
1st-Class 50s scored: 4
1st-Class 100s scored: 1
One-Day 50s: 3
Place in batting averages: 181st
av. 19.84 (1988 153rd av. 23.42)
Place in bowling averages: —
(1988 98th av. 32.52)
1st-Class catches 1989: 1 (career 11)
Parents: William and Margaret
Marital status: Single
Family links with cricket: Father played club cricket, 'Mother a demon
watcher, and sandwich-maker!'
Education: St Mark's Primary School; Worsley Wardley High; Eccles Col-
lege; Carnegie College, Leeds
Qualifications: 8 O-levels, 3 A-levels, BA(Hons) Human Movement
Jobs outside cricket: Lecturing in winter, 'and working in a friend's chip shop.'
Off-season 1989–90: 'Mending a broken thumb, losing weight, working in
friend's chip shop, and lecturing on human movement and aerobics.'
Cricketing superstitions or habits: 'Left sock on first. Count to three between
every ball. Don't like being on 99!'
Cricketers particularly learnt from: Father and Geoff Ogden (Worsley CC),
Nick Speak, Fred Trueman ('through listening'), David Hughes
Cricketers particularly admired: 'Harry Pilling's ability to play while not
feeling well!' Graeme Hick
Other sports played: Golf, squash, rugby, fives
Other sports followed: Archery, Manchester United FC
Injuries 1989: Broke thumb really badly in July
Relaxations: Walking dogs. Keep two hamsters. Dining out
Extras: Scored a record 197 runs whilst playing for North of England v South,
Southampton 1982. Represented NAYC v MCC 1982. Holds record number

of runs for Lancashire Cricket Fed. U-19 (av. 105.00), 1982. Holds record number of runs in Manchester & District Cricket Association League, whilst playing for Worsley CC in 1984: 1193 runs (av. 70.17). Represented Greater Manchester U-19 County at football 1981–82. Released by Lancashire at the end of 1989 season and joined Somerset on a three-year contract, 1990.

Opinions on cricket: '2nd XI cricket should be played on better pitches if that cricket is to be a successful grounding for future 1st XI players. Pitches should be uncovered. There is too much cricket. Should play one-day games in coloured clothing. Fielders should wear gloves.'

Best batting performance: 107 Lancashire v Derbyshire, Derby 1988
Best bowling performance: 4-27 Lancashire v Middlesex, Old Trafford 1987

LAST SEASON: BATTING

	I.	N.O.	R.	H.S.	AV.
TEST					
1ST-CLASS	15	2	258	40	19.84
INT					
RAL	5	1	82	29	20.50
NAT.W.					
B & H	3	0	20	13	6.66

LAST SEASON: BOWLING

	O.	M.	R.	W.	AV.
TEST					
1ST-CLASS	52	12	166	4	41.50
INT					
RAL	1	0	7	0	–
NAT.W.					
B & H	11.5	3	27	1	27.00

CAREER: BATTING

	I.	N.O.	R.	H.S.	AV.
TEST					
1ST-CLASS	63	6	1185	107	20.78
INT					
RAL	30	5	695	84	27.80
NAT.W.	6	1	148	49	29.60
B & H	7	0	36	13	5.14

CAREER: BOWLING

	O.	M.	R.	W.	AV.
TEST					
1ST-CLASS	505.4	93	1644	49	33.55
INT					
RAL	190.3	7	989	18	54.94
NAT.W.	71.5	6	265	9	29.44
B & H	46.5	6	177	7	25.28

84. Against which county did Mark Ramprakash hit his maiden century?

HAYNES, D. L.   Middlesex

Full Name: Desmond Leo
Haynes
Role: Right-hand bat, right-arm
bowler
Born: 15 February 1956, St James,
Barbados, West Indies
County debut: 1989
County cap: 1989
Test debut: 1977–78
No. of Tests: 85
No. on One-Day Internationals:
158
1000 runs in a season: 1
1st-Class 50s scored: 87
1st-Class 100s scored: 26
1st-Class 200s scored: 1
One-Day 50s: 40
One-Day 100s: 14
Place in batting averages: 21st
av. 45.18
1st-Class catches 1989: 12 (career 128
+ 1 stumping)
Education: Federal HS, Barbados
Overseas teams played for: Barbados 1976–89; clubs: Carlton (West Indies),
Melbourne (Australia); played for Scotland in B&H Cup
Overseas tours: World Series Cricket (Kerry Packer) 1978–79; West Indies to
Australia 1979–80, 1981–82, 1984–85, 1988–89; West Indies to New Zealand
1979–80, 1987; West Indies to England 1980, 1984, 1988; West Indies to

LAST SEASON: BATTING

	I.	N.O.	R.	H.S.	AV.
TEST					
1ST-CLASS	37	5	1446	206*	45.18
INT					
RAL	10	0	198	56	19.80
NAT.W.	5	0	301	88	60.20
B & H	1	0	59	59	59.00

CAREER: BATTING

	I.	N.O.	R.	H.S.	AV.
TEST	146	17	5340	184	41.39
1ST-CLASS	218	23	8762	206*	44.93
INT	157	20	5884	152*	42.94
RAL	10	0	198	56	19.80
NAT.W.	5	0	301	88	60.20
B & H	4	0	131	59	32.75

LAST SEASON: BOWLING

	O.	M.	R.	W.	AV.
TEST					
1ST-CLASS	6	3	13	0	–
INT					
RAL	3	0	19	0	–
NAT.W.					
B & H					

CAREER: BOWLING

	O.	M.	R.	W.	AV.
TEST	3	0	8	1	8.00
1ST-CLASS	23	4	77	4	19.25
INT	5	0	24	0	–
RAL	3	0	19	0	–
NAT.W.					
B & H	18	4	32	1	32.00

Pakistan 1980–81; West Indies B to Zimbabwe 1981; West Indies to India 1983, 1987–88
Best batting performance: 206* Middlesex v Kent, Uxbridge 1989
Best bowling performance: 1-2 West Indies v Pakistan, Lahore 1980–81

HEGG, W. K. Lancashire

Full Name: Warren Kevin Hegg
Role: Right-hand bat, wicket-keeper
Born: 23 February 1968, Radcliffe, Lancashire
Height: 5′ 8″ **Weight:** 11st
Nickname: Chucky, Chutch, The Admiral
County debut: 1986
1st-Class 50s scored: 6
1st-Class 100s scored: 1
Place in batting averages: 184th av. 19.82 (1988 219th av. 16.10)
Parents: Kevin and Glenda
Marital status: Single
Family links with cricket: Father played as opening bat in local leagues, as does brother Martin as an opening bowler
Education: Unsworth High School; Stand College, Whitefield
Qualifications: 5 O-levels, 7 CSEs; qualified coach
Jobs outside cricket: Groundsman at Old Trafford; worked at warehouse (involved in textiles)
Off-season 1989–90: Playing and coaching in Tasmania
Cricketing superstitions or habits: Left pad on first. Always wears a hat when keeping wicket
Overseas tours: North of England U-19 to Bermuda 1985; England Young Cricketers to Sri Lanka; England Youth to World Cup in Australia 1988; Lancashire to Jamaica 1986–87, 1987–88; Lancashire to Zimbabwe 1989
Overseas teams played for: Sheffield CC, Tasmania 1987–88, 1988–89, 1989–90
Cricketers particularly learnt from: Father, Jim Kenyon (old pro), Clive Lloyd, Alan Knott
Cricketers particularly admired: Clive Lloyd, Phil DeFreitas ('good competitor'), Gehan Mendis ('superb technique')
Other sports played: Football, golf, tennis

236

Other sports followed: Football, rugby league

Relaxations: Watching TV, sleeping, walking dog, fishing

Extras: First player to make County debut from Lytham CC. Holds Lancashire Schools U-19 record for most dismissals in a match – 6 (previous holder Graeme Fowler). Youngest player to score a 100 for Lancashire for 30 years, 130 v Northamptonshire in fourth 1st-class game

Opinions on cricket: 'Sunday League run-ups back to 15 yards. Three two-hour sessions.'

Best batting performance: 130 Lancashire v Northamptonshire, Northampton 1987

LAST SEASON: BATTING

	I.	N.O.	R.	H.S.	AV.
TEST					
1ST-CLASS	39	4	694	86	19.82
INT					
RAL	7	2	25	8	5.00
NAT.W.	3	0	65	29	21.66
B & H	3	1	28	13	14.00

CAREER: BATTING

	I.	N.O.	R.	H.S.	AV.
TEST					
1ST-CLASS	100	13	1598	130	18.36
INT					
RAL	16	6	57	9*	5.70
NAT.W.	5	0	91	29	18.20
B & H	5	1	40	13	10.00

LAST SEASON: WICKET KEEPING

	C.	ST.			
TEST					
1ST-CLASS	77	2			
INT					
RAL	19	2			
NAT.W.	1	–			
B & H	7	–			

CAREER: WICKET KEEPING

	C.	ST.			
TEST					
1ST-CLASS	159	24			
INT					
RAL	41	6			
NAT.W.	2	–			
B & H	14	–			

85. What did Tuppy Owen-Smith and Clive Van Ryneveld have in common?

HEMMINGS, E. E. Nottinghamshire

Full Name: Edward Ernest
Hemmings
Role: Right-hand bat, off-break
bowler
Born: 20 February 1949,
Leamington Spa, Warwickshire
Height: 5′ 10″ **Weight:** 13st
Nickname: Eddie
County debut: 1966 (Warwickshire),
1979 (Nottinghamshire)
County cap: 1974 (Warwickshire),
1980 (Nottinghamshire)
Benefit: 1987
Test debut: 1982
No. of Tests: 9

No. of One-Day Internationals: 13
50 wickets in a season: 13
1st-Class 50s scored: 24
1st-Class 100s scored: 1
1st-Class 5 w. in innings: 61
1st-Class 10 w. in match: 14
One-Day 50s: 1
Place in batting averages: 178th av. 20.20 (1988 217th av. 16.33)
Place in bowling averages: 64th av. 29.65 (1988 89th av. 31.23)
Strike rate 1989: 68.62 (career 65.79)
1st-Class catches 1989: 6 (career 184)
Parents: Edward and Dorothy Phyliss
Wife and date of marriage: Christine Mary, 23 October 1971
Children: Thomas Edward, 26 July 1977; James Oliver, 9 September 1979
Family links with cricket: Father and father's father played Minor Counties
and League cricket
Education: Campion School, Leamington Spa
Off-season 1989–90: Touring West Indies with England
Overseas tours: Derrick Robins' XI tour to South Africa 1975; International
XI tour to Pakistan 1981 and West Indies 1982–83; England to Australia and
New Zealand 1982–83; World Cup, Pakistan, Australia and New Zealand
1987–88; England to West Indies 1990
Cricketers particularly learnt from: John Jameson, Clive Rice
Cricketers particularly admired: Tim Robinson
Other sports played: 'Only golf now!'
Relaxations: 'Watching football at any level – especially junior. Dining out
with my wife. Golf, real ale – and sleeping it off!'

Extras: No longer wears glasses, plays in contact lenses. Started his career as a medium-pacer, and was thought of as a successor to Tom Cartwright. 'I was even known as "Tommy's Ghost" around Edgbaston.' Suffers from asthma. Took a hat-trick for Warwickshire in 1977 but had to wait four years to receive the inscribed match ball, when he had moved to Nottinghamshire. Hit first century – 127* v Yorkshire at Worksop, July 1982 – after 16 years in first-class game. When playing in a benefit game in Blackpool with Tim Robinson, spotted the potential of Franklyn Stephenson and recommended him to Nottinghamshire as a successor to Richard Hadlee

Best batting performance: 127* Nottinghamshire v Yorkshire, Worksop 1982
Best bowling performance: 10-175 International XI v West Indies XI, Kingston 1982–83

LAST SEASON: BATTING

	I.	N.O.	R.	H.S.	AV.
TEST	2	0	73	38	36.50
1ST-CLASS	30	7	432	58*	18.78
INT					
RAL	6	2	58	20*	14.50
NAT.W.	–	–	–	–	–
B & H	5	3	14	6*	7.00

LAST SEASON: BOWLING

	O.	M.	R.	W.	AV.
TEST	33	8	81	0	–
1ST-CLASS	630.2	163	1639	58	28.25
INT					
RAL	64	5	274	8	34.25
NAT.W.	12	5	27	1	27.00
B & H	75.3	10	241	9	26.77

CAREER: BATTING

	I.	N.O.	R.	H.S.	AV.
TEST	14	3	280	95	25.45
1ST-CLASS	555	128	8377	127*	19.61
INT	3	1	8	4*	4.00
RAL	157	47	1486	44*	13.50
NAT.W.	26	9	230	31*	13.52
B & H	47	15	464	61*	14.50

CAREER: BOWLING

	O.	M.	R.	W.	AV.
TEST	421.4	120	957	16	59.81
1ST-CLASS	13384.2	3786	35645	1243	28.67
INT	119.2	9	538	20	26.90
RAL	1529	101	7070	240	29.45
NAT.W.	413.1	70	1361	40	34.02
B & H	749.1	98	2333	68	34.30

---

86. Which town or city, after London, has produced the most English Test players?

HEPWORTH, P. N.   Leicestershire

Full Name: Peter Nash Hepworth
Role: Right-hand opening bat,
occasional off-break bowler
Born: 4 May 1967, Ackworth,
West Yorkshire
Height: 6′ 1″ **Weight:** 11st 11lbs
Nickname: Nash, Heppers
County debut: 1988
1st-Class 50s scored: 1
1st-Class catches 1989: 3 (career 3)
Parents: George and Zena
Marital status: Single
Family links with cricket: Father and
uncle played cricket for Ackworth
Education: Ackworth & Hemsworth
Junior/Middle Schools, High School
Qualifications: 8 CSEs, MCC Part 1
Coaching Certificate

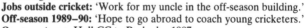

Jobs outside cricket: 'Work for my uncle in the off-season building.'
Off-season 1989–90: 'Hope to go abroad to coach young cricketers.'
Overseas tours: Hull CC to Barbados 1987
Cricketers particularly learnt from: Geoff Boycott, Father, Doug Lloyd,
John Lawrence, Ian Steen, Ken Higgs, and the senior Leicestershire players
Cricketers particularly admired: David Gower, Geoff Boycott, Don Wilson,
MCC Coach for his attitude with young players
Other sports played: Football
Other sports followed: Rugby League
Injuries 1989: Bad groin injury – off for three weeks
Relaxations: Watching sport, music
Extras: Started playing for Ackworth Cricket Club following the likes of Neil
Lloyd, Graham Stevenson, Geoff Boycott
Opinions on cricket: 'Pitches should be made to last and to encourage stroke
play. Bowlers would have to bowl line and length and not rely on assistance
from the pitches.'
Best batting performance: 51 Leicestershire v Sussex, Leicester 1988

LAST SEASON: BATTING

	I.	N.O.	R.	H.S.	AV.
TEST					
1ST-CLASS	8	0	63	17	7.87
INT					
RAL	1	1	20	20*	–
NAT.W.					
B & H					

CAREER: BATTING

	I.	N.O.	R.	H.S.	AV.
TEST					
1ST-CLASS	14	0	195	51	13.92
INT					
RAL	4	1	89	38	29.66
NAT.W.					
B & H					

240

HICK, G. A.   Worcestershire

Full Name: Graeme Ashley Hick
Role: Right-hand bat, off-break
bowler, slip and gully fielder
Born: 23 May 1966, Salisbury,
Rhodesia
Height: 6′ 3″ **Weight:** 14½st
Nickname: Hicky, Hickery
County debut: 1984
County cap: 1986
1000 runs in a season: 5
1st-Class 50s scored: 42
1st-Class 100s scored: 40
1st-Class 200s scored: 6
1st-Class 5 w. in innings: 2
1st-Class 10 w. in match: 1
One-Day 50s: 27
One-Day 100s: 7
Place in batting averages: 7th
av. 57.00 (1988 2nd av. 77.51)

Place in bowling averages: 12th av. 19.96 (1988 85th av. 30.57)
Strike rate 1989: 57.61 (career 72.85)
1st-Class catches 1989: 43 (career 163)
Parents: John and Eve
Marital status: Single
Family links with cricket: Father connected with cricket administration since
1972 and in 1984 elected to Zimbabwe Cricket Union Board of Control
Education: Banket Primary; Prince Edward Boys' High School, Zimbabwe
Qualifications: 4 O-levels, NCA coaching award
Jobs outside cricket: Zimbabwe Cricket Union coach
Off-season 1989–90: Taking the whole winter as a rest from cricket
Cricketing superstitions or habits: Left pad on first
Overseas tours: Zimbabwe XI 1983 World Cup; Zimbabwe to Sri Lanka
1983–84; Zimbabwe U-23 Triangular Tournament to Zambia; Zimbabwe to
UK 1985
Overseas teams played for: Old Harrarians, Zimbabwe 1982–86; Northern
Districts 1987–89
Cricketers particularly learnt from: David Houghton, Basil D'Oliveira,
Father
Cricketers particularly admired: Duncan Fletcher (Zimbabwe captain) for
approach and understanding of the game
Other sports played: Golf, tennis, squash, indoor hockey
Other sports followed: Follows Liverpool FC

Relaxations: Watching movies, television, listening to music

Extras: Youngest player participating in 1983 Prudential World Cup (aged 17); youngest player to represent Zimbabwe. Scored 1234 runs in 1984 Birmingham League season; scored 964 runs in 1984 2nd XI for Worcestershire; scored 185 in Birmingham League – highest score since the War; scored 11 centuries (including six in a row) in both above competitions. Scored 108* when only 6 years old for school team, Banket Junior. Played hockey for Zimbabwe, on tour in England, Holland and Germany. In 1986, at age 20, he became the youngest player to score 2000 runs in an English season. One of *Wisden*'s Five Cricketers of the Year, 1986. Hit 405* v Somerset, 1988, the highest individual score in England since 1895. Scored 1000 first-class runs by end of May 1988, taking century off West Indies to complete it. Hit record of 410 runs in April, 1988. Decided to qualify for England but following the meeting of the TCCB in December 1988, has to wait until 1991. Hit most sixes, 29, in 1989 English first-class season. Took a rest from cricket for the whole 1989–90 season

Opinions on cricket: 'The four-day game proved to be a winner. A closer look should be given to the pitches. Surely some of them cannot be good for cricket?'

Best batting performance: 405* Worcestershire v Somerset, Taunton 1988
Best bowling performance: 5-52 Worcestershire v Essex, Colchester 1989

LAST SEASON: BATTING

	I.	N.O.	R.	H.S.	AV.
TEST					
1ST-CLASS	38	6	1824	173*	57.00
INT					
RAL	15	1	435	84	31.07
NAT.W.	4	2	228	90*	114.00
B & H	4	0	170	109	42.50

LAST SEASON: BOWLING

	O.	M.	R.	W.	AV.
TEST					
1ST-CLASS	214.4	65	519	26	19.96
INT					
RAL	36	0	197	6	32.83
NAT.W.	15	0	67	0	–
B & H	10	0	50	0	–

CAREER: BATTING

	I.	N.O.	R.	H.S.	AV.
TEST					
1ST-CLASS	234	25	12733	405*	60.92
INT					
RAL	69	11	2258	111	38.93
NAT.W.	15	4	788	172*	71.63
B & H	19	3	867	109	54.18

CAREER: BOWLING

	O.	M.	R.	W.	AV.
TEST					
1ST-CLASS	1165.4	271	3547	96	36.94
INT					
RAL	149.1	1	799	27	29.59
NAT.W.	66.3	4	225	9	25.00
B & H	33	1	135	3	45.00

HINKS, S. G.   Kent

Full Name: Simon Graham Hinks
Role: Left-hand bat, bat/pad fielder
Born: 12 October 1960,
Northfleet, Kent
Height: 6' 2" **Weight:** 13st 4lbs
Nickname: Hinksy
County debut: 1982
County cap: 1985
1000 runs in a season: 2
1st-Class 50s scored: 27
1st-Class 100s scored: 7
One-Day 50s: 14
Place in batting averages: 87th
av. 32.12 (1988 98th av. 29.38)
1st-Class catches 1989: 8 (career 82)
Parents: Mary and Graham
Marital status: Single
Family links with cricket: Father
captained Gravesend CC and is now

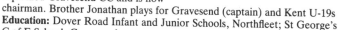

chairman. Brother Jonathan plays for Gravesend (captain) and Kent U-19s
Education: Dover Road Infant and Junior Schools, Northfleet; St George's
C of E School, Gravesend
Qualifications: 5 O-levels, 1 A-level
Jobs outside cricket: Worked for Reed Corrugated Cases for last two years as
a sales representative; coach
Cricketing superstitions or habits: Puts gear on in set order
Overseas tours: Troubadors XI to Argentina 1989
Overseas teams played for: Pirates, Johannesburg 1981–82; University of
Tasmania 1983–86
Cricketers particularly learnt from: 'Learnt from my father and members of
local club, Gravesend; and past and present members of county.'
Cricketers particularly admired: 'Admire Clive Lloyd's style and power and
anyone who has proved themselves over a long period.'
Other sports played: Most ball games
Injuries 1989: Fourteen stitches in top lip after being hit by Devon Malcolm
Relaxations: TV, music, papers, books, DIY, gardening
Opinions on cricket: 'Young players are still very dependent on going abroad
during the winter months as counties still do very little, if anything, to find
them winter employment. Players, particularly bowlers, therefore do not
have time to recover from injury or rest sufficiently playing overseas, as they
would with the benefit of a winter rest and stable employment. They would
also be able to afford mortgages (at present the wages for six months are so

243

low they can't afford one) and so feel more secure in the cricketing life, and be more able to commit themselves to one particular county, rather than going to the highest bidder.'

Best batting performance: 138 Kent v Oxford University, Oxford 1988
Best bowling performance: 2-18 Kent v Nottinghamshire, Trent Bridge 1989

LAST SEASON: BATTING

	I.	N.O.	R.	H.S.	AV.
TEST					
1ST-CLASS	36	4	1028	104*	32.12
INT					
RAL	13	1	306	80*	25.50
NAT.W.	1	0	62	62	62.00
B & H	5	0	102	49	20.40

CAREER: BATTING

	I.	N.O.	R.	H.S.	AV.
TEST					
1ST-CLASS	210	13	5706	138	28.96
INT					
RAL	71	6	1423	99	21.89
NAT.W.	8	2	322	95	53.66
B & H	27	1	701	85	26.96

LAST SEASON: BOWLING

	O.	M.	R.	W.	AV.
TEST					
1ST-CLASS	4	0	18	2	9.00
INT					
RAL					
NAT.W.					
B & H					

CAREER: BOWLING

	O.	M.	R.	W.	AV.
TEST					
1ST-CLASS	81.3	9	307	6	51.16
INT					
RAL	25	1	139	4	34.75
NAT.W.					
B & H	41	0	198	5	39.60

HODGSON, G. D.   Gloucestershire

Full Name: Geoffrey Dean Hodgson
Role: Right-hand bat
Born: 22 October 1966, Carlisle
Height: 6′ 1″ **Weight:** 12st 4lbs
Nickname: Deano, Ocko
County debut: 1987 (Warwickshire), 1989 (Gloucestershire)
Parents: John Geoffrey and Dorothy Elizabeth
Marital status: Single
Education: Nelson Thomlinson Comprehensive, Wigton; Loughborough University
Qualifications: 11 GCE O-levels (6 As, 3 Bs, 2 Cs), 4 GCE A-levels (3 As, 1 B), BSc Honours Human Biological Sciences (2:1), NCA Qualified Cricket Coach, PFA Qualified Football Coach, LTA Qualified Tennis Coach

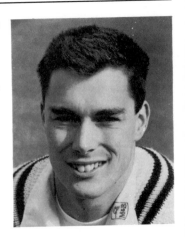

Off-season 1989–90: Working for a finance company in Birmingham

Cricketing superstitions or habits: 'Always put left pad and left batting glove on before the right pad and batting glove.'

Overseas tours: NCA England North to International Youth Tournament in Bermuda 1985; Geoff Humpage Benefit Tour to Barbados 1987

Overseas teams played for: Southern Districts, Queensland, Australia September 1988–March 1989

Cricketers particularly learnt from: Dennis Amiss

Cricketers particularly admired: Dennis Amiss, Martin Crowe, Mohinder Armanath, Sunil Gavaskar

Other sports played: Football, tennis, table tennis

Other sports followed: Football, international rugby, major golf tournaments, tennis, American football

Relaxations: Listening to music (various types). Reading thrillers and autobiographies. Watching comedies and old John Wayne and Clint Eastwood films. Dancing at clubs/discos. Keeping fit in winter skiing.

Opinions on cricket: '16 four-day Championship matches on good covered wickets. Less one-day cricket. Both Benson & Hedges and NatWest Trophy should be knockouts. Co-ordinating one- and four-day matches to reduce amount of travelling throughout the season. Regionalised Sunday League, i.e. north and south. Play-offs for top two in each division. This would mean less Sunday cricket which is least beneficial to producing Test cricketers.'

Best batting performance: 25 Gloucestershire v Somerset, Bristol 1989

LAST SEASON: BATTING

	I.	N.O.	R.	H.S.	AV.
TEST					
1ST-CLASS	4	0	60	25	15.00
INT					
RAL	3	0	63	39	21.00
NAT.W.					
B & H					

CAREER: BATTING

	I.	N.O.	R.	H.S.	AV.
TEST					
1ST-CLASS	4	0	60	25	15.00
INT					
RAL	4	0	75	39	18.75
NAT.W.	1	0	35	35	35.00
B & H					

87. Which England Test captain was born in Peru?

HOLDING, M. A. Derbyshire

Full Name: Michael Anthony Holding
Role: Right-hand bat, right-arm
fast bowler
Born: 16 February 1954, Kingston,
Jamaica
Nickname: Whispering Death, Mickey
County debut: 1981 (Lancashire),
1983 (Derbyshire)
County cap: 1983 (Derbyshire)
Test debut: 1975–76
No. of Tests: 60
No. of One-Day Internationals: 102
50 wickets in a season: 3
1st-Class 50s scored: 14
1st-Class 5 w. in innings: 39
1st-Class 10 w. in match: 5
One-Day 50s: 7
Place in batting averages: 262nd av. 10.00 (1988 242nd av. 12.90)
Place in bowling averages: 74th av. 30.82 (1988 110th av. 34.45)
Strike rate 1989: 55.32 (career 47.46)
1st-Class catches 1989: 8 (career 125)
Overseas tours: With West Indies to Australia 1975–76, 1979–80, 1981–82,
1984–85, 1986–87; to England 1976, 1980, 1984; to Pakistan 1980–81; to India
1983–84; to New Zealand 1979–80, 1986–87; International team to Pakistan
1981–82
Overseas teams played for: Jamaica 1972–88; Tasmania 1982–83; Canterbury, New Zealand 1987–88

LAST SEASON: BATTING

	I.	N.O.	R.	H.S.	AV.
TEST					
1ST-CLASS	13	4	90	34	10.00
INT					
RAL	11	2	97	33*	10.77
NAT.W.	2	0	38	32	19.00
B & H	3	0	23	12	7.66

CAREER: BATTING

	I.	N.O.	R.	H.S.	AV.
TEST	76	10	910	73	13.78
1ST-CLASS	207	33	2690	80	15.45
INT	42	11	282	64	9.09
RAL	61	6	788	58	14.32
NAT.W.	10	1	108	32	12.00
B & H	17	4	279	69	21.46

LAST SEASON: BOWLING

	O.	M.	R.	W.	AV.
TEST					
1ST-CLASS	258.1	46	863	28	30.82
INT					
RAL	97	9	321	16	20.06
NAT.W.	21	4	49	3	16.33
B & H	39.4	7	117	6	19.50

CAREER: BOWLING

	O.	M.	R.	W.	AV.
TEST	140.5 1925.5	15 395	5898	249	23.68
1ST-CLASS	56 3887	5 953	12335	519	23.76
INT	912.1	97	3034	142	21.36
RAL	543.5	51	2148	100	21.48
NAT.W.	150.4	30	377	26	14.50
B & H	251	39	768	35	21.94

Extras: One of *Wisden*'s Five Cricketers of the Year, 1976. Played for Lancashire in 1981. Moved to Derbyshire in 1983. Has 'deepest voice in county cricket'. Retired from Test cricket in 1987. Retired from Derbyshire at end of 1989 season
Best batting performance: 80 Derbyshire v Yorkshire, Chesterfield 1985
Best bowling performance: 8-92 West Indies v England, The Oval 1976

HOLMES, G. C. — Glamorgan

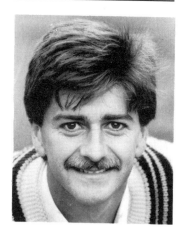

Full Name: Geoffrey Clark Holmes
Role: Right-hand bat, right-arm medium bowler, cover fielder
Born: 16 September 1958, Newcastle-on-Tyne
Height: 5′ 10″ **Weight:** 11st 2lbs
County debut: 1978
County cap: 1985
1000 runs in a season: 3
1st-Class 50s scored: 31
1st-Class 100s scored: 8
1st-Class 5 w. in innings: 2
One-Day 50s: 13
Place in batting averages: 194th av. 18.72 (1988 56th av. 35.67)
Place in bowling averages: — (1988 123rd av. 40.45)
1st-Class catches 1989: 6 (career 79)
Parents: George and Rita
Wife: Christine
Children: Victoria
Family links with cricket: Father played in the Northumberland League
Education: West Denton High School
Qualifications: 6 O-levels, 2 A-levels; Advanced Cricket Coach
Jobs outside cricket: Trainee estimator; has worked as milkman
Cricketing superstitions or habits: 'When things are going well I try to keep my preparations on the next day as similar as possible.'
Overseas teams played for: Villa CC, Antigua 1980–81; Bathurst RUCC, New South Wales 1983–84; Fish Hoek, South Africa 1984–85
Cricketers particularly learnt from: Javed Miandad
Cricketers particularly admired: Geoff Boycott, John Snow
Other sports played: Soccer, snooker

Injuries 1989: Broken thumb resulted in missing first two months of the season

Relaxations: Reading (especially cricket books), TV, sport, 3-card brag

Extras: Scored a century in each innings v Somerset at Taunton, 1988

Opinions on cricket: 'I think we play too much county cricket and would like to see 16 Championship matches per season with no extra one-day cricket. I would like to see one of the one-day competitions to be played as day–night matches, under floodlights.'

Best batting performance: 117 Glamorgan v Gloucestershire, Bristol 1988

Best bowling performance: 5-38 Glamorgan v Essex, Colchester 1988

LAST SEASON: BATTING

	I.	N.O.	R.	H.S.	AV.
TEST					
1ST-CLASS	21	3	337	38	18.72
INT					
RAL	11	1	213	63*	21.30
NAT.W.	2	0	51	26	25.50
B & H					

CAREER: BATTING

	I.	N.O.	R.	H.S.	AV.
TEST					
1ST-CLASS	302	45	6928	117	26.95
INT					
RAL	105	18	2048	73	23.54
NAT.W.	14	0	280	57	20.00
B & H	23	6	543	70	31.94

LAST SEASON: BOWLING

	O.	M.	R.	W.	AV.
TEST					
1ST-CLASS	63.4	10	195	4	48.75
INT					
RAL	28	0	200	4	50.00
NAT.W.	4	0	22	1	22.00
B & H					

CAREER: BOWLING

	O.	M.	R.	W.	AV.
TEST					
1ST-CLASS	1113.2	213	3831	84	45.60
INT					
RAL	453.1	13	2445	96	25.46
NAT.W.	82	15	220	11	20.00
B & H	137.2	14	558	22	25.36

88. Which England Test captain was born in Italy?

HOUSEMAN, I. J.   Yorkshire

Full Name: Ian James Houseman
Role: Right-hand bat, right-arm fast bowler
Born: 12 October 1969, Harrogate, North Yorkshire
Height: 5′ 10″ **Weight:** 11½st
Nickname: Acid
County debut: 1989
Parents: Eric and Jennifer
Marital status: Single
Family links with cricket: Father Eric a Yorkshire committee man; sister Fiona played for Yorkshire Ladies U-19
Education: Harrogate Grammar School, Loughborough University
Qualifications: 10 O-levels, 5 A-levels
Off-season 1989–90: 'At University.'
Cricketers particularly learnt from: Steve Oldham, Doug Padgett, Peter Kippax, Arnie Sidebottom
Cricketers particularly admired: Michael Holding, Fred Trueman, Richard Hadlee, Dennis Lillee
Other sports played: Golf, rugby union
Other sports followed: Rugby league, boxing
Injuries 1989: Torn side muscle – out 3 weeks in August
Relaxations: 'Various types of pop/rock music – mainly oldies 60s/70s – e.g. Van Morrison, The Doors.'
Extras: Young England 1989/ESCA 19's 1986–88, U-15s 1985
Opinions on cricket: 'From a fast bowler's viewpoint I feel the English game would benefit at all levels from playing slightly less cricket on faster, better, uncovered pitches. Although this is obviously difficult to achieve it would hopefully lead to (i) the revival of attacking spin bowling and more overs bowled by spinners (ii) more genuinely fast English bowlers i.e. more chance

LAST SEASON: BATTING

	I.	N.O.	R.	H.S.	AV.
TEST					
1ST-CLASS	1	0	18	18	18.00
INT					
RAL					
NAT.W.					
B & H					

CAREER: BATTING

	I.	N.O.	R.	H.S.	AV.
TEST					
1ST-CLASS	1	0	18	18	18.00
INT					
RAL					
NAT.W.					
B & H					

to recover from niggles and fresher bowlers throughout the season (iii) improved batting techniques (iv) faster over rates and generally more keenly contested cricket (v) increased crowds and revenue?'
Best batting performance: 18 Yorkshire v Sussex, Middlesbrough 1989

HUGHES, D. P.   Lancashire

Full Name: David Paul Hughes
Role: Right-hand bat, slow left-arm bowler
Born: 13 May 1947, Newton-le-Willows
Height: 5′ 11″ **Weight:** 12st
Nickname: Yozzer
County debut: 1967
County cap: 1970
Benefit: 1981
1000 runs in a season: 2
50 wickets in a season: 4
1st-Class 50s scored: 43
1st-Class 100s scored: 8
1st-Class 5 w. in innings: 20
1st-Class 10 w. in match: 2
One-Day 50s: 10
Place in batting averages: 166th av. 21.73 (1988 205th av. 17.40)
Place in bowling averages: 41st av. 25.25
Strike rate 1989: 51.08 (career 65.95)
1st-Class catches 1989: 18 (career 308)

Parents: Both deceased
Wife and date of marriage: Christine, March 1973
Children: James, July 1975
Family links with cricket: Father, Lloyd, a professional with Bolton League club Walkden, before and after Second World War
Education: Newton-le-Willows Grammar School
Qualifications: NCA Coaching Certificate
Overseas tours: With Derrick Robins' XI to South Africa 1972–73; England Counties side to West Indies 1974–75; Lancashire to West Indies 1986–87, 1987–88; Lancashire to Zimbabwe 1988–89
Overseas teams played for: Tasmania while coaching there in 1975–76 and 1976–77
Cricketers particularly learnt from: 'At the start of my career I spoke to all the leading left-arm spin bowlers in the game for help.'

Relaxations: Golf

Extras: Coached in South Africa 1977–78; coached in Tasmania 1978–79 and 1979–80. Gillette Cup 'specialist'. Hit 24 runs off John Mortimer v Gloucestershire in penultimate over in Gillette semi-final in 1972. Hit 26 runs off last over of innings v Northamptonshire in Gillette Final at Lord's, 1976. Bowled 13 consecutive maiden overs v Gloucestershire at Bristol, 1980. Appointed Lancashire captain 1987. One of *Wisden*'s Five Cricketers of the Year, 1987

Best batting performance: 153 Lancashire v Glamorgan, Old Trafford 1983
Best bowling performance: 7-24 Lancashire v Oxford University, Oxford 1970

LAST SEASON: BATTING

	I.	N.O.	R.	H.S.	AV.
TEST					
1ST-CLASS	24	5	413	50*	21.73
INT					
RAL	12	2	146	32	14.60
NAT.W.	3	1	9	6	4.50
B & H	3	1	17	12	8.50

CAREER: BATTING

	I.	N.O.	R.	H.S.	AV.
TEST					
1ST-CLASS	561	99	10071	153	21.79
INT					
RAL	215	48	3005	92	17.99
NAT.W.	40	16	810	71	33.75
B & H	57	14	977	52	22.72

LAST SEASON: BOWLING

	O.	M.	R.	W.	AV.
TEST					
1ST-CLASS	102.1	27	303	12	25.25
INT					
RAL					
NAT.W.					
B & H					

CAREER: BOWLING

	O.	M.	R.	W.	AV.
TEST					
1ST-CLASS	6850.2	2117	18695	626	29.86
INT					
RAL	809.1	62	3568	169	21.11
NAT.W.	300.2	29	1166	44	26.50
B & H	237.2	40	754	29	26.00

89. Which England Test captain was born in Lanarkshire?

HUGHES, S. P.　　　　　　Middlesex

Full Name: Simon Peter Hughes
Role: Right-hand bat, right-arm
fast-medium bowler
Born: 20 December 1959, Kingston,
Surrey
Height: 5' 10" **Weight:** 11st 7lbs
Nickname: Yozzer, Spam, Yule
County debut: 1980
County cap: 1981
50 wickets in a season: 2
1st-Class 50s scored: 1
1st-Class 5 w. in innings: 8
Place in batting averages: 258th av.
10.52 (1988 193rd av. 20.06)
Place in bowling averages: 19th
av. 21.41 (1988 130th av. 46.59)
Strike rate 1989: 47.91 (career 55.73)
1st-Class catches 1989: 4 (career 38)
Parents: Peter and Erica

Marital status: Single
Family links with cricket: Father very keen coach and player who owned indoor cricket school. 'Uncle once hit a ball over the school pavilion!'
Education: Latymer Upper School, Hammersmith; Durham University
Qualifications: 10 O-levels, 4 A-levels, BA General Studies
Jobs outside cricket: Writes regular sports column in local weekly paper, and monthly for *The Cricketer*. Also contributes a weekly cricket column to *The Independent*
Off-season 1989–90: 'At home, getting my fingers into as many pies as possible.'
Overseas tours: Personal overseas spell playing in Sri Lanka 1979; Middlesex CCC tour to Zimbabwe winter 1980; with Overseas XI (captained by J. M. Brearley) to Calcutta (v Indian XI) 1980–81; International Ambassador tour to India 1985; Fred Rumsey's Cricket Festival, Barbados 1987; Bristol University to Sri Lanka 1987–88
Overseas teams played for: Colts CC, Colombo, Sri Lanka, and Sri Lanka Board President's XI; Northern Transvaal 1982–83; Grosvenor-Fynaland 1983–84; Auckland University 1984–85; Fremantle CC (Perth) 1985–86; Sydney University 1987; Grafton CC (Auckland) 1988–89
Cricketers particularly learnt from: Father, Jack Robertson, Mike Brearley, Mike Selvey, Gubby Allen
Cricketers particularly admired: John Emburey, Clive Radley, Malcolm Marshall, Richard Hadlee

252

Other sports played: Soccer (for university), tennis, golf
Injuries 1989: Dislocated left elbow at Abergavenny
Relaxations: Travelling, slapstick films, jazz and blues piano, eating curry, broadcasting and journalism
Extras: Took 4-82 v Kent on Championship debut, plus played in County Championship and Gillette Cup winning sides (Lord's Final) in 1980 in first season. Selected for England U-25 XI v Sri Lanka (Trent Bridge) July 1981. Awarded cap after only 20 matches. Middlesex/Austin Reed Player of the Year 1986. Won a free holiday as Middlesex leading wicket-taker 1986
Opinions on cricket: 'It's about time county cricket was promoted as a present-day sport, and not as a nineteenth-century one.'
Best batting performance: 53 Middlesex v Cambridge University, Cambridge 1988
Best bowling performance: 7-35 Middlesex v Surrey, The Oval 1986

LAST SEASON: BATTING

	I.	N.O.	R.	H.S.	AV.
TEST					
1ST-CLASS	28	7	221	31	10.52
INT					
RAL	7	4	28	8	9.33
NAT.W.	3	2	25	11	25.00
B & H	3	2	20	15*	20.00

CAREER: BATTING

	I.	N.O.	R.	H.S.	AV.
TEST					
1ST-CLASS	170	56	1387	53	12.16
INT					
RAL	34	18	236	22*	14.75
NAT.W.	12	7	45	11	9.00
B & H	13	7	47	15*	7.83

LAST SEASON: BOWLING

	O.	M.	R.	W.	AV.
TEST					
1ST-CLASS	463.2	120	1242	58	21.41
INT					
RAL	104.2	5	495	22	22.50
NAT.W.	53	9	182	10	18.20
B & H	28	1	126	10	12.60

CAREER: BOWLING

	O.	M.	R.	W.	AV.
TEST					
1ST-CLASS	3576.3	711	11240	385	29.19
INT					
RAL	561.3	14	2747	102	26.93
NAT.W.	222.2	28	812	37	21.94
B & H	155.1	14	620	29	21.37

90. How many Welsh-born players had played for England, up to the end of 1989: 7, 10, or 16?

HUMPAGE, G. W.　　　　Warwickshire

Full Name: Geoffrey William
Humpage
Role: Right-hand bat, wicket-
keeper; can also bowl right-arm
medium
Born: 24 April 1954, Birmingham
Height: 5′ 9″ **Weight:** 12st 7lbs
Nickname: Farsley
County debut: 1974
County cap: 1976
Benefit: 1987
No. of One-Day Internationals: 3
1000 runs in a season: 11
1st-Class 50s scored: 92
1st-Class 100s scored: 27
1st-Class 200s scored: 2
One-Day 50s: 35
One-Day 100s: 3
Place in batting averages: 45th
av. 38.55 (1988 216th av. 16.44)
1st-Class catches 1989: 6 (career 641 + 72 stumpings)
Parents: Ernest and Mabel

LAST SEASON: BATTING

	I.	N.O.	R.	H.S.	AV.
TEST					
1ST-CLASS	34	7	1041	183	38.55
INT					
RAL	10	0	111	26	11.10
NAT.W.	5	0	175	65	35.00
B & H	3	0	37	17	12.33

CAREER: BATTING

	I.	N.O.	R.	H.S.	AV.
TEST					
1ST-CLASS	552	72	17470	254	36.39
INT	2	0	11	6	5.50
RAL	181	24	3913	109*	24.92
NAT.W.	36	4	908	77	28.37
B & H	58	7	1346	100*	26.39

LAST SEASON: WICKET KEEPING

	C.	ST.			
TEST					
1ST-CLASS	35	4			
INT					
RAL	6	–			
NAT.W.	5	1			
B & H	5	–			

LAST SEASON: BOWLING

	O.	M.	R.	W.	AV.
TEST					
1ST-CLASS	27	7	56	3	18.66
INT					
RAL					
NAT.W.					
B & H					

CAREER: BOWLING

	O.	M.	R.	W.	AV.
TEST					
1ST-CLASS	162.2	24	518	13	39.84
INT					
RAL	97.5	2	556	15	37.06
NAT.W.					
B & H	27	2	123	3	41.00

CAREER: WICKET KEEPING

	C.	ST.			
TEST					
1ST-CLASS	641	72			
INT	2	–			
RAL	123	20			
NAT.W.	39	8			
B & H	72	3			

Wife and date of marriage: Valerie Anne, 14 September 1983 (2nd marriage)
Children: Philip Andrew Guy, 16 November 1977
Education: Golden Hillock Comprehensive School, Birmingham
Jobs outside cricket: Former police cadet, then police constable, Birmingham City Police. Coach, Scarborough CC, Western Australia 1978–79. Sports executive for Pace Insurance Consultants, Birmingham
Overseas tours: With South African Breweries to South Africa 1981–82
Overseas teams played for: Orange Free State 1981–82
Other sports played: Soccer, squash, tennis, swimming, golf, snooker, table tennis
Relaxations: Reading, listening to E.L.O.
Extras: Good impressionist, particularly of Frankie Howerd. Took part in record Warwickshire and English first-class 4th wicket partnership of 470 v Lancashire at Southport, July 1982, with Kallicharran (230*). Humpage made 254 including 13 sixes. Previous 4th wicket record was 448 for Surrey at The Oval v Yorkshire in 1899, by R. Abel and T. W. Hayward. Joined England Rebels in South Africa in 1982. One of *Wisden*'s Five Cricketers of the Year, 1984
Best batting performance: 254 Warwickshire v Lancashire, Southport 1982
Best bowling performance: 2-13 Warwickshire v Gloucestershire, Edgbaston 1980

HUSSAIN, N.   Essex

Full Name: Nasser Hussain
Role: Right-hand bat
Born: 28 March 1968, Madras, India
Height: 6' 1"
Nickname: Bunny
County debut: 1987
1st-Class 50s scored: 5
1st-Class 100s scored: 4
One-Day 50s: 4
One-day 100s: 1
Place in batting averages: 17th av. 47.14
1st-Class catches 1989: 23 (career 30)
Parents: Jainad and Shireen
Marital status: Single
Family links with cricket: Father played for Madras in Ranji Trophy 1966–67. Uncle played for Combined Indian Universities.

Brother Amel on Hampshire staff in 1983 and 1984. Brother Abbas played for Essex 2nd XI
Education: Forest School; Durham University
Qualifications: 9 O-levels, 3 A-levels; BSc(Hons) in Geology; NCA Cricket Coaching Award
Jobs outside cricket: Worked at Morgan Guaranty Bank during holidays
Off-season 1989–90: Touring with England to India for Nehru Trophy, and to West Indies
Overseas tours: Young England to Sri Lanka 1987; Young England to Australia for Youth World Cup 1988; England to India for Nehru Trophy 1989; England to West Indies 1990
Overseas teams played for: Madras 1986–87
Cricketers particularly learnt from: Father, Ray East, Graham Saville
Cricketers particularly admired: 'They are all in the Essex dressing-room, plus David Gower.'
Other sports played: Golf, football
Other sports followed: Golf, football, American football
Relaxations: Music, TV
Extras: Played for England Schools U-15 for two years (one as captain). Youngest player to play for Essex Schools U-11 at the age of 8 and U-15 at the age of 12. At 15, was considered the best young leg-spin bowler in the country. Does not drink. Played for Ilford CC; Cricket Writers' Society Cricketer of the Year 1989. Selected for England's tour of West Indies 1990
Opinions on cricket: 'Better pitches, please!'
Best batting performance: 165* Essex v Leicestershire, Chelmsford 1988

LAST SEASON: BATTING

	I.	N.O.	R.	H.S.	AV.
TEST					
1ST-CLASS	24	3	990	141	47.14
INT					
RAL	7	2	163	63*	32.60
NAT.W.	1	0	24	24	24.00
B & H	5	0	237	118	47.40

CAREER: BATTING

	I.	N.O.	R.	H.S.	AV.
TEST					
1ST-CLASS	40	6	1508	165*	44.35
INT					
RAL	17	3	362	63*	25.85
NAT.W.	1	0	24	24	24.00
B & H	12	2	450	118	45.00

HUTCHINSON, I. J. F.
Middlesex

Full Name: Ian James Frederick Hutchinson

Role: Right-hand opening bat, right-arm medium pace bowler

Born: 31 October 1964, Welshpool

Height: 6′ **Weight:** 13st 7lbs

Nickname: Hutch, Bradders

County debut: 1987

1st-Class 100s: 2

1st-Class 200s: 1

Place in batting averages: 16th av. 48.73

1st-Class catches 1989: 14 (career 14)

Parents: Ann and Michael

Wife and date of marriage: Louise, 19 September 1987

Family links with cricket: Grandfather played for Leicestershire 2nd XI. Father played club cricket

Education: Kingsland Grange Preparatory School; Shrewsbury School

Qualifications: 10 O-levels, 2 A-levels, cricket coach part 1

Jobs outside cricket: Financial adviser. Coach of Eton fives at eight London public schools

Off-season 1989–90: Working in London as a financial adviser

Cricketing superstitions or habits: Left pad on first

Overseas tours: La Manga with Middlesex 1985

Overseas teams played for: Bathurst Rugby and Cricket Club, Australia 1984

Cricketers particularly learnt from: Wilf Slack, Roland Butcher, Clive Radley

Cricketers particularly admired: Geoff Boycott, Barry Richards

Other sports played: Eton fives, tennis

Other sports followed: 'Any apart from horses!'

Relaxations: 'At home with Louise. Eating out. Gardening. Studying new products from work.'

LAST SEASON: BATTING

	I.	N.O.	R.	H.S.	AV.
TEST					
1ST-CLASS	18	3	731	201*	48.73
INT					
RAL	6	0	38	13	6.33
NAT.W.	1	0	1	1	1.00
B & H					

CAREER: BATTING

	I.	N.O.	R.	H.S.	AV.
TEST					
1ST-CLASS	22	3	779	201*	41.00
INT					
RAL	7	1	60	22*	10.00
NAT.W.	1	0	1	1	1.00
B & H					

257

Extras: Played for Shropshire 1984–85. On MCC groundstaff 1984–86. Was substitute fielder for England v New Zealand at Lord's 1986
Opinions on cricket: 'None – apart from the fact that I don't see how sides (especially Middlesex) can bowl so slowly per hour. Surely the crowds won't come back to watch 13 overs per hour.'
Best batting performance: 201* Middlesex v Oxford University, Oxford 1989

IBADULLA, K. B.   Gloucestershire

Full Name: Kassem Ben Ibadulla
Role: Right-hand bat, off-break bowler
Born: 13 October 1964, Birmingham
Height: 5′ 6″ **Weight:** 11st 5lbs
Nickname: Kass
County debut: 1987
1st-Class 50s scored: 2
1st-Class 100s scored: 1
1st-Class 5 w. in innings: 1
1st-Class catches 1989: 0 (career 9)
Parents: Khalid and Gertrude
Marital status: Single
Family links with cricket: Father Khalid 'Billy' Ibadulla played for Warwickshire and Pakistan
Education: Springfield Primary School, Birmingham; St Dunstan's Preparatory School, Catford; Otago Boys High School, New Zealand

LAST SEASON: BATTING

	I.	N.O.	R.	H.S.	AV.
TEST					
1ST-CLASS					
INT					
RAL	2	2	17	9*	–
NAT.W.					
B & H	1	0	0	0	0.00

CAREER: BATTING

	I.	N.O.	R.	H.S.	AV.
TEST					
1ST-CLASS	32	8	579	107	24.12
INT					
RAL	3	2	29	12	29.00
NAT.W.					
B & H	1	0	0	0	0.00

LAST SEASON: BOWLING

	O.	M.	R.	W.	AV.
TEST					
1ST-CLASS					
INT					
RAL	4	1	14	0	–
NAT.W.					
B & H	4	0	22	0	–

CAREER: BOWLING

	O.	M.	R.	W.	AV.
TEST					
1ST-CLASS	239.4	54	763	19	40.15
INT					
RAL	4	1	14	0	–
NAT.W.					
B & H	4	0	22	0	–

Qualifications: School Certificate and OE New Zealand. Qualified coach
Off-season 1989–90: Playing in New Zealand
Overseas teams played for: Otago, New Zealand 1981, 1990
Cricketers particularly learnt from: Father and all at Gloucester
Cricketers particularly admired: Geoff Boycott
Other sports played: Billiards
Relaxations: Fishing, sleeping, music
Extras: Scored maiden first-class hundred for Otago in New Zealand. Played for Cheshire in 1986
Best batting performance: 107 Otago v Central Districts, New Plymouth 1987–88
Best bowling performance: 5-22 Otago v Canterbury, Invercargill 1982–83

IGGLESDEN, A. P. Kent

Full Name: Alan Paul Igglesden
Role: Right-hand bat, right-arm fast bowler, outfielder
Born: 8 October 1964, Farnborough, Kent
Height: 6′ 6″ **Weight:** 14st 3lbs
Nickname: Iggy, Norman
County debut: 1986
Test debut: 1989
No. of Tests: 1
50 wickets in a season: 2
1st-Class 5 w. in innings: 9
1st-Class 10 w. in match: 2
Place in bowling averages: 90th av. 34.87 (1988 22nd av. 21.75)

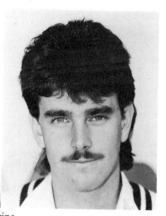

Strike rate 1989: 62.66 (career 48.71)
1st-Class catches 1989: 5 (career 14)
Parents: Alan Trevor and Gillian Catharine
Wife and date of marriage: Hilary Moira, 20 January 1990
Family links with cricket: Brother Kevin plays for Holmesdale in the Kent League
Education: St Mary's Primary School, Westerham; Hosey School, Westerham; Churchill Secondary School, Westerham
Qualifications: 9 CSEs, Coaching Certificate
Jobs outside cricket: 'Since I left school I have had a couple of jobs to fit in with my cricket at Kent.'
Off-season 1989–90: Touring Zimbabwe with England A. Watching Crystal Palace

Cricketing superstitions or habits: 'Like to be at the ground early. Try to keep to the same match build-up if things are going well. Try to keep pre-match practice. Always leave the dressing-room after the wicket-keeper.'

Overseas tours: With England to Zimbabwe 1990

Overseas teams played for: Avendale CC 1985–89; Western Province 1987–88, 1988–89

Cricketers particularly learnt from: Terry Alderman, Bob Woolmer, Colin Page, Stuart Leary, Colin Tomlin, Stan Topliss

Cricketers particularly admired: Terry Alderman, Dennis Lillee, Ian Botham, Imran Khan, Chris Penn, Mark Benson, Roy Pienaar

Other sports played: Golf, football, snooker, darts

Other sports followed: Football – 'go to watch Crystal Palace with the lads whenever I can.'

Relaxations: Listening to music, sleeping, watching sport on TV (except horse-racing), crosswords

Extras: 'I didn't play any schools representative cricket.'

Opinions on cricket: 'We play far too much cricket.'

Best batting performance: 41 Kent v Surrey, Canterbury 1988

Best bowling performance: 6-34 Kent v Surrey, Canterbury 1988

LAST SEASON: BATTING

	I.	N.O.	R.	H.S.	AV.
TEST	1	1	2	2*	–
1ST-CLASS	21	8	115	32*	8.84
INT					
RAL	5	3	2	1*	1.00
NAT.W.	1	0	2	2	2.00
B & H	2	1	3	2*	3.00

CAREER: BATTING

	I.	N.O.	R.	H.S.	AV.
TEST	1	1	2	2*	–
1ST-CLASS	55	16	378	41	9.69
INT					
RAL	8	4	27	13*	6.75
NAT.W.	1	0	2	2	2.00
B & H	3	2	8	5*	8.00

LAST SEASON: BOWLING

	O.	M.	R.	W.	AV.
TEST	37	3	146	3	48.66
1ST-CLASS	547.5	98	1807	53	34.09
INT					
RAL	97	8	347	23	15.08
NAT.W.	17	1	67	2	33.50
B & H	62	6	243	9	27.00

CAREER: BOWLING

	O.	M.	R.	W.	AV.
TEST	37	3	146	3	48.66
1ST-CLASS	1481.1	254	4900	184	26.63
INT					
RAL	150.5	13	564	32	17.62
NAT.W.	36	6	127	6	21.16
B & H	85	8	335	11	30.45

ILLINGWORTH, R. K.　Worcestershire

Full Name: Richard Keith Illingworth
Role: Right-hand bat, slow
left-arm bowler
Born: 23 August 1963, Bradford
Height: 6' **Weight:** 13st 7lbs
Nickname: Lucy, Harry
County debut: 1982
County cap: 1986
50 wickets in a season: 2
1st-Class 50s scored: 6
1st-Class 100s scored: 1
1st-Class 5 w. in innings: 14
1st-Class 10 w. in match: 4
Place in batting averages: 230th
av. 13.87 (1988 163rd av. 22.44)
Place in bowling averages: 22nd
av. 21.78 (1988 24th av. 21.96)
Strike rate 1989: 65.21 (career 77.75)
1st-Class catches 1989: 11 (career 80)
Parents: Keith and Margaret
Wife and date of marriage: Anne, 20 September 1985
Children: Miles Jonathan, 28 August 1987, Thomas Lynden, 20 April 1989
Family links with cricket: Father plays Bradford League cricket
Education: Wrose Brow Middle; Salts Grammar School ('same school as the
late Jim Laker')
Qualifications: 6 O-levels, senior coaching award holder
Jobs outside cricket: Civil servant; working for Golding Pipework Services
Off-season 1989–90: Touring Zimbabwe with England A
Overseas tours: Denmark Youth Tournament NAYC 1981; Whitbread scholarship playing for Colts CC, Brisbane 1982–83; Wisden Cricket XI, Barbados
1983; University of St Heliers, Auckland, New Zealand 1986–87, 1987–88;
Zingari CC, Pietermaritzburg, and Natal 1988–89; England A to Zimbabwe
1989–90
Cricketers particularly learnt from: Father
Other sports played: Golf, football
Other sports followed: Football (follows Leeds United, Bradford City and
Bradford Northern)
Injuries 1989: 'Sore knees throughout season, but did not miss a game
through injury.'
Relaxations: 'Listening to music. Reading cricket autobiographies. DIY
around the house and garden, and playing with Miles and Thomas.'
Extras: Took 11 for 108 on South African first-class debut for Natal B v

Boland 1988. Scored 120 not out as a night-watchman for Worcestershire v Warwickshire 1988

Opinions on cricket: 'Counties should be limited to one overseas player on the staff in any one year.'

Best batting performance: 120* Worcestershire v Warwickshire, Worcester 1987

Best bowling performance: 7-50 Worcestershire v Oxford University, Oxford 1985

LAST SEASON: BATTING

	I.	N.O.	R.	H.S.	AV.
TEST					
1ST-CLASS	26	2	333	71	13.87
INT					
RAL	4	2	49	22	24.50
NAT.W.	1	0	1	1	1.00
B & H	3	2	19	11	19.00

CAREER: BATTING

	I.	N.O.	R.	H.S.	AV.
TEST					
1ST-CLASS	185	48	2548	120*	18.59
INT					
RAL	39	20	180	22	9.47
NAT.W.	7	2	48	22	9.60
B & H	11	7	78	17*	19.50

LAST SEASON: BOWLING

	O.	M.	R.	W.	AV.
TEST					
1ST-CLASS	445.4	179	893	41	21.78
INT					
RAL	88.4	5	374	19	19.68
NAT.W.	47	4	165	6	27.50
B & H	22	3	76	1	76.00

CAREER: BOWLING

	O.	M.	R.	W.	AV.
TEST					
1ST-CLASS	4535.5	1356	11329	350	32.36
INT					
RAL	473.4	25	2178	99	22.00
NAT.W.	150.1	21	460	15	30.66
B & H	165	21	598	20	29.90

ILOTT, M. C. Essex

Full Name: Mark Christopher Ilott
Role: Left-hand bat, left-arm fast bowler
Born: 27 August 1970, Watford
Height: 6′ 2″ **Weight:** 12st
Nickname: Ramble, Muke, Bambi
County debut: 1988
Place in bowling averages: 95th av. 36.50
Strike rate 1989: 65.40 (career 72.92)
1st-Class catches 1989: 1 (career 1)
Parents: John and Glenys
Marital status: Single
Family links with cricket: Father long-time President of Watford Town CC. Brother is vice-captain of Watford CC, and represents Hertfordshire CCC. Grandfather played for Ruislip Manor for many years

Education: Francis Combe School

Qualifications: 8 O-levels, 2 A/O-levels, 2 A-levels

Jobs outside cricket: Storeman for R. S. Kennedys, civil and electrical engineers

Off-season 1989–90: Playing in Adelaide, Australia

Overseas teams played for: East Torrens District CC in Adelaide, Australia 1989–90

Cricketers particularly learnt from: John Lever, Ray East, Nick King, Dennis Lillee

Cricketers particularly admired: John Lever, Graham Gooch, Malcolm Marshall, Richard Hadlee

Other sports played: 'None competitively but all for fun!'

Other sports followed: Tennis, football, American football

Relaxations: Reading, listening to music

Opinions on cricket: 'Lbw should be given if no shot is played and ball pitches outside leg stump and would have hit the wicket.'

Best batting performance: 13* Essex v Surrey, Oval 1989

Best bowling performance: 4-26 Essex v Cambridge University, Cambridge 1989

LAST SEASON: BATTING

	I.	N.O.	R.	H.S.	AV.
TEST					
1ST-CLASS	4	4	22	13*	–
INT					
RAL	1	0	4	4	4.00
NAT.W.					
B & H					

CAREER: BATTING

	I.	N.O.	R.	H.S.	AV.
TEST					
1ST-CLASS	5	4	28	13*	28.00
INT					
RAL	1	0	4	4	4.00
NAT.W.					
B & H					

LAST SEASON: BOWLING

	O.	M.	R.	W.	AV.
TEST					
1ST-CLASS	109	22	365	10	36.50
INT					
RAL	8	0	27	0	–
NAT.W.					
B & H					

CAREER: BOWLING

	O.	M.	R.	W.	AV.
TEST					
1ST-CLASS	158	37	476	13	36.61
INT					
RAL	8	0	27	0	–
NAT.W.					
B & H					

JAMES, K. D.   Hampshire

Full Name: Kevan David James
Role: Left-hand bat, left-arm
fast-medium bowler, fields
'anywhere but short leg'
Born: 18 March 1961, Lambeth,
South London
Height: 6' ½" **Weight:** 12st 6lbs
Nickname: Jambo, Jaimo
County debut: 1980 (Middlesex),
1985 (Hampshire)
County cap: 1989
1st-Class 50s scored: 9
1st-Class 100s scored: 4
1st-Class 5 w. in innings: 7
One-Day 50s: 2
Place in batting averages: 109th

av. 28.88 (1988 220th av.16.00)
Place in bowling averages: 84th
av. 33.02 (1988 23rd av. 21.80)
Strike rate 1989: 67.37 (career 61.94)
1st-Class catches 1989: 6 (career 28)
Parents: David and Helen
Wife and date of marriage: Debbie, October 1987
Family links with cricket: Late father played club cricket in North London
Education: Edmonton County High School
Qualifications: 5 O-levels; qualified coach
Overseas tours: Young England tour of Australia 1978–79; Young England
tour of West Indies 1979–80

LAST SEASON: BATTING

	I.	N.O.	R.	H.S.	AV.
TEST					
1ST-CLASS	37	3	982	162	28.88
INT					
RAL	12	5	243	66	34.71
NAT.W.	3	0	70	42	23.33
B & H	3	1	94	45	47.00

CAREER: BATTING

	I.	N.O.	R.	H.S.	AV.
TEST					
1ST-CLASS	121	23	2802	162	28.59
INT					
RAL	44	18	708	66	27.23
NAT.W.	8	2	132	42	22.00
B & H	15	2	252	45	19.38

LAST SEASON: BOWLING

	O.	M.	R.	W.	AV.
TEST					
1ST-CLASS	415.3	91	1222	37	33.02
INT					
RAL	111.3	11	379	17	22.29
NAT.W.	42	6	167	6	27.83
B & H	35.2	5	149	3	49.66

CAREER: BOWLING

	O.	M.	R.	W.	AV.
TEST					
1ST-CLASS	1682.5	395	5019	163	30.79
INT					
RAL	503.1	29	2109	63	33.47
NAT.W.	113.4	12	472	16	29.50
B & H	199.1	21	752	22	34.18

Overseas teams played for: Canterbury Province U-23, New Zealand 1980; Sydenham CC, Christchurch, New Zealand 1980–81; Wellington, New Zealand 1982–83, 1984–85; Eden-Roskill, Auckland 1987–88
Cricketers particularly learnt from: Don Bennett (Middlesex coach)
Other sports played: Soccer
Other sports followed: Watches American football, follows Spurs
Relaxations: DIY and making money. Wrote two columns, one in *The Club Cricketer*, the other in a local Southampton paper. 'It would be nice just to have time to relax.'
Extras: Released by Middlesex at end of 1984 season and joined Hampshire
Best batting performance: 162 Hampshire v Glamorgan, Cardiff 1989
Best bowling performance: 6-22 Hampshire v Australia, Southampton 1985

JAMES, S. P. Glamorgan

Full Name: Stephen Peter James
Role: Right-hand bat
Born: 7 September 1967, Lydney
Height: 6' **Weight:** 12st
Nickname: Jamer, Douggie, Pedro, Sid
County debut: 1985
1st-Class 50s scored: 3
1st-Class 100s scored: 3
One-Day 50s: 1
Place in batting averages: 66th av. 35.46
1st-Class catches 1989: 9 (career 13)
Parents: Peter and Margaret
Marital status: Single
Family links with cricket: Father played for Gloucestershire 2nd XI
Education: Monmouth School; University College, Swansea; Cambridge University
Qualifications: BA(Hons) Classics
Off-season 1989–90: Finishing Land Economy degree at Cambridge
Cricketing superstitions or habits: 'Always put left pad on first. Never change clothing when I've done well.'
Overseas tours: Welsh Schools (captain) to Barbados 1984. Monmouth School (captain) to Sri Lanka 1985

Cricketers particularly learnt from: 'Sonny' Avery, Graham 'Budgie' Burgess, Alan Jones, Graham Saville

Cricketers particularly admired: Geoff Boycott

Other sports played: Rugby (for Lydney, Gloucestershire and Cambridge University), squash

Other sports followed: All sports

Relaxations: Music, films

Extras: Scored maiden century in only second first-class game. Made debut in 1985 v Sussex but did not get onto field. Played for Combined Universities in Benson & Hedges Cup 1989 but was unable to play in quarter-final v Somerset because of an exam. Cambridge Blue

Best batting performance: 151* Cambridge University v Warwickshire, Cambridge 1989

LAST SEASON: BATTING

	I.	N.O.	R.	H.S.	AV.
TEST					
1ST-CLASS	27	1	922	151*	35.46
INT					
RAL	3	0	30	13	10.00
NAT.W.					
B & H	4	0	105	65	26.25

CAREER: BATTING

	I.	N.O.	R.	H.S.	AV.
TEST					
1ST-CLASS	40	2	1168	151*	30.73
INT					
RAL	3	0	30	13	10.00
NAT.W.					
B & H	4	0	105	65	26.25

JARVIS, K. B. S.   Gloucestershire

Full Name: Kevin Bertram Sidney Jarvis

Role: Right-hand bat, right-arm fast-medium bowler

Born: 23 April 1953, Dartford, Kent

Height: 6' 3" **Weight:** 13st

Nickname: Jarvo, Ferret, KJ

County debut: 1975 (Kent), 1988 (Gloucestershire)

County cap: 1977 (Kent)

Benefit: 1987 (£48,485)

50 wickets in a season: 7

1st-Class 5 w. in innings: 20

1st-Class 10 w. in match: 3

Place in bowling averages: 37th av. 25.78

Strike rate 1989: 49.77 (career 56.25)

1st-Class catches 1989: 3 (career 59)

Parents: Herbert John and Margaret Elsie
Wife and date of marriage: Margaret Anne, 16 September 1978
Children: Simon Martin, 16 April 1985; Laura Emily, 6 January 1988
Family links with cricket: Son very keen; father played club cricket; Simon Hinks is a distant relative
Education: Springhead School, Northfleet, Kent; Thames Polytechnic
Qualifications: 6 O-levels, 3 A-levels, NCA coach, ISMA, MAMSA
Jobs outside cricket: Accountancy, insurance, clerical
Cricketing superstitions or habits: 'Take guard at least one foot outside the off-stump, to allow for natural tendency to end up some distance outside leg.'
Overseas tours: Derrick Robins' XI to Far East 1977; International XI to Jamaica 1982
Overseas teams played for: Played and coached for South Melbourne, 1979 and 1981; Tooronga 1978
Cricketers particularly learnt from: Derek Underwood, Bob Woolmer
Cricketers particularly admired: Richard Hadlee, Dennis Lillee
Other sports played: Squash, badminton, tennis, football, hockey, darts
Other sports followed: 'Watch everything except synchronised swimming.'
Extras: Released by Kent at end of 1987 season. Joined Gloucestershire on a two-year contract in 1988. 'Surpassed my previous highest score in 1989 – an achievement thought by many to be the equivalent of running a three-minute mile.'
Opinions on cricket: 'There are too many people with too many opinions on cricket.'
Best batting performance: 32 Gloucestershire v Hampshire, Portsmouth 1989
Best bowling performance: 8-97 Kent v Worcestershire, Worcester 1978

LAST SEASON: BATTING

	I.	N.O.	R.	H.S.	AV.
TEST					
1ST-CLASS	14	3	65	32	5.90
INT					
RAL	4	0	19	11	4.75
NAT.W.	–	–	–	–	–
B & H					

CAREER: BATTING

	I.	N.O.	R.	H.S.	AV.
TEST					
1ST-CLASS	197	85	402	32	3.58
INT					
RAL	53	30	78	11	3.39
NAT.W.	11	5	16	5*	2.66
B & H	24	15	16	4*	1.77

LAST SEASON: BOWLING

	O.	M.	R.	W.	AV.
TEST					
1ST-CLASS	298.4	69	928	36	25.78
INT					
RAL	90.4	9	430	9	47.77
NAT.W.	22.4	2	57	8	7.12
B & H					

CAREER: BOWLING

	O.	M.	R.	W.	AV.
TEST					
1ST-CLASS	6290.4	1378	19856	671	29.59
INT					
RAL	1170.3	97	4956	203	24.41
NAT.W.	259.3	31	931	45	20.68
B & H	532.2	78	1885	86	21.91

JARVIS, P. W. Yorkshire

Full Name: Paul William Jarvis
Role: Right-hand bat, right-arm
fast-medium bowler
Born: 29 June 1965, Redcar,
North Yorkshire
Height: 5′ 11″ **Weight:** 12st 5lbs
Nickname: Jarv, Beaver, Gnasher
County debut: 1981
County cap: 1986
Test debut: 1987–88
No. of Tests: 6
No. of One-Day Internationals: 5
50 wickets in a season: 3
1st-Class 50s scored: 1
1st-Class 5 w. in innings: 17
1st-Class 10 w. in match: 3
Place in batting averages: 249th
av. 11.80
Place in bowling averages: 33rd
av. 25.31 (1988 6th av. 17.59)
Strike rate 1989: 48.75 (career 49.99)
1st-Class catches 1989: 2 (career 32)
Parents: Malcolm and Marjorie
Wife: Wendy
Children: Alexander Michael, 13 July 1989
Family links with cricket: Father has played league cricket for 30 years with Marske CC; brother Andrew played for English Schools U-15s, and also had trials for Northamptonshire and Derbyshire
Education: Bydales Comprehensive School, Marske
Qualifications: 4 O-levels
Jobs outside cricket: Trainee groundsman, Marske Cricket Club
Off-season 1989–90: Touring South Africa with unofficial English team
Cricketing superstitions or habits: The number 111
Overseas tours: Channel Islands April 1986 and Ireland June 1986 with Yorkshire; St Lucia and Barbados, 1987, with Yorkshire; with England to World Cup, Pakistan, Australia and New Zealand 1987–88
Overseas teams played for: Mosman Middle Harbour CC, Sydney 1984–85; Avendale CC, Cape Town 1985–86
Cricketers particularly learnt from: Maurice Hill, Phil Carrick, Geoff Boycott, Albert Padmore
Cricketers particularly admired: Dennis Lillee, Richard Hadlee
Other sports played: Football, running and fitness, golf, squash

Other sports followed: Most sports

Relaxations: Fishing, music, golf

Extras: Youngest player ever to play for Yorkshire 1st XI in John Player League and County Championship (16 years, 2 months, 1 day in John Player League; 16 years, 2 months, 13 days for County Championship). Youngest player to do hat-trick in JPL and Championship. Played for Young England v West Indies 1982 and Australia 1983. Selected for TCCB XI v New Zealand 1986

Opinions on cricket: 'Only people actually born in England should be permitted to play for England. County cricket should be divided into two divisions, 10 in either division. The tables would be chosen on merit and run on a similar basis to the football league, the additional teams would come from either the minor counties, e.g. Northumberland, or counties having two teams in the league. Three-day cricket would be played between the 10 teams in each league – a total of 18 matches as you would play each other home and away. Two top (2nd division) and two bottom (1st division) would be promoted and relegated each season. The B & H Cup and NWT would be run exactly as it is now and the RAL would be played in its divisions – the two winners and runners up in each division (4 teams) would then play off for the overall champions cup – the winners of each division would also win their respective (A division and B division) league cups. This system would make the cricket much more interesting for more teams – nearly every team rather than just a few at the end of a season will have something to play for – encouraging better cricket to play and making it more interesting for the spectators to follow. Four-day cricket should be scrapped.' Regarding the 1989–90 tour of South Africa, and his responsibilities to his wife, son, and £66,500 mortgage: 'I would have to play in every Test match at home and away for the next six years to earn as much as £80,000 after tax. As a fast bowler with a history of injuries, I do not think that is possible. I have had back and circulation problems, and I could be injured and out of the game for a long spell and no-one would care.'

LAST SEASON: BATTING

	I.	N.O.	R.	H.S.	AV.
TEST	3	0	33	22	11.00
1ST-CLASS	22	5	203	59*	11.94
INT					
RAL	7	4	37	15*	12.33
NAT.W.	2	1	21	15*	21.00
B & H	2	0	4	4	2.00

CAREER: BATTING

	I.	N.O.	R.	H.S.	AV.
TEST	9	2	98	29*	14.00
1ST-CLASS	114	37	1050	59*	13.63
INT	2	1	5	5*	5.00
RAL	31	16	157	29*	10.46
NAT.W.	6	2	56	16	14.00
B & H	7	1	44	20	7.33

LAST SEASON: BOWLING

	O.	M.	R.	W.	AV.
TEST	69.2	4	290	2	145.00
1ST-CLASS	548.1	128	1634	74	22.08
INT					
RAL	99.2	12	395	17	23.23
NAT.W.	24	1	98	1	98.00
B & H	33	9	84	8	10.50

CAREER: BOWLING

	O.	M.	R.	W.	AV.
TEST	224.3	41	708	14	50.57
1ST-CLASS	2767	566	8827	345	25.58
INT	47.5	4	187	6	31.16
RAL	475.1	36	2079	98	21.21
NAT.W.	128.5	15	462	16	28.87
B & H	186	35	590	34	17.35

Best batting performance: 59* Yorkshire v Nottinghamshire, Trent Bridge 1989
Best bowling performance: 7-55 Yorkshire v Surrey, Leeds 1986

JEAN-JACQUES, M. Derbyshire

Full Name: Martin Jean-Jacques
Role: Right-hand bat, right-arm fast-medium pace bowler
Born: 2 August 1960, Soufriere, St Mark, Dominica
Height: 5′ 11″ **Weight:** 12st 7lbs
Nickname: JJ
County debut: 1986
1st-Class 50s scored: 1
1st-Class 5 w. in innings: 1
1st-Class 10 w. in match: 1
1st-Class catches 1989: 1 (career 10)
Education: Scotts Head Primary, Dominica; Aylestone High School, Kensal Green, London
Qualifications: Approved electrician
Jobs outside cricket: Electrician
Off-season 1989–90: 'Back on a building site, as an electrician.'
Overseas tours: With the Troubadors to Argentina and Brazil 1987; Buckinghamshire CCC to Australia 1989

LAST SEASON: BATTING

	I.	N.O.	R.	H.S.	AV.
TEST					
1ST-CLASS	8	1	34	16*	4.85
INT					
RAL	–	–	–	–	–
NAT.W.					
B & H					

CAREER: BATTING

	I.	N.O.	R.	H.S.	AV.
TEST					
1ST-CLASS	44	8	439	73	12.19
INT					
RAL	12	1	69	15	6.27
NAT.W.	5	3	28	16	14.00
B & H	2	1	4	2*	4.00

LAST SEASON: BOWLING

	O.	M.	R.	W.	AV.
TEST					
1ST-CLASS	90.2	11	359	15	23.93
INT					
RAL	1	0	7	0	–
NAT.W.					
B & H					

CAREER: BOWLING

	O.	M.	R.	W.	AV.
TEST					
1ST-CLASS	675.3	102	2354	73	32.24
INT					
RAL	131	2	716	20	35.80
NAT.W.	74	7	310	12	25.83
B & H	30	0	164	5	32.80

Cricketers particularly learnt from: Michael Holding
Cricketers particularly admired: Michael Holding
Other sports followed: Football
Relaxations: Listening to music – reggae and soul
Extras: Played Minor Counties cricket for Buckinghamshire since 1983. Formerly played for Shepherds Bush CC. On debut for Derbyshire (v Yorkshire) put on 132 with A. Hill for the 10th wicket – a new Derbyshire record
Best batting performance: 73 Derbyshire v Yorkshire, Sheffield 1986
Best bowling performance: 8-77 Derbyshire v Kent, Derby 1986

JEFFERIES, S. T. Hampshire

Full Name: Stephen Thomas Jefferies
Role: Left-hand bat, left-arm fast-medium bowler
Born: 8 December 1959, Cape Town, South Africa
Nickname: Jeffo
County debut: 1982 (Derbyshire), 1983 (Lancashire), 1988 (Hampshire)
1st-Class 50s scored: 14
1st-Class 5 w. in innings: 16
1st-Class 10 w. in match: 3
Place in batting averages: 69th av. 35.00 (1988 72nd av. 33.00)
Place in bowling averages: 122nd av. 58.50 (1988 114th av. 35.76)
Strike rate 1989: 99.83 (career 58.27)
1st-Class catches 1989: 7 (career 53)
Education: Plumstead High School
Jobs outside cricket: Physical training instructor with South African Navy
Off-season 1989–90: Playing in South Africa
Overseas teams played for: Western Province, South Africa 1978–89
Extras: Professional with Crompton in Central Lancashire League. Played for South African Schools XI in 1978. With Derbyshire in 1982. Left Lancashire staff 1985. Man of the Match B & H Final 1988. Released by Hampshire at the end of 1989 season
Best batting performance: 93 Lancashire v Sussex, Old Trafford 1985

Best bowling performance: 10-59 Western Province v Orange Free State, Cape Town 1987–88

LAST SEASON: BATTING

	I.	N.O.	R.	H.S.	AV.
TEST					
1ST-CLASS	13	6	245	42	35.00
INT					
RAL	6	2	96	26	24.00
NAT.W.					
B & H	3	1	14	7	7.00

LAST SEASON: BOWLING

	O.	M.	R.	W.	AV.
TEST					
1ST-CLASS	199.4	30	702	12	58.50
INT					
RAL	53.4	4	284	12	23.66
NAT.W.					
B & H	38.1	0	171	5	34.20

CAREER: BATTING

	I.	N.O.	R.	H.S.	AV.
TEST					
1ST-CLASS	174	36	3629	93	26.29
INT					
RAL	30	9	592	39	28.19
NAT.W.	6	1	106	39	21.20
B & H	8	1	95	39	13.57

CAREER: BOWLING

	O.	M.	R.	W.	AV.
TEST					
1ST-CLASS	4205.3	905	12232	433	28.24
INT					
RAL	247.4	20	1103	44	25.06
NAT.W.	69.5	3	292	11	26.54
B & H	196.1	22	709	35	20.25

JESTY, T. E.   Lancashire

Full Name: Trevor Edward Jesty
Role: Right-hand bat, right-arm medium bowler
Born: 2 June 1948, Gosport, Hampshire
Height: 5′ 9″ **Weight:** 11st 10lbs
Nickname: Jets
County debut: 1966 (Hampshire), 1985 (Surrey), 1988 (Lancashire)
County cap: 1971 (Hampshire), 1985 (Surrey)
Benefit: 1982
No. of One-Day Internationals: 10
1000 runs in a season: 10
50 wickets in a season: 2
1st-Class 50s scored: 103
1st-Class 100s scored: 32
1st-Class 200s scored: 2
1st-Class 5 w. in innings: 19
One-Day 50s: 43
One-Day 100s: 7
Place in batting averages: 52nd av. 36.78 (1988 105th av. 28.87)
1st-Class catches 1989: 6 (career 259 + 1 stumping)

Parents: Aubrey Edward and Sophia

Wife and date of marriage: Jacqueline, 12 September 1970

Children: Graeme Barry, 27 September 1972; Lorna Samantha, 7 November 1976

Family links with cricket: Brother, Aubrey Jesty, wicket-keeper and left-hand bat, could have joined Hampshire staff, but decided to continue with his apprenticeship

Education: Privet County Secondary Modern, Gosport

Jobs outside cricket: Representative for wine company

Overseas tours: International XI to West Indies 1982–83; Lancashire to West Indies 1987–88; Lancashire to Zimbabwe 1988–89

Overseas teams played for: Border in 1973–74, and Griqualand West in 1974–75 and 1975–76 in the Currie Cup Competition, South Africa; Canterbury, New Zealand 1979–80

Cricketers particularly learnt from: Barry Richards

Other sports played: Soccer, golf

Relaxations: Watching soccer, gardening

Extras: Took him 10 years to score maiden first-class century. Missed most of 1980 season through injury. Made vice-captain of Hampshire in 1981. Considered to be most unlucky not to be chosen for England tour of Australia 1982–83 after brilliant 1982 season, then was called in as a replacement. One of *Wisden*'s Five Cricketers of the Year, 1982. Left Hampshire at end of 1984 when not appointed captain. Took over captaincy of Surrey in 1985. Replaced as captain in 1986. Released by Surrey at end of 1987 season. Joined Lancashire 1988

Best batting performance: 248 Hampshire v Cambridge University, Cambridge 1984

Best bowling performance: 7-75 Hampshire v Worcestershire, Southampton 1976

LAST SEASON: BATTING

	I.	N.O.	R.	H.S.	AV.
TEST					
1ST-CLASS	35	7	1030	93*	36.78
INT					
RAL	9	1	171	51	21.37
NAT.W.	2	0	19	13	9.50
B & H	4	1	77	34	25.66

CAREER: BATTING

	I.	N.O.	R.	H.S.	AV.
TEST					
1ST-CLASS	751	99	21005	248	32.21
INT	10	4	127	52*	21.16
RAL	259	36	5554	166*	24.90
NAT.W.	35	2	976	118	29.57
B & H	71	11	2150	105	35.83

LAST SEASON: BOWLING

	O.	M.	R.	W.	AV.
TEST					
1ST-CLASS	12.5	2	43	0	–
INT					
RAL	3	0	31	0	–
NAT.W.					
B & H	5	2	7	0	–

CAREER: BOWLING

	O.	M.	R.	W.	AV.
TEST					
1ST-CLASS	6138	1634	16048	584	27.47
INT	18	0	93	1	93.00
RAL	1300.3	76	6126	248	24.70
NAT.W.	314	52	1038	39	26.61
B & H	519.4	64	1797	74	24.28

JOHNSON, P.   Nottinghamshire

Full Name: Paul Johnson
Role: Right-hand bat, right-arm occasional bowler
Born: 24 April 1965, Newark
Height: 5′ 8″ **Weight:** 12st
Nickname: Johno, Dwarf, Gus, Midge
County debut: 1982
County cap: 1986
1000 runs in a season: 3
1st-Class 50s scored: 35
1st-Class 100s scored: 14
One-Day 50s: 10
One-Day 100s: 1
Place in batting averages: 112th av. 28.75 (1988 57th av. 35.61)
1st-Class catches 1989: 20 (career 105 + 1 stumping)
Parents: Donald Edward and Joyce
Wife and date of marriage: Hazel Katrina, 17 October 1987
Family links with cricket: Father played local cricket and is a qualified coach
Education: Grove Comprehensive School, Newark
Qualifications: 9 CSEs, senior coaching certificate
Cricketing superstitions or habits: Left pad on first
Overseas tours: Keith Pont Benefit tour to Barbados 1987
Overseas teams played for: RAU, Johannesburg 1985–86; Hutt DCC, New Zealand 1988–89
Cricketers particularly learnt from: Most of Nottinghamshire staff, Clive Rice, Mike Harris
Cricketers particularly admired: 'Too many to mention!'
Other sports played: Football referee, golf (14 handicap), bowls, '– most ball games'
Other sports followed: Watches ice-hockey (Nottingham Panthers), football (Forest and County)
Relaxations: 'Driving, easy crosswords, sleeping, eating, and company of good friends.'
Extras: Played for English Schools cricket in 1980–81 season. Youngest member ever to join the Nottinghamshire CCC staff. Hit 16 sixes in School County Cup game v Joseph Whittaker, scoring 195*. Played for Young England U-19, 1982 and 1983. Made 235 for Nottinghamshire 2nd XI, July 1982, aged 17. Won man of match award in first NatWest game (101* v Staffordshire); missed 1985 final due to appendicitis

Opinions on cricket: 'Counties should be left to prepare wickets and not have restrictions put upon them, e.g. uncovered pitches, no heavy rollers. It seems to be a trial and error exercise at the players' inconvenience, as always! England's cricket media should give more backing to its players. There is enough pressure on players without trash being raked up. This also applies to the coverage on TV with so-called expert views which only seem to belittle today's players which wouldn't have happened in the "experts" day.'

Best batting performance: 140 Nottinghamshire v Hampshire, Basingstoke 1988

Best bowling performance: 1–9 Nottinghamshire v Oxford University, Trent Bridge 1984

LAST SEASON: BATTING

	I.	N.O.	R.	H.S.	AV.
TEST					
1ST-CLASS	36	3	949	109*	28.75
INT					
RAL	11	3	180	41	22.50
NAT.W.	1	0	47	47	47.00
B & H	3	0	63	54	21.00

CAREER: BATTING

	I.	N.O.	R.	H.S.	AV.
TEST					
1ST-CLASS	237	23	7127	140	33.30
INT					
RAL	78	10	1503	90	22.10
NAT.W.	15	2	333	101*	25.61
B & H	21	2	310	54	16.31

LAST SEASON: BOWLING

	O.	M.	R.	W.	AV.
TEST					
1ST-CLASS	4.2	0	64	0	–
INT					
RAL					
NAT.W.					
B & H					

CAREER: BOWLING

	O.	M.	R.	W.	AV.
TEST					
1ST-CLASS	61.2	7	417	3	139.00
INT					
RAL					
NAT.W.	2	0	16	0	–
B & H					

91. How many Scottish-born players had played for England, up to the end of 1989: 6, 11, or 14?

92. How many Irish-born players had played for England, up to the end of 1989: 0, 4, or 11?

JONES, A. N.   Somerset

Full Name: Adrian Nicholas Jones
Role: Left-hand bat, right-arm
fast bowler, outfielder
Born: 22 July 1961, Woking
Height: 6' 2" **Weight:** 14st
Nickname: Quincy, Jonah
County debut: 1981 (Sussex),
1987 (Somerset)
County cap: 1986 (Sussex),
1987 (Somerset)
50 wickets in a season: 3
1st-Class 5 w. in innings: 8
1st-Class 10 w. in match: 1
Place in batting averages: 226th
av. 14.30 (1988 263rd av. 10.00)
Place in bowling averages: 58th
av. 28.36 (1988 83rd av. 30.14)
Strike rate 1989: 50.98 (career 52.24)
1st-Class catches 1989: 8 (career 34)

Parents: William Albert and Emily Doris
Wife and date of marriage: Elizabeth Antoinette, 1 October 1988
Family links with cricket: Father and brother, Glynne, both fine club
cricketers
Education: Forest Grange Preparatory School; Seaford College
Qualifications: 8 O-levels, 2 A-levels, NCA coaching qualification, financial
planning and advising qualifications
Jobs outside cricket: Financial consultant/adviser; car salesman
Cricketing superstitions or habits: 'Always salute a magpie.'
Overseas teams played for: Old Selbournians and Bohemians, South Africa
1981–82; Border 1981–82; Red and White CC, Haarlem, Holland 1980;
Orange Free State 1986
Cricketers particularly learnt from: Father, Ian Greig, Geoff Arnold, Imran
Khan, Garth le Roux
Cricketers particularly admired: Imran Khan, Geoff Arnold, Garth le Roux,
Jimmy Cook, Chris Tavaré, Tony Pigott
Other sports played: 'Golf badly; hockey slightly better; rugby like an
animal.'
Relaxations: 'UB40, watching Laurel and Hardy films, walking, eating, good
wine and port.'
Extras: Played for Young England in 1981. Left Sussex to join Somerset at
end of 1986 season
Opinions on cricket: 'There should be an alternative system for the awarding

276

of a benefit than the present haphazard method. Perhaps an endowment scheme taken out when the player is capped. Too much notice is taken of averages.'

Best batting performance: 43* Somerset v Leicestershire, Taunton 1989
Best bowling performance: 7-30 Somerset v Hampshire, Southampton 1988

LAST SEASON: BATTING

	I.	N.O.	R.	H.S.	AV.
TEST					
1ST-CLASS	23	10	186	43*	14.30
INT					
RAL	9	5	55	37	13.75
NAT.W.	2	0	9	7	4.50
B & H	1	0	25	25	25.00

CAREER: BATTING

	I.	N.O.	R.	H.S.	AV.
TEST					
1ST-CLASS	111	46	714	43*	10.98
INT					
RAL	22	16	138	37	23.00
NAT.W.	4	2	13	7	6.50
B & H	10	4	67	25	11.16

LAST SEASON: BOWLING

	O.	M.	R.	W.	AV.
TEST					
1ST-CLASS	603.2	119	2014	71	28.36
INT					
RAL	111.3	12	587	24	24.45
NAT.W.	21.5	2	94	4	23.50
B & H	62.3	11	250	17	14.70

CAREER: BOWLING

	O.	M.	R.	W.	AV.
TEST					
1ST-CLASS	2472.5	426	8425	284	29.66
INT					
RAL	448.1	27	2244	109	20.58
NAT.W.	133.3	13	358	13	27.53
B & H	177.1	21	743	24	30.95

KALLICHARRAN, A. I.   Warwickshire

Full Name: Alvin Isaac Kallicharran
Role: Left-hand bat, right-arm off-spin bowler
Born: 21 March 1949, Guyana
Height: 5′ 4″
Nickname: Kalli
County debut: 1971
County cap: 1972
Benefit: 1983 (£34,094)
Test debut: 1971–72
No. of Tests: 66
No. of One-Day Internationals: 31
1000 runs in a season: 12
1st-Class 50s scored: 158
1st-Class 100s scored: 81
1st-Class 200s scored: 6
1st-Class 5 w. in innings: 1
One-Day 50s: 59
One-Day 100s: 12
Place in batting averages: 126th av. 26.52 (1988 92nd av. 29.85)

1st-Class catches 1989: 8 (career 318)
Marital status: Married
Children: One son, Rohan
Family links with cricket: Brother, Derek Isaac, played for Guyana
Overseas tours: With West Indies to England in 1973, 1976, 1980; India, Sri Lanka and Pakistan 1974–75; Australia 1975–76 and 1979–80; India and Sri Lanka 1978–79 as captain; New Zealand 1979–80; Pakistan 1980; West Indies XI to South Africa 1982–83, 1983–84
Overseas teams played for: Guyana 1966–81 in Shell Shield competition; Queensland in 1977–78 Sheffield Shield competition; Transvaal 1981–84, and Orange Free State 1984–88
Extras: Scored 100* and 101 in first two innings in Test matches v New Zealand in 1971. Signed for World Series Cricket but resigned before playing. He has made his home in England. With Geoff Humpage took part in record – for Warwickshire and for all English counties – 4th wicket stand of 470 v Lancashire at Southport in July 1982. Kallicharran made 230*, Humpage 254*. Previous record was 448 by Abel and Hayward for Surrey v Yorkshire at The Oval in 1899. Top of Warwickshire batting averages in 1981, 1982 and 1983. Banned from playing in West Indies for going to South Africa. One of *Wisden*'s Five Cricketers of the Year, 1982. Has captained both Transvaal and Orange Free State
Opinions on cricket: 'There is so much hypocrisy from politicians over South Africa. Sport should always be free of political pressure. If sportsmen were left alone to maintain their links with all other nations, this world might be a better place for it. Sport brings people of all colours and persuasions together – it doesn't drive people apart as political extremists do. Sport allows ordinary people to see we are all the same underneath. Cutting South Africa off from that sort of contact cannot possibly help the situation there.'
Best batting performance: 243* Warwickshire v Glamorgan, Edgbaston 1983
Best bowling performance: 5-45 Transvaal v Western Province, Cape Town 1982–83

LAST SEASON: BATTING

	I.	N.O.	R.	H.S.	AV.
TEST					
1ST-CLASS	25	2	610	119	26.52
INT					
RAL	12	0	489	104	40.75
NAT.W.	4	1	162	93*	54.00
B & H	4	0	175	62	43.75

LAST SEASON: BOWLING

	O.	M.	R.	W.	AV.
TEST					
1ST-CLASS	28.5	8	55	2	27.50
INT					
RAL	4	0	34	0	–
NAT.W.					
B & H					

CAREER: BATTING

	I.	N.O.	R.	H.S.	AV.
TEST	109	10	4399	187	44.43
1ST-CLASS	714	75	28030	243*	43.86
INT	28	4	826	78	34.41
RAL	172	18	4829	104	31.35
NAT.W.	29	3	1331	206	51.19
B & H	60	7	2315	122*	43.67

CAREER: BOWLING

	O.	M.	R.	W.	AV.
TEST	3.1 63.3	1 13	158	4	39.50
1ST-CLASS	1104.2	166	3872	80	48.40
INT	17	3	64	3	21.33
RAL	165.1	5	914	14	65.28
NAT.W.	92.4	9	319	4	79.75
B & H	34	0	153	0	–

KELLEHER, D. J. M.   Kent

Full Name: Daniel John Michael
Kelleher
Role: Right-hand bat, right-arm
medium bowler, outfielder
Born: 5 May 1966, London
Height: 6′ **Weight:** 12st 13lbs
Nickname: Donk, Shots
County debut: 1987
1st-Class 50s scored: 2
1st-Class 5 w. in innings: 2
Place in batting averages: 203rd
av. 17.63
Place in bowling averages: 104th
av. 40.87
Strike rate 1989: 70.95 (career 60.79)
1st-Class catches 1989: 3 (career 6)
Parents: John and Joan
Marital status: Single
Family links with cricket: Uncle
played county cricket for Surrey and Northants. Father played club cricket
Education: St Mary's Grammar School, Sidcup; Erith College of Technology
Qualifications: O-levels
Jobs outside cricket: Gardener
Cricketing superstitions or habits: Always puts gear on in set order
Overseas tours: Kent Schools U-17 to Vancouver and Victoria, Canada 1984;
UK Upsetters to Trinidad and Tobago 1986
Overseas teams played for: Doncaster CC, Melbourne 1984–85; Avendale
CC, Cape Town 1986–87

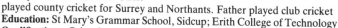

LAST SEASON: BATTING

	I.	N.O.	R.	H.S.	AV.
TEST					
1ST-CLASS	14	3	194	53*	17.63
INT					
RAL	5	1	27	10	6.75
NAT.W.	–				
B & H	2	2	15	11*	–

CAREER: BATTING

	I.	N.O.	R.	H.S.	AV.
TEST					
1ST-CLASS	33	16	425	53*	25.00
INT					
RAL	10	2	53	19	6.62
NAT.W.	1	1	0	0*	–
B & H	3	3	15	11*	–

LAST SEASON: BOWLING

	O.	M.	R.	W.	AV.
TEST					
1ST-CLASS	283.5	63	981	24	40.87
INT					
RAL	68	5	234	3	78.00
NAT.W.					
B & H	32	4	113	3	37.66

CAREER: BOWLING

	O.	M.	R.	W.	AV.
TEST					
1ST-CLASS	678.5	158	2088	67	31.16
INT					
RAL	130	8	486	10	48.60
NAT.W.	17.2	2	79	2	39.50
B & H	76	7	269	6	44.83

Cricketers particularly learnt from: My father, Claude Lewis, Alan Spencer, Colin Page
Cricketers particularly admired: Ian Botham, David Gower, Richard Davis, David Sabine
Other sports played: Golf, skiing
Other sports followed: Rugby, American football, women's tennis
Relaxations: Watching TV, music, watching Richard Davis bat
Extras: Played for Kent Schools from U-11 to U-19. At school played rugby and cricket for Kent
Opinions on cricket: 'Too much cricket is played.'
Best batting performance: 53* Kent v Derbyshire, Dartford 1989
Best bowling performance: 6-109 Kent v Somerset, Bath 1987

KELLETT, S. A. Yorkshire

Full Name: Simon Andrew Kellett
Role: Opening bat; occasional right-arm fast-medium bowler
Born: 16 October 1967, Mirfield
Height: 6' 2" **Weight:** 13st
Nickname: Kell
County debut: 1989
1st-Class catches 1989: 1 (career 1)
Parents: Brian and Valerie
Marital status: Single
Family links with cricket: Father played local league cricket
Education: Whitcliffe Mount High School; Huddersfield Technical College
Qualifications: 2 O-levels (Maths and Economics)
Jobs outside cricket: Worked in sports centre, and last winter had a driving job
Off-season 1989–90: Playing club cricket in New Zealand
Cricketing superstitions or habits: Puts left pad on first
Overseas tours: Bradford Junior Cricket League to Barbados; Yorkshire pre-season tour to La Manga
Cricketers particularly learnt from: Doug Padgett (coach), Ian Steen, Billy Rhodes
Cricketers particularly admired: Martyn Moxon, Graeme Hick, Geoff Boycott, Graham Gooch

Other sports played: Golf, squash
Other sports followed: Rugby League (very keen Bradford Northern fan), horse racing
Injuries 1989: Groin strain – missed 4 weeks
Relaxations: Playing sport, or watching TV (good comedy shows, Fawlty Towers, Only Fools and Horses)
Extras: Captained NAYC against MCC; captained Yorkshire U-19s to Cambridge Festival win. Out first ball in county cricket (faced Malcolm Marshall on King pair)
Opinions on cricket: 'More four-day cricket to improve technique for Test cricket. Improve the state of wickets.'
Best batting performance: 5 Yorkshire v Hampshire, Southampton 1989

LAST SEASON: BATTING

	I.	N.O.	R.	H.S.	AV.
TEST					
1ST-CLASS	3	0	5	5	1.66
INT					
RAL					
NAT.W.					
B & H					

CAREER: BATTING

	I.	N.O.	R.	H.S.	AV.
TEST					
1ST-CLASS	3	0	5	5	1.66
INT					
RAL					
NAT.W.					
B & H					

KENDRICK, N. M. Surrey

Full Name: Neil Michael Kendrick
Role: Right-hand bat, left-arm spin bowler, slip fielder
Born: 11 November 1967, Bromley
Height: 5' 11" **Weight:** 11st 7lbs
Nickname: Kendo, The Rat
County debut: 1988
1st-Class catches 1989: 3 (career 4)
Parents: Michael Hall and Anne Patricia
Marital status: Single
Family links with cricket: Father plays club cricket for Old Wilsonians, and sister has represented Kent Ladies
Education: Hayes Primary; Wilson's Grammar School
Qualifications: 7 O-levels, 1 A-level; cricket coach certificate
Jobs outside cricket: Stockbroker, hospital porter, labourer, shepherd

Off-season 1989–90: Working in advertising
Overseas tours: Australia, 1985–86 with Surrey U-19; Dubai, 1988–89 with Surrey
Cricketing superstitions or habits: 'Any that I have seem to disappear when I'm doing badly! Never follow Keith Medlycott in anything, or anybody he touches.'
Cricketers particularly learnt from: Alec Stewart, Neil Stewart, Mickey Stewart, Chris Waller, Geoff Arnold, Mike Kendrick
Cricketers particularly admired: Phil Edmonds, Bishen Bedi, 'for the way they made it look so easy'
Other sports played: Football, golf
Other sports followed: Most ball sports
Relaxations: 'Working in my spare time as a shepherd.'
Opinions on cricket: 'Four-day cricket is a must. But it must be played on the best pitches possible. Bowlers and batters will become better cricketers if they play on good wickets.'
Best batting performance: 11* Surrey v Kent, The Oval 1989
Best bowling performance: 3-50 Surrey v Somerset, Guildford 1989

LAST SEASON: BATTING

	I.	N.O.	R.	H.S.	AV.
TEST					
1ST-CLASS	3	1	17	11*	8.50
INT					
RAL					
NAT.W.					
B & H					

LAST SEASON: BOWLING

	O.	M.	R.	W.	AV.
TEST					
1ST-CLASS	62	21	139	6	23.16
INT					
RAL					
NAT.W.					
B & H					

CAREER: BATTING

	I.	N.O.	R.	H.S.	AV.
TEST					
1ST-CLASS	4	2	25	11*	12.50
INT					
RAL					
NAT.W.					
B & H					

CAREER: BOWLING

	O.	M.	R.	W.	AV.
TEST					
1ST-CLASS	90.5	28	236	7	33.71
INT					
RAL					
NAT.W.					
B & H					

93. Who played only once for England in a Test match, but was captain?

KIMBER, S. J. S.   Sussex

Full Name: Simon Julian Spencer
Kimber
Role: Right-hand bat, right-arm
fast-medium bowler
Born: 6 October 1963, Ormskirk,
Lancashire
Height: 6′ 2″ **Weight:** 13st
Nickname: Kew
County debut: 1985 (Worcestershire),
1987 (Sussex)
1st-Class 50s scored: 1
1st-Class catches 1989: 0 (career 5)
Parents: Ron and Joan (deceased)
Marital status: Single
Family links with cricket: Father
played good standard of club cricket
in England and West Indies
(Jamaica) for three years
Education: Thomas More School,
Kloof, South Africa
Qualifications: School matriculation in South Africa
Jobs outside cricket: Insurance broker
Off-season 1989–90: Playing for Durban Collegians, South Africa
Overseas teams played for: Durban Collegians, South Africa 1984–85 to
1989–90; Natal B 1986–87
Cricketers particularly learnt from: Father
Cricketers particularly admired: Richard Hadlee
Other sports played: Soccer, rugby, tennis, squash, golf

LAST SEASON: BATTING

	I.	N.O.	R.	H.S.	AV.
TEST					
1ST-CLASS	2	0	46	25	23.00
INT					
RAL					
NAT.W.					
B & H					

LAST SEASON: BOWLING

	O.	M.	R.	W.	AV.
TEST					
1ST-CLASS	30	6	91	2	45.50
INT					
RAL					
NAT.W.					
B & H					

CAREER: BATTING

	I.	N.O.	R.	H.S.	AV.
TEST					
1ST-CLASS	21	7	312	54	22.28
INT					
RAL	9	4	60	15*	12.00
NAT.W.	1	0	0	0	0.00
B & H	3	1	26	15	13.00

CAREER: BOWLING

	O.	M.	R.	W.	AV.
TEST					
1ST-CLASS	364.1	61	1282	33	38.84
INT					
RAL	107.1	2	578	9	64.22
NAT.W.					
B & H	32	4	112	5	22.40

Other sports followed: Soccer, rugby, tennis, athletics
Relaxations: Music, watching sport and films, eating out
Opinions on cricket: 'I feel more four-day cricket should be phased in, forcing more results; and giving lower-middle order batsmen more chance to bat, and less experienced bowlers more bowling.'
Best batting performance: 54 Sussex v Nottinghamshire, Eastbourne 1987
Best bowling performance: 4-76 Natal B v Eastern Province B, Uitenhage 1986–87

KRIKKEN, K. M. Derbyshire

Full Name: Karl Matthew Krikken
Role: Right-hand bat, wicket-keeper
Born: 9 April 1969, Bolton
Height: 5' 10" **Weight:** 12st 6lbs
Nickname: Krikk, Wizard
County debut: 1987 (Sunday League), 1989 (First Class)
1st-Class catches 1989: 1 (career 2)
Parents: Brian and Irene
Marital status: Single
Family links with cricket: Father played for Lancashire and Worcestershire in 1960s as wicket-keeper
Education: Horwich Parish Church School, Rivington; Blackrod High School
Qualifications: 6 O-levels, 3 A-levels; qualified coach
Jobs outside cricket: 'Joined Derbyshire straight from school.'
Off-season 1989–90: Working in England
Overseas tours: Kimberley, Griqualand West, South Africa 1988–89
Overseas teams played for: CBC Old Boys, Kimberley, Griqualand West Cricket Union v Eastern Province B 1988–89
Cricketers particularly learnt from: Father, Phil Russell, Alan Hill, 'plus a lot of the cricketers at Derby'
Cricketers particularly admired: Alan Knott, Bob Taylor, Rod Marsh
Other sports played: Squash, badminton, running etc, most ball games
Other sports followed: Football (Wigan Athletic), Rugby League (Wigan)
Injuries 1989: Spiral fracture of little finger on left hand – missed last three weeks of season

Relaxations: Music, videos, good food, 'anything that you can do sitting down.'

Extras: During time in South Africa lost half a metre of colon (small intestine) in a major operation. Played first first-class game in South Africa as an overseas professional, and did not play in normal position of wicket-keeper. Had to wait till fifth first-class game in fact to be picked as wicket-keeper

Best batting performance: 37 Derbyshire v Leicestershire, Leicester 1989

LAST SEASON: BATTING

	I.	N.O.	R.	H.S.	AV.
TEST					
1ST-CLASS	8	3	88	37	17.60
INT					
RAL	1	0	16	16	16.00
NAT.W.					
B & H					

LAST SEASON: WICKET KEEPING

	C.	ST.			
TEST					
1ST-CLASS	3	1			
INT					
RAL					
NAT.W.					
B & H					

CAREER: BATTING

	I.	N.O.	R.	H.S.	AV.
TEST					
1ST-CLASS	10	3	108	37	15.42
INT					
RAL	1	0	16	16	16.00
NAT.W.					
B & H					

CAREER: WICKET KEEPING

	C.	ST.			
TEST					
1ST-CLASS	3	1			
INT					
RAL		1			
NAT.W.					
B & H					

LAMB, A. J.   Northamptonshire

Full Name: Allan Joseph Lamb
Role: Right-hand bat, right-arm medium bowler. Captain
Born: 20 June 1954, Langebaanweg, Cape Province, South Africa
Height: 5′ 9″ **Weight:** 12st 7lbs
Nickname: Lambie, Legger
County debut: 1978
County cap: 1978
Benefit: 1988 (£134,000)
Test debut: 1982
No. of Tests: 57
No. of One-Day Internationals: 83
1000 runs in a season: 9
1st-Class 50s scored: 121
1st-Class 100s scored: 57
1st-Class 200s scored: 1
One-Day 50s: 60

One-Day 100s: 14
Place in batting averages: 16th av. 52.35 (1988 11th av. 52.86)
1st-Class catches 1989: 11 (career 256)
Parents: Michael and Joan
Wife and date of marriage: Lindsay St Leger, 8 December 1979
Children: Katie-Ann, 1987
Family links with cricket: Father played in the Boland League. Brother played for Western Province B. Brother-in-law, Tony Bucknall, won 10 caps for England at rugger
Education: Wynberg Boys' High School; Abbotts College
Qualifications: Matriculation
Jobs outside cricket: Timber representative. Promotions and selling
Off-season 1989–90: Touring India and West Indies with England, as vice-captain. 'Getting fit, and having a holiday with my family.'
Overseas tours: With England to Australia and New Zealand 1982–83; New Zealand and Pakistan 1983–84; India and Australia 1984–85; West Indies 1986; World Cup 1987; India and West Indies 1989–90
Overseas teams played for: Western Province in Currie Cup Competition, 1972–81; Orange Free State 1987–88
Cricketers particularly learnt from: 'Hylton Ackerman, Eddie Barlow, my father.'
Cricketers particularly admired: Mike Procter, Dennis Lillee
Other sports played: Squash, golf, cresta run, hunting, skiing
Other sports followed: Tennis
Relaxations: Shooting, fishing
Injuries 1989: Fractured and broke right index finger v Leicestershire on 20 July – out for rest of season
Extras: Made first-class debut for Western Province in 1972–73 Currie Cup. Applied to be registered as English in 1980 but application deferred. Was top of batting averages 1980. Was primarily a bowler when first played schoolboy cricket in South Africa. One of *Wisden*'s Five Cricketers of the Year, 1980.

LAST SEASON: BATTING

	I.	N.O.	R.	H.S.	AV.
TEST	2	0	129	125	64.50
1ST-CLASS	13	1	604	171	50.33
INT	3	1	135	100*	67.50
RAL	5	1	121	80*	30.25
NAT.W.	2	0	107	103	53.50
B & H	4	2	220	87*	110.00

LAST SEASON: BOWLING

	O.	M.	R.	W.	AV.
TEST					
1ST-CLASS					
INT					
RAL					
NAT.W.					
B & H					

CAREER: BATTING

	I.	N.O.	R.	H.S.	AV.
TEST	100	9	3098	137*	34.04
1ST-CLASS	463	79	19391	294	50.49
INT	81	15	2859	118	43.31
RAL	120	18	3946	132*	38.68
NAT.W.	30	1	1122	103	38.68
B & H	50	9	1989	126*	48.51

CAREER: BOWLING

	O.	M.	R.	W.	AV.
TEST	5		23	1	23.00
1ST-CLASS	41.1	10	141	5	28.20
INT	1	0	3	0	–
RAL					
NAT.W.	1.2	0	12	1	12.00
B & H	1	0	11	1	11.00

Missed two years of first-class cricket because of military training. Qualified to play for England 1982. Appointed Northamptonshire captain 1989

Opinions on cricket: 'The TCCB must be more strict with clubs on the wickets produced. The loss of 25 points is a good fine. The quicker four-day cricket comes, the better!'

Best batting performance: 294 Orange Free State v Eastern Province, Bloemfontein 1987–88

Best bowling performance: 1-1 Northamptonshire v Derbyshire, Derby 1978

LAMPITT, S. R.　　　Worcestershire

Full Name: Stuart Richard Lampitt
Role: Right-hand bat, right-arm fast-medium bowler
Born: 29 July 1966, Wolverhampton
Height: 5′ 11″ **Weight:** 13st
Nickname: Jed (after Jed Clampitt in Beverly Hillbillies)
County debut: 1985
County cap: 1989
1st-Class 5 w. in innings: 2
Place in bowling averages: 4th av. 16.96
Strike rate 1989: 42.54 (career 54.20)
1st-Class catches 1989: 5 (career 11)
Parents: Joseph Charles and Muriel Ann
Marital status: Single
Education: Kingswinford Secondary School; Dudley College of Technology

LAST SEASON: BATTING

	I.	N.O.	R.	H.S.	AV.
TEST					
1ST-CLASS	7	2	99	46	19.80
INT					
RAL	3	0	30	21	10.00
NAT.W.	2	1	9	9*	9.00
B & H					

CAREER: BATTING

	I.	N.O.	R.	H.S.	AV.
TEST					
1ST-CLASS	23	6	221	46	13.00
INT					
RAL	5	1	45	21	11.25
NAT.W.	2	1	9	9*	9.00
B & H					

LAST SEASON: BOWLING

	O.	M.	R.	W.	AV.
TEST					
1ST-CLASS	219.5	57	526	31	16.96
INT					
RAL	45	0	236	9	26.22
NAT.W.	28	1	114	4	28.50
B & H					

CAREER: BOWLING

	O.	M.	R.	W.	AV.
TEST					
1ST-CLASS	307.1	69	821	34	24.14
INT					
RAL	65	1	353	13	27.15
NAT.W.	28	1	114	4	28.50
B & H					

Qualifications: 7 O-levels; Diploma in Business Studies (just)
Jobs outside cricket: Steel sheerer winter 1984–85; warehouseman 1988–89
Off-season 1989–90: 'Working at home.' Playing soccer for Sandwell Borough
Cricketing superstitions or habits: 'Always check guard when new bowler comes on.'
Overseas tours: NCA England South to Bermuda 1986
Overseas teams played for: Mangore CC, Auckland, New Zealand 1986–87, 1987–88
Cricketers particularly learnt from: Ron Headley, Mark Scott, Basil D'Oliveira
Cricketers particularly admired: Ian Botham, Viv Richards
Other sports played: Football, golf, 'most ball sports.'
Other sports followed: 'All except show-jumping and bowls.'
Relaxations: 'Watching TV, listening to music, going out with mates for a FEW drinks.'
Extras: Won Cockspur Cup with Stourbridge 1987. Took 5 wickets and made 42 in Final at Lord's
Opinions on cricket: 'Maybe 16 four-day games, each starting on a Monday, would be better, and play one-day cricket at weekends where more people would be able to watch. Fridays off.'
Best batting performance: 46 Worcestershire v Warwickshire, Worcester 1989
Best bowling performance: 5-32 Worcestershire v Kent, Worcester 1989

LARKINS, W.   Northamptonshire

Full Name: Wayne Larkins
Role: Right-hand bat, right-arm medium bowler
Born: 22 November 1953
Height: 5′ 11″ **Weight:** 12st
Nickname: Ned
County debut: 1972
County cap: 1976
Benefit: 1986
Test debut: 1979–80
No. of Tests: 6
No. of One-Day Internationals: 6
1000 runs in a season: 11
1st-Class 50s scored: 89
1st-Class 100s scored: 43
1st-Class 200s scored: 2
1st-Class 5 w. in innings: 1
One-Day 50s: 45

One-Day 100s: 12
Place in batting averages: 31st av. 42.54 (1988 126th av. 26.25)
1st-Class catches 1989: 20 (career 221)
Parents: Mavis (father deceased)
Wife and date of marriage: Jane Elaine, 22 March 1975
Children: Philippa Jane, 30 May 1981
Family links with cricket: Father was umpire. Brother, Melvin, played for Bedford Town for many years
Education: Bushmead, Eaton Socon, Huntingdon
Jobs outside cricket: Farming
Off-season 1989–90: Touring with England in West Indies
Overseas tours: England to Australia and India 1979–80; England to India and West Indies 1989–90
Cricketers particularly learnt from: Mushtaq Mohammad
Other sports played: Golf, football (currently with Buckingham and was on Notts County's books), squash
Relaxations: Gardening
Extras: With Peter Willey, received 2016 pints of beer (seven barrels) from a Northampton brewery as a reward for their efforts in Australia in 1979–80. Hat-trick for Northamptonshire v Combined Universities, Benson & Hedges Cup, 1980. Banned from English Test Cricket for three years for joining rebel tour of South Africa in 1982. Recalled to Test team 1986 but withdrew due to thumb injury. Missed another Test recall in 1987 due to injury sustained whilst playing football. Took over county captaincy following Allan Lamb's injury mid-season, 1989
Best batting performance: 252 Northamptonshire v Glamorgan, Cardiff 1983
Best bowling performance: 5-59 Northamptonshire v Worcestershire, Worcester 1984

LAST SEASON: BATTING

	I.	N.O.	R.	H.S.	AV.
TEST					
1ST-CLASS	45	3	1787	126	42.54
INT					
RAL	13	0	285	101	21.92
NAT.W.	3	0	20	19	6.66
B & H	5	0	153	54	30.60

CAREER: BATTING

	I.	N.O.	R.	H.S.	AV.
TEST	11	0	176	34	16.00
1ST-CLASS	641	40	20877	252	34.73
INT	6	0	84	34	14.00
RAL	211	13	5391	172*	27.22
NAT.W.	37	3	1269	121*	37.32
B & H	63	3	1911	132	31.85

LAST SEASON: BOWLING

	O.	M.	R.	W.	AV.
TEST					
1ST-CLASS	14	2	47	0	–
INT					
RAL	4	0	18	1	18.00
NAT.W.	6	0	26	0	–
B & H					

CAREER: BOWLING

	O.	M.	R.	W.	AV.
TEST	2	0	21	0	–
1ST-CLASS	559.1	119	1807	42	43.02
INT					
RAL	325.5	9	1599	55	29.07
NAT.W.	79.5	9	274	4	68.50
B & H	112.3	14	444	16	27.75

LAWRENCE, D. V.   Gloucestershire

Full Name: David Valentine
Lawrence
Role: Right-hand bat, right-arm
fast bowler, slip fielder
Born: 28 January 1964, Gloucester
Height: 6′ 3″ **Weight:** 15st 7lbs
Nickname: Syd, Bruno
County debut: 1981
County cap: 1985
Test debut: 1988
No. of Tests: 1
50 wickets in a season: 3
1st-Class 50s scored: 1
1st-Class 5 w. in innings: 14
Place in batting averages: 225th
av. 14.41
Place in bowling averages: 90th
av. 34.88 (1988 65th av. 27.33)
Strike rate 1989: 60.73 (career 54.22)
1st-Class catches 1989: 6 (career 32)
Parents: Joseph and Joyce
Education: Linden School, Gloucester
Qualifications: 3 CSEs

Overseas tours: England B to Sri Lanka 1986; Gloucestershire CCC to Sri
Lanka 1986–87
Overseas teams played for: Scarborough CC, Perth, Western Australia
Cricketers particularly learnt from: Michael Holding, Richard Hadlee,
Dennis Lillee

LAST SEASON: BATTING

	I.	N.O.	R.	H.S.	AV.
TEST					
1ST-CLASS	17	5	173	45	14.41
INT					
RAL	2	0	16	16	8.00
NAT.W.					
B & H	1	0	0	0	0.00

CAREER: BATTING

	I.	N.O.	R.	H.S.	AV.
TEST	1	0	4	4	4.00
1ST-CLASS	152	31	1209	65*	9.99
INT					
RAL	14	5	95	21*	10.55
NAT.W.	7	3	4	2*	1.00
B & H	9	5	43	22*	10.75

LAST SEASON: BOWLING

	O.	M.	R.	W.	AV.
TEST					
1ST-CLASS	344.1	60	1186	34	34.88
INT					
RAL	29	2	123	5	24.60
NAT.W.					
B & H	44	4	164	5	32.80

CAREER: BOWLING

	O.	M.	R.	W.	AV.
TEST	36	9	111	3	37.00
1ST-CLASS	3262.3	479	12082	362	33.37
INT					
RAL	305	4	1607	52	30.90
NAT.W.	149.4	14	621	20	31.05
B & H	214	14	877	30	29.23

Cricketers particularly admired: Viv Richards
Other sports played: Rugby football. 'Was offered terms to play professional rugby league winter 1985–86, but turned them down.'
Relaxations: 'Like listening to jazz, funk and dancing.'
Best batting performance: 65* Gloucestershire v Glamorgan, Swansea 1987
Best bowling performance: 7-47 Gloucestershire v Surrey, Cheltenham 1988

LEATHERDALE, D. A. Worcestershire

Full Name: David Anthony Leatherdale
Role: Right-hand bat, right-arm medium bowler
Born: 26 November 1967, Bradford
Height: 5' 10½" **Weight:** 11st
Nickname: Lugs, Jimmy, Spock
County debut: 1988
One-Day 50s scored: 2
Place in batting averages: 237th av. 13.28 (1988 203rd av. 18.21)
1st-Class catches 1989: 13 (career 16)
Parents: Paul Anthony and Rosalyn
Marital status: Single
Family links with cricket: Brother plays in Bradford League. Brother-in-law played for Young England in 1979 (toured Canada)
Education: Bolton Royd Primary School, Pudsey; Pudsey Grammar School
Qualifications: 8 O-levels, 2 A-levels; NCA Coaching Award (Stage 1)
Jobs outside cricket: Sales assistant, Merlin Sports and Leisure Ltd, Pudsey
Off-season 1989–90: Organising charity auction for Radio Wyvern
Cricketing superstitions or habits: 'Left pad on first as do 80 per cent of all cricketers. After taking guard I take a stroll and tap the wicket on a few pitch marks to settle myself.'
Overseas tours: Barbados 1985 with Bradford Junior League side
Overseas teams played for: Pretoria Police CC 1987–89
Cricketers particularly learnt from: Mark Scott, George Batty, Peter Kippax
Other sports played: Golf (Yorkshire schools), football, squash
Relaxations: Listening to music, writing letters
Opinions on cricket: 'A full circuit of 2nd XI cricket as with the 1st XI will only improve the standards of 2nd-class cricket in England, and make it easier for 2nd XI players to adapt to the move up into 1st-class cricket.'

Best batting performance: 34* Worcestershire v Kent, Folkestone 1988
Best bowling performance: 1-12 Worcestershire v Northamptonshire, Worcester 1988

LAST SEASON: BATTING

	I.	N.O.	R.	H.S.	AV.
TEST					
1ST-CLASS	8	1	93	25	13.28
INT					
RAL	3	1	18	11*	9.00
NAT.W.	2	0	16	11	8.00
B & H					

CAREER: BATTING

	I.	N.O.	R.	H.S.	AV.
TEST					
1ST-CLASS	23	2	348	34*	16.57
INT					
RAL	8	3	146	62*	29.20
NAT.W.	6	1	94	43	18.80
B & H					

LAST SEASON: BOWLING

	O.	M.	R.	W.	AV.
TEST					
1ST-CLASS					
INT					
RAL					
NAT.W.					
B & H					

CAREER: BOWLING

	O.	M.	R.	W.	AV.
TEST					
1ST-CLASS	7	3	20	1	20.00
INT					
RAL					
NAT.W.					
B & H					

LENHAM, N. J.   Sussex

Full Name: Neil John Lenham
Role: Right-hand bat, right-arm medium bowler
Born: 17 December 1965, Worthing
Height: 5′ 11″ **Weight:** 11st
Nickname: Archie, Pin
County debut: 1984
1st-Class 50s scored: 12
1st-Class 100s scored: 2
One-Day 50s: 2
Place in batting averages: 127th av. 26.37 (1988 144th av. 24.43)
1st-Class catches 1989: 7 (career 27)
Parents: Leslie John and Valerie Anne
Marital status: Single
Family links with cricket: Father ex-Sussex county cricketer and now NCA National Coach
Education: Broadwater Manor House Prep School; Brighton College
Qualifications: 5 O-levels, 2 A-levels, Advanced Cricket Coach
Jobs outside cricket: Teacher, grease monkey in a garage

Off-season 1989–90: Playing and coaching in Tasmania
Cricketing superstitions or habits: 'Adjusting all equipment to obtain comfort before every delivery.'
Overseas tours: 1981 tour to Barbados with Sussex U-16; 1982 tour to Barbados with Sussex Young Cricketers; 1985 England Young Cricketers tour to West Indies (as captain)
Overseas teams played for: Port Elizabeth CC, South Africa 1988–89; Brighton CC, Tasmania 1989–90
Cricketers particularly learnt from: Father, John Spencer, Norman Gifford
Cricketers particularly admired: Ken McEwan, Barry Richards, Ralph Dellor
Other sports played: Hockey, squash, golf, 'and cards, badly.'
Other sports followed: Golf, rugby
Injuries 1989: 'None, unbelievably.'
Relaxations: Music, reading, keeping tropical fish, fishing
Extras: Made debut for Young England 1983. Broke record for number of runs scored in season at a public school in 1984 (1534 av. 80.74). Youngest player to appear for County 2nd XI at 14 years old
Opinions on cricket: 'A full season of four-day first-class cricket should now be seriously considered.'
Best batting performance: 116 Sussex v Surrey, Hove 1989
Best bowling performance: 4-85 Sussex v Leicestershire, Leicester 1986

LAST SEASON: BATTING

	I.	N.O.	R.	H.S.	AV.
TEST					
1ST-CLASS	27	3	633	116	26.37
INT					
RAL	5	0	49	26	9.80
NAT.W.	1	0	17	17	17.00
B & H					

LAST SEASON: BOWLING

	O.	M.	R.	W.	AV.
TEST					
1ST-CLASS	38	5	127	4	31.75
INT					
RAL	8	0	59	3	19.66
NAT.W.					
B & H					

CAREER: BATTING

	I.	N.O.	R.	H.S.	AV.
TEST					
1ST-CLASS	110	15	2540	116	26.73
INT					
RAL	16	7	216	39	24.00
NAT.W.	2	0	23	17	11.50
B & H	9	2	225	82	32.14

CAREER: BOWLING

	O.	M.	R.	W.	AV.
TEST					
1ST-CLASS	197.5	34	637	16	39.81
INT					
RAL	28	0	146	5	29.20
NAT.W.	9	0	48	1	48.00
B & H	9	0	46	1	46.00

94. Who has played most Test matches for England?

LEVER, J. K.   Essex

Full Name: John Kenneth Lever
Role: Right-hand bat, left-arm
fast-medium bowler
Born: 24 February 1949, Stepney
Height: 6' **Weight:** 13st
Nickname: Jake, JK, Stanley
County debut: 1967
County cap: 1970
Benefit: 1980 (£66,250) and
Testimonial, 1989
Test debut: 1976–77
No. of Tests: 21
No. of One-Day Internationals: 22

50 wickets in a season: 17
1st-Class 50s scored: 3
1st-Class 5 w. in innings: 85
1st-Class 10 w. in match: 12
Place in bowling averages: 61st
av. 29.00 (1988 84th av. 26.04)
Strike rate 1989: 60.69 (career 52.97)
1st-Class catches 1989: 4 (career 187)
Parents: Ken and Doris
Wife and date of marriage: Chris, 30 July 1983
Children: Jocelyn Jennifer, 9 January 1985; James, 4 March 1988
Education: Highlands Junior; Dane County Secondary School
Qualifications: 3 O-levels, 3 RSAs
Jobs outside cricket: Clerk with Access Social Club; Byron Shipping;
Dominion Insurance
Off-season 1989–90: Working at Bancroft's School
Cricketing superstitions or habits: 'Too many to mention.'
Overseas tours: With Derrick Robins' XI to South Africa 1972–73, 1973–74;
India, Sri Lanka and Australia 1976–77; Pakistan and New Zealand 1977–78;
Derrick Robins' XI to Sri Lanka 1977–78; Australia 1978–79 and 1979–80;
Overseas XI to India 1980–81; South African Breweries XI to South Africa
1981–82
Overseas teams played for: Natal 1982–85
Cricketers particularly learnt from: 'The Essex team.' Bill Morris
Cricketers particularly admired: Sir Gary Sobers
Other sports played: Football, golf
Injuries 1989: Back spasms – causing him to miss what should have been his
last match for Essex, the Refuge Cup Final v Nottinghamshire
Relaxations: Indian food, real ale

294

Extras: Took 10 wickets on his Test debut in 1976 v India at Delhi. Took 106 wickets at an average of 15.80 in 1978, and 106 wickets at an average of 17.30 in 1979, and 106 wickets at an average of 16.28 in 1983. President of Blythswood CC. Member of Ilford CC since the age of 14. One of *Wisden's* Five Cricketers of the Year, 1978. Has reputation of 'not breaking down'. On the executive of the Cricketers' Association. Banned from Test Cricket for three years for joining rebel tour of South Africa in 1982. Recalled to England side in 1986 after four-year absence. Published his autobiography *J. K. Lever, A Cricketer's Cricketer*, in 1989. Retired at the end of the 1989 season, to become games master at Bancroft's School. At the time of his retirement was the first and only bowler to bowl 2000 Sunday League overs, and was the leading wicket-taker with 386

Opinions on cricket: 'Pitches to be improved if four-day cricket is here to stay. There have been enormous changes during my career. Some of them have been all to the good, and have made the game far more professional, much better organised, and even financially prosperous. Others, to be frank, I have found quite distasteful. I am not too bothered about bowlers who rant and rave, and tell the batsman where to go when they get him out. After all, bowlers have always shouted their appeals *to* the umpire, although why they have to point and scream so ferociously *at* the umpire these days is beyond me. In spite of that I do not think there is too much verbal abuse in the game, and what I am really concerned about is the far more subtle use of gamesmanship which has crept in. Batsmen who nick the ball to the wicket-keeper and do not walk when they know that they are out are symptomatic of a desire to win at all costs which is not helping anybody – least of all umpires. It was a reflection of the sharp practices which have gone on when a new regulation was introduced in 1988, delaying the appearance of a substitute for five overs after a player had gone off, in order to stop unscrupulous sides replacing an old and not so agile fielder with a younger, more fleet-footed one. It started in

LAST SEASON: BATTING

	I.	N.O.	R.	H.S.	AV.
TEST					
1ST-CLASS	10	0	56	27	5.60
INT					
RAL	3	2	7	5*	7.00
NAT.W.	1	1	3	3*	–
B & H	–	–	–	–	–

CAREER: BATTING

	I.	N.O.	R.	H.S.	AV.
TEST	31	5	306	53	11.76
1ST-CLASS	541	192	3678	91	10.53
INT	11	4	56	27*	8.00
RAL	116	70	409	23	8.89
NAT.W.	27	19	97	15*	12.12
B & H	26	18	104	13	13.00

LAST SEASON: BOWLING

	O.	M.	R.	W.	AV.
TEST					
1ST-CLASS	263.1	55	754	26	29.00
INT					
RAL	113	23	389	21	18.52
NAT.W.	12	1	42	0	–
B & H	52	12	175	6	29.16

CAREER: BOWLING

	O.	M.	R.	W.	AV.
TEST	166.7 516.2	27 113	1951	73	26.72
1ST-CLASS	210.4 14184.3	40 3171	39819	1649	24.14
INT	33 148	5 15	713	24	29.70
RAL	2044.1	234	7619	386	19.73
NAT.W.	456.3	106	1219	70	17.41
B & H	904.1	172	2789	149	18.71

international cricket, but it was the counties who had to suffer, even though we have not had too many problems with it. I am sure that the umpires would have been able to stamp it out, if they had been given the authority to do so.'

Best batting performance: 91 Essex v Glamorgan, Cardiff 1970
Best bowling performance: 8-37 Essex v Gloucestershire, Bristol 1984

LEWIS, C. C. — Leicestershire

Full Name: Christopher Clairmonte Lewis
Role: Right-hand bat, right-arm medium bowler
Born: 14 February 1968, Georgetown, Guyana
Height: 6′ 2½″ **Weight:** 13st
Nickname: Carl
County debut: 1987
1st-Class 50s scored: 2
1st-Class 5 w. in innings: 5
1st-Class 10 w. in match: 1
One-Day 50s scored: 2
Place in batting averages: 220th av. 15.38 (1988 181st av. 21.05)
Place in bowling averages: 23rd av. 21.91 (1988 71st av. 28.80)
Strike rate 1989: 40.06 (career 49.25)
1st-Class catches 1989: 12 (career 23)
Parents: Philip and Patricia
Marital status: Single
Education: Willesden High School
Qualifications: 2 O-levels
Off-season 1989–90: Touring Zimbabwe with England A
Overseas tours: Young England to Australia 1987; Zimbabwe with England A 1990
Cricketers particularly learnt from: Ted Jackson, Paddy Clift
Cricketers particularly admired: Richard Hadlee
Other sports played: Snooker, football
Other sports followed: Snooker, football, darts, American football
Injuries 1989: Blood circulation problem, Raynaud's Phenomenon – off early June to late August
Relaxations: Music, sleeping
Best batting performance: 69 Leicestershire v Kent, Canterbury 1989

Best bowling performance: 6-22 Leicestershire v Oxford University, Oxford 1988

LAST SEASON: BATTING

	I.	N.O.	R.	H.S.	AV.
TEST					
1ST-CLASS	19	1	277	69	15.38
INT					
RAL	12	2	238	50	23.80
NAT.W.	1	0	5	5	5.00
B & H	3	2	48	23*	48.00

LAST SEASON: BOWLING

	O.	M.	R.	W.	AV.
TEST					
1ST-CLASS	300.3	59	986	45	21.91
INT					
RAL	54	6	231	11	21.00
NAT.W.					
B & H	40.3	2	162	6	27.00

CAREER: BATTING

	I.	N.O.	R.	H.S.	AV.
TEST					
1ST-CLASS	46	5	730	69	17.80
INT					
RAL	22	8	365	50	26.07
NAT.W.	5	0	101	53	20.20
B & H	6	4	71	23*	30.50

CAREER: BOWLING

	O.	M.	R.	W.	AV.
TEST					
1ST-CLASS	755.1	151	2363	92	25.68
INT					
RAL	143.4	8	639	22	29.04
NAT.W.	51	4	189	6	31.50
B & H	68.3	4	271	10	27.10

LILLEY, A. W.   Essex

Full Name: Alan William Lilley
Role: Right-hand bat, right-arm medium bowler, cover fielder
Born: 8 May 1959, Ilford, Essex
Height: 6′ 2″ **Weight:** 14st
Nickname: Lil
County debut: 1978
County cap: 1986
1st-Class 50s scored: 24
1st-Class 100s scored: 3
One-Day 50s: 8
One-Day 100s: 2
Place in batting averages: 142nd av. 24.52 (1988 120th av. 26.76)
1st-Class catches 1989: 11 (career 67)
Parents: Min and Ron
Wife and date of marriage: Helen, 6 October 1984 (separated)
Family links with cricket: Father played for Osborne CC as a bowler for 18 years
Education: Caterham High School, Ilford
Jobs outside cricket: Shipping broker

Off-season 1989–90: Coaching at Essex CCC Indoor Cricket School
Overseas teams played for: Perth CC, Western Australia 1979–80
Cricketers particularly learnt from: Stuart Turner, Bill Morris
Other sports played: 'Most ball games.'
Extras: Was on MCC Young Pro staff at Lord's one season after leaving school. Scored century in second innings of debut v Nottinghamshire. Has broken every finger of both hands, twice. One of the strongest men on the county circuit, in the class of Willey and Botham
Best batting performance: 113* Essex v Derbyshire, Chesterfield 1989
Best bowling performance: 3-116 Essex v Glamorgan, Swansea 1985

LAST SEASON: BATTING

	I.	N.O.	R.	H.S.	AV.
TEST					
1ST-CLASS	27	2	613	113*	24.52
INT					
RAL	8	1	112	33	16.00
NAT.W.					
B & H	6	1	174	95*	34.80

CAREER: BATTING

	I.	N.O.	R.	H.S.	AV.
TEST					
1ST-CLASS	189	15	4494	113*	25.82
INT					
RAL	110	10	1616	60	16.16
NAT.W.	15	2	352	113	27.07
B & H	35	4	711	119	22.93

LAST SEASON: BOWLING

	O.	M.	R.	W.	AV.
TEST					
1ST-CLASS	6	0	53	1	53.00
INT					
RAL					
NAT.W.					
B & H					

CAREER: BOWLING

	O.	M.	R.	W.	AV.
TEST					
1ST-CLASS	85.3	4	558	8	69.75
INT					
RAL	4.3	0	23	3	7.66
NAT.W.	8	3	33	2	16.50
B & H	1	0	4	1	4.00

95. Who has played most consecutive Test matches?

96. Who is the oldest man to play Test cricket?

LLONG, N. J.   Kent

Full Name: Nigel James Llong
Role: Left-hand bat, right-arm
off-break bowler
Born: 11 February 1969, Ashford
Height: 6' **Weight:** 11½st
Nickname: The Nidge, Jack, Lloydie
County debut: 1989 (RAL only)
Parents: Richard and Peggy
Marital status: Single
Family links with cricket: Father
played local club cricket
Education: The North School for
Boys, Essella Road, Ashford, Kent
Qualifications: 6 CSEs
Jobs outside cricket: Assistant
groundsman
Off-season 1989–90: Working for
local company (storeman)
Cricketing superstitions or habits:
'Thigh pad on first, left pad first; always bat in spikes.'
Overseas teams played for: Crusaders, Melbourne, Australia November
to March 1988; Ashburton CC, Melbourne, Australia November to March
1988
Cricketers particularly learnt from: Colin Page, Alan Ealham, Mark Dobson
Cricketers particularly admired: David Gower, John Emburey, Phil
Edmonds, Roger Harper
Other sports played: Golf, squash
Other sports followed: Football, horse racing

LAST SEASON: BATTING

	I.	N.O.	R.	H.S.	AV.
TEST					
1ST-CLASS					
INT					
RAL	1	1	0	0*	–
NAT.W.					
B & H					

CAREER: BATTING

	I.	N.O.	R.	H.S.	AV.
TEST					
1ST-CLASS					
INT					
RAL	1	1	0	0*	–
NAT.W.					
B & H					

LAST SEASON: BOWLING

	O.	M.	R.	W.	AV.
TEST					
1ST-CLASS					
INT					
RAL	3	0	20	1	20.00
NAT.W.					
B & H					

CAREER: BOWLING

	O.	M.	R.	W.	AV.
TEST					
1ST-CLASS					
INT					
RAL	3	0	20	1	20.00
NAT.W.					
B & H					

Injuries 1989: Strained tendons and ligaments in right ankle in July – off for 2 weeks
Relaxations: Horse racing, fishing
Opinions on cricket: 'All Championship games should be four days, and all cup and one-day games played at the weekend. I think this would help players concentrate more on longer innings, instead of breaking a three-day game to play a Sunday League game.'

LLOYD, G. D. Lancashire

Full Name: Graham David Lloyd
Role: Right-hand bat
Born: 1 July 1969, Accrington
Height: 5′ 9″ **Weight:** 11st 7lbs
Nickname: Bumble
County debut: 1988
1st-Class 100s scored: 3
Place in batting averages: 40th
av. 40.18
1st-Class catches 1989: 2 (career 3)
Parents: David and Susan
Marital status: Single
Family links with cricket: Father
played for Lancashire and England
Education: Hollins County High
School, Accrington
Qualifications: 3 O-levels; cricket
coach
Off-season 1989–90: Playing cricket
in Queensland
Cricketing superstitions or habits: Puts left pad on first
Overseas teams played for: Balmain, Sydney 1986–87, 1987–88
Cricketers particularly learnt from: Terry Holt (local coach), Dad, Graeme Fowler
Cricketers particularly admired: Graeme Hick, Allan Lamb, David Makinson

LAST SEASON: BATTING

	I.	N.O.	R.	H.S.	AV.
TEST					
1ST-CLASS	12	1	442	117	40.18
INT					
RAL					
NAT.W.					
B & H					

CAREER: BATTING

	I.	N.O.	R.	H.S.	AV.
TEST					
1ST-CLASS	14	1	464	117	35.69
INT					
RAL					
NAT.W.					
B & H					

Other sports played: Tennis, golf
Other sports followed: All sports
Best batting performance: 117 Lancashire v Nottinghamshire, Worksop 1989

LLOYD, T. A. Warwickshire

Full Name: Timothy Andrew Lloyd
Role: Left-hand bat, off-break bowler. Captain
Born: 5 November 1956, Oswestry
Height: 5′ 11″ **Weight:** 12st
Nickname: Towser
County debut: 1977
County cap: 1980
Benefit: 1990
Test debut: 1984
No. of Tests: 1
No. of One-Day Internationals: 3
1000 runs in a season: 8
1st-Class 50s scored: 68
1st-Class 100s scored: 27
1st-Class 200s scored: 1
One-Day 50s: 45
One-Day 100s: 2
Place in batting averages: 54th
av. 36.70 (1988 49th av. 36.20)
1st-Class catches 1989: 9 (career 125)
Parents: John Romer and Gwen
Wife: Gilly
Children: Georgia, Sophie
Education: Oswestry Boys' High School; Dorset College of Higher Education
Qualifications: O-levels, 2 A-levels, HND Tourism, NCA Advanced Coach
Jobs outside cricket: Business entertainment/corporate hospitality executive
Off-season 1989–90: Working with Elite Promotions
Overseas tours: Derrick Robins' XI to South America 1979; Warwickshire CCC to Zambia 1977; Warwickshire Wanderers to Barbados 1978; English Counties XI to Zimbabwe 1984–85
Overseas teams played for: Orange Free State 1978–79, 1979–80; Zingari CC, Waverley CC
Cricketers particularly learnt from: Dennis Amiss
Cricketers particularly admired: Allan Border
Other sports played: Soccer, golf, tennis, table tennis, squash
Other sports followed: 'Most sports, but particularly racing.'

Relaxations: 'Enjoying my home, drinking good wine and beer, eating various cuisines, greyhounds. Also playing golf and walking.'

Extras: Scored 202* for Shropshire Schools v Worcestershire. Played for Shropshire and Warwickshire 2nd XI, both in 1975. Has been captain of Warwickshire since 1988

Opinions on cricket: 'After-match arrangements at some grounds must be looked into more closely. Hygiene and refreshment seem low on some counties' list of priorities.'

Best batting performance: 208* Warwickshire v Gloucestershire, Edgbaston 1983

Best bowling performance: 3-62 Warwickshire v Surrey, Edgbaston 1985

LAST SEASON: BATTING

	I.	N.O.	R.	H.S.	AV.
TEST					
1ST-CLASS	33	2	1138	183	36.70
INT					
RAL	14	1	312	56*	24.00
NAT.W.	5	0	169	57	33.80
B & H	4	0	61	37	15.25

CAREER: BATTING

	I.	N.O.	R.	H.S.	AV.
TEST	1	1	10	10*	–
1ST-CLASS	443	39	14524	208*	35.95
INT	3	0	101	49	33.66
RAL	137	13	3575	90	28.83
NAT.W.	28	3	1066	121	42.64
B & H	41	3	1214	137*	31.94

LAST SEASON: BOWLING

	O.	M.	R.	W.	AV.
TEST					
1ST-CLASS	29	7	111	1	111.00
INT					
RAL					
NAT.W.					
B & H					

CAREER: BOWLING

	O.	M.	R.	W.	AV.
TEST					
1ST-CLASS	293	49	1300	16	81.25
INT					
RAL	23.1	0	149	1	149.00
NAT.W.	9	1	47	2	23.50
B & H	15	1	76	0	–

97. Who was the oldest man to play Test cricket for Australia?

LLOYDS, J. W.   Gloucestershire

Full Name: Jeremy William Lloyds
Role: Left-hand bat, off-break
bowler, close fielder
Born: 17 November 1954, Penang,
Malaya
Height: 5′ 11″ **Weight:** 12st
Nickname: Jo'burg, JJ or Jerry
County debut: 1979 (Somerset),
1985 (Gloucestershire)
County cap: 1982 (Somerset),
1985 (Gloucestershire)
1000 runs in a season: 3
1st-Class 50s scored: 50
1st-Class 100s scored: 10
1st-Class 5 w. in innings: 12
1st-Class 10 w. in match: 1
One-Day 50s: 3

Place in batting averages: 113th
av. 28.66 (1988 186th av. 20.61)
Place in bowling averages: 83rd av. 33.00 (1988 132nd av. 58.23)
Strike rate 1989: 66.90 (career 67.79)
1st-Class catches 1989: 19 (career 192)
Parents: Edwin William and Grace Cicely
Marital status: Single
Family links with cricket: Father played for Blundell's 1st XI 1932–35, selected for Public Schools Rest v Lord's Schools at Lord's 1935. Played Inter-State cricket in Malaya and Singapore 1950–55. Brother, Christopher Edwin Lloyds, played for Blundell's 1st XI 1964–66 and Somerset 2nd XI in 1966
Education: St Dunstan's Prep School; Blundell's School
Qualifications: 10 O-levels, NCA Advanced Coach
Jobs outside cricket: Lloyds Bank, Taunton, for 1½ years. MCC Young Professionals at Lord's 1975 for 4 years
Overseas tours: With Somerset to Antigua 1981; with Gloucestershire to Barbados 1985; Sri Lanka 1987
Overseas teams played for: St Stithian's Old Boys, Johannesburg 1978–80; Toombul DCC, Brisbane 1980–82; North Sydney District 1982–83; Orange Free State 1983–84; Preston (Victoria) 1986
Cricketers particularly learnt from: Don Wilson, Derek Taylor, Brian Davison
Cricketers particularly admired: John Hampshire, Graeme Pollock, Viv Richards, Ian Botham, Derek Underwood, Brian Davison
Other sports played: Golf, swimming, windsurfing

Other sports followed: Motor racing, tennis, American football

Relaxations: Music, cinema, driving, reading

Extras: Scored 132* and 102* for Somerset in same Championship match, June 1982. Took 30 catches in 1982 season for Somerset. Moved to Gloucestershire for 1985 season

Opinions on cricket: 'Coloured clothing worn for all one-day cricket. Covered wickets at all times. If another TV channel wants to cover full Sunday cricket and one-day games, let them. The five over substitute law (which does not affect Test cricket – caused by certain Test countries abusing the rule in one-day cricket in 1987) should be scrapped, for reasons obvious to those who know and play the game!'

Best batting performance: 132* Somerset v Northamptonshire, Northampton 1982

Best bowling performance: 7-88 Somerset v Essex, Chelmsford 1982

LAST SEASON: BATTING

	I.	N.O.	R.	H.S.	AV.
TEST					
1ST-CLASS	39	3	1032	71	28.66
INT					
RAL	12	0	224	65	18.66
NAT.W.	2	0	33	28	16.50
B & H	1	1	9	9*	–

CAREER: BATTING

	I.	N.O.	R.	H.S.	AV.
TEST					
1ST-CLASS	339	46	9037	132*	30.84
INT					
RAL	82	11	1007	65	14.18
NAT.W.	15	3	214	40	17.83
B & H	20	3	270	51	15.88

LAST SEASON: BOWLING

	O.	M.	R.	W.	AV.
TEST					
1ST-CLASS	255.2	55	726	22	33.00
INT					
RAL	9	0	54	0	–
NAT.W.	10	1	39	0	–
B & H	1	0	3	0	–

CAREER: BOWLING

	O.	M.	R.	W.	AV.
TEST					
1ST-CLASS	3106.1	663	9864	274	36.00
INT					
RAL	101.2	6	515	11	46.81
NAT.W.	48.3	5	159	3	53.00
B & H	30.2	2	100	4	25.00

98. How old was W. G. Grace when he last played for England?

LONGLEY, J. I. — Kent

Full Name: Jonathan Ian Longley
Role: Right-hand bat
Born: 12 April 1969,
New Brunswick, USA
Height: 5′ 8″ **Weight:** 11½st
Nickname: Tufty
County debut: 1989
One-Day 50s scored: 1
Parents: Dick and Helen
Marital status: Single
Education: Tonbridge School,
Durham University
Qualifications: 9 O-levels, 3 A-levels
Off-season 1989–90: At university
Cricketers particularly learnt from:
Howard Mutton, David Walsh,
mother, father, brother, Tunbridge
Wells Cricket Club, Kent playing
members

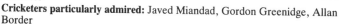

Cricketers particularly admired: Javed Miandad, Gordon Greenidge, Allan
Border
Other sports played: Rugby, squash
Other sports followed: Rugby, golf
Relaxations: Music, walking the dogs
Extras: Member of Combined Universities team that reached the quarter-
finals of B & H Cup in 1989
Opinions on cricket: 'The cricketers themselves should have more say in the
way cricket is run in this country. Most cricketers agree that too much first-
class cricket is played which dilutes the quality of the game, and is reflected
in low interest shown by the public in county cricket. More time should be
given to practising specific skills. I also believe that there are too many professionals. Cricket in this country can't support them properly.'
Best batting performance: 17 Kent v Essex, Southend 1989

LAST SEASON: BATTING

	I.	N.O.	R.	H.S.	AV.
TEST					
1ST-CLASS	8	0	42	17	5.25
INT					
RAL	4	0	96	57	24.00
NAT.W.					
B & H	5	1	119	49	29.75

CAREER: BATTING

	I.	N.O.	R.	H.S.	AV.
TEST					
1ST-CLASS	8	0	42	17	5.25
INT					
RAL	4	0	96	57	24.00
NAT.W.					
B & H	5	1	119	49	29.75

LORD, G. J.   Worcestershire

Full Name: Gordon John Lord
Role: Left-hand bat, slow left-arm
bowler, specialist third-man
Born: 25 April 1961, Birmingham
Height: 5' 10" **Weight:** 'Variable
and confidential!'
Nickname: Plum
County debut: 1983 (Warwickshire),
1987 (Worcestershire)
1st-Class 50s scored: 10
1st-Class 100s scored: 2
One-Day 50s: 1
One-Day 100s: 1
Place in batting averages: 195th
av. 18.71 (1988 112th av. 27.80)
1st-Class catches 1989: 2 (career 15)
Parents: Michael David and
Christine Frances
Marital status: Single
Family links with cricket: Uncle Charles Watts played for Leicestershire
Education: Warwick School; Durham University
Qualifications: 7 O-levels, 4 A-levels, BA General Studies, NCA Coaching
Award
Jobs outside cricket: Personnel trainee, Lucas Engineering and Systems;
Assistant Manager, Worcester Country Club
Off-season 1989–90: Working at Worcester Country Club
Overseas tours: England U-19 to Australia 1978–79 and West Indies 1979–80
Cricketers particularly learnt from: Allan Wilkins (school coach), Neal
Abberley (2nd XI coach), Norman Graham (University coach), Peter
Stringer, Tim Curtis, Basil D'Oliveira
Cricketers particularly admired: Dennis Amiss, Graeme Hick
Other sports played: Squash
Other sports followed: Watches rugby, squash, snooker
Relaxations: All forms of music, particularly church organ music; astronomy,
reading, people, Indian cooking and eating

LAST SEASON: BATTING

	I.	N.O.	R.	H.S.	AV.
TEST					
1ST-CLASS	16	2	262	80	18.71
INT					
RAL	–	–	–	–	–
NAT.W.	–	–	–	–	–
B & H	2	0	18	18	9.00

CAREER: BATTING

	I.	N.O.	R.	H.S.	AV.
TEST					
1ST-CLASS	94	8	1985	199	23.08
INT					
RAL	13	1	249	103	20.75
NAT.W.	1	0	0	0	0.00
B & H	6	0	41	18	6.83

Extras: Released by Warwickshire at end of 1986 season. Joined Worcestershire in 1987

Best batting performance: 199 Warwickshire v Yorkshire, Edgbaston 1985

LOVE, J. D.   Yorkshire

Full Name: James Derek Love
Role: Right-hand bat, right-arm medium bowler
Born: 22 April 1955, Leeds
Height: 6′ 2″ **Weight:** 14st
Nickname: Jim
County debut: 1975
County cap: 1980
Benefit: 1989
No. of One-Day Internationals: 3
1000 runs in a season: 2
1st-Class 50s scored: 56
1st-Class 100s scored: 13
One-Day 50s: 18
One-Day 100s: 4
Place in batting averages: 177th av. 20.30 (1988 104th av. 28.88)
1st-Class catches 1989: 6 (career 125)
Parents: Derek Oliver and Betty
Wife and date of marriage: Janice Hazel, 28 February 1986
Children: Thomas James, 4 March 1988
Family links with cricket: Father played local cricket; brother Robert plays for Tadcaster CC in Yorkshire League
Education: Brudenell County Secondary, Leeds
Jobs outside cricket: Civil servant for three years until left to become professional cricketer
Overseas tours: Yorkshire CCC to West Indies 1986–87
Overseas teams played for: Whitbread Scholarship to Mosman Middle Harbour and District CC in 1977–78; Scarborough CC, Perth, Western Australia 1978–79; Mosman Middle Harbour and District CC 1982–83, 1984–85
Cricketers particularly learnt from: Doug Padgett (county coach)
Other sports played: Local football, golf
Other sports followed: Rugby League
Relaxations: Shooting
Extras: Man of the Match in Yorkshire's victory in B & H Cup Final 1987. Awarded Benefit 1989. Released by Yorkshire at end of 1989 season

307

Opinions on cricket: 'I wish employment could be found for more cricketers when the season ends.'
Best batting performance: 170* Yorkshire v Worcestershire, Worcester 1979
Best bowling performance: 2-0 Yorkshire v Windward Islands, Castries 1986–87

LAST SEASON: BATTING

	I.	N.O.	R.	H.S.	AV.
TEST					
1ST-CLASS	15	2	264	53	20.30
INT					
RAL	10	1	197	65	21.88
NAT.W.	1	0	8	8	8.00
B & H	4	0	44	30	11.00

LAST SEASON: BOWLING

	O.	M.	R.	W.	AV.
TEST					
1ST-CLASS	4	1	20	2	10.00
INT					
RAL					
NAT.W.					
B & H					

CAREER: BATTING

	I.	N.O.	R.	H.S.	AV.
TEST					
1ST-CLASS	391	59	10327	170*	31.10
INT	3	0	61	43	20.33
RAL	146	18	2919	118*	22.80
NAT.W.	18	3	266	67	17.73
B & H	39	12	1113	118*	41.22

CAREER: BOWLING

	O.	M.	R.	W.	AV.
TEST					
1ST-CLASS	235.3	38	835	12	69.58
INT					
RAL	19	1	83	3	27.66
NAT.W.	12	3	39	2	19.50
B & H	1	0	7	0	–

LYNCH, M. A. Surrey

Full Name: Monte Allan Lynch
Role: Right-hand bat, right-arm medium and off-break bowler
Born: 21 May 1958, Georgetown, Guyana
Weight: 12st
Nickname: Mont
County debut: 1977
County cap: 1982
No. of One-Day Internationals: 3
1000 runs in a season: 6
1st-Class 50s scored: 56
1st-Class 100s scored: 29
One-Day 50s: 29
One-Day 100s: 4
Place in batting averages: 10th av. 54.71 (1988 35th av. 39.84)
1st-Class catches 1989: 6 (career 222)
Parents: Lawrence and Doreen Austin

Marital status: Single

Family links with cricket: 'Father and most of family played at some time or another.'

Education: Ryden's School, Walton-on-Thames

Overseas tours: West Indies XI to South Africa 1983–84; International XI to Pakistan 1981–82

Overseas teams played for: Guyana 1982–83

Other sports played: Football, table tennis

Injuries 1989: Damaged right leg in a pre-season charity football match; and had to have an operation on his right knee

Extras: Hitting 141* for Surrey v Glamorgan at Guildford in August 1982, off 78 balls in 88 minutes, one six hit his captain's, Roger Knight, car, denting it. Repeated trick in 1983 v Worcestershire in John Player League. Joined West Indies Rebels in South Africa 1983–84, although qualified for England. Appeared in all three One-Day Internationals v West Indies 1988

Best batting performance: 172* Surrey v Kent, Oval 1989

Best bowling performance: 3-6 Surrey v Glamorgan, Swansea 1981

LAST SEASON: BATTING

	I.	N.O.	R.	H.S.	AV.
TEST					
1ST-CLASS	9	2	383	172*	54.71
INT					
RAL					
NAT.W.					
B & H					

LAST SEASON: BOWLING

	O.	M.	R.	W.	AV.
TEST					
1ST-CLASS	1	1	0	0	–
INT					
RAL					
NAT.W.					
B & H					

CAREER: BATTING

	I.	N.O.	R.	H.S.	AV.
TEST					
1ST-CLASS	394	46	12343	172*	35.46
INT	3	0	8	6	2.66
RAL	134	20	3339	136	29.28
NAT.W.	24	4	597	129	29.85
B & H	37	3	975	112*	28.67

CAREER: BOWLING

	O.	M.	R.	W.	AV.
TEST					
1ST-CLASS	295.5	56	1116	24	46.50
INT					
RAL	11.5	0	95	5	19.00
NAT.W.	23	6	80	2	40.00
B & H	6	0	42	0	–

99. Which two England Test captains were born in Trinidad?

MAHER, B. J. M.   Derbyshire

Full Name: Bernard Joseph Michael
Maher
Role: Right-hand bat, wicket-keeper
Born: 11 February 1958, Hillingdon
Height: 5′ 9½″ **Weight:** 11st 7lbs
Nickname: 'Tends to vary but all
derogatory!' B.J.
County debut: 1981
County cap: 1987
1st-Class 50s scored: 17
1st-Class 100s scored: 4
One-Day 50s: 2
Place in batting averages: 202nd
av. 17.67 (1988 96th av. 29.51)
Parents: Francis J. (deceased) and
Mary Ann
Marital status: Single
Family links with cricket: Brother
kept wicket for school. Father
followed Derbyshire CCC quite closely
Education: St Bernadette's Primary; Abbotsfield Comprehensive; Bishops-
malt Grammar; Loughborough University
Qualifications: 10 O-levels, 3 A-levels, BSc Hons in Economics and Account-
ancy, NCA Coaching Award. Qualified to professional stage 2 of certified
accountancy exams
Jobs outside cricket: Accountant. Has also worked in public relations for
Owen Products and Latham's Car and Truck Sales
Off-season 1989–90: Playing in Otago, New Zealand
Cricketing superstitions or habits: 'I like to take leg stump guard when I have
not faced the bowling for some time.'
Overseas tours: With the Middlesex Cricket League touring team to Trinidad
and Tobago 1978; Amsterdam with Loughborough University 1981
Overseas teams played for: Zingari CC, Pietermaritzburg 1982–83, 1983–84;
Ellerslie CC, Auckland, New Zealand 1984–85; Kamo CC and Northland,
New Zealand 1985–86; Northern Districts B 1986–87; Taieri CC, New
Zealand
Cricketers particularly learnt from: Bob Taylor, Alan Knott, John Wright
Cricketers particularly admired: Malcolm Marshall, Richard Hadlee,
Gordon Greenidge
Other sports played: Badminton
Other sports followed: Athletics, rugby, tennis, boxing
Injuries 1989: Missed two games at start of season with an injured thumb

Relaxations: Scuba-diving, fell-walking, coarse- and fly-fishing

Extras: Caught five catches in innings on debut v Gloucestershire. Topped wicket-keepers' dismissals list in 1987 with 76 victims

Opinions on cricket: 'A "transfer system" should operate in cricket allowing both clubs and players to make money. A transfer system would also indirectly improve youth cricket, because young talent will be sought and coached more effectively, because of the possible earnings potential for county clubs. Television coverage of the Refuge Assurance League is declining in favour of other sports. I believe coloured clothing and floodlights should be used, along with other gimmicks to ensure the public and television coverage on Sundays is maintained. To ensure the best national cricket team is selected a paid national selector should be appointed to watch every county game. A lot has been written and said about ways in which to stop fast bowlers intimidating batsmen by bowling short. Restrictions on the number of short balls per over etc. do not appear to have worked. I believe there should be no restrictions on the bowler, but possibly the answer could be by making the glove no longer part of the bat, i.e. balls which leap at a batsman's throat are often fended away by a player's gloves. By making a player caught off the glove not out it will allow batsmen to defend themselves without fear of getting out.'

Best batting performance: 126 Derbyshire v New Zealand, Derby 1986

Best bowling performance: 2-69 Derbyshire v Glamorgan, Abergavenney 1986

LAST SEASON: BATTING

	I.	N.O.	R.	H.S.	AV.
TEST					
1ST-CLASS	40	6	601	97	17.67
INT					
RAL	12	3	141	49*	15.66
NAT.W.	2	0	17	14	8.50
B & H	4	1	111	42*	37.00

CAREER: BATTING

	I.	N.O.	R.	H.S.	AV.
TEST					
1ST-CLASS	199	35	3662	126	22.32
INT					
RAL	61	12	772	78	15.75
NAT.W.	9	1	99	44	12.37
B & H	13	2	256	50	23.27

LAST SEASON: WICKET KEEPING

	C.	ST.		
TEST				
1ST-CLASS	57	2		
INT				
RAL	17	–		
NAT.W.	3	–		
B & H	7	–		

LAST SEASON: BOWLING

	O.	M.	R.	W.	AV.
TEST					
1ST-CLASS	12	0	83	1	83.00
INT					
RAL					
NAT.W.					
B & H					

CAREER: BOWLING

	O.	M.	R.	W.	AV.
TEST					
1ST-CLASS	45	2	234	4	58.50
INT					
RAL					
NAT.W.					
B & H					

CAREER: WICKET KEEPING

	C.	ST.		
TEST				
1ST-CLASS	280	14		
INT				
RAL	57	9		
NAT.W.	17	0		
B & H	25	1		

MALCOLM, D. E.   Derbyshire

Full Name: Devon Eugene Malcolm
Role: Right-hand bat, right-arm
fast bowler
Born: 22 February 1963, Kingston,
Jamaica
Height: 6′ 3″ **Weight:** 14st 7lbs
Nickname: Dude
County debut: 1984
Test debut: 1989
No. of Tests: 1
50 wickets in a season: 1
1st-Class 50s scored: 1
1st-Class 5 w. in innings: 3
Place in batting averages: 173rd
av. 20.66
Place in bowling averages: 35th
av. 23.87 (1988 81st av. 29.92)
Strike rate 1989: 38.02 (career 48.77)
1st-Class catches 1989: 1 (career 12)
Parents: Albert and Brendalee (deceased)
Marital status: Single
Education: St Elizabeth Technical High School; Richmond College
Qualifications: College certificates, O-levels, coaching certificate
Jobs outside cricket: Coaching
Off-season 1989–90: Touring West Indies with England
Overseas tours: England to West Indies 1989–90
Overseas teams played for: Ellerslie CC, New Zealand 1985–86
Cricketers particularly learnt from: M. Holding, P. Russell, K. Barnett

LAST SEASON: BATTING

	I.	N.O.	R.	H.S.	AV.
TEST	2	0	14	9	7.00
1ST-CLASS	14	7	172	51	24.57
INT					
RAL	1	0	0	0	0.00
NAT.W.	2	0	10	6	5.00
B & H					

LAST SEASON: BOWLING

	O.	M.	R.	W.	AV.
TEST	44	2	166	1	166.00
1ST-CLASS	253.5	38	956	46	20.78
INT					
RAL	24	0	90	4	22.50
NAT.W.	19	1	80	4	20.00
B & H					

CAREER: BATTING

	I.	N.O.	R.	H.S.	AV.
TEST	2	0	14	9	7.00
1ST-CLASS	67	21	411	51	8.93
INT					
RAL	2	0	16	16	8.00
NAT.W.	5	0	11	6	2.20
B & H	2	1	0	0*	0.00

CAREER: BOWLING

	O.	M.	R.	W.	AV.
TEST	44	2	166	1	166.00
1ST-CLASS	1386.4	240	5051	175	28.86
INT					
RAL	40	0	177	7	25.28
NAT.W.	51	4	205	6	34.16
B & H	47	4	149	8	18.62

Cricketers particularly admired: Michael Holding, Richard Hadlee
Other sports played: Football
Other sports followed: Football, table tennis
Relaxations: Reggae, funk and soul music
Extras: Wears spectacles when batting and bowling. Became eligible to play for England in 1987. Has a photograph on display in his house of Geoffrey Boycott's bat coming down too late as his middle stump is knocked out of the ground, bowled by Malcolm playing for Yorkshire League XI v Yorkshire in 1983. Played league cricket for Sheffield Works and Sheffield United
Best batting performance: 51 Derbyshire v Surrey, Derby 1989
Best bowling performance: 6-68 Derbyshire v Warwickshire, Derby 1988

MALLENDER, N. A.   Somerset

Full Name: Neil Alan Mallender
Role: Right-hand bat, right-arm fast-medium bowler
Born: 13 August 1961, Kirk Sandall, Nr Doncaster
Height: 6′ **Weight:** 13st
Nickname: Ghostie
County debut: 1980 (Northamptonshire), 1987 (Somerset)
County cap: 1984 (Northamptonshire), 1987 (Somerset)
50 wickets in a season: 4
1st-Class 50s scored: 4
1st-Class 5 w. in innings: 16
1st-Class 10 w. in match: 3
Place in batting averages: 237th
av. 13.28 (1988 248th av. 12.15)
Place in bowling averages: 53rd av. 27.78 (1988 17th av. 20.74)
Strike rate 1989: 61.78 (career 58.66)
1st-Class catches 1989: 8 (career 86)
Parents: Ron and Jean
Wife and date of marriage: Caroline, 1 October 1984
Children: Kirstie Jane, 18 May 1988
Family links with cricket: Brother Graham used to play good representative cricket before joining the RAF
Education: Beverley Grammar School, East Yorkshire
Qualifications: 7 O-levels

313

Off-season 1989–90: Playing for Otago in New Zealand
Cricketing superstitions or habits: Left boot on first
Overseas tours: Young England to West Indies 1980
Overseas teams played for: Belmont DCC, NSW 1980–81; Bathurst, NSW 1982–83; Otago and Kaikorai CC, New Zealand 1983–89
Cricketers particularly learnt from: Peter Willey, Warren Lees, Martin Crowe, Dennis Lillee
Cricketers particularly admired: Richard Hadlee, Dennis Lillee
Other sports played: Golf
Other sports followed: Rugby League (especially Hull RFC), most sports
Injuries 1989: Strained hamstring – out for three games in July
Relaxations: Watching sports
Extras: Signed a 3-year contract to play for Somerset in 1987. Took hat-trick in first round of 1987 B & H Cup v Combined Universities
Best batting performance: 88 Otago v Central Districts, Oamaru 1984–85
Best bowling performance: 7-27 Otago v Auckland, Auckland 1984–85

LAST SEASON: BATTING

	I.	N.O.	R.	H.S.	AV.
TEST					
1ST-CLASS	18	4	186	48*	13.28
INT					
RAL	10	6	70	21*	17.50
NAT.W.					
B & H	2	1	2	1*	2.00

CAREER: BATTING

	I.	N.O.	R.	H.S.	AV.
TEST					
1ST-CLASS	259	82	2551	88	14.41
INT					
RAL	53	28	294	23*	11.76
NAT.W.	9	3	43	11*	7.16
B & H	14	5	42	16*	4.66

LAST SEASON: BOWLING

	O.	M.	R.	W.	AV.
TEST					
1ST-CLASS	514.5	121	1389	50	27.78
INT					
RAL	83.4	3	302	12	25.16
NAT.W.					
B & H	64	8	245	8	30.62

CAREER: BOWLING

	O.	M.	R.	W.	AV.
TEST					
1ST-CLASS	5729.2	1290	16430	586	28.03
INT					
RAL	780.2	46	3498	138	25.34
NAT.W.	199.4	28	575	30	19.16
B & H	355.3	43	1303	48	27.14

100. What do Cyril Washbrook, Paul Parker, Trevor Bailey, and Douglas Jardine have in common, as county cricketers?

MARKS, V. J. Somerset

Full Name: Victor James Marks
Role: Right-hand bat, off-break bowler
Born: 25 June 1955, Middle Chinnock, Somerset
Height: 5′ 9″ **Weight:** 11st 8lbs
Nickname: Vic
County debut: 1975
County cap: 1979
Benefit: 1988
Test debut: 1982
No. of Tests: 6
No. of One-Day Internationals: 34
1000 runs in a season: 2
50 wickets in a season: 8
1st-Class 50s scored: 73
1st-Class 100s scored: 5
1st-Class 5 w. in innings: 40
1st-Class 10 w. in match: 5
One-Day 50s: 14
Place in batting averages: 39th av. 41.10 (1988 138th av. 24.79)
Place in bowling averages: 116th av. 47.91 (1988 74th av. 29.13)
Strike rate 1989: 107.72 (career 73.70)
1st-Class catches 1989: 7 (career 143)
Parents: Harold and Joan
Wife and date of marriage: Anna, 9 September 1978
Children: Amy, 27 November 1979; Rosie, 8 November 1987
Family links with cricket: 'Father a dangerous village cricketer.'
Education: Blundell's School; Oxford University
Qualifications: MA Classics
Off-season 1989–90: Working for *The Observer* as cricket correspondent
Jobs outside cricket: Teaching – but not since March 1981
Overseas tours: Derrick Robins' XI to Canada 1977; England to Australia and New Zealand 1982–83, New Zealand and Pakistan 1983–84, India and Australia 1984–85; Christians in Sport to India 1985
Overseas teams played for: Grade cricket with Bayswater Morley CC in Perth, Western Australia 1981–82, Western Australia 1986–87
Cricketers particularly learnt from: Tom Cartwright, Arthur Milton
Cricketers particularly admired: Colin Dredge
Other sports played: Squash, golf
Extras: Half-blue for rugby fives at Oxford University. Debut for Oxford

University CC 1975. Blue 1975–76–77–78. Captain 1976–77. Somerset vice-captain 1984. Author of *Somerset County Cricket Scrapbook* (1984), *Marks Out of XI* (1985), *TCCB Guide to Better Cricket* (1987) and *The Ultimate One-Day Cricket Match* (1988) with Robin Drake. Took over as captain when Peter Roebuck was injured in August 1988. Appointed captain for 1989 season. Retired at end of 1989 season to become cricket correspondent for *The Observer*

Opinions on cricket: 'We play too much.'

Best batting performance: 134 Somerset v Worcestershire, Weston-super-Mare 1984

Best bowling performance: 8-17 Somerset v Lancashire, Bath 1985

LAST SEASON: BATTING

	I.	N.O.	R.	H.S.	AV.
TEST					
1ST-CLASS	32	12	822	89*	41.10
INT					
RAL	16	2	282	67*	20.14
NAT.W.	2	1	55	36*	55.00
B & H	4	2	56	15*	28.00

CAREER: BATTING

	I.	N.O.	R.	H.S.	AV.
TEST	10	1	249	83	27.66
1ST-CLASS	490	89	12170	134	30.34
INT	24	3	285	44	13.57
RAL	138	33	2299	80	21.89
NAT.W.	25	8	527	55	31.00
B & H	49	10	1024	81*	26.25

LAST SEASON: BOWLING

	O.	M.	R.	W.	AV.
TEST					
1ST-CLASS	843.5	245	2252	47	47.91
INT					
RAL	127.2	7	573	24	23.87
NAT.W.	24	1	76	4	19.00
B & H	66	13	192	5	38.40

CAREER: BOWLING

	O.	M.	R.	W.	AV.
TEST	180.2	54	484	11	44.00
1ST-CLASS	10371.2	2856	28107	848	33.14
INT	306.2	28	1135	44	25.79
RAL	977	61	4007	154	26.01
NAT.W.	250.2	42	761	25	30.44
B & H	559.4	95	1717	52	33.01

101. Which current county cricketer was born in Malaysia?

MARSH, S. A.   Kent

Full Name: Steven Andrew Marsh
Role: Right-hand bat, wicket-keeper
Born: 27 January 1961, Westminster
Height: 5′ 11″ **Weight:** 12st
County debut: 1982
County cap: 1986
Nickname: Marshy
1st-Class 50s scored: 14
1st-Class 100s scored: 2
One-Day 50s scored: 1
Place in batting averages: 141st
av. 24.56 (1988 140th av. 24.58)
Parents: Melvyn Graham and Valerie
Ann
Wife and date of marriage: Julie,
27 September 1986
Family links with cricket: Father
played local cricket for Lordswood.
Father-in-law, Bob Wilson, played
for Kent 1954–66
Education: Walderslade Secondary School for Boys; Mid-Kent College of
Higher and Further Education
Qualifications: 6 O-levels, 2 A-levels, OND in Business Studies
Jobs outside cricket: Office clerk, cricket coach, computer operator
Off-season 1989–90: 'Working for my car sponsor, Swale Motor Co., as a
computer operator and accounts clerk.'
Cricketing superstitions or habits: 'When batting, getting into double figures.'
Overseas tours: Lordswood CC, Kent to Barbados 1979; Fred Rumsey's tour
to Barbados 1987, 1988

LAST SEASON: BATTING

	I.	N.O.	R.	H.S.	AV.
TEST					
1ST-CLASS	31	1	614	90*	24.56
INT					
RAL	12	1	217	53	19.72
NAT.W.	1	0	6	6	6.00
B & H	5	2	75	41*	25.00

CAREER: BATTING

	I.	N.O.	R.	H.S.	AV.
TEST					
1ST-CLASS	143	28	2775	120	24.13
INT					
RAL	40	8	451	53	14.09
NAT.W.	3	1	31	24*	15.50
B & H	15	4	144	41*	13.09

LAST SEASON: WICKET KEEPING

	C.	ST.
TEST		
1ST-CLASS	40	1
INT		
RAL	20	2
NAT.W.	2	–
B & H	7	–

CAREER: WICKET KEEPING

	C.	ST.
TEST		
1ST-CLASS	209	14
INT		
RAL	66	9
NAT.W.	13	1
B & H	29	2

Overseas teams played for: Avendale CC, South Africa 1985–86
Cricketers particularly learnt from: Alan Igglesden ('I have learnt to keep to leg-side bowling!'), Bob Woolmer
Cricketers particularly admired: Gary Sobers, Alan Knott
Other sports played: Golf, snooker, soccer, horse riding
Relaxations: Horse racing, eating and sleeping
Extras: Once swallowed one of Graham Cowdrey's contact lenses, when Cowdrey left it in a glass of water overnight and Marsh drank the water
Best batting performance: 120 Kent v Essex, Chelmsford 1988

MARSHALL, M. D. Hampshire

Full Name: Malcolm Denzil Marshall
Role: Right-hand bat, right-arm fast bowler
Born: 18 April 1958, Barbados
Height: 5' 10½" **Weight:** 12st 8lbs
Nickname: Macko
County debut: 1979
County cap: 1981
Benefit: 1987 (£61,006)
Test debut: 1978–79
No. of Tests: 66
No. of One-Day Internationals: 100
50 wickets in a season: 8
1st-Class 50s scored: 37
1st-Class 100s scored: 4
1st-Class 5 w. in innings: 78
1st-Class 10 w. in match: 11
One-Day 50s: 3
Place in batting averages: 132nd av. 25.75 (1988 78th av. 32.11)
Place in bowling averages: 3rd av. 16.67 (1988 1st av. 13.16)
Strike rate 1989: 46.81 (career 42.43)
1st-Class catches 1989: 2 (career 110)
Parents: Mrs Eleanor Inniss
Children: Shelly, 24 November 1984
Family links with cricket: Cousin Errol Yearwood plays for Texaco in Barbados as a fast bowler
Education: St Giles Boys' School; Parkinson Comprehensive School, Barbados

Qualifications: School passes in Maths and English
Jobs outside cricket: Working for Banks Brewery
Off-season 1989–90: Playing in and for the West Indies
Overseas tours: With West Indies to India and Sri Lanka 1978–79; Australia 1979–80, 1981–82, 1984–85, 1988–89; Pakistan 1980–81; India 1983–84; England 1980, 1984, 1988; Zimbabwe 1981; New Zealand 1979–80
Overseas teams played for: Barbados 1977–90
Cricketers particularly learnt from: Wes Hall, Gary Sobers
Other sports played: Tennis, darts, pool, golf
Injuries 1989: Broke wrist at home pre-season which delayed his appearance at start of season
Relaxations: Soul music, reggae
Extras: Took nine wickets in debut match v Glamorgan in May 1979. Scored his first first-class century (109) in Zimbabwe, October 1981, for the West Indies against Zimbabwe. Most wickets in the Shell Shield Competition (25) by a Barbadian. Broke record of number of wickets taken in a 22-match season (i.e. since 1969) with 133. Published autobiography *Marshall Arts* (1987). Nearly chose to become a wicket-keeper. 'Even now I wish sometimes I was in Jeff Dujon's place behind the stumps.' £61,006 from his benefit was a record for a West Indian in county cricket. One of *Wisden*'s Five Cricketers of the Year, 1982
Opinions on cricket: 'Cricket has been my life since I could stand upright and hold a cricket bat or at least our home-made apology, built from anything that looked like one. I played morning, noon and night every day of my life. Not even school could get in the way of my obsession with the game. There was no question of playing football, or anything else, for very long. It was cricket, cricket and more cricket.'
Best batting performance: 116* Hampshire v Lancashire, Southampton 1982
Best bowling performance: 8-71 Hampshire v Worcestershire, Southampton 1982

LAST SEASON: BATTING

	I.	N.O.	R.	H.S.	AV.
TEST					
1ST-CLASS	21	5	412	68*	25.75
INT					
RAL	5	0	119	36	23.80
NAT.W.	2	1	20	17*	20.00
B & H					

LAST SEASON: BOWLING

	O.	M.	R.	W.	AV.
TEST					
1ST-CLASS	428.3	115	1067	64	16.67
INT					
RAL	66.5	4	224	10	22.40
NAT.W.	46.1	9	136	7	19.42
B & H					

CAREER: BATTING

	I.	N.O.	R.	H.S.	AV.
TEST	84	8	1438	92	18.92
1ST-CLASS	295	41	6219	116*	24.48
INT	55	15	667	66	16.67
RAL	64	16	861	46	17.93
NAT.W.	15	8	214	51	30.57
B & H	23	1	285	34	12.95

CAREER: BOWLING

	O.	M.	R.	W.	AV.
TEST	2477.5	520	6699	326	20.54
1ST-CLASS	6800.4	1875	17024	986	17.26
INT	885.5	100	2980	127	23.46
RAL	765.3	72	2628	114	23.05
NAT.W.	236.5	45	631	25	25.24
B & H	265.1	51	737	37	19.91

MARTIN, P. J. Lancashire

Full Name: Peter James Martin
Role: Right-hand bat, right-arm
fast-medium bowler
Born: 15 November 1968,
Accrington
Height: 6′ 4½″ **Weight:** 15st
Nickname: Digger, Boofe, Maurice
County debut: 1989
1st-Class catches 1989: 1 (career 1)
Parents: Keith and Catherine Una
Marital status: Single
Education: Danum Grammar
School, Doncaster
Qualifications: 6 O-levels, 2 A-levels
Jobs outside cricket: Played cricket
straight from school
Off-season 1989–90: Playing and
coaching in Launceston, Tasmania
Cricketing superstitions or habits:
Always ready at the last minute, fielding and batting
Overseas tours: Young England Youth World Cup to Australia 1988
Overseas teams played for: Southern Districts CC, Queensland 1988–89
Cricketers particularly learnt from: Peter Lever, Paul Allott, John Abrahams, coaches at Lancashire
Cricketers particularly admired: Dennis Lillee, Ian Botham
Other sports played: Football (at school) for South Yorkshire U-19, basketball, golf (badly) and 'a bit of squash'
Relaxations: Music, bit of reading, Bailey's Irish Cream, eating out

LAST SEASON: BATTING

	I.	N.O.	R.	H.S.	AV.
TEST					
1ST-CLASS	2	0	20	16	10.00
INT					
RAL					
NAT.W.					
B & H					

LAST SEASON: BOWLING

	O.	M.	R.	W.	AV.
TEST					
1ST-CLASS	43	6	133	1	133.00
INT					
RAL					
NAT.W.					
B & H					

CAREER: BATTING

	I.	N.O.	R.	H.S.	AV.
TEST					
1ST-CLASS	2	0	20	16	10.00
INT					
RAL					
NAT.W.					
B & H					

CAREER: BOWLING

	O.	M.	R.	W.	AV.
TEST					
1ST-CLASS	43	6	133	1	133.00
INT					
RAL					
NAT.W.					
B & H					

Opinions on cricket: 'Water hogs should not be used at any stage in a cricket match.'
Best batting performance: 16 Lancashire v Australians, Old Trafford 1989
Best bowling performance: 1-46 Lancashire v Australians, Old Trafford 1989

MARTINDALE, D. J. R.
Nottinghamshire

Full Name: Duncan John Richardson Martindale
Role: Right-hand bat, cover fielder
Born: 13 December 1963, Harrogate
Height: 5' 11½" **Weight:** 12st
Nickname: Blowers
County debut: 1985
1st-Class 50s scored: 5
1st-Class 100s scored: 2
One-Day 50s scored: 1
Place in batting averages: 179th
av. 20.09 (1988 192nd av. 20.07)
1st-Class catches 1989: 6 (career 18)
Parents: Don and Isabel
Marital status: Single
Family links with cricket: Father
and grandfather played club cricket
in Nottingham; great uncle played
for Nottinghamshire 2nd XI

Education: Lymm Grammar School; Trent Polytechnic
Qualifications: 9 O-levels, 2 A-levels, HND Business Studies, NCA Coaching Award
Off-season 1989–90: Working at Nottinghamshire CCC with Christians in Sport
Overseas tours: International Ambassadors XI to India 1985
Overseas teams played for: Prospect and District CC, Adelaide 1985–86, 1986–87; Mt Lawley CC, Perth 1988–89
Cricketers particularly learnt from: 'The batsmen at Nottinghamshire in particular.'
Cricketers particularly admired: Richard Hadlee, Clive Rice, Vic Marks
Other sports played: All sports, particularly long-distance running, squash and golf

Relaxations: Reading, listening to all types of music, meeting people, good food, travelling
Extras: Scored a century (104*) in fifth first-class innings. First one-day match was 1985 NatWest Final. Member of Christians in Sport
Opinions on cricket: 'I believe that cricket has to improve its public appeal. That is, it must generate interest among the "general" public. More of an emphasis on quality not quantity.'
Best batting performance: 104* Nottinghamshire v Lancashire, Old Trafford 1985

LAST SEASON: BATTING

	I.	N.O.	R.	H.S.	AV.
TEST					
1ST-CLASS	11	0	221	78	20.09
INT					
RAL	6	1	191	53	38.20
NAT.W.	1	0	47	47	47.00
B & H					

CAREER: BATTING

	I.	N.O.	R.	H.S.	AV.
TEST					
1ST-CLASS	56	6	1106	104*	22.12
INT					
RAL	11	1	275	53	27.50
NAT.W.	2	1	67	47	67.00
B & H					

MARU, R. J. Hampshire

Full Name: Rajesh Jamnadass Maru
Role: Right-hand bat, slow left-arm bowler, close fielder
Born: 28 October 1962, Nairobi
Height: 5′ 6″ **Weight:** 10st 7lbs
Nickname: Raj
County debut: 1980 (Middlesex), 1984 (Hampshire)
County cap: 1986 (Hampshire)
50 wickets in a season: 3
1st-Class 50s scored: 2
1st-Class 5 w. in innings: 12
1st-Class 10 w. in match: 1
Place in batting averages: 253rd av. 11.29 (1988 245th av. 12.58)
Place in bowling averages: 87th av. 33.89 (1988 115th av. 35.84)
Strike rate 1989: 79.90 (career 69.45)
1st-Class catches 1989: 21 (career 140)
Parents: Jamnadass and Prabhavati
Family links with cricket: Brother Pradip has played for Middlesex 2nd XI and now plays for Wembley in Middlesex League

322

Education: Harrow College (Pinner Sixth Form); Rooks Heath High; Okington Manor

Qualifications: NCA Senior cricket coach

Off-season 1989–90: 'Having a winter off from playing, but doing some private coaching.'

Cricketing superstitions or habits: Nelsons: 111, 222 and 333

Overseas tours: Young England tour of West Indies 1980; NCA tour of Canada 1979; Barbican International XI to Dubai; Middlesex to Zimbabwe 1980–81; Hampshire to Barbados 1987, 1988; Hampshire to Dubai 1989

Overseas teams played for: Blenheim CC, New Zealand 1985–86, 1986–87

Cricketers particularly learnt from: Jack Robertson, Derek Underwood, David Graveney, Malcolm Marshall, Les Lenham

Cricketers particularly admired: Malcolm Marshall, Mike Gatting, Derek Underwood, Phil Edmonds, Gordón Greenidge

Other sports played: Badminton, table tennis, squash, swimming, hockey

Other sports followed: Football, rugby union, 'and all the sports above that I play'

Relaxations: Music, reading, TV

Extras: Played for Middlesex 1980–83. Joined Hampshire in 1984

Opinions on cricket: 'If we are going to play four-day cricket, then the wickets have to improve, so that they last the full four days. Practice wickets when you play away from home should be prepared so that you can have decent practice before the game.'

Best batting performance: 74 Hampshire v Gloucestershire, Gloucester 1988

Best bowling performance: 7-79 Hampshire v Middlesex, Bournemouth 1984

LAST SEASON: BATTING

	I.	N.O.	R.	H.S.	AV.
TEST					
1ST-CLASS	25	8	192	29	11.29
INT					
RAL	2	1	9	8*	9.00
NAT.W.	–	–	–	–	–
B & H					

CAREER: BATTING

	I.	N.O.	R.	H.S.	AV.
TEST					
1ST-CLASS	133	38	1322	74	13.91
INT					
RAL	5	4	18	8*	18.00
NAT.W.	–	–	–	–	–
B & H					

LAST SEASON: BOWLING

	O.	M.	R.	W.	AV.
TEST					
1ST-CLASS	586	162	1491	44	33.89
INT					
RAL	22.1	2	113	2	56.50
NAT.W.	24	1	54	1	54.00
B & H					

CAREER: BOWLING

	O.	M.	R.	W.	AV.
TEST					
1ST-CLASS	4121	1145	11033	356	30.99
INT					
RAL	82.1	5	401	11	36.45
NAT.W.	26	1	59	3	19.66
B & H					

MAYNARD, M. P.　　　　Glamorgan

Full Name: Matthew Peter Maynard
Role: Right-hand bat, right-arm
medium bowler, slip fielder
Born: 21 March 1966, Oldham
Height: 5′ 10½″ **Weight:** 12st 9lbs
Nickname: The Kid
County debut: 1985
County cap: 1987
Test debut: 1988
No. of Tests: 1
1000 runs in a season: 4
1st-Class 50s scored: 33
1st-Class 100s scored: 9
One-Day 50s: 9
One-Day 100s: 2
Place in batting averages: 116th
av. 27.97 (1988 32nd av. 41.25)
1st-Class catches 1989: 23 (career 89)
Parents: Pat and Ken (deceased)
Wife and date of marriage: Susan, 27 September 1986
Children: Thomas, 25 March 1989
Family links with cricket: Father pro'd for Duckinfield. Brother played club
cricket. Brother Charles plays for St Fagans
Education: Ysgol David Hughes, Anglesey
Qualifications: Cricket coach
Jobs outside cricket: Sales rep for Bangor City FC; barman, burger-bar chef,
labourer on site
Off-season 1989–90: Touring South Africa with unofficial English team
Cricketing superstitions or habits: 'Left pad on first.'
Overseas tours: Barbados with North Wales XI 1982; Barbados with Glam-
organ CCC 1989; unofficial England XI to South Africa 1989–90
Overseas teams played for: St Josephs, Whakatane 1986–87, 1987–88; Gos-
nells CC, Perth, Western Australia 1988–89
Cricketers particularly learnt from: Father, Colin Page, Bill Clutterbuck,
John Steele and 'everyone at Glamorgan'
Cricketers particularly admired: Richard Hadlee, Ian Botham, Barry
Richards
Other sports played: Golf, snooker
Other sports followed: Rugby, golf
Relaxations: 'Socialising, playing golf, and spending time with my wife and
son.'
Extras: Scored century on debut v Yorkshire at Swansea. Also youngest

centurion for Glamorgan. Scored 1000 runs in first full season, and in four consecutive seasons. Fastest ever 50 for Glamorgan (14 mins) v Yorkshire. Youngest player to be awarded Glamorgan cap. Fastest TV 50 in Refuge Assurance League 1987. Leading 6-hitter in Championship in 1987. Three B & H Gold Awards. Voted Young Cricketer of the Year 1988 by the Cricket Writers Club

Opinions on cricket: 'We should play 16 four-day matches.'

Best batting performance: 191* Glamorgan v Gloucestershire, Cardiff 1989

Best bowling performance: 3-21 Glamorgan v Oxford University, Oxford 1987

LAST SEASON: BATTING

	I.	N.O.	R.	H.S.	AV.
TEST					
1ST-CLASS	40	3	1035	191*	27.97
INT					
RAL	15	1	269	61*	19.21
NAT.W.	2	0	68	56	34.00
B & H	4	1	80	43*	26.66

CAREER: BATTING

	I.	N.O.	R.	H.S.	AV.
TEST	2	0	13	10	6.50
1ST-CLASS	162	18	5333	191*	37.03
INT					
RAL	57	3	1162	92*	21.51
NAT.W.	9	0	221	64	24.55
B & H	15	3	516	115	43.00

LAST SEASON: BOWLING

	O.	M.	R.	W.	AV.
TEST					
1ST-CLASS	26	5	72	0	–
INT					
RAL					
NAT.W.					
B & H	2	0	26	0	–

CAREER: BOWLING

	O.	M.	R.	W.	AV.
TEST					
1ST-CLASS	75.1	13	233	4	58.25
INT					
RAL					
NAT.W.					
B & H	4	0	32	0	–

102. Which current county cricketer was born in Osnabruck, West Germany?

103. Which current county cricketer is nicknamed Zorro?

McEWAN, S. M.　　　　Worcestershire

Full Name: Steven Michael
McEwan
Role: Right-hand bat, right-arm
fast-medium bowler, slip fielder
Born: 5 May 1962, Worcester
Height: 6' 1" **Weight:** 13st 7lbs
Nickname: Mac, Maciz, Freddy
County debut: 1985
County cap: 1989
50 wickets in a season: 1
1st-Class 5 w. in innings: 3
Place in batting averages: 152nd
av. 23.16
Place in bowling averages: 9th
av. 19.21
Strike rate 1989: 42.51 (career 53.42)
1st-Class catches 1989: 3 (career 12)
Parents: Michael James and
Valerie Jeanette

Marital status: Single
Family links with cricket: Father and uncle played club cricket
Education: Worcester Royal Grammar School
Qualifications: 6 O-levels, 3 A-levels. Technician's certificate in building
Jobs outside cricket: Assistant buyer, building trade; cricket coach
Overseas teams played for: Birkenhead City, Auckland 1985–87; Springs,
Johannesburg 1988–89
Cricketers particularly learnt from: Dipak Patal, Basil D'Oliveira, Kapil
Dev

LAST SEASON: BATTING

	I.	N.O.	R.	H.S.	AV.
TEST					
1ST-CLASS	9	3	139	28*	23.16
INT					
RAL	2	2	7	7*	–
NAT.W.	1	0	6	6	6.00
B & H					

CAREER: BATTING

	I.	N.O.	R.	H.S.	AV.
TEST					
1ST-CLASS	23	11	184	28*	15.33
INT					
RAL	7	5	20	7*	10.00
NAT.W.	1	0	6	6	6.00
B & H					

LAST SEASON: BOWLING

	O.	M.	R.	W.	AV.
TEST					
1ST-CLASS	368.3	80	999	52	19.21
INT					
RAL	43	0	210	5	42.00
NAT.W.	11	3	51	3	17.00
B & H					

CAREER: BOWLING

	O.	M.	R.	W.	AV.
TEST					
1ST-CLASS	899.2	159	2880	101	28.51
INT					
RAL	153	2	796	26	30.61
NAT.W.	11	3	51	3	17.00
B & H					

Cricketers particularly admired: Richard Hadlee, Malcolm Marshall
Other sports played: Soccer
Other sports followed: American football
Relaxations: TV, reading
Extras: Took 10 wickets for 13 runs in an innings in 1983 for Worcester Nomads against Moreton-in-Marsh. Also broke school bowling record, 60 wickets, at WRGS, 1982
Opinions on cricket: 'In favour of four-day county cricket.'
Best batting performance: 28* Worcestershire v Warwickshire, Worcester 1989
Best bowling performance: 6-34 Worcestershire v Leicestershire, Kidderminster 1989

MEDLYCOTT, K. T. Surrey

Full Name: Keith Thomas Medlycott
Role: Right-hand bat, slow left-arm bowler, slip fielder
Born: 12 May 1965, Whitechapel
Height: 5' 11" **Weight:** 13st
Nickname: Medders
County debut: 1984
County cap: 1988
50 wickets in a season: 2
1st-Class 50s scored: 17
1st-Class 100s scored: 2
1st-Class 5 w. in innings: 13
1st-Class 10 w. in match: 5
Place in batting averages: 93rd av. 30.93 (1988 157th av. 23.08)
Place in bowling averages: 96th av. 33.32 (1988 43rd av. 24.05)
Strike rate 1989: 66.70 (career 61.30)
1st-Class catches 1989: 19 (career 69)
Parents: Thomas Alfred (deceased) and June Elizabeth
Marital status: Single
Family links with cricket: 'Father played club cricket for Colposa. Twin brother Paul plays *very* occasionally!'
Education: Parmiters Grammar School; Wandsworth Comprehensive
Qualifications: 2 O-levels
Jobs outside cricket: Coaching

327

Off-season 1989–90: Touring West Indies with England
Cricketing superstitions or habits: 'Bad habit of talking rubbish before batting, which definitely annoys the coach!'
Overseas tours: Barbados, 1981, with London Schools; Barbados with Grahame Clinton's Benefit 1989
Overseas teams played for: Oostelikes CC 1983–88; Harlequins CC 1984–85
Cricketers particularly learnt from: Geoff Arnold, T. Sheppard, Chris Waller, Don Wilson
Cricketers particularly admired: Tom Medlycott, David Ward – 'always plays with a smile.'
Other sports played: Football, rugby
Other sports followed: Rugby, football, 'try to watch Andy Jones of Charlton.'
Relaxations: 'Sport in general.'
Extras: Scored 100 on debut (117* v Cambridge University) in 1984. Took first hat-trick of career against Hampshire 2nd XI, 1988. Capped in last game of season, against Kent. Did not play cricket at his first school. Spent season on Lord's ground staff. Offered a contract by Northamptonshire in 1984. Directed to Surrey by Mickey Stewart
Opinions on cricket: 'We should have four-day cricket. The TCCB should pay groundsmen instead of the clubs, and then sack the bad ones!'
Best batting performance: 153 Surrey v Kent, The Oval 1987
Best bowling performance: 8-52 Surrey v Sussex, Hove 1988

LAST SEASON: BATTING

	I.	N.O.	R.	H.S.	AV.
TEST					
1ST-CLASS	38	8	928	86*	30.93
INT					
RAL	13	3	102	33	10.20
NAT.W.	3	2	27	18	27.00
B & H	2	0	13	11	6.50

CAREER: BATTING

	I.	N.O.	R.	H.S.	AV.
TEST					
1ST-CLASS	125	27	2626	153	26.79
INT					
RAL	21	4	195	34	11.47
NAT.W.	3	2	27	18	27.00
B & H	2	0	13	11	6.50

LAST SEASON: BOWLING

	O.	M.	R.	W.	AV.
TEST					
1ST-CLASS	722.4	181	2166	65	33.32
INT					
RAL	71	3	345	19	18.15
NAT.W.	26	5	94	1	94.00
B & H	4.3	0	37	2	18.50

CAREER: BOWLING

	O.	M.	R.	W.	AV.
TEST					
1ST-CLASS	2390.5	631	7007	234	29.94
INT					
RAL	91	3	477	23	20.73
NAT.W.	26	5	94	1	94.00
B & H	4.3	0	37	2	18.50

MENDIS, G. D. Lancashire

Full Name: Gehan Dixon Mendis
Role: Right-hand opening bat
Born: 24 April 1955, Colombo, Ceylon
Height: 5′ 8″ **Weight:** 11st
Nickname: Mendo, Dix
County debut: 1974 (Sussex), 1986 (Lancashire)
County cap: 1980 (Sussex), 1986 (Lancashire)
1000 runs in a season: 10
1st-Class 50s scored: 90
1st-Class 100s scored: 29
1st-Class 200s scored: 3
One-Day 50s: 32
One-Day 100s: 6
Place in batting averages: 25th av. 44.09 (1988 54th av. 35.89)
1st-Class catches 1989: 5 (career 116 + 1 stumping)
Parents: Sam Dixon Charles and Sonia Marcelle (both deceased)
Children: Hayley, 11 December 1982
Education: St Thomas College, Mount Lavinia, Sri Lanka; Brighton, Hove & Sussex Grammar School; Bede College, Durham University
Qualifications: BEd Mathematics, Durham; NCA Coaching Certificate
Jobs outside cricket: Teacher at Rosemead School, Littlehampton, Sussex; Richard Ellis, Perth, Western Australia; City Sales & Marketing Ltd, London. Self-employed
Overseas tours: Maharaja Organisation XI to India 1980; Rohan Kanhai's Invitation XI to Pakistan 1981; numerous international teams to West Indies; Lancashire CCC to West Indies 1986–87, 1987–88; Lancashire to Zimbabwe 1988–89
Overseas teams played for: Maharaja Organisation XI in Sri Lanka 1980–81; Colombo CC; Sebastianites CC, and Mount Lawley CC, Western Australia; Nedlands CC Perth
Cricketers particularly admired: Barry Richards, Richard Hadlee
Other sports played: 'None any more!'
Other sports followed: Formula One motor racing
Relaxations: Music, 'getting away from cricket'
Extras: Played for TCCB XI in 1981. Has twice turned down invitations to play for Sri Lanka in order to be free to be chosen for England. Left Sussex at end of 1985 to join Lancashire. Played table tennis for Sussex at junior level

Opinions on cricket: 'None, any more, as cricketers and/or captains have not much say in the running of the game. Sign of old age, I guess!'
Best batting performance: 209* Sussex v Somerset, Hove 1984
Best bowling performance: 1-65 Sussex v Yorkshire, Hove 1985

LAST SEASON: BATTING

	I.	N.O.	R.	H.S.	AV.
TEST					
1ST-CLASS	34	3	1367	118	44.09
INT					
RAL	11	0	300	66	27.27
NAT.W.	3	0	81	46	27.00
B & H	5	1	158	82*	39.50

CAREER: BATTING

	I.	N.O.	R.	H.S.	AV.
TEST					
1ST-CLASS	523	49	17247	209*	36.38
INT					
RAL	161	14	4120	125*	28.02
NAT.W.	33	2	1032	141*	33.29
B & H	54	2	1467	109	28.21

LAST SEASON: BOWLING

	O.	M.	R.	W.	AV.
TEST					
1ST-CLASS	2	0	5	0	–
INT					
RAL					
NAT.W.					
B & H					

CAREER: BOWLING

	O.	M.	R.	W.	AV.
TEST					
1ST-CLASS	29.3	2	158	1	158.00
INT					
RAL					
NAT.W.					
B & H					

MERRICK, T. A.   Warwickshire

Full Name: Tyrone Anthony Merrick
Role: Right-hand bat, right-arm fast-medium bowler
Born: 10 June 1963, Antigua
Height: 6′
County debut: 1987
County cap: 1988
50 wickets in a season: 2
1st-Class 50s scored: 2
1st-Class 5 w. in innings: 14
1st-Class 10 w. in match: 2
One-Day 50s: 1
Place in batting averages: —
(1988 234th av. 14.22)
Place in bowling averages: —
(1988 26th av. 22.10)
1st-Class catches 1989: 0 (career 25)
Children: Anthea, 6 January 1987
Education: All Saints Primary and Secondary Schools
Jobs outside cricket: Physical Education Teacher

330

Off-season 1989–90: Playing in West Indies
Overseas tours: West Indies Youth Team to England 1982; West Indies B to Zimbabwe 1986
Overseas teams played for: Leeward Islands 1982–90
Cricketers particularly learnt from: Andy Roberts, Eldine Baptiste
Other sports followed: Soccer, lawn tennis
Relaxations: Listening to music
Extras: Played for Rawtenstall in Lancashire League 1985 and 1986. Released by Warwickshire at end of 1989 season
Best batting performance: 74* Warwickshire v Gloucestershire, Edgbaston 1987
Best bowling performance: 7-45 Warwickshire v Lancashire, Edgbaston 1987

LAST SEASON: BATTING

	I.	N.O.	R.	H.S.	AV.
TEST					
1ST-CLASS	3	0	40	31	13.33
INT					
RAL	3	2	22	21*	22.00
NAT.W.					
B & H					

CAREER: BATTING

	I.	N.O.	R.	H.S.	AV.
TEST					
1ST-CLASS	80	15	995	74*	15.30
INT					
RAL	11	3	126	59	15.75
NAT.W.	2	0	15	13	7.50
B & H	4	1	27	13*	9.00

LAST SEASON: BOWLING

	O.	M.	R.	W.	AV.
TEST					
1ST-CLASS	110.4	29	320	12	26.66
INT					
RAL	19.2	2	85	5	17.00
NAT.W.					
B & H					

CAREER: BOWLING

	O.	M.	R.	W.	AV.
TEST					
1ST-CLASS	1780.2	224	5643	233	24.21
INT					
RAL	139.3	18	543	25	21.72
NAT.W.	21	7	39	3	13.00
B & H	49	8	127	5	25.40

104. When did Sri Lanka play their first Test match?

METCALFE, A. A.   Yorkshire

Full Name: Ashley Anthony Metcalfe
Role: Right-hand bat, off-break bowler
Born: 25 December 1963, Horsforth, Leeds
Height: 5′ 9½″ **Weight:** 11st 7lbs
County debut: 1983
County cap: 1986
1000 runs in a season: 4
1st-Class 50s scored: 33
1st-Class 100s scored: 14
1st-Class 200s scored: 1
One-Day 50s: 24
One-Day 100s: 1
Place in batting averages: 74th av. 34.44 (1988 44th av. 37.71)
1st-Class catches 1989: 8 (career 40)
Parents: Tony and Ann
Wife and date of marriage: Diane, 20 April 1986
Family links with cricket: Father played in local league; father-in-law Ray Illingworth (Yorkshire and England)
Education: Ladderbanks Middle School; Bradford Grammar School; University College, London
Qualifications: 9 O-levels, 3 A-levels, NCA Coaching Certificate
Jobs outside cricket: Worked for Grattan Mail Order Co, Paul Madeley's DIY
Overseas tours: NCA tour of Denmark 1981; Yorkshire CCC to West Indies 1986–87
Overseas teams played for: Ringwood CC, Melbourne 1985–87; Orange Free State 1988–89
Cricketers particularly learnt from: Doug Padgett, Ray Illingworth, Don Wilson
Cricketers particularly admired: Barry Richards
Other sports played: Golf
Other sports followed: Most
Relaxations: 'Relaxing at home with my wife.'
Extras: 'I made 122 on my debut for Yorkshire against Nottinghamshire at Park Avenue in 1983. I was the youngest ever Yorkshire player to do so and it was the highest ever score by a Yorkshireman on debut.'
Opinions on cricket: 'Politics should not interfere with sport – South Africa should be eligible for Test cricket.'

Best batting performance: 216* Yorkshire v Middlesex, Headingley 1988
Best bowling performance: 2-18 Yorkshire v Warwickshire, Scarborough 1987

LAST SEASON: BATTING

	I.	N.O.	R.	H.S.	AV.
TEST					
1ST-CLASS	37	1	1230	138	34.16
INT					
RAL	16	0	367	76	22.93
NAT.W.	2	0	90	50	45.00
B & H	4	0	144	77	36.00

CAREER: BATTING

	I.	N.O.	R.	H.S.	AV.
TEST					
1ST-CLASS	201	11	6426	216*	33.82
INT					
RAL	77	2	2001	115*	26.68
NAT.W.	12	1	409	85	37.18
B & H	17	3	735	94*	52.50

LAST SEASON: BOWLING

	O.	M.	R.	W.	AV.
TEST					
1ST-CLASS	13.4	3	33	0	–
INT					
RAL					
NAT.W.					
B & H					

CAREER: BOWLING

	O.	M.	R.	W.	AV.
TEST					
1ST-CLASS	53.1	8	205	4	51.25
INT					
RAL					
NAT.W.	7	0	44	2	22.00
B & H					

METSON, C. P.   Glamorgan

Full Name: Colin Peter Metson
Role: Right-hand bat, wicket-keeper
Born: 2 July 1963, Cuffley, Hertfordshire
Height: 5′ 6″ **Weight:** 10st 9lbs
Nickname: Dempster, Reggie, Jazzer
County debut: 1981 (Middlesex), 1987 (Glamorgan)
County cap: 1987 (Glamorgan)
1st-Class 50s scored: 3
Place in batting averages: 216th av. 15.96 (1988 223rd av. 15.95)
Parents: Denis Alwyn and Jean Mary
Marital status: Single
Family links with cricket: Father played good club cricket and for MCC; brother plays club cricket for Winchmore Hill CC

Education: Stanborough School, Welwyn Garden City; Enfield Grammar School; Durham University

Qualifications: 10 O-levels, 5 A-levels, BA Hons Economic History, NCA Senior Coaching Award

Jobs outside cricket: Accounts clerk

Off-season 1989–90: 'At home in London.'

Cricketing superstitions or habits: 'Always put right pad on before left; always wear a sun hat; try to use the same equipment right through the season if possible, especially wicket-keeping gloves. Try not to watch the cricket as a wicket always falls when I do.'

Overseas teams played for: Payeham CC, Adelaide 1985–86, 1986–87; Rostrevor CC 1987–88

Cricketers particularly learnt from: Jack Robertson, Bob Taylor, Father, Don Bennett, Paul Downton

Cricketers particularly admired: Bob Taylor, Mike Brearley

Other sports played: Football, golf, tennis

Other sports followed: American football, golf, football, all sports except wrestling

Injuries 1989: 'No injuries serious enough to make me miss any game.'

Relaxations: *Daily Telegraph* crossword, reading, drinking good wine, Mexican food, watching most sports programmes

Extras: Young Wicket-keeper of the Year 1981. Three Young England Tests v India 1981. Captain Durham University 1984, losing finalists in UAU competition. Beat Cambridge University twice. Middlesex 2nd XI Player of the Year 1984. Left Middlesex in March 1987 to replace Terry Davies at Glamorgan

Opinions on cricket: 'Cricket must find ways to market itself better, and in finding the sponsors, must give them value for money. Four-day cricket in 1988 looked to be a success, so I would encourage 16 four-day games, as long as the pitches lasted at least three days. Playing sessions could then be two hours long, with perhaps 100 overs minimum in the day.'

Best batting performance: 96 Middlesex v Gloucestershire, Uxbridge 1984

LAST SEASON: BATTING

	I.	N.O.	R.	H.S.	AV.
TEST					
1ST-CLASS	33	8	399	47	15.96
INT					
RAL	11	4	74	21*	10.57
NAT.W.	1	0	6	6	6.00
B & H	3	0	19	12	6.33

CAREER: BATTING

	I.	N.O.	R.	H.S.	AV.
TEST					
1ST-CLASS	131	32	1669	96	16.85
INT					
RAL	36	19	259	23*	15.23
NAT.W.	4	1	10	6	3.33
B & H	7	0	46	12	6.57

LAST SEASON: WICKET KEEPING

	C.	ST.
TEST		
1ST-CLASS	57	6
INT		
RAL	11	2
NAT.W.	1	–
B & H	1	–

CAREER: WICKET KEEPING

	C.	ST.
TEST		
1ST-CLASS	206	22
INT		
RAL	55	17
NAT.W.	6	–
B & H	7	2

MIDDLETON, T. C.   Hampshire

Full Name: Tony Charles Middleton
Role: Right-hand bat, slow left-arm
bowler
Born: 1 February 1964, Winchester
Height: 5′ 11″ **Weight:** 11st
Nickname: Roo, Midders, TC
County debut: 1984
1st-Class 50s scored: 3
Place in batting averages: 121st
av. 27.40
1st-Class catches 1989: 8 (career
16)
Parents: Peter and Molly
Marital status: Single
Family links with cricket: Brother
plays local club cricket in
Hampshire
Education: Weeke Infants and
Junior Schools; Montgomery of
Alamein Comprehensive, Winchester; Peter Symonds Sixth Form College,
Winchester
Qualifications: 1 A-level, 5 O-levels
Jobs outside cricket: Worked for two winters as an electrical engineer
Cricketing superstitions or habits: 'Always wear spikes to bat in.'
Overseas teams played for: Club cricket for Durban Police, South Africa
1984–85 and 1985–86
Cricketers particularly learnt from: 'Too many to name.'
Cricketers particularly admired: Barry Richards, Gordon Greenidge

LAST SEASON: BATTING

	I.	N.O.	R.	H.S.	AV.
TEST					
1ST-CLASS	11	1	274	69	27.40
INT					
RAL	1	1	4	4*	–
NAT.W.					
B & H					

CAREER: BATTING

	I.	N.O.	R.	H.S.	AV.
TEST					
1ST-CLASS	30	4	640	69	24.61
INT					
RAL	1	1	4	4*	–
NAT.W.					
B & H					

LAST SEASON: BOWLING

	O.	M.	R.	W.	AV.
TEST					
1ST-CLASS	3	0	26	1	26.00
INT					
RAL					
NAT.W.					
B & H					

CAREER: BOWLING

	O.	M.	R.	W.	AV.
TEST					
1ST-CLASS	12	1	74	2	37.00
INT					
RAL					
NAT.W.					
B & H					

Other sports played: Squash, football, badminton
Other sports followed: Football, rugby union
Relaxations: Watching and playing other sports
Extras: Played for England Schools 1982
Opinions on cricket: 'Sunday League should be increased to 50 overs with normal run ups and only one knock-out plus play-offs for top Sunday League sides. Hopefully the introduction of a full four-day Championship in the near future will put an end to contrived results and "result" wickets.'
Best batting performance: 69 Hampshire v Glamorgan, Cardiff 1989
Best bowling performance: 1-13 Hampshire v Middlesex, Lord's 1986

MIKE, G. W.   Nottinghamshire

Full Name: Gregory Wentworth Mike
Role: Right-hand bat, right-arm fast-medium bowler
Born: 14 August 1966, Nottingham
Height: 6' 1" **Weight:** 14½st
Nickname: Esther
County debut: 1988 (RAL), 1989 (First-Class)
1st-Class 50s scored: 1
Parents: Clinton and Kathleen
Marital status: Single
Family links with cricket: 'My father played.'
Education: Claremount Comprehensive; Basford Hall College
Qualifications: 2 O-levels, 4 CSEs
Jobs outside cricket: Youth work
Off-season 1989–90: In Barbados
Overseas teams played for: Yorkshire, Barbados 1988
Cricketers particularly learnt from: Franklyn Stephenson, Mike Bore
Cricketers particularly admired: Ian Botham, Viv Richards
Other sports played: Squash, snooker, cycling 'and just keeping fit'
Other sports followed: Snooker, boxing
Injuries 1989: 'Side injuries – off three weeks.'
Relaxations: Listening to music, playing snooker
Opinions on cricket: 'Great game!'

Best batting performance: 56* Nottinghamshire v Cambridge University, Cambridge 1989

LAST SEASON: BATTING

	I.	N.O.	R.	H.S.	AV.
TEST					
1ST-CLASS	2	1	71	56*	71.00
INT					
RAL	3	1	25	25*	12.50
NAT.W.					
B & H	1	0	29	29	29.00

CAREER: BATTING

	I.	N.O.	R.	H.S.	AV.
TEST					
1ST-CLASS	2	1	71	56*	71.00
INT					
RAL	4	1	25	25*	8.33
NAT.W.					
B & H	1	0	29	29	29.00

LAST SEASON: BOWLING

	O.	M.	R.	W.	AV.
TEST					
1ST-CLASS	28	5	107	2	53.50
INT					
RAL	14.3	0	74	2	37.00
NAT.W.					
B & H					

CAREER: BOWLING

	O.	M.	R.	W.	AV.
TEST					
1ST-CLASS	28	5	107	2	53.50
INT					
RAL	26.3	1	155	3	51.66
NAT.W.					
B & H					

MILLER, G.   Derbyshire

Full Name: Geoffrey Miller
Role: Right-hand bat, off-break bowler
Born: 8 September 1952, Chesterfield
Height: 6′ 2″ **Weight:** 11st 6lbs
Nickname: Dusty
County debut: 1973 (Derbyshire), 1987 (Essex)
County cap: 1976 (Derbyshire), 1988 (Essex)
Benefit: 1985
Test debut: 1976
No. of Tests: 34
No. of One-Day Internationals: 25
50 wickets in a season: 4
1st-Class 50s scored: 72
1st-Class 100s scored: 2
1st-Class 5 w. in innings: 38
1st-Class 10 w. in match: 7
One-Day 50s: 17

Place in batting averages: 91st av. 31.45 (1988 168th av. 22.17)
Place in bowling averages: 115th av. 46.40 (1988 78th av. 29.56)
Strike rate 1989: 115.00 (career 66.18)
1st-Class catches 1989: 7 (career 302)

Parents: Keith and Gwen
Wife: Carol
Children: Helen Jane; Anna Louise; James Daniel
Family links with cricket: Father played local cricket in Chesterfield. Brother plays for Chesterfield CC
Education: Chesterfield Grammar School
Qualifications: 5 O-levels
Jobs outside cricket: Owner of two sports shops
Off-season 1989–90: 'Running my sports shops.'
Overseas tours: With England Young Cricketers to India 1970–71 and West Indies 1972; toured with England to India, Sri Lanka, Australia 1976–77; Pakistan and New Zealand 1977–78; Australia 1978–79 and 1979–80 but had to return December 1979 through injury; West Indies 1981; Australia and New Zealand 1982–83
Overseas teams played for: Natal 1983–84
Cricketers particularly learnt from: Eddie Barlow, Ray Illingworth, Fred Titmus
Cricketers particularly admired: 'The late Ken Barrington.'
Other sports played: Golf, table tennis, football
Relaxations: 'Crosswords, reading, television, family life. Watching Chesterfield FC particularly, and all sports in general. Driving. Running my business. Indian food. Doing VAT.'
Extras: Became captain of Derbyshire halfway through 1979 season, but relinquished it halfway through 1981 season in favour of Barry Wood. Declined to sign for Derbyshire for 1982 season, and was released. Negotiated with several other counties, but signed again. Eventually left at end of 1986 season and joined Essex for 1987. Played table tennis for Derbyshire. Released by Essex at end of 1989 season, and returned to Derbyshire
Best batting performance: 130 Derbyshire v Lancashire, Old Trafford 1984
Best bowling performance: 8-70 Derbyshire v Leicestershire, Coalville 1982

LAST SEASON: BATTING

	I.	N.O.	R.	H.S.	AV.
TEST					
1ST-CLASS	14	3	346	61	31.45
INT					
RAL	6	3	90	44*	30.00
NAT.W.	1	0	15	15	15.00
B & H	2	1	20	20	20.00

LAST SEASON: BOWLING

	O.	M.	R.	W.	AV.
TEST					
1ST-CLASS	191.4	60	464	10	46.40
INT					
RAL	66	2	302	8	37.75
NAT.W.	12	1	42	0	–
B & H	19	0	94	1	94.00

CAREER: BATTING

	I.	N.O.	R.	H.S.	AV.
TEST	51	4	1213	98*	25.80
1ST-CLASS	483	82	10581	130	26.38
INT	18	2	136	46	8.50
RAL	157	34	2564	84	20.84
NAT.W.	20	4	357	59*	22.31
B & H	54	13	1027	88*	25.04

CAREER: BOWLING

	O.	M.	R.	W.	AV.
TEST	280.1 484.4	79 140	1859	60	30.98
1ST-CLASS	256.2 8210.1	48 2314	21687	793	27.34
INT	13 194	1 19	813	25	32.52
RAL	1002.3	68	4206	146	28.80
NAT.W.	238.3	53	639	22	29.04
B & H	544	102	1599	61	26.21

MILLNS, D. J.   Nottinghamshire

Full Name: David James Millns
Role: Left-hand bat, right-arm
fast medium bowler, 1st slip fielder
Born: 27 February 1965, Mansfield
Height: 6′ 3″ **Weight:** 14st
Nickname: Ming, Rocket Man, Bulb
Head
County debut: 1988
1st-Class catches 1989: 2 (career 6)
Parents: Bernard and Brenda
Marital status: Single
Family links with cricket: Father
and elder brother Paul both play
for Clipstone WCC in Bassettlaw
League
Education: Garibaldi Comprehensive
Qualifications: 9 CSEs; Qualified
junior coach
Jobs outside cricket: Worked for
British Coal for three years as a linesman on the surveying staff at Clipstone
Colliery
Off-season 1989–90: Playing for Birkinhead CC, Auckland, and coaching
during the week
Cricketing superstitions or habits: 'Always try and walk out onto field behind
the captain.'
Overseas teams played for: Uitenhage CC, South Africa 1988–89; Birkinhead
CC, Auckland, New Zealand
Cricketers particularly learnt from: John Birch – 'epitomises total profession-
alism.'
Cricketers particularly admired: Clive Rice – 'always backed himself or any of
his players in any situation.'
Other sports played: Football, snooker, golf ('to a poor standard')
Other sports followed: American football, skiing, Formula One motor racing
Injuries 1989: 'Cracked cartilage in right knee, and had operation to remove
this in early September. Torn tricep in left arm in early August ended the
season.'
Relaxations: Watching films, sleeping, eating out
Extras: Had two operations on each leg to cure shin sores in November
1987
Opinions on cricket: 'Opinions of professional cricketers do not seem to be
worth printing, because the people in charge of this great game do not seem to
take much notice.'

Best batting performance: 9 Nottinghamshire v Australians, Trent Bridge 1989
Best bowling performance: 4-86 Nottinghamshire v Australians, Trent Bridge 1989

LAST SEASON: BATTING

	I.	N.O.	R.	H.S.	AV.
TEST					
1ST-CLASS	3	1	16	9	8.00
INT					
RAL	1	1	0	0*	–
NAT.W.					
B & H					

LAST SEASON: BOWLING

	O.	M.	R.	W.	AV.
TEST					
1ST-CLASS	118	22	399	8	49.87
INT					
RAL	6	0	34	0	–
NAT.W.					
B & H					

CAREER: BATTING

	I.	N.O.	R.	H.S.	AV.
TEST					
1ST-CLASS	15	6	36	9	4.00
INT					
RAL	2	2	0	0*	–
NAT.W.					
B & H					

CAREER: BOWLING

	O.	M.	R.	W.	AV.
TEST					
1ST-CLASS	297	44	1082	27	40.07
INT					
RAL	29	0	179	3	59.66
NAT.W.					
B & H					

MOLES, A. J. Warwickshire

Full Name: Andrew James Moles
Role: Right-hand opening bat, right-arm medium bowler
Born: 12 February 1961, Solihull
Height: 5′ 10″ **Weight:** 13½st
Nickname: Molar
County debut: 1986
County cap: 1987
1000 runs in a season: 2
1st-Class 50s scored: 29
1st-Class 100s scored: 14
1st-Class 200s scored: 2
One-Day 50s: 8
One-Day 100s: 1
Place in batting averages: 73rd
av. 34.48 (1988 70th av. 33.37)
1st-Class catches 1989: 18 (career 66)
Parents: Stuart Francis and Gillian Margaret
Wife and date of marriage: Jacquie, 17 December 1988
Family links with cricket: Brother plays for Solihull in the Midland Championship

Education: Finham Park Comprehensive, Coventry; Henley College of Further Education; Butts College of Further Education
Qualifications: 3 O-levels, 4 CSEs, Toolmaker/Standard Room Inspector City & Guilds 205 Pts I, II, III
Jobs outside cricket: Standard Room Inspector
Cricketing superstitions or habits: 'Put left pad on first. Never look back at stumps after being bowled.'
Overseas teams played for: Griqualand West Cricket Union, South Africa 1985–86, 1987–88
Cricketers particularly learnt from: Dennis Amiss, Fred Gardner
Cricketers particularly admired: Dennis Amiss, Martin Crowe
Other sports played: Football
Relaxations: Listening to music or a meal with friends and talking about cricket
Best batting performance: 230* Griqualand West v Northern Transvaal B, Verwoerdburn 1988–89
Best bowling performance: 3-21 Warwickshire v Oxford University, Oxford 1987

LAST SEASON: BATTING

	I.	N.O.	R.	H.S.	AV.
TEST					
1ST-CLASS	38	5	1138	130*	34.48
INT					
RAL	4	0	51	19	12.75
NAT.W.	5	0	131	61	26.20
B & H	4	0	91	65	22.75

CAREER: BATTING

	I.	N.O.	R.	H.S.	AV.
TEST					
1ST-CLASS	168	17	6264	230*	41.48
INT					
RAL	31	2	628	85	21.65
NAT.W.	11	0	310	127	28.18
B & H	12	0	319	72	26.58

LAST SEASON: BOWLING

	O.	M.	R.	W.	AV.
TEST					
1ST-CLASS	24	3	136	1	136.00
INT					
RAL					
NAT.W.					
B & H	7	0	36	0	–

CAREER: BOWLING

	O.	M.	R.	W.	AV.
TEST					
1ST-CLASS	443	95	1384	31	44.64
INT					
RAL	63	0	358	7	51.14
NAT.W.	15	0	81	0	–
B & H	31	0	151	2	75.50

105. Who was born in Ireland, played in the first ever Test match, and captained Australia twice?

MOORES, P.

Sussex

Full Name: Peter Moores
Role: Right-hand bat, wicket-keeper
Born: 18 December 1962,
Macclesfield, Cheshire
Height: 6′ **Weight:** 13st
Nickname: Stumper, Billy
County debut: 1983 (Worcestershire),
1985 (Sussex)
1st-Class 50s scored: 5
1st-Class 100s scored: 1
Place in batting averages: 130th
av. 26.20 (1988 204th av. 17.95)
Parents: Bernard and Winifred
Wife and date of marriage: Karen,
28 September 1989
Family links with cricket: Three
brothers, Anthony, Stephen and
Robert, all play local cricket
Education: King Edward VI School,
Macclesfield
Qualifications: 7 O-levels, 3 A-levels. Senior NCA Coaching Award
Overseas teams played for: Old Hararians, Zimbabwe 1983–84; Harare
Sports Club 1984–85; Rovers CC, South Africa 1986–87, 1987–88; Orange
Free State, South Africa 1988–89
Cricketers particularly learnt from: Don Wilson, Basil D'Oliveira, Norman
Gifford, Dave Hill, Ian Wilson, Anthony Moores
Cricketers particularly admired: Bob Taylor, Farouk Engineer, Alan Knott
Other sports played: Squash, football, swimming and most ball games

LAST SEASON: BATTING

	I.	N.O.	R.	H.S.	AV.
TEST					
1ST-CLASS	30	6	629	116	26.20
INT					
RAL	9	2	51	21	7.28
NAT.W.	2	0	25	20	12.50
B & H	3	1	4	3	2.00

CAREER: BATTING

	I.	N.O.	R.	H.S.	AV.
TEST					
1ST-CLASS	94	13	1674	116	20.66
INT					
RAL	26	11	177	34	11.80
NAT.W.	4	1	48	20	16.00
B & H	3	1	4	3	2.00

LAST SEASON: WICKET KEEPING

	C.	ST.			
TEST					
1ST-CLASS	56	2			
INT					
RAL	13	7			
NAT.W.	1	1			
B & H	5	1			

CAREER: WICKET KEEPING

	C.	ST.			
TEST					
1ST-CLASS	129	11			
INT					
RAL	34	12			
NAT.W.	6	1			
B & H	6	1			

Other sports followed: Football, gymnastics, athletics
Relaxations: Old films, music, photography
Extras: On the MCC groundstaff in 1982 before joining Worcestershire in latter half of 1982 season. Joined Sussex in 1985. Organises county pre-season fitness training, and takes pre-match warm-ups
Opinions on cricket: 'County programme should be 16 four-day games, which would allow more genuine results. Also, counties would have to have more depth, as lower order batsmen would have plenty of time to bat, and fourth and fifth change bowlers would have more opportunity.'
Best batting performance: 116 Sussex v Somerset, Hove 1989

MORRIS, H. Glamorgan

Full Name: Hugh Morris
Role: Left-hand bat, right-arm medium bowler, slip fielder
Born: 5 October 1963, Cardiff
Height: 5′ 8″ **Weight:** 12st 4lbs
Nickname: H, Banacek, Grimsdale
County debut: 1981
County cap: 1986
1000 runs in a season: 3
1st-Class 50s scored: 35
1st-Class 100s scored: 9
One-Day 50s: 15
One-Day 100s: 4
Place in batting averages: 79th av. 32.95 (1988 113th av. 27.73)
1st-Class catches 1989: 18 (career 70)
Parents: Roger and Anne
Marital status: Single
Family links with cricket: Brother played for Wales U-19 and Glamorgan U-19. Father played league cricket. Cousin played for Welsh Schools U-15
Education: Blundell's School; South Glamorgan Institute of HE
Qualifications: 9 O-levels, 3 A-levels, 1 AO-level, BA(Hons), NCA Coaching Award
Jobs outside cricket: Marketing Department, Glamorgan CCC; Sales Representative; Recruitment Consultant
Off-season 1989–90: Working for Keltec Recruitment Agency
Cricketing superstitions or habits: 'Getting off 111. Put right pad on first.'
Overseas tours: With English Public Schoolboy tour to West Indies 1980–81; to Sri Lanka 1982–83; to USA (Los Angeles) with Haverfordwest CC 1984

Cricketers particularly learnt from: Alan Jones, Tom Cartwright, Kevin Lyons
Cricketers particularly admired: Ian Botham, Javed Miandad, Viv Richards
Other sports played: Rugby, golf
Other sports followed: Most sports
Relaxations: Music, watching movies, having a few quiet pints, travelling, and a holiday at the end of the season
Extras: Highest schoolboy cricket average in 1979 (89.71), 1981 (184.6) and 1982 (149.2). Captain of England U-19 Schoolboys in 1981 and 1982. Played for Young England v Young West Indies 1982, and captained Young England v Australia. Won Gray-Nicholls 'Most Promising Schoolboy' Award 1981, and Young Cricketer of 1982. Played first-class rugby for Aberavon 1984–85 and South Glamorgan Institute scoring over 150 points. Appointed Glamorgan captain 1986 – the youngest ever for county. Scored most runs in Sunday League by a Glamorgan player – 586. Resigned as captain of Glamorgan during 1989 season. First Glamorgan player to score a century in each of the four competitions
Best batting performance: 143 Glamorgan v Oxford University, Oxford 1987
Best bowling performance: 1-6 Glamorgan v Oxford University, Oxford 1987

LAST SEASON: BATTING

	I.	N.O.	R.	H.S.	AV.
TEST					
1ST-CLASS	43	2	1351	133	32.95
INT					
RAL	14	2	349	83	29.08
NAT.W.	2	1	207	154*	207.00
B & H	4	1	154	143*	51.33

LAST SEASON: BOWLING

	O.	M.	R.	W.	AV.
TEST					
1ST-CLASS	8.5	0	33	0	–
INT					
RAL					
NAT.W.					
B & H					

CAREER: BATTING

	I.	N.O.	R.	H.S.	AV.
TEST					
1ST-CLASS	228	23	6388	143	31.16
INT					
RAL	69	8	1838	100	30.13
NAT.W.	11	2	484	154*	53.77
B & H	18	2	439	143*	27.43

CAREER: BOWLING

	O.	M.	R.	W.	AV.
TEST					
1ST-CLASS	47.1	6	261	2	130.50
INT					
RAL					
NAT.W.					
B & H	2	0	14	1	14.00

MORRIS, J. E.   Derbyshire

Full Name: John Edward Morris
Role: Right-hand bat, right-arm medium bowler
Born: 1 April 1964, Crewe
Height: 5′ 10½″ **Weight:** 13st 6lbs
Nickname: Animal
County debut: 1982
County cap: 1986
1000 runs in a season: 4
1st-Class 50s scored: 40
1st-Class 100s scored: 17
One-Day 50s: 11
One-Day 100s: 3
Place in batting averages: 28th
av. 43.10 (1988 45th av. 37.62)
1st-Class catches 1989: 8 (career 64)
Parents: George (Eddie) and Jean
Marital status: Single
Family links with cricket: Father
played for Crewe CC for many years as an opening bowler
Education: Shavington Comprehensive School; Dane Bank College of Further Education
Qualifications: O-levels
Jobs outside cricket: Worked as a carpet fitter. PR officer for indoor cricket centre
Off-season 1989–90: Full-time training
Overseas teams played for: Subiaco Floreat CC, Perth, Western Australia 1986–87; Griqualand West 1988–89

LAST SEASON: BATTING

	I.	N.O.	R.	H.S.	AV.
TEST					
1ST-CLASS	43	5	1638	156	43.10
INT					
RAL	13	3	419	112*	41.90
NAT.W.	2	0	4	4	2.00
B & H	2	0	13	13	6.50

CAREER: BATTING

	I.	N.O.	R.	H.S.	AV.
TEST					
1ST-CLASS	250	18	8339	191	35.94
INT					
RAL	88	8	2180	112*	27.25
NAT.W.	13	2	182	43*	16.54
B & H	23	3	453	65	22.65

LAST SEASON: BOWLING

	O.	M.	R.	W.	AV.
TEST					
1ST-CLASS	10	2	38	0	–
INT					
RAL					
NAT.W.					
B & H					

CAREER: BOWLING

	O.	M.	R.	W.	AV.
TEST					
1ST-CLASS	91.3	11	540	3	180.00
INT					
RAL					
NAT.W.					
B & H					

Cricketers particularly learnt from: Tony Borrington, Phil Russell, Father
Other sports played: Football, basketball, snooker
Other sports followed: Athletics, motor racing
Relaxations: Movies, music, good food, fly-fishing
Best batting performance: 191 Derbyshire v Kent, Derby 1986
Best bowling performance: 1-13 Derbyshire v Yorkshire, Harrogate 1987

MORTENSEN, O. H.   Derbyshire

Full Name: Ole Henrik Mortensen
Role: Right-hand bat, right-arm
fast-medium bowler
Born: 29 January 1958, Vejle,
Denmark
Height: 6' 4" **Weight:** 14st 2lbs
Nickname: Stan (coined by Bob
Taylor after England footballer
Stan Mortenson), Blood-
Axe
County debut: 1983
County cap: 1986
50 wickets in a season: 2
1st-Class 50s scored: 1
1st-Class 5 w. in innings: 13
1st-Class 10 w. in match: 1
Place in batting averages: —
(1988 252nd av. 11.50)
Place in bowling averages: 14th
av. 20.41 (1988 2nd av. 13.64)
Strike rate 1989: 46.69 (career 50.61)
1st-Class catches 1989: 5 (career 31)
Parents: Will Ernst and Inge Wicka
Wife: Jette Jepmond
Children: Julie Jepmond, 30 August 1982
Family links with cricket: 'My small brother, Michael, used to play cricket. He
is now a professional tennis player, and has played in Davis Cup for
Denmark.'
Education: Brondbyoster School; Avedore School
Jobs outside cricket: Worked as a tax assistant in Denmark
Overseas tours: East Africa in 1976 with the Danish national side, and
Scotland, Wales, Ireland and Holland
Overseas teams played for: Ellerslie, Auckland, New Zealand 1983–84;
Brighton CC, Melbourne 1985–86; Svanholm CC, Denmark

Cricketers particularly learnt from: Torben Jensen, Jorgen Janson, Peter Hargreaves and many others
Cricketers particularly admired: Dennis Lillee, Bob Taylor
Other sports played: Tennis, golf, football
Relaxations: Music, books, movies
Extras: *Derbyshire's Dane* by Peter Hargreaves, published 1984. Has played for Denmark. Only Dane currently playing first-class cricket
Opinions on cricket: 'Too much cricket; seam bowlers turn into robots by August.'
Best batting performance: 74* Derbyshire v Yorkshire, Chesterfield 1987
Best bowling performance: 6-27 Derbyshire v Yorkshire, Sheffield 1983

LAST SEASON: BATTING

	I.	N.O.	R.	H.S.	AV.
TEST					
1ST-CLASS	19	8	79	20*	8.77
INT					
RAL	5	3	25	11	12.50
NAT.W.	2	1	5	4*	5.00
B & H	2	1	1	1	1.00

CAREER: BATTING

	I.	N.O.	R.	H.S.	AV.
TEST					
1ST-CLASS	118	61	540	74*	9.47
INT					
RAL	35	24	65	11	5.90
NAT.W.	9	6	24	11	8.00
B & H	6	3	6	3*	2.00

LAST SEASON: BOWLING

	O.	M.	R.	W.	AV.
TEST					
1ST-CLASS	334.4	64	878	43	20.41
INT					
RAL	102	17	294	19	15.47
NAT.W.	24	6	60	6	10.00
B & H	44	9	108	6	18.00

CAREER: BOWLING

	O.	M.	R.	W.	AV.
TEST					
1ST-CLASS	2488.2	597	6709	295	22.74
INT					
RAL	632.3	67	2327	90	25.85
NAT.W.	124	32	339	22	15.40
B & H	228.2	32	666	35	19.02

106. Who topped the Derbyshire batting averages last season?
107. Who topped the Essex batting averages last season?

MOXON, M. D. Yorkshire

Full Name: Martyn Douglas Moxon
Role: Right-hand bat, right-arm medium bowler, slip fielder
Born: 4 May 1960, Barnsley
Height: 6′ 1″ **Weight:** 13st 7lbs
Nickname: Frog
County debut: 1981
County cap: 1984
Test debut: 1986
No. of Tests: 10
No. of One-Day Internationals: 8
1000 runs in a season: 5
1st-Class 50s scored: 56
1st-Class 100s scored: 22
One-Day 50s: 24
One-Day 100s: 1
Place in batting averages: 64th

av. 35.57 (1988 32nd av. 41.25)
1st-Class catches 1989: 21 (career 145)
Parents: Audrey and Derek (deceased)
Wife and date of marriage: Sue, October 1985
Family links with cricket: Father and grandfather played local league cricket. Father was coach to Wombwell Cricket Lovers' Society
Education: Holgate Grammar School, Barnsley
Qualifications: 8 O-levels, 3 A-levels, HNC in Business Studies, NCA Coaching Award
Off-season 1989–90: Running coaching clinics in Yorkshire
Jobs outside cricket: Bank clerk with Barclays Bank for two years before turning professional full-time
Cricketing superstitions or habits: 'Always put left pad on first.'
Overseas tours: Captain of North of England U-19 tour of Canada 1979; with England to India and Australia 1984–85, England B tour to Sri Lanka 1986; Yorkshire to West Indies 1986–87; England to Pakistan and New Zealand 1987–88
Overseas teams played for: Griqualand West, South Africa 1982–83 and 1983–84
Cricketers particularly learnt from: Doug Padgett, Phil Carrick, Steve Oldham
Cricketers particularly admired: Viv Richards
Other sports played: Football in the local league in the winter, and golf
Other sports followed: 'Am a keen supporter of Barnsley FC.'

348

Injuries 1989: Broke left fore-arm in pre-season practice, missing first six weeks of season

Relaxations: Listening to most types of music, having a drink with friends

Extras: Captained Yorkshire Schools U-15s and North of England U-15s. Played for Yorkshire Cricket Federation U-19s. Captained Yorkshire Senior Schools. Like Yorkshire colleagues, G. Stevenson and A. Sidebottom, he played for Wombwell Cricket Lovers' Society U-18 side which competes in the Joe Lumb U-18 Competition. At the time, made the highest score by a player on his Yorkshire debut – 116 v Essex (since overtaken by Ashley Metcalfe). First Yorkshire player to make centuries on his first two Championship games in Yorkshire: 116 v Essex at Headingley and 111 v Derbyshire at Sheffield. Changed from spectacles to contact lenses in 1981. Scored 153 in first 'Roses' innings. Picked for Lord's Test of 1984 v West Indies, but had to withdraw through injury and had to wait until 1986 to make Test debut

Best batting performance: 191 Yorkshire v Northamptonshire, Scarborough 1988

Best bowling performance: 3-24 Yorkshire v Hampshire, Southampton 1989

LAST SEASON: BATTING

	I.	N.O.	R.	H.S.	AV.
TEST	2	0	18	18	9.00
1ST-CLASS	32	1	1156	162*	37.29
INT					
RAL	10	0	243	59	24.30
NAT.W.	2	0	73	59	36.50
B & H					

LAST SEASON: BOWLING

	O.	M.	R.	W.	AV.
TEST					
1ST-CLASS	50	9	165	5	33.00
INT					
RAL	44.3	1	227	6	37.83
NAT.W.	11	4	34	2	17.00
B & H					

CAREER: BATTING

	I.	N.O.	R.	H.S.	AV.
TEST	17	1	455	99	28.43
1ST-CLASS	279	18	10092	191	38.66
INT	8	0	174	70	21.75
RAL	63	5	1633	86	28.15
NAT.W.	15	4	573	82*	52.09
B & H	26	4	1057	106*	48.04

CAREER: BOWLING

	O.	M.	R.	W.	AV.
TEST	8	2	30	0	–
1ST-CLASS	358.4	60	1235	23	53.69
INT					
RAL	111.3	3	610	10	61.00
NAT.W.	19	4	66	3	22.00
B & H	42	1	168	4	42.00

MUNTON, T. A.   Warwickshire

Full Name: Timothy Alan Munton
Role: Right-hand bat, right-arm
fast-medium bowler
Born: 30 July 1965, Melton Mowbray
Height: 6′ 6″ **Weight:** 14st
Nickname: Tiny, Herman
County debut: 1985
50 wickets in a season: 1
1st-Class 5 w. in innings: 5
Place in bowling averages: 39th
av. 26.06 (1988 31st av. 22.76)
Strike rate 1989: 62.40 (career 57.50)
1st-Class catches 1989: 11 (career 17)
Parents: Alan and Brenda
Wife and date of marriage: Helen,
20 September 1986
Education: Sarson High School, King Edward VII Upper School
Qualifications: 8 O-levels, 1 A-level; cricket coach
Overseas teams played for: Victoria University, Wellington, New Zealand
1985–86; Witswatersrand University, Johannesburg 1986–87
Cricketers particularly learnt from: Ken Hughes
Cricketers particularly admired: Bob Willis, Clive Rice, Richard Hadlee
Other sports played: Basketball, soccer
Relaxations: Listening to music
Extras: Appeared for Leicestershire 2nd XI 1982–84
Best batting performance: 38 Warwickshire v Yorkshire, Scarborough 1987
Best bowling performance: 6-21 Warwickshire v Worcestershire, Edgbaston
1988

LAST SEASON: BATTING

	I.	N.O.	R.	H.S.	AV.
TEST					
1ST-CLASS	20	11	43	7	4.77
INT					
RAL	5	5	10	4*	–
NAT.W.	1	1	1	1*	–
B & H	1	0	13	13	13.00

CAREER: BATTING

	I.	N.O.	R.	H.S.	AV.
TEST					
1ST-CLASS	73	29	348	38	7.90
INT					
RAL	13	11	33	7*	16.50
NAT.W.	2	2	1	1*	–
B & H	5	4	22	13	22.00

LAST SEASON: BOWLING

	O.	M.	R.	W.	AV.
TEST					
1ST-CLASS	613.4	178	1538	59	26.06
INT					
RAL	109.3	14	429	12	35.75
NAT.W.	44	7	132	6	22.00
B & H	41	5	140	5	28.00

CAREER: BOWLING

	O.	M.	R.	W.	AV.
TEST					
1ST-CLASS	1686.4	444	4517	176	25.66
INT					
RAL	327.3	33	1338	43	31.11
NAT.W.	71.4	10	237	8	29.62
B & H	116	10	394	12	32.83

Full Name: Anthony John Murphy
Role: Right-hand bat, right-arm medium bowler
Born: 6 August 1962, Manchester
Height: 5′ 11¾″ **Weight:** 14st
Nickname: Audi, Headless, Tramp, Compo
County debut: 1985 (Lancashire), 1989 (Surrey)
50 wickets in a season: 1
1st-Class 5 w. in innings: 2
Place in bowling averages: 75th av. 30.89
Strike rate 1989: 57.50 (career 61.41)
1st-Class catches 1989: 1 (career 7)
Parents: John Desmond and Elizabeth Catherine
Marital status: Single
Family links with cricket: Brother plays club cricket for Cheadle
Education: Xaverian College, Manchester; Swansea University
Qualifications: 9 O-levels, 4 A-levels
Jobs outside cricket: Computer operator for Barclays Bank. Part-time store detective. Wool tester. Transport Consultant
Off-season 1989–90: Coaching in Tasmania for Ulverston CC
Overseas tours: Minor Counties U-25s to Kenya 1986; Lancashire to West Indies 1986–87
Overseas teams played for: Central Districts & Taradale CC, New Zealand 1985–88; Ulverston CC, Tasmania 1988–89, 1989–90
Cricketers particularly learnt from: G. Fowler, G. G. Arnold, Steve O'Shaughnessy
Cricketers particularly admired: Clive Lloyd, Michael Holding ('both great ambassadors for cricket as well as great exponents of the game')
Other sports played: Fishing, cards, golf
Other sports followed: 'Football – English, American and Australian.'
Relaxations: 'Sleep as often as possible!'
Opinions on cricket: 'I feel four-day cricket can only succeed if the standard of wickets improves dramatically. At the moment, too many games do not last to their expected duration due to bad or under-prepared wickets. This is not helping English cricket, especially in the batting department. I also think that the ICC should make a decision, one way or the other, as to whether or not cricketers with links in South Africa can compete in international cricket or

not, and this ruling should be adhered to by all members of the ICC, thus avoiding another farce like the on-off winter tour of India.'

Best batting performance: 38 Surrey v Gloucestershire, Oval 1989
Best bowling performance: 6-97 Surrey v Derbyshire, Derby 1989

LAST SEASON: BATTING

	I.	N.O.	R.	H.S.	AV.
TEST					
1ST-CLASS	21	8	78	38	6.00
INT					
RAL	5	1	4	3	1.00
NAT.W.	–	–	–	–	–
B & H	3	1	5	5*	2.50

CAREER: BATTING

	I.	N.O.	R.	H.S.	AV.
TEST					
1ST-CLASS	40	15	103	38	4.12
INT					
RAL	6	2	6	3	1.50
NAT.W.	–	–	–	–	–
B & H	3	1	5	5*	3.50

LAST SEASON: BOWLING

	O.	M.	R.	W.	AV.
TEST					
1ST-CLASS	623	127	2008	65	30.89
INT					
RAL	110	6	467	21	22.23
NAT.W.	35	4	134	4	33.50
B & H	27	2	96	0	–

CAREER: BOWLING

	O.	M.	R.	W.	AV.
TEST					
1ST-CLASS	1003.1	75	3276	98	33.42
INT					
RAL	116	6	500	22	22.72
NAT.W.	35	4	134	4	33.50
B & H	27	2	96	0	–

NEALE, P. A. Worcestershire

Full Name: Phillip Anthony Neale
Role: Right-hand bat, cover fielder
Born: 5 June 1954, Scunthorpe
Height: 5′ 11″ **Weight:** 11st 10lbs
Nickname: Phil
County debut: 1975
County cap: 1978
Benefit: 1988 (£153,005)
1000 runs in a season: 8
1st-Class 50s scored: 84
1st-Class 100s scored: 26
One-Day 50s: 30
One-Day 100s: 2
Place in batting averages: 42nd
av. 40.04 (1988 35th av. 39.84)
1st-Class catches 1989: 5 (career 115)
Parents: Geoff and Margaret
Wife and date of marriage: Christine,
26 September 1976

Children: Kelly Joanne, 9 November 1979; Craig Andrew, 11 February 1982

Education: Frederick Gough Grammar School, Scunthorpe; John Leggot Sixth Form College, Scunthorpe; Leeds University

Qualifications: 10 O-levels, 2 A-levels, BA Hons Russian. Preliminary football and cricket coaching awards

Jobs outside cricket: Teacher, former professional footballer

Off-season 1989–90: Marketing Manager for P.-E. Inbucon, management consultants

Cricketing superstitions or habits: Left pad on first

Cricketers particularly learnt from: 'Most county players – you learn by watching.'

Cricketers particularly admired: Basil D'Oliveira, Norman Gifford, Alan Ormrod

Other sports played: Squash, golf ('badly')

Other sports followed: Most sports – mainly via TV

Injuries 1989: Glandular fever – off for five weeks from April to May

Relaxations: 'Reading, spending time with my family, trying to learn to play golf.'

Extras: Played for Lincolnshire 1973–74. Scored 100 runs before lunch v Warwickshire at Worcester, 1979. Captain 1983–. Testimonial season with Lincoln City 1984–85. Retired from full-time football 1985. Celebrated his benefit season by captaining Worcestershire to a County Championship and Sunday League double

Best batting performance: 167 Worcestershire v Sussex, Kidderminster, 1988

Best bowling performance: 1-15 Worcestershire v Derbyshire, Worcester 1976

LAST SEASON: BATTING

	I.	N.O.	R.	H.S.	AV.
TEST					
1ST-CLASS	32	8	961	98	40.04
INT					
RAL	14	7	285	49*	40.71
NAT.W.	3	2	74	43*	74.00
B & H	1	0	3	3	3.00

CAREER: BATTING

	I.	N.O.	R.	H.S.	AV.
TEST					
1ST-CLASS	514	78	15903	167	36.47
INT					
RAL	186	45	4195	102	29.75
NAT.W.	29	3	901	98	34.65
B & H	52	6	1387	128	30.15

LAST SEASON: BOWLING

	O.	M.	R.	W.	AV.
TEST					
1ST-CLASS	1	0	8	0	–
INT					
RAL					
NAT.W.					
B & H					

CAREER: BOWLING

	O.	M.	R.	W.	AV.
TEST					
1ST-CLASS	60.5	4	283	1	283.00
INT					
RAL	8.2	0	50	2	25.00
NAT.W.					
B & H					

NEWELL, M.   Nottinghamshire

Full Name: Michael Newell
Role: Right-hand opening bat,
leg-break bowler, occasional
wicket-keeper, short leg
Born: 25 February 1965, Blackburn
Height: 5′ 8″ **Weight:** 11st
Nickname: Sam, Tricky, Mott,
Merrick
County debut: 1984
County cap: 1987
1000 runs in a season: 1
1st-Class 50s scored: 17
1st-Class 100s scored: 4
1st-Class 200s scored: 1
One-Day 50s: 2
Place in batting averages: 156th
av. 22.70 (1988 170th av. 21.76)
1st-Class catches 1989: 18
(career 86 + 1 stumping)
Parents: Barry and Janet
Wife and date of marriage: Jayne, 23 September 1989
Family links with cricket: Father chairman of Notts Unity CC. Brother Paul
plays for Loughborough University
Education: West Bridgford Comprehensive
Qualifications: 8 O-levels, 3 A-levels. NCA Advanced Coach
Jobs outside cricket: Part-time barman, has worked in children's home;
packer at Gunn and Moore. Selling kit at Trent Bridge. Journalist
Off-season 1989–90: Doing football and rugby reports for newspapers
Cricketing superstitions or habits: 'Always put right pad on first; always bat
in short sweater and long-sleeved shirt. Wear the same whites if I am in
form.'
Overseas tours: NCA U-19 tour to Holland 1983
Overseas teams played for: Nedland CC, Perth 1985–86
Cricketers particularly learnt from: Tim Robinson, Eddie Hemmings
Cricketers particularly admired: Franklyn Stephenson, John Birch
Other sports played: Football ('of a low standard'), indoor cricket
Other sports followed: Watches rugby union and football, horse racing
Relaxations: Good films, music and drinking at the Trent Bridge Inn
Extras: Carried his bat through the Nottinghamshire innings v Warwickshire,
scoring 10 out of Nottinghamshire's 44 – the sixth-lowest individual score by a
batsman playing all through an innings
Opinions on cricket: 'I feel that individuals should not be prevented from

playing in South Africa, though rebel team tours are undoubtedly a danger to the future of Test cricket.'

Best batting performance: 203* Nottinghamshire v Derbyshire, Derby 1987
Best bowling performance: 2-38 Nottinghamshire v Sri Lankans, Trent Bridge 1988

LAST SEASON: BATTING

	I.	N.O.	R.	H.S.	AV.
TEST					
1ST-CLASS	26	2	545	99	22.70
INT					
RAL	4	0	82	47	20.50
NAT.W.					
B & H	5	0	91	39	18.20

CAREER: BATTING

	I.	N.O.	R.	H.S.	AV.
TEST					
1ST-CLASS	147	22	3619	203*	28.95
INT					
RAL	13	1	297	58	24.75
NAT.W.	3	0	97	60	32.33
B & H	8	1	174	39	24.85

LAST SEASON: WICKET KEEPING

	C.	ST.		
TEST				
1ST-CLASS				
INT				
RAL				
NAT.W.				
B & H				

LAST SEASON: BOWLING

	O.	M.	R.	W.	AV.
TEST					
1ST-CLASS	8	0	44	0	–
INT					
RAL					
NAT.W.					
B & H					

CAREER: BOWLING

	O.	M.	R.	W.	AV.
TEST					
1ST-CLASS	52.1	6	247	6	41.16
INT					
RAL					
NAT.W.	1	0	10	0	–
B & H					

CAREER: WICKET KEEPING

	C.	ST.		
TEST				
1ST-CLASS				
INT				
RAL	4	–		
NAT.W.				
B & H				

108. Who topped the Glamorgan batting averages last season?
109. Who topped the Gloucestershire batting averages last season?

NEWMAN, P. G.   Derbyshire

Full Name: Paul Geoffrey Newman
Role: Right-hand bat, right-arm
fast-medium bowler
Born: 10 January 1959, Leicester
Height: 6′ 2″ **Weight:** 14st
Nickname: Judge
County debut: 1980
County cap: 1986
50 wickets in a season: 2
1st-Class 50s scored: 5
1st-Class 100s scored: 1
1st-Class 5 w. in innings: 6
One-Day 50s: 2
Place in batting averages: 223rd
av. 14.71 (1988 232nd av. 14.38)
Place in bowling averages: 97th
av. 37.55 (1988 63rd av. 27.14)
Strike rate 1989: 74.18 (career 57.52)
1st-Class catches 1989: 11 (career 36)
Wife and date of marriage: Karen, 24 September 1988
Education: Alderman Newton's Grammar School, Leicester
Qualifications: 6 O-levels
Jobs outside cricket: Various temporary jobs
Off-season 1989–90: 'Deciding my future.'
Cricketing superstitions or habits: Always wears wrist bands to bowl. Puts left
pad on first
Overseas tours: English Counties XI to Zimbabwe 1985
Overseas teams played for: Queensland Cricket Association Colts XI 1981–
82; Old Collegians and Pietermaritzburg, South Africa 1983–84 and 1985–86;
Green Point, Cape Town 1987–88
Cricketers particularly admired: John Snow, Richard Hadlee, Dennis Lillee
Other sports played: Golf, 8-a-side indoor cricket
Other sports followed: Leicester City FC
Injuries 1989: 'Missed the odd game with minor injuries.'
Relaxations: Collecting cricket memorabilia, especially cigarette cards
Extras: Played for Leicestershire 2nd XI in 1978 and 1979, but was released.
As a schoolboy, was a wicket-keeper. Took 50 wickets in his first season with
Derbyshire. Won Commercial Union U-23 Bowling Award for 1981. Won
Whitbread Scholarship to Brisbane, Australia 1981–82. Resigned from
Derbyshire CCC in September 1989
Opinions on cricket: 'The reduction of overseas players to one only is a great
move, especially for the average county cricketer like myself.'

356

Best batting performance: 115 Derbyshire v Leicestershire, Chesterfield 1985
Best bowling performance: 8-29 Derbyshire v Yorkshire, Leeds 1988

LAST SEASON: BATTING

	I.	N.O.	R.	H.S.	AV.
TEST					
1ST-CLASS	25	4	309	86*	14.71
INT					
RAL	7	3	53	24	13.25
NAT.W.	2	0	29	25	14.50
B & H	3	1	40	26*	20.00

LAST SEASON: BOWLING

	O.	M.	R.	W.	AV.
TEST					
1ST-CLASS	333.5	73	1014	27	37.55
INT					
RAL	78	8	321	14	22.92
NAT.W.	15	1	97	2	48.50
B & H	41	9	125	2	62.50

CAREER: BATTING

	I.	N.O.	R.	H.S.	AV.
TEST					
1ST-CLASS	170	33	2152	115	15.70
INT					
RAL	58	19	552	52*	14.15
NAT.W.	10	2	137	35	17.12
B & H	21	9	248	56*	20.66

CAREER: BOWLING

	O.	M.	R.	W.	AV.
TEST					
1ST-CLASS	2991.3	580	9736	312	31.20
INT					
RAL	654.2	35	2914	100	29.14
NAT.W.	145.3	21	481	20	24.05
B & H	328.1	42	1184	36	32.88

NEWPORT, P. J. Worcestershire

Full Name: Philip John Newport
Role: Right-hand bat, right-arm fast-medium bowler, outfielder
Born: 11 October 1962, High Wycombe
Height: 6′ 2″ **Weight:** 13st 7lbs
Nickname: Newps, Spike, Schnozz
County debut: 1982
County cap: 1986
Test debut: 1988
No. of Tests: 2
50 wickets in a season: 2
1st-Class 50s scored: 6
1st-Class 5 w. in innings: 19
1st-Class 10 w. in match: 3
Place in batting averages: 231st av. 13.80 (1988 124th av. 26.29)
Place in bowling averages: 24th av. 22.00 (1988 12th av. 19.82)
Strike rate 1989: 40.95 (career 47.37)
1st-Class catches 1989: 3 (career 38)
Parents: John and Sheila Diana

Wife and date of marriage: Christine, 26 October 1985

Family links with cricket: 'Father is a good club cricketer, my younger brother Stewart played for High Wycombe CC.'

Education: Royal Grammar School, High Wycombe; Portsmouth Polytechnic

Qualifications: 8 O-levels, 3 A-levels, BA (Hons) Geography, basic coaching qualification

Jobs outside cricket: Schoolmaster at Worcester Royal Grammar School 1985–86

Cricketing superstitions or habits: 'Always put a 10p piece in left pocket when batting.'

Overseas tours: With NCA to Denmark 1981

Overseas teams played for: Avis Vogelconn, New Plymouth, New Zealand 1986–87; Boland and Kraalfontein, Cape Town, South Africa 1987–88

Cricketers particularly admired: Batting of Graeme Hick; bowling of Malcolm Marshall; fielding of Gordon Lord

Other sports played: Soccer, rugby union, badminton, tennis, golf

Other sports followed: American football, sport in general

Injuries 1989: After second Test, achilles tendon failed to respond to treatment, and he missed the rest of the season

Relaxations: Listening to music, reading; in New Zealand surfing, water-skiing, horse riding

Extras: Had trial as schoolboy for Southampton FC. Played cricket for NAYC England Schoolboys 1981. Also for Buckinghamshire in Minor Counties in 1981. Took part in Minor Counties final 1982. Wears contact lens in left eye only. Chosen to tour with England on cancelled tour of India 1988–89

Opinions on cricket: 'Championship should be solely four-day cricket. Points be deducted for poor pitches, determined by umpires' report. One overseas player per county only to be replaced if injury rules him out for rest of season. Overseas tour for an England B/U-25 side each winter. Better construction

LAST SEASON: BATTING

	I.	N.O.	R.	H.S.	AV.
TEST	2	0	44	36	22.00
1ST-CLASS	10	2	94	27	11.75
INT					
RAL	2	1	11	10*	11.00
NAT.W.					
B & H	3	0	14	12	4.66

CAREER: BATTING

	I.	N.O.	R.	H.S.	AV.
TEST	3	0	70	36	23.33
1ST-CLASS	133	43	2241	86	24.90
INT					
RAL	29	12	205	26*	12.05
NAT.W.	7	2	60	25	12.00
B & H	12	3	70	15	7.77

LAST SEASON: BOWLING

	O.	M.	R.	W.	AV.
TEST	44	7	175	2	87.50
1ST-CLASS	235.5	35	727	39	18.64
INT					
RAL	30.2	0	109	8	13.62
NAT.W.					
B & H	38	4	138	4	34.50

CAREER: BOWLING

	O.	M.	R.	W.	AV.
TEST	91.3	18	339	9	37.66
1ST-CLASS	2751.1	444	9099	351	25.92
INT					
RAL	340.2	3	1566	56	27.96
NAT.W.	126.2	14	400	12	33.33
B & H	153	12	514	23	22.34

of cricketers' helmets and grilles. Names or numbers on players' shirts to help identification on Sundays only.'

Best batting performance: 86 Boland v Transvaal B, Stellenbosch 1987–88
Best bowling performance: 8-52 Worcestershire v Middlesex, Lord's 1988

NICHOLAS, M. C. J. Hampshire

Full Name: Mark Charles Jefford Nicholas
Role: Right-hand bat, right-arm medium bowler, slip fielder, captain
Born: 29 September 1957, London
Height: 5' 11½" **Weight:** 12st 7lbs
Nickname: Skip, MCJ, Dougie
County debut: 1978
County cap: 1982
1000 runs in a season: 7
1st-Class 50s scored: 48
1st-Class 100s scored: 26
1st-Class 200s scored: 1
1st-Class 5 w. in innings: 2
One-Day 50s: 27
One-Day 100s: 1
Place in batting averages: 59th av. 36.25 (1988 94th av. 29.56)
Place in bowling averages: 35th av. 25.60
Strike rate 1989: 49.06 (career 75.10)
1st-Class catches 1989: 20 (career 165)
Parents: Anne
Marital status: Single
Family links with cricket: Grandfather (F.W.H.) played for Essex as batsman and wicket-keeper and toured with MCC. Father played for Navy
Education: Fernden Prep School; Bradfield College
Qualifications: 9 O-levels, 3 A-levels
Jobs outside cricket: Worked in Classified Advertising for *The Observer*. Selling for agencies. Writing for papers and magazines. PR agency
Off-season 1989–90: Writing a book; touring Zimbabwe as captain of England A; some golf
Cricketing superstitions or habits: 'Kit must fit. Not many susperstitions left: too few runs – though I do have favourite batting trousers and put my left pad on first and . . .'

Overseas tours: Toured South Africa with Dragons (Public Schools team) 1976–77 as captain; with MCC to Bangladesh February 1981; and to East and Central Africa October 1981; Dubai with *Cricketer* International XI November 1981; Dubai and Bahrain with 'England XI' March 1981; English Counties XI to Zimbabwe 1984–85; Sri Lanka with England B 1986 as captain; Zimbabwe with England A 1989–90

Overseas teams played for: Captain of Southern Lakes in Australia 1978–79 and Grosvenor/Fynnland, Durban 1982–83, 1983–84

Cricketers particularly learnt from: Barry Richards, Jimmy Gray, Dean Jones

Cricketers particularly admired: Barry Richards, John Snow

Other sports played: Regular football with Old Bradfieldians (Arthurian League), golf, fives, squash

Relaxations: Theatre, contemporary music, restaurants and wine

Extras: Appointed Hampshire captain 1985; captain of England 'A' team touring Zimbabwe, 1989–90

Opinions on cricket: 'We really are playing and travelling too much for anyone's good – players, spectators, marketing people, everyone. You don't ask Lendl, Ballesteros, Jehangir Khan, Gullit to play on bad pitches, so, for crying out loud, do something about ours!'

Best batting performance: 206* Hampshire v Oxford University, Oxford 1982

Best bowling performance: 6-37 Hampshire v Somerset, Southampton 1989

LAST SEASON: BATTING

	I.	N.O.	R.	H.S.	AV.
TEST					
1ST-CLASS	40	5	1269	140	36.25
INT					
RAL	15	1	382	57	27.28
NAT.W.	4	2	155	71	77.50
B & H	4	0	49	32	12.25

CAREER: BATTING

	I.	N.O.	R.	H.S.	AV.
TEST					
1ST-CLASS	418	50	12050	206*	32.74
INT					
RAL	128	19	2909	108	26.68
NAT.W.	28	3	739	71	29.56
B & H	42	4	891	74	23.44

LAST SEASON: BOWLING

	O.	M.	R.	W.	AV.
TEST					
1ST-CLASS	122.4	16	384	15	25.60
INT					
RAL	36.1	3	175	7	25.00
NAT.W.	2	0	17	0	–
B & H	21	1	89	2	44.50

CAREER: BOWLING

	O.	M.	R.	W.	AV.
TEST					
1ST-CLASS	801.1	159	2543	64	39.73
INT					
RAL	301.1	5	1661	58	28.63
NAT.W.	83.2	8	332	9	36.88
B & H	165	10	730	21	34.76

NICHOLSON, N. G.   Yorkshire

Full Name: Neil George Nicholson
Role: Left-hand bat
Born: 17 October 1963, Danby,
Whitby, North Yorkshire
Height: 5′ 8″ **Weight:** 12st 7lbs
Nickname: Lorry
County debut: 1988
1st-Class 50s scored: 1
1st-Class catches 1989: 5 (career
8)
Parents: George and Jean
Wife and date of marriage: Alison,
27 October 1984
Children: Michael Neil, 5 February
1985; Ian John, 28 May 1986
Family links with cricket: Father
played local league cricket around
Danby
Education: Danby School; Eskdale
School; Whitby School
Qualifications: 5 O-levels, Process Operation Part I
Jobs outside cricket: Used to work for ICI as a storeman
Cricketers particularly learnt from: Martin McGuire, Maurice Hill, Doug
Padgett
Cricketers particularly admired: Clive Lloyd
Other sports played: Golf, football
Other sports followed: Any but showjumping
Relaxations: Watching TV and gardening
Opinions on cricket: 'Cricketers should be allowed to play wherever they
choose, i.e. in South Africa, and be sure of having no problems in the future,
from any type of playing ban.'
Best batting performance: 56* Yorkshire v Warwickshire, Leeds 1989

LAST SEASON: BATTING

	I.	N.O.	R.	H.S.	AV.
TEST					
1ST-CLASS	4	2	87	56*	43.50
INT					
RAL	2	1	1	1*	1.00
NAT.W.					
B & H					

CAREER: BATTING

	I.	N.O.	R.	H.S.	AV.
TEST					
1ST-CLASS	8	3	134	56*	26.80
INT					
RAL	2	1	1	1*	1.00
NAT.W.					
B & H					

NIXON, P. A.   Leicestershire

Full Name: Paul Andrew Nixon
Role: Left-hand bat, wicket-keeper
Born: 21 October 1970, Carlisle
Height: 6′ **Weight:** 12½st
Nickname: Nico
County debut: 1989
Parents: Brian and Sylvia
Marital status: Single
Family links with cricket:
'Grandfather and father played local
league cricket for Edenhall CC and
Penrith in the North Lancashire
League. Mum made teas.'
Education: Langwathby Primary,
Ullswater High
Qualifications: 2 O-levels, 6 CSEs,
NCA Cricket Coaching Certificate
Jobs outside cricket: Working on
father's farm
Off-season 1989–90: '6 months' holiday in Aussie!'
Cricketing superstitions or habits: 'Too many to mention. All the usuals.'
Overseas tours: Cumbria Schools to Denmark 1986
Cricketers particularly learnt from: Allan Knott, Don Wilson
Cricketers particularly admired: Allan Knott, Bob Taylor, David Gower, Viv
Richards
Other sports played: Football, golf, rugby, basketball
Other sports followed: Football – Carlisle and Spurs FC
Relaxations: Music, eating out

LAST SEASON: BATTING

	I.	N.O.	R.	H.S.	AV.
TEST					
1ST-CLASS	7	3	87	24*	21.75
INT					
RAL	1	0	1	1	1.00
NAT.W.					
B & H					

LAST SEASON: WICKET KEEPING

	C.	ST.		
TEST				
1ST-CLASS	12	2		
INT				
RAL	1	–		
NAT.W.				
B & H				

CAREER: BATTING

	I.	N.O.	R.	H.S.	AV.
TEST					
1ST-CLASS	7	3	87	24*	21.75
INT					
RAL	1	0	1	1	1.00
NAT.W.					
B & H					

CAREER: WICKET KEEPING

	C.	ST.		
TEST				
1ST-CLASS	12	2		
INT				
RAL	1	–		
NAT.W.				
B & H				

Extras: MCC Young Pro 1988 season, Minor Counties for Cumberlang at 16
Opinions on cricket: 'Politics should be kept out of sport. 2nd XI cricket should be played on first-class grounds as much as possible.'
Best batting performance: 24* Leicestershire v Sussex, Eastbourne 1989

NOON, W. M.　　　Northamptonshire

Full Name: Wayne Michael Noon
Role: Right-hand bat, wicket-keeper
Born: 5 February 1971, Grimsby
Height: 5' 9" **Weight:** 11½st
Nickname: Spoon Head, Noonie, Matt
County debut: 1988 (RAL), 1989 (First-Class)
Parents: Trafford and Rosemary
Marital status: Single
Education: Caistor Grammar School
Qualifications: 5 O-levels
Jobs outside cricket: Duck farmer
Off-season 1989–90: Young England Tour to Australia as captain
Cricketing superstitions or habits: 'Always put right pad on first. Never walk onto the field 6th.'

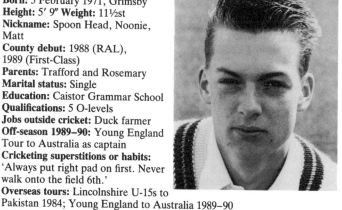

Overseas tours: Lincolnshire U-15s to Pakistan 1984; Young England to Australia 1989–90
Cricketers particularly learnt from: Bob Carter (Northamptonshire coach), Brian Reynolds

LAST SEASON: BATTING

	I.	N.O.	R.	H.S.	AV.
TEST					
1ST-CLASS	2	0	37	37	18.50
INT					
RAL					
NAT.W.					
B & H	–	–	–	–	–

CAREER: BATTING

	I.	N.O.	R.	H.S.	AV.
TEST					
1ST-CLASS	2	0	37	37	18.50
INT					
RAL	2	1	15	9*	15.00
NAT.W.					
B & H	–	–	–	–	–

LAST SEASON: WICKET KEEPING

	C.	ST.			
TEST					
1ST-CLASS	3	1			
INT					
RAL					
NAT.W.					
B & H					

CAREER: WICKET KEEPING

	C.	ST.			
TEST					
1ST-CLASS	3	1			
INT					
RAL	2	–			
NAT.W.					
B & H					

Cricketers particularly admired: Ian Botham, Bob Taylor, Jack Russell, Geoff Cook

Other sports played: Football, table tennis

Other sports followed: Support Lincoln City FC

Relaxations: 'Listening to rock music; having a complete day's break from cricket.'

Extras: Played for Young England 1989

Opinions on cricket: 'I think that the tea interval should be as long as the lunch interval. I think there is far too much cricket packed into six months. It should be spread over a longer time. And clubs should do more to help the lads find jobs in the winter.'

Best batting performance: 37 Northamptonshire v Australians, Northampton 1989

NORTH, P. D.   Glamorgan

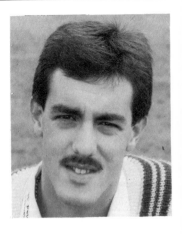

Full Name: Philip David North

Role: Right-hand bat, slow left-arm bowler

Born: 16 May 1965, Newport, Gwent

Height: 5' 5" **Weight:** 10st

Nickname: Knobbler

County debut: 1985

1st-Class catches 1989: 3 (career 7)

Parents: Arthur and Audrey

Wife and date of marriage: Natalie, 21 April 1990

Family links with cricket: Father and uncles played club cricket

Education: St Julian's Comprehensive; Nash College of Further Education

Qualifications: 5 O-levels, OND in Mechanical Engineering, qualified toolmaker

Jobs outside cricket: Toolmaker with brake manufacturer (Lucas Girling in Cwmbran). Gardener and window cleaner in Australia. Indoor cricket umpire. Landscape gardener. Roofer

Off-season 1989–90: 'Looking for a new career.'

Overseas tours: With Glamorgan CCC to Barbados 1989

Overseas teams played for: Southport CC, Brisbane 1985–86; Penrith CC, Sydney 1986–87, 1987–88

Cricketers particularly learnt from: Don Shepherd, John Steele, Bill Pippen (Australia)

Cricketers particularly admired: Richard Hadlee, Graeme Hick, Matthew Maynard – 'I taught him everything I know about slogging!'

Other sports played: Golf, squash

Other sports followed: Soccer, golf, most sports except horse-racing

Injuries 1989: Cartilage removed in left knee – off seven weeks

Relaxations: Films, socialising, eating out, driving, quiet drinking. 'Spending time with my family. I've just bought a new flat so I'd better enjoy decorating and gardening.'

Extras: 'Nothing to do with cricket but when I was an apprentice with Lucas Girling, I machined three or four disc brakes that were on Richard Noble's "Thrust II" world land speed record-breaking car.' Released by Glamorgan at the end of the 1989 season

Opinions on cricket: 'Second XI games should *all* be played at the respective county grounds. The standard of wickets, covering, and facilities are quite often sub-standard at "out-grounds".'

Best batting performance: 41* Glamorgan v Northamptonshire, Wellingborough 1988

Best bowling performance: 4-43 Glamorgan v Worcestershire, Neath 1987

LAST SEASON: BATTING

	I.	N.O.	R.	H.S.	AV.
TEST					
1ST-CLASS	5	0	32	17	16.40
INT					
RAL					
NAT.W.					
B & H					

CAREER: BATTING

	I.	N.O.	R.	H.S.	AV.
TEST					
1ST-CLASS	25	7	200	41*	11.11
INT					
RAL	1	0	0	0	0.00
NAT.W.					
B & H					

LAST SEASON: BOWLING

	O.	M.	R.	W.	AV.
TEST					
1ST-CLASS	108.3	34	229	5	45.80
INT					
RAL					
NAT.W.					
B & H					

CAREER: BOWLING

	O.	M.	R.	W.	AV.
TEST					
1ST-CLASS	412.3	113	1009	24	42.04
INT					
RAL	23	3	101	5	20.20
NAT.W.					
B & H					

110. Who topped the Hampshire batting averages last season?

O'GORMAN, T. J. G.   Derbyshire

Full Name: Timothy Joseph Gerard
O'Gorman
Role: Right-hand bat
Born: 15 May 1967, Woking
Height: 6′ 2″ **Weight:** 11st 7lbs
County debut: 1987
1st-Class 50s scored: 1
1st-Class 100s scored: 2
Place in batting averages: 46th
av. 38.50 (1988 211th av. 16.88)
1st-Class catches 1989: 2 (career 9)
Parents: Brian and Kathleen
Marital status: Single
Family links with cricket:
Grandfather played for Surrey;
father played for Nigeria, for Sussex
2nd XI and Middlesex 2nd XI
Education: St George's College,
Weybridge, Surrey; Durham
University
Qualifications: 12 O-levels, 3 A-levels; Honours Law Degree, Durham
Jobs outside cricket: Working in solicitors' office during holidays
Off-season 1989–90: 'Attending Law School in Guildford.'
Overseas tours: St George's College to Zimbabwe 1984; Troubadours to
Argentina and Brazil 1987
Cricketers particularly learnt from: Father, Mike Edwards (Surrey)
Cricketers particularly admired: David Gower, Greg Chappell
Other sports played: Hockey (England Schools U-16s and U-18s trialist),
rugby (England Schools U-18 final trialist), tennis, golf
Other sports followed: Tennis, football, golf
Relaxations: Arts, theatre, music, movies
Extras: Surrey Young Cricketer of the Year 1984. Captained Surrey Young
Cricketers for three years (1986 winners of Hilda Overy Trophy)
Best batting performance: 124 Derbyshire v Gloucestershire, Cheltenham
1989

LAST SEASON: BATTING

	I.	N.O.	R.	H.S.	AV.
TEST					
1ST-CLASS	14	2	462	124	38.50
INT					
RAL	5	2	86	46*	28.66
NAT.W.					
B & H	2	0	9	9	4.50

CAREER: BATTING

	I.	N.O.	R.	H.S.	AV.
TEST					
1ST-CLASS	27	3	633	124	26.37
INT					
RAL	6	2	100	46*	25.00
NAT.W.					
B & H	6	0	117	43	19.50

OLDHAM, S. Yorkshire

Full Name: Stephen Oldham
Role: Right-hand bat, right-arm
fast-medium bowler
Born: 26 July 1948, High Green,
Sheffield
Height: 6′ 1″ **Weight:** 14st (summer),
15st (winter)
Nickname: Esso
County debut: 1974 (Yorkshire),
1980 (Derbyshire)
County cap: 1980 (Derbyshire)
50 wickets in a season: 1
1st-Class 50s scored: 1
1st-Class 5 w. in innings: 4
Parents: Robert and Kathleen
Wife: Linda
Children: Sally and Katherine
Education: Crossfield High Green
School
Qualifications: 6 O-levels, 2 A-levels
Jobs outside cricket: Qualified engineer. Assistant works manager
Cricketing superstitions or habits: 'Always play back to fast bowling.'
Cricketers particularly learnt from: Chris Old, Mike Hendrick
Cricketers particularly admired: Geoff Boycott
Other sports played: Football, golf
Relaxations: 'Helping to run my local football club. Drinking Tetley's.'
Extras: Best man at Graham Stevenson's wedding. Debut for Yorkshire 1974
and left after 1979 season. Returned to Yorkshire in 1984 and 1989

LAST SEASON: BATTING

	I.	N.O.	R.	H.S.	AV.
TEST					
1ST-CLASS					
INT					
RAL	1	1	4	4*	–
NAT.W.					
B & H	2	0	0	0	0.00

CAREER: BATTING

	I.	N.O.	R.	H.S.	AV.
TEST					
1ST-CLASS	98	41	648	50	11.36
INT					
RAL	42	23	214	38*	11.26
NAT.W.	7	3	42	19	10.50
B & H	14	4	18	4*	1.80

LAST SEASON: BOWLING

	O.	M.	R.	W.	AV.
TEST					
1ST-CLASS					
INT					
RAL	16	2	53	1	53.00
NAT.W.					
B & H	40	8	148	4	37.00

CAREER: BOWLING

	O.	M.	R.	W.	AV.
TEST					
1ST-CLASS	3021	647	8919	273	32.67
INT					
RAL	878.5	54	3774	154	24.50
NAT.W.	150.5	16	561	25	22.44
B & H	377.4	62	1230	61	20.16

Best batting performance: 50 Yorkshire v Sussex, Hove 1979
Best bowling performance: 7-78 Derbyshire v Warwickshire, Edgbaston 1982

ONTONG, R. C. Glamorgan

Full Name: Rodney Craig Ontong
Role: Right-hand bat, off-break
bowler
Born: 9 September 1955,
Johannesburg
County debut: 1975
County cap: 1979
Benefit: 1989
1000 runs in a season: 5
50 wickets in a season: 5
1st-Class 50s scored: 76
1st-Class 100s scored: 19
1st-Class 200s scored: 1
1st-Class 5 w. in innings: 32
1st-Class 10 w. in match: 4
One-Day 50s: 17
One-Day 100s: 1
Place in batting averages: —
(1988 26th av. 43.17)
Place in bowling averages: —
(1988 127th av. 43.38)
1st-Class catches 1989: 3 (career 178)
Education: Selbourne College, East London, South Africa
Overseas teams played for: Made debut in 1972–73 for Border in Currie Cup

LAST SEASON: BATTING

	I.	N.O.	R.	H.S.	AV.
TEST					
1ST-CLASS	5	0	54	48	10.80
INT					
RAL	5	1	127	44	31.75
NAT.W.					
B & H	1	0	40	40	40.00

LAST SEASON: BOWLING

	O.	M.	R.	W.	AV.
TEST					
1ST-CLASS	133.5	22	361	6	60.16
INT					
RAL	34	0	177	6	29.50
NAT.W.					
B & H	6	0	36	0	–

CAREER: BATTING

	I.	N.O.	R.	H.S.	AV.
TEST					
1ST-CLASS	587	85	14896	204*	29.67
INT					
RAL	142	20	2898	100	23.75
NAT.W.	17	3	528	64	37.71
B & H	40	6	938	81	27.58

CAREER: BOWLING

	O.	M.	R.	W.	AV.
TEST					
1ST-CLASS	8722.2	2014	25334	823	30.78
INT					
RAL	966	52	4387	136	32.25
NAT.W.	173	24	648	15	43.20
B & H	389.4	62	1273	48	26.52

Competition. Transferred to Transvaal for 1976–77 season, before returning to Border. Northern Transvaal 1985–88

Injuries 1989: Injured knee ligaments in a car crash in August 1988, and never fully recovered, missing much of 1989 season

Extras: Took over Glamorgan captaincy during 1984, but resigned during 1986. Retired at end of 1989 season

Best batting performance: 204* Glamorgan v Middlesex, Swansea 1984

Best bowling performance: 8-67 Glamorgan v Nottinghamshire, Trent Bridge 1985

O'SHAUGHNESSY, S. J. Worcestershire

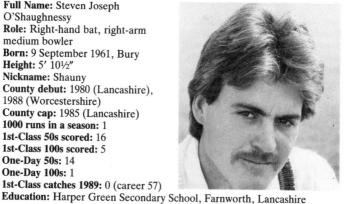

Full Name: Steven Joseph O'Shaughnessy
Role: Right-hand bat, right-arm medium bowler
Born: 9 September 1961, Bury
Height: 5′ 10½″
Nickname: Shauny
County debut: 1980 (Lancashire), 1988 (Worcestershire)
County cap: 1985 (Lancashire)
1000 runs in a season: 1
1st-Class 50s scored: 16
1st-Class 100s scored: 5
One-Day 50s: 14
One-Day 100s: 1
1st-Class catches 1989: 0 (career 57)
Education: Harper Green Secondary School, Farnworth, Lancashire

LAST SEASON: BATTING

	I.	N.O.	R.	H.S.	AV.
TEST					
1ST-CLASS	2	0	11	7	5.50
INT					
RAL	8	1	162	69	23.14
NAT.W.	–	–	–	–	–
B & H	2	0	18	14	9.00

LAST SEASON: BOWLING

	O.	M.	R.	W.	AV.
TEST					
1ST-CLASS					
INT					
RAL	30	0	193	4	48.25
NAT.W.	4	0	14	0	–
B & H					

CAREER: BATTING

	I.	N.O.	R.	H.S.	AV.
TEST					
1ST-CLASS	181	28	3720	159*	24.31
INT					
RAL	92	17	1784	101*	23.78
NAT.W.	18	4	386	62	27.57
B & H	28	1	614	90	22.74

CAREER: BOWLING

	O.	M.	R.	W.	AV.
TEST					
1ST-CLASS	1196.3	220	4108	114	36.03
INT					
RAL	508.1	14	2605	67	38.88
NAT.W.	142	13	592	13	45.53
B & H	184	32	671	25	26.84

Overseas tours: Canada 1979 with NCA U-19 XI; West Indies 1980 with England Young Cricketers
Relaxations: Snooker
Extras: Scored 100 in 35 minutes v Leicestershire, 11 September 1983 to equal fastest first-class century scored by Percy Fender in 1920. Released at end of 1987 season. Joined Worcestershire in 1988. Released by Worcestershire at the end of 1989 season
Best batting performance: 159* Lancashire v Somerset, Bath 1984
Best bowling performance: 4-66 Lancashire v Nottinghamshire, Trent Bridge 1982

PALMER, G. V. Somerset

Full Name: Gary Vincent Palmer
Role: Right-hand bat, right-arm fast-medium bowler
Born: 1 November 1965, Taunton
Height: 6' 1" **Weight:** 11st 7lbs
Nickname: Pedlar
County debut: 1982
1st-Class 50s scored: 3
1st-Class 5 w. in innings: 1
One-Day 50s: 1
1st-Class catches 1989: 0 (career 30)
Parents: Kenneth Ernest and Joy Valerie
Marital status: Single
Family links with cricket: Father, K. E. Palmer, played for Somerset and England. Toured Pakistan with Commonwealth team, 1963. Test Umpire. Coach at Somerset CCC in winter. Grandfather did the double for 13 consecutive seasons in club cricket, and scored 25 centuries for Devizes CC
Education: North Town Junior School; Queen's College, Junior and Senior
Qualifications: SRA Part 1 Squash Coaching Certificate, NCA Cricket Coaching Award, GCEs
Jobs outside cricket: Squash coaching
Overseas tours: English Schools U-19 to Zimbabwe 1982–83; England Young Cricketers to West Indies 1984–85
Cricketers particularly learnt from: 'Learnt from my father from an early age.'
Cricketers particularly admired: Viv Richards, Joel Garner, Ian Botham

Other sports played: Squash

Relaxations: 'Listening to music – the up-to-date variety.'

Extras: Somerset U-19 Squash champion. Youngest professional ever; had summer contract with Somerset at 14. Captain of England U-15. English Schools U-16 Cricketer of the Year. Possibly youngest cricketer to play for England U-19. Made debut for Somerset 1st XI at 16. Opened his first-class career v Leicestershire by bowling two maidens. Released by Somerset at end of 1989 season

Best batting performance: 78 Somerset v Gloucestershire, Bristol 1983

Best bowling performance: 5-38 Somerset v Warwickshire, Taunton 1983

LAST SEASON: BATTING

	I.	N.O.	R.	H.S.	AV.
TEST					
1ST-CLASS					
INT					
RAL	4	3	22	9*	22.00
NAT.W.					
B & H					

LAST SEASON: BOWLING

	O.	M.	R.	W.	AV.
TEST					
1ST-CLASS					
INT					
RAL	23	1	137	3	45.66
NAT.W.					
B & H					

CAREER: BATTING

	I.	N.O.	R.	H.S.	AV.
TEST					
1ST-CLASS	70	11	903	78	15.30
INT					
RAL	36	18	294	33	16.33
NAT.W.	2	1	27	17	27.00
B & H	9	3	101	53	16.83

CAREER: BOWLING

	O.	M.	R.	W.	AV.
TEST					
1ST-CLASS	1128.2	182	4107	92	44.64
INT					
RAL	313	3	1698	60	28.30
NAT.W.	33	3	134	4	33.50
B & H	95.2	7	431	11	39.18

111. Who topped the Kent batting averages last season?

112. Who topped the Lancashire batting averages last season?

PARKER, P. W. G.   Sussex

Full Name: Paul William Giles Parker

Role: Right-hand bat, leg-break bowler, cover fielder, captain
Born: 15 January 1956, Bulawayo, Rhodesia
Height: 5′ 10½″ **Weight:** 12st
Nickname: Porky, Polly
County debut: 1976
County cap: 1979
Benefit: 1988 (£59,400)
Test debut: 1981
No. of Tests: 1
1000 runs in a season: 8
1st-Class 50s scored: 69
1st-Class 100s scored: 37
1st-Class 200s scored: 1
One-Day 50s: 45
One-Day 100s: 5
Place in batting averages: 49th av. 37.84 (1988 39th av. 38.82)
1st-Class catches 1989: 12 (career 211)
Parents: Anthony John and Margaret Edna
Wife and date of marriage: Teresa, 25 January 1980
Children: James William Ralph, 6 November 1980; Jocelyn Elizabeth, 10 September 1984
Family links with cricket: Father played for Essex 2nd XI. Uncle, David Green, played for Northamptonshire and Worcestershire. Two brothers, Guy and Rupert, 'very keen and active cricketers'. Father wrote *The Village Cricket Match* and was sports editor of ITN
Education: Collyer's Grammar School; St Catharine's College, Cambridge
Qualifications: MA (Cantab.)
Jobs outside cricket: Winter employment with Messrs Laing & Cruickshank (Stockbrokers), London
Overseas tours: Combined Oxford & Cambridge XI tour of Australia 1979–80
Overseas teams played for: Sturt CC, Adelaide, Australia 1979–80; Natal, South Africa 1980–81
Cricketers particularly learnt from: J. Denman, Sussex CCC
Other sports played: 'Most ball games.'
Injuries 1989: Pulled hamstring – missed all June and some of July
Relaxations: Reading, crosswords, bridge, music
Extras: Was selected for Cambridge for Varsity rugby match in 1977 but had

to withdraw through injury. Was first reserve for England on Australia tour 1979–80. Appointed captain of Sussex 1988

Best batting performance: 215 Cambridge University v Essex, Cambridge 1976

Best bowling performance: 2-21 Sussex v Surrey, Guildford 1984

LAST SEASON: BATTING

	I.	N.O.	R.	H.S.	AV.
TEST					
1ST-CLASS	29	3	984	136	37.84
INT					
RAL	9	1	183	67	22.87
NAT.W.	2	1	141	87*	141.00
B & H	3	1	145	85*	72.50

CAREER: BATTING

	I.	N.O.	R.	H.S.	AV.
TEST	2	0	13	13	6.50
1ST-CLASS	513	71	15559	215	35.20
INT					
RAL	161	24	4236	121*	30.91
NAT.W.	33	5	1041	109	37.17
B & H	56	5	1337	85*	26.21

LAST SEASON: BOWLING

	O.	M.	R.	W.	AV.
TEST					
1ST-CLASS	7	2	17	0	–
INT					
RAL	1	0	10	0	–
NAT.W.					
B & H					

CAREER: BOWLING

	O.	M.	R.	W.	AV.
TEST					
1ST-CLASS	150.5	26	599	11	54.45
INT					
RAL	6.3	0	38	2	19.00
NAT.W.	2	0	17	1	17.00
B & H	1.2	0	6	2	3.00

PARKS, R. J.   Hampshire

Full Name: Robert James Parks
Role: Right-hand bat, wicket-keeper
Born: 15 June 1959, Cuckfield, Sussex
Height: 5′ 7¾″ **Weight:** 10st 7lbs
Nickname: Bobby
County debut: 1980
County cap: 1982
1st-Class 50s scored: 14
Place in batting averages: 137th av. 25.11 (1988 226th av. 15.55)
Parents: James and Irene
Wife and date of marriage: Amanda, 30 January 1982
Family links with cricket: Father, Jim Parks, played for Sussex and England, as did his grandfather, J. H. Parks. Uncle, H. W. Parks, also played for Sussex
Education: Eastbourne

Grammar School; Southampton Institute of Technology
Qualifications: 9 O-levels, 1 A-level, OND and HND in Business Studies
Jobs outside cricket: Training in accountancy, working for Jardine Air Cargo; LEP International
Off-season 1989–90: Working for computer software company, Capsco Software Europe Ltd
Cricketing superstitions or habits: Left pad on first
Overseas tours: English Counties XI to Zimbabwe 1985
Cricketers particularly learnt from: Alan Knott, John Rice
Cricketers particularly admired: Bob Taylor, Nick Pocock
Other sports played: Squash, football, golf
Other sports followed: 'Keen follower of Spurs, especially when they beat Arsenal.'
Relaxations: Stamp collecting, crosswords
Extras: Broke the Hampshire record for the number of dismissals in a match, v Derbyshire, 1982 (10 catches). Took over from Bob Taylor as stand-in wicket-keeper for England v New Zealand at Lord's after injury to Bruce French
Opinions on cricket: 'There is a serious danger that cricketers representing their countries are playing far too much international cricket which is proving detrimental to their fitness and performance at county level.'
Best batting performance: 89 Hampshire v Cambridge University, Cambridge 1984

LAST SEASON: BATTING

	I.	N.O.	R.	H.S.	AV.
TEST					
1ST-CLASS	29	12	427	76*	25.11
INT					
RAL	10	3	55	25	7.85
NAT.W.	1	0	0	0	0.00
B & H	1	1	4	4*	–

CAREER: BATTING

	I.	N.O.	R.	H.S.	AV.
TEST					
1ST-CLASS	253	69	3559	89	19.34
INT					
RAL	54	28	524	38*	20.15
NAT.W.	11	4	88	25	12.57
B & H	25	9	164	23*	10.25

LAST SEASON: WICKET KEEPING

	C.	ST.			
TEST					
1ST-CLASS	67	4			
INT					
RAL	14	–			
NAT.W.	5	1			
B & H	4	–			

CAREER: WICKET KEEPING

	C.	ST.			
TEST					
1ST-CLASS	568	66			
INT					
RAL	143	27			
NAT.W.	33	7			
B & H	51	5			

PARSONS, G. J. — Leicestershire

Full Name: Gordon James Parsons
Role: Left-hand bat, right-arm
medium bowler, outfielder
Born: 17 October 1959, Slough
Height: 6' 1" **Weight:** 13st 7lbs
'– about half a stone too heavy!'
Nickname: Bullhead
County debut: 1978 (Leicestershire),
1986 (Warwickshire),
1989 (Leicestershire)
County cap: 1984 (Leicestershire),
1987 (Warwickshire)
50 wickets in a season: 2
1st-Class 50s scored: 20
1st-Class 5 w. in innings: 13
1st-Class 10 w. in match: 1
Place in batting averages: 128th
av. 26.33 (1988 197th av. 19.33)
Place in bowling averages: 92nd
av. 35.48 (1988 9th av. 19.06)
Strike rate 1989: 64.67 (career 59.44)
1st-Class catches 1989: 11 (career 67)
Parents: Dave and Evelyn
Marital status: Engaged
Family links with cricket: Father played club cricket
Education: Woodside County Secondary School, Slough
Qualifications: 5 O-levels
Jobs outside cricket: Worked as clerk at T. L. Bennett, Ratby, Leicester.
Coaching
Off-season 1989–90: Playing for Orange Free State in South Africa
Cricketing superstitions or habits: 'None – touch wood!'
Overseas tours: England Schools tour to India 1977–78; Australasia with
Derrick Robins' U-23 XI 1979–80; Zimbabwe with Leicestershire 1981
Overseas teams played for: Maharaja in Sri Lanka 1979, 1981–82, 1982–83;
Boland, South Africa 1983–84; Griqualand 1984–85, 1985–86; Orange Free
State 1988–89, 1989–90
Cricketers particularly learnt from: 'Ramsay Benson, Alf Gover, Ken Higgs,
Roger Tolchard and Andy Roberts have given me plenty of good advice plus
too many to mention – particularly in the team.'
Cricketers particularly admired: Jonathan Agnew, Mike Garnham, David
Allett, Peter Hepworth, Richard Edmunds 'and Andrew Roseberry for his
northern grit.'

375

Other sports played: Golf, squash

Extras: Played for Leicester 2nd XI since 1976 and also for Buckinghamshire in 1977. Left Leicestershire after 1985 season and joined Warwickshire. Capped by Warwickshire while in plaster and on crutches. Released by Warwickshire at end of 1988 season and returned to his old county Leicestershire

Opinions on cricket: 'Would be nice to see 16 four-day matches, played on "good cricket wickets", with a certain number of overs per day rather than 110 overs and over-rate fines.'

Best batting performance: 76 Boland v Western Province B, Cape Town 1984–85

Best bowling performance: 9-72 Boland v Transvaal B, Johannesburg 1984–85

LAST SEASON: BATTING

	I.	N.O.	R.	H.S.	AV.
TEST					
1ST-CLASS	26	8	474	69	26.33
INT					
RAL	9	3	79	20	13.16
NAT.W.	1	1	16	16*	–
B & H	1	1	63	63*	–

LAST SEASON: BOWLING

	O.	M.	R.	W.	AV.
TEST					
1ST-CLASS	334.1	79	1100	31	35.48
INT					
RAL	99	6	482	9	53.55
NAT.W.	20	1	118	0	–
B & H	40	8	146	6	24.33

CAREER: BATTING

	I.	N.O.	R.	H.S.	AV.
TEST					
1ST-CLASS	281	61	4271	76	19.41
INT					
RAL	66	21	508	26*	11.28
NAT.W.	12	3	121	23	13.44
B & H	20	9	252	63*	22.90

CAREER: BOWLING

	O.	M.	R.	W.	AV.
TEST					
1ST-CLASS	4844.5	1036	15124	489	30.92
INT					
RAL	778.2	39	3468	108	32.11
NAT.W.	195.1	25	755	16	47.18
B & H	367.3	46	1306	47	27.78

113. Who topped the Leicestershire batting averages last season?

PATEL, M. M.   Kent

Full Name: Minal Mahesh Patel
Role: Right-hand bat, left-arm spinner
Born: 7 August 1970, Bombay, India
Height: 5′ 9″ **Weight:** 9st
Nickname: Min
County debut: 1989
1st-Class catches 1989: 1 (career 1)
Parents: Mahesh and Aruna
Marital status: Single
Family links with cricket: 'Dad played good club cricket in India, Africa and England.'
Education: Dartford Grammar School; Erith College of Technology
Qualifications: 6 O-levels, 3 A-levels (Maths, Chemistry, Geography)
Off-season 1989–90: Studying for a (BA) Economics Degree
Cricketing superstitions or habits: 'Put kit on in same order.'
Overseas tours: School tour to Barbados 1988
Cricketers particularly learnt from: Colin Page, R. Davis
Cricketers particularly admired: Bishen Bedi, Derek Underwood, Sunil Gavaskar
Other sports played: Football, squash, swimming
Other sports followed: 'All except anything to do with horses!'
Relaxations: 'Listening to soul and hip-hop music. Going to concerts.'

LAST SEASON: BATTING

	I.	N.O.	R.	H.S.	AV.
TEST					
1ST-CLASS	1	0	3	3	3.00
INT					
RAL					
NAT.W.					
B & H					

LAST SEASON: BOWLING

	O.	M.	R.	W.	AV.
TEST					
1ST-CLASS	10	2	34	1	34.00
INT					
RAL					
NAT.W.					
B & H					

CAREER: BATTING

	I.	N.O.	R.	H.S.	AV.
TEST					
1ST-CLASS	1	0	3	3	3.00
INT					
RAL					
NAT.W.					
B & H					

CAREER: BOWLING

	O.	M.	R.	W.	AV.
TEST					
1ST-CLASS	10	2	34	1	34.00
INT					
RAL					
NAT.W.					
B & H					

Extras: Played for ESCA 1988, 1989, and NCA England South 1989. Kent League Young Player of the Year 1987, playing for Blackheath CC
Opinions on cricket: 'There should be more four-day cricket.'
Best batting performance: 3 Kent v Middlesex, Canterbury 1989
Best bowling performance: 1-34 Kent v Middlesex, Canterbury 1989

PATTERSON, B. P.   Lancashire

Full Name: Balfour Patrick Patterson
Role: Right-hand bat, right-arm fast bowler, outfielder
Born: 15 September 1961, Portland, Jamaica
Height: 6' 2½" **Weight:** 14st
Nickname: Balf, Pato
County debut: 1984
County cap: 1987
Test debut: 1985–86
No. of Tests: 17
No. of One-Day Internationals: 27
50 wickets in a season: 1
1st-Class 5 w. in innings: 18
1st-Class 10 w. in match: 2
Place in bowling averages: 11th av. 19.31 (1988 50th av. 25.28)
Strike rate 1989: 39.46 (career 48.72)
1st-Class catches 1989: 1 (career 21)
Parents: Maurice and Emelda
Marital status: Single
Family links with cricket: Father and grandfather played for parish in Jamaica
Education: Happy Grove High School; Wolmers High School for Boys
Qualifications: Jamaica School Certificates, O-levels
Jobs outside cricket: Accounts clerk
Off-season 1989–90: Playing in West Indies
Overseas tours: West Indies to Pakistan 1986–87; to New Zealand 1986–87; to India 1987–88; to England 1988
Overseas teams played for: Tasmania 1984–85; Jamaica 1982–90
Cricketers particularly learnt from: Anderson Roberts
Cricketers particularly admired: Present West Indian team, Dennis Lillee
Other sports played: Basketball, football, squash and table tennis for fitness and pleasure
Other sports followed: Watches football
Relaxations: Swimming, listening to music, watching television

Best batting performance: 29 Lancashire v Northamptonshire, Northampton 1987
Best bowling performance: 7-24 Jamaica v Guyana, Kingston 1985–86

LAST SEASON: BATTING

	I.	N.O.	R.	H.S.	AV.
TEST					
1ST-CLASS	9	5	15	4*	3.75
INT					
RAL					
NAT.W.					
B & H					

LAST SEASON: BOWLING

	O.	M.	R.	W.	AV.
TEST					
1ST-CLASS	210.3	43	618	32	19.31
INT					
RAL					
NAT.W.					
B & H					

CAREER: BATTING

	I.	N.O.	R.	H.S.	AV.
TEST	21	11	88	21*	8.80
1ST-CLASS	99	35	375	29	5.85
INT	5	5	20	13*	–
RAL	2	2	5	3*	–
NAT.W.					
B & H	2	2	18	15*	–

CAREER: BOWLING

	O.	M.	R.	W.	AV.
TEST	449.2	62	1759	59	29.81
1ST-CLASS	2417.1	394	7800	294	26.53
INT	235.3	17	1042	51	20.43
RAL	22.2	0	98	5	19.60
NAT.W.					
B & H	31	4	108	4	27.00

PENBERTHY, A. L.   Northamptonshire

Full Name: Anthony Leonard Penberthy
Role: Left-hand bat, right-arm medium-pace bowler
Born: 1 September 1969, Troon, Cornwall
Height: 6′ 1″ **Weight:** 11½st
Nickname: Berth, Penbers
County debut: 1989
1st-Class catches 1989: 4 (career 4)
Parents: Gerald and Wendy
Marital status: Single
Family links with cricket: Father played in local leagues in Cornwall and is now a qualified umpire instructor
Education: Troon County Primary; Camborne Comprehensive
Qualifications: 3 O-levels, 3 CSEs, coaching certificate
Jobs outside cricket: Worked in factory making surgical supports
Off-season 1989–90: Working back home in Cornwall

Cricketing superstitions or habits: 'Always put right pad on first.'
Cricketers particularly learnt from: Brian Reynolds, Bob Carter, Dennis Lillee
Cricketers particularly admired: Ian Botham, David Gower, Geoff Boycott, Viv Richards, Dennis Lillee
Other sports played: Football, snooker, golf
Other sports followed: Rugby
Relaxations: Listening to music, watching videos and comedy programmes
Extras: Had trials for Plymouth Argyle at football but came to Northampton for cricket trials instead. Took wicket with first ball in first-class cricket, Mark Taylor caught behind against Australians June 1989. Played for Young England 1989
Opinions on cricket: 'Too much one-day cricket which breeds bad habits in Championship cricket and Test cricket. Think that good cricket wickets should be produced and not doctored pitches which give a false impression of the ability of the cricketer.'
Best batting performance: 27 Northamptonshire v Nottinghamshire, Northampton 1989
Best bowling performance: 3-56 Northamptonshire v Australians, Northampton 1989

LAST SEASON: BATTING

	I.	N.O.	R.	H.S.	AV.
TEST					
1ST-CLASS	8	0	75	27	9.37
INT					
RAL	3	0	46	35	15.33
NAT.W.					
B & H					

CAREER: BATTING

	I.	N.O.	R.	H.S.	AV.
TEST					
1ST-CLASS	8	0	75	27	9.37
INT					
RAL	3	0	46	35	15.33
NAT.W.					
B & H					

LAST SEASON: BOWLING

	O.	M.	R.	W.	AV.
TEST					
1ST-CLASS	48	7	162	3	54.00
INT					
RAL	12	1	50	3	16.66
NAT.W.					
B & H					

CAREER: BOWLING

	O.	M.	R.	W.	AV.
TEST					
1ST-CLASS	48	7	162	3	54.00
INT					
RAL	12	1	50	3	16.66
NAT.W.					
B & H					

PENN, C.   Kent

Full Name: Christopher Penn
Role: Left-hand bat, right-arm
medium bowler
Born: 19 June 1963, Dover
Height: 6′ 1″ **Weight:** 14st
Nickname: Penny, Gazza
County debut: 1982
County cap: 1987
50 wickets in a season: 1
1st-Class 50s scored: 5
1st-Class 100s scored: 1
1st-Class 5 w. in innings: 9
Place in batting averages: 196th
av. 18.64 (1988 159th av. 22.94)
Place in bowling averages: 109th
av. 43.70 (1988 45th av. 24.55)
Strike rate 1989: 82.97 (career 60.84)
1st-Class catches 1989: 4 (career 43)
Parents: Reg and Brenda
Wife and date of marriage: Caroline
Ann, 22 March 1986
Children: Matthew Thomas, 14 October 1987
Family links with cricket: Father played club cricket for Dover CC for 26
years; father-in-law keen Kent follower
Education: River Primary School; Dover Grammar School
Qualifications: 9 O-levels, 2 A-levels
Jobs outside cricket: Farm worker, car cleaner for hire company, financial
planning consultant ('retired very quickly'), lumberjack
Off-season 1989–90: Coaching in Kent; working for the County on ground
Cricketing superstitions or habits: 'Eat baked beans for breakfast – otherwise
none, luckily!'
Overseas tours: NCA tour of Denmark 1981; Whitbread Scholarship to
Australia 1982–83
Overseas teams played for: Koohinore Crescents, Johannesburg 1981–82 and
1983–84; West Perth 1982–83; Johannesburg Municipals 1983–84; Wits
University 1984–85
Cricketers particularly learnt from: 'My father, Colin Page, Brian Luckhurst,
Barney Lock and many others.'
Cricketers particularly admired: Alan Knott, Dennis Lillee, Cliff Jamieson,
Terry Alderman
Other sports played: Rugby, football, golf, squash
Other sports followed: All sports

Injuries 1989: 'Sore heels and ankles due to hard ground, and injuries due to general over-use.'

Relaxations: Music, art and art history, Indian food, local sport

Extras: Played for Young England and England Schools. Took hat-trick in first 2nd XI match v Middlesex when 16 years old. Bowled two consecutive overs v Sussex 2nd XI, 1982, bowling last over at night, and first over next morning, 'which John Langridge noticed too late.' Kent Player of the Year 1988

Opinions on cricket: 'Too much car travel which could lead to a serious accident. Not a long enough break between games, which leads to stale cricket and stale bodies.'

Best batting performance: 115 Kent v Lancashire, Old Trafford 1984

Best bowling performance: 7-70 Kent v Middlesex, Lord's 1988

LAST SEASON: BATTING

	I.	N.O.	R.	H.S.	AV.
TEST					
1ST-CLASS	21	4	317	60	18.64
INT					
RAL	4	2	47	18	23.50
NAT.W.	1	0	3	3	3.00
B & H	4	2	43	24*	21.50

CAREER: BATTING

	I.	N.O.	R.	H.S.	AV.
TEST					
1ST-CLASS	108	28	1582	115	19.77
INT					
RAL	31	8	211	40	9.17
NAT.W.	3	0	8	5	2.66
B & H	14	6	89	24*	11.12

LAST SEASON: BOWLING

	O.	M.	R.	W.	AV.
TEST					
1ST-CLASS	567	101	1792	41	43.70
INT					
RAL	53.3	5	227	5	45.40
NAT.W.	18	1	69	2	34.50
B & H	60.3	12	197	5	39.40

CAREER: BOWLING

	O.	M.	R.	W.	AV.
TEST					
1ST-CLASS	2180.1	413	7057	215	32.82
INT					
RAL	351.4	14	1692	56	30.21
NAT.W.	62	8	180	8	22.50
B & H	191.1	19	740	23	32.17

114. Who topped the Middlesex batting averagges last season?

PETERS, N. H. Surrey

Full Name: Nicholas Howard Peters
Role: Right-hand bat, right-arm
fast-medium bowler
Born: 21 February 1968, Guildford
Height: 6′ 3″ **Weight:** 13st 7lbs
Nickname: Bond-Machine, OO
County debut: 1988
1st-Class 5 w. in innings: 1
1st-Class 10 w. in match: 1
Place in batting averages: —
(1988 249th av. 12.14)
Place in bowling averages: —
(1988 67th av. 28.05)
1st-Class catches 1989: 2 (career 7)
Parents: Howard and Rosalind
Marital status: Single
Education: Humpty Dumpty Junior
School; Cranmore Preparatory
School, East Horsley; Sherborne
School, Dorset
Qualifications: 8 O-levels, 2 A-levels; at present doing a degree in sports
science/history
Jobs outside cricket: Factory cleaner
Off-season 1989–90: Studying
Overseas tours: Surrey U-19s to Australia 1985
Cricketers particularly learnt from: Geoff Arnold
Cricketers particularly admired: Bill Wyman, Ian Botham
Other sports played: Basketball, cross-country, table tennis, tennis

LAST SEASON: BATTING

	I.	N.O.	R.	H.S.	AV.
TEST					
1ST-CLASS	3	0	16	15	5.33
INT					
RAL	1	1	1	1*	—
NAT.W.					
B & H					

CAREER: BATTING

	I.	N.O.	R.	H.S.	AV.
TEST					
1ST-CLASS	18	8	101	25*	10.10
INT					
RAL	5	3	6	4*	3.00
NAT.W.	–	–	–	–	–
B & H	1	1	1	1*	—

LAST SEASON: BOWLING

	O.	M.	R.	W.	AV.
TEST					
1ST-CLASS	82.1	11	292	6	48.66
INT					
RAL	10	0	51	1	51.00
NAT.W.					
B & H					

CAREER: BOWLING

	O.	M.	R.	W.	AV.
TEST					
1ST-CLASS	360.3	61	1246	40	31.15
INT					
RAL	40.5	1	181	7	25.85
NAT.W.	21	3	78	3	26.00
B & H	30	3	101	3	33.66

Relaxations: 'General relaxing, talking to Mark Frost and Graeme Brown who both have an unbelievable insight into present day cricket.'
Extras: Played for England Schools and NAYC
Opinions on cricket: '"No pain no gain." It is essential to always set yourself both short-term and long-term goals with maximum commitment and specificity.'
Best batting performance: 25* Surrey v Leicestershire, The Oval 1988
Best bowling performance: 6-31 Surrey v Warwickshire, The Oval 1988

PICK, R. A.   Nottinghamshire

Full Name: Robert Andrew Pick
Role: Left-hand bat, right-arm fast-medium bowler
Born: 19 November 1963, Nottingham
Height: 5′ 10″ **Weight:** 13st
Nickname: Dad, Picky
County debut: 1983
County cap: 1987
50 wickets in a season: 1
1st-Class 50s scored: 2
1st-Class 5 w. in innings: 4
1st-Class 10 w. in match: 1
Place in bowling averages: 89th av. 34.47
Strike rate 1989: 58.61 (career 60.28)
1st-Class catches 1989: 2 (career 16)
Parents: Bob and Lillian
Wife and date of marriage: Jennie Ruth, 8 April 1989
Family links with cricket: Father, uncles and cousins all play local cricket for Thrumpton CC
Education: Alderman Derbyshire Comprehensive; High Pavement College
Qualifications: 7 O-levels, 1 A-level, coaching qualification
Jobs outside cricket: Labourer; van driver; warehouse work
Off-season 1989–90: Playing in New Zealand
Overseas tours: Barbados with Keith Pont Benefit 1986
Overseas teams played for: Upper Hutt CC, New Zealand 1984–85; Taita CC, New Zealand 1986–87, 1987–88
Cricketers particularly admired: Bob White, Mike Hendrick, Mike Harris, Franklyn Stephenson
Other sports played: Football, fishing

Other sports followed: Ice-hockey, American football
Relaxations: 'As much fishing as possible and listening to a wide range of music; eating and drinking; going to the pictures.'
Extras: Played three Tests for Young England v Young Australia 1983. Played soccer for Nottingham Schoolboys
Injuries 1989: Torn side muscle – off for month of July
Opinions on cricket: 'Coloured clothing should be introduced for all one-day cricket.'
Best batting performance: 63 Nottinghamshire v Warwickshire, Nuneaton 1985
Best bowling performance: 6-52 Nottinghamshire v Oxford University, Oxford 1989

LAST SEASON: BATTING

	I.	N.O.	R.	H.S.	AV.
TEST					
1ST-CLASS	13	2	64	17	5.81
INT					
RAL	2	1	6	6	6.00
NAT.W.					
B & H	2	1	3	2*	3.00

CAREER: BATTING

	I.	N.O.	R.	H.S.	AV.
TEST					
1ST-CLASS	82	21	885	63	14.50
INT					
RAL	20	9	117	24	10.63
NAT.W.	8	6	63	34*	31.50
B & H	9	5	17	4	4.25

LAST SEASON: BOWLING

	O.	M.	R.	W.	AV.
TEST					
1ST-CLASS	205.1	34	724	21	34.47
INT					
RAL	46	2	246	7	35.14
NAT.W.					
B & H	41	4	162	7	23.14

CAREER: BOWLING

	O.	M.	R.	W.	AV.
TEST					
1ST-CLASS	1778.3	330	6203	177	35.04
INT					
RAL	396.2	14	2098	66	31.78
NAT.W.	156.1	17	572	22	26.00
B & H	177.5	16	720	25	28.80

115. Who were the only two Gloucestershire batsmen to score 1000 first-class runs last season?

PICKLES, C. S.

Full Name: Christopher Stephen Pickles
Role: Right-hand bat, right-arm medium bowler
Born: 30 January 1966, Cleckheaton
Height: 6' 1" **Weight:** 13st
Nickname: Pick, Piccolo
County debut: 1985
1st-Class 50s scored: 2
Place in batting averages: 155th av. 22.82
Place in bowling averages: 102nd av. 40.58
Strike rate 1989: 71.86 (career 84.02)
1st-Class catches 1989: 10 (career 14)
Parents: Ronald Albert and Christine Mary
Wife and date of marriage: Janet Elizabeth, 22 October 1988
Children: Samantha Janet, 10 October 1989
Family links with cricket: Father and brother both play local league cricket
Education: Whitcliffe Mount Comprehensive; West End Middle, Heaton Avenue
Qualifications: Qualified cricket coach
Jobs outside cricket: Work in textiles
Off-season 1989–90: Working for Heckmondwike FB industrial carpet manufacturers
Overseas tours: NCA U-19 to Bermuda 1985

LAST SEASON: BATTING

	I.	N.O.	R.	H.S.	AV.
TEST					
1ST-CLASS	24	7	388	66	22.82
INT					
RAL	7	3	39	19	9.75
NAT.W.	1	0	3	3	3.00
B & H	2	0	9	5	4.50

CAREER: BATTING

	I.	N.O.	R.	H.S.	AV.
TEST					
1ST-CLASS	29	9	443	66	22.15
INT					
RAL	15	8	94	19	13.42
NAT.W.	1	0	3	3	3.00
B & H	3	1	22	13*	11.00

LAST SEASON: BOWLING

	O.	M.	R.	W.	AV.
TEST					
1ST-CLASS	347.2	79	1177	29	40.58
INT					
RAL	100.4	4	529	17	31.11
NAT.W.	12	1	41	1	41.00
B & H	38	8	142	1	142.00

CAREER: BOWLING

	O.	M.	R.	W.	AV.
TEST					
1ST-CLASS	490.1	97	1620	35	46.28
INT					
RAL	180.4	10	887	27	32.85
NAT.W.	12	1	41	1	41.00
B & H	49	11	170	1	170.00

Overseas teams played for: City Cricket Club, Whangerai, New Zealand 1986–87
Cricketers particularly learnt from: Ian Steen, Doug Padgett, Steve Oldham
Cricketers particularly admired: Michael Holding
Other sports played: Rugby union
Other sports followed: Cleckheaton RFC
Relaxations: 'Going out for a pint and then having some fish and chips.' Music, videos
Opinions on cricket: 'Nobody should qualify as English unless they were born in this country.'
Best batting performance: 66 Yorkshire v Somerset, Taunton 1989
Best bowling performance: 4-92 Yorkshire v Northamptonshire, Northampton 1989

PIENAAR, R. F.   Kent

Full Name: Roy Francois Pienaar
Role: Right-hand opening bat, right-arm fast-medium bowler
Born: 17 July 1961, Johannesburg
Height: 6′ 2″ **Weight:** 13st
Nickname: Vitas
County debut: 1987
County cap: 1988
1000 runs in a season: 2
1st-Class 50s scored: 40
1st-Class 100s scored: 13
1st-Class 5 w. in innings: 3
One-Day 50s: 3
One-Day 100s scored: 1
Place in batting averages: 14th av. 52.84 (1988 47th av. 37.21)
Place in bowling averages: —
(1988 97th av. 32.27)
1st-Class catches 1989: 8 (career 54)
Parents: Ron and Heather
Marital status: Single
Education: St Stithian's College, Johannesburg
Qualifications: Matriculation (Higher Grade); Bachelor of Commerce, University of Cape Town
Jobs outside cricket: Partner in import/export business
Off-season 1989–90: Playing in South Africa, and helping run business
Cricketing superstitions or habits: Puts left pad on first

Overseas tours: Wanderers' Club to England 1977

Overseas teams played for: Transvaal B 1977–78; Western Province 1984–85; Northern Transvaal 1985–88; Transvaal 1988–90. For South Africa v Australian unofficial team 1985–86, 1986–87

Cricketers particularly learnt from: Peter Stringer, John Inverarity, Colin Tomlin ('for his fitness'), Colin Bland ('for his fielding')

Cricketers particularly admired: Barry Richards, Graeme Pollock, Mark Harman

Other sports played: Tennis, swimming, jogging

Other sports followed: Tennis, golf, rugby, athletics – 'one particular athlete, Claudine Tomlin'

Injuries 1989: 'Operations on both my knees – out for first two months of the season.'

Relaxations: Keeping fit, music, movies, wildlife

Extras: South African Cricketer of the Year 1983. Shared in record One-Day opening stand for South Africa v Australia of 154 with Jimmy Cook. Played for Worcestershire 2nd XI and Kidderminster in Birmingham League. Joined Kent mid-season in 1987 as their overseas player in place of the injured Eldine Baptiste

Opinions on cricket: 'We should play four-day cricket, and each team once, on good wickets. To raise the standard of cricket, players and coaches should be more inquisitive as to how the body and mind works in the performance of the skills required.'

Best batting performance: 153 Kent v Derbyshire, Derby 1987

Best bowling performance: 5-24 Western Province v Natal, Durban 1981–82

LAST SEASON: BATTING

	I.	N.O.	R.	H.S.	AV.
TEST					
1ST-CLASS	29	4	1321	134*	52.84
INT					
RAL	7	0	238	119	34.00
NAT.W.	2	0	100	90	50.00
B & H	2	0	43	36	21.50

CAREER: BATTING

	I.	N.O.	R.	H.S.	AV.
TEST					
1ST-CLASS	217	15	6938	153	34.34
INT					
RAL	19	1	510	119	28.33
NAT.W.	4	1	192	90	64.00
B & H	2	0	43	36	21.50

LAST SEASON: BOWLING

	O.	M.	R.	W.	AV.
TEST					
1ST-CLASS	11	3	43	0	–
INT					
RAL					
NAT.W.	5	1	16	2	8.00
B & H					

CAREER: BOWLING

	O.	M.	R.	W.	AV.
TEST					
1ST-CLASS	1699	338	4683	143	32.74
INT					
RAL	79	1	383	14	27.35
NAT.W.	46	8	120	9	13.33
B & H					

PIERSON, A. R. K.   Warwickshire

Full Name: Adrian Roger Kirshaw Pierson
Role: Right-hand bat, off-break bowler
Born: 21 July 1963, Enfield, Middlesex
Height: 6′ 4½″ **Weight:** 12st
Nickname: Skirlog, Stick
County debut: 1985
1st-Class 5 w. in innings: 2
Place in bowling averages: 96th av. 37.40
Strike rate 1989: 71.96 (career 82.89)
1st-Class catches 1989: 8 (career 15)
Parents: Patrick Blake Kirshaw and Patricia Margaret
Marital status: Engaged
Education: Lochinver House Primary; Kent College, Canterbury; Hatfield Polytechnic
Qualifications: 8 O-levels, 2 A-levels, NCA Senior Coach
Jobs outside cricket: Light aircraft engineer
Off-season 1989–90: Coaching and playing in Zimbabwe
Cricketing superstitions or habits: Always puts left pad on first
Overseas tours: Barbados 1985 with Dennis Amiss Testimonial XI
Overseas teams played for: Walmer CC, Port Elizabeth, South Africa 1985–89

LAST SEASON: BATTING

	I.	N.O.	R.	H.S.	AV.
TEST					
1ST-CLASS	20	4	126	18	7.87
INT					
RAL	3	2	17	9	17.00
NAT.W.	–	–	–	–	–
B & H	2	0	1	1	0.50

CAREER: BATTING

	I.	N.O.	R.	H.S.	AV.
TEST					
1ST-CLASS	49	20	315	42*	10.86
INT					
RAL	15	8	78	21*	11.14
NAT.W.	1	1	1	1*	–
B & H	6	2	19	11	4.75

LAST SEASON: BOWLING

	O.	M.	R.	W.	AV.
TEST					
1ST-CLASS	383.5	79	1197	32	37.40
INT					
RAL	32	1	185	6	30.83
NAT.W.	17	3	55	4	13.75
B & H	40	5	136	1	136.00

CAREER: BOWLING

	O.	M.	R.	W.	AV.
TEST					
1ST-CLASS	773.4	160	2509	56	44.80
INT					
RAL	166.2	7	789	16	49.31
NAT.W.	41	8	111	4	27.75
B & H	78	10	258	6	43.00

Cricketers particularly learnt from: Don Wilson, Neal Abberley, Harry Birrell, Norman Gifford, Eddie Hemmings
Cricketers particularly admired: John Emburey, Phil Edmonds, Tony Greig
Other sports played: Hockey, golf, tennis
Other sports followed: All sports '– except horse racing'
Injuries 1989: Tendonitis in right shoulder – missed last six weeks of season
Relaxations: Music, driving, reading
Extras: On Lord's groundstaff 1984–85
Opinions on cricket: 'Banning cricketers from playing in South Africa will only affect apartheid in cricket. This has now undergone change. Overthrows should not be counted against the bowler: perhaps they should be entered as extras.'
Best batting performance: 42* Warwickshire v Northamptonshire, Northampton 1986
Best bowling performance: 6-82 Warwickshire v Derbyshire, Nuneaton 1989

PIGOTT, A. C. S. Sussex

Full Name: Anthony Charles Shackleton Pigott
Role: Right-hand bat, right-arm fast bowler, slip fielder
Born: 4 June 1958, London
Height: 6' 1" **Weight:** 13st
Nickname: Lester
County debut: 1978
County cap: 1982
Test debut: 1983–84
No. of Tests: 1
50 wickets in a season: 4
1st-Class 50s scored: 14
1st-Class 100s scored: 1
1st-Class 5 w. in innings: 19
1st-Class 10 w. in match: 1
One-Day 50s: 2
Place in batting averages: 134th
av. 25.27 (1988 131st av. 25.69)
Place in bowling averages: 81st av. 31.57 (1988 68th av. 28.08)
Strike rate 1989: 61.74 (career 52.57)
1st-Class catches 1989: 21 (career 95)
Parents: Tom and Juliet
Marital status: Divorced
Children: Elliot Sebastian, 15 March 1983

Family links with cricket: Father captained club side
Education: Harrow School
Qualifications: 5 O-levels, 2 A-levels; Junior Coaching Certificate
Jobs outside cricket: Sportsmaster at Claremont Prep School, Hastings. Owner of squash club at county ground
Off-season 1989–90: Running the squash club
Overseas tours: With Derrick Robins' XI to Australasia 1980; part of England tour to New Zealand 1983–84
Overseas teams played for: Waverley CC, Sydney, Australia 1976–77, 1977–78, 1979–80; Wellington, New Zealand 1982–83 and 1983–84; Claremont, Cape Town 1980–81, 1981–82
Cricketers particularly learnt from: Geoff Arnold, Norman Gifford
Cricketers particularly admired: Ian Botham, John Snow
Other sports played: Squash, racquets, football, golf
Other sports followed: Football, golf, squash, tennis – 'all of them'
Injuries 1989: 'Hamstring – but played through it.'
Relaxations: Squash club. 'Spending time with my son.'
Extras: Public Schools Racquets champion 1975. Had operation on back, April 1981, missing most of season, and was told by a specialist he would never play cricket again. First three wickets in first-class cricket were a hat-trick. Postponed wedding to make Test debut when called into England party on tour of New Zealand. Originally going to Somerset for 1984 season, but then remained with Sussex. Was diagnosed as a diabetic after he lost 11lbs in two weeks in 1987, but recovered to take 74 wickets in 1988 season
Opinions on cricket: 'We should start playing total four-day cricket.'
Best batting performance: 104* Sussex v Warwickshire, Edgbaston 1986
Best bowling performance: 7-74 Sussex v Northamptonshire, Eastbourne 1982

LAST SEASON: BATTING

	I.	N.O.	R.	H.S.	AV.
TEST					
1ST-CLASS	27	5	556	91	25.27
INT					
RAL	9	3	234	51*	39.00
NAT.W.	2	0	18	13	9.00
B & H	3	2	64	49*	64.00

CAREER: BATTING

	I.	N.O.	R.	H.S.	AV.
TEST	2	1	12	8*	12.00
1ST-CLASS	210	45	3478	104*	21.07
INT					
RAL	55	23	670	51*	20.93
NAT.W.	8	0	152	53	19.00
B & H	18	7	125	49*	11.36

LAST SEASON: BOWLING

	O.	M.	R.	W.	AV.
TEST					
1ST-CLASS	679.1	130	2084	66	31.57
INT					
RAL	94	4	405	17	23.82
NAT.W.	36	4	162	3	54.00
B & H	41	6	152	5	30.40

CAREER: BOWLING

	O.	M.	R.	W.	AV.
TEST	17	7	75	2	37.50
1ST-CLASS	4215.2	755	13889	481	28.87
INT					
RAL	696.1	23	3352	153	21.90
NAT.W.	144.4	20	526	20	26.30
B & H	234	28	993	36	27.58

PIPER, K. J.   Warwickshire

Full Name: Keith John Piper
Role: Right-hand bat, wicket-keeper
Born: 18 December 1969
Height: 5′ 6″ **Weight:** 10½st
Nickname: Tubbsy, Tuba
County debut: 1989
Place in batting averages: 215th av. 16.00
Parents: John and Charlotte
Marital status: Single
Family links with cricket: 'Dad plays club cricket in Leicester.'
Education: Seven Sisters Junior; Somerset Senior
Qualifications: Cricket Coaching Award, Basketball Coaching Award
Off-season 1989–90: Labouring
Cricketing superstitions or habits:
'Run out to get the ball before anyone when keeping. Put left pad on first.'
Overseas tours: Haringey Cricket College to Barbados 1986; Trinidad 1987; Jamaica 1988, 1989
Cricketers particularly learnt from: Andy Brassington, Dermot Reeve, Alan Knott
Cricketers particularly admired: Jack Russell, Andy Brassington, Dermot Reeve, Paul Smith, Viv Richards, Desmond Haynes
Other sports played: Football, squash
Other sports followed: Snooker, football

LAST SEASON: BATTING

	I.	N.O.	R.	H.S.	AV.
TEST					
1ST-CLASS	15	2	208	41	16.00
INT					
RAL	5	2	46	20	15.33
NAT.W.	–	–	–	–	–
B & H					

CAREER: BATTING

	I.	N.O.	R.	H.S.	AV.
TEST					
1ST-CLASS	15	2	208	41	16.00
INT					
RAL	5	2	46	20	15.33
NAT.W.	–	–	–	–	–
B & H					

LAST SEASON: WICKET KEEPING

	C.	ST.			
TEST					
1ST-CLASS	26	1			
INT					
RAL	3	–			
NAT.W.	2	–			
B & H					

CAREER: WICKET KEEPING

	C.	ST.			
TEST					
1ST-CLASS	26	1			
INT					
RAL	3	–			
NAT.W.	2	–			
B & H					

Relaxations: 'Music, videos, eating a bit.'
Best batting performance: 41 Warwickshire v Surrey, Edgbaston 1989 (on debut)

POLLARD, P.   Nottinghamshire

Full Name: Paul Pollard
Role: Left-hand bat, right-arm medium bowler
Born: 24 September 1968, Carlton, Nottinghamshire
Height: 5' 10" **Weight:** 12st
Nickname: Polly
County debut: 1987
1000 runs in a season: 1
1st-Class 50s scored: 6
1st-Class 100s scored: 3
One-Day 50s scored: 1
One-Day 100s scored: 2
Place in batting averages: 78th
av. 33.25 (1988 121st av. 26.75)
1st-Class catches 1989: 19 (career 29)
Parents: Eric and Mary
Education: Gedling Comprehensive
Jobs outside cricket: Trainee pub manager; labouring
Off-season 1989–90: Playing for North Perth CC, Australia
Cricketing superstitions or habits: 'Always bat in some kind of headgear.'
Overseas tours: Chesterfield CC to Barbados 1986
Overseas teams played for: Southern Districts, Brisbane, Australia 1987–88; North Perth CC 1989–90
Cricketers particularly learnt from: Clive Rice, Mike Bore, Gordon Stringfellow (the Nottinghamshire 2nd XI scorer and local cricketer)
Cricketers particularly admired: Clive Rice, Graeme Pollock, Richard Hadlee, David Gower
Other sports played: Golf, snooker
Other sports followed: Ice-hockey, golf, football
Relaxations: Watching videos, playing golf, 'spending time with my girlfriend'
Extras: Made debut for Nottinghamshire 2nd XI in 1985. Worked in Nottinghamshire CCC office on a Youth Training Scheme. Shared stands of 222 and 282 with Tim Robinson v Kent 1988. Youngest player to reach 1000 runs for Nottinghamshire. First player to claim on the Western Australian Cricket Association medical insurance scheme

393

Best batting performance: 153 Nottinghamshire v Cambridge University, Cambridge 1989

LAST SEASON: BATTING

	I.	N.O.	R.	H.S.	AV.
TEST					
1ST-CLASS	32	0	1064	153	33.25
INT					
RAL	10	1	350	123*	38.88
NAT.W.	2	0	27	23	13.50
B & H	5	0	95	77	19.00

CAREER: BATTING

	I.	N.O.	R.	H.S.	AV.
TEST					
1ST-CLASS	56	1	1624	153	29.52
INT					
RAL	14	1	435		33.46
NAT.W.	2	0	27	23	13.50
B & H	5	0	95	77	19.00

POOLEY, J. C. Middlesex

Full Name: Jason Calvin Pooley
Role: Left-hand bat, slow right-arm bowler, cover fielder
Born: 8 August 1969, Hammersmith
Height: 6′ **Weight:** 12st 13lbs
County debut: 1989
Parents: Dave and Kath
Marital status: Single
Family links with cricket: Father and older brother play club cricket; younger brother Gregg plays for Middlesex YC and Second XI
Education: Acton High School
Jobs outside cricket: Helping in father's building firm
Off-season 1989–90: Working for father
Cricketing superstitions or habits: Always puts right pad on first
Overseas teams played for: St George's, Sydney, Australia 1988–89
Cricketers particularly learnt from: Father, David Green, Don Bennett, Clive Radley
Cricketers particularly admired: David Gower, Mike Gatting, Clive Radley
Other sports played: Football and most sports
Other sports followed: Horse racing and Portsmouth FC
Relaxations: Studying horse racing, sport and music
Extras: Won Rapid Cricket Line Second XI Player of Year 1989, in first year as professional. Not related to Gloucestershire's Malcolm Pooley

394

Opinions on cricket: 'All Championship matches should be four-day games.'
Best batting performance: 14 Middlesex v Kent, Canterbury 1989

LAST SEASON: BATTING

	I.	N.O.	R.	H.S.	AV.
TEST					
1ST-CLASS	1	0	14	14	14.00
INT					
RAL					
NAT.W.					
B & H					

CAREER: BATTING

	I.	N.O.	R.	H.S.	AV.
TEST					
1ST-CLASS	1	0	14	14	14.00
INT					
RAL					
NAT.W.					
B & H					

POOLEY, M. W.　　　Gloucestershire

Full Name: Malcolm William Pooley
Role: Right-hand bat, right-arm
medium bowler, out-fielder
Born: 27 July 1969, Truro
Height: 5' 11" **Weight:** 12st 2lbs
Nickname: 'The Boy', Mally,
Gel-boy
County debut: 1988
Place in batting averages: —
(1988 201st av. 18.62)
Place in bowling averages: —
(1988 77th av. 29.53)
1st-Class catches 1989: 1 (career 5)
Parents: Douglas John and
Christine Wendy
Marital status: Single
Education: Poole Secondary School;
Cornwall College
Qualifications: 4 O-levels, 6 CSE and
City and Guilds in Sport and Recreation; NCA Coaching Certificate
Jobs outside cricket: Assistant PE teacher (YTS)
Off-season 1989–90: Working in local brewery
Cricketing superstitions or habits: Puts left pad on first
Overseas tours: NCA tour of Ireland, in International Youth Tournament,
1987; England Young Cricketers to Australia for Youth World Cup 1988
Cricketers particularly learnt from: Graham Wiltshire and John Shepherd –
Gloucestershire coaches
Cricketers particularly admired: Viv Richards, Ian Botham, Kevin Curran
Other sports played: Cornwall Schools U-16 football and rugby

Other sports followed: All sports. Plymouth Argyle FC
Relaxations: Music, old comedy films
Extras: Man of the tournament at the IYT in Ireland
Opinions on cricket: 'Lunch and tea break should be extended to an hour and half an hour respectively.'
Best batting performance: 38 Gloucestershire v Middlesex, Lord's 1988
Best bowling performance: 4-80 Gloucestershire v Kent, Bristol 1988

LAST SEASON: BATTING

	I.	N.O.	R.	H.S.	AV.
TEST					
1ST-CLASS	3	1	6	3	3.00
INT					
RAL	8	5	29	8	9.66
NAT.W.	–	–	–	–	–
B & H	–	–	–	–	–

LAST SEASON: BOWLING

	O.	M.	R.	W.	AV.
TEST					
1ST-CLASS	35	6	113	0	–
INT					
RAL	87.5	5	401	16	25.06
NAT.W.	12	2	35	0	–
B & H	41	3	156	3	52.00

CAREER: BATTING

	I.	N.O.	R.	H.S.	AV.
TEST					
1ST-CLASS	16	6	155	38	15.50
INT					
RAL	9	6	30	8	10.00
NAT.W.	–	–	–	–	–
B & H	–	–	–	–	–

CAREER: BOWLING

	O.	M.	R.	W.	AV.
TEST					
1ST-CLASS	163.4	36	497	13	38.23
INT					
RAL	103.5	5	480	19	25.26
NAT.W.	12	2	35	0	–
B & H	41	3	156	3	52.00

POTTER, L.   Leicestershire

Full Name: Laurie Potter
Role: Right-hand bat, slow left-arm bowler, slip fielder
Born: 7 November 1962, Bexleyheath, Kent
Height: 6' 1" **Weight:** 14st
Nickname: Pottsie
County debut: 1981 (Kent), 1986 (Leicestershire)
County cap: 1988 (Leicestershire)
1000 runs in a season: 1
1st-Class 50s scored: 31
1st-Class 100s scored: 6
One-Day 50s: 11
One-Day 100s: 2
Place in batting averages: 86th av. 32.14 (1988 74th av. 32.77)
Place in bowling averages: 72nd av. 30.66

Strike rate 1989: 64.33 (career 71.79)
1st-Class catches 1989: 25 (career 124)
Parents: Ronald Henry Ernest and Audrey Megan
Wife and date of marriage: Helen Louise, October 1989
Family links with cricket: Father-in-law Kent 2nd XI scorer
Education: Kelmscott Senior High School, Perth, Western Australia
Qualifications: Australian leaving exams
Off-season 1989–90: 'At home. Some PE at Leicester Grammar, and coaching at county ground.'
Overseas tours: With Australian U-19 team to Pakistan 1981
Overseas teams played for: Australia U-19 team, West Perth CC 1977–82; Griqualand West 1984–85 and 1985–86 as captain; Harmony CC, South Africa 1987–88; Orange Free State 1987–88; Gosnells CC, Perth 1989
Cricketers particularly learnt from: Norman O'Neill, Alan Beukas (Griqualand West), Brian Luckhurst, Peter Willey, Derek Underwood, Alan Knott
Cricketers particularly admired: Derek Underwood, Alan Knott
Other sports played: Rugby
Other sports followed: Rugby
Relaxations: Home and family; following sports
Extras: Captained Australia U-19 team to Pakistan 1981. Played for Young England v Young India 1981. Parents emigrated to Australia when he was 4. His mother wrote to Kent in 1978 asking for trial for him. Captained Young Australia as well as Young England. Decided to leave Kent after 1985 season and joined Leicestershire
Opinions on cricket: 'As no doubt others have said, wickets in general need improving. Good pace and bounce is not always easy to obtain, but is so important for attractive cricket.'
Best batting performance: 165* Griqualand West v Border, East London 1984–85
Best bowling performance: 4-52 Griqualand West v Boland, Stellenbosch 1985–86

LAST SEASON: BATTING

	I.	N.O.	R.	H.S.	AV.
TEST					
1ST-CLASS	39	5	1093	121*	32.14
INT					
RAL	15	1	182	34	13.00
NAT.W.	2	1	21	17	21.00
B & H	3	1	66	23	33.00

CAREER: BATTING

	I.	N.O.	R.	H.S.	AV.
TEST					
1ST-CLASS	226	27	5682	165*	28.55
INT					
RAL	82	7	1888	105	25.17
NAT.W.	9	1	187	45	23.37
B & H	17	2	407	112	27.13

LAST SEASON: BOWLING

	O.	M.	R.	W.	AV.
TEST					
1ST-CLASS	160.5	34	460	15	30.66
INT					
RAL	14.2	2	66	4	16.50
NAT.W.	5	0	33	0	–
B & H	8	3	22	1	22.00

CAREER: BOWLING

	O.	M.	R.	W.	AV.
TEST					
1ST-CLASS	1088.5	263	3085	91	33.90
INT					
RAL	116.1	6	544	24	22.66
NAT.W.	31	7	99	2	49.50
B & H	51	6	219	4	54.75

PRICHARD, P. J. Essex

Full Name: Paul John Prichard
Role: Right-hand bat,
cover/mid-wicket fielder
Born: 7 January 1965, Brentwood
Height: 5′ 10″ **Weight:** 12st 7lbs
Nickname: Prich, Pablo, Digger,
Middis
County debut: 1984
County cap: 1986
1000 runs in a season: 2
1st-Class 50s scored: 41
1st-Class 100s scored: 3
One-Day 50s: 8
One-Day 100s: 1
Place in batting averages: 104th
av. 29.65 (1988 40th av. 38.77)
1st-Class catches 1989: 20 (career 79)
Parents: John and Margaret
Marital status: Separated
Family links with cricket: Father played club cricket in Essex
Education: Brentwood County High School
Qualifications: NCA Senior Coaching Award
Jobs outside cricket: Worked for shipping company
Off-season 1989–90: Playing for Waverley CC, Sydney, Australia
Overseas tours: Kingfishers tour of South Africa 1981
Overseas teams played for: VOB Cavaliers, Cape Town 1981–82; Sutherland
CC, Sydney 1985–86, 1987–88; Waverley OCC 1988–89, 1989–90
Cricketers particularly learnt from: All at Essex 'and by watching others'
Cricketers particularly admired: 'Admire and respect all pros'
Other sports played: Golf
Other sports followed: Rugby Union, football, American football
Relaxations: 'Sailing my boat, listening to music, having a few quiet beers.'
Opinions on cricket: 'None that will make any difference!'
Best batting performance: 147* Essex v Nottinghamshire, Chelmsford 1986

LAST SEASON: BATTING

	I.	N.O.	R.	H.S.	AV.
TEST					
1ST-CLASS	36	4	949	128	29.65
INT					
RAL	13	2	159	37*	14.45
NAT.W.	1	0	17	17	17.00
B & H	6	3	216	73*	72.00

CAREER: BATTING

	I.	N.O.	R.	H.S.	AV.
TEST					
1ST-CLASS	198	24	5594	147*	32.14
INT					
RAL	49	5	890	103*	20.22
NAT.W.	9	0	267	94	29.66
B & H	21	6	546	73*	36.40

PRIDGEON, A. P.   Worcestershire

Full Name: Alan Paul Pridgeon
Role: Right-hand bat, right-arm medium bowler
Born: 22 February 1954, Wall Heath, Staffordshire
Height: 6′ 3″ **Weight:** 13st 2lbs
Nickname: Pridge
County debut: 1972
County cap: 1980
Benefit: 1989
50 wickets in a season: 6
1st-Class 50s scored: 1
1st-Class 5 w. in innings: 10
1st-Class 10 w. in match: 1
Place in bowling averages: —
(1988 93rd av. 31.52)
1st-Class catches 1989: 1 (career 83)
Parents: Albert Ernest and Sybil Ruby
Wife and date of marriage: Jane, 7 October 1978
Children: Laura, 8 August 1983; Benjamin Mark, 8 August 1985
Education: Summerhill Secondary Modern, Kingswinford, West Midlands
Qualifications: 6 CSEs, Qualified FA Coach, Qualified NCA Coach
Jobs outside cricket: Semi-professional footballer, salesman; has worked for Manpower Commission
Cricketing superstitions or habits: 'Hate batting while Sylvester Clarke is bowling.'
Overseas tours: Worcestershire CC to Barbados 1980

LAST SEASON: BATTING

	I.	N.O.	R.	H.S.	AV.
TEST					
1ST-CLASS	5	1	24	19*	6.00
INT					
RAL	1	1	4	4*	—
NAT.W.					
B & H	–	–	–	–	–

CAREER: BATTING

	I.	N.O.	R.	H.S.	AV.
TEST					
1ST-CLASS	221	84	1188	67	8.67
INT					
RAL	51	29	148	17	6.72
NAT.W.	10	7	38	13*	12.66
B & H	20	11	81	13*	9.00

LAST SEASON: BOWLING

	O.	M.	R.	W.	AV.
TEST					
1ST-CLASS	65.5	17	149	4	37.25
INT					
RAL	31	1	173	7	24.71
NAT.W.					
B & H	26.1	3	88	1	88.00

CAREER: BOWLING

	O.	M.	R.	W.	AV.
TEST					
1ST-CLASS	6017.3	1251	17367	530	32.76
INT					
RAL	1084	52	4860	167	29.10
NAT.W.	175.2	31	517	16	32.31
B & H	442.3	51	1683	35	48.08

Overseas teams played for: Howick and Pakuranga, New Zealand 1983–84
Cricketers particularly learnt from: Viv Richards, Dennis Lillee, Norman Gifford
Cricketers particularly admired: Steve Perryman
Other sports played: Semi-professional footballer for Dudley Town FC, West Midlands League; golf, snooker, tennis
Other sports followed: Horse racing
Relaxations: Horse racing, taking dog (Muffin) for walks
Extras: He was the county's longest-serving player. Finished top of Refuge Assurance League bowling averages in 1988. Released by Worcestershire at end of 1989 season
Best batting performance: 67 Worcestershire v Warwickshire, Worcester 1984
Best bowling performance: 7-35 Worcestershire v Oxford University, Oxford 1976

PRIESTLEY, I. M. Yorkshire

Full Name: Iain Martin Priestley
Role: Right-hand bat, right-arm
fast-medium bowler
Born: 25 September 1967, Leeds
Height: 6' 3" **Weight:** 12½st
Nickname: Imp
County debut: 1989
1st-Class catches 1989: 1 (career 1)
Parents: Colin and Florence
Marital status: Single
Family links with cricket: Father is
an NCA coach and umpire
Education: Calverley C of E School;
Priesthorpe Comprehensive School
Jobs outside cricket: Joiner
Off-season 1989–90: Coaching and
playing cricket in Bundeburgh,
Australia
Overseas tours: Bradford Junior
Team U-17 (captain) to Barbados April 1986; Bradford Youth Team (captain) to Barbados April 1988
Overseas teams played for: Witamatta, Auckland, New Zealand September 1988 to March 1989
Cricketers particularly learnt from: Phil Carrick, Steve Oldham, David Bairstow

400

Cricketers particularly admired: Ian Botham, Geoff Boycott, 'and most of the West Indies players'

Other sports played: Pool

Other sports followed: Rugby League

Injuries 1989: Tore groin muscle – off first-class cricket for three weeks in July. Re-occurred end July – no first-class cricket after this, only club cricket

Relaxations: 'Discos and the odd pint.'

Extras: Played at Farsley CC, Bradford League as junior with Tim Boon, Ashley Metcalfe, Steve Rhodes and David Ripley

Opinions on cricket: 'Super game – socially as well as playing – but politics sometimes spoil the international aspect.'

Best batting performance: 23 Yorkshire v Northamptonshire, Northampton 1989

Best bowling performance: 4-27 Yorkshire v Nottinghamshire, Leeds 1989

LAST SEASON: BATTING

	I.	N.O.	R.	H.S.	AV.
TEST					
1ST-CLASS	4	2	25	23	12.50
INT					
RAL					
NAT.W.					
B & H					

LAST SEASON: BOWLING

	O.	M.	R.	W.	AV.
TEST					
1ST-CLASS	30	6	119	4	29.75
INT					
RAL					
NAT.W.					
B & H					

CAREER: BATTING

	I.	N.O.	R.	H.S.	AV.
TEST					
1ST-CLASS	4	2	25	23	12.50
INT					
RAL					
NAT.W.					
B & H					

CAREER: BOWLING

	O.	M.	R.	W.	AV.
TEST					
1ST-CLASS	30	6	119	4	29.75
INT					
RAL					
NAT.W.					
B & H					

116. Who topped the Northamptonshire batting averages last season?

PRINGLE, D. R.   Essex

Full Name: Derek Raymond Pringle
Role: Right-hand bat, right-arm
fast-medium bowler, 1st slip fielder.
Vice-captain
Born: 18 September 1958, Nairobi
Height: 6′ 5″ **Weight:** 15¾st
Nickname: Ignell, Suggs
County debut: 1978
County cap: 1982
Test debut: 1982
No. of Tests: 21
No. of One-Day Internationals: 23
50 wickets in a season: 6
1st-Class 50s scored: 33
1st-Class 100s scored: 8
1st-Class 5 w. in innings: 21
1st-Class 10 w. in match: 3
One-Day 50s: 21
Place in batting averages: 163rd

av. 22.15 (1988 198th av. 19.11)
Place in bowling averages: 7th av. 18.64 (1988 58th av. 26.17)
Strike rate 1989: 42.65 (career 57.70)
1st-Class catches 1989: 6 (career 117)
Parents: Donald James (deceased) and Doris May
Marital status: Single
Family links with cricket: Father represented Kenya and East Africa (played
in World Cup 1975)
Education: St Mary's School, Nairobi; Felsted School, Essex; Cambridge
University (Fitzwilliam College)
Qualifications: 8 O-levels, 3 A-levels, MA Cantab.
Jobs outside cricket: T-shirt designer
Off-season 1989–90: Touring Zimbabwe with England A
Cricketing superstitions or habits: 'None now; too many ducks have seen to
that.'
Overseas tours: With England Schools to India 1978–79; Oxbridge tour of
Australia 1979–80; England to Australia and New Zealand 1982–83; England
B tour to Sri Lanka 1986; England A to Zimbabwe 1990
Cricketers particularly learnt from: My father, Gordon Barker, 'Tonker'
Taylor, Keith Fletcher
Cricketers particularly admired: 'Neil Foster for his flexible philosophy about
bowling and life.'
Other sports played: Squash, golf

402

Other sports followed: Watches rugby union

Relaxations: 'Modern music, especially The Smiths, New Order, Billy Bragg and The The, photography, conchology, pub discussions over a pint of Adnams. Good novels: Kunderg, Naipaul, Garcia Marquez etc.'

Extras: 'Took all ten wickets for Nairobi Schools U-13½ v Up Country Schools U-13½. Captain of Cambridge 1982 season. Extra in *Chariots of Fire*. Once went shark hunting with Chris Smith of Hampshire (a recklessly brave fellow) in the Maldive Islands.'

Opinions on cricket: 'If four-day cricket will allow more days off in order to mentally prepare oneself for each match, then I'm all for it. Uncovered wickets don't suit our batsmen so scrap that idea. Our spinners have also bowled far less than normal, so wet wickets don't always equal more spin. Inception of up-to-date technologies in order to reduce umpiring errors, as there is too much at stake (particularly at international level) to merely grin and accept bad decisions, i.e. off-the-field panel of three watching replays, electrode implants in ball, pads, bat etc, anything to aid the umpires who are now in a very high-pressure situation.'

Best batting performance: 128 Essex v Kent, Chelmsford 1988

Best bowling performance: 7-18 Essex v Glamorgan, Swansea 1989

LAST SEASON: BATTING

	I.	N.O.	R.	H.S.	AV.
TEST	3	0	33	27	11.00
1ST-CLASS	20	4	388	81*	24.25
INT	3	1	34	25*	17.00
RAL	6	1	88	46*	17.60
NAT.W.	1	0	4	4	4.00
B & H	5	2	81	44*	27.00

LAST SEASON: BOWLING

	O.	M.	R.	W.	AV.
TEST	86.2	12	306	5	61.20
1ST-CLASS	582	151	1447	89	16.25
INT	29.3	3	107	3	35.66
RAL	91.3	6	432	18	24.00
NAT.W.	12	1	53	1	53.00
B & H	75	10	279	15	18.60

CAREER: BATTING

	I.	N.O.	R.	H.S.	AV.
TEST	36	3	512	63	15.51
1ST-CLASS	286	56	6465	128	28.10
INT	19	7	318	49*	26.50
RAL	77	18	1504	81*	25.49
NAT.W.	21	5	429	80*	26.81
B & H	48	9	1158	68	29.69

CAREER: BOWLING

	O.	M.	R.	W.	AV.
TEST	625	133	1807	48	37.64
1ST-CLASS	4982.1	1216	13384	539	24.83
INT	217.5	23	959	23	41.69
RAL	690.5	32	3253	117	27.80
NAT.W.	217.2	40	667	26	25.65
B & H	537	60	1944	80	24.30

117. Who topped the Nottinghamshire batting averages last season?

PRINGLE, N. J.   Somerset

Full Name: Nicholas John Pringle
Role: Right-hand bat, right-arm
medium bowler, cover fielder,
short leg
Born: 20 September 1966,
Weymouth, Dorset
Height: 5′ 11″ **Weight:** 12st
Nickname: Pring
County debut: 1986
1st-Class 50s scored: 3
Place in batting averages: —
(1988 166th av. 22.18)
1st-Class catches 1989: 5 (career 14)
Parents: Marion and Guy Pease
Marital status: Single
Education: Priorswood
Comprehensive, Taunton;
Taunton School
Qualifications: 8 O-levels, 1 A-level.
NCA Coaching Certificate
Off-season 1989–90: Playing and coaching for Harvey CC, in Bunbury &
District League, Western Australia
Overseas tours: Taunton School to Sri Lanka 1983
Overseas teams played for: Mossman CC, Sydney 1986–87; Napier Tech. CC,
Hawkes's Bay, New Zealand 1987–88, 1988–89; Harvey CC, Western Aus-
tralia 1989–90
Cricketers particularly learnt from: Martin Crowe, Don Wilson, John
Jameson. 'Learning all the time from various cricketers and coaches.'
Cricketers particularly admired: Martin Crowe, Richard Hadlee, Viv
Richards, Greg Chappell, – 'and anyone who plays first-class cricket for a
great length of time.'
Other sports played: Football, squash, running, and general fitness
Other sports followed: Rugby, anything except horse racing
Relaxations: Gardeners Arms, Taunton, reading Jeffrey Archer novels,
listening to music, sport
Extras: On Lord's ground staff 1986. Called up from there by Somerset for his
debut
Opinions on cricket: 'Abolish Benson & Hedges Cup to reduce the amount
of cricket, and allow the development of the three- and four-day game.
The Sunday League and NatWest should continue as the major one-day
competitions.'
Best batting performance: 79 Somerset v Warwickshire, Edgbaston 1987

404

Best bowling performance: 2-35 Somerset v Glamorgan, Weston-super-Mare 1987

LAST SEASON: BATTING

	I.	N.O.	R.	H.S.	AV.
TEST					
1ST-CLASS	9	1	50	12*	6.25
INT					
RAL					
NAT.W.					
B & H					

LAST SEASON: BOWLING

	O.	M.	R.	W.	AV.
TEST					
1ST-CLASS	26	2	122	0	–
INT					
RAL					
NAT.W.					
B & H					

CAREER: BATTING

	I.	N.O.	R.	H.S.	AV.
TEST					
1ST-CLASS	44	6	662	79	17.42
INT					
RAL	6	1	71	22	14.20
NAT.W.	1	0	17	17	17.00
B & H					

CAREER: BOWLING

	O.	M.	R.	W.	AV.
TEST					
1ST-CLASS	142	17	551	5	110.20
INT					
RAL	5	0	28	0	–
NAT.W.					
B & H					

PRITCHARD, N. M. A   Gloucestershire

Full Name: Neil Michael Albert Pritchard
Role: Right-hand bat
Born: 4 July 1967, Thornbury, Avon
Height: 5′ 10″ **Weight:** 11st
Nickname: Pritch
County debut: 1989 (RAL)
Parents: Michael and Sandra
Marital status: Single
Family links with cricket: Father played for Gloucestershire club and ground, and 2nd XI
Education: St Helens Primary; Marlwood School; Swansea University
Qualifications: 8 O-levels, 2 A-levels, BSc(Hons) Economics
Jobs outside cricket: Insurance clerk, labouring
Off-season 1989–90: Playing in Australia
Overseas teams played for: Durban Collegians January 1986–March 1986
Cricketers particularly learnt from: 'My father, Graham Wiltshire, David Allen, John Sheppard, and the senior players at Gloucestershire.'

Cricketers particularly admired: Graeme Hick, Barry Richards
Other sports played: Football, golf, squash
Other sports followed: Football, golf, rugby, athletics, ski-ing
Relaxations: Cinema, music, books, ski-ing
Opinions on cricket: 'There does seem to be a problem with three-day cricket in that games sometimes have to be manufactured rather than left to their natural progression.'

LAST SEASON: BATTING

	I.	N.O.	R.	H.S.	AV.
TEST					
1ST-CLASS					
INT					
RAL	1	0	9	9	9.00
NAT.W.					
B & H					

CAREER: BATTING

	I.	N.O.	R.	H.S.	AV.
TEST					
1ST-CLASS					
INT					
RAL	1	0	9	9	9.00
NAT.W.					
B & H					

RADFORD, N. V.   Worcestershire

Full Name: Neal Victor Radford
Role: Right-hand bat, right-arm fast-medium bowler, gully fielder
Born: 7 June 1957, Luanshya, Zambia
Height: 5′ 11″ **Weight:** 12st 4lbs
Nickname: Radiz, Vic
County debut: 1980 (Lancashire), 1985 (Worcestershire)
County cap: 1985 (Worcestershire)
Test debut: 1986
No. of Tests: 3
No. of One-Day Internationals: 6
50 wickets in a season: 5
1st-Class 50s scored: 5
1st-Class 5 w. in innings: 39
1st-Class 10 w. in match: 6
Place in batting averages: 209th av. 23.00 (1988 165th av. 22.22)
Place in bowling averages: 30th av. 23.00 (1988 48th av. 24.92)
Strike rate 1989: 45.18 (career 47.78)
1st-Class catches 1989: 13 (career 107)
Parents: Victor Reginald and Edith Joyce
Wife: Lynne

Children: Luke Anthony, 20th November 1988
Family links with cricket: Brother Wayne pro for Gowerton (SWCA) and Glamorgan 2nd XI. Also played for Orange Free State in Currie Cup
Education: Athlone Boys High School, Johannesburg
Qualifications: Matriculation and university entrance. NCA Advanced Coach
Jobs outside cricket: Auditor
Off-season 1989–90: 'I shall be wintering in England, working for Cascade pools.'
Cricketing superstitions or habits: 'Nelson and left pad on first.'
Overseas teams played for: Transvaal 1979–89; South African Schools XI; South African Army
Overseas tours: With England to New Zealand and Australia 1987–88
Cricketers particularly admired: Vincent van der Bijl
Other sports played: Golf, squash
Other sports followed: All sports
Injuries 1989: 'Severe groin injury – kept me out of the last six championship games.'
Relaxations: Music, TV, films
Extras: Only bowler to take 100 first-class wickets in 1985. First player to 100 wickets in 1987. Took most first-class wickets in 1987 with 109. One of *Wisden*'s Five Cricketers of the Year, 1985
Opinions on cricket: 'We play too much cricket! A cut down will result in better standard all round. Have a day off for travelling as the majority of injuries and stiffness are caused by travelling hundreds of miles immediately after matches. I do feel as a professional working person, one should be entitled to accept work where one so desires.'
Best batting performance: 76* Lancashire v Derbyshire, Blackpool 1981
Best bowling performance: 9-70 Worcestershire v Somerset, Worcestershire 1986

LAST SEASON: BATTING

	I.	N.O.	R.	H.S.	AV.
TEST					
1ST-CLASS	21	2	325	66*	17.10
INT					
RAL	9	3	162	38*	27.00
NAT.W.	2	1	0	0*	0.00
B & H	3	2	48	39*	48.00

CAREER: BATTING

	I.	N.O.	R.	H.S.	AV.
TEST	4	1	21	12*	7.00
1ST-CLASS	206	47	2583	76*	16.24
INT	3	2	0	0*	0.00
RAL	56	27	615	48*	21.20
NAT.W.	11	2	90	37	10.00
B & H	18	9	195	39*	21.66

LAST SEASON: BOWLING

	O.	M.	R.	W.	AV.
TEST					
1ST-CLASS	572.4	119	1725	75	23.00
INT					
RAL	82.2	8	314	22	14.27
NAT.W.	44	13	105	3	35.00
B & H	28	3	89	6	14.83

CAREER: BOWLING

	O.	M.	R.	W.	AV.
TEST	113	15	351	4	87.75
1ST-CLASS	6059.5	1195	18809	771	24.39
INT	58	5	230	2	115.00
RAL	613.2	32	2717	129	21.06
NAT.W.	222	36	692	29	23.86
B & H	244	31	840	35	24.00

RAMPRAKASH, M. R.   Middlesex

Full Name: Mark Ravin Ramprakash
Role: Right-hand bat
Born: 5 September 1969,
Bushey, Herts
Height: 5′ 9″ **Weight:** 11½st
Nickname: Ramps
County debut: 1987
1000 runs in a season: 1
1st-Class 50s scored: 12
1st-Class 100s scored: 1
One-Day 50s: 3
Place in batting averages: 58th
av. 36.27
1st-Class catches 1989: 14 (career 22)
Parents: Jennifer and Deo
Marital status: Single
Family links with cricket: Father
played club cricket in Guyana
Education: Gayton High School;
Harrow Weald College
Qualifications: 5 O-levels

Cricketing superstitions or habits: Left pad on first
Overseas tours: England U-19s to Sri Lanka 1987
Cricketers particularly learnt from: Jack Robertson, Don Bennett
Cricketers particularly admired: All the great all-rounders
Other sports played: Football
Other sports followed: Snooker, tennis
Relaxations: Watching good comedy films and westerns
Extras: Won Best U-15 Schoolboy of 1985 by Cricket Society. Won Gray Nicholls Award for Best Young Cricketer 1986. Did not begin to play cricket until he was nine years old. Made debut for Middlesex age 17 in April 1987 v Yorkshire, making 17 and 63*. Played for Middlesex Under-11s and Under-13s. Played for Bessborough CC at age 13. Played for ESCA Under-15s v Public Schools, 1984. Played in NCA Guernsey Festival Tournament and scored 204*. Played for Young England in the last two Tests against Sri Lanka in 1986. Played for Middlesex 2nd XI at age 16. In one weekend in June 1986, he scored 148* on the Saturday and 140 on the Sunday for Bessborough CC. In 1987, played for Stanmore CC and made 186* on his debut. Opportunities to play for Middlesex were severely restricted during 1987 and 1988 by the fact that he was still at school studying for A-levels. Man of the Match in Middlesex's NatWest Trophy Final win 1988, on his debut in the competition. Cricket Society's Most Promising Player of the Year 1988

Opinions on cricket: 'Wickets should be covered at all times.'
Best batting performance: 128 Middlesex v Yorkshire, Leeds 1989

LAST SEASON: BATTING

	I.	N.O.	R.	H.S.	AV.
TEST					
1ST-CLASS	34	5	1052	128	36.27
INT					
RAL	12	3	264	47*	29.33
NAT.W.	5	0	81	43	16.20
B & H	4	1	48	24*	16.00

CAREER: BATTING

	I.	N.O.	R.	H.S.	AV.
TEST					
1ST-CLASS	61	12	1794	128	36.61
INT					
RAL	20	4	454	82*	28.37
NAT.W.	6	0	137	56	22.83
B & H	4	1	48	24*	16.00

RANDALL, D. W.   Nottinghamshire

Full Name: Derek William Randall
Role: Right-hand bat, cover fielder
Born: 24 February 1951, Retford, Nottinghamshire
Height: 5′ 8½″ **Weight:** 11st
Nickname: Arkle, Rags
County debut: 1972
County cap: 1973
Benefit: 1983 (£42,000)
Test debut: 1976–77
No. of Tests: 47
No. of One-Day Internationals: 49
1000 runs in a season: 12
1st-Class 50s scored: 144
1st-Class 100s scored: 41
1st-Class 200s scored: 3
One-Day 50s: 59
One-Day 100s: 6
Place in batting averages: 41st
av. 40.13 (1988 38th av. 38.97)
1st-Class catches 1989: 14 (career 315)
Parents: Frederick and Mavis
Wife and date of marriage: Elizabeth, September 1973
Children: Simon, June 1977
Family links with cricket: Father played local cricket – 'tried to bowl fast off a long run and off the wrong foot too!'
Education: Sir Frederick Milner Secondary Modern School, Retford
Qualifications: ONC mechanical engineering, mechanical draughtsman
Jobs outside cricket: Coaching
Overseas tours: Derrick Robins' XI to South Africa 1975–76; England to

India, Sri Lanka and Australia 1976–77; Pakistan and New Zealand 1977–78; Australia 1978–79, Australia and India 1979–80; Australia and New Zealand 1982–83; New Zealand and Pakistan 1983–84; England B to Zimbabwe 1985–86

Overseas teams played for: North Perth, Australia

Cricketers particularly learnt from: Sir Gary Sobers, Tom Graveney ('boyhood idol'), Reg Simpson

Other sports played: Football, squash, golf

Relaxations: Listening to varied selection of tapes. Family man

Extras: Played in one John Player League match in 1971 for Nottinghamshire. Before joining Nottinghamshire staff, played for Retford CC in the Bassetlaw League, and helped in Championship wins of 1968 and 1969. One of the finest fielders in cricket. Scored 174 in Centenary Test v Australia 1977. Renowned for his untidiness in the dressing room. One of *Wisden*'s Five Cricketers of the Year, 1979

Best batting performance: 237 Nottinghamshire v Derbyshire, Trent Bridge 1988

Best bowling performance: 3-15 Nottinghamshire v MCC, Lord's 1982

LAST SEASON: BATTING

	I.	N.O.	R.	H.S.	AV.
TEST					
1ST-CLASS	43	6	1485	130	40.13
INT					
RAL	12	2	342	70*	34.20
NAT.W.	2	0	29	29	14.50
B & H	7	1	219	57*	36.50

LAST SEASON: BOWLING

	O.	M.	R.	W.	AV.
TEST					
1ST-CLASS	1	0	3	0	–
INT					
RAL					
NAT.W.					
B & H					

CAREER: BATTING

	I.	N.O.	R.	H.S.	AV.
TEST	79	5	2470	174	33.37
1ST-CLASS	647	63	22270	237	38.13
INT	45	5	1067	88	26.68
RAL	205	28	5685	123	32.11
NAT.W.	36	5	887	149*	28.61
B & H	80	12	2363	103*	34.75

CAREER: BOWLING

	O.	M.	R.	W.	AV.
TEST	2	0	3	0	–
1ST-CLASS	70.5	5	383	12	31.91
INT	0.2	0	2	1	2.00
RAL	0.5	0	9	0	–
NAT.W.	2	0	23	0	–
B & H	2.5	0	5	0	–

118. Who topped the Somerset batting averages last season?

RATCLIFFE, J. D.　　Warwickshire

Full Name: Jason David Ratcliffe
Role: Opening bat, right-arm
medium-pace bowler, slip fielder
Born: 19 June 1969, Solihull
Height: 6' 3" **Weight:** 12st 7lbs
Nickname: Ratters, Roland
County debut: 1988
1st-Class 50s scored: 2
1st-Class 100s scored: 1
One-Day 50s: 1
Place in batting averages: 61st
av. 35.68
1st-Class catches 1989: 5 (career 7)
Parents: David and Sheila
Marital status: Single
Family links with cricket: Father
(D. P. Ratcliffe) played for
Warwickshire 1956–62
Education: Meadow Green Primary
School; Sharmons Cross Secondary School; Solihull Sixth Form College
Qualifications: 6 O-levels; Advanced Cricket Coach
Jobs outside cricket: PA at printing company
Off-season 1989–90: Coaching at Edgbaston Indoor School
Overseas teams played for: Westend CC, Kimberley 1987–88
Cricketers particularly learnt from: Father, Warwickshire coaches and play-
ing staff
Cricketers particularly admired: Geoff Boycott, Dennis Amiss
Other sports played: Football, squash, snooker

LAST SEASON: BATTING

	I.	N.O.	R.	H.S.	AV.
TEST					
1ST-CLASS	20	4	571	127*	35.68
INT					
RAL	4	1	47	37	15.33
NAT.W.	1	0	59	59	59.00
B & H					

CAREER: BATTING

	I.	N.O.	R.	H.S.	AV.
TEST					
1ST-CLASS	24	4	602	127*	30.10
INT					
RAL	4	1	47	37	15.33
NAT.W.	1	0	59	59	59.00
B & H					

LAST SEASON: BOWLING

	O.	M.	R.	W.	AV.
TEST					
1ST-CLASS	27	6	82	1	82.00
INT					
RAL	9.1	0	58	2	29.00
NAT.W.					
B & H					

CAREER: BOWLING

	O.	M.	R.	W.	AV.
TEST					
1ST-CLASS	27	6	82	1	82.00
INT					
RAL	9.1	0	58	2	29.00
NAT.W.					
B & H					

Other sports followed: Most sports
Relaxations: 'Listening to music, reading, walking my dogs (three Golden Retrievers), eating out.'
Best batting performance: 127* Warwickshire v Cambridge University, Cambridge 1989
Best bowling performance: 1-15 Warwickshire v Yorkshire, Leeds 1989

REDPATH, I. Derbyshire

Full Name: Ian Redpath
Role: Right-hand bat, right-arm leg-spin/medium bowler, cover fielder
Born: 12 September 1965, Basildon
Height: 5' 9" **Weight:** 11½st
Nickname: Redders
County debut: 1987 (Essex), 1989 (Derbyshire)
1st-Class catches 1989: 0 (career 2)
Parents: Bill and Sheila
Marital status: Single
Family links with cricket: Father played for local club side
Education: Woodlands School, Bastable VIth Form
Qualifications: 6 O-levels, 2 A-levels, Senior Coaching Award
Jobs outside cricket: Trainee computer programmer, assistant manager at indoor cricket centre
Off-season 1989–90: Playing on the Gold Coast, Queensland, Australia
Overseas teams played for: Penrith, NSW 1985–86, 1986–87; Werribee, Melbourne 1987–88; Surfers Paradise, Gold Coast 1988–89
Cricketers particularly learnt from: John Lever, Ray East
Cricketers particularly admired: John Lever, Graham Gooch, Steve Waugh
Other sports played: Football, squash
Other sports followed: Football occasionally

LAST SEASON: BATTING

	I.	N.O.	R.	H.S.	AV.
TEST					
1ST-CLASS	6	2	88	43*	22.00
INT					
RAL	1	0	9	9	9.00
NAT.W.					
B & H					

CAREER: BATTING

	I.	N.O.	R.	H.S.	AV.
TEST					
1ST-CLASS	18	3	216	46	14.40
INT					
RAL	2	1	20	11*	20.00
NAT.W.					
B & H					

Relaxations: Music, sleep
Opinions on cricket: 'Still believe too much cricket is played by professionals in this country. I am sure there must be a better balance for players to perform to a higher standard and still obtain the financial reward that is essential for clubs to survive.'
Best batting performance: 46 Essex v Northamptonshire, Ilford 1987

REEVE, D. A. Warwickshire

Full Name: Dermot Alexander Reeve
Role: Right-hand bat, right-arm fast-medium bowler, fields anywhere
Born: 2 April 1963, Hong Kong
Height: 6' **Weight:** 12st
Nickname: Legend, Motte
County debut: 1983 (Sussex), 1988 (Warwickshire)
County cap: 1986 (Sussex), 1989 (Warwickshire)
50 wickets in a season: 2
1st-Class 50s scored: 15
1st-Class 100s scored: 2
1st-Class 5 w. in innings: 5
One-Day 50s: 4
Place in batting averages: 23rd av. 44.69 (1988 174th av. 21.55)
Place in bowling averages: — (1988 90th av. 31.25)
1st-Class catches 1989: 13 (career 75)
Parents: Alexander James and Monica
Wife and date of marriage: Julie, 20 December 1986
Children: Emily Kaye, 14 September 1988
Family links with cricket: Father captain of school XI, brother Mark an improving club cricketer and captains Stanmore 3rd XI
Education: King George V School, Kowloon, Hong Kong
Qualifications: 7 O-levels
Jobs outside cricket: Cricket coach
Off-season 1989–90: Playing and coaching in Perth, Western Australia 'for eighth successive winter'
Cricketing superstitions or habits: 'Hot bath every morning.'
Overseas tours: Hong Kong to Malaysia and Singapore 1980; Hong Kong British Forces to Malaysia 1982; MCC to Holland and Denmark 1983

Overseas teams played for: Claremont-Cottesloe CC, Western Australia 1982–85, 1989–90; Mount Lawley CC, Perth 1985–88

Cricketers particularly learnt from: Don Wilson, David Clinton, John Barclay, Colin Wells, Bob Cottam

Cricketers particularly admired: John Barclay, Chris Cowdrey, Tim Minton, Alan Donald

Other sports played: Golf – 'as often as I'm allowed'

Other sports followed: Most sports '– except motor-racing and horse racing. Love watching rugby union and gymnastics.'

Injuries 1989: 'Still recovering from a shoulder operation I had in September 1988.'

Relaxations: Music, videos, swimming, Perth beaches, Italian food

Extras: Formerly on Lord's groundstaff. Represented Hong Kong in the ICC Trophy competition June 1982. Hong Kong Cricketer of the Year 1980–81. Hong Kong's Cricket Sports Personality of the Year 1981. Man of the Match in 1986 NatWest Final. Silk Cut Challenge Finalist. Moved from Sussex to Warwickshire in 1988

Opinions on cricket: 'Four-day cricket on covered wickets. 100 overs a day, 16 matches. More one-day internationals in England. Over rate fines too strict. I would also like to see coloured clothing for Sunday cricket.'

Best batting performance: 119 Sussex v Surrey, Guildford 1984

Best bowling performance: 7-37 Sussex v Lancashire, Lytham 1987

LAST SEASON: BATTING

	I.	N.O.	R.	H.S.	AV.
TEST					
1ST-CLASS	17	4	581	97*	44.69
INT					
RAL	14	5	375	70*	41.66
NAT.W.	5	1	111	45	27.75
B & H					

CAREER: BATTING

	I.	N.O.	R.	H.S.	AV.
TEST					
1ST-CLASS	141	38	2773	119	26.92
INT					
RAL	52	18	780	70*	22.94
NAT.W.	13	6	187	45	26.71
B & H	15	7	152	30*	19.00

LAST SEASON: BOWLING

	O.	M.	R.	W.	AV.
TEST					
1ST-CLASS	97.4	35	163	11	14.81
INT					
RAL	23.4	0	111	1	111.00
NAT.W.	47	11	131	4	32.75
B & H					

CAREER: BOWLING

	O.	M.	R.	W.	AV.
TEST					
1ST-CLASS	2886.1	754	7641	274	27.88
INT					
RAL	499.1	15	2325	88	26.42
NAT.W.	173.5	39	488	20	24.40
B & H	153.4	16	667	18	37.05

REMY, C. C.

Sussex

Full Name: Carlos Charles Remy
Role: Right-hand bat, right-arm medium bowler
Born: 24 July 1968, St Lucia, Windward Islands, West Indies
1st-Class catches 1989: 1 (career 1)
Education: St Aloyious School, Archway, London; Haringey Cricket College
Extras: Played for Middlesex 2nd XI 1987–88. Plays club cricket for Littlehampton in the Sussex League
Best bowling performance:
1-22 Sussex v Hampshire, Hove 1989

LAST SEASON: BATTING

	I.	N.O.	R.	H.S.	AV.
TEST					
1ST-CLASS	1	0	0	0	0.00
INT					
RAL					
NAT.W.					
B & H					

CAREER: BATTING

	I.	N.O.	R.	H.S.	AV.
TEST					
1ST-CLASS	1	0	0	0	0.00
INT					
RAL					
NAT.W.					
B & H					

LAST SEASON: BOWLING

	O.	M.	R.	W.	AV.
TEST					
1ST-CLASS	15	3	33	1	33.00
INT					
RAL					
NAT.W.					
B & H					

CAREER: BOWLING

	O.	M.	R.	W.	AV.
TEST					
1ST-CLASS	15	3	33	1	33.00
INT					
RAL					
NAT.W.					
B & H					

RHODES, S. J.　　　　　Worcestershire

Full Name: Steven John Rhodes
Role: Right-hand bat, wicket-keeper
Born: 17 June 1964, Bradford
Height: 5′ 8″ **Weight:** 11st 10lbs
Nickname: Wilf, Bumpy
County debut: 1981 (Yorkshire),
1985 (Worcestershire)
County cap: 1988 (Worcestershire)
No. of One-Day Internationals: 3
1st-Class 50s scored: 12
1st-Class 100s scored: 1
One-Day 50s: 2
Place in batting averages: 71st
av. 34.61 (1988 129th av. 25.95)
Parents: Bill and Norma
Marital status: Single
Family links with cricket: Father
played for Nottinghamshire 1961–64
Education: Bradford Moor Junior
School; Lapage St Middle; Carlton-Bolling Comprehensive, Bradford
Qualifications: 4 O-levels, cricket coaching certificate
Jobs outside cricket: Trainee manager in sports retailer in winters of 1980–81
and 1981–82. Cucumber picker in Queensland. Worked at New Road in off-
season 1988–89 organising commemorative items for 1988 season
Off-season 1989–90: Touring Zimbabwe with England A
Cricketing superstitions or habits: 'I like to make sure I am not last out of the
changing room when fielding.'
Overseas tours: England 'B' to Sri Lanka 1986; picked for cancelled England
tour of India 1988–89; England A to Zimbabwe 1990
Overseas teams played for: Past Brothers Cricket Club, Bundaberg, Queens-
land, Australia 1982–83 and 1983–84, and Bundaberg Cricket Association;
Avis Vogeltown CC, New Plymouth, New Zealand 1987–88
Cricketers particularly learnt from: Phil Carrick, Doug Padgett, Tim Curtis,
Father
Cricketers particularly admired: Alan Knott ('seemed to have lots of time
with his keeping'), Bob Taylor, Graeme Hick
Other sports played: Golf
Other sports followed: Rugby league (Bradford Northern)
Relaxations: 'Playing (and paying) golf with Tim (Bandit) Curtis.' Tropical
fish
Extras: Played for Young England v Young Australia in 1983. Youngest
wicket-keeper to play for Yorkshire. Holds record for most victims in an

innings for Young England. Played for England Schools U-15s. Released by Yorkshire to join Worcestershire at end of 1984 season. Record 29 Sunday League dismissals in 1988

Opinions on cricket: 'Play four-day matches on good pitches. The TCCB should pay the groundsman. Scrap the 25-point deduction rule as wickets should be good if TCCB employ groundsmen! Do away with one one-day competition to reduce cricket, and keep players fresh. All one-dayers should be a maximum of 50 overs.'

Best batting performance: 108 Worcestershire v Derbyshire, Derby 1988

LAST SEASON: BATTING

	I.	N.O.	R.	H.S.	AV.
TEST					
1ST-CLASS	31	13	623	83	34.61
INT	2	1	9	8	9.00
RAL	7	2	108	48*	21.60
NAT.W.	2	0	64	61	32.00
B & H	4	1	74	42*	24.66

CAREER: BATTING

	I.	N.O.	R.	H.S.	AV.
TEST					
1ST-CLASS	168	58	3144	108	28.58
INT	2	1	9	8	9.00
RAL	52	12	890	48*	22.25
NAT.W.	14	6	152	61	19.00
B & H	20	5	329	51*	21.93

LAST SEASON: WICKET KEEPING

	C.	ST.			
TEST					
1ST-CLASS	61	6			
INT	2	–			
RAL	16	6			
NAT.W.	1	1			
B & H	1	1			

CAREER: WICKET KEEPING

	C.	ST.			
TEST					
1ST-CLASS	306	34			
INT	2	–			
RAL	87	21			
NAT.W.	22	4			
B & H	29	5			

119. Who topped the Surrey batting averages last season?

120. Who topped the Sussex batting averages last season?

RIPLEY, D.   Northamptonshire

Full Name: David Ripley
Role: Right-hand bat, wicket-keeper
Born: 13 September 1966, Leeds
Height: 5′ 11″ **Weight:** 12st
Nickname: Rips, Spud, Sheridan
County debut: 1984
County cap: 1987
1st-Class 50s scored: 2
1st-Class 100s scored: 3
Place in batting averages: 147th
av. 23.55 (1988 212th av. 16.70)
Parents: Arthur and Brenda
Wife and date of marriage: Jackie,
24 September 1988
Family links with cricket: 'My Mum
once made the teas at Farsley CC.'
Education: Woodlesford Primary;
Royds High, Leeds
Qualifications: 5 O-levels, NCA
Coaching Certificate
Jobs outside cricket: Director of Gard Sports, Northampton
Off-season 1989–90: Working in Gard Sports Shop, Northampton

LAST SEASON: BATTING

	I.	N.O.	R.	H.S.	AV.
TEST					
1ST-CLASS	36	9	636	123	23.55
INT					
RAL	8	4	55	18*	13.75
NAT.W.	3	2	28	21*	28.00
B & H	3	2	32	22*	32.00

CAREER: BATTING

	I.	N.O.	R.	H.S.	AV.
TEST					
1ST-CLASS	143	32	2226	134*	20.05
INT					
RAL	36	18	337	36*	18.72
NAT.W.	9	4	72	27*	14.40
B & H	13	5	183	33	22.87

LAST SEASON: WICKET KEEPING

	C.	ST.			
TEST					
1ST-CLASS	57	6			
INT					
RAL	16	1			
NAT.W.	6	–			
B & H	6	–			

LAST SEASON: BOWLING

	O.	M.	R.	W.	AV.
TEST					
1ST-CLASS					
INT					
RAL					
NAT.W.					
B & H					

CAREER: BOWLING

	O.	M.	R.	W.	AV.
TEST					
1ST-CLASS	9	0	89	2	44.50
INT					
RAL					
NAT.W.					
B & H					

CAREER: WICKET KEEPING

	C.	ST.			
TEST					
1ST-CLASS	236	42			
INT					
RAL	38	9			
NAT.W.	18	2			
B & H	20	3			

418

Cricketing superstitions or habits: 'If having a good run will not have my hair cut; left pad on first. Like to be last out of changing room. The number 111.'
Overseas tours: To West Indies with England Young Cricketers 1984–85
Overseas teams played for: Poverty Bay Cricket Association, New Zealand 1985–86
Cricketers particularly learnt from: Brian Reynolds, Jim Yardley, Ian Stein, Billy Rhodes, Roy Wills
Cricketers particularly admired: Alan Knott, Bob Taylor, Ian Botham, Dennis Lillee
Other sports played: Soccer, golf, pool
Other sports followed: Soccer (Leeds United) and rugby league (Castleford)
Relaxations: Music, eating out
Extras: Finished top of wicket-keepers' dismissals list for 1988 with 87 victims
Best batting performance: 134* Northamptonshire v Yorkshire, Scarborough 1986
Best bowling performance: 2-89 Northamptonshire v Essex, Ilford 1987

ROBERTS, A. R.   Northamptonshire

Full Name: Andrew Richard Roberts
Role: Mid-order right-hand bat, leg-spin bowler
Born: 16 April 1971, Kettering
Height: 5′ 6″ **Weight:** 10st 4lbs
Nickname: Reggie, Andy
County debut: 1989
1st-Class catches 1989: 1 (career 1)
Parents: David and Shirley
Marital status: Single
Family links with cricket: 'Dad (Dave) had a couple of games on trial at Northampton.'
Education: Our Ladys, Kettering; and Bishop Stopford, Kettering
Qualifications: 3 O-levels, 5 CSEs
Jobs outside cricket: General assistant in sports centre; labourer on site
Off-season 1989–90: 'Playing cricket in Christchurch, New Zealand.'
Cricketers particularly learnt from: Bob Carter, Brian Reynolds, Dennis Brookes, John Malfait
Cricketers particularly admired: Richard Williams, Wayne Larkins, Malcolm Marshall, Derek Randall

419

Other sports played: Badminton, golf
Other sports followed: Football
Injuries 1989: Strained a hamstring – out for two weeks
Relaxations: 'Music, swimming and a pint!'
Opinions on cricket: 'Better pitches to encourage seam bowlers to bowl line and length and to help batsmen build a decent innings.'
Best batting performance: 8* Northamptonshire v Glamorgan, Swansea 1989
Best bowling performance: 1-40 Northamptonshire v Glamorgan, Swansea 1989

LAST SEASON: BATTING

	I.	N.O.	R.	H.S.	AV.
TEST					
1ST-CLASS	3	1	22	8*	11.00
INT					
RAL					
NAT.W.					
B & H					

LAST SEASON: BOWLING

	O.	M.	R.	W.	AV.
TEST					
1ST-CLASS	34	2	157	2	78.50
INT					
RAL					
NAT.W.					
B & H					

CAREER: BATTING

	I.	N.O.	R.	H.S.	AV.
TEST					
1ST-CLASS	3	1	22	8*	11.00
INT					
RAL					
NAT.W.					
B & H					

CAREER: BOWLING

	O.	M.	R.	W.	AV.
TEST					
1ST-CLASS	34	2	157	2	78.50
INT					
RAL					
NAT.W.					
B & H					

121. Who topped the Warwickshire batting averages last season?

ROBERTS, B.   Derbyshire

Full Name: Bruce Roberts
Role: Right-hand bat, right-arm
medium bowler, slip fielder,
occasional wicket-keeper
Born: 30 May 1962, Lusaka,
Zambia
Height: 6′ 1″ **Weight:** 14st
County debut: 1984
County cap: 1986
1000 runs in a season: 2
1st-Class 50s scored: 36
1st-Class 100s scored: 11
1st-Class 5 w. in innings: 1
One-Day 50s: 15
One-Day 100s: 2
Place in batting averages: 172nd
av. 20.80 (1988 125th av. 26.25)
1st-Class catches 1989: 18
(career 142 + 1 stumping)
Parents: Arthur William and Sara Ann
Wife: Ingrid
Family links with cricket: Father played for Country Districts
Education: Ruzawi, Peterhouse, and Prince Edward, Zimbabwe
Qualifications: O-levels, Coaching qualifications
Jobs outside cricket: Working in family sports shop
Off-season 1989–90: 'In England, working on a farm, and doing odd jobs.'
Overseas teams played for: Transvaal A and B, 1982–89
Cricketers particularly learnt from: 'My father and Ali Bacher.'

LAST SEASON: BATTING

	I.	N.O.	R.	H.S.	AV.
TEST					
1ST-CLASS	27	1	541	102	20.80
INT					
RAL	9	1	145	35*	18.12
NAT.W.	2	1	77	64*	77.00
B & H	3	1	76	30	38.00

LAST SEASON: BOWLING

	O.	M.	R.	W.	AV.
TEST					
1ST-CLASS	9	0	30	0	–
INT					
RAL	5	0	32	1	32.00
NAT.W.					
B & H	8.1	2	38	1	38.00

CAREER: BATTING

	I.	N.O.	R.	H.S.	AV.
TEST					
1ST-CLASS	293	25	7994	184	29.82
INT					
RAL	75	13	1858	101*	29.96
NAT.W.	12	2	297	64*	29.70
B & H	25	6	661	100	34.78

CAREER: BOWLING

	O.	M.	R.	W.	AV.
TEST					
1ST-CLASS	879.1	158	2896	86	33.67
INT					
RAL	139.4	2	918	41	22.39
NAT.W.	23	2	104	2	52.00
B & H	43.1	5	201	5	40.20

Cricketers particularly admired: Javed Miandad, Allan Border, Clive Rice
Other sports played: Swimming, squash, golf, riding
Other sports followed: Rugby
Injuries 1989: Cracked index finger in right hand in July
Relaxations: 'Family, spending time with friends, watching movies, going to the theatre.'
Best batting performance: 184 Derbyshire v Sussex, Chesterfield 1987
Best bowling performance: 5-68 Transvaal B v Northern Transvaal B, Johannesburg 1986–87

ROBERTS, M. L.　　　　Glamorgan

Full Name: Martin Leonard Roberts
Role: Right-hand bat, wicket-keeper
Born: 12 April 1966, Mullion, Cornwall
Height: 5' 11" **Weight:** 11½st
Nickname: Henry, Mert
County debut: 1985
Parents: Leonard and Marian
Wife and date of marriage: Susan, 20 September 1986
Children: Christopher, 18 May 1989
Family links with cricket: Brother Kevin plays for Helston in the Senior Division in Cornwall; father also played in the Senior Division
Education: Helston Comprehensive School
Qualifications: 5 O-levels; qualified cricket coach
Jobs outside cricket: Worked at W. H. Smith & Son for two winters. Also worked as an administrative assistant at the Cardiff Crown Court for one winter. Worked for Minerva Dental for two winters
Off-season 1989–90: Working for an employment agency in Cardiff
Cricketing superstitions or habits: 'Always put left pad on first.'
Overseas tours: NAYC to Holland 1984
Cricketers particularly learnt from: Alan Jones, John Steele, Terry Davies, Jesse Laurie (ex-Cornwall wicket-keeper), 'and most of all my dad'
Cricketers particularly admired: Bob Taylor, Jack Russell
Other sports played: Football, golf, snooker
Other sports followed: 'Like watching rugby union internationals.'

Relaxations: 'Eating out occasionally, watching television and spending time with my wife and baby.'
Extras: Awarded 2nd XI Player of the Year 1989
Best batting performance: 8 Glamorgan v Northamptonshire, Northampton 1986

LAST SEASON: BATTING

	I.	N.O.	R.	H.S.	AV.
TEST					
1ST-CLASS					
INT					
RAL	1	1	1	1*	–
NAT.W.					
B & H					

LAST SEASON: WICKET KEEPING

	C.	ST.			
TEST					
1ST-CLASS					
INT					
RAL					
NAT.W.					
B & H					

CAREER: BATTING

	I.	N.O.	R.	H.S.	AV.
TEST					
1ST-CLASS	3	0	14	8	4.66
INT					
RAL	2	2	7	6*	–
NAT.W.					
B & H					

CAREER: WICKET KEEPING

	C.	ST.			
TEST					
1ST-CLASS	4	1			
INT					
RAL	1	–			
NAT.W.					
B & H					

ROBINSON, J. D.   Surrey

Full Name: Jonathan David Robinson
Role: Left-hand bat, right-arm medium bowler, cover or slip fielder
Born: 3 August 1966, Epsom, Surrey
Height: 5' 10½" **Weight:** 12st 4lbs
Nickname: Robbo, Johnny Yamamoto
County debut: 1988
Place in batting averages: 188th av. 19.44
1st-Class catches 1989: 2 (career 3)
Parents: Peter and Wendy
Marital status: Single
Family links with cricket: Father played for Cambridge University and Esher CC; 'Mother bowled at me in the garden!'
Education: Danes Hill Preparatory School; Lancing College; West Sussex Institute of Higher Education

Qualifications: 6 O-levels, 3 A-levels, BA degree in Sports Studies, Cricket Coaching Award

Jobs outside cricket: Marketing/sales executive at Video Arts Ltd; stand-up comedian and impressionist; 'making machines that go ping'

Off-season 1989–90: Playing cricket for Manley CC, Sydney, Australia

Cricketing superstitions or habits: Left pad on first, lucky shirt. 'Talk about anything except cricket when batting – helps concentration.'

Overseas tours: Lancing College 1st XI to Holland 1981; to Jersey 1982; to Melbourne, Sydney and Adelaide 1983; Esher CC to Barbados 1988

Overseas teams played for: Manley CC, Australia 1989–90

Cricketers particularly learnt from: Father, David Smith, Geoff Arnold, Don Smith, Chris Waller, Peter Robinson, James Boiling, Nick Peters

Cricketers particularly admired: Ian Botham, David Gower, Robin Smith, James Boiling, Bobby Lowe

Other sports played: Soccer, squash, tennis, swimming, jogging, rugby

Other sports followed: Rugby, squash, soccer, horse racing (brother Michael is a trainer)

Injuries 1989: Four stitches in left eyebrow at Grace Road in August – out for three days. Broken little finger on left hand at Grace Road in September – out for one day. 'I love Grace Road!'

Relaxations: Theatre, restaurants, TV, music, pubs, all sports, cinema, clubs, friends, travel

Extras: Did a major study at college about the commercialisation of cricket

Opinions on cricket: 'Four-day championship matches can only be beneficial to English cricket, as a build-up to the ultimate kind of cricket – the Test Match. One-day matches, however, are a lot of fun to play in, and for spectators.'

Best batting performance: 38* Surrey v Oxford University, Oxford 1989

Best bowling performance: 2-37 Surrey v Leicestershire, Leicester 1989

LAST SEASON: BATTING

	I.	N.O.	R.	H.S.	AV.
TEST					
1ST-CLASS	11	2	175	38*	19.44
INT					
RAL	8	3	57	18*	11.40
NAT.W.					
B & H	1	0	0	0	0.00

LAST SEASON: BOWLING

	O.	M.	R.	W.	AV.
TEST					
1ST-CLASS	30.2	5	120	3	40.00
INT					
RAL	29	0	139	2	69.50
NAT.W.					
B & H					

CAREER: BATTING

	I.	N.O.	R.	H.S.	AV.
TEST					
1ST-CLASS	16	4	230	38*	19.16
INT					
RAL	9	3	71	18*	11.83
NAT.W.					
B & H	1	0	0	0	0.00

CAREER: BOWLING

	O.	M.	R.	W.	AV.
TEST					
1ST-CLASS	52.2	9	225	6	37.50
INT					
RAL	38.2	0	209	2	104.50
NAT.W.					
B & H					

ROBINSON, M. A.   Northamptonshire

Full Name: Mark Andrew Robinson
Role: Right-hand bat, right-arm fast-medium bowler
Born: 23 November 1966, Hull
Height: 6' 3" **Weight:** 12st 12lbs
Nickname: Smokey, Coddy, Robbo
County debut: 1987
Place in bowling averages: 73rd av. 30.78 (1988 34th av. 22.93)
Strike rate 1989: 66.67 (career 62.77)
1st-Class catches 1989: 3 (career 9)
Parents: Joan Margaret and Malcolm
Marital status: Single
Family links with cricket: Maternal grandfather an established local cricketer. Father was hostile cricketer in back ten-foot
Education: Fifth Avenue Primary; Endike Junior High; Hull Grammar School
Qualifications: 6 O-levels, 2 A-levels, 1st NCA Cricket Coaching Award
Jobs outside cricket: Jeweller, sports shop assistant, employee at Hull Indoor Cricket Stadium, cricket coach
Off-season 1989–90: Working at Hull Indoor Cricket Stadium
Cricketing superstitions or habits: Refuses to walk on the pitch sixth in line
Overseas tours: North of England U-19s to Bermuda 1985
Overseas teams played for: East Christchurch-Shirley CC 1987–88; Canterbury Province, New Zealand 1989
Cricketers particularly learnt from: Fred Cowell, Ken Lake, Doug Ferguson, Dave Rees, Bob Carter (NCCC), Duncan Wild, Dennis Lillee
Cricketers particularly admired: Dennis Lillee, Richard Hadlee, Winston Davis, Neil Foster, Mike Gatting, John Emburey
Other sports played: Football (Hull Schools and Humberside U-19), indoor cricket (National League), tennis
Other sports followed: Hull City FC ('The Tigers'), and all sports
Injuries 1989: 'Thigh strain lasting six weeks, but managed to play with it.'
Relaxations: Cinema, soap operas, reading, music, hot baths
Extras: Took part in Leeds to London relay run around all county headquarters, in aid of Leukaemia Research. Took hat-trick with first three balls of innings in Yorkshire League, playing for Hull v Doncaster. First time this has been done for 71 years. First player to win Yorkshire U-19s

425

Bowler of the Season Award in two successive years. Won player of the month award August/September 1988. NCCC Uncapped Player of the Year 1989

Opinions on cricket: 'The rebel tour of South Africa has been brought about by the governing bodies of all cricketing nations refusing to accept the advances made by the SACU. Second-team cricket is a pale shadow of the first-class game. Young players are supposed to learn the game while playing on wickets without bounce or pace, and often with sub-standard balls.'

Best batting performance: 19* Northamptonshire v Essex, Chelmsford 1988
Best bowling performance: 4-19 Northamptonshire v Glamorgan, Wellingborough 1988

LAST SEASON: BATTING

	I.	N.O.	R.	H.S.	AV.
TEST					
1ST-CLASS	23	10	17	9	1.30
INT					
RAL	4	0	2	2	0.50
NAT.W.	–	–	–	–	–
B & H	–	–	–	–	–

LAST SEASON: BOWLING

	O.	M.	R.	W.	AV.
TEST					
1ST-CLASS	411.1	81	1139	37	30.78
INT					
RAL	81	4	309	8	38.62
NAT.W.	23.4	4	62	5	12.40
B & H	44	5	110	5	22.00

CAREER: BATTING

	I.	N.O.	R.	H.S.	AV.
TEST					
1ST-CLASS	52	22	69	19*	2.30
INT					
RAL	8	1	3	2	0.42
NAT.W.	–	–	–	–	–
B & H	–	–	–	–	–

CAREER: BOWLING

	O.	M.	R.	W.	AV.
TEST					
1ST-CLASS	1161.2	231	3304	111	29.76
INT					
RAL	136.1	5	589	11	53.54
NAT.W.	23.4	4	62	5	12.40
B & H	44	5	110	5	22.00

122. Who topped the Worcestershire batting averages last season?

ROBINSON, P. E.　　　　　Yorkshire

Full Name: Phillip Edward
Robinson
Role: Right-hand middle-order bat,
slip or cover fielder
Born: 3 August 1963, Keighley
Height: 5′ 9″ **Weight:** 13st
Nickname: Robbo, Billy, Red
County debut: 1984
County cap: 1988
1000 runs in a season: 1
1st-Class 50s scored: 24
1st-Class 100s scored: 4
One-Day 50s: 9
Place in batting averages: 106th
av. 28.92 (1988 79th av. 31.70)
1st-Class catches 1989: 11 (career 56)
Parents: Keith and Lesley
Wife: Jane, 1986
Family links with cricket: Father
played and brothers play in Bradford League
Education: Long Lee Primary; Hartington Middle; Greenhead Grammar
Qualifications: 2 O-levels
Off-season 1989–90: Playing for Eden Roskill CC, Auckland, New Zealand
Cricketing superstitions or habits: 'Always put my left pad on first.'
Overseas teams played for: Southland, New Zealand 1987–88; Eden Roskill
CC, Auckland, New Zealand 1989–90
Cricketers particularly learnt from: 'I learn from all cricketers.'
Cricketers particularly admired: Gary Sobers, Geoff Boycott, Michael
Holding
Other sports played: Football, golf, squash
Other sports followed: Keighley Rugby League, and Manchester United and
Meadowbank football teams
Relaxations: Crosswords, reading, playing sports, watching TV
Extras: Scored the highest score by a Yorkshire 2nd XI player of 233 in 1983 v
Kent at Canterbury

LAST SEASON: BATTING

	I.	N.O.	R.	H.S.	AV.
TEST					
1ST-CLASS	31	4	781	147	28.92
INT					
RAL	15	2	267	55	20.53
NAT.W.					
B & H	4	0	67	37	16.75

CAREER: BATTING

	I.	N.O.	R.	H.S.	AV.
TEST					
1ST-CLASS	137	17	3973	147	33.10
INT					
RAL	71	8	1636	78*	25.96
NAT.W.	3	0	66	66	22.00
B & H	9	0	166	42	18.44

Opinions on cricket: 'There should not be any overseas professionals playing in county cricket.'
Best batting performance: 147 Yorkshire v Kent, Scarborough 1989

ROBINSON, R. T.   Nottinghamshire

Full Name: Robert Timothy Robinson
Role: Right-hand opening bat, cover fielder, captain
Born: 21 November 1958, Sutton-in-Ashfield, Nottinghamshire
Height: 5′ 11½″ **Weight:** 12st 4lbs
Nickname: Robbo, Chop
County debut: 1978
County cap: 1983
Test debut: 1984–85
No. of Tests: 29
No. of One-Day Internationals: 26
1000 runs in a season: 7
1st-Class 50s scored: 70
1st-Class 100s scored: 34
1st-Class 200s scored: 1
One-Day 50s: 36
One-Day 100s: 3
Place in batting averages: 35th av. 42.11 (1988 42nd av. 38.51)
1st-Class catches 1989: 31 (career 153)
Parents: Eddy and Christine
Wife and date of marriage: Patricia, 2 November 1985
Children: Philip, 14 December 1986
Family links with cricket: Father, uncle, cousin and brother all played local cricket. Brother played for Nottinghamshire Schoolboys
Education: Dunstable Grammar School; High Pavement College, Nottingham; Sheffield University
Qualifications: Degree in Accounting and Financial Management
Jobs outside cricket: Trainee accountant. Working in Commercial Department, Nottinghamshire CCC. After-dinner speaking. Promotional work for Gunn & Moore
Off-season 1989–90: Touring South Africa with unofficial English team
Cricketing superstitions or habits: Always puts left pad on first
Overseas tours: NCA U-19 tour 1976; England to India and Australia 1984–85, 1987–88; West Indies 1986; World Cup, India, Pakistan and New Zealand 1987–88

Overseas teams played for: Durban Collegians, South Africa 1980–81
Cricketers particularly learnt from: Clive Rice, Mike Harris
Cricketers particularly admired: Geoffrey Boycott
Other sports played: Squash
Other sports followed: Soccer, rugby
Relaxations: Television, reading, spending time with family
Extras: Played for Northants 2nd XI in 1974–75 and for Nottinghamshire 2nd XI in 1977. Had soccer trials with Portsmouth, Chelsea and QPR. Plays in contact lenses. One of *Wisden*'s Five Cricketers of the Year, 1985
Opinions on cricket: 'Fewer overseas players, four-day county championship, and better batting wickets.'
Best batting performance: 207 Nottinghamshire v Warwickshire, Trent Bridge 1983
Best bowling performance: 1-22 Nottinghamshire v Northamptonshire, Northampton 1982

LAST SEASON: BATTING

	I.	N.O.	R.	H.S.	AV.
TEST	2	0	12	12	6.00
1ST-CLASS	40	6	1504	146*	44.23
INT					
RAL	14	3	439	97*	39.90
NAT.W.	2	0	33	24	16.50
B & H	7	0	263	86	37.57

CAREER: BATTING

	I.	N.O.	R.	H.S.	AV.
TEST	49	0	1601	175	32.67
1ST-CLASS	372	47	13463	207	41.42
INT	26	0	597	83	22.96
RAL	117	12	3255	100	31.00
NAT.W.	24	2	915	139	41.59
B & H	46	3	1430	120	33.25

LAST SEASON: BOWLING

	O.	M.	R.	W.	AV.
TEST					
1ST-CLASS	6	0	46	0	–
INT					
RAL					
NAT.W.					
B & H					

CAREER: BOWLING

	O.	M.	R.	W.	AV.
TEST	1	1	0	0	–
1ST-CLASS	30	0	211	2	105.50
INT					
RAL					
NAT.W.					
B & H					

123. Who topped the Yorkshire batting averages last season?

ROEBUCK, P. M. Somerset

Full Name: Peter Michael Roebuck
Role: Right-hand bat, right-arm 'fast off-break bowler', slip fielder
Born: 6 March 1956, Oxford
Height: 6′ **Weight:** 13st 5lbs
Nickname: Professor
County debut: 1974
County cap: 1978
1000 runs in a season: 8
1st-Class 50s scored: 82
1st-Class 100s scored: 29
1st-Class 200s scored: 1
1st-Class 5 w. in innings: 1
One-Day 50s: 32
One-Day 100s: 5
Place in batting averages: 38th
av. 41.14 (1988 109th av. 28.37)
Place in bowling averages: 80th
av. 31.54
Strike rate 1989: 76.90 (career 104.20)
1st-Class catches 1989: 8 (career 151)
Parents: James and Elizabeth
Marital status: Single
Family links with cricket: Mother and sister both played for Oxford University Ladies. Younger brother Paul played for ESCA U-15 and now plays for Glamorgan
Education: Park School, Bath; Millfield School; Emmanuel College, Cambridge University
Qualifications: 1st Class Hons degree in law
Jobs outside cricket: Teacher, author and freelance journalist
Off-season 1989–90: 'Working for *Sydney Morning Herald* and *Age* in Australia, and preparing for my benefit.'
Cricketing superstitions or habits: 'We cranky old pros feel only contempt for those who rely on luck. We do well because we are tried and trusted. Touch wood!'
Overseas tours: Toured in Australia with Combined Oxford & Cambridge XI 1979–80
Overseas teams played for: Played in Perth, Australia 1979–80; also in Corfu, Sydney and Fiji
Cricketers particularly learnt from: Viv Richards, Martin Crowe
Cricketers particularly admired: R. J. O. Meyer, Keith Fletcher
Other sports played: 'Tennis, kayaking, soccer with Somerset CCC soccer

430

team (apart from heading, trapping, tackling and shooting, I play OK).'

Other sports followed: 'Not synchronised swimming – I follow Bath Rugby (since 12 years of age) and Somerset cricket.'

Injuries 1989: 'Missed one game with gammy finger.'

Relaxations: 'Reginald Perrin books, Clint Eastwood films, music of all kinds from Fauré Requiem to the works of Mr Springsteen. Plotting.'

Extras: Cambridge blue 1975–76–77. Plays in spectacles. Youngest Minor County cricketer, playing for Somerset 2nd XI at age of 13. Shared in 4th wicket partnership record for county of 251 with I. V. A. Richards v Surrey at Weston-super-Mare in 1977. Books: *Slice of Cricket*, *It Never Rains* and *It Sort of Clicks* (with Ian Botham). Articles in *Sunday Times*, *Independent*, *Guardian*, 'and anyone else who asks'. Founder member of campaign for fair play. Appointed captain in 1986. One of *Wisden*'s Five Cricketers of the Year, 1988. Resigned captaincy during 1988 season. Writing a history of Somerset cricket

Opinions on cricket: 'It is a great shame that bowlers consider me vulnerable to the flier directed at my head rather than, say, the slow half-volley on the leg stump.'

Best batting performance: 221* Somerset v Nottinghamshire, Trent Bridge 1986

Best bowling performance: 6-50 Cambridge University v Kent, Canterbury 1977

LAST SEASON: BATTING

	I.	N.O.	R.	H.S.	AV.
TEST					
1ST-CLASS	37	3	1399	149	41.14
INT					
RAL	13	1	272	63	22.66
NAT.W.	2	0	120	102	51.00
B & H	6	0	266	102	44.33

CAREER: BATTING

	I.	N.O.	R.	H.S.	AV.
TEST					
1ST-CLASS	495	73	15585	221*	36.93
INT					
RAL	151	23	3844	105	30.03
NAT.W.	33	2	925	102	29.83
B & H	56	6	1468	120	29.36

LAST SEASON: BOWLING

	O.	M.	R.	W.	AV.
TEST					
1ST-CLASS	141	35	347	11	31.54
INT					
RAL	36.4	0	186	12	15.50
NAT.W.	10	0	55	2	27.50
B & H	15	2	61	4	15.25

CAREER: BOWLING

	O.	M.	R.	W.	AV.
TEST					
1ST-CLASS	955.1	238	2696	55	49.01
INT					
RAL	49.1	0	251	14	17.92
NAT.W.	10	0	55	2	27.50
B & H	23.2	3	84	6	14.00

ROMAINES, P. W. Gloucestershire

Full Name: Paul William Romaines
Role: Right-hand opening bat,
off-break bowler
Born: 25 December 1955, Bishop
Auckland, Co Durham
Height: 6′ **Weight:** 12st 8lbs
Nickname: Canny, Human
County debut: 1975 (Northampton-
shire), 1982 (Gloucestershire)
County cap: 1983 (Gloucestershire)
1000 runs in a season: 3
1st-Class 50s scored: 39
1st-Class 100s scored: 13
One-Day 50s: 20
One-Day 100s: 2
Place in batting averages: 180th
av. 20.00 (1988 122nd av. 26.52)
1st-Class catches 1989: 2 (career 65)
Parents: George and Freda
Wife and date of marriage: Julie Anne, 1979
Children: Claire Louise
Family links with cricket: Father played local cricket and is still an avid
watcher. Grandfather, W. R. Romaines, represented Durham in Minor
Counties cricket, and played v Australia in 1926
Education: Leeholme School, Bishop Auckland
Qualifications: 8 O-levels, NCA Qualified Coach
Jobs outside cricket: Sales representative
Overseas tours: Gloucestershire CCC to Sri Lanka 1986–87
Overseas teams played for: Gordon CC, Sydney 1981–2, 1982–3; Griqualand
West 1984–85; De Beers CC 1984–85
Cricketers particularly learnt from: Peter Willey, Barry Dudleston, David
Graveney
Cricketers particularly admired: Zaheer Abbas, Graham Gooch, Clive
Radley, Gordon Greenidge
Other sports played: Squash, golf, soccer
Other sports followed: Athletics
Injuries 1989: Cracked index finger of left hand – out for three weeks in June
Relaxations: 'Listening to music, having a good pint, antiques, people, writing
letters, good conversation.'
Extras: Debut for Northamptonshire 1975. Played Minor County cricket with
Durham 1977–1981. Joined Gloucestershire in 1982
Opinions on cricket: 'In favour of four-day cricket. Not in favour of the

Reader Ball. Four-foot line on the wicket should be extended to five feet. Over rate fines are too stiff and should be abolished.'

Best batting performance: 186 Gloucestershire v Warwickshire, Nuneaton 1982

Best bowling performance: 3-42 Gloucestershire v Surrey, The Oval 1985

LAST SEASON: BATTING

	I.	N.O.	R.	H.S.	AV.
TEST					
1ST-CLASS	11	0	220	77	20.00
INT					
RAL	9	1	84	31	10.50
NAT.W.					
B & H	4	0	109	76	27.25

CAREER: BATTING

	I.	N.O.	R.	H.S.	AV.
TEST					
1ST-CLASS	293	21	7790	186	28.63
INT					
RAL	89	8	2257	105	27.86
NAT.W.	15	2	380	82	29.23
B & H	20	1	663	125	34.89

LAST SEASON: BOWLING

	O.	M.	R.	W.	AV.
TEST					
1ST-CLASS					
INT					
RAL					
NAT.W.					
B & H					

CAREER: BOWLING

	O.	M.	R.	W.	AV.
TEST					
1ST-CLASS	36.5	2	217	3	72.33
INT					
RAL					
NAT.W.					
B & H					

ROSE, G. D.   Somerset

Full Name: Graham David Rose
Role: Right-hand bat, right-arm fast-medium bowler, 1st slip
Born: 12 April 1964, Tottenham
Height: 6' 4" **Weight:** 14st 7lbs
Nickname: Rosie
County debut: 1985 (Middlesex), 1987 (Somerset)
County cap: 1988
50 wickets in a season: 1
1st-Class 50s scored: 4
1st-Class 5 w. in innings: 3
One-Day 50s: 3
Place in batting averages: 183rd av. 19.84 (1988 189th av. 20.26)
Place in bowling averages: 38th av. 24.31 (1988 61st av. 26.77)
Strike rate 1989: 53.40 (career 51.15)
1st-Class catches 1989: 4 (career 25)
Parents: William and Edna

Wife and date of marriage: Teresa Julie, 19 September 1987
Family links with cricket: Father and brother played club cricket in North London
Education: Northumberland Park School, Tottenham
Qualifications: 6 O-levels, 4 A-levels. NCA Coaching Certificate
Jobs outside cricket: 'Many and various – for example, bricklayer's mate, tele-researcher, wool sampler.'
Overseas tours: ESCA U-19 to Zimbabwe; NCA South to Holland 1983; Haringey Cricket College to West Indies 1986
Overseas teams played for: Carey Park, Western Australia 1984–85; Fremantle, Perth 1986–87; Paarl CC, South Africa 1988–89
Cricketers particularly learnt from: Jack Robertson, Ted Jackson, Father, Ron Booth
Cricketers particularly admired: Steve Waugh, Wayne Daniel, Richard Hadlee
Other sports played: Golf, squash
Other sports followed: 'Follow Spurs for my sins.'
Relaxations: Music – Dire Straits, Beatles, Pink Floyd, U2
Extras: Played for Young England v Young Australia 1983. Took 6 wickets for 41 on Middlesex debut. Joined Somerset for 1987 season and scored 95 on debut
Opinions on cricket: 'Four-day cricket is definitely a success, but something has to be done about the state of the pitches to see that games can last four days. Over-rate fines should not be levied if quotas are reached by 6.30 pm. Counties should do more to find winter employment for their players, especially the younger ones.'
Best batting performance: 95 Somerset v Lancashire, Taunton 1987
Best bowling performance: 6-41 Middlesex v Worcestershire, Worcester 1985

LAST SEASON: BATTING

	I.	N.O.	R.	H.S.	AV.
TEST					
1ST-CLASS	20	7	258	50*	19.84
INT					
RAL	9	2	160	61*	22.85
NAT.W.					
B & H	2	1	11	7*	11.00

CAREER: BATTING

	I.	N.O.	R.	H.S.	AV.
TEST					
1ST-CLASS	76	18	1206	95	20.79
INT					
RAL	38	7	702	93*	22.64
NAT.W.	3	0	37	26	12.33
B & H	10	2	117	42	14.62

LAST SEASON: BOWLING

	O.	M.	R.	W.	AV.
TEST					
1ST-CLASS	418.2	104	1143	47	24.31
INT					
RAL	75.1	10	284	19	14.94
NAT.W.					
B & H	58.2	6	210	4	52.50

CAREER: BOWLING

	O.	M.	R.	W.	AV.
TEST					
1ST-CLASS	1347	294	4064	158	25.72
INT					
RAL	336.4	21	1409	51	27.62
NAT.W.	32.5	7	103	4	25.75
B & H	153.2	13	593	18	32.94

ROSEBERRY, M. A. Middlesex

Full Name: Michael Anthony Roseberry
Role: Right-hand bat, right-arm occasional off-break and swing bowler, close-to-wicket fielder
Born: 28 November 1966, Houghton-le-Spring, Sunderland
Height: 6′ **Weight:** 14st
Nickname: Zorro
County debut: 1985
1st-Class 50s scored: 9
1st-Class 100s scored: 1
One-Day 50s scored: 1
Place in batting averages: 77th av. 33.41 (1988 176th av. 21.44)
1st-Class catches 1989: 14 (career 27)
Parents: Matthew and Jean
Marital status: Single
Family links with cricket: Uncle, Peter Wyness, played for Royal Navy; brother Andrew has just joined Leicester
Education: Tonstall Preparatory School; Durham School
Qualifications: 5 O-levels, 1 A-level
Jobs outside cricket: 'Last winter I coached rugby at my old school as well as basketball.'
Cricketing superstitions or habits: 'Tend to put my front batting pad on first.'
Overseas tours: Durham School 1st XI to Barbados 1983; Young England to West Indies 1985; Kenya with Minor Counties U-25, 1986
Overseas teams played for: Fremantle, Perth, Western Australia 1986; Melville CC, Perth
Cricketers particularly learnt from: Alec Coxon (ex-England and Yorkshire bowler), Don Wilson and Gordon Jenkins (MCC Indoor School), Mike Gatting
Cricketers particularly admired: Ian Botham, Geoff Boycott
Other sports played: 'Rugby, squash, snooker and whatever takes my fancy.'
Other sports followed: Football, golf
Relaxations: Snooker, music
Extras: Won Lord's Taverners/MCC Cricketer of the Year 1983. Won Sunday Sun/Dixon Sport Cricketer of the Year 1983. Won Cricket Societies' Wetherall Award 1983, 1984. Won Cricket Societies' Award for Best Young

Cricketer of the Year 1984 and Frank Morris Memorial Award 1984. Won Cricket Society award for best all-rounder in schools cricket twice. Played in Durham League as a professional while still at school. At age 16, playing for Durham School v St Bees, he hit 216 in 160 minutes. When not playing for Middlesex, he turns out for Richmond

Opinions on cricket: 'The position on overseas players should be tightened up as it has got well out of hand. Hopefully four-day cricket will come in on a permanent basis.'

Best batting performance: 101 Middlesex v Oxford University, Oxford 1989

Best bowling performance: 1-1 Middlesex v Sussex, Hove 1988

LAST SEASON: BATTING

	I.	N.O.	R.	H.S.	AV.
TEST					
1ST-CLASS	29	5	804	101*	33.50
INT					
RAL	9	2	199	83*	28.42
NAT.W.	3	0	64	26	21.33
B & H					

LAST SEASON: BOWLING

	O.	M.	R.	W.	AV.
TEST					
1ST-CLASS	14.5	5	47	0	–
INT					
RAL					
NAT.W.					
B & H					

CAREER: BATTING

	I.	N.O.	R.	H.S.	AV.
TEST					
1ST-CLASS	72	12	1634	101*	27.23
INT					
RAL	18	2	376	83*	23.50
NAT.W.	3	0	64	26	21.33
B & H	2	0	8	6	4.00

CAREER: BOWLING

	O.	M.	R.	W.	AV.
TEST					
1ST-CLASS	31.3	6	133	2	66.50
INT					
RAL					
NAT.W.					
B & H					

124. Who topped Derbyshire's bowling averages last season?

RUSSELL, R. C.   Gloucestershire

Full Name: Robert Charles Russell
Role: Left-hand bat, wicket-keeper
Born: 15 August 1963, Stroud
Height: 5′ 8½″ **Weight:** 9st 8lbs
Nickname: Jack, Bob (after great
England wicket-keeper, Bob Taylor),
Whispering Gloves
County debut: 1981
County cap: 1985
Test debut: 1988
No. of Tests: 7
No. of One-Day Internationals: 2
1st-Class 50s scored: 18
1st-Class 100s scored: 1
One-Day 50s: 3
One-Day 100s: 1
Place in batting averages: 124th
av. 26.63 (1988 82nd av. 30.96)
Parents: John and Jennifer
Wife and date of marriage: Aileen Ann, 6 March 1985
Children: Stepson, Marcus Anthony; Elizabeth Ann, March 1988; Victoria, 1989
Education: Uplands County Primary School; Archway Comprehensive School
Qualifications: 7 O-levels, 2 A-levels
Jobs outside cricket: Carpet fitter, ran own carpet business, but has had to give it up because of cricket commitments; professional artist
Off-season 1989–90: Touring with England to India and to West Indies. Working as an artist
Cricketing superstitions or habits: 'The numbers 37 and 87. In general try to make clothing and equipment last as long as possible.' Keeps a lucky handkerchief in right-hand trouser pocket. Changes his clothes completely when batting, as opposed to fielding. Has worn the same hat in every first-class match since 1982
Overseas tours: Denmark with NCA Young Cricketers 1981; with Gloucestershire to Barbados 1985; Mendip Acorns Pacific tour 1984; Gloucestershire to Sri Lanka 1987; England to Pakistan 1987; to India and West Indies 1989–90
Overseas teams played for: Takapuna CC, New Zealand 1983–85
Cricketers particularly learnt from: Alan Knott, Bob Taylor
Cricketers particularly admired: Alan Knott, Bob Taylor
Other sports played: 'Occasional football; snooker, when time!'

Other sports followed: Football ('a Tottenham Hotspur supporter, but only on television'), snooker

Relaxations: Drawing, sketching, painting (oil and watercolour). Watching comedy, Rory Bremner and Phil Cool especially

Extras: Spotted at age 9 by Gloucestershire coach, Graham Wiltshire. Record for most dismissals in a match for first-class debut: 8 (7 caught, 1 stumped) for Gloucestershire v Sri Lankans at Bristol, 1981. Youngest wicket-keeper for Gloucestershire (17 years 307 days). Represented Young England v Young West Indies in the Agatha Christie 'Test Match' series, 1982. Played for Duchess of Norfolk's XI v West Indies at Arundel in 1984. Joint holder of world record for hat-trick of catches (v Surrey at The Oval 1986). Youngest wicket-keeper to score Sunday League hundred (v Worcestershire at Hereford 1986). Had a three-week exhibition of his drawings in Bristol 1988. Published a book of his work entitled *A Cricketer's Art* (1988). Was chosen as England's Man of the Test Series, England v Australia 1989. Commissioned by Dean of Gloucester to do a drawing of Gloucester Cathedral to raise funds for 900th Anniversary. Still turns out for his original club, Stroud CC, whenever he can. Runs six miles a day to keep fit. Drinks anything up to 20 cups of tea a day, and actually had a cup of tea during the drinks interval during the Gloucestershire v Glamorgan game at Bristol 1989

Best batting performance: 128* England v Australia, Old Trafford 1989

LAST SEASON: BATTING

	I.	N.O.	R.	H.S.	AV.
TEST	11	3	314	128*	39.25
1ST-CLASS	18	4	272	59*	19.42
INT					
RAL	9	3	93	39	15.50
NAT.W.	1	1	42	42*	–
B & H	4	3	56	44	56.00

LAST SEASON: WICKET KEEPING

	C.	ST.			
TEST	14	4			
1ST-CLASS	37	3			
INT					
RAL	14	2			
NAT.W.	2	–			
B & H	5	–			

CAREER: BATTING

	I.	N.O.	R.	H.S.	AV.
TEST	12	3	408	128*	45.33
1ST-CLASS	214	52	3841	72	23.70
INT	1	1	2	2*	–
RAL	58	19	906	108	23.23
NAT.W.	12	4	188	42*	23.50
B & H	18	6	182	44	15.16

CAREER: WICKET KEEPING

	C.	ST.			
TEST	17	4			
1ST-CLASS	344	65			
INT	3	–			
RAL	72	17			
NAT.W.	18	5			
B & H	29	7			

SADIQ, Z. A.   Surrey

Full Name: Zahid Asa Sadiq
Role: Right-hand bat
Born: 6 May 1965, Nairobi
Height: 5′ 11″ **Weight:** 11st 2lbs
Nickname: Zeidi, Munch, Shag
County debut: 1987
1st-Class 50s scored: 1
One-Day 50s: 1
1st-Class catches 1989: 3 (career 5)
Parents: Mohammed Sadiq
Marital status: Single
Education: Rutlish School
Qualifications: 2 O-levels
Cricketing superstitions or habits:
Left pad on first
Overseas teams played for:
Claremont CC, Australia 1986–87;
Wembley CC, Australia 1987–88
Cricketers particularly learnt from:
Monte Lynch, Chris Waller, Geoff Arnold
Cricketers particularly admired: Viv Richards, Monte Lynch, Imran Khan
Other sports played: Squash, rugby
Other sports followed: Rugby
Relaxations: Listening to music, parties
Extras: Released by Surrey at end of 1989 season
Best batting performance: 64 Surrey v Cambridge University, Cambridge
1988

LAST SEASON: BATTING

	I.	N.O.	R.	H.S.	AV.
TEST					
1ST-CLASS	5	0	78	36	15.60
INT					
RAL	8	0	87	34	10.87
NAT.W.					
B & H	2	0	10	9	5.00

CAREER: BATTING

	I.	N.O.	R.	H.S.	AV.
TEST					
1ST-CLASS	11	0	213	64	19.36
INT					
RAL	18	0	241	53	13.38
NAT.W.					
B & H	2	0	10	9	5.00

SALISBURY, I. D. K.   Sussex

Full Name: Ian David Kenneth
Salisbury
Role: Right-hand bat, right-arm leg
spinner
Born: 2 January 1970, Northampton
Height: 5′ 11″ **Weight:** 12st
Nickname: Budgie, Sals, Santa,
Buster
County debut: 1989
Place in batting averages: 260th
av. 10.33
Place in bowling averages: 123rd
av. 62.13
Strike rate 1989: 111.06 (career
111.06)
1st-Class catches 1989: 4 (career 4)
Parents: Dave and Margaret
Marital status: Single
Family links with cricket: Father is a
sportsfield maintenance contractor
Education: Moulton Comprehensive, Northampton
Qualifications: 7 O-levels; NCA Coaching Certificate
Off-season 1989–90: 'Abroad in Zimbabwe, coaching in schools, and playing
at weekends.'
Cricketers particularly learnt from: Don Wilson, Norman Gifford
Cricketers particularly admired: David Smith, Paul Parker, Peter Moores
Other sports played: Football, golf, snooker
Other sports followed: 'All sports.'

LAST SEASON: BATTING

	I.	N.O.	R.	H.S.	AV.
TEST					
1ST-CLASS	10	4	62	37	10.33
INT					
RAL					
NAT.W.					
B & H					

CAREER: BATTING

	I.	N.O.	R.	H.S.	AV.
TEST					
1ST-CLASS	10	4	62	37	10.33
INT					
RAL					
NAT.W.					
B & H					

LAST SEASON: BOWLING

	O.	M.	R.	W.	AV.
TEST					
1ST-CLASS	277.4	61	932	15	62.13
INT					
RAL					
NAT.W.					
B & H					

CAREER: BOWLING

	O.	M.	R.	W.	AV.
TEST					
1ST-CLASS	277.4	61	932	15	62.13
INT					
RAL					
NAT.W.					
B & H					

Relaxations: Good food and music

Opinions on cricket: 'Spin bowlers are becoming a dying breed in county cricket, due to some people thinking they aren't necessary, and that extra seamers are because there are a lot of green wickets, one-day cricket, and pressure of having always to keep the runs down as opposed to taking wickets.'

Best batting performance: 37 Sussex v Essex, Horsham 1989

Best bowling performance: 3-75 Sussex v Somerset, Hove 1989

SARGEANT, N. F. Surrey

Full Name: Neil Fredrick Sargeant
Role: Right-hand bat, wicket-keeper
Born: 8 November 1965, Hammersmith
Height: 5' 7" **Weight:** 10st 7lbs
Nickname: Sarge, Bilko, Dusty
County debut: 1989
Parents: Barry and Christine
Marital status: Single
Education: Grange Primary School; Whitmore High School
Qualifications: 2 O-levels
Jobs outside cricket: 'Working for my father's building company.'
Off-season 1989–90: Playing cricket abroad
Cricketing superstitions or habits: 'Always put left keeping pad on first.'

LAST SEASON: BATTING

	I.	N.O.	R.	H.S.	AV.
TEST					
1ST-CLASS	3	1	26	16	13.00
INT					
RAL					
NAT.W.					
B & H					

CAREER: BATTING

	I.	N.O.	R.	H.S.	AV.
TEST					
1ST-CLASS	3	1	26	16	13.00
INT					
RAL					
NAT.W.					
B & H					

LAST SEASON: WICKET KEEPING

	C.	ST.		
TEST				
1ST-CLASS	4	1		
INT				
RAL				
NAT.W.				
B & H				

CAREER: WICKET KEEPING

	C.	ST.		
TEST				
1ST-CLASS	4	1		
INT				
RAL				
NAT.W.				
B & H				

Overseas teams played for: Green Point CC 1987–88, 1988–89
Cricketers particularly learnt from: Hylton Ackerman, Robin Jackman, Ian Greig, John Farrell
Cricketers particularly admired: Alan Knott, Bob Taylor, Ray Jennings
Other sports played: Football, golf
Other sports followed: Football, golf, horse racing
Relaxations: Horse racing, music
Extras: Played football for Tottenham Hotspur Youth Team
Best batting performance: 16 Surrey v Gloucestershire, The Oval 1989

SAXELBY, K. — Nottinghamshire

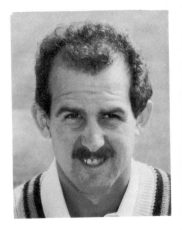

Full Name: Kevin Saxelby
Role: Right-hand bat, right-arm fast medium bowler
Born: 23 February 1959, Worksop
Height: 6' 2" **Weight:** 14st
Nickname: Sax, Sacko
County debut: 1978
County cap: 1984
1st-Class 50s scored: 1
1st-Class 5 w. in innings: 6
1st-Class 10 w. in match: 1
Place in batting averages: 213th av. 16.20
Place in bowling averages: 107th av. 42.11 (1988 131st av. 49.23)
Strike rate 1989: 78.55 (career 61.72)
1st-Class catches 1989: 3 (career 27)
Parents: George Kenneth and Hilda Margaret
Wife: Peta Jean Wendy
Children: Craig Robert, 6 June 1985
Family links with cricket: Father played in local league cricket. Brother played for NAYC and Nottinghamshire
Education: Magnus Grammar School, Newark
Qualifications: 10 O-levels, 4 A-levels
Jobs outside cricket: Farmer
Off-season 1989–90: Working on family farm
Overseas teams played for: North Perth, Australia 1979–80; Durban Collegians, South Africa 1980–81; Alma-Marist, Cape Town 1982–83
Cricketers particularly admired: Dennis Lillee, John Snow
Other sports played: Rugby union

Other sports followed: 'Most sports except soccer and anything to do with horses.'

Relaxations: Gardening, DIY

Opinions on cricket: 'I believe there should be no limit on over rates in four-day cricket, in order to encourage quick bowling as opposed to seam bowling.'

Best batting performance: 59* Nottinghamshire v Derbyshire, Chesterfield 1982

Best bowling performance: 6-49 Nottinghamshire v Sussex, Trent Bridge 1987

LAST SEASON: BATTING

	I.	N.O.	R.	H.S.	AV.
TEST					
1ST-CLASS	11	6	81	19	16.20
INT					
RAL	6	4	15	6*	7.50
NAT.W.	1	0	1	1	1.00
B & H	–	–	–	–	–

LAST SEASON: BOWLING

	O.	M.	R.	W.	AV.
TEST					
1ST-CLASS	235.4	65	758	18	42.11
INT					
RAL	90.5	1	473	29	16.31
NAT.W.	12	0	70	3	23.33
B & H	19.4	1	96	3	32.00

CAREER: BATTING

	I.	N.O.	R.	H.S.	AV.
TEST					
1ST-CLASS	131	42	1069	59*	12.01
INT					
RAL	37	25	153	23*	12.75
NAT.W.	5	3	26	12	13.00
B & H	12	7	53	13*	10.60

CAREER: BOWLING

	O.	M.	R.	W.	AV.
TEST					
1ST-CLASS	3014	715	9386	293	32.03
INT					
RAL	678.5	25	3368	137	24.58
NAT.W.	195.1	22	753	30	25.10
B & H	298.2	33	1159	45	25.75

SAXELBY, M.   Nottinghamshire

Full Name: Mark Saxelby

Role: Left-hand bat, right-arm medium bowler

Born: 4 January 1969, Newark

Height: 6′ 3″ **Weight:** 14st

Nickname: Sax, Steffi

County debut: 1989

Parents: George Kenneth and Hilda Margaret

Marital status: Single

Family links with cricket: Brother plays for Nottinghamshire; father played local cricket

Education: Nottingham High School

Qualifications: 7 O-levels, 2 A-levels

Jobs outside cricket: Lab technician

Off-season 1989–90: Working as lab technician
Cricketers particularly learnt from: John Birch, Kevin Saxelby
Cricketers particularly admired: Richard Hadlee, Derek Randall
Other sports played: Rugby union
Other sports followed: Rugby union and league, football, American football
Injuries 1989: 'Never missed a game through injury, but had some trouble with my shoulder and had an operation in October.'
Relaxations: All sports, cinema, pubs
Opinions on cricket: 'Would like to see four-day games through the week, one day off, then one-day games on Saturday and Sunday. Sunday League games should be hyped up (e.g. coloured clothing, advertising) to bring new spectators into cricket.'
Best batting performance: 32* Nottinghamshire v Cambridge University, Cambridge 1989
Best bowling performance: 2-25 Nottinghamshire v Cambridge University, Cambridge 1989

LAST SEASON: BATTING

	I.	N.O.	R.	H.S.	AV.
TEST					
1ST-CLASS	2	1	36	32*	36.00
INT					
RAL					
NAT.W.					
B & H					

CAREER: BATTING

	I.	N.O.	R.	H.S.	AV.
TEST					
1ST-CLASS	2	1	36	32*	36.00
INT					
RAL					
NAT.W.					
B & H					

LAST SEASON: BOWLING

	O.	M.	R.	W.	AV.
TEST					
1ST-CLASS	16	3	50	2	25.00
INT					
RAL					
NAT.W.					
B & H					

CAREER: BOWLING

	O.	M.	R.	W.	AV.
TEST					
1ST-CLASS	16	3	50	2	25.00
INT					
RAL					
NAT.W.					
B & H					

125. Who topped Essex's bowling averages last season?

SCOTT, C. W.　　Nottinghamshire

Full Name: Christopher Wilmot Scott
Role: Right-hand bat, wicket-keeper
Born: 23 January 1964, Lincoln
Height: 5′ 8″ **Weight:** 11st
Nickname: George, Ginge
County debut: 1981
County cap: 1988
1st-Class 50s scored: 4
Place in batting averages: 189th
av. 19.42 (1988 210th av. 16.95)
Parents: Kenneth and Kathleen
Wife and date of marriage:
Jacqueline, 18 March 1989
Family links with cricket: Father
and brothers play for Collingham CC
Education: Robert Pattinson
Comprehensive School, North
Hykeham, Lincoln
Qualifications: 4 O-levels, 2 CSEs,
coaching certificate
Jobs outside cricket: Farming; cricket coach
Off-season 1989–90: Coaching in Rotorua, New Zealand
Cricketing superstitions or habits: 'I never say anything to the outgoing batsman as I walk in to bat.'
Overseas teams played for: Poverty Bay CC, New Zealand 1983–84; Queensland University, Australia 1985–86, 1987–88
Cricketers particularly learnt from: Bruce French, Pasty Harris, Bob White

LAST SEASON: BATTING

	I.	N.O.	R.	H.S.	AV.
TEST					
1ST-CLASS	10	3	136	51	19.42
INT					
RAL	2	1	11	11*	11.00
NAT.W.					
B & H	–	–	–	–	–

CAREER: BATTING

	I.	N.O.	R.	H.S.	AV.
TEST					
1ST-CLASS	69	16	1152	78	21.73
INT					
RAL	10	4	94	26	15.66
NAT.W.	–	–	–	–	–
B & H	3	1	28	18	14.00

LAST SEASON: WICKET KEEPING

	C.	ST.		
TEST				
1ST-CLASS	15	2		
INT				
RAL	2	–		
NAT.W.				
B & H	–	–		

CAREER: WICKET KEEPING

	C.	ST.		
TEST				
1ST-CLASS	131	9		
INT				
RAL	22	1		
NAT.W.	4	–		
B & H	1	–		

Cricketers particularly admired: Ian Botham above all, Clive Rice, but many others
Other sports played: Rugby union
Other sports followed: Soccer
Injuries 1989: Sprained ankle, and missed first game of the season
Relaxations: Watching films, eating out
Extras: One of the youngest players to play for Nottinghamshire in County Championship team – made debut at 17 years 157 days. Ten catches against Derbyshire, May 1988, broke Nottinghamshire record for catches in a match
Opinions on cricket: 'I find four-day cricket very long and boring especially having to bowl 110 overs a day. I would like the three-day game to stay.'
Best batting performance: 78 Nottinghamshire v Cambridge University, Cambridge 1983

SCOTT, R. J. Hampshire

Full Name: Richard James Scott
Role: Left-hand bat, right-arm medium pace bowler
Born: 2 November 1963, Bournemouth
Height: 5′ 11″ **Weight:** 14st 'at the start of the season – but usually 16st after a season with Robin Smith!'
Nickname: Gazza, Scotty-Boy
County debut: 1986
1st-Class 50s scored: 4
1st-Class 100s scored: 1
One-Day 50s: 2
One-Day 100s: 1
Place in batting averages: 170th av. 21.00 (1988 136th av. 24.93)
1st-Class catches 1989: 7 (career 17)
Parents: Andrew and Ann
Marital status: Engaged
Family links with cricket: 'Dad played for Colehill. Two brothers also play for same side in Dorset League.'
Education: Queen Elizabeth School, Wimborne
Qualifications: 2 O-levels, CSEs, coaching award
Jobs outside cricket: Worked for father's building firm before turning professional
Off-season 1989–90: Playing for South Perth CC

Cricketing superstitions or habits: 'Always put right pad on first. Never have a big night out before batting.'

Overseas tours: Bournemouth CC to California 1989

Overseas teams played for: Glenwood Old Boys, Durban 1984–85, 1985–86; Pirates CC, Durban 1987–88, 1988–89; South Perth CC 1989–90

Cricketers particularly learnt from: Chris and Robin Smith, and father

Cricketers particularly admired: Ian Botham, Malcolm Marshall

Other sports played: Golf (with a hefty slice), football, snooker

Other sports followed: Golf, football

Injuries 1989: Had appendix out in July – off for a month

Relaxations: 'Like to relax down any nice pub testing out local brews. Also like taking dog for walks deep in Dorset countryside.'

Extras: Played Minor Counties cricket for Dorset since 1981. Represented Minor Counties Cricket Association in 1985

Opinions on cricket: 'Four-day game a revelation. Best side will always win Championship.'

Best batting performance: 107* Hampshire v Sri Lankans, Southampton 1988

LAST SEASON: BATTING

	I.	N.O.	R.	H.S.	AV.
TEST					
1ST-CLASS	20	1	399	77	21.00
INT					
RAL	9	1	249	116*	31.12
NAT.W.	1	0	22	22	22.00
B & H	3	0	123	69	41.00

CAREER: BATTING

	I.	N.O.	R.	H.S.	AV.
TEST					
1ST-CLASS	36	2	773	107*	22.73
INT					
RAL	15	2	338	116*	26.00
NAT.W.	2	0	22	22	11.00
B & H	4	0	164	69	41.00

126. Who topped Glamorgan's bowling averages last season?

SCRIVEN, T. J. A.　　　　Somerset

Full Name: Timothy John Adam
Scriven
Role: Right-hand bat, slow left-arm
bowler
Born: 15 December 1965,
High Wycombe
Height: 6′ 3″ **Weight:** 14st
Nickname: Sammy, Spiv
County debut: 1988
Parents: John Richard and
Hilary Margaret
Marital status: Single
Family links with cricket: Father
played 2nd XI cricket for Hampshire
as well as Minor County cricket for
Buckinghamshire. Brother Jeremy
plays club cricket
Education: RGS, High Wycombe
Qualifications: 6 O-levels; qualified
cricket coach
Jobs outside cricket: Insurance clerk, groundsman at a sports centre
Cricketing superstitions or habits: Left pad on first
Overseas teams played for: Marist CC, New Plymouth, New Zealand 1986–
87; Marist CC and Taranaki 1987–88
Cricketers particularly learnt from: Father, Richard Williams, Peter Robinson
Cricketers particularly admired: Wayne Larkins, Steve Waugh, Barry
Richards, Phil Edmonds, Steven Boock

LAST SEASON: BATTING

	I.	N.O.	R.	H.S.	AV.
TEST					
1ST-CLASS	–	–	–	–	–
INT					
RAL					
NAT.W.					
B & H					

LAST SEASON: BOWLING

	O.	M.	R.	W.	AV.
TEST					
1ST-CLASS	43.1	8	155	4	38.75
INT					
RAL					
NAT.W.					
B & H					

CAREER: BATTING

	I.	N.O.	R.	H.S.	AV.
TEST					
1ST-CLASS	2	0	11	7	5.50
INT					
RAL					
NAT.W.	1	0	2	2	2.00
B & H					

CAREER: BOWLING

	O.	M.	R.	W.	AV.
TEST					
1ST-CLASS	139.1	33	392	7	56.00
INT					
RAL					
NAT.W.	12	0	27	0	–
B & H					

448

Other sports played: Golf, football, hockey
Other sports followed: Likes to watch and follow most sports
Relaxations: Watching films, music, going for a drink
Extras: On the Northamptonshire staff 1985–87. Released by Somerset at end of 1989 season
Opinions on cricket: '16 four-day games should be played in the County Championship. Spinners should be given every encouragement by the counties, with slow bowling clinics being organised, etc.'
Best batting performance: 7 Somerset v Derbyshire, Weston-super-Mare 1988
Best bowling performance: 2-67 Somerset v Lancashire, Taunton 1989

SHAHID, N.   Essex

Full Name: Nadeem Shahid
Role: Right-hand bat, right-arm leg spin googly bowler, all-rounder
Born: 23 April 1969, Karachi
Height: 5′ 11½″ **Weight:** 11st 6lbs
Nickname: Prince, Nad, Nasser
County debut: 1989
1st-Class 50s scored: 1
Place in batting averages: 55th av. 36.42
1st-Class catches 1989: 6 (career 6)
Parents: Ahmed and Salma
Marital status: Single
Family links with cricket: Brother plays in the local league
Education: Stoke & Northgate High; Ipswich School
Qualifications: 6 O-levels, 1 A-level
Off-season 1989–90: Playing for

Gosnells CC in Perth, Western Australia
Cricketing superstitions or habits: 'Having my collars up when batting. When bowling, I always have my right collar up, and left collar down.'
Overseas tours: Ipswich School to Barbados 1987
Overseas teams played for: Gosnells CC, Perth, Western Australia 1989–90
Cricketers particularly learnt from: Keith Fletcher, Ray East, Bob Cunnell
Cricketers particularly admired: Abdul Qadir, Ian Botham
Other sports played: Golf, badminton, tennis, table tennis, snooker
Other sports followed: Tennis, rugby, American football

Injuries 1989: Split nail on second finger in right hand – off for one week in May. Broken nose – off for one week after operation

Relaxations: 'I enjoy listening to music (mainly pop and soul), watching TV comedies, and a few soaps, and cricket videos. And staying in bed for as long as possible – on my off days!'

Extras: Youngest player to play for Suffolk at the age of 17. 'Learnt most of my cricket at Copdock CC.' Played for HMC, MCC Schools, ESCA U-19, NCA Young Cricketers (Lord's and International Youth tournament in Belfast), and at every level for Suffolk. Won various awards including National Young TSB Player of the Year 1986, twice winner of *Daily Telegraph* bowling award 1987, 1988, and Cricket Societies Wetherell Award 1988 etc.

Opinions on cricket: 'Would like to see higher wages for young players coming new onto the staff. The 25 points deduction rule should be changed – as the preparation of the pitches has nothing to do with the players themselves so why should they suffer. Perhaps a fining system should be introduced.'

Best batting performance: 52 Essex v Surrey, Chelmsford 1989
Best bowling performance: 2-40 Essex v Leicestershire, Chelmsford 1989

LAST SEASON: BATTING

	I.	N.O.	R.	H.S.	AV.
TEST					
1ST-CLASS	9	2	255	52	36.42
INT					
RAL	1	0	11	11	11.00
NAT.W.					
B & H					

LAST SEASON: BOWLING

	O.	M.	R.	W.	AV.
TEST					
1ST-CLASS	81.1	13	326	8	40.75
INT					
RAL					
NAT.W.					
B & H					

CAREER: BATTING

	I.	N.O.	R.	H.S.	AV.
TEST					
1ST-CLASS	9	2	255	52	36.42
INT					
RAL	1	0	11	11	11.00
NAT.W.					
B & H					

CAREER: BOWLING

	O.	M.	R.	W.	AV.
TEST					
1ST-CLASS	81.1	13	326	8	40.75
INT					
RAL					
NAT.W.					
B & H					

127. Who topped Gloucestershire's bowling averages last season?

SHARMA, R. Derbyshire

Full Name: Rajesh Sharma
Role: Right-hand bat, off-break
bowler, slip or short-leg fielder
Born: 27 June 1962, Kenya
Height: 6′ 3″ **Weight:** 13st
Nickname: Reg
County debut: 1985
1st-Class 50s scored: 9
1st-Class 100s scored: 1
1st-Class 5 w. in innings: 2
One-Day 50s: 1
Place in batting averages: 146th
av. 23.59 (1988 107th av. 28.63)
Place in bowling averages: 49th
av. 27.35
Strike rate 1989: 57.55 (career 85.69)
1st-Class catches 1989: 17 (career 61)
Parents: M. R. and R. D.
Marital status: Single
Family links with cricket: Younger brother has played 2nd XI cricket for Kent
Education: Parkland School for Boys
Qualifications: CSEs and O-levels
Jobs outside cricket: Family business (retail trade)
Overseas teams played for: Mudgreeba, Queensland 1982–83; Helensvale,
Queensland 1983–84
Cricketers particularly learnt from: Ron Harland (played for Bexley CC)
Cricketers particularly admired: Viv Richards
Other sports played: Snooker and golf

LAST SEASON: BATTING

	I.	N.O.	R.	H.S.	AV.
TEST					
1ST-CLASS	37	5	755	77	23.59
INT					
RAL	12	0	100	28	8.33
NAT.W.	2	0	60	50	30.00
B & H	2	0	5	5	2.50

CAREER: BATTING

	I.	N.O.	R.	H.S.	AV.
TEST					
1ST-CLASS	107	20	2196	111	25.24
INT					
RAL	35	6	403	37	13.89
NAT.W.	7	0	110	50	15.71
B & H	3	0	7	5	2.33

LAST SEASON: BOWLING

	O.	M.	R.	W.	AV.
TEST					
1ST-CLASS	191.5	50	547	20	27.35
INT					
RAL	46	5	201	12	16.75
NAT.W.	0.4	0	0	1	–
B & H	6.2	0	27	0	–

CAREER: BOWLING

	O.	M.	R.	W.	AV.
TEST					
1ST-CLASS	757	178	2187	53	41.26
INT					
RAL	126	13	611	21	29.09
NAT.W.	46.4	7	146	6	24.33
B & H	6.2	0	27	0	–

Other sports followed: Football and snooker
Relaxations: 'Spending lots of time with my dogs, Simba, Sable and Bruno.'
Opinions on cricket: 'I believe that overseas players have improved the standard of county cricket and their experience has helped younger players. However, I fail to understand the fairness of one county being allowed to have more overseas players than others. When each county is allowed an equal number of overseas players the standards will improve even more.'
Best batting performance: 111 Derbyshire v Yorkshire, Chesterfield 1987
Best bowling performance: 6-80 Derbyshire v Gloucestershire, Bristol 1987

SHARP, K. Yorkshire

Full Name: Kevin Sharp
Role: Left-hand bat, off-break bowler
Born: 6 April 1959, Leeds
Height: 5' 10" **Weight:** 12st 9lbs
Nickname: Lambsy, Poodle
County debut: 1976
County cap: 1982
Benefit: 1991
1000 runs in a season: 1
1st-Class 50s scored: 46
1st-Class 100s scored: 14
One-Day 50s: 26
One-Day 100s: 3
Place in batting averages: 75th av. 34.13 (1988 162nd av. 22.52)
1st-Class catches 1989: 9 (career 106)
Parents: Gordon and Joyce
Wife and date of marriage: Karen, 1 October 1983
Children: Amy Lauren, 28 December 1985
Family links with cricket: Father played with Woodhouse in Leeds League for many years. Young brother David now playing local cricket
Education: Abbey Grange C of E High School, Leeds
Qualifications: CSE Grade I Religious Education. Coaching award
Jobs outside cricket: Plasterer's labourer, warehouseman, driver for film company; working for Credit Collections UK Ltd
Off-season 1989–90: Working in commercial debt collection
Overseas tours: Derrick Robins' XI to Australasia 1980; Yorkshire to West Indies 1986–87

Overseas teams played for: Subiaco Floreat CC, Perth, Australia; De Beers CC, Griqualand West 1981–84
Cricketers particularly learnt from: Doug Padgett, Geoff Boycott, Phil Carrick
Cricketers particularly admired: Richard Hadlee, Malcolm Marshall
Other sports played: Golf, squash
Other sports followed: Snooker, soccer
Injuries 1989: Burst eardrum – off for one week in June. Fractured thumb – off for two weeks in August–September
Relaxations: Decorating and maintaining the house
Extras: 260* v Young West Indies 1977. Rested during latter part of 1980 season on medical advice. Captain of England U-19 v West Indies U-19 1978 at Worcester. Winston Churchill Travelling Fellowship to Australia for two months, 1978. 'I took the first wicket of my career in 1984 – a feat I never thought possible.'
Opinions on cricket: 'Would like to see more Englishmen playing for England. Why should English players be made scapegoats when South Africans are left well alone?'
Best batting performance: 181 Yorkshire v Gloucestershire, Harrogate 1986
Best bowling performance: 2-13 Yorkshire v Glamorgan, Bradford 1984

LAST SEASON: BATTING

	I.	N.O.	R.	H.S.	AV.
TEST					
1ST-CLASS	19	4	512	78	34.13
INT					
RAL	8	0	256	80	32.00
NAT.W.	1	0	15	15	15.00
B & H	1	0	5	5	5.00

CAREER: BATTING

	I.	N.O.	R.	H.S.	AV.
TEST					
1ST-CLASS	348	33	9644	181	30.61
INT					
RAL	126	11	3108	114	27.02
NAT.W.	13	2	228	50	20.72
B & H	39	3	1073	105*	29.80

LAST SEASON: BOWLING

	O.	M.	R.	W.	AV.
TEST					
1ST-CLASS	14	0	85	0	–
INT					
RAL					
NAT.W.					
B & H					

CAREER: BOWLING

	O.	M.	R.	W.	AV.
TEST					
1ST-CLASS	210.2	43	887	12	73.91
INT					
RAL	0.1	0	1	0	–
NAT.W.	10	0	47	4	11.75
B & H					

SHASTRI, R.   Glamorgan

Full Name: Ravishankar Shastri
Role: Right-hand bat, slow
left-arm bowler, close fielder
Born: 27 May 1962, Bombay
Height: 6′ 3½″ **Weight:** 13st 1lb
Nickname: Shas
County debut: 1987
County cap: 1988
Test debut: 1980–81
No. of Tests: 65
No. of One-Day Internationals: 110
1000 runs in a season: 1
1st-Class 50s scored: 47
1st-Class 100s scored: 18
1st-Class 200s scored: 1
1st-Class 5 w. in innings: 14
1st-Class 10 w. in match: 3
One-Day 50s: 25
One-Day 100s: 2
Place in batting averages: — (1988 66th av. 33.82)
Place in bowling averages: — (1988 113th av. 33.45)
1st-Class catches 1989: 14 (career 103)
Parents: Jayadritha and Lakshmi
Marital status: Single
Qualifications: Bachelor of Commerce, Bombay University
Jobs outside cricket: Public relations executive
Off-season 1989–90: Playing in India
Cricketing superstitions or habits: Left pad and left boot on first
Overseas tours: Young India to Sri Lanka 1980 and England 1981; India to England 1982, 1983, 1986; to West Indies 1983, 1988–89; to New Zealand 1981; to Australia 1985–86; to Pakistan 1982–83, 1984–85; to Sri Lanka 1985; to Zimbabwe 1984
Overseas teams played for: Bombay 1979–89
Cricketers particularly learnt from: Chandu Borde, Sunil Gavaskar, Gary Sobers
Cricketers particularly admired: Imran Khan, Viv Richards, Richard Hadlee, Gundappa Vishwanath, Gary Sobers, Gordon Greenidge
Other sports played: Swimming, tennis, chess
Other sports followed: Tennis, athletics
Relaxations: Watching sports, films, listening to music
Extras: Has batted at every number for India except No. 11. Hit six sixes in an over off Tank Raj for Bombay v Baroda at Bombay 1984–85 on the way to

highest first-class score of 200*. Played in MCC Bicentenary Test. Fined £1450 by Indian Cricket Board for playing in North America after West Indian tour in 1989

Opinions on cricket: 'We must have neutral umpires.'
Best batting performance: 200* Bombay v Baroda, Bombay 1984–85
Best bowling performance: 9-101 Bombay v Rest of India, Indore 1981–82

LAST SEASON: BATTING

	I.	N.O.	R.	H.S.	AV.
TEST					
1ST-CLASS	27	5	1004	127	45.63
INT					
RAL	10	0	311	92	31.10
NAT.W.	2	0	17	13	8.50
B & H	2	0	34	25	17.00

CAREER: BATTING

	I.	N.O.	R.	H.S.	AV.
TEST	97	13	2872	142	34.19
1ST-CLASS	162	28	5852	200*	43.67
INT	89	16	2235	102	30.61
RAL	36	7	1073	92	37.00
NAT.W.	7	2	157	59*	31.40
B & H	11	2	201	55	22.33

LAST SEASON: BOWLING

	O.	M.	R.	W.	AV.
TEST					
1ST-CLASS	282.2	66	780	11	70.90
INT					
RAL	55	2	251	7	35.85
NAT.W.	24	5	56	3	18.66
B & H	22	0	82	0	–

CAREER: BOWLING

	O.	M.	R.	W.	AV.
TEST	2370.4	623	5387	139	38.75
1ST-CLASS	3521.5	910	8227	273	30.13
INT	865.2	48	3602	103	34.97
RAL	206	7	911	24	37.95
NAT.W.	58.1	8	164	12	13.66
B & H	116	8	414	4	103.50

SHINE, K. J.   Hampshire

Full Name: Kevin James Shine
Role: Right-hand bat, right-arm medium bowler
Born: 22 February 1969, Bracknell, Berkshire
County debut: 1989
Extras: Plays club cricket for Reading. Hampshire 2nd XI debut in 1986
Best batting performance: 26* Hampshire v Middlesex, Lords 1989
Best bowling performance: 1-6 Hampshire v Middlesex, Lords 1989

LAST SEASON: BATTING

	I.	N.O.	R.	H.S.	AV.
TEST					
1ST-CLASS	2	1	29	26*	29.00
INT					
RAL					
NAT.W.					
B & H					

CAREER: BATTING

	I.	N.O.	R.	H.S.	AV.
TEST					
1ST-CLASS	2	1	29	26*	29.00
INT					
RAL					
NAT.W.					
B & H					

LAST SEASON: BOWLING

	O.	M.	R.	W.	AV.
TEST					
1ST-CLASS	32.2	8	88	3	29.33
INT					
RAL					
NAT.W.					
B & H					

CAREER: BOWLING

	O.	M.	R.	W.	AV.
TEST					
1ST-CLASS	32.2	8	88	3	29.33
INT					
RAL					
NAT.W.					
B & H					

SIDEBOTTOM, A.   Yorkshire

Full Name: Arnold Sidebottom
Role: Right-hand bat, right-arm
fast-medium bowler, outfielder
Born: 1 April 1954, Barnsley
Height: 6′ 2″ **Weight:** 13st 10lbs
Nickname: Woofer, Red Setter,
Arnie
County debut: 1973
County cap: 1980
Benefit: 1988: £103,240
Test debut: 1985
No. of Tests: 1
50 wickets in a season: 4
1st-Class 50s scored: 13
1st-Class 100s scored: 1
1st-Class 5 w. in innings: 23
1st-Class 10 w. in match: 3
One-Day 50s: 1
Place in batting averages: 199th
av. 18.10 (1988 116th av. 27.21)
Place in bowling averages: 32nd av. 23.38 (1988 16th av. 20.68)
Strike rate 1989: 50.82 (career 51.19)
1st-Class catches 1989: 10 (career 61)
Parents: Jack and Florence
Wife and date of marriage: Gillian, 17 June 1977
Children: Ryan Jay, 1978; Dale, 1980

Family links with cricket: Father good cricketer
Education: Barnsley Broadway Grammar School
Jobs outside cricket: Professional footballer with Manchester United for five years, Huddersfield Town for two years and Halifax Town
Overseas teams played for: Orange Free State 1981–84
Overseas tours: Rebel England team to South Africa 1982; Yorkshire to West Indies 1986–87
Cricketers particularly learnt from: Father, Doug Padgett, Geoff Boycott
Cricketers particularly admired: Steve Oldham, David Bairstow, Graham Stevenson
Other sports played: Professional football, tennis, table tennis, badminton
Other sports followed: Most sports
Relaxations: Watching television, horse racing, playing with sons
Extras: Banned from Test cricket for three years for joining rebel team to South Africa in 1982. Injured toe during Test debut in 1985 and not picked for England again. Yorkshire Player of the Year 1989
Best batting performance: 124 Yorkshire v Glamorgan, Cardiff 1977
Best bowling performance: 8-72 Yorkshire v Leicestershire, Middlesbrough 1986

LAST SEASON: BATTING

	I.	N.O.	R.	H.S.	AV.
TEST					
1ST-CLASS	24	5	344	45*	18.10
INT					
RAL	7	5	47	20	23.50
NAT.W.	2	0	8	8	4.00
B & H					

LAST SEASON: BOWLING

	O.	M.	R.	W.	AV.
TEST					
1ST-CLASS	576	129	1590	68	23.38
INT					
RAL	81.3	8	317	10	31.70
NAT.W.	24	6	66	1	66.00
B & H					

CAREER: BATTING

	I.	N.O.	R.	H.S.	AV.
TEST	1	0	2	2	2.00
1ST-CLASS	257	61	4384	124	22.36
INT					
RAL	78	29	797	52*	16.26
NAT.W.	15	5	191	45	19.10
B & H	25	8	235	32	13.82

CAREER: BOWLING

	O.	M.	R.	W.	AV.
TEST	18.4	3	65	1	65.00
1ST-CLASS	5020.2	1110	14277	590	24.19
INT					
RAL	982.4	48	4216	140	30.11
NAT.W.	222.2	33	624	35	17.82
B & H	425.4	68	1372	65	21.10

SIMMONS, J.   Lancashire

Full Name: Jack Simmons
Role: Right-hand bat, off-break bowler, slip fielder
Born: 28 March 1941, Clayton-le-Moors, nr Accrington
Height: 6' 1" **Weight:** 15st 7lbs
Nickname: Simmo, Flat Jack
County debut: 1968
County cap: 1971
Benefit: 1980 (£128,000)
50 wickets in a season: 9
1st-Class 50s scored: 41
1st-Class 100s scored: 6
1st-Class 5 w. in innings: 41
1st-Class 10 w. in match: 6
One-Day 50s: 6
Place in batting averages: —
(1988 191st av. 20.11)
Place in bowling averages: —
(1988 46th av. 24.57)
1st-Class catches 1989: 4 (career 341)
Parents: Robert and Ada
Wife and date of marriage: Jacqueline, 23 March 1963
Children: Kelly Louise, 28 January 1979
Family links with cricket: Father, Robert, played for Enfield in Lancashire League. Grandfather, Robert, also played for Enfield from 1887, giving 92 years' association with the same club
Education: Accrington Technical School; Blackburn Technical College
Qualifications: 5 O-levels, ONC, City & Guilds in Quantities
Jobs outside cricket: Draughtsman with Accrington Brick & Tile Co Ltd, and Lancashire County Surveyors' Department. Sports Agency (Jack Simmons Ltd). Travel company with Murray Birnie. Director of Bowlers Leisure Centre and Conference Centre, with six indoor cricket courts, eight bowling lanes, two 5-a-side pitches, 16 snooker tables, new hi-tech gym and four bars, in Trafford Park, Manchester
Off-season 1989–90: Working at Bowlers
Cricketing superstitions or habits: 'I always like to be last on the field. To do the same things again if successful once, i.e. clothes or eating habits.'
Overseas tours: Zimbabwe and South Africa with Whitbread Wanderers 1975; Mike Brearley Invitation XI to Calcutta 1981; New York 1985 with C. Lloyd Lancashire XI; MCC to Bermuda 1987; Lancashire to West Indies 1987–88; Lancashire to Zimbabwe 1988–89

Overseas teams played for: Tasmania 1972–79 (where he is 'a bit of a folk hero'). Captained Tasmania to Gillette Cup for first time in 1979, and when they first entered Sheffield Shield (1978)

Cricketers particularly learnt from: 'Coached by Clyde Walcott when I was a youngster. Learnt from Clive Lloyd with Lancashire. Jack Bond, Ray Illingworth, plus many more off-spinners.'

Cricketers particularly admired: 'Clive Lloyd (great team man), Viv Richards, Chappell brothers, and great bowlers, Dennis Lillee and Michael Holding.'

Other sports played: Golf, indoor cricket

Other sports followed: Football, horse racing

Relaxations: Soccer, golf, horse racing, eating, playing cards, watching television and going on holiday

Extras: 'I didn't play for a couple of years because I broke my leg three times in ten months and the previous year broke my arm quite badly, all playing soccer – except one broken leg, which was broken going down to the football ground just after I had it out of plaster for the first time.' Made debut for 2nd XI in 1959. Hat-trick v Nottinghamshire, Liverpool 1977. Director of Burnley FC. Published autobiography *Flat Jack* in 1986. One of *Wisden*'s Five Cricketers of the Year, 1984. Reached 1000 first-class wickets in career in 1988. Retired at end of 1989 season

Opinions on cricket: 'Cricket fines can become a farce, with players thinking of fines when they should be concentrating on cricket. If four-day cricket comes in throughout the season, there are, on average, too many result pitches, especially for quick bowlers. I would like to see the lbw law changed to encourage leg-spinners.'

Best batting performance: 112 Lancashire v Sussex, Hove 1970

Best bowling performance: 7-59 Tasmania v Queensland, Brisbane 1978–79

LAST SEASON: BATTING

	I.	N.O.	R.	H.S.	AV.
TEST					
1ST-CLASS	9	5	56	16	14.00
INT					
RAL	1	1	1	1*	–
NAT.W.	2	2	2	2*	–
B & H	1	1	7	7*	–

LAST SEASON: BOWLING

	O.	M.	R.	W.	AV.
TEST					
1ST-CLASS	100	17	309	3	103.00
INT					
RAL	85	2	398	17	23.41
NAT.W.	30	8	68	2	34.00
B & H	53	9	161	3	53.66

CAREER: BATTING

	I.	N.O.	R.	H.S.	AV.
TEST					
1ST-CLASS	564	146	9417	112	22.52
INT					
RAL	179	57	1925	65	15.77
NAT.W.	38	16	462	54*	21.00
B & H	53	22	672	64	21.67

CAREER: BOWLING

	O.	M.	R.	W.	AV.
TEST					
1ST-CLASS	446.2 10535.4	94 2473	28084	1033	27.18
INT					
RAL	1918.2	138	8102	307	26.39
NAT.W.	618.5	114	1795	78	23.01
B & H	731.2	143	2144	78	27.48

SMALL, G. C.   Warwickshire

Full Name: Gladstone Cleophas Small
Role: Right-hand bat, right-arm fast-medium bowler
Born: 18 October 1961, St George, Barbados
Height: 5' 11" **Weight:** 12st
Nickname: Gladys
County debut: 1980
County cap: 1982
Test debut: 1986
No. of Tests: 6
No. of One-Day Internationals: 25
50 wickets in a season: 6
1st-Class 50s scored: 5
1st-Class 5 w. in innings: 25
1st-Class 10 w. in match: 2
Place in batting averages: 224th av. 14.55 (1988 134th av. 25.18)
Place in bowling averages: 34th av. 25.45 (1988 13th av. 20.06)
Strike rate 1989: 58.58 (career 54.54)
1st-Class catches 1989: 4 (career 57)
Parents: Chelston and Gladys
Marital status: Married
Family links with cricket: Cousin, Milton Small, toured England with West Indies in 1984
Education: Mosely School; Hall Green Technical College, Birmingham
Qualifications: 2 O-levels
Off-season 1989–90: Touring with England in India and West Indies
Overseas tours: With Young England to New Zealand 1979–80; Derrick Robins' XI tour of Australia, Tasmania and New Zealand 1980; Rohan Kanhai International XI tour of Pakistan 1981; England to Australia 1986–87; World Cup 1987; England to Pakistan, Australia and New Zealand 1987–88; England to India and West Indies 1989–90
Overseas teams played for: Balwyn CC, Melbourne 1982–83, 1984–85; South Australia and West Torrens, Adelaide 1985–86
Cricketers particularly learnt from: David Brown (manager at Warwickshire)
Cricketers particularly admired: Dennis Lillee, Malcolm Marshall, Richard Hadlee, Bob Willis
Other sports played: Golf, tennis
Other sports followed: Athletics, golf, tennis, soccer

Relaxations: 'Playing a round of golf really relaxes me; listening to music and relaxing with my wife.'

Extras: In 1980, became youngest bowler to take five JPL wickets in one innings. Was called up for England Test squad v Pakistan at Edgbaston, July 1982, but did not play. Bowled 18-ball over v Middlesex in August 1982, with 11 no balls

Opinions on cricket: 'The introduction of four-day Championship cricket will improve the first-class game in that teams would have to bowl out the opposition twice instead of relying on contrived results. For four-day cricket to be successful, clubs must be made to produce good, hard cricketing wickets that would be beneficial to both batsmen and bowlers.'

Best batting performance: 70 Warwickshire v Lancashire, Old Trafford 1988

Best bowling performance: 7-15 Warwickshire v Nottinghamshire, Edgbaston 1988

LAST SEASON: BATTING

	I.	N.O.	R.	H.S.	AV.
TEST	1	0	59	59	59.00
1ST-CLASS	23	4	232	34	12.21
INT					
RAL	6	1	37	10	7.40
NAT.W.	2	1	19	15	19.00
B & H	3	1	19	11	9.50

CAREER: BATTING

	I.	N.O.	R.	H.S.	AV.
TEST	8	3	120	59	24.00
1ST-CLASS	256	58	2902	70	14.65
INT	10	5	33	8*	6.60
RAL	56	18	295	40*	7.76
NAT.W.	14	6	135	33	16.87
B & H	22	6	98	19*	6.12

LAST SEASON: BOWLING

	O.	M.	R.	W.	AV.
TEST	60	12	198	4	49.50
1ST-CLASS	477	122	1202	51	23.56
INT					
RAL	97	5	428	12	35.66
NAT.W.	52	8	134	5	26.80
B & H	43	10	156	7	22.28

CAREER: BOWLING

	O.	M.	R.	W.	AV.
TEST	240.3	61	652	24	27.16
1ST-CLASS	5223	1101	15887	577	27.53
INT	237	15	941	27	34.85
RAL	784	52	3535	153	23.10
NAT.W.	240.1	43	771	28	27.53
B & H	327.2	57	1206	41	29.41

128. Who topped the Hampshire bowling averages last season?

SMITH, C. L. Hampshire

Full Name: Christopher Lyall Smith
Role: Right-hand bat, off-spin bowler
Born: 15 October 1958, Durban, South Africa
Height: 5′ 11″ **Weight:** 13st 10lbs
Nickname: Kippy
County debut: 1979 (Glamorgan), 1980 (Hampshire)
County cap: 1981 (Hampshire)
Benefit: 1990
Test debut: 1983
No. of Tests: 8
No. of One-Day Internationals: 4
1000 runs in a season: 8
1st-Class 50s scored: 69
1st-Class 100s scored: 36
1st-Class 200s scored: 1
1st-Class 5 w. in innings: 1
One-Day 50s: 32
One-Day 100s: 5
Place in batting averages: 32nd av. 42.41 (1988 53rd av. 35.90)
1st-Class catches 1989: 19 (career 157)
Parents: John Arnold and Elaine Jessie
Wife and date of marriage: Julie Owen, August 1989
Family links with cricket: Grandfather, Vernon Lyall Shearer, played for Natal; brother Robin also plays for Hampshire and England
Education: Northlands High School, Durban, South Africa
Qualifications: Matriculation (2 A-level equivalents)
Jobs outside cricket: 'Running Chris Smith Sports Entertainment which specialises in corporate entertaining. Also run a travel business and am involved with Car Phone Group's activities around Hampshire.'
Overseas tours: Toured UK with Kingsmead Mynahs (Natal U-25s under another name) 1976; with England to New Zealand and Pakistan 1983–84; England B to Sri Lanka 1986
Overseas teams played for: Kingsmead Mynahs; Natal Schools 1975; South African Schools 1976; Natal B (debut 1978)
Cricketers particularly admired: Barry Richards, Grayson Heath (coach in South Africa)
Other sports played: League squash, golf (15 handicap)
Other sports followed: Watches football (Southampton FC)
Relaxations: Walking in the countryside with my dog or lying on the beach, swimming, listening to music

462

Extras: Made debut for Glamorgan in 1979. Played for Gorseinon in South Wales League in 1979. Made Hampshire debut 1980. Captained Hampshire 2nd XI in 1981. Became eligible to play for England in 1983. One of *Wisden*'s Five Cricketers of the Year, 1983

Opinions on cricket: 'Still feel the game is undersold and that too few clubs employ successful, proven, get-up-and-go marketing managers. Welcome four-day cricket as it should help to produce more potential Test players.'

Best batting performance: 217 Hampshire v Warwickshire, Edgbaston 1987

Best bowling performance: 5-69 Hampshire v Sussex, Southampton 1988

LAST SEASON: BATTING

	I.	N.O.	R.	H.S.	AV.
TEST					
1ST-CLASS	33	4	1230	143*	42.41
INT					
RAL	11	3	155	45	19.37
NAT.W.	4	0	293	159	73.25
B & H	1	0	4	4	4.00

CAREER: BATTING

	I.	N.O.	R.	H.S.	AV.
TEST	14	1	392	91	30.15
1ST-CLASS	387	49	14197	217	42.00
INT	4	0	109	70	27.25
RAL	99	20	2933	95	37.12
NAT.W.	24	4	1049	159	52.45
B & H	26	4	651	82*	29.59

LAST SEASON: BOWLING

	O.	M.	R.	W.	AV.
TEST					
1ST-CLASS	35	13	72	2	36.00
INT					
RAL					
NAT.W.					
B & H					

CAREER: BOWLING

	O.	M.	R.	W.	AV.
TEST	17	4	39	3	13.00
1ST-CLASS	678.5	130	2486	42	59.19
INT	6	0	28	2	14.00
RAL	3.3	1	10	2	5.00
NAT.W.	15	3	59	5	11.80
B & H					

129. Who topped the Kent bowling averages last season?

130. Who topped the Lancashire bowling averages last season?

SMITH, D. M.   Sussex

Full Name: David Mark Smith
Role: Left-hand bat, right-arm
fast-medium bowler
Born: 9 January 1956, Balham
Height: 6′ 4″ **Weight:** 15st
Nickname: Smudger, Tom
County debut: 1973 (Surrey),
1984 (Worcestershire),
1989 (Sussex)
County cap: 1980 (Surrey),
1984 (Worcestershire)
Test debut: 1985–86
No. of Tests: 2
No. of One-Day Internationals: 1
1000 runs in a season: 5
1st-Class 50s scored: 54
1st-Class 100s scored: 23
One-Day 50s: 29
One-Day 100s: 4
Place in batting averages: 22nd av. 45.00 (1988 18th av. 48.86)
1st-Class catches 1989: 13 (career 155)
Parents: Dennis Henry and Tina
Wife and date of marriage: Jacqui, 7 January 1977
Children: Sarah Jane Louise, 4 April 1982
Family links with cricket: Father plays cricket for the BBC
Education: Battersea Grammar School
Qualifications: 3 O-levels
Jobs outside cricket: Two years with insurance company, one year with Harrods, one year spent in Zimbabwe, two years with building firm. Contracts manager, painting and decorating firm
Cricketing superstitions or habits: 'No room for them all.'
Overseas tours: West Indies with England 1986
Overseas teams played for: Sydney University, Australia 1980–81, 1982–83
Cricketers particularly learnt from: Mickey Stewart, Graham Roope
Cricketers particularly admired: Graham Gooch, Malcolm Marshall, Ian Botham
Other sports played: Football, motor racing
Relaxations: 'I own my own racing car.'
Extras: Played for Surrey 2nd XI in 1972. Was not retained after 1977 but was re-instated in 1978. Top of Surrey first-class batting averages in 1982. Sacked by Surrey during 1983 season. Joined Worcestershire in 1984. Rejoined

Surrey in 1987. Released by Surrey at end of 1988 season. Joined Sussex for 1989

Best batting performance: 189* Worcestershire v Kent, Worcester 1984
Best bowling performance: 3-40 Surrey v Sussex, The Oval 1976

LAST SEASON: BATTING

	I.	N.O.	R.	H.S.	AV.
TEST					
1ST-CLASS	35	6	1305	184	45.00
INT					
RAL	11	1	296	56	29.60
NAT.W.	3	1	175	99*	87.50
B & H	4	0	55	41	13.75

LAST SEASON: BOWLING

	O.	M.	R.	W.	AV.
TEST					
1ST-CLASS	4.1	0	21	0	–
INT					
RAL					
NAT.W.					
B & H					

CAREER: BATTING

	I.	N.O.	R.	H.S.	AV.
TEST	4	0	80	47	20.00
1ST-CLASS	388	77	11390	189*	36.62
INT	1	1	10	10*	–
RAL	135	27	3004	87*	27.81
NAT.W.	30	6	1202	109	50.08
B & H	54	9	1605	126	35.66

CAREER: BOWLING

	O.	M.	R.	W.	AV.
TEST					
1ST-CLASS	460.1	96	1541	30	51.36
INT					
RAL	124.5	6	606	12	50.50
NAT.W.	31	6	118	4	29.50
B & H	56	4	266	8	33.25

SMITH, G.   Warwickshire

Full Name: Gareth Smith
Role: Right-hand bat, left-arm fast-medium bowler, cover fielder
Born: 20 July 1966, Jarrow, County Durham
Height: 6′ 1″ **Weight:** 12st
Nickname: Smudger, Headless ('thanks lads!')
County debut: 1986
1st-Class 5 w. in innings: 1
1st-Class catches 1989: 0 (career 2)
Parents: John and Patricia
Marital status: Engaged
Family links with cricket: Father on selection committee at Boldon CC
Education: Boldon Comprehensive School; South Tyneside College
Qualifications: 6 O-levels, B.Tec ONC/OND in Computer Studies
Jobs outside cricket: Worked in sports shop in Newcastle (1985–86); worked for Mailforce Ltd as a computer operator/computer programmer

Off-season 1989–90: Working for Mailforce Ltd as a computer operator/computer programmer

Cricketing superstitions or habits: 'If any – putting on left pad or left boot first; wear sweatband around right forearm.'

Overseas teams played for: Belgrano CC, Argentina 1986–87, Uitenhage CC, South Africa 1987–88

Cricketers particularly learnt from: Bob Carter (Northamptonshire CCC), David Capel ('for his wholehearted, 100%, aggression on the pitch'), George Latham (Boldon CC), Keith Judd (Boldon CC), Dennis Lillee, Wayne Larkins, Geoff Cook

Other sports played: Golf (socially), football

Other sports followed: Golf, football (Sunderland FC)

Relaxations: 'Music (any type – mainly Kate Bush or Bon Jovi), reading, going to the theatre, walking. Watching Rik Mayall (of "Young Ones" fame). Having a pint.'

Extras: Took wicket with only second ball in first-class cricket – of S. M. Gavaskar. Took part in round the country relay to raise money for leukemia research. 'Would like to thank most sincerely Bob Carter for everything he did for me at Northamptonshire CC over the last 4–5 years. Sincerely hope that Durham become a first-class county.'

Best batting performance: 29* Northamptonshire v Lancashire, Old Trafford 1987

Best bowling performance: 6-72 Northamptonshire v Sussex, Hove 1987

LAST SEASON: BATTING

	I.	N.O.	R.	H.S.	AV.
TEST					
1ST-CLASS	3	1	6	6	3.00
INT					
RAL	–	–	–	–	–
NAT.W.					
B & H				·	

CAREER: BATTING

	I.	N.O.	R.	H.S.	AV.
TEST					
1ST-CLASS	10	2	60	29*	7.50
INT					
RAL	–	–	–	–	–
NAT.W.					
B & H					

LAST SEASON: BOWLING

	O.	M.	R.	W.	AV.
TEST					
1ST-CLASS	31	5	112	2	56.00
INT					
RAL	7	0	63	0	–
NAT.W.					
B & H					

CAREER: BOWLING

	O.	M.	R.	W.	AV.
TEST					
1ST-CLASS	152	23	552	17	32.47
INT					
RAL	11	0	80	0	–
NAT.W.					
B & H					

SMITH, I.   Glamorgan

Full Name: Ian Smith
Role: Right-hand bat, right-arm
medium bowler, slip fielder
Born: 11 March 1967, Consett,
County Durham
Height: 6′ 3″ **Weight:** 14½st
Nickname: Smudga
County debut: 1985
1st-Class 50s scored: 3
1st-Class 100s scored: 2
One-Day 50s: 1
Place in batting averages: 81st
av. 32.75
Place in bowling averages: 106th
av. 41.96
Strike rate 1989: 59.38 (career 68.61)
1st-Class catches 1989: 8 (career 16)
Parents: Jim and Mary
Marital status: Single
Family links with cricket: Father NCA Coach
Education: Ryton Comprehensive
Qualifications: 4 O-levels, CSE
Off-season 1989–90: Coaching in New Zealand
Cricketing superstitions or habits: 'Never walk on the field third.'
Overseas tours: Young England to West Indies; Glamorgan to Barbados
Overseas teams played for: Papatoetoe, New Zealand 1986–87–88
Cricketers particularly learnt from: John Steele, John Hampshire, father
Cricketers particularly admired: Ian Botham

LAST SEASON: BATTING

	I.	N.O.	R.	H.S.	AV.
TEST					
1ST-CLASS	28	4	786	116	32.75
INT					
RAL	11	2	186	56*	20.66
NAT.W.	1	0	33	33	33.00
B & H	1	0	9	9	9.00

LAST SEASON: BOWLING

	O.	M.	R.	W.	AV.
TEST					
1ST-CLASS	257.2	28	1091	26	41.96
INT					
RAL	35	1	234	6	39.00
NAT.W.	8	0	25	0	–
B & H					

CAREER: BATTING

	I.	N.O.	R.	H.S.	AV.
TEST					
1ST-CLASS	58	9	1101	116	22.46
INT					
RAL	24	6	300	56*	16.66
NAT.W.	2	0	38	33	19.00
B & H	3	0	15	9	5.00

CAREER: BOWLING

	O.	M.	R.	W.	AV.
TEST					
1ST-CLASS	537.3	82	2113	47	44.95
INT					
RAL	94	4	498	14	35.57
NAT.W.	12	0	43	1	43.00
B & H	14	0	69	1	69.00

Other sports played: Football, golf
Other sports followed: All sports
Relaxations: 'Having the odd pint.'
Extras: Glamorgan Young Player of the Year 1989
Best batting performance: 116 Glamorgan v Kent, Canterbury 1989
Best bowling performance: 3-48 Glamorgan v Hampshire, Cardiff 1989

SMITH, N. M. K. Warwickshire

Full Name: Neil Michael Knight
Smith
Role: Right-hand bat, off-spin
bowler, slip fielder
Born: 27 July 1967, Solihull
Height: 6′ 1″ **Weight:** 12st 10lbs
Nickname: Gurt
County debut: 1987
1st-Class 100s scored: 1
1st-Class catches 1989: 2 (career 3)
Parents: Mike (M.J.K.) and Diana
Marital status: Single
Family links with cricket: Father
captained Warwickshire and England
Education: Warwick School
Qualifications: 3 O-levels (Maths,
English, French); cricket coach
Grade 1
Off-season 1989–90: 'In Perth for six
months, coaching and playing.'

LAST SEASON: BATTING

	I.	N.O.	R.	H.S.	AV.
TEST					
1ST-CLASS	11	2	248	161	27.55
INT					
RAL	7	2	48	14	9.60
NAT.W.	3	2	31	16*	31.00
B & H					

CAREER: BATTING

	I.	N.O.	R.	H.S.	AV.
TEST					
1ST-CLASS	16	3	307	161	23.61
INT					
RAL	11	2	75	22	8.33
NAT.W.	3	2	31	16*	31.00
B & H					

LAST SEASON: BOWLING

	O.	M.	R.	W.	AV.
TEST					
1ST-CLASS	130.4	27	427	11	38.81
INT					
RAL	66	2	334	6	55.66
NAT.W.	11	0	39	2	19.50
B & H					

CAREER: BOWLING

	O.	M.	R.	W.	AV.
TEST					
1ST-CLASS	177.4	35	599	15	39.93
INT					
RAL	77	2	398	7	56.85
NAT.W.	11	0	39	2	19.50
B & H					

Cricketing superstitions or habits: 'I always say see you in a minute when leaving the pavilion to go out to bat.'
Overseas tours: South America 1987; Barbados 1987–88
Cricketers particularly learnt from: Father
Cricketers particularly admired: David Gower, John Emburey
Other sports played: Rugby, squash, golf, tennis
Other sports followed: Any sport 'except horse racing'
Relaxations: Films, music, watching sport
Best batting performance: 161 Warwickshire v Yorkshire, Leeds 1989
Best bowling performance: 3-62 Warwickshire v Yorkshire, Leeds 1989

SMITH, P. A. Warwickshire

Full Name: Paul Andrew Smith
Role: Right-hand number 5 bat, right-arm fast-medium bowler, 'Dogsbody in the field.'
Born: 15 April 1964, Newcastle-on-Tyne
Height: 6′ 2″ **Weight:** 12st
Nickname: Smithy, Jim
County debut: 1982
County cap: 1986
1000 runs in a season: 2
1st-Class 50s scored: 39
1st-Class 100s scored: 3
1st-Class 5 w. in innings: 1
One-Day 50s: 8
Place in batting averages: 70th av. 34.63 (1988 152nd av. 23.56)
Place in bowling averages: 48th av. 27.21 (1988 39th av. 23.47)
Strike rate 1989: 49.57 (career 57.42)
1st-Class catches 1989: 6 (career 44)
Parents: Kenneth and Joy

Wife and date of marriage: Caroline, 31 July 1987
Children: Oliver James, 5 February 1988
Family links with cricket: Father played for Leicestershire and Northumberland. Both brothers played for Warwickshire
Education: Heaton Grammar School, Newcastle
Qualifications: 5 O-levels
Jobs outside cricket: Warehouseman 1985–86. Worked for *Birmingham Post and Mail* in winters

Cricketing superstitions or habits: 'I dislike watching whilst waiting to bat. Like to wear lucky kit if I'm having a good run.'

Overseas teams played for: Florida, Johannesburg 1982–83; Belgrano CC, Argentina 1983–84; Carlton, Melbourne 1984–85. 'I haven't spent a full winter away for five years. I feel that playing cricket 12 months of the year kills you mentally.'

Cricketers particularly learnt from: Father, Dennis Amiss, Bob Willis, 'and most, but not all, at Warwickshire'

Cricketers particularly admired: Ian Botham, David (Vic) Thorne, Wayne Larkins, Dennis Amiss, 'I admire most players who play professionally, as it's not easy.'

Other sports played: Occasional squash, 'and trying to learn golf'

Other sports followed: 'Not a great spectator but I suppose I enjoy watching Mike Tyson boxing.'

Injuries 1989: 'Top-edged C. Walsh into my nose, resulting in 21 stitches. A lot of my nose is now fibre-glass and plastic surgery. Told to rest till April 1990, but played 13 days later in NatWest semi-final against Worcestershire.'

Relaxations: Music, videos, records, tapes, etc. Likes reading autobiographies connected with music and cricket. American cars of the 1960s and 70s

Extras: Along with Andy Moles set a new world record for most consecutive 50+ partnerships in first 12 innings together. During 1987 and 1988 seasons had more new helmets than bats. In 1989, scored 140 v Worcestershire, during which scored 100 out of partnership of 123 with D. Reeve. In 1989, took a hat-trick against Northamptonshire. Writes a column for local newspaper

Opinions on cricket: 'I think four-day cricket is a really good idea, *but* wickets for those games must be good and not green fliers. Bensons is played too early in the season (– that is, the early rounds). I do not believe that averages always tell the truth. People must look deeper into where individuals bat, or when they were brought on to bowl.'

LAST SEASON: BATTING

	I.	N.O.	R.	H.S.	AV.
TEST					
1ST-CLASS	26	4	762	140	34.63
INT					
RAL	12	1	479	93*	43.54
NAT.W.	3	0	31	24	10.33
B & H	4	1	143	74	47.66

LAST SEASON: BOWLING

	O.	M.	R.	W.	AV.
TEST					
1ST-CLASS	272.4	37	898	33	27.21
INT					
RAL	65.1	1	335	5	67.00
NAT.W.	25	0	115	5	23.00
B & H	37.5	6	139	5	27.80

CAREER: BATTING

	I.	N.O.	R.	H.S.	AV.
TEST					
1ST-CLASS	239	28	6014	140	28.50
INT					
RAL	80	19	1558	93*	25.54
NAT.W.	17	2	301	79	20.06
B & H	25	4	442	74	21.04

CAREER: BOWLING

	O.	M.	R.	W.	AV.
TEST					
1ST-CLASS	1560	196	6326	163	38.80
INT					
RAL	367.3	10	1973	55	35.87
NAT.W.	107.4	6	432	17	25.41
B & H	110.2	10	481	15	32.06

Best batting performance: 140 Warwickshire v Worcestershire, Worcester 1989
Best bowling performance: 5-82 Warwickshire v Surrey, Edgbaston 1989

SMITH, R. A.   Hampshire

Full Name: Robin Arnold Smith
Role: Right-hand bat, wrist spinner, gully fielder
Born: 13 September 1963, Durban, South Africa
Height: 5′ 11¾″ **Weight:** 15st 3lbs
Nickname: The Judge
County debut: 1982
County cap: 1985
Test debut: 1988
No. of Tests: 8
No. of One-Day Internationals: 4
1000 runs in a season: 4
1st-Class 50s scored: 35
1st-Class 100s scored: 20
1st-Class 200s scored: 1
One-Day 50s: 17
One-Day 100s: 6
Place in batting averages: 4th
av. 58.40 (1988 24th av. 39.88)
1st-Class catches 1989: 11 (career 98)
Parents: John Arnold and Elaine Jessie
Wife and date of marriage: Katherine, 21 September 1988
Family links with cricket: Grandfather played for Natal in Currie Cup. Brother Chris plays for Hampshire, Natal and England
Education: Northlands Boys High, Durban
Qualifications: 'Highly qualified.'
Jobs outside cricket: Financial adviser
Off-season 1989–90: Touring with England in India and West Indies
Overseas tours: England to India and West Indies 1989–90
Overseas teams played for: Natal in South African Currie Cup season 1980–84; Perth, Western Australia
Cricketers particularly learnt from: Brother Chris, Barry Richards, Mike Procter
Cricketers particularly admired: Malcolm Marshall, Allan Border, Graeme Hick

Other sports played: Squash, golf, snow and water skiing. Plays full-back for Romsey RFC

Other sports followed: Soccer, athletics, most sports

Relaxations: 'Reading Jeffrey Archer novels, trout fishing, siestas, keeping fit and spending as much time as possible with my lovely wife.'

Extras: Played rugby for Natal Schools, 1980. South Africa Schools Cricket, 1979–80. Still holds nineteen school athletics records and two South African schools records in shot putt and 100 metre hurdles

Opinions on cricket: 'I think four-day cricket so far has been a great success. I think the standard of umpiring in England is of a very high quality in comparison to umpiring in other parts of the world.'

Best batting performance: 209* Hampshire v Essex, Southampton 1987

Best bowling performance: 2-11 Hampshire v Surrey, Southampton 1985

LAST SEASON: BATTING

	I.	N.O.	R.	H.S.	AV.
TEST	10	1	553	143	61.44
1ST-CLASS	19	1	1024	182	56.88
INT	3	0	59	35	19.66
RAL	9	1	226	131	28.25
NAT.W.	3	2	240	125*	240.00
B & H	4	2	292	155*	146.00

CAREER: BATTING

	I.	N.O.	R.	H.S.	AV.
TEST	16	2	698	143	49.85
1ST-CLASS	241	42	8212	209*	41.26
INT	4	0	68	35	17.00
RAL	63	10	1958	131	36.94
NAT.W.	14	3	656	125*	59.63
B & H	21	5	779	155*	48.68

LAST SEASON: BOWLING

	O.	M.	R.	W.	AV.
TEST					
1ST-CLASS	15	3	72	0	
INT					
RAL					
NAT.W.					
B & H					

CAREER: BOWLING

	O.	M.	R.	W.	AV.
TEST					
1ST-CLASS	115.2	18	515	9	57.22
INT					
RAL					
NAT.W.	2.5	0	13	2	6.50
B & H	1	0	2	0	–

131. Who topped the Leicestershire bowling averages last season?

132. Who topped the Middlesex bowling averages last season?

SOMAIA, K.   Glamorgan

Full Name: Kamal Somaia
Role: Right-hand bat, left-arm orthodox spin bowler, all-rounder
Born: 22 July 1968, London
Height: 6' 1" **Weight:** 11st
Nickname: Kamakaze
County debut: 1989
1st-Class 5 w. in innings: 1
1st-Class catches 1989: 1 (career 1)
Parents: Anil and Zacna
Marital status: Single
Family links with cricket: 'My father says he was a bit of a legend in the leagues in Tanzania. Played school cricket tanga.'
Education: 'Studied my primary/ secondary and university in Melbourne, Australia.'
Qualifications: Finished HSC in Australia and 2 years of accountancy
Jobs outside cricket: Salesman in fabrics and fashion garments
Off-season 1989–90: 'I play District cricket for a club called Ringwood in Melbourne, Australia.'
Cricketing superstitions or habits: 'Changes from each county and each ground.'
Overseas teams played for: CCI Cricket Club, Bombay, India 1987; Ringwood, Melbourne, Australia 1989–90
Cricketers particularly learnt from: 'Gary Sobers (coached by him from 12 years–15 years old). John Steele (helped me a lot in my first year with Glamorgan). Jack Berkinshaw.'
Cricketers particularly admired: Sunil Gavaskar, Gary Sobers, Ian Botham, Kiran More, Ravi Shastri, Allan Border
Other sports played: Tennis, table tennis
Other sports followed: Australian rules football
Injuries 1989: 'Strained the ligaments in my right ankle, August 1989 – out for four weeks.'
Relaxations: 'Love listening to music, going to nightclubs and socializing with mates. Also when in Melbourne, I enjoy spending time with my family who live there.'
Opinions on cricket: 'I feel there should be more four-day games or have one four-day game a week and one Sunday league game. Less cricket would allow players to concentrate more and probably get better crowds.'

473

Best batting performance: 15 Glamorgan v Gloucestershire, Bristol 1989
Best bowling performance: 5-87 Glamorgan v Leicestershire, Cardiff 1989

LAST SEASON: BATTING

	I.	N.O.	R.	H.S.	AV.
TEST					
1ST-CLASS	6	0	50	15	8.33
INT					
RAL	1	0	0	0	0.00
NAT.W.					
B & H					

LAST SEASON: BOWLING

	O.	M.	R.	W.	AV.
TEST					
1ST-CLASS	78.4	19	245	8	30.62
INT					
RAL	12	0	88	1	88.00
NAT.W.					
B & H					

CAREER: BATTING

	I.	N.O.	R.	H.S.	AV.
TEST					
1ST-CLASS	6	0	50	15	8.33
INT					
RAL	1	0	0	0	0.00
NAT.W.					
B & H					

CAREER: BOWLING

	O.	M.	R.	W.	AV.
TEST					
1ST-CLASS	78.4	19	245	8	30.62
INT					
RAL	12	0	88	1	88.00
NAT.W.					
B & H					

SPEAK, N. J.   Lancashire

Full Name: Nicholas Jason Speak
Role: Right-hand opening bat,
off-spin bowler
Born: 21 October 1966, Manchester
Height: 6′ **Weight:** 11st 7lbs
Nickname: Speaky
County debut: 1986–87 in Jamaica
1st-Class 50s scored: 1
Place in batting averages: 173rd
av. 20.66
1st-Class catches 1989: 4 (career 6)
Parents: John and Irene
Marital status: Single
Family links with cricket: Father was
league professional in Lancashire and
Yorkshire
Education: Parrs Wood High School
and Sixth Form College
Qualifications: 5 O-levels; NCA
Coaching Certificate
Jobs outside cricket: YTS with Lancashire CCC (1986)
Off-season 1989–90: Playing and coaching in Canberra
Cricketing superstitions or habits: Puts left pad on first

Overseas tours: NAYC North (for International Youth Competition) to Bermuda 1985; Lancashire CCC pre-season tour to Jamaica 1987, Zimbabwe 1989

Overseas teams played for: Taradale CC, Napier, New Zealand 1985; Napier Old Boys CC (contracted player), New Zealand 1986 and 1987

Cricketers particularly learnt from: 'My father, and all the staff at Lancashire.'

Cricketers particularly admired: Martin Crowe, Dexter Fitton

Other sports played: Lacrosse, snooker

Other sports followed: 'Most sports.'

Relaxations: General interest in all sports, music, reading, eating out, preferably Indian

Opinions on cricket: 'One overseas player per county, with a minimum of a five-year contract. The return of spin bowlers to county and Test cricket. To have more U-25 matches at county level. To see return of South Africa to Test cricket. To see Holland reach Test level, along with Zimbabwe.'

Best batting performance: 64 Lancashire v Essex, Old Trafford 1989

LAST SEASON: BATTING

	I.	N.O.	R.	H.S.	AV.
TEST					
1ST-CLASS	10	1	186	64	20.66
INT					
RAL					
NAT.W.					
B & H					

CAREER: BATTING

	I.	N.O.	R.	H.S.	AV.
TEST					
1ST-CLASS	14	1	235	64	18.07
INT					
RAL	1	0	13	13	13.00
NAT.W.					
B & H					

133. Who topped the Northamptonshire bowling averages last season?

134. Who topped the Nottinghamshire bowling averages last season?

SPEIGHT, M. P.   Sussex

Full Name: Martin Peter Speight
Role: Right-hand bat,
wicket-keeper/close fielder
Born: 24 October 1967, Walsall
Height: 5' 10½" **Weight:** 11st
Nickname: Sprog, Hoover, Ginger
County debut: 1986
1st-Class 50s scored: 5
One-Day 50s: 3
Place in batting averages: 125th
av. 26.56 (1988 195th av. 19.84)
1st-Class catches 1989: 9 (career 20)
Parents: Peter John and Valerie
Marital status: Single
Education: Hassocks' Infants School;
The Windmill's School, Hassocks;
Hurstpierpoint College Junior and
Senior Schools; Durham University
Qualifications: 13 O-levels,
3 A-levels; BA Hons. Dunelm
Off-season 1989–90: Playing cricket and coaching in Wellington, New Zealand
Cricketing superstitions or habits: Right pad on first
Overseas tours: NCA to Bermuda 1985; Hurstpierpoint College to India 1985–86; England YCs Tour to Sri Lanka 1987
Overseas teams played for: Wellington CC, New Zealand
Cricketers particularly learnt from: Derek Semmence (coach at Hurstpierpoint College), Paul Parker, Johnny Longley, Tim O'Gorman

LAST SEASON: BATTING

	I.	N.O.	R.	H.S.	AV.
TEST					
1ST-CLASS	17	1	425	88	26.56
INT					
RAL	7	1	236	74	39.33
NAT.W.	2	0	55	48	27.50
B & H	5	0	110	30	22.00

LAST SEASON: WICKET KEEPING

	C.	ST.			
TEST					
1ST-CLASS					
INT					
RAL					
NAT.W.					
B & H	4	1			

CAREER: BATTING

	I.	N.O.	R.	H.S.	AV.
TEST					
1ST-CLASS	32	1	704	88	22.70
INT					
RAL	11	1	323	74	32.30
NAT.W.	2	0	55	48	27.50
B & H	11	0	261	83	23.72

CAREER: WICKET KEEPING

	C.	ST.			
TEST					
1ST-CLASS					
INT					
RAL	1	–			
NAT.W.					
B & H	10	1			

476

Cricketers particularly admired: Nasser Hussain, James Boiling
Other sports played: Hockey, squash, rowing, golf, rugby, football, canoeing, fives
Other sports followed: Golf, tennis, football
Relaxations: Music, TV, drawing, oil paintings (landscapes)
Extras: 148* v Sutton Valence Old Boys, Brewer's Cup Final 1988; Member of Durham University UAU Winners 1987, Runners Up 1988; Member of Combined Universities' XI in B & H Cup 1987, 1988; Member of Durham University's men's hockey team to Barbados 1988. Sussex CCC's Most Promising Player 1989
Opinions on cricket: 'It's only a game!'
Best batting performance: 88 Sussex v Leicester, Hove 1989
Best bowling performance: 1-2 Sussex v Middlesex, Hove 1988

STANLEY, N. A.   Northamptonshire

Full Name: Neil Alan Stanley
Role: Right-hand bat, right-arm off-spin bowler
Born: 16 May 1968, Bedford
Height: 6′ 3″ **Weight:** 14st 4lbs
Nickname: Giz
County debut: 1988
1st-Class 50s scored: 4
1st-Class catches 1989: 0 (career 4)
Parents: Jack and Julie Margaret
Marital status: Single
Education: Bedford Modern School
Qualifications: 7 O-levels, NCA senior coaching award
Jobs outside cricket: Postman, chicken farmer
Off-season 1989–90: Playing for Sydenham CC, Christchurch, New Zealand
Cricketing superstitions or habits: 'Change bats if not scoring runs; left pad first.'
Overseas tours: Bedford Modern School to Barbados 1983; Young England to Youth World Cup, Australia 1988
Overseas teams played for: Sydenham CC, Christchurch, New Zealand 1989–90
Cricketers particularly learnt from: Bob Carter, Brian Reynolds, all at Northampton

Cricketers particularly admired: Ian Botham, Wayne Larkins
Other sports played: Table tennis (for Bedfordshire), football
Other sports followed: Snooker, golf
Injuries 1989: Cracked bone in left wrist in mid-August – off for the rest of the season
Relaxations: Listening to Sigue Sigue Sputnik and other loud bands, watching Clint Eastwood films
Opinions on cricket: 'Politics should be kept out of sport. A higher percentage of Second XI games should be played on First XI grounds. Too much cricket is played.'
Best batting performance: 75 Northamptonshire v Leicestershire, Leicester 1989

LAST SEASON: BATTING

	I.	N.O.	R.	H.S.	AV.
TEST					
1ST-CLASS	6	0	187	75	31.16
INT					
RAL	1	0	13	13	13.00
NAT.W.					
B & H	–	–	–	–	–

CAREER: BATTING

	I.	N.O.	R.	H.S.	AV.
TEST					
1ST-CLASS	18	2	450	75	28.12
INT					
RAL	8	3	78	18	15.60
NAT.W.					
B & H	2	0	13	8	6.50

STANWORTH, J. Lancashire

Full Name: John Stanworth
Role: Right-hand bat, wicket-keeper
Born: 30 September 1960, Oldham, Lancashire
Height: 5′ 10″ **Weight:** 10st 7lbs
Nickname: Stanny, Stick
County debut: 1983
1st-Class 50s scored: 1
Parents: Robert and Freda
Marital status: Single
Education: Chadderton Grammar School; North Cheshire College, Warrington
Qualifications: 8 O-levels, 1 A-level, BEd Physical Education
Jobs outside cricket: Health and fitness programmer, PE teacher
Off-season 1989–90: Teaching PE

Overseas tours: British Colleges Sports Association to West Indies 1981

Cricketers particularly learnt from: 'Bob Blair (ex-New Zealand and Wellington) gave me a kick up the pants in my formative years.'

Cricketers particularly admired: Alan Knott, for his dedication. Bob Taylor for his 'ease' behind the wicket

Other sports followed: Rugby

Relaxations: Car mechanics, TV, music and films

Extras: Instigated pre-season training for the squad

Best batting performance: 50* Lancashire v Gloucestershire, Bristol 1985

LAST SEASON: BATTING

	I.	N.O.	R.	H.S.	AV.
TEST					
1ST-CLASS	–	–	–	–	–
INT					
RAL					
NAT.W.					
B & H					

LAST SEASON: WICKET KEEPING

	C.	ST.			
TEST					
1ST-CLASS	2	–			
INT					
RAL					
NAT.W.					
B & H					

CAREER: BATTING

	I.	N.O.	R.	H.S.	AV.
TEST					
1ST-CLASS	38	11	236	50*	8.74
INT					
RAL	4	2	7	4*	3.50
NAT.W.	1	0	0	0	0.00
B & H	3	2	17	8*	17.00

CAREER: WICKET KEEPING

	C.	ST.			
TEST					
1ST-CLASS	51	8			
INT					
RAL	10	1			
NAT.W.	6	1			
B & H	4	–			

135. How many wickets did Franklyn Stephenson take last season: 71, 91, or 101?

136. Who topped the Somerset bowling averages last season?

STEPHENSON, F. D.   Nottinghamshire

Full Name: Franklyn Dacosta Stephenson
Role: Right-arm fast bowler, right-hand bat
Born: 8 April 1959, Barbados
Height: 6' 4" **Weight:** 13st 7lbs
Nickname: Cookie, Stevo
County debut: 1982 (Gloucestershire), 1988 (Nottinghamshire)
County cap: 1988 (Nottinghamshire)
1000 runs in a season: 1
50 wickets in a season: 2
1st-Class 50s scored: 16
1st-Class 100s scored: 3
1st-Class 5 w. in innings: 23
1st-Class 10 w. in match: 6
One-Day 50s: 2
Place in batting averages: 164th
av. 22.11 (1988 102nd av. 29.08)
Place in bowling averages: 8th av. 18.77 (1988 8th av. 18.31)
Strike rate 1989: 38.65 (career 41.03)
1st-Class catches 1989: 7 (career 36)
Parents: Leonard Young and Violet
Wife: Julia
Children: Amanda, Orissa
Education: St John Baptist Mixed School; Samuel Jackson Prescod Polytechnic
Jobs outside cricket: Hotel porter. Golf pro in Barbados
Off-season 1989–90: 'Training to regain my place in the Barbados cricket side, and playing golf.'
Overseas tours: With West Indies U-19s to England 1978; with rebel West Indies team to South Africa 1983, 1983–84
Overseas teams played for: Tasmania 1981–82; Barbados 1981–82
Cricketers particularly learnt from: Charlie Griffith
Cricketers particularly admired: Sir Garfield Sobers, Lawrence Rowe, Sylvester Clarke, Collis King
Other sports played: Lawn tennis, golf (off scratch)
Other sports followed: Athletics, golf
Injuries 1989: Hamstring trouble – out for seven first-class games
Relaxations: 'Playing golf, listening to music, spending time with my wife and kids.'

480

Extras: Toured England with West Indies U-19 in 1978. After being introduced to English League Cricket in 1979 with Littleborough in the Central Lancashire League, had three consecutive success-filled championships. In 1980 with Royton, took 100 wickets and scored 621 runs (first time in 66 years); with Rawtenstall in 1981 and 1982, took 105 wickets and 559 runs, and over 100 wickets and over 500 runs respectively; and also participated in Barbados 10th Shell Shield championship victory in 16 years in 1982. Hit 165 for Barbados in 1982 having been sent in as night-watchman. Took 10 wickets in match on debut for Tasmania. Top of Gloucestershire first-class bowling averages in 1982. In 1988, did the double when he scored 1018 first-class runs and took 125 first-class wickets. Britannic Assurance Player of the Year, 1988. One of *Wisden*'s Players of the Year 1988. Now eligible to play again for West Indies, having been banned for playing in South Africa

Opinions on cricket: 'I fail to see how the further limitation of overseas players can be the answer to the lack of outstanding English players; or, for that matter, the low gate receipts being experienced by the county clubs. I think that a lot more can be done to promote and sell the game in England; and along those lines I think that the English officials can take a hint from Australian cricket authorities especially with Test tours etc. I don't think it will do much for the players–officials relationship when the umpires are asked to run to Lord's shouting "dissent" every time a player sneezes too hard on the field of play.'

Best batting performance: 165 Barbados v Leeward Islands, Basseterre 1981–82

Best bowling performance: 8-47 Nottinghamshire v Essex, Trent Bridge 1989

LAST SEASON: BATTING

	I.	N.O.	R.	H.S.	AV.
TEST					
1ST-CLASS	30	3	597	81	22.11
INT					
RAL	11	3	264	69	33.00
NAT.W.	2	1	33	22	33.00
B & H	6	2	115	54	28.75

CAREER: BATTING

	I.	N.O.	R.	H.S.	AV.
TEST					
1ST-CLASS	112	8	2588	165	24.88
INT					
RAL	30	8	503	69	22.86
NAT.W.	3	1	40	22	20.00
B & H	9	2	136	54	19.42

LAST SEASON: BOWLING

	O.	M.	R.	W.	AV.
TEST					
1ST-CLASS	592.4	135	1727	92	18.77
INT					
RAL	105.5	9	412	20	20.60
NAT.W.	24	4	48	2	24.00
B & H	56	10	183	10	18.30

CAREER: BOWLING

	O.	M.	R.	W.	AV.
TEST					
1ST-CLASS	2236.2	503	6577	327	20.11
INT					
RAL	265.5	25	1119	56	19.98
NAT.W.	68	15	184	9	20.44
B & H	99.2	16	296	16	18.50

STEPHENSON, J. P. — Essex

Full Name: John Patrick Stephenson
Role: Right-hand opening bat,
right-arm medium bowler
Born: 14 March 1965, Stebbing
Height: 6′ 1″ **Weight:** 12½st
Nickname: Stanley, Svensson
County debut: 1985
Test debut: 1989
No. of Tests: 1
1000 runs in a season: 1
1st-Class 50s scored: 19
1st-Class 100s scored: 5
One-Day 50s: 3
Place in batting averages: 50th
av. 37.61 (1988 100th av. 29.29)
1st-Class catches 1989: 11 (career 44)
Parents: Patrick and Eve
Marital status: Single
Family links with cricket: 'Father
member of Rugby Meteors Cricketer Cup winning side in 1973. Three
brothers in Felstead 1st XI; Guy played for Essex 2nd XI; Mark and Paul play
for Rickling Green and Felstead Robins, as does Father; Mum does my
whites!'
Education: Felstead Prep School; Felstead Senior School; Durham University
Qualifications: 7 O-levels, 3 A-levels; NCA Coaching Award; General Arts BA
Jobs outside cricket: Refrigeration engineering with Cullen and Sons 1987;
resident tutor Melbourne CEGS 1987–88; groundsman, Fitzroy CC, 1984
Off-season 1989–90: England 'A' tour to Zimbabwe
Cricketing superstitions or habits: 'They change with my form.'
Overseas tours: Zimbabwe 1982–83 with ESCA U-19s; Barbados with Keith
Pont Benefit 1986; Zimbabwe with England A 1989–90
Overseas teams played for: Fitzroy CC, Melbourne 1983–84; Fitzroy-
Doncaster 1987–88; Crusaders CC 1983–84, 1987–88; Boland 1988–89
Cricketers particularly learnt from: Gordon Barker, Ray East, Keith
Fletcher, Graham Gooch
Cricketers particularly admired: Graham Gooch, Brian Hardie and many
others
Other sports played: Squash, hockey, snooker, golf
Other sports followed: Most except horse racing and synchronised swimming
Relaxations: Modern Literature. Modern music, e.g. The Pixies, REM

Extras: Scored 1100 runs in 2nd XI and 791 in 1st XI in 1988. Awarded 2nd XI cap in 1984 when leading run-scorer with Essex 2nd XI. Young Player of the Year 1985 for Essex CCC. Captained Durham University to victory in UAU Competition 1986. Captain of Combined Universities team 1987 in the first year that it was drawn from all universities

Opinions on cricket: 'Four-day cricket to stay and hopefully take over as long as wickets improve across the country. Less 40-over cricket. Abolish 5-over rule for substitute fielders. One registered overseas player per county. No restraint of trade.'

Best batting performance: 171 Essex v Lancashire, Lytham 1989

Best bowling performance: 3-48 Boland v Natal B, Pietermaritzburg 1988–89

LAST SEASON: BATTING

	I.	N.O.	R.	H.S.	AV.
TEST	2	0	36	25	18.00
1ST-CLASS	37	3	1318	171	38.76
INT					
RAL	9	2	98	30	14.00
NAT.W.	1	0	6	6	6.00
B & H	5	1	169	63*	42.25

CAREER: BATTING

	I.	N.O.	R.	H.S.	AV.
TEST	2	0	36	25	18.00
1ST-CLASS	130	12	3727	171	31.58
INT					
RAL	26	6	358	45	17.90
NAT.W.	5	1	98	55	24.50
B & H	8	1	288	75	41.14

LAST SEASON: BOWLING

	O.	M.	R.	W.	AV.
TEST					
1ST-CLASS	93	20	307	7	43.85
INT					
RAL	67	1	305	9	33.88
NAT.W.	4	1	22	0	–
B & H	31	3	107	6	17.83

CAREER: BOWLING

	O.	M.	R.	W.	AV.
TEST					
1ST-CLASS	268.1	53	849	21	40.42
INT					
RAL	85.2	2	397	10	39.70
NAT.W.	4	1	22	0	–
B & H	47	3	182	8	22.75

137. How many first-class wickets did Peter Roebuck take last season: 1, 10, or 21?

138. Who topped the Surrey bowling averages last season?

STEWART, A. J.   Surrey

Full Name: Alec James Stewart
Role: Right-hand bat, right-arm
medium bowler, occasional
wicket-keeper
Born: 8 April 1963, Merton
Nickname: Stewie
Height: 5' 10" **Weight:** 12st
County debut: 1981
County cap: 1985
1000 runs in a season: 5
1st-Class 50s scored: 44
1st-Class 100s scored: 13
1st-Class 200s scored: 1
One-Day 50s: 17
One-Day 100s: 3
Place in batting averages: 24th
av. 44.51 (1988 62nd av. 34.68)
1st-Class catches 1989: 55 (career 180
+ 6 stumpings)

Parents: Michael James and Sheila Marie Macdonald
Marital status: Single
Family links with cricket: Father played for England (1962–64) and Surrey
(1954–72). Brother Neil plays club cricket and captains Malden Wanderers
CC (the 1989 Surrey Championship champions), and Surrey 2nd XI; sister,
Judy, plays for Malden Wanderers Ladies XI
Education: Tiffin School
Qualifications: 4 O-levels
Jobs outside cricket: Sales rep for Slater-Gartrell Sports, Western Australia
Off-season 1989–90: Touring India and West Indies with England
Cricketing superstitions or habits: 'Always put left foot on to cricket field first,
when going out to bat.'
Overseas tours: Surrey U-19 tour of Australia 1980–81; England to India
1989; England to West Indies 1990
Overseas teams played for: Midland-Guildford CC, Western Australia
1981–89
Cricketers particularly learnt from: Geoff Arnold, Kevin Gartrell
Cricketers particularly admired: Geoff Boycott, Alan Knott, Tony Mann,
'Animal Samuel'
Other sports played: All sports
Other sports followed: All sports, watches Chelsea FC
Injuries 1989: Broken finger – did not keep wicket for five weeks
Relaxations: Eating out, good music, sun-bathing, visiting the Durham area

484

Opinions on cricket: 'Need 16 four-day games, played on top quality pitches. This will improve the standard of our first-class cricket, and prepare players better for Test cricket.'

Best batting performance: 206* Surrey v Essex, The Oval 1989

Best bowling performance: 1-7 Surrey v Lancashire, Old Trafford 1989

LAST SEASON: BATTING

	I.	N.O.	R.	H.S.	AV.
TEST					
1ST-CLASS	42	5	1647	206*	44.51
INT					
RAL	16	1	691	119	46.06
NAT.W.	3	0	80	55	26.66
B & H	4	0	75	44	18.75

CAREER: BATTING

	I.	N.O.	R.	H.S.	AV.
TEST					
1ST-CLASS	225	24	7676	206*	38.18
INT					
RAL	80	8	1955	119	27.15
NAT.W.	14	2	500	107*	41.66
B & H	20	2	393	63*	21.83

LAST SEASON: WICKET KEEPING

	C.	ST.			
TEST					
1ST-CLASS	55	3			
INT					
RAL	10	3			
NAT.W.	1	–			
B & H	5	2			

LAST SEASON: BOWLING

	O.	M.	R.	W.	AV.
TEST					
1ST-CLASS	21.4	0	120	2	60.00
INT					
RAL					
NAT.W.					
B & H					

CAREER: BOWLING

	O.	M.	R.	W.	AV.
TEST					
1ST-CLASS	49.5	5	263	3	87.66
INT					
RAL	0.3	0	4	0	–
NAT.W.					
B & H					

CAREER: WICKET KEEPING

	C.	ST.			
TEST					
1ST-CLASS					
INT					
RAL	14	4			
NAT.W.	1	–			
B & H	5	2			

139. Who topped the Sussex bowling averages last season?

140. Who topped the Warwickshire bowling averages last season?

STOVOLD, A. W. Gloucestershire

Full Name: Andrew Willis-Stovold
Role: Right-hand bat, wicket-keeper
Born: 19 March 1953, Bristol
Height: 5' 7" **Weight:** 12st 4lbs
Nickname: Stumper, Squeak, Stov,
Stovers, Stubble
County debut: 1973
County cap: 1976
Benefit: 1987 (£75,000)
1000 runs in a season: 8
1st-Class 50s scored: 96
1st-Class 100s scored: 19
1st-Class 200s scored: 1
One-Day 50s: 35
One-Day 100s: 4
Place in batting averages: 227th
av. 14.15 (1988 60th av. 35.02)
1st-Class catches 1989: 5 (career 289
+ 45 stumpings)
Parents: Lancelot Walter and Dorothy Patricia
Wife and date of marriage: Kay Elizabeth, 30 September 1978
Children: Nicholas, 18 June 1981; Neil, 24 February 1983
Family links with cricket: Father played local club cricket for Old Down CC.
Brother Martin also played county cricket for Gloucestershire
Education: Filton High School; Loughborough College of Education
Qualifications: Certificate of Education
Jobs outside cricket: Teacher at Tockington Manor Prep School
Cricketing superstitions or habits: 'Keeping the same routine until I have a
bad run, then trying something else. Always prepare for batting in the same
order.'
Overseas tours: England Schools to India 1970–71; England Young
Cricketers to West Indies 1972; Gloucestershire to Sri Lanka 1986–87
Overseas teams played for: Orange Free State 1974–76
Cricketers particularly admired: Mike Procter, Barry Richards, Richard
Hadlee
Other sports played: Football, golf
Other sports followed: Rugby, hunting, horse racing
Relaxations: Gardening, walking
Extras: Writes a weekly article for *Gloucestershire Echo*. His 1987 benefit
produced a record £75,000 for a Gloucestershire player
Opinions on cricket: 'Worried about the sudden increase in player "trans-
fers". We must not let it get too much like football.'

Best batting performance: 212* Gloucestershire v Northamptonshire, Northampton 1982
Best bowling performance: 1-0 Gloucestershire v Derbyshire, Bristol 1976

LAST SEASON: BATTING

	I.	N.O.	R.	H.S.	AV.
TEST					
1ST-CLASS	13	0	184	36	14.15
INT					
RAL	4	0	92	38	23.00
NAT.W.	1	0	49	49	49.00
B & H	5	0	197	90	39.40

CAREER: BATTING

	I.	N.O.	R.	H.S.	AV.
TEST					
1ST-CLASS	626	35	17601	212*	29.78
INT					
RAL	180	21	3795	98*	23.86
NAT.W.	33	3	1138	104*	37.93
B & H	65	8	2134	123	37.43

LAST SEASON: WICKET KEEPING

	C.	ST.	
TEST			
1ST-CLASS			
INT			
RAL			
NAT.W.			
B & H			

LAST SEASON: BOWLING

	O.	M.	R.	W.	AV.
TEST					
1ST-CLASS					
INT					
RAL					
NAT.W.					
B & H					

CAREER: BOWLING

	O.	M.	R.	W.	AV.
TEST					
1ST-CLASS	52.3	8	218	4	54.50
INT					
RAL					
NAT.W.					
B & H					

CAREER: WICKET KEEPING

	C.	ST.	
TEST			
1ST-CLASS			
INT			
RAL	58	13	
NAT.W.	17	5	
B & H	38	4	

141. Who topped the Worcestershire bowling averages last season?
142. Who topped the Yorkshire bowling averages last season?

SUCH, P. M.   Leicestershire

Full Name: Peter Mark Such
Role: Right-hand bat, off-spin bowler
Born: 12 June 1964, Helensburgh, Scotland
Height: 6′ 1″ **Weight:** 11st 7lbs
Nickname: Suchy
County debut: 1982 (Nottinghamshire), 1987 (Leicestershire)
1st-Class 5 w. in innings: 6
Place in bowling averages: 105th av. 41.06 (1988 106th av. 34.00)
Strike rate 1989: 97.73 (career 67.47)
1st-Class catches 1989: 2 (career 39)
Parents: John and Margaret
Marital status: Single
Family links with cricket: Father and brother village cricketers
Education: Lantern Lane Primary School; Harry Carlton Comprehensive, East Leake

Qualifications: 9 O-levels, 3 A-levels, Qualified Cricket Coach (Senior)
Jobs outside cricket: Van driver, handyman, tax office clerk, TV installer
Off-season 1989–90: Playing and coaching in Zimbabwe
Cricketing superstitions or habits: 'Stick to a successful routine.'
Overseas tours: Fred Rumsey's tour to Barbados 1987
Overseas teams played for: Kempton Park CC, South Africa 1982–83; Bathurst CC, New South Wales 1985–86
Cricketers particularly learnt from: Bob White, Eddie Hemmings
Cricketers particularly admired: Richard Hadlee
Other sports played: Hockey, golf
Other sports followed: American football and most other sports
Relaxations: Music, reading, watching most sports and good movies
Extras: Played for Young England v Young Australia in three 'Tests' in 1983. Represented TCCB v New Zealand 1986. Left Nottinghamshire at end of 1986 season. Joined Leicestershire in 1987 and released at the end of 1989
Opinions on cricket: 'County cricket is basically an entertainment industry, so what does the membership think of the game? The majority find it tedious and lacking in variety, so can the game's ruling body ignore the demands of one of its benefactors? Are we going to repay members' loyalty with slow over-rates? If the current trend continues we will become increasingly dependent on the generosity of sponsors.

What can be done to remedy the situation? Is some form of legislation required to force the hands of county captains? A solution needs to be found to change the thinking and approach to the game. The win at all costs whatever the surface attitude needs to be replaced, making it more enjoyable for players and spectators alike. The game needs to be played on a good surface which evens up the contest between bat and ball, giving both players and public the necessary variety.'

Best batting performance: 16 Nottinghamshire v Middlesex, Lord's 1984

Best bowling performance: 6-123 Nottinghamshire v Kent, Trent Bridge 1983

LAST SEASON: BATTING

	I.	N.O.	R.	H.S.	AV.
TEST					
1ST-CLASS	8	2	18	14	3.00
INT					
RAL	2	1	8	8*	8.00
NAT.W.					
B & H	–	–	–	–	–

CAREER: BATTING

	I.	N.O.	R.	H.S.	AV.
TEST					
1ST-CLASS	81	30	127	16	2.49
INT					
RAL	3	2	8	8*	8.00
NAT.W.					
B & H	–	–	–	–	–

LAST SEASON: BOWLING

	O.	M.	R.	W.	AV.
TEST					
1ST-CLASS	244.2	70	616	15	41.06
INT					
RAL	25	1	134	3	44.66
NAT.W.					
B & H	11	2	35	1	35.00

CAREER: BOWLING

	O.	M.	R.	W.	AV.
TEST					
1ST-CLASS	2328	619	6371	207	30.77
INT					
RAL	67	2	408	8	51.00
NAT.W.					
B & H	44	3	186	5	37.20

143. Who bowled the most first-class county overs last season?

144. Who bowled the second most first-class county overs last season?

SWALLOW, I. G.   Yorkshire

Full Name: Ian Geoffrey Swallow
Role: Right-hand bat, off-break
bowler, cover or slip fielder
Born: 18 December 1962, Barnsley
Height: 5′ 7″ **Weight:** 10st
Nickname: Chicken, Swal
County debut: 1983
1st-Class 50s scored: 2
1st-Class 100s scored: 1
1st-Class 5 w. in innings: 1
Place in batting averages: 217th
av. 15.94 (1988 183rd av. 20.70)
Place in bowling averages: 113th
av. 45.50
Strike rate 1989: 84.37 (career 101.32)
1st-Class catches 1989: 5 (career 28)
Parents: Geoffrey and Joyce
Marital status: Single
Family links with cricket: Father and brother both played for Elsecar Village
CC
Education: Hayland Kirk, Balk, Comprehensive School; Barnsley Technical
College
Qualifications: 3 O-levels
Jobs outside cricket: Storeman
Cricketing superstitions or habits: Always puts left pad on first
Overseas teams played for: Sunshine CC, Melbourne 1985–86, 1986–87
Cricketers particularly learnt from: Doug Padgett, Phil Carrick, Steve
Oldham

LAST SEASON: BATTING

	I.	N.O.	R.	H.S.	AV.
TEST					
1ST-CLASS	20	2	287	64	15.94
INT					
RAL	–	–	–	–	–
NAT.W.	1	1	17	17*	–
B & H					

CAREER: BATTING

	I.	N.O.	R.	H.S.	AV.
TEST					
1ST-CLASS	82	18	1296	114	20.25
INT					
RAL	1	0	2	2	2.00
NAT.W.	1	1	17	17*	–
B & H	3	2	18	10*	18.00

LAST SEASON: BOWLING

	O.	M.	R.	W.	AV.
TEST					
1ST-CLASS	225	56	728	16	45.50
INT					
RAL					
NAT.W.	4	0	16	0	–
B & H					

CAREER: BOWLING

	O.	M.	R.	W.	AV.
TEST					
1ST-CLASS	1080.5	249	3270	64	51.09
INT					
RAL	4	0	31	0	–
NAT.W.	4	0	16	0	–
B & H	36	4	151	2	75.50

Cricketers particularly admired: Viv Richards, John Emburey
Other sports played: Football and most sports for fun
Other sports followed: Barnsley FC, all sports
Relaxations: Sports in general
Extras: Took hat-trick v Warwickshire 2nd XI 1984. Figures: 4-3-2-4. Released by Yorkshire at end of 1989 season
Best batting performance: 114 Yorkshire v MCC, Scarborough 1987
Best bowling performance: 7-95 Yorkshire v Nottinghamshire, Trent Bridge 1987

SYKES, J. F. Middlesex

Full Name: James Frederick Sykes
Role: Right-hand bat, off-break bowler, slip or gully fielder
Born: 30 December 1965, Shoreditch
Height: 6′ 2″ **Weight:** 13st 7lbs
Nickname: Eric, Sykesy
County debut: 1983
1st-Class 50s scored: 3
1st-Class 100s scored: 1
One-Day 50s: 1
Place in batting averages: —
(1988 146th av. 24.33)
1st-Class catches 1989: 1 (career 16)
Parents: James and Kathleen
Education: Bow Comprehensive
Qualifications: 1 O-level
Jobs outside cricket: Coaching in South Africa for 2 weeks

LAST SEASON: BATTING

	I.	N.O.	R.	H.S.	AV.
TEST					
1ST-CLASS	4	1	41	19	13.66
INT					
RAL	6	1	112	38	22.40
NAT.W.					
B & H	2	1	54	38	54.00

CAREER: BATTING

	I.	N.O.	R.	H.S.	AV.
TEST					
1ST-CLASS	38	7	696	126	22.45
INT					
RAL	22	5	308	57	18.11
NAT.W.					
B & H	3	1	78	38	39.00

LAST SEASON: BOWLING

	O.	M.	R.	W.	AV.
TEST					
1ST-CLASS	30	14	47	4	11.75
INT					
RAL	13	1	85	4	21.25
NAT.W.					
B & H	4	0	18	1	18.00

CAREER: BOWLING

	O.	M.	R.	W.	AV.
TEST					
1ST-CLASS	396.2	92	1157	30	38.56
INT					
RAL	143.1	4	651	24	27.12
NAT.W.					
B & H	4	0	18	1	18.00

Cricketing superstitions or habits: 49, 99
Overseas tours: England U-19 to West Indies 1984–85
Cricketers particularly learnt from: John Emburey, Don Bennett, Graham Barlow, Wayne Daniel
Cricketers particularly admired: Clive Radley, Neil Williams
Other sports played: Squash, football
Best batting performance: 126 Middlesex v Cambridge University, Cambridge 1985
Best bowling performance: 4-49 Middlesex v Glamorgan, Cardiff 1987

TAVARÉ, C. J.   Somerset

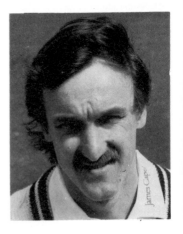

Full Name: Christopher James Tavaré
Role: Right-hand bat, off-break bowler, slip fielder
Born: 27 October 1954, Orpington
Height: 6′ 1½″ **Weight:** 12st 12lbs
Nickname: Tav, Rowdy
County debut: 1974 (Kent), 1989 (Somerset)
County cap: 1978 (Kent), 1989 (Somerset)
Benefit: 1988 (£92,318), (Kent)
Test debut: 1980
No. of Tests: 31
No. of One-Day Internationals: 29
1000 runs in a season: 13
1st-Class 50s scored: 111
1st-Class 100s scored: 36
One-Day 50s: 50
One-Day 100s: 12
Place in batting averages: 57th av. 36.29 (1988 28th av. 42.02)
1st-Class catches 1989: 18 (career 346)
Parents: Andrew and June
Wife and date of marriage: Vanessa, 22 March 1980
Family links with cricket: Father, Uncle Jack Tavaré, and Uncle Derrick Attwood, all played school and club cricket, father and Uncle Jack at Chatham House, father and Uncle Derrick at Bickley Park CC. Elder brother Stephen and younger brother Jeremy both play cricket
Education: Sevenoaks School; Oxford University
Qualifications: Zoology degree
Jobs outside cricket: Consultant, N. M. Schroder Financial Management Ltd

Off-season 1989–90: Working for Ministry of Agriculture, Fisheries & Food, in Exeter
Overseas tours: England to India and Sri Lanka 1981–82; Australia and New Zealand 1982–83; New Zealand and Pakistan 1983–84
Overseas teams played for: University of Western Australia, Perth 1977–78; West Perth CC for half a season 1978–79
Other sports played: Golf
Other sports followed: 'Take an interest in most sports, especially American football in winter.'
Relaxations: Music, zoology, films, gardening, woodwork, golf
Extras: Played for England Schools v All-India Schools at Birmingham in 1973, scoring 124*. Oxford University cricket blue 1975–76–77. Whitbread Scholarship to Perth, Australia, 1978–79. Suffers from asthma and hay-fever. Was top-scorer with 82* and Man of the Match, on debut for England in 55-over match v West Indies at Headingley, May 1980. Captain of Kent 1983–84. Rejected Kent's offer of a new contract for 1989 and joined Somerset as vice-captain. Vic Marks, captain of Somerset, was Tavaré's captain at Oxford, 1976 and 1977. Somerset captain for 1990
Best batting performance: 168* Kent v Essex, Chelmsford 1982
Best bowling performance: 1-3 Kent v Hampshire, Canterbury 1986

LAST SEASON: BATTING

	I.	N.O.	R.	H.S.	AV.
TEST	1	0	2	2	2.00
1ST-CLASS	38	2	1341	153	37.25
INT					
RAL	15	1	467	120*	33.35
NAT.W.	2	1	180	101	180.00
B & H	6	3	346	104*	115.33

CAREER: BATTING

	I.	N.O.	R.	H.S.	AV.
TEST	56	2	1755	149	32.50
1ST-CLASS	535	59	18127	168*	38.08
INT	28	2	720	83*	27.69
RAL	171	24	4758	136*	32.36
NAT.W.	30	5	1106	118*	44.24
B & H	76	7	2224	143	32.23

LAST SEASON: BOWLING

	O.	M.	R.	W.	AV.
TEST					
1ST-CLASS					
INT					
RAL					
NAT.W.					
B & H					

CAREER: BOWLING

	O.	M.	R.	W.	AV.
TEST	5	3	11	0	–
1ST-CLASS	105.5	15	514	5	102.80
INT	2	0	3	0	–
RAL					
NAT.W.					
B & H					

TAYLOR, L. B. Leicestershire

Full Name: Leslie Brian Taylor
Role: Right-hand bat, right-arm
fast-medium bowler
Born: 25 October 1953, Earl Shilton,
Leicestershire
Height: 6′ 3½″ **Weight:** 14st 7lbs
Nickname: Les
County debut: 1977
County cap: 1981
Benefit: 1989
Test debut: 1985
No. of Tests: 2
No. of One-Day Internationals: 2
1st-Class 50s scored: 1
1st-Class 5 w. in innings: 18
1st-Class 10 w. in match: 1
Place in bowling averages: 94th
av. 36.29 (1988 66th av. 27.62)
Strike rate 1989: 67.66 (career 54.09)
1st-Class catches 1989: 5 (career 53)
Parents: Peggy and Cyril
Wife and date of marriage: Susan, 12 July 1973
Children: Jamie, 24 June 1976; Donna, 10 November 1978; Suzy, 3 June 1981
Family links with cricket: Relation of the late Sam Coe, holder of highest
individual score for Leicestershire, 252* v Northamptonshire at Leicester in
1914
Education: Heathfield High School, Earl Shilton
Qualifications: Qualified carpenter and joiner

LAST SEASON: BATTING

	I.	N.O.	R.	H.S.	AV.
TEST					
1ST-CLASS	18	8	60	27	6.00
INT					
RAL	5	3	8	3*	4.00
NAT.W.	–	–	–	–	–
B & H					

CAREER: BATTING

	I.	N.O.	R.	H.S.	AV.
TEST	1	1	1	1*	–
1ST-CLASS	198	85	1060	60	9.38
INT	1	1	1	1*	–
RAL	39	27	117	15*	9.75
NAT.W.	6	5	18	6*	18.00
B & H	10	5	18	5	3.60

LAST SEASON: BOWLING

	O.	M.	R.	W.	AV.
TEST					
1ST-CLASS	270.4	53	871	24	36.29
INT					
RAL	55	1	232	13	17.84
NAT.W.	23	0	107	2	53.50
B & H					

CAREER: BOWLING

	O.	M.	R.	W.	AV.
TEST	63.3	11	178	4	44.50
1ST-CLASS	5174.2	1227	14436	577	25.01
INT	14	3	47	0	–
RAL	860.5	59	3775	178	21.20
NAT.W.	146.1	23	496	30	16.53
B & H	302	57	984	51	19.29

494

Overseas tours: Derrick Robins' XI to South America 1978–79; England to West Indies 1985–86
Overseas teams played for: Natal 1981–84
Other sports played: Swimming and football
Relaxations: Game-shooting, fox-hunting with the Atherstone Hunt
Extras: Was banned from Test cricket for three years for joining rebel England tour of South Africa in 1982
Opinions on cricket: 'We should not be subjected to over-rate fines in one-day cricket.'
Best batting performance: 60 Leicestershire v Essex, Chelmsford 1988
Best bowling performance: 7-28 Leicestershire v Derbyshire, Leicester 1981

TAYLOR, N. R. Kent

Full Name: Neil Royston Taylor
Role: Right-hand bat, off-break bowler, outfielder
Born: 21 July 1959, Farnborough, Kent
Height: 6' 1" **Weight:** 13st 10lbs
Nickname: Map
County debut: 1979
County cap: 1982
1000 runs in a season: 6
1st-Class 50s scored: 46
1st-Class 100s scored: 23
One-Day 50s: 16
One-Day 100s: 4
Place in batting averages: 30th av. 42.71 (1988 117th av. 27.20)
1st-Class catches 1989: 9 (career 110)
Parents: Leonard and Audrey
Wife and date of marriage: Jane Claire, 25 September 1982
Children: Amy Louise, 7 November 1985; Lauren, 21 July 1988
Family links with cricket: Brother Colin played for Kent U-19s. Father played club cricket
Education: Cray Valley Technical High School
Qualifications: 8 O-levels, 2 A-levels, NCA Coaching Certificate
Jobs outside cricket: Insurance broker, and working in Civil Service
Off-season 1989–90: Coaching for Kent CCC
Cricketing superstitions or habits: Always puts batting gear on in same order. Wears same gear when scoring runs

Overseas tours: With England Schools Team to India 1977–78; Kent to Vancouver 1979

Overseas teams played for: Randburg, Johannesburg 1980–86; coach at St Stithian's College 1981–86

Cricketers particularly learnt from: Bob Woolmer, Mark Benson, Chris Tavaré

Cricketers particularly admired: Alan Knott, Gary Sobers, Barry Richards

Other sports played: Rugby (played for Kent U-21 XV), golf

Other sports followed: 'Anything – but not horses!'

Relaxations: Listening to records, lying in bed reading the Sunday newspapers. Reading autobiographies, Robert Ludlum, Frederick Forsyth, Wilbur Smith. Listening to music: Level 42, Phil Collins, U2; watching TV

Extras: Made 110 on debut for Kent CCC v Sri Lanka, 1979. Won four Man of the Match awards in first five matches. Scored highest score by Kent player in Benson & Hedges cricket: 121 v Sussex and Somerset. Scored three successive centuries in B & H. Played for England B v Pakistan, 1982. Fielded twice as 12th man for England v India in 1982 and West Indies in 1988, both matches at The Oval

Opinions on cricket: 'The type of pitches we play on must be improved. Perhaps the groundsmen could be employed by the TCCB, so that they do not feel pressured by their county club. They can then produce their best pitch, instead of inferior ones!'

Best batting performance: 155* Kent v Glamorgan, Cardiff 1983

Best bowling performance: 2-20 Kent v Somerset, Canterbury 1985

LAST SEASON: BATTING

	I.	N.O.	R.	H.S.	AV.
TEST					
1ST-CLASS	41	6	1495	118	42.71
INT					
RAL	11	2	271	56	30.11
NAT.W.	2	0	42	29	21.00
B & H	6	0	159	64	26.50

LAST SEASON: BOWLING

	O.	M.	R.	W.	AV.
TEST					
1ST-CLASS	2	0	13	0	–
INT					
RAL					
NAT.W.	6.5	0	29	3	9.66
B & H					

CAREER: BATTING

	I.	N.O.	R.	H.S.	AV.
TEST					
1ST-CLASS	342	45	10329	155*	34.77
INT					
RAL	80	8	1925	85	26.73
NAT.W.	16	0	413	85	25.81
B & H	31	1	1253	137	41.76

CAREER: BOWLING

	O.	M.	R.	W.	AV.
TEST					
1ST-CLASS	238.3	41	808	15	53.86
INT					
RAL					
NAT.W.	15.5	3	48	3	16.00
B & H	2	1	5	0	–

TAZELAAR, D.   Surrey

Full Name: Dirk Tazelaar
Role: Right-hand bat, left-arm
fast-medium bowler
Born: 13 January 1963, Ipswich,
Queensland, Australia
County debut: 1989
1st-Class 50s scored: 1
1st-Class 5 w. in innings: 5
1st-Class 10 w. in match: 1
1st-Class catches 1989: 1 (career 17)
Overseas teams played for:
Queensland 1985–89
Extras: Returned to Australia
mid-season owing to injury
Best batting performance: 56
Queensland v New South Wales,
Brisbane 1987–88
Best bowling performance: 6-52
Queensland v Western Australia,
Brisbane 1987–88

LAST SEASON: BATTING

	I.	N.O.	R.	H.S.	AV.
TEST					
1ST-CLASS	4	1	65	29	21.66
INT					
RAL					
NAT.W.					
B & H					

CAREER: BATTING

	I.	N.O.	R.	H.S.	AV.
TEST					
1ST-CLASS	48	19	603	56	20.79
INT					
RAL					
NAT.W.					
B & H					

LAST SEASON: BOWLING

	O.	M.	R.	W.	AV.
TEST					
1ST-CLASS	127.4	24	417	10	41.70
INT					
RAL					
NAT.W.					
B & H					

CAREER: BOWLING

	O.	M.	R.	W.	AV.
TEST					
1ST-CLASS	1343.1	270	3941	138	28.55
INT					
RAL					
NAT.W.					
B & H					

TEDSTONE, G. A.   Gloucestershire

Full Name: Geoffrey Alan Tedstone
Role: Right-hand bat, wicket-keeper
Born: 19 January 1961, Southport
Height: 5′ 6½″ **Weight:** 10½st
Nickname: Ted, Super
County debut: 1982 (Warwickshire), 1989 (Gloucestershire)
1st-Class 50s scored: 4
One-Day 50s: 1
Place in batting averages: 233rd av. 13.73 (1988 200th av. 18.87)
Parents: Ken and Win
Wife and date of marriage: Jane, 17 September 1988
Family links with cricket: Sister, Janet Aspinall, plays for England Ladies. Father played club cricket for Leamington. Brother Roger plays for Leamington

Education: Warwick School; St Pauls College, Cheltenham
Qualifications: 6 O-levels, 4 A-levels, BEd degree, qualified teacher, FA coach
Jobs outside cricket: PE teacher
Off-season 1989–90: Teaching at Emscote Lawn School, Warwick
Overseas tours: Young England to West Indies 1980; British Colleges to West Indies 1981; Dennis Amiss XI to Barbados 1985; Geoff Humpage Benefit tour to Barbados 1987

LAST SEASON: BATTING

	I.	N.O.	R.	H.S.	AV.
TEST					
1ST-CLASS	17	2	206	50	13.73
INT					
RAL	5	2	28	12	9.33
NAT.W.					
B & H					

LAST SEASON: WICKET KEEPING

	C.	ST.			
TEST					
1ST-CLASS	24	3			
INT					
RAL	2	–			
NAT.W.					
B & H					

CAREER: BATTING

	I.	N.O.	R.	H.S.	AV.
TEST					
1ST-CLASS	62	9	847	67*	15.98
INT					
RAL	10	4	102	31*	17.00
NAT.W.	1	1	55	55*	–
B & H	–	–	–	–	–

CAREER: WICKET KEEPING

	C.	ST.			
TEST					
1ST-CLASS	73	13			
INT					
RAL	12	2			
NAT.W.					
B & H	–	–			

Overseas teams played for: Union High School, South Africa 1982–83
Cricketers particularly learnt from: Father, David 'Stan' Smith, ex-Warwickshire, now Hertfordshire
Cricketers particularly admired: Dennis Amiss, Bob Taylor
Other sports played: Hockey for Coventry and Warwickshire
Other sports followed: Soccer (Wolverhampton Wanderers FC)
Relaxations: Playing or watching most sports, listening to music, watching films, being sociable
Extras: 'I changed in 1988 from being a tireless medium pace net bowler into a tiresome non-turning off-spin net bowler!'
Best batting performance: 67* Warwickshire v Cambridge University, Cambridge 1983

TENNANT, L.   Leicestershire

Full Name: Lloyd Tennant
Role: Right-hand bat, right-arm medium bowler, outfielder
Born: 9 April 1968, Walsall
Height: 5' 11" **Weight:** 12st 7lbs
Nickname: Charmaine (after the Tennent Lager advert)
County debut: 1986
1st-Class catches 1989: 0 (career 1)
Parents: Dennis and Jean
Marital status: Single
Family links with cricket: Father played local club cricket as opening bowler
Education: Shellfield Comprehensive School
Qualifications: 8 CSEs
Jobs outside cricket: Fencing and bricklaying

Off-season 1989–90: Working for GBG Fencing Ltd. To Zimbabwe after Christmas to play cricket
Cricketing superstitions or habits: 'Wearing favourite gear. Always put left boot on first.'
Overseas tours: England U-19 to Sri Lanka 1986–87
Cricketers particularly learnt from: Ken Higgs, Alan Townsend
Cricketers particularly admired: Ian Botham, Malcolm Marshall
Other sports played: Football
Relaxations: Listening to music, watching TV

Opinions on cricket: 'Politics should be kept out of the game.'
Best batting performance: 12* Leicestershire v Sussex, Leicester 1986
Best bowling performance: 1-0 Leicestershire v Warwickshire, Edgbaston 1988

LAST SEASON: BATTING

	I.	N.O.	R.	H.S.	AV.
TEST					
1ST-CLASS					
INT					
RAL	2	1	14	13	14.00
NAT.W.					
B & H					

LAST SEASON: BOWLING

	O.	M.	R.	W.	AV.
TEST					
1ST-CLASS					
INT					
RAL	6	0	39	0	–
NAT.W.					
B & H					

CAREER: BATTING

	I.	N.O.	R.	H.S.	AV.
TEST					
1ST-CLASS	4	2	16	12*	8.00
INT					
RAL	7	5	44	17*	22.00
NAT.W.					
B & H					

CAREER: BOWLING

	O.	M.	R.	W.	AV.
TEST					
1ST-CLASS	34	6	110	3	36.66
INT					
RAL	81	5	354	11	32.18
NAT.W.					
B & H					

TERRY, V. P.　　　　　Hampshire

Full Name: Vivian Paul Terry
Role: Right-hand bat, right-arm medium bowler, slip or cover fielder
Born: 14 January 1959, Osnabruck, West Germany
Height: 6′ **Weight:** 13st 6lbs
County debut: 1978
County cap: 1983
Test debut: 1984
No. of Tests: 2
1000 runs in a season: 6
1st-Class 50s scored: 53
1st-Class 100s scored: 17
One-Day 50s: 27
One-Day 100s: 6
Place in batting averages: 88th av. 31.92 (1988 95th av. 29.55)
1st-Class catches 1989: 39 (career 195)
Parents: Michael and Patricia
Wife and date of marriage: Bernadette, 4 June 1986

Children: Siobhan Catherine, 13 September 1987

Education: Durlston Court, Barton-on-Sea, Hampshire; Millfield School, Somerset

Qualifications: 8 O-levels, 1 A-level, advanced cricket coach

Jobs outside cricket: Worked in a fish factory, apple picker, estate agent, coach

Off-season 1989–90: 'In the main, coaching in Hampshire.'

Overseas tours: ESCA tour to India 1977–78; Gordon Greenidge benefit tour to Paris and Isle of Wight; English Counties tour to Zimbabwe 1985; Hampshire CCC to Dubai 1989

Overseas teams played for: Sydney 1978–79; in New Zealand 1980–81; Durban Collegians 1982–83

Cricketers particularly learnt from: Chris Smith

Cricketers particularly admired: Gordon Greenidge, Chris Smith, Viv and Barry Richards, Malcolm Marshall, Gary Sobers

Other sports played: Golf, squash, soccer

Other sports followed: Most sports

Relaxations: Music, sport

Opinions on cricket: 'Why don't the authorities do what most people feel should be done – 16 four-day games? It's obvious we play too much cricket, and because of this one tends to "drift" at times. In such circumstances, every game does not seem crucial.'

Best batting performance: 190 Hampshire v Sri Lankans, Southampton 1988

LAST SEASON: BATTING

	I.	N.O.	R.	H.S.	AV.
TEST	–	–	–	–	–
1ST-CLASS	41	2	1245	180	31.92
INT					
RAL	14	1	332	79*	25.53
NAT.W.	4	0	110	99	27.50
B & H	4	0	184	76	46.00

CAREER: BATTING

	I.	N.O.	R.	H.S.	AV.
TEST	3	0	16	8	5.33
1ST-CLASS	289	30	8923	190	34.45
INT					
RAL	114	15	2975	142	30.05
NAT.W.	21	1	789	165*	39.45
B & H	35	3	1185	109	37.03

145. Who bowled the third most first-class overs last season?

THOMAS, J. G.   Northamptonshire

Full Name: John Gregory Thomas
Role: Right-hand bat, right-arm
fast bowler
Born: 12 August 1960, Trebanos,
Swansea
Height: 6′ 3″ **Weight:** 14st
Nickname: Blodwen
County debut: 1979 (Glamorgan),
1989 (Northamptonshire)
County cap: 1986 (Glamorgan)
Test debut: 1985–86
No. of Tests: 5
No. of One-Day Internationals: 3
50 wickets in a season: 1
1st-Class 50s scored: 6
1st-Class 100s scored: 2
1st-Class 5 w. in innings: 15
1st-Class 10 w. in match: 1
Place in batting averages: 248th
av. 11.93 (1988 142nd av. 24.52)
Place in bowling averages: 62nd av. 29.04 (1988 94th av. 31.89)
Strike rate 1989: 48.02 (career 77.76)
1st-Class catches 1989: 3 (career 59)
Parents: Illtyd and Margaret
Marital status: Single
Family links with cricket: Father played village cricket
Education: Cwmtawe Comprehensive School; South Glamorgan Institute of
Higher Education

LAST SEASON: BATTING

	I.	N.O.	R.	H.S.	AV.
TEST					
1ST-CLASS	32	3	346	35	11.93
INT					
RAL	6	1	67	23	13.40
NAT.W.	1	0	1	1	1.00
B & H	3	0	7	3	2.33

CAREER: BATTING

	I.	N.O.	R.	H.S.	AV.
TEST	10	4	83	31*	13.83
1ST-CLASS	217	35	2976	110	16.35
INT	3	2	1	1*	1.00
RAL	69	15	657	37	12.16
NAT.W.	11	3	151	34	18.87
B & H	20	2	162	32	9.00

LAST SEASON: BOWLING

	O.	M.	R.	W.	AV.
TEST					
1ST-CLASS	536.2	79	1946	67	29.04
INT					
RAL	90	4	394	17	23.17
NAT.W.	28	0	114	8	14.25
B & H	43.2	7	135	8	16.87

CAREER: BOWLING

	O.	M.	R.	W.	AV.
TEST	129	18	504	10	50.40
1ST-CLASS	3898	690	13556	455	29.79
INT	26	2	144	3	48.00
RAL	560.1	35	2660	104	25.57
NAT.W.	107.5	7	406	17	23.88
B & H	238.2	32	896	33	27.15

Qualifications: Qualified teacher, advanced cricket coach
Off-season 1989–90: Touring South Africa with unofficial England team
Cricketing superstitions or habits: The number 111
Overseas tours: British Colleges to West Indies 1982; England to West Indies 1985–86; unofficial England tour to South Africa 1990
Overseas teams played for: Border Cricket Union, South Africa 1983–87; Eastern Province 1987–89
Other sports followed: Watches rugby
Relaxations: Any sport, music
Extras: Bowling award for four wickets or more most times in 1983. Having never hit a first-class century before, hit two in August 1988. Signed for Northamptonshire in 1989
Best batting performance: 110 Glamorgan v Warwickshire, Edgbaston 1988
Best bowling performance: 6-53 Northamptonshire v Leicestershire, Northampton 1989

THORNE, D. A.   Warwickshire

Full Name: David Anthony Thorne
Role: Right-hand bat, left-arm medium bowler, slip fielder
Born: 12 December 1964, Coventry
Height: 5′ 11″ **Weight:** 12st
Nickname: Strop, Thorney
County debut: 1983
1st-Class 50s scored: 16
1st-Class 100s scored: 2
1st-Class 5 w. in innings: 1
One-Day 50s: 1
Place in batting averages: 235th av. 13.40 (1988 151st av. 23.58)
1st-Class catches 1989: 5 (career 54)
Parents: Dennis and Barbara
Marital status: Single
Family links with cricket: Father is a qualified coach in Warwickshire area, and was a very good club player. Brothers, Robert and Philip, both played for Warwickshire Schools. Mother played for Hinckley Ladies
Education: Bablake School, Coventry; Keble College, Oxford
Qualifications: 10 O-levels, 3 A-levels, BA (2.1) in Modern History; MCC coaching certificate

503

Jobs outside cricket: Components packager for Quinton Hazell car components. Worked as a labourer on building site pre-season 1983. Teaching
Cricketing superstitions or habits: 'Always left pad on first. If I get runs I try to wear the same shirt and trousers no matter how dirty until I fail again.'
Overseas tours: Oxbridge to Hong Kong and Australia 1985–86. Barbados tours with Dennis Amiss 1985, and Geoff Humpage 1987
Cricketers particularly learnt from: 'Dennis Amiss, Dermot Reeve, Dean Hoffmann and above all my Father.'
Cricketers particularly admired: Rob Weir, Dennis Amiss, Paul Smith, Norman Gifford
Other sports played: Rugby, golf, football
Other sports followed: 'Football, any sports except horse racing.'
Relaxations: Listening to music, reading biographies and non-fiction. Watching good films
Extras: Hit for 26 in 3rd over in first John Player League game by Trevor Jesty. Was out first ball on first-class debut v Oxford University. Once took 7 for 7 in a school's first XI match including a hat-trick and all seven bowled. Secretary OUCC 1985, captain 1986. Scored unbeaten 100 in 1986 Varsity Match only to lose off last ball to a leg-bye
Opinions on cricket: 'There is too much cricket played in this country. Four-day cricket is an excellent idea, but the pitches must be improved. That is what is wrong, above all, with English cricket at the moment. There should only be one overseas player per county.'
Best batting performance: 124 Oxford University v Zimbabwe, Oxford 1985
Best bowling performance: 5-39 Oxford University v Cambridge University, Lord's 1984

LAST SEASON: BATTING

	I.	N.O.	R.	H.S.	AV.
TEST					
1ST-CLASS	10	0	134	41	13.40
INT					
RAL	6	0	70	28	11.66
NAT.W.	1	1	2	2*	–
B & H	4	2	121	57*	60.50

LAST SEASON: BOWLING

	O.	M.	R.	W.	AV.
TEST					
1ST-CLASS	6	2	13	0	–
INT					
RAL					
NAT.W.					
B & H					

CAREER: BATTING

	I.	N.O.	R.	H.S.	AV.
TEST					
1ST-CLASS	113	15	2523	124	25.74
INT					
RAL	35	10	479	59*	19.16
NAT.W.	5	1	72	21	18.00
B & H	19	5	325	57*	23.21

CAREER: BOWLING

	O.	M.	R.	W.	AV.
TEST					
1ST-CLASS	705.5	156	2078	41	50.68
INT					
RAL	95.5	1	580	13	44.61
NAT.W.	1	0	4	0	–
B & H	60.3	4	251	1	251.00

THORPE, G. P.   Surrey

Full Name: Graham Paul Thorpe
Role: Left-hand bat, right-arm medium bowler
Born: 1 August 1969, Farnham
Height: 5′ 10″ **Weight:** 12st
Nickname: Chalky
County debut: 1988
1000 runs in a season: 1
1st-Class 50s scored: 8
1st-Class 100s scored: 3
One-Day 50s: 4
Place in batting averages: 20th av. 45.28
1st-Class catches 1989: 12 (career 15)
Parents: Geoff and Toni
Marital status: Single
Family links with cricket: 'Both brothers play cricket, so does Dad. Mother a qualified scorer.'
Education: Weydon Comprehensive; Farnham Sixth-Form College
Qualifications: 6 O-levels, PE Diploma
Jobs outside cricket: Working for wine merchants. British Telecom
Off-season 1989–90: Touring Zimbabwe with England A. Working for British Telecom, and selling wine
Overseas tours: Surrey CCC to Dubai 1988, 1989; England A to Zimbabwe 1990
Cricketers particularly learnt from: Graham Clinton, David Smith, Alec Stewart

LAST SEASON: BATTING

	I.	N.O.	R.	H.S.	AV.
TEST					
1ST-CLASS	30	5	1132	154	45.28
INT					
RAL	12	1	349	80	31.72
NAT.W.	3	0	83	74	27.66
B & H	1	0	22	22	22.00

CAREER: BATTING

	I.	N.O.	R.	H.S.	AV.
TEST					
1ST-CLASS	36	7	1290	154	44.48
INT					
RAL	13	1	364	80	30.33
NAT.W.	3	0	83	74	27.66
B & H	1	0	22	22	22.00

LAST SEASON: BOWLING

	O.	M.	R.	W.	AV.
TEST					
1ST-CLASS	55	5	205	4	51.25
INT					
RAL	17	0	100	2	50.00
NAT.W.	2	0	12	0	–
B & H	11	2	35	3	11.66

CAREER: BOWLING

	O.	M.	R.	W.	AV.
TEST					
1ST-CLASS	85	8	282	8	35.25
INT					
RAL	21	1	125	2	62.50
NAT.W.	2	0	12	0	–
B & H	11	2	35	3	11.66

Cricketers particularly admired: Ian Botham, Viv Richards, Mark Ramprakash
Other sports played: Football, squash, snooker, table tennis
Other sports followed: Football, American football
Relaxations: 'Talking to Graham Clinton and James Boiling. Seeing my girlfriend. Reading cricket books, and watching old videos of the war.'
Extras: Played England Schools cricket U-15 and U-19 and England Schools football U-18
Opinions on cricket: 'There should be 16 four-day matches, with two limited-overs competitions.'
Best batting performance: 154 Surrey v Kent, The Oval 1989
Best bowling performance: 2-31 Surrey v Essex, The Oval 1989

TOLLEY, C. M.   Worcestershire

Full Name: Christopher Mark Tolley
Role: Right-hand bat, left-arm medium bowler
Born: 30 December 1967, Kidderminster
Height: 5' 9" **Weight:** 10st 8lbs
Nickname: Frog, Clyde
County debut: 1989
Parents: Ray and Elisabeth
Marital status: Single
Family links with cricket: Father played local league; brother Richard plays for Stourbridge in the Birmingham League (he has played Youth Representative Cricket for Worcestershire)
Education: Oldswinford Primary School; Redhill Comprehensive School; King Edward VI College, Stourbridge; 'doing my third year at Loughborough University.'
Qualifications: 9 O-levels, 3 A-levels, sitting finals for BSc PE Sports Science and Recreation Management
Jobs outside cricket: Builder's labourer
Off-season 1989–90: 'I will be doing my finals at Loughborough University.'
Cricketing superstitions or habits: 'I put on my batting kit in the same order every time.'
Overseas tours: The British Universities Sports Federation tour to Barbados October 1989

Cricketers particularly learnt from: 'My father, Basil D'Oliveira (coach), Dave Collins (club coach), Mark Scott.'
Cricketers particularly admired: Ian Botham, Richard Hadlee, Graeme Hick
Other sports played: Hockey, football, tennis, table tennis
Relaxations: Listening to music, watching sport (either live or on TV)
Extras: Played for ESCA U-19 in 1986; played for the Combined Universities 1989
Best batting performance: 37 Worcestershire v Kent, Worcester 1989
Best bowling performance: 1-21 Worcestershire v Somerset, Worcester 1989

LAST SEASON: BATTING

	I.	N.O.	R.	H.S.	AV.
TEST					
1ST-CLASS	6	2	120	37	30.00
INT					
RAL	–	–	–	–	–
NAT.W.					
B & H	4	1	30	22	10.00

CAREER: BATTING

	I.	N.O.	R.	H.S.	AV.
TEST					
1ST-CLASS	6	2	120	37	30.00
INT					
RAL	–	–	–	–	–
NAT.W.					
B & H	4	1	30	22	10.00

LAST SEASON: BOWLING

	O.	M.	R.	W.	AV.
TEST					
1ST-CLASS	61	16	138	1	138.00
INT					
RAL	13	1	37	1	37.00
NAT.W.					
B & H	49	8	167	4	41.75

CAREER: BOWLING

	O.	M.	R.	W.	AV.
TEST					
1ST-CLASS	61	16	138	1	138.00
INT					
RAL	13	1	37	1	37.00
NAT.W.					
B & H	49	8	167	4	41.75

146. Who scored the most first-class county runs last season?

147. Who were the only two Derbyshire batsmen to score 1000 runs last season for Derbyshire?

148. Who hit the second most first-class county runs last season?

TOPLEY, T. D.   Essex

Full Name: Thomas Donald Topley
Role: Right-hand bat, right-arm
fast-medium bowler
Born: 25 February 1964, Canterbury
Height: 6' 3" **Weight:** 13st 8lbs
Nickname: Toppers, Baldrick,
Wimble, Jack
County debut: 1985 (Surrey),
1985 (Essex)
County cap: 1988 (Essex)
50 wickets in a season: 2
1st-Class 50s scored: 2
1st-Class 5 w. in innings: 11
1st-Class 10 w. in match: 2
Place in batting averages: 243rd
av. 12.59 (1988 230th av. 14.68)
Place in bowling averages: 37th
av. 24.03 (1988 53rd av. 25.60)
Strike rate 1989: 47.20 (career 49.84)
1st-Class catches 1989: 14 (career 38)
Parents: Tom and Rhoda
Marital status: Single
Family links with cricket: Brother Peter played for Kent (1972–75). Father
played for Royal Navy
Education: Royal Hospital School, Holbrook, Suffolk
Qualifications: 6 O-levels, NCA Coach at Intermediate level
Jobs outside cricket: Progress Officer at C. K. & P., exporting to the Gulf
States, 1984–85. Shipping agent, Brightlingsea Port Ltd, 1988–89
Off-season 1989–90: 'Staying in England and hibernating!'
Cricketing superstitions or habits: 'Trying to avoid changing next to Pringle!'
Overseas tours: Keith Pont Benefit tour to Barbados 1986
Overseas teams played for: Natal Midlands & Noodsburg, South Africa 1985–
86; Roodeport City CC 1986–87; Griqualand West, South Africa 1987–88
Cricketers particularly learnt from: Don Wilson, Geoff Arnold, and all at
Essex
Cricketers particularly admired: John Lever, Graham Gooch
Other sports played: Rugby, football, badminton and all ball sports
Other sports followed: Rugby, soccer
Injuries 1989: Sliced finger in early season, by a letter box. Shin soreness
returned in September
Relaxations: Photography, food, travelling
Extras: Spent three years prior to joining Essex on the MCC Young

Professionals at Lord's. As 12th man held famous Test match one-handed 'catch' for England v West Indies at Lord's: unfortunately, did not count as he fell over rope in taking it. Played for Surrey during 1985

Opinions on cricket: 'I am in favour of four-day cricket, but only if the wickets will last; hence the need to improve wickets. Abolish the 25 point system for bad wickets, and instead "heavily" fine the club.'

Best batting performance: 66 Essex v Yorkshire, Leeds 1987

Best bowling performance: 7-75 Essex v Derbyshire, Chesterfield 1988

LAST SEASON: BATTING

	I.	N.O.	R.	H.S.	AV.
TEST					
1ST-CLASS	26	4	277	49	12.59
INT					
RAL	5	2	33	12*	11.00
NAT.W.					
B & H	–	–	–	–	–

CAREER: BATTING

	I.	N.O.	R.	H.S.	AV.
TEST					
1ST-CLASS	88	20	1038	66	15.26
INT					
RAL	20	7	110	23	8.46
NAT.W.	3	1	25	15*	12.50
B & H	2	2	9	6*	–

LAST SEASON: BOWLING

	O.	M.	R.	W.	AV.
TEST					
1ST-CLASS	606.5	143	1851	77	24.03
INT					
RAL	87	2	383	16	23.93
NAT.W.					
B & H	40	12	101	6	16.83

CAREER: BOWLING

	O.	M.	R.	W.	AV.
TEST					
1ST-CLASS	2078	434	6214	250	24.85
INT					
RAL	314	16	1330	57	23.33
NAT.W.	61.2	9	188	12	15.66
B & H	138	24	445	22	20.22

TREMLETT, T. M.   Hampshire

Full Name: Timothy Maurice Tremlett
Role: Right-hand bat, right-arm medium bowler
Born: 26 July 1956, Wellington, Somerset
Height: 6′ 2″ **Weight:** 13st 7lbs
Nickname: Hurricane, Trooper, R2
County debut: 1976
County cap: 1983
50 wickets in a season: 4
1st-Class 50s scored: 17
1st-Class 100s scored: 1
1st-Class 5 w. in innings: 11
Place in batting averages: 120th av. 27.50 (1988 336th av. 13.87)
Place in bowling averages: 25th av. 22.25 (1988 36th av. 23.28)

Strike rate 1989: 60.00 (career 58.66)

1st-Class catches 1989: 0 (career 72)

Parents: Maurice Fletcher and Melina May

Wife and date of marriage: Carolyn Patricia, 28 September 1979

Children: Christopher Timothy, 2 September 1981; Alastair Jonathan, 1 February 1983; Benjamin Paul, 2 May 1984

Family links with cricket: Father played for Somerset and for England against West Indies in the West Indies 1947–48. Captained Somerset 1958–60. Younger brother plays local club cricket for Deanery CC

Education: Bellemoor Secondary Modern; Richard Taunton Sixth-Form College

Qualifications: 5 O-levels, 1 A-level. Advanced Coaching Certificate

Jobs outside cricket: One winter spent labouring on building site for muscle-building ('did not seem to work'). Furrier in father-in-law's business. 'I am still registered to play cricket for Hampshire, although I am now employed full-time as coaching/cricket administrator.'

Cricketing superstitions or habits: 'I always like to be the last to leave the dressing room when taking the field plus always walk round the large table on the right-hand side in our dressing room before taking the field. This has replaced leaving the dressing room last as most of our players rarely get out on time!'

Overseas tours: English Counties tour to Zimbabwe 1985; England B to Sri Lanka 1986

Overseas teams played for: Oudtshoorn Teachers' Training College, Western Cape, South Africa 1978–79

Cricketers particularly learnt from: 'My father, and in general watching and listening to other cricketers, first-class or club players.'

Cricketers particularly admired: Vincent van der Bijl, Mike Hendrick, Malcolm Marshall, Richard Hadlee

Other sports played: Golf (7 handicap), table tennis, squash, swimming, badminton

Injuries 1989: Dislocated right thumb – off for ten days in May

Relaxations: Collecting cricket books and records, gardening, cinema

Extras: Member of local cricket club, Deanery. Batted in almost every position for Hants in batting order from 1 to 11 in 1979. Captained both his school and sixth-form college at cricket. Writes a weekly column in *Portsmouth Sports Mail*. Appointed captain of Hampshire 2nd XI for 1990

Opinions on cricket: 'With ever increasing numbers of top-class cricketers withdrawing from international fixtures, the cricketing authorities will hopefully begin to reduce the amount of cricket played in this country, especially one-day cricket. With the emphasis still geared towards one-day matches, specialists are still outnumbered heavily by bits-and-pieces performers, with young spin-bowlers particularly at a disadvantage. To ensure that the highest standards are maintained, the structure of English first-class cricket is in further need of streamlining.'

Best batting performance: 102* Hampshire v Somerset, Taunton 1985
Best bowling performance: 6-53 Hampshire v Somerset, Weston-super-Mare 1987

LAST SEASON: BATTING

	I.	N.O.	R.	H.S.	AV.
TEST					
1ST-CLASS	8	4	110	40*	27.50
INT					
RAL	1	1	7	7*	–
NAT.W.					
B & H					

LAST SEASON: BOWLING

	O.	M.	R.	W.	AV.
TEST					
1ST-CLASS	160	49	356	16	22.25
INT					
RAL	16	1	72	3	24.00
NAT.W.					
B & H					

CAREER: BATTING

	I.	N.O.	R.	H.S.	AV.
TEST					
1ST-CLASS	244	63	3719	102*	20.54
INT					
RAL	55	25	321	35	10.70
NAT.W.	13	4	142	43*	15.77
B & H	25	10	213	36*	14.20

CAREER: BOWLING

	O.	M.	R.	W.	AV.
TEST					
1ST-CLASS	4292.3	1239	10366	439	23.61
INT					
RAL	892.4	37	4155	164	25.33
NAT.W.	213.2	37	697	28	24.89
B & H	325.5	50	1063	46	23.10

TRUMP, H. R. J.   Somerset

Full Name: Harvey Russell John Trump
Role: Right-hand bat, off-spin bowler
Born: 11 October 1968, Taunton
Height: 6′ 2″ **Weight:** 13st 3lbs
Nickname: Trumpton
County debut: 1988
Place in bowling averages: 110th av. 45.00 (1988 72nd av. 29.00)
Strike rate 1989: 99.84 (career 84.00)
1st-Class catches 1989: 6 (career 13)
Marital status: Single
Family links with cricket: Father played for Somerset 2nd XI and captained Devon
Education: Edgarley Hall (Millfield Jnr School); Millfield School; Chester College of Higher Education
Qualifications: 7 O-levels, 2 A-levels
Off-season 1989–90: Doing last year of degree at Chester
Cricketing superstitions or habits: 'Too numerous to mention.'

511

Overseas tours: England Young Cricketers to Sri Lanka; to Australia for Junior World Cup; NCA (South) to Northern Ireland for U-19 ICC Tournament

Cricketers particularly learnt from: Vic Marks, Steve Waugh, Jimmy Cook

Cricketers particularly admired: John Emburey, Vic Marks, Viv Richards

Other sports played: Hockey especially, and most other ball games

Other sports followed: Hockey

Relaxations: Reading, walking, swimming, 'helping disabled children when possible'

Extras: Played county hockey for Somerset U-19s. Qualified lifeguard, attaining bronze medallion lifesaving award. Preliminary teacher of disabled swimming certificate

Opinions on cricket: 'As most cricketers believe, something has to be done about the over-rate fining system. We must improve our respective county coaching systems wherever possible, to ensure that youngsters of high quality remain in their home county and are assembled occasionally as a group in their own age-groups, for assessment and progress reports – especially in the winter. This enables an eye to be kept on promising talent, and their promise possibly enhanced.'

Best batting performance: 48 Somerset v Hampshire, Taunton 1988

Best bowling performance: 4-17 Somerset v Kent, Canterbury 1988

LAST SEASON: BATTING

	I.	N.O.	R.	H.S.	AV.
TEST					
1ST-CLASS	15	2	94	31*	7.23
INT					
RAL	2	0	2	2	1.00
NAT.W.	1	0	0	0	0.00
B & H					

LAST SEASON: BOWLING

	O.	M.	R.	W.	AV.
TEST					
1ST-CLASS	416	93	1125	25	45.00
INT					
RAL	70	2	301	8	37.62
NAT.W.	21	0	73	2	36.50
B & H					

CAREER: BATTING

	I.	N.O.	R.	H.S.	AV.
TEST					
1ST-CLASS	26	3	156	48	6.78
INT					
RAL	3	0	6	4	2.00
NAT.W.	1	0	0	0	0.00
B & H					

CAREER: BOWLING

	O.	M.	R.	W.	AV.
TEST					
1ST-CLASS	686	167	1821	49	37.16
INT					
RAL	70	2	301	8	37.62
NAT.W.	21	0	73	2	36.50
B & H					

149. Who hit the third most first-class county runs last season?

TUFNELL, P. C. R.   Middlesex

Full Name: Philip Clive Roderick
Tufnell
Role: Right-hand bat, slow left-arm
spinner
Born: 29 April 1966, Hadley Wood,
Hertfordshire
Height: 6′ **Weight:** 11st 8lbs
Nickname: Tuffers, Brucie
County debut: 1986
50 wickets in a season: 1
1st-Class 5 w. in innings: 4
Place in bowling averages: 60th
av. 28.43 (1988 126th av. 42.32)
Strike rate 1989: 65.69 (career
77.19)
1st-Class catches 1989: 9 (career 20)
Parents: Sylvia and Alan
Wife and date of marriage: Alison
Jane, 5 October 1986
Education: Highgate School; Southgate School
Qualifications: O-level in Art; City & Guilds Silversmithing
Jobs outside cricket: Silversmith, mini-cabbing
Overseas tours: Young England tour to the West Indies 1985
Cricketers particularly learnt from: Jack Robertson, Gordon Jenkins, Don
Wilson
Cricketers particularly admired: Clive Radley, Derek Underwood
Other sports played: Snooker, hack around at golf
Other sports followed: American football

LAST SEASON: BATTING

	I.	N.O.	R.	H.S.	AV.
TEST					
1ST-CLASS	11	3	54	12	6.75
INT					
RAL	1	1	13	13*	–
NAT.W.	–	–	–	–	–
B & H					

CAREER: BATTING

	I.	N.O.	R.	H.S.	AV.
TEST					
1ST-CLASS	38	12	151	20	5.80
INT					
RAL	1	1	13	13*	–
NAT.W.	–	–	–	–	–
B & H					

LAST SEASON: BOWLING

	O.	M.	R.	W.	AV.
TEST					
1ST-CLASS	602.1	160	1564	55	28.43
INT					
RAL	10	0	44	1	44.00
NAT.W.	12	1	50	1	50.00
B & H					

CAREER: BOWLING

	O.	M.	R.	W.	AV.
TEST					
1ST-CLASS	1518.1	386	4085	118	34.61
INT					
RAL	24	1	106	2	53.00
NAT.W.	24	4	79	4	19.75
B & H					

Relaxations: 'Taking Alison and her friend Elaine shopping. Finding excuses to get out of buying a round.'
Extras: MCC Young Cricketer of the Year 1984. Middlesex uncapped Bowler of the Year 1987
Opinions on cricket: 'Tea should be longer. Keep uncovered wickets.'
Best batting performance: 20 Middlesex v Kent, Lord's 1988
Best bowling performance: 6-60 Middlesex v Kent, Canterbury 1987

TURNER, D. R.   Hampshire

Full Name: David Roy Turner
Role: Left-hand bat, right-arm slow medium bowler, out-fielder
Born: 5 February 1949, Corsham, nr Chippenham, Wiltshire
Height: 5′ 6″ **Weight:** 11st 8lbs
Nickname: Birdy, Fossil
County debut: 1966
County cap: 1970
Benefit: 1981 (£23,011)
1000 runs in a season: 9
1st-Class 50s scored: 90
1st-Class 100s scored: 28
One-Day 50s: 60
One-Day 100s: 5
Place in batting averages: 115th av. 28.00 (1988 58th av. 35.41)
1st-Class catches 1989: 2 (career 191)
Parents: Robert Edward and Evelyn Peggy
Wife and date of marriage: Henriette, 18 February 1977
Children: Nicola Marianna, 15 March 1984
Education: Chippenham Boys' High School
Qualifications: 5 O-levels
Off-season 1989–90: Becoming involved in the shoe business
Overseas tours: With Derrick Robins' XI to South Africa 1972–73
Overseas teams played for: Western Province in the winning 1977–78 Currie Cup Competition side; player-coach for Paarl Cricket Club, South Africa 1972–80, 1982–85
Cricketers particularly learnt from: Roy Marshall
Cricketers particularly admired: Mike Procter
Other sports played: Golf, football, athletics
Injuries 1989: 'Split little finger on right hand, which required several stitches.

514

Out of action for seven to ten days, missing first two matches of the season. Was taken ill in mid-July, and missed a week. Had an operation on an infected finger/hand injury on left hand, missing two to three weeks in late August to early September.'

Relaxations: Chess, gardening, reading, television, watching war films

Extras: Played for Wiltshire in 1965. Took a hat-trick in a Lambert & Butler 7-a-side floodlit tournament at Ashton Gate, Bristol on 17 September 1981 v Glamorgan. Captained school at soccer, rugger and cricket. Also ran for school in cross-country and athletics. Shared in an unbeaten partnership of 283 with C. G. Greenidge, a record in any one-day competition, in Benson & Hedges Cup, Hampshire v Minor Counties South at Amersham in 1973. Scored a career best 184* v Gloucestershire in 1987, 18 years since previous best Championship score

Opinions on cricket: 'I would like the cricket authorities to try for one season, 16 four-day Championship matches, coupled with a Saturday 60-overs limited cricket league, along with the usual Sunday League. There should be tighter controls on overseas players. They should scrap the no-substitute rule. Perhaps substitutes should only be allowed at the discretion of the umpires. In four-day cricket, they should increase the follow-on figure from 150 to 175. Also, captains should be given the chance to choose any roller they wish.'

Best batting performance: 184* Hampshire v Gloucestershire, Gloucester 1987

Best bowling performance: 2-7 Hampshire v Glamorgan, Bournemouth 1981

LAST SEASON: BATTING

	I.	N.O.	R.	H.S.	AV.
TEST					
1ST-CLASS	17	4	364	65*	28.00
INT					
RAL	9	0	210	66	23.33
NAT.W.	1	1	22	22*	–
B & H	4	1	81	40*	27.00

CAREER: BATTING

	I.	N.O.	R.	H.S.	AV.
TEST					
1ST-CLASS	696	74	19005	184*	30.55
INT					
RAL	248	23	6639	114	29.50
NAT.W.	38	5	985	100*	29.84
B & H	76	12	2164	123*	33.81

LAST SEASON: BOWLING

	O.	M.	R.	W.	AV.
TEST					
1ST-CLASS	4.2	1	11	0	–
INT					
RAL					
NAT.W.					
B & H					

CAREER: BOWLING

	O.	M.	R.	W.	AV.
TEST					
1ST-CLASS	104.2	28	357	9	39.66
INT					
RAL	1.3	0	11	0	–
NAT.W.	1	0	4	0	–
B & H	0.2	0	4	0	–

TURNER, I. J.   Hampshire

Full Name: Ian John Turner
Role: Right-hand bat, slow left-arm bowler
Born: 18 July 1968, Denmead
Height: 6' 1" **Weight:** 14st
Nickname: Turns
County debut: 1989
Parents: Robert and Sheila
Marital status: Single
Family links with cricket: 'Dad plays for Hambledon CC.'
Education: Cowplain Comprehensive School; South Downs College
Qualifications: 7 CSEs, pass in BTec General Diploma in Business Studies
Jobs outside cricket: Bank clerk
Off-season 1989–90: 'Going to Australia to play for Waverley in Sydney.'
Cricketing superstitions or habits: 'Always put on left pad first.'
Cricketers particularly learnt from: Peter Sainsbury, Robert 'Topsy' Turner (father)
Cricketers particularly admired: Sir Garfield Sobers, Malcolm Marshall, Robin Smith
Other sports played: 'Anything and everything within reason.'
Other sports followed: 'Football – especially Liverpool – and look at Portsmouth scores.'

LAST SEASON: BATTING

	I.	N.O.	R.	H.S.	AV.
TEST					
1ST-CLASS	2	1	9	9*	9.00
INT					
RAL					
NAT.W.					
B & H					

LAST SEASON: BOWLING

	O.	M.	R.	W.	AV.
TEST					
1ST-CLASS	35	21	48	4	12.00
INT					
RAL					
NAT.W.					
B & H					

CAREER: BATTING

	I.	N.O.	R.	H.S.	AV.
TEST					
1ST-CLASS	2	1	9	9*	9.00
INT					
RAL					
NAT.W.					
B & H					

CAREER: BOWLING

	O.	M.	R.	W.	AV.
TEST					
1ST-CLASS	35	21	48	4	12.00
INT					
RAL					
NAT.W.					
B & H					

516

Injuries 1989: Had an operation on ligaments in left knee – off for three months. Started again in middle of July
Relaxations: Listening to music
Opinions on cricket: 'State of pitches in 2nd XI cricket is inadequate. Why not put the games on County pitches?'
Best batting performance: 9* Hampshire v Glamorgan, Southampton 1989
Best bowling performance: 3-20 Hampshire v Glamorgan, Southampton 1989

TWOSE, R. G.   Warwickshire

Full Name: Roger Graham Twose
Role: Left-hand bat, right-arm fast-medium bowler
Born: 17 April 1968, Torquay ('in a car!')
Height: 6′ **Weight:** 14st
Nickname: Twosey, Buffalo, Rhino
County debut: 1989
Place in batting averages: 152nd av. 23.16
1st-Class catches 1989: 2 (career 2)
Parents: Paul Francis Worth and Patricia Ann
Marital status: Single
Family links with cricket: Father played for Devon, brother Richard plays for Devon, uncles – Roger Tolchard played for Leicestershire and England, Jeff Tolchard played for Leicestershire
Education: Wolborough Hill, Newton Abbot, Devon; King's College, Taunton, Somerset
Qualifications: 7 O-levels, 2 A-levels, NCA Coaching Certificate
Jobs outside cricket: Potato picker, baker, water meter reading
Off-season 1989–90: Playing cricket in Auckland, New Zealand
Cricketing superstitions or habits: 'Not listening to Ratters! (Jason Ratcliffe).'
Overseas tours: King's College, Taunton to Barbados, West Indies 1984
Overseas teams played for: Combined Colleges & Horowhenua, New Zealand 1986, 1988; Papakura & Counties, New Zealand 1989
Cricketers particularly learnt from: Ken Rogers, Roy Marshall, Roger Tolchard, Jeff Tolchard, John Poustie

517

Cricketers particularly admired: 'My brother Richard, Ian Botham, Viv Richards, Vince Baines, Haydon Gray.'

Other sports played: Rugby, hockey, soccer, golf, all sports

Other sports followed: 'Ali Babar wrestling and chess.'

Injuries 1989: 'Tore ligaments in left ankle – off for 5 weeks in June and July.'

Relaxations: Fishing, travelling, skiing etc

Extras: 'Once took all ten wickets in an innings whilst playing in New Zealand (much to Geoff Humpage's amusement)!'

Opinions on cricket: 'Night games under floodlights should be introduced with coloured clothing and individual names on shirts, commercializing the game – even if it meant hiring football grounds and laying down temporary wickets, play through the rain if need be, anything for the paying public.'

Best batting performance: 37 Warwickshire v Hampshire, Bournemouth 1989

Best bowling performance: 1-54 Warwickshire v Yorkshire, Leeds 1989

LAST SEASON: BATTING

	I.	N.O.	R.	H.S.	AV.
TEST					
1ST-CLASS	9	3	139	37	23.16
INT					
RAL	6	1	79	28	15.80
NAT.W.	1	0	9	9	9.00
B & H					

CAREER: BATTING

	I.	N.O.	R.	H.S.	AV.
TEST					
1ST-CLASS	9	3	139	37	23.16
INT					
RAL	6	1	79	28	15.80
NAT.W.	1	0	9	9	9.00
B & H					

LAST SEASON: BOWLING

	O.	M.	R.	W.	AV.
TEST					
1ST-CLASS	38.5	3	143	1	143.00
INT					
RAL	24	0	128	3	42.66
NAT.W.	10	0	31	1	31.00
B & H					

CAREER: BOWLING

	O.	M.	R.	W.	AV.
TEST					
1ST-CLASS	38.5	3	143	1	143.00
INT					
RAL	24	0	128	3	42.66
NAT.W.	10	0	31	1	31.00
B & H					

150. Who was the oldest Test player on his debut?

151. What is the lowest ever Test team total?

UDAL, S. D.   Hampshire

Full Name: Shaun David Udal
Role: Right-hand bat, off-spin
bowler, field in the deep
Born: 18 March 1969, Farnborough
Height: 6′ 2″ **Weight:** 11½st
Nickname: Prawn
County debut: 1989
Parents: Robin and Mary
Marital status: Single
Family links with cricket:
Grandfather played for Middlesex
and Leicestershire; father played
for Surrey Colts, and for Camberley
CC for thirty-five years
Education: Tower Hill Infant and
Junior Schools; Cove County
Secondary School

Qualifications: 8 CSEs, qualified print finisher
Jobs outside cricket: Print finisher
Off-season 1989–90: Playing for Hamilton CC in Newcastle, Sydney,
Australia
Cricketing superstitions or habits: Left pad on first, tap corner of crease when
batting
Overseas teams played for: Hamilton CC, Sydney 1989
Cricketers particularly learnt from: Grandfather, father, Peter Sainsbury
Cricketers particularly admired: Ian Botham, Malcolm Marshall
Other sports played: Football, golf, snooker
Other sports followed: Aldershot FC
Relaxations: Watching videos, going out for a drink, going to nightclubs
Extras: Has taken two hat-tricks in club cricket, and scored a double hundred
in a 40-over club game
Opinions on cricket: 'Too much one-day cricket, and too many bad 2nd XI
pitches.'

LAST SEASON: BOWLING

	O.	M.	R.	W.	AV.
TEST					
1ST-CLASS	11	6	21	0	–
INT					
RAL	5	0	36	1	36.00
NAT.W.					
B & H					

CAREER: BOWLING

	O.	M.	R.	W.	AV.
TEST					
1ST-CLASS	11	6	21	0	–
INT					
RAL	5	0	36	1	36.00
NAT.W.					
B & H					

UNWIN, P. D.

Somerset

Full Name: Paul David Unwin
Role: Right-hand bat, occasional bowler
Born: 9 June 1967, Waidawa, New Zealand
County debut: 1989
1st-Class 5 w. in innings: 1
1st-Class 10 w. in match: 1
1st-Class catches 1989: 0 (career 18)
Overseas teams played for: Central Districts, New Zealand 1986–89
Best batting performance: 34 Central Districts v Auckland, Palmerston North 1986–87
Best bowling performance: 6-42 Central Districts v Otago, Palmerston North 1986–87

LAST SEASON: BATTING

	I.	N.O.	R.	H.S.	AV.
TEST					
1ST-CLASS	1	1	4	4*	–
INT					
RAL					
NAT.W.					
B & H					

CAREER: BATTING

	I.	N.O.	R.	H.S.	AV.
TEST					
1ST-CLASS	15	6	156	34	17.33
INT					
RAL					
NAT.W.					
B & H					

LAST SEASON: BOWLING

	O.	M.	R.	W.	AV.
TEST					
1ST-CLASS	36	6	116	5	23.20
INT					
RAL					
NAT.W.					
B & H					

CAREER: BOWLING

	O.	M.	R.	W.	AV.
TEST					
1ST-CLASS	463.1	82	1703	40	42.57
INT					
RAL					
NAT.W.					
B & H					

WALKER, A.   Northamptonshire

Full Name: Alan Walker
Role: Left-hand bat, right-arm fast-medium bowler, outfielder
Born: 7 July 1962, Emley, nr Huddersfield
Height: 5′ 11″ **Weight:** 12st 7lbs
Nickname: Walks, Wacky
County debut: 1983
County cap: 1987
1st-Class 5 w. in innings: 2
Place in batting averages: —
(1988 179th av. 21.30)
Place in bowling averages: —
(1988 52nd av. 25.55)
1st-Class catches 1989: 3 (career 35)
Parents: Malcolm and Enid
Wife and date of marriage: Janice, 17 September 1983
Education: Emley Junior School; Kirkburton Middle School; Shelley High School
Qualifications: 2 O-levels, 4 CSEs, qualified coal-face worker
Jobs outside cricket: Miner; worked in iron foundry
Off-season 1989–90: Ground work for local builder
Cricketing superstitions or habits: Puts right pad on first, wears the same thing next day if successful the day before
Overseas tours: Denmark with NCA U-19s (North of England) 1980
Overseas teams played for: Uitenhage, South Africa 1984–85, 1986–87
Cricketers particularly learnt from: David Steele, Nick Cook, Winston Davis, Dennis Lillee
Cricketers particularly admired: Dennis Lillee, Richard Hadlee, Malcolm Marshall
Other sports played: Football
Other sports followed: Rugby league (Wakefield Trinity), football (Huddersfield Town)
Injuries 1989: Strained ligament on kneecap – off one week; torn calf – off two weeks; torn hamstring – off two weeks; back strain – off four weeks
Relaxations: 'Watching TV, listening to music, DIY, gardening, cooking, socialising.'
Extras: Took part in a sponsored drive to every first-class headquarters, including Oxford, Cambridge and Arundel, in one day, with four other members of the club, raising money for Cat-scan appeal and the cricket club

Best batting performance: 41* Northamptonshire v Warwickshire, Edgbaston 1987
Best bowling performance: 6-50 Northamptonshire v Lancashire, Northampton 1986

LAST SEASON: BATTING

	I.	N.O.	R.	H.S.	AV.
TEST					
1ST-CLASS	7	4	46	14*	15.33
INT					
RAL	3	3	5	4*	–
NAT.W.	–	–	–	–	–
B & H					

LAST SEASON: BOWLING

	O.	M.	R.	W.	AV.
TEST					
1ST-CLASS	75	13	274	5	54.80
INT					
RAL	32.4	5	109	7	15.57
NAT.W.	12	4	29	1	29.00
B & H					

CAREER: BATTING

	I.	N.O.	R.	H.S.	AV.
TEST					
1ST-CLASS	85	44	589	41*	14.36
INT					
RAL	14	8	56	13	9.33
NAT.W.	3	1	11	7	5.50
B & H	6	5	30	15*	30.00

CAREER: BOWLING

	O.	M.	R.	W.	AV.
TEST					
1ST-CLASS	2079.1	424	6461	212	30.47
INT					
RAL	451.2	27	2044	84	24.33
NAT.W.	112.4	19	382	15	25.46
B & H	184.1	13	819	23	35.60

WALSH, C. A.   Gloucestershire

Full Name: Courtney Andrew Walsh
Role: Right-hand bat, right-arm fast bowler
Born: 30 October 1962, Kingston, Jamaica
Height: 6′ 5½″ **Weight:** 14st 7lbs
Nickname: Mark, Walshy, Cuddy
County debut: 1984
County cap: 1985
Test debut: 1984–85
No. of Tests: 34
No. of One-Day Internationals: 68
50 wickets in a season: 4
1st-Class 50s scored: 2
1st-Class 5 w. in innings: 40
1st-Class 10 w. in match: 6
Place in batting averages: 200th av. 18.00
Place in bowling averages: 15th av. 20.67 (1988 111th av. 34.55)
Strike rate 1989: 46.49 (career 45.82)

1st-Class catches 1989: 2 (career 47)
Parents: Eric and Joan Wollaston
Marital status: Single
Education: Excelsior High School
Qualifications: GCE and CXL
Off-season 1989–90: Playing for the West Indies
Overseas tours: West Indies Young Cricketers to Zimbabwe 1983; West Indies to England 1984; to Australia 1984–85, 1986–87; to Pakistan 1986; to India 1987–88; World Cup 1987; to England 1988
Overseas teams played for: Jamaica 1981–88
Cricketers particularly learnt from: Michael Holding, Andy Roberts, Malcolm Marshall, George Headley
Cricketers particularly admired: Michael Holding, Viv Richards, Lawrence Rowe, Richard Hadlee, Clive Lloyd, Imran Khan
Other sports played: Football, basketball, tennis
Other sports followed: Basketball, track and field events
Injuries 1989: Injured right arm – off from 22 June until 5 July; and again from 12 July to 26 July
Relaxations: Swimming, reading and listening to music
Extras: Took record 10-43 in Jamaican school cricket in 1979. Played in MCC Bicentenary Test 1987. On tour, he has the reputation as an insatiable collector of souvenirs. David Graveney, when captaining Gloucestershire, reckoned Walsh was the 'best old-ball bowler in the world'. One of *Wisden*'s Five Cricketers of the Year, 1986. Took hat-trick for West Indies v Australia
Best batting performance: 52 Gloucestershire v Yorkshire, Bristol 1986
Best bowling performance: 9-72 Gloucestershire v Somerset, Bristol 1986

LAST SEASON: BATTING

	I.	N.O.	R.	H.S.	AV.
TEST					
1ST-CLASS	25	5	360	47	18.00
INT					
RAL	6	2	37	18*	9.25
NAT.W.	1	1	9	9*	–
B & H	3	0	43	28	14.33

CAREER: BATTING

	I.	N.O.	R.	H.S.	AV.
TEST	43	16	277	30*	10.25
1ST-CLASS	164	39	1521	52	12.16
INT	20	9	77	18	7.00
RAL	27	6	185	35	8.80
NAT.W.	7	3	56	25*	14.00
B & H	9	3	73	28	12.16

LAST SEASON: BOWLING

	O.	M.	R.	W.	AV.
TEST					
1ST-CLASS	627.4	134	1675	81	20.67
INT					
RAL	55.5	4	234	13	18.00
NAT.W.	12	2	27	1	27.00
B & H	29	6	93	3	31.00

CAREER: BOWLING

	O.	M.	R.	W.	AV.
TEST	1102.5	239	2958	122	24.24
1ST-CLASS	4128.3	727	12498	563	22.19
INT	609.3	53	2317	76	30.48
RAL	328.4	24	1355	66	20.53
NAT.W.	105	13	345	15	23.00
B & H	143.3	19	500	17	29.41

WARD, D. M.   Surrey

Full Name: David Mark Ward
Role: Right-hand bat, off-break
bowler, gully fielder
Born: 10 February 1961, Croydon
Height: 6′ **Weight:** 13st 2lbs
Nickname: Cocker, Wardy, Jaws,
Gnasher
County debut: 1985
1st-Class 50s scored: 8
1st-Class 100s scored: 3
One-Day 50s: 6
Place in batting averages: 133rd
av. 25.33 (1988 79th av. 31.40)
1st-Class catches 1989: 24 (career 55,
inc. catches taken as wicket-keeper)
Parents: Thomas and Dora Kathleen
Marital status: Single
Education: Haling Manor High
School; Croydon Technical College
Qualifications: 2 O-levels, Advanced City and Guilds in Carpentry and
Joinery
Jobs outside cricket: Carpenter. Working in Chinese take-away
Off-season 1989–90: 'In the sun!'
Cricketing superstitions or habits: Marks across corner of non-striking crease
with bat
Overseas tours: Barbados 1985 with Surrey; Dubai 1988 with Surrey
Overseas teams played for: Caulfield CC, Australia 1984–85, 1985–86 and
1986–87; Sunshine CC, Australia 1987–88

LAST SEASON: BATTING

	I.	N.O.	R.	H.S.	AV.
TEST					
1ST-CLASS	26	2	608	145	25.33
INT					
RAL	16	2	409	76	29.21
NAT.W.	3	0	198	97	66.00
B & H	4	0	34	14	8.50

LAST SEASON: WICKET KEEPING

	C.	ST.			
TEST					
1ST-CLASS	14	–			
INT					
RAL	1	–			
NAT.W.	1	–			
B & H					

CAREER: BATTING

	I.	N.O.	R.	H.S.	AV.
TEST					
1ST-CLASS	88	12	2107	145	27.72
INT					
RAL	53	10	1074	76	24.97
NAT.W.	7	0	231	97	33.00
B & H	7	0	46	14	6.57

CAREER: WICKET KEEPING

	C.	ST.			
TEST					
1ST-CLASS	14	–			
INT					
RAL	4	–			
NAT.W.	1	–			
B & H					

Cricketers particularly learnt from: Geoff Arnold, Chris Waller, Rehan Alikhan, Keith Ebdon

Cricketers particularly admired: Graham Gooch, Ian Botham, Viv Richards, John Goodey (Banstead CC), Neil Silberry

Other sports played: Football, snooker, table tennis

Other sports followed: Charlton FC – 'seem to spend most of the time with my hands over my eyes!'

Relaxations: Eating out, watching TV, movies, jazz, golf, greyhound racing

Opinions on cricket: 'Why can't we work where we want?'

Best batting performance: 145 Surrey v Oxford University, Oxford 1989

WARD, T. R.   Kent

Full Name: Trevor Robert Ward

Role: Right-hand bat; occasional off-spin bowler

Born: 18 January 1968, Farningham, Kent

Height: 5′ 11″ **Weight:** 12st 11lbs

Nickname: Wardy, Gwondwana Butts

County debut: 1986

1000 runs in a season: 1

1st-Class 50s scored: 12

1st-Class 100s scored: 1

One-Day 50s: 2

Place in batting averages: 60th av. 35.91 (1988 80th av. 21.29)

1st-Class catches 1989: 12 (career 21)

Parents: Robert Henry and Hazel Ann

Marital status: Engaged

Family links with cricket: Father played a little village cricket with Farningham

Education: Anthony Roper County Primary; Hextable Comprehensive

Qualifications: 7 O-levels

Jobs outside cricket: Worked in building trade; sports shop assistant

Off-season 1989–90: Working in Kent

Cricketing superstitions or habits: Puts left pad on first

Overseas tours: NCA to Bermuda 1985; Young England to Sri Lanka 1987; Young England to Australia 1988 for Youth World Cup

Overseas teams played for: Scarborough CC, Perth, Western Australia 1985–86

Cricketers particularly learnt from: Alan Ealham, Derek Aslett, Colin Page, Graham Saville

Cricketers particularly admired: Graham Gooch, Mike Gatting, Ian Botham, Gordon Greenidge, Roy Pienaar – 'for his athleticism and awareness in the field.'

Other sports played: Football, golf, squash

Other sports followed: Football, most sports

Relaxations: Watching films, fishing

Opinions on cricket: 'Less cricket, with more four-day games. And with four-day cricket, there must be better batting wickets, to ensure the matches go the full distance. Counties must try to find employment for players through the winter.'

Best batting performance: 104 Kent v Somerset, Bath 1989

Best bowling performance: 1-84 Kent v Nottinghamshire, Trent Bridge 1989

LAST SEASON: BATTING

	I.	N.O.	R.	H.S.	AV.
TEST					
1ST-CLASS	40	5	1257	104	35.91
INT					
RAL	15	0	301	54	20.06
NAT.W.	2	0	101	83	50.50
B & H	6	1	118	37	23.60

LAST SEASON: BOWLING

	O.	M.	R.	W.	AV.
TEST					
1ST-CLASS	41.5	8	157	1	157.00
INT					
RAL	23	0	98	3	32.66
NAT.W.	12	0	58	1	58.00
B & H	2	0	10	0	–

CAREER: BATTING

	I.	N.O.	R.	H.S.	AV.
TEST					
1ST-CLASS	61	6	1679	104	30.52
INT					
RAL	20	0	357	54	17.85
NAT.W.	4	0	136	83	34.00
B & H	6	1	118	37	23.60

CAREER: BOWLING

	O.	M.	R.	W.	AV.
TEST					
1ST-CLASS	45.5	9	161	1	161.00
INT					
RAL	23	0	98	3	32.66
NAT.W.	12	0	58	1	58.00
B & H	2	0	10	0	–

152. Which Test wicket-keeper made the most dismissals in his career: R. W. Marsh of Australia, or A. P. E. Knott of England?

153. Which wicket-keeper holds the record for the most dismissals in a Test?

WARNER, A. E.   Derbyshire

Full Name: Allan Esmond Warner
Role: Right-hand bat, right-arm
fast bowler, outfielder
Born: 12 May 1959, Birmingham
Height: 5′ 8″ **Weight:** 10st
Nickname: Esis
County debut: 1982 (Worcestershire),
1985 (Derbyshire)
County cap: 1987
1st-Class 50s scored: 13
1st-Class 5 w. in innings: 2
One-Day 50s: 1
Place in batting averages: 222nd
av. 14.88 (1988 224th av. 15.78)
Place in bowling averages: 33rd
av. 23.45 (1988 57th av. 26.15)
Strike rate 1989: 56.77 (career 61.30)
1st-Class catches 1989: 4 (career 30)
Parents: Edgar and Sarah
Children: Alvin, 6 September 1980
Education: Tabernacle School, St Kitts, West Indies
Qualifications: CSE Maths
Jobs outside cricket: Bricklaying
Cricketers particularly learnt from: John Browny, Henry Benjamin
Cricketers particularly admired: Malcolm Marshall, Michael Holding
Other sports played: Football, table tennis
Other sports followed: Football, boxing and athletics
Relaxations: Watching movies, music (soul, reggae and calypso)

LAST SEASON: BATTING

	I.	N.O.	R.	H.S.	AV.
TEST					
1ST-CLASS	23	6	253	46	14.88
INT					
RAL	5	1	95	40	23.75
NAT.W.	1	0	0	0	0.00
B & H	2	1	5	5*	5.00

LAST SEASON: BOWLING

	O.	M.	R.	W.	AV.
TEST					
1ST-CLASS	331.1	80	821	35	23.45
INT					
RAL	62.4	1	277	7	39.57
NAT.W.	12	2	60	1	60.00
B & H	22	4	62	5	12.40

CAREER: BATTING

	I.	N.O.	R.	H.S.	AV.
TEST					
1ST-CLASS	173	33	2384	91	17.02
INT					
RAL	58	13	595	68	13.22
NAT.W.	6	0	66	32	11.00
B & H	17	6	107	24*	9.72

CAREER: BOWLING

	O.	M.	R.	W.	AV.
TEST					
1ST-CLASS	2319.2	464	7158	227	31.53
INT					
RAL	504.1	11	2629	87	30.21
NAT.W.	85.3	11	354	8	44.25
B & H	250.2	22	1046	38	27.52

Extras: Released by Worcestershire at end of 1984 and joined Derbyshire
Best batting performance: 91 Derbyshire v Leicestershire, Chesterfield 1986
Best bowling performance: 5-27 Worcestershire v Glamorgan, Worcester 1984

WASIM AKRAM Lancashire

Full Name: Wasim Akram
Role: Left-hand bat, left-arm fast-medium bowler
Born: 3 June 1966, Lahore, Pakistan
Height: 6′ 3″ **Weight:** 12st 7lbs
County debut: 1988
Test debut: 1984–85
No. of Tests: 25
No. of One-Day Internationals: 58
50 wickets in a season: 1
1st-Class 50s scored: 7
1st-Class 100s scored: 1
1st-Class 5 w. in innings: 16
1st-Class 10 w. in match: 3
One-Day 50s: 1
Place in batting averages: 175th av. 20.58 (1988 81st av. 31.00)
Place in bowling averages: 5th av. 17.73 (1988 20th av. 21.48)
Strike rate 1989: 44.49 (career 58.94)
1st-Class catches 1989: 3 (career 25)

LAST SEASON: BATTING

	I.	N.O.	R.	H.S.	AV.
TEST					
1ST-CLASS	20	3	350	49	20.58
INT					
RAL	13	4	210	44*	23.33
NAT.W.	3	0	38	19	12.66
B & H	4	1	126	52	42.00

CAREER: BATTING

	I.	N.O.	R.	H.S.	AV.
TEST	31	6	410	66	16.40
1ST-CLASS	58	11	1153	116*	24.53
INT	35	6	298	48*	10.27
RAL	20	6	336	44*	24.00
NAT.W.	5	0	61	19	12.20
B & H	7	1	168	52	28.00

LAST SEASON: BOWLING

	O.	M.	R.	W.	AV.
TEST					
1ST-CLASS	467.1	103	1117	63	17.73
INT					
RAL	104.3	6	399	27	14.77
NAT.W.	29	6	114	2	57.00
B & H	55	8	217	13	16.69

CAREER: BOWLING

	O.	M.	R.	W.	AV.
TEST	829	206	2098	76	27.60
1ST-CLASS	1277.5	280	3235	146	22.15
INT	474.2	46	1826	71	25.71
RAL	170	9	663	41	16.17
NAT.W.	49	8	179	6	29.83
B & H	85.4	9	326	16	20.37

Education: Islamia College
Off-season 1989–90: Playing in and for Pakistan
Overseas tours: Pakistan U-23 to Sri Lanka 1984–85; Pakistan to New Zealand 1984–85; Sri Lanka 1985–86; India 1986–87; England 1987; West Indies 1987–88
Overseas teams played for: PACO 1984–86; Lahore Whites 1985–86
Extras: His second first-class match was playing for Pakistan on tour in New Zealand. Imran Khan wrote of him: 'I have great faith in Wasim Akram. I think he will become a great all-rounder, as long as he realises how much hard work is required. His batting needs attention, but he has the advantage of thinking like a lower order batsman: he doesn't have the problems of being a frustrated opening bat. As a bowler he is extremely gifted, and has it in him to be the best left-armer since Alan Davidson.'
Best batting performance: 116* Lancashire v Somerset, Old Trafford 1988
Best bowling performance: 7-42 World XI v MCC XI, Scarborough 1989

WATKIN, S. L. Glamorgan

Full Name: Steven Llewellyn Watkin
Role: Right-hand bat, right-arm fast-medium bowler
Born: 13 September 1964, Duffryn, Rhondda, nr Port Talbot
Height: 6′ 6″ **Weight:** 13st 4lbs
Nickname: Watty, Banger
County debut: 1986
County cap: 1989
50 wickets in a season: 1
1st-Class 5 w. in innings: 10
1st-Class 10 w. in match: 3
Place in bowling averages: 40th av. 25.10 (1988 87th av. 30.93)
Strike rate 1989: 50.56 (career 56.43)
1st-Class catches 1989: 7 (career 8)
Parents: John and Sandra

Wife and date of marriage: Bronwyn, February 1989
Family links with cricket: 'Brother plays for Maesteg, and Mum makes the teas.'
Education: Cymer Afan Comprehensive; Swansea College of Further Education; South Glamorgan Institute of Higher Education
Qualifications: 8 O-levels, 2 A-levels, BA degree in Human Movement Studies, BA in Modern Dance and Drama

Jobs outside cricket: Delivering telephone directories. Busking in Cardiff High Street
Off-season 1989–90: Touring Zimbabwe with England A
Cricketing superstitions or habits: 'Like to get on the front foot first ball. Don't like to spend too long at the crease!'
Overseas tours: British Colleges to West Indies 1987; Zimbabwe with England 1990
Overseas teams played for: Potchefstroom University, South Africa 1987–88
Cricketers particularly learnt from: Tom Cartwright, Alan Jones, Barry Lloyd, Edward Bevan
Cricketers particularly admired: Richard Hadlee, Dennis Lillee
Other sports played: Football, tennis, basketball, orienteering, motor racing
Other sports followed: All sports except horse racing
Relaxations: Watching TV, listening to music, a few beers
Opinions on cricket: 'Four-day cricket is here to stay. It produces better cricket, and less results coming from captain's agreements.'
Best batting performance: 31 Glamorgan v Leicestershire, Leicester 1989
Best bowling performance: 8-59 Glamorgan v Warwickshire, Edgbaston 1988

LAST SEASON: BATTING

	I.	N.O.	R.	H.S.	AV.
TEST					
1ST-CLASS	29	5	134	31	5.58
INT					
RAL	6	2	49	28*	12.25
NAT.W.	1	1	2	2*	–
B & H	3	2	5	3*	5.00

LAST SEASON: BOWLING

	O.	M.	R.	W.	AV.
TEST					
1ST-CLASS	792.1	170	2359	94	25.10
INT					
RAL	90.4	6	453	13	34.84
NAT.W.	18	5	40	2	20.00
B & H	35.3	10	121	3	40.33

CAREER: BATTING

	I.	N.O.	R.	H.S.	AV.
TEST					
1ST-CLASS	48	12	249	31	6.91
INT					
RAL	8	3	57	28*	11.40
NAT.W.	1	1	2	2*	–
B & H	4	3	9	4*	9.00

CAREER: BOWLING

	O.	M.	R.	W.	AV.
TEST					
1ST-CLASS	1335.4	300	3864	142	27.21
INT					
RAL	131.4	8	633	21	30.14
NAT.W.	18	5	40	2	20.00
B & H	38.3	10	146	3	48.66

154. Which rugger international played Minor Counties cricket last season?

WATKINSON, M. — Lancashire

Full Name: Michael Watkinson
Role: Right-hand bat, right-arm medium or off-break bowler
Born: 1 August 1961, Westhoughton
Height: 6′ 1½″ **Weight:** 13st
Nickname: Winker
County debut: 1982
County cap: 1987
50 wickets in a season: 2
1st-Class 50s scored: 25
1st-Class 100s scored: 1
1st-Class 5 w. in innings: 14
One-Day 50s: 6
Place in batting averages: 162nd av. 22.31 (1988 173rd av. 21.68)
Place in bowling averages: 54th av. 28.06 (1988 109th av. 34.21)
Strike rate 1989: 54.96 (career 63.47)
1st-Class catches 1989: 12 (career 73)
Parents: Albert and Marian
Wife and date of marriage: Susan, 12 April 1986
Education: Rivington and Blackrod High School, Horwich
Qualifications: 8 O-levels, HTC Civil Engineering
Jobs outside cricket: Draughtsman
Overseas tours: Lancashire CCC to West Indies 1987–88
Overseas teams played for: Woder Valley CC, Canberra 1984–85
Cricketers particularly learnt from: Paul Allott, Steve O'Shaughnessy
Cricketers particularly admired: Clive Lloyd, Imran Khan

LAST SEASON: BATTING

	I.	N.O.	R.	H.S.	AV.
TEST					
1ST-CLASS	39	6	733	70	22.21
INT					
RAL	14	3	249	57	22.63
NAT.W.	3	1	82	62	41.00
B & H	3	0	10	7	3.33

CAREER: BATTING

	I.	N.O.	R.	H.S.	AV.
TEST					
1ST-CLASS	209	29	4198	106	23.32
INT					
RAL	74	24	1089	58	21.78
NAT.W.	15	4	245	62	22.27
B & H	18	3	200	70*	13.33

LAST SEASON: BOWLING

	O.	M.	R.	W.	AV.
TEST					
1ST-CLASS	503.5	109	1540	55	28.00
INT					
RAL	98.4	3	430	13	33.07
NAT.W.	28	2	114	2	57.00
B & H	52	8	221	2	110.50

CAREER: BOWLING

	O.	M.	R.	W.	AV.
TEST					
1ST-CLASS	3110.3	660	9557	294	32.50
INT					
RAL	628.3	32	2955	94	31.43
NAT.W.	195.5	18	774	16	48.37
B & H	263.1	26	1102	29	38.00

Other sports played: Football
Extras: Played for Cheshire CCC in Minor Counties, and NatWest Trophy (v Middlesex) 1982. Man of the Match in the first ever Refuge Assurance Cup Final 1988
Best batting performance: 106 Lancashire v Surrey, Southport 1985
Best bowling performance: 7-25 Lancashire v Sussex, Lytham 1987

WAUGH, M. E.   Essex

Full Name: Mark Edward Waugh
Role: Right-hand bat, right-arm fast-medium pace bowler
Born: 2 June 1965, Canterbury, New South Wales
Height: 5′ 9¾″ **Weight:** 13st 7lbs
Nickname: Tugger, Junior
County debut: 1988
No. of One-Day Internationals: 6
1000 runs in a season: 1
1st-Class 50s scored: 20
1st-Class 100s scored: 10
One-Day 50s: 3
One-Day 100s: 2
Place in batting averages: 26th av. 43.91
Place in bowling averages: 63rd av. 29.64
Strike rate 1989: 50.28 (career 63.08)
1st-Class catches 1989: 31 (career 70)
Parents: Rodger and Beverley
Marital status: Single
Family links with cricket: Uncle a 1st Grade cricketer in Sydney for Bankstown/Canterbury. Twin-brother Steve plays for Australia and played for Somerset in 1988. Younger brother Dean played in Bolton League with Astley Bridge in 1989
Education: East Hills Boys High School
Qualifications: Higher School Certificate, cricket coach
Jobs outside cricket: Sales assistant, ML Sporting Goods 1983; Sales and Promotions, Kingsgrove Sports Store 1984–88
Off-season 1989–90: Playing cricket for New South Wales
Cricketing superstitions or habits: 'Almost always wear a short-sleeved jumper when batting.'
Overseas tours: With New South Wales to Zimbabwe 1986, 1987; to New Zealand 1986

Overseas teams played for: New South Wales 1985–90
Cricketers particularly learnt from: Bob Simpson, especially for his fielding techniques. 'Generally watching cricket you learn.'
Cricketers particularly admired: 'Allan Border for his guts and determination. Viv Richards for his natural aggression and flair.'
Other sports played: 'Any – but mainly golf and tennis.'
Other sports followed: Any – especially horse racing
Relaxations: Horse racing, eating, sleeping
Extras: Only twins to score hundreds in the same innings of a first-class match (Steve and Mark). Chosen as New South Wales Cricketer of the Year, 1988 and Sheffield Shield Cricketer of the Year, jointly with D. Tazelaar of Queensland and Surrey. Only batsman – so far – to score a century on his Sunday League debut
Opinions on cricket: 'Too much cricket is played, resulting in tiredness and injuries. Wickets must improve.'
Best batting performance: 165 Essex v Leicestershire, Leicester 1988–89
Best bowling performance: 4-130 New South Wales v Queensland 1985–86

LAST SEASON: BATTING

	I.	N.O.	R.	H.S.	AV.
TEST					
1ST-CLASS	39	4	1537	165	43.91
INT					
RAL	15	6	494	112*	54.88
NAT.W.	1	0	0	0	0.00
B & H	6	0	212	93	35.33

LAST SEASON: BOWLING

	O.	M.	R.	W.	AV.
TEST					
1ST-CLASS	117.2	19	415	14	29.64
INT					
RAL	19	0	104	4	26.00
NAT.W.					
B & H	2	0	20	0	–

CAREER: BATTING

	I.	N.O.	R.	H.S.	AV.
TEST					
1ST-CLASS	100	13	3767	165	43.29
INT	5	0	126	42	25.20
RAL	18	6	614	112*	51.16
NAT.W.	1	0	0	0	0.00
B & H	6	0	212	93	35.33

CAREER: BOWLING

	O.	M.	R.	W.	AV.
TEST					
1ST-CLASS	398	78	1308	35	37.37
INT					
RAL	32	1	172	6	28.66
NAT.W.					
B & H	2	0	20	0	–

155. What is the younger brother of Steve and Mark Waugh called?

WELLS, A. P.   Sussex

Full Name: Alan Peter Wells
Role: Right-hand bat, right-arm
medium bowler, cover fielder
Born: 2 October 1961, Newhaven
Height: 6′ **Weight:** 12st 4lbs
Nickname: Morph, Bomber
County debut: 1981
County cap: 1986
1000 runs in a season: 4
1st-Class 50s scored: 43
1st-Class 100s scored: 10
One-Day 50s: 18
Place in batting averages: 15th
av. 52.54 (1988 61st av. 34.75)
1st-Class catches 1989: 10 (career
86)
Parents: Ernest William Charles and
Eunice Mae
Marital status: Single
Family links with cricket: Father
played for many years for local club. Eldest brother Ray plays club cricket.
Brother of C. M. Wells of Sussex
Education: Tideway Comprehensive, Newhaven
Qualifications: 5 O-levels, NCA Coaching Certificate
Jobs outside cricket: Laboratory assistant. Coached in South Africa
Off-season 1989–90: Touring South Africa with unofficial England team
Cricketing superstitions or habits: 'Have to put bat at junction of return and
popping crease at the end of each over. Never stand inside the return crease

LAST SEASON: BATTING

	I.	N.O.	R.	H.S.	AV.
TEST					
1ST-CLASS	38	7	1629	153	52.54
INT					
RAL	15	0	393	72	26.20
NAT.W.	2	1	141	87*	141.00
B & H	4	0	55	20	13.75

CAREER: BATTING

	I.	N.O.	R.	H.S.	AV.
TEST					
1ST-CLASS	263	44	7485	161*	34.17
INT					
RAL	100	12	2165	72	24.60
NAT.W.	15	4	288	87*	26.18
B & H	26	2	638	72	26.58

LAST SEASON: BOWLING

	O.	M.	R.	W.	AV.
TEST					
1ST-CLASS	11.1	2	54	0	–
INT					
RAL					
NAT.W.					
B & H					

CAREER: BOWLING

	O.	M.	R.	W.	AV.
TEST					
1ST-CLASS	81.1	7	376	5	75.20
INT					
RAL	10.2	0	69	4	17.25
NAT.W.	1	0	1	0	–
B & H	10	1	72	3	24.00

when backing up. When repairing wicket count how many times I tap ground. Double whirl of arms with bat when going in to bat. Plus many more.'
Overseas tours: NCA U-19 tour of Canada 1979; unofficial England XI to South Africa 1989–90
Overseas teams played for: Border, South Africa 1981–82
Cricketers particularly learnt from: Father, Chris Waller, Roger Marshall, Les Lenham
Other sports played: Table tennis, squash, darts, snooker, tennis
Relaxations: Listening to music, eating out, drinking in country pubs
Extras: Played for England Young Cricketers v India 1981
Best batting performance: 161* Sussex v Kent, Hove 1987
Best bowling performance: 3-67 Sussex v Worcestershire, Worcester 1987

WELLS, C. M. Sussex

Full Name: Colin Mark Wells
Role: Right-hand bat, right-arm medium bowler
Born: 3 March 1960, Newhaven
Height: 6' **Weight:** 13st
Nickname: Bomber, Dougie
County debut: 1979
County cap: 1982
No. of One-Day Internationals: 2
1000 runs in a season: 6
50 wickets in a season: 2
1st-Class 50s scored: 51
1st-Class 100s scored: 17
1st-Class 200s scored: 1
1st-Class 5 w. in innings: 6
One-Day 50s: 21
One-Day 100s: 3
Place in batting averages: 80th

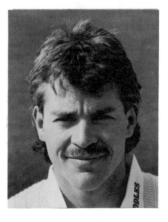

av. 32.93 (1988 141st av. 24.54)
Place in bowling averages: 51st av. 27.57 (1988 108th av. 34.16)
Strike rate 1989: 69.16 (career 69.60)
1st-Class catches 1989: 10 (career 77)
Parents: Ernest William Charles and Eunice Mae
Wife and date of marriage: Celia, 25 September 1982
Children: Jessica Louise, 2 October 1987
Family links with cricket: Father, Billy, had trials for Sussex and played for Sussex Cricket Association. Eldest brother Ray plays club cricket and youngest brother Alan plays for Sussex

Education: Tideway Comprehensive School, Newhaven
Qualifications: 9 O-levels, 2 CSEs, 1 A-level, MCC Intermediate Coaching Certificate
Jobs outside cricket: Working as a cellular telephone salesman for F. Smith & Co. of Horsham
Off-season 1989–90: Running sub-contract assembly and wiring business with father and brother, Alan
Cricketing superstitions or habits: Left boot and left pad on first
Overseas tours: With England to Sharjah 1985
Overseas teams played for: Border 1980–81; Western Province 1984–85
Other sports played: Football, rugby, hockey, basketball, tennis, table tennis
Relaxations: Sea-angling, philately, listening to music
Injuries 1989: Achilles heel problem – out for one game in August
Extras: Played in three John Player League matches in 1978. Was recommended to Sussex by former Sussex player, Ian Thomson. Highest 4th wicket partnership of 256 for Sussex v Glamorgan with Imran Khan. Vice captain since 1988
Opinions on cricket: 'Should play four-day cricket as soon as possible. Strongly believe that we cram in too much cricket, which must have a detrimental effect on all, especially the fast bowlers, particularly long term.'
Best batting performance: 203 Sussex v Hampshire, Hove 1984
Best bowling performance: 6-34 Sussex v Lancashire, Lytham 1987

LAST SEASON: BATTING

	I.	N.O.	R.	H.S.	AV.
TEST					
1ST-CLASS	36	4	1054	84*	32.93
INT					
RAL	15	2	314	63	24.15
NAT.W.	2	0	10	8	5.00
B & H	4	0	188	117	47.00

LAST SEASON: BOWLING

	O.	M.	R.	W.	AV.
TEST					
1ST-CLASS	564.5	152	1351	49	27.57
INT					
RAL	98	9	374	9	41.55
NAT.W.	34	1	121	0	–
B & H	42	6	182	8	22.75

CAREER: BATTING

	I.	N.O.	R.	H.S.	AV.
TEST					
1ST-CLASS	375	57	10634	203	33.44
INT	2	0	22	17	11.00
RAL	135	21	3201	104*	28.07
NAT.W.	22	3	415	76	21.84
B & H	41	4	1024	117	27.67

CAREER: BOWLING

	O.	M.	R.	W.	AV.
TEST					
1ST-CLASS	4025.2	957	11206	347	32.29
INT					
RAL	785.2	61	2918	105	27.79
NAT.W.	189.4	24	564	12	47.00
B & H	230	32	859	32	26.84

WELLS, V. J.   Kent

Full Name: Vincent John Wells
Role: Right-hand bat, right-arm
medium pace bowler, wicket-keeper
Born: 6 August 1965, Dartford
Height: 6′ **Weight:** 13st
Nickname: Wellsy
County debut: 1987
1st-Class catches 1989: 1 (career 2)
Parents: Pat and Jack
Wife and date of marriage: Debbie,
14 October 1989
Family links with cricket: Brother
plays club cricket in Kent League
Education: Downs School, Dartford;
Sir William Nottidge School,
Whitstable
Qualifications: 1 O-level, 8 CSEs
Jobs outside cricket: Ex-manager of
sportshop
Off-season 1989–90: 'Staying in England.'
Cricketing superstitions or habits: 'Put left pad on first. Never put right glove
on until I'm inside the boundary rope.'
Overseas teams played for: Parsnell CC, Auckland, New Zealand 1986;
Avendale CC 1986–87, 1988–89
Cricketers particularly learnt from: Colin Page, Bob Woolmer, Richard
Ellison
Cricketers particularly admired: David Gower, Ian Botham
Other sports played: Football. 'Enjoy most sports.'

LAST SEASON: BATTING

	I.	N.O.	R.	H.S.	AV.
TEST					
1ST-CLASS	4	1	37	22	12.33
INT					
RAL					
NAT.W.					
B & H					

LAST SEASON: BOWLING

	O.	M.	R.	W.	AV.
TEST					
1ST-CLASS	14	2	61	1	61.00
INT					
RAL			-		
NAT.W.					
B & H					

CAREER: BATTING

	I.	N.O.	R.	H.S.	AV.
TEST					
1ST-CLASS	6	1	43	22	8.60
INT					
RAL	2	1	12	10*	12.00
NAT.W.					
B & H	1	1	15	15*	–

CAREER: BOWLING

	O.	M.	R.	W.	AV.
TEST					
1ST-CLASS	28	6	112	2	56.00
INT					
RAL	22	1	68	7	9.71
NAT.W.					
B & H	7	1	33	0	–

Relaxations: 'Eating out; reading.'
Extras: Was a schoolboy footballer with Leyton Orient
Opinions on cricket: 'Sunday run-ups should return to shorter ones. Something should be done to make the Sunday League more exciting, and more of a family day out. For example, maybe coloured pads or gloves or clothing.'
Best batting performance: 22 Kent v Lancashire, Old Trafford 1989
Best bowling performance: 1-11 Kent v Derbyshire, Dartford 1989

WESTON, M. J.   Worcestershire

Full Name: Martin John Weston
Role: Right-hand bat, right-arm medium bowler
Born: 8 April 1959, Worcester
Height: 6' 1" **Weight:** 15st
Nickname: Wesso
County debut: 1979
County cap: 1986
1000 runs in a season: 1
1st-Class 50s scored: 26
1st-Class 100s scored: 3
One-Day 50s: 11
One-Day 100s: 1
Place in batting averages: 138th av. 24.89 (1988 118th av. 27.05)
Place in bowling averages: 68th av. 30.41 (1988 60th av. 26.33)
Strike rate 1989: 70.75 (career 79.52)
1st-Class catches 1989: 8 (career 70)
Parents: John Franklyn and Sheila Margaret
Marital status: Single
Family links with cricket: 'Father was a pretty useful all-rounder for the British Waterways team.'
Education: St George's C of E Junior; Samuel Southall Secondary Modern, '– and Worcester's Pavilion Bar!'
Qualifications: City & Guilds and Advance Crafts in Bricklaying
Jobs outside cricket: Coaching, bricklaying, finance executive
Off-season 1989–90: Working in finance
Cricketing superstitions or habits: 'Have a bacon sandwich before a game.'
Overseas tours: 1980 tour to Barbados with Worcestershire CCC
Cricketers particularly learnt from: Basil D'Oliveira

Other sports played: Football, squash
Other sports followed: Horse racing
Injuries 1989: Fractured index finger; torn thigh muscle; haemorrhoids
Relaxations: Reading *Sporting Life*
Opinions on cricket: 'Four-day cricket is a must. Certain one-day games should be played in coloured clothing, with a white ball.'
Best batting performance: 145* Worcestershire v Northamptonshire, Worcester 1984
Best bowling performance: 4-24 Worcestershire v Warwickshire, Edgbaston 1988

LAST SEASON: BATTING

	I.	N.O.	R.	H.S.	AV.
TEST					
1ST-CLASS	22	3	473	74	24.89
INT					
RAL	11	2	249	72	27.66
NAT.W.	4	0	142	50	35.50
B & H	3	1	34	19*	17.00

CAREER: BATTING

	I.	N.O.	R.	H.S.	AV.
TEST					
1ST-CLASS	229	19	5189	145*	24.70
INT					
RAL	91	14	1603	109	20.81
NAT.W.	17	4	419	50	32.23
B & H	29	1	535	56	19.10

LAST SEASON: BOWLING

	O.	M.	R.	W.	AV.
TEST					
1ST-CLASS	141.3	44	365	12	30.41
INT					
RAL	89	6	313	13	24.07
NAT.W.	30	2	104	1	104.00
B & H	12	1	39	1	39.00

CAREER: BOWLING

	O.	M.	R.	W.	AV.
TEST					
1ST-CLASS	1021.1	251	2924	77	37.97
INT					
RAL	397.3	17	1694	57	29.71
NAT.W.	104.2	13	390	10	39.00
B & H	90.1	8	325	11	29.54

156. Which Prime Minister described Lord's as the 'cathedral of cricket'?

157. Which legendary England fast bowler was awarded an OBE by the Queen in the 1989 Birthday Honours?

WHITAKER, J. J.　　Leicestershire

Full Name: John James Whitaker
Role: Right-hand bat, off-break
bowler
Born: 5 May 1962, Skipton,
Yorkshire
Height: 6' **Weight:** 13st
County debut: 1983
County cap: 1986
Test debut: 1986–87
No. of Tests: 1
No. of One-Day Internationals: 2
1000 runs in a season: 6
1st-Class 50s scored: 41
1st-Class 100s scored: 18
1st-Class 200s scored: 1
One-Day 50s: 13
One-Day 100s: 3
Place in batting averages: 48th
av. 37.88 (1988 52nd av. 35.97)

1st-Class catches 1989: 14 (career 98)
Parents: John and Anne
Family links with cricket: Father plays club cricket for Skipton
Education: Uppingham School
Qualifications: 7 O-levels
Jobs outside cricket: Employee of Whitakers Chocolates Ltd; groundsman,
Adelaide 1982–83; cricket coach and farmer, Tasmania 1983
Off-season 1989–90: Touring Zimbabwe with England A
Overseas tours: Australia 1981–82 with Uppingham School; England to
Australia 1986–87; England A to Zimbabwe 1990
Overseas teams played for: Glenelg CC, Adelaide 1982–83; Old Scotch CC,
Tasmania 1983–84; Somerset West, South Africa 1984–85
Cricketers particularly learnt from: Maurice Hallam (coach at Uppingham),
Brian Davison
Cricketers particularly admired: Geoff Boycott, Dennis Amiss
Other sports played: Rugby, hockey, tennis, golf, squash
Other sports followed: Football, Leicester Tigers rugby
Relaxations: Discos, music, reading, eating out
Extras: One of *Wisden*'s Five Cricketers of the Year, 1986
Opinions on cricket: 'Too many wickets are sub-standard. There is too much
first-class cricket.'
Best batting performance: 200* Leicestershire v Nottinghamshire, Leicester
1986

Best bowling performance: 1-41 Leicestershire v Essex, Leicester 1986

LAST SEASON: BATTING

	I.	N.O.	R.	H.S.	AV.
TEST					
1ST-CLASS	39	3	1364	138	37.88
INT					
RAL	14	2	413	81	34.41
NAT.W.	2	0	42	36	21.00
B & H	3	0	107	48	35.66

LAST SEASON: BOWLING

	O.	M.	R.	W.	AV.
TEST					
1ST-CLASS					
INT					
RAL					
NAT.W.					
B & H					

CAREER: BATTING

	I.	N.O.	R.	H.S.	AV.
TEST	1	0	11	11	11.00
1ST-CLASS	237	31	8066	200*	39.15
INT	2	1	48	44*	48.00
RAL	72	10	2031	132	32.75
NAT.W.	13	0	479	155	36.84
B & H	22	2	471	73*	23.55

CAREER: BOWLING

	O.	M.	R.	W.	AV.
TEST					
1ST-CLASS	20.2	2	168	1	168.00
INT					
RAL	0.2	0	4	0	–
NAT.W.	4	0	9	0	–
B & H					

WHITTICASE, P.   Leicestershire

Full Name: Philip Whitticase
Role: Right-hand bat, wicket-keeper
Born: 15 March 1965, Birmingham
Height: 5′ 8″ **Weight:** 10st 7lbs
Nickname: Jasper, Tracy,
Roland Rat
County debut: 1984
County cap: 1987
1st-Class 50s scored: 11
Place in batting averages: 102nd
av. 29.73 (1988 128th av. 21.31)
Parents: Larry Gordon and Ann
Marital status: Single
Family links with cricket:
Grandfather and Father club
cricketers (both wicket-keepers)
Education: Buckpool Secondary;
Crestwood Comprehensive
Qualifications: 5 O-levels, 4 CSEs,
coaching certificate
Jobs outside cricket: Inland Revenue, Linkbronze Ltd
Overseas teams played for: South Bunbury, Western Australia 1984–86
Cricketers particularly learnt from: D. Collins (Stourbridge CC), members of
Leicestershire staff

Cricketers particularly admired: Bob Taylor, Alan Knott, Philip DeFreitas, Dennis Amiss

Other sports played: Football, table tennis, golf. Used to be on schoolboy forms with Birmingham City FC

Relaxations: Football, golf, listening to music. 'I'm interested in most sports. Playing cards is amusing especially when Les Taylor and John Agnew are involved. A good night out.'

Extras: Played for MCC v Scotland 1985. Took two catches in Paddy Clift's hat-trick v Derby at Chesterfield 1985. Was Derek Underwood's last first-class victim

Opinions on cricket: 'I would like to see 16 four-day games, so that you play every county just once, during the week. Have the weekends purely for one-day cricket, Refuge League on a Sunday, and have a new competition on a Saturday, possibly involving coloured clothing.'

Best batting performance: 71 Leicestershire v Somerset, Leicester 1988

LAST SEASON: BATTING

	I.	N.O.	R.	H.S.	AV.
TEST					
1ST-CLASS	29	6	684	61	29.73
INT					
RAL	9	0	98	23	10.88
NAT.W.	1	0	0	0	0.00
B & H	2	2	50	36*	–

CAREER: BATTING

	I.	N.O.	R.	H.S.	AV.
TEST					
1ST-CLASS	127	29	2242	71	22.87
INT					
RAL	27	5	230	29*	10.45
NAT.W.	6	1	67	32	13.40
B & H	9	4	137	36*	27.40

LAST SEASON: WICKET KEEPING

	C.	ST.			
TEST					
1ST-CLASS	41	2			
INT					
RAL	10	–			
NAT.W.	2	–			
B & H	3	1			

CAREER: WICKET KEEPING

	C.	ST.			
TEST					
1ST-CLASS	227	9			
INT					
RAL	45	4			
NAT.W.	12	–			
B & H	19	1			

158. Who captained the Combined Universities last season?

WILD, D. J.   Northamptonshire

Full Name: Duncan James Wild
Role: Left-hand bat, right-arm
medium bowler
Born: 28 November 1962,
Northampton
Height: 6′ **Weight:** 12st 7lbs
Nickname: Oscar, Wildy, Spunko
County debut: 1980
County cap: 1986
1st-Class 50s scored: 13
1st-Class 100s scored: 5
One-Day 50s: 7
Place in batting averages: 187th
av. 19.53 (1988 218th av. 16.26)
Place in bowling averages: — (1988
91st av. 31.27)
1st-Class catches 1989: 7 (career 40)
Parents: John and Glenys
Marital status: Single
Family links with cricket: Father played for Northamptonshire
Education: Cherry Orchard Middle; Northampton School for Boys
Qualifications: 7 O-levels. Diploma in international trade
Jobs outside cricket: Law costs draughtsman, manufacturer's agent, proprietor of promotional clothing business
Off-season 1989–90: Running own business in Northampton
Overseas tours: England Young Cricketers to West Indies 1980
Cricketers particularly learnt from: Wayne Larkins, Bob Carter, Allan Lamb

LAST SEASON: BATTING

	I.	N.O.	R.	H.S.	AV.
TEST					
1ST-CLASS	15	0	293	121	19.53
INT					
RAL	10	3	210	54	30.00
NAT.W.	1	0	38	38	38.00
B & H	1	0	3	3	3.00

CAREER: BATTING

	I.	N.O.	R.	H.S.	AV.
TEST					
1ST-CLASS	163	21	3608	144	25.40
INT					
RAL	67	22	1008	91	22.40
NAT.W.	10	0	86	38	8.60
B & H	20	7	232	48	17.84

LAST SEASON: BOWLING

	O.	M.	R.	W.	AV.
TEST					
1ST-CLASS					
INT					
RAL	3	0	29	0	–
NAT.W.					
B & H					

CAREER: BOWLING

	O.	M.	R.	W.	AV.
TEST					
1ST-CLASS	878	79	2836	65	43.63
INT					
RAL	432.1	13	2094	73	28.68
NAT.W.	122.3	16	424	14	30.28
B & H	101.5	5	398	14	28.42

Cricketers particularly admired: David Gower, Richard Hadlee, Geoff Cook, Martin Crowe
Other sports played: Squash, golf
Other sports followed: Rugby, soccer
Relaxations: 'Shopping at Tesco's; drinking Guinness.'
Extras: Played for England Young Cricketers v Young India in 3-Test series 1981. Also for Young England v Young West Indies, 1982
Opinions on cricket: 'Play all four-day games; play each county once; start games on a Saturday. Sunday League the same as now. Benson & Hedges, and NatWest the same as now, except have two days to cover the game instead of three.'
Best batting performance: 144 Northamptonshire v Lancashire, Southport 1984
Best bowling performance: 4-4 Northamptonshire v Cambridge University, Cambridge 1986

WILLEY, P.   Leicestershire

Full Name: Peter Willey
Role: Right-hand bat, off-break bowler, all-rounder
Born: 6 December 1949, Sedgefield, Co Durham
Height: 6′ 1″ **Weight:** 13st
Nickname: Chin, Will
County debut: 1966 (Northamptonshire), 1984 (Leicestershire)
County cap: 1971 (Northamptonshire), 1984 (Leicestershire)
Benefit: 1981 (£31,400)
Test debut: 1976
No. of Tests: 26
No. of One-Day Internationals: 26
1000 runs in a season: 9
50 wickets in a season: 2
1st-Class 50s scored: 96
1st-Class 100s scored: 41
1st-Class 200s scored: 1
1st-Class 5 w. in innings: 26
1st-Class 10 w. in match: 3
One-Day 50s: 60
One-Day 100s: 9

544

Place in batting averages: 108th av. 28.94 (1988 135th av. 25.07)
Place in bowling averages: 44th av. 26.62 (1988 125th av. 42.26)
Strike rate 1989: 69.91 (career 74.23)
1st-Class catches 1989: 11 (career 219)
Parents: Oswald and Maisie
Wife and date of marriage: Charmaine, 23 September 1971
Children: Heather Jane, 11 September 1985
Family links with cricket: Father played local club cricket in County Durham
Education: Secondary School, Seaham, County Durham
Jobs outside cricket: Has worked as a groundsman, labourer and in a shoe factory
Overseas tours: Toured Australia with England 1979–80; West Indies 1981 and 1986; India 1979–80; with Derrick Robins' XI to South Africa 1972–73; to Sri Lanka 1977–78; with unofficial England XI to South Africa 1981–82
Overseas teams played for: Eastern Province, South Africa 1982–85
Cricketers particularly learnt from: Bishan Bedi, Geoffrey Boycott
Other sports played: Golf, shooting
Other sports followed: Football, golf, rugby
Relaxations: Reading, taking Irish Setter for long walks and shooting, gardening
Extras: With Wayne Larkins, received 2016 pints of beer (seven barrels) from a brewery in Northampton as a reward for their efforts in Australia with England in 1978–79. Hit a six off his first ball v Middlesex in JPL, 26 July 1981. Shared in 4th wicket partnership record for county, 370 with R. T. Virgin v Somerset at Northampton in 1976. Youngest player ever to play for Northamptonshire CCC at 16 years 180 days v Cambridge in 1966. Banned from Test cricket for three years for joining England rebel tour of South Africa in 1982. Left Northamptonshire at end of 1983 and moved to Leicestershire as vice-captain. Appointed Leicestershire captain for 1987. Resigned captaincy at end of season. Was the choice of former England captain, Mike Brearley,

LAST SEASON: BATTING

	I.	N.O.	R.	H.S.	AV.
TEST					
1ST-CLASS	37	2	1013	99	28.94
INT					
RAL	11	0	119	31	10.81
NAT.W.	2	0	132	89	66.00
B & H	2	0	64	41	32.00

CAREER: BATTING

	I.	N.O.	R.	H.S.	AV.
TEST	50	6	1184	102*	26.90
1ST-CLASS	810	104	21810	227	30.89
INT	24	1	538	64	23.39
RAL	246	18	6094	107	26.72
NAT.W.	46	6	1407	154*	35.17
B & H	62	11	1640	88*	32.15

LAST SEASON: BOWLING

	O.	M.	R.	W.	AV.
TEST					
1ST-CLASS	431.1	136	985	37	26.62
INT					
RAL	77	6	299	11	27.18
NAT.W.	24	3	72	2	36.00
B & H	33	4	104	2	52.00

CAREER: BOWLING

	O.	M.	R.	W.	AV.
TEST	181.5	49	456	7	65.14
1ST-CLASS	32.6 8963.4	13 2498	21412	721	29.69
INT	171.5	9	659	13	50.69
RAL	1450.2	124	5864	217	27.02
NAT.W.	455.3	60	1403	34	41.26
B & H	584.3	92	1625	44	36.93

to lead England v West Indies on the 1989–90 tour, but the selectors thought otherwise.

Opinions on cricket: 'Wickets must improve at every ground. It is the only way to get good cricketers. Four-day cricket won't make people better cricketers. Young players have things made too easy for them.'

Best batting performance: 227 Northamptonshire v Somerset, Northampton 1976

Best bowling performance: 7-37 Northamptonshire v Oxford University, Oxford 1975

WILLIAMS, N. F.　　　　　　Middlesex

Full Name: Neil Fitzgerald Williams
Role: Right-hand bat, right-arm fast-medium bowler
Born: 2 July 1962, Hopewell, St Vincent, West Indies
Height: 5' 11" **Weight:** 11st 7lbs
Nickname: Joe
County debut: 1982
County cap: 1984
50 wickets in a season: 2
1st-Class 50s scored: 7
1st-Class 5 w. in innings: 6
1st-Class 10 w. in match: 1
Place in batting averages: 158th av. 22.64 (1988 184th av. 20.66)
Place in bowling averages: 78th av. 31.29 (1988 5th av. 17.03)
Strike rate 1989: 63.35 (career 52.97)
1st-Class catches 1989: 4 (career 30)
Parents: Alexander and Aldreta
Marital status: Single

Family links with cricket: 'Uncle Joe was 12th man for St Vincent and plays 1st Division cricket.'

Education: Cane End Primary School, St Vincent; Acland Burghley School, Tufnell Park

Qualifications: School Leavers Certificate, 6 O-levels, 1 A-level

Overseas tours: English Counties to Zimbabwe 1985

Overseas teams played for: Windward Islands 1982–83; Tasmania 1983–84

Cricketers particularly learnt from: Wilf Slack, Roland Butcher, Wayne Daniel

Cricketers particularly admired: Viv Richards, Andy Roberts, Michael Holding, Dennis Lillee, Malcolm Marshall, Lawrence Rowe
Other sports followed: Most
Relaxations: Reggae, soca, soul, cinema
Extras: Was on stand-by for England in New Zealand and Pakistan 1983–84
Best batting performance: 69* Middlesex v Hampshire, Lord's 1989
Best bowling performance: 7-55 English Counties XI v Zimbabwean XI, Harare 1984–85

LAST SEASON: BATTING

	I.	N.O.	R.	H.S.	AV.
TEST					
1ST-CLASS	19	5	317	69*	22.64
INT					
RAL	3	0	22	22	7.33
NAT.W.					
B & H	2	0	6	4	3.00

LAST SEASON: BOWLING

	O.	M.	R.	W.	AV.
TEST					
1ST-CLASS	327.2	58	970	31	31.29
INT					
RAL	62	5	241	10	24.10
NAT.W.					
B & H	23.2	4	108	2	54.00

CAREER: BATTING

	I.	N.O.	R.	H.S.	AV.
TEST					
1ST-CLASS	141	35	2140	69*	20.18
INT					
RAL	33	11	331	43	15.04
NAT.W.	7	3	36	10	9.00
B & H	17	3	154	29*	11.00

CAREER: BOWLING

	O.	M.	R.	W.	AV.
TEST					
1ST-CLASS	2904.4	546	9644	329	29.31
INT					
RAL	450.3	16	1988	78	25.48
NAT.W.	89.1	15	301	13	23.15
B & H	275	30	1072	28	38.28

WILLIAMS, R. G.　　Northamptonshire

Full Name: Richard Grenville Williams
Role: Right-hand bat, off-break bowler, all-rounder
Born: 10 August 1957, Bangor, Caernarvonshire
Height: 5′ 6″ **Weight:** 12st
Nickname: Chippy
County debut: 1974
County cap: 1979
Benefit: 1989
1000 runs in a season: 6
1st-Class 50s scored: 51
1st-Class 100s scored: 17
1st-Class 5 w. in innings: 9
One-Day 50s: 21
Place in batting averages: 145th av. 23.71 (1988 67th av. 33.80)

Place in bowling averages: — (1988 80th av. 29.69)
1st-Class catches 1989: 3 (career 92)
Parents: Gordon and Rhianwen
Wife and date of marriage: Helen Laura, 24 April 1982
Family links with cricket: Father played for Caernarvonshire and North Wales
Education: Ellesmere Port Grammar School
Jobs outside cricket: Qualified carpenter (self-employed)
Off-season 1989–90: 'Number One priority is to overcome the knee injury which kept me out of cricket most of last season.'
Overseas tours: West Indies with England Young Cricketers 1976; Australasia in 1980 with Derrick Robins' U-23 XI; Zimbabwe with English Counties 1985
Overseas teams played for: Stockton CC and Belmont CC in Sydney, Australia on Whitbread Scholarship. Papagostoe CC, Auckland, New Zealand
Other sports played: Golf
Injuries 1989: Knee operation from end of May onwards: patella tendon
Relaxations: Fly fishing, shooting, fly tying
Extras: Debut for 2nd XI in 1972 aged 14 years 11 months. Made maiden century in 1979 and then scored four centuries in five innings. Hat-trick v Gloucestershire, at Northampton 1980. Was first player to score a century against the 1980 West Indies touring team. Was stand-by for England in India 1981
Best batting performance: 175* Northamptonshire v Leicestershire, Leicester 1980
Best bowling performance: 7-73 Northamptonshire v Cambridge University, Cambridge 1980

LAST SEASON: BATTING

	I.	N.O.	R.	H.S.	AV.
TEST					
1ST-CLASS	8	1	166	71	23.71
INT					
RAL	–	–	–	–	–
NAT.W.					
B & H	3	1	40	30	20.00

CAREER: BATTING

	I.	N.O.	R.	H.S.	AV.
TEST					
1ST-CLASS	407	57	10998	175*	31.42
INT					
RAL	124	21	2371	82	23.01
NAT.W.	26	5	492	94	23.42
B & H	37	9	899	83	32.10

LAST SEASON: BOWLING

	O.	M.	R.	W.	AV.
TEST					
1ST-CLASS	22.1	7	44	2	22.00
INT					
RAL	8	0	33	2	16.50
NAT.W.					
B & H	26	5	147	4	36.75

CAREER: BOWLING

	O.	M.	R.	W.	AV.
TEST					
1ST-CLASS	3947.4	1005	11176	337	33.16
INT					
RAL	427.2	25	2043	75	27.24
NAT.W.	165	29	501	26	19.26
B & H	227	32	826	27	30.59

WOOD, J. R.   Hampshire

Full Name: Julian Ross Wood
Role: Left-hand bat, right-arm
medium bowler
Born: 21 November 1968,
Winchester, Hampshire
Height: 5' 8" **Weight:** 13st 7lbs
Nickname: Woody or Fred (as in
Flintstone)
County debut: 1989
1st-Class 50s scored: 4
One-Day 50s: 1
Place in batting averages: 53rd
av. 36.75
1st-Class catches 1989: 6 (career 6)
Parents: Ross and Susan Keysell
Marital status: Single
Family links with cricket: Father –
NCA coach, ACU umpire, also
played in local league
Education: St Barts Prep School; Priors Court School; Leighton Park
School
Qualifications: CSE, NCA Coaching Certificate
Jobs outside cricket: Coaching all sports at schools and clubs, sheep farming,
forestry
Off-season 1989–90: 'Coaching all sports and assisting at Gosfield School,
Essex.'
Cricketing superstitions or habits: 'Always put right pad on first, try to wear
the same kit which has given me previous success.'
Overseas tours: Berkshire U-19 to Sri Lanka 1985–86; MCC YC to Hong
Kong 1987
Overseas teams played for: Newcastle City CC, NSW, Australia 1988–89
Cricketers particularly learnt from: Mark Simmons (captain of Berkshire),
Don Wilson (head coach at Lord's), Richard Hadlee
Cricketers particularly admired: Ian Botham, Robin Smith, Malcolm
Marshall
Other sports played: Football, rugby, hockey
Other sports followed: All sports
Relaxations: 'Having a few beers with my mates, watching videos, music,
keeping fit.'
Extras: Hit first ball in first-class cricket for four – scored 58 on debut v Sussex.
Scored 65 v Australians. England Schools U-15, U-19. MCC Young Profes-
sionals groundstaff

Opinions on cricket: 'Counties should be restricted to one overseas player. More 4-day games so our batsmen can prepare themselves for Test matches.'
Best batting performance: 96 Hampshire v Northamptonshire, Northampton 1989
Best bowling performance: 1-5 Hampshire v Sussex, Southampton 1989

LAST SEASON: BATTING

	I.	N.O.	R.	H.S.	AV.
TEST					
1ST-CLASS	18	2	588	96	36.75
INT					
RAL	4	0	90	66	22.50
NAT.W.	1	1	3	3*	–
B & H					

LAST SEASON: BOWLING

	O.	M.	R.	W.	AV.
TEST					
1ST-CLASS	4.3	0	21	1	21.00
INT					
RAL					
NAT.W.					
B & H					

CAREER: BATTING

	I.	N.O.	R.	H.S.	AV.
TEST					
1ST-CLASS	18	2	588	96	36.75
INT					
RAL	4	0	90	66	22.50
NAT.W.	1	1	3	3*	–
B & H					

CAREER: BOWLING

	O.	M.	R.	W.	AV.
TEST					
1ST-CLASS	4.3	0	21	1	21.00
INT					
RAL					
NAT.W.					
B & H					

WREN, T. N.   Kent

Full Name: Timothy Neil Wren
Role: Right-hand bat, left-arm medium bowler
Born: 26 March 1970, Folkestone
Height: 6′ 3″ **Weight:** 14st 7lbs
Nickname: Cell, Blockhead
County debut: 1989 (RAL only)
Parents: James and Gillian
Marital status: Single
Family links with cricket: Father and brother played for local village teams
Education: Lyminge Primary; Folkestone Grammar School
Qualifications: 6 O-levels
Jobs outside cricket: Worked as a plumber for father in close season
Off-season 1989–90: 'Playing club cricket in Zimbabwe.'
Cricketing superstitions or habits: 'Always put on gear in certain order.'

Cricketers particularly learnt from: Alan Ealham, Colin Page, Richard Ellison
Cricketers particularly admired: John Lever, Ian Botham, Richard Hadlee
Other sports played: Rugby, golf
Other sports followed: American football, rugby, golf
Relaxations: Listening to music, good food, films, reading
Opinions on cricket: 'Too much cricket played; more four-day cricket (each county once?).'

LAST SEASON: BOWLING

	O.	M.	R.	W.	AV.
TEST					
1ST-CLASS					
INT					
RAL	7.3	0	41	1	41.00
NAT.W.					
B & H					

CAREER: BOWLING

	O.	M.	R.	W.	AV.
TEST					
1ST-CLASS					
INT					
RAL	7.3	0	41	1	41.00
NAT.W.					
B & H					

WRIGHT, A. J. Gloucestershire

Full Name: Anthony John Wright
Role: Right-hand bat, off-break bowler, slip fielder
Born: 27 July 1962, Stevenage
Height: 6' **Weight:** '13st in April, 14st in September.'
Nickname: Billy, Horace
County debut: 1982
County cap: 1987
1000 runs in a season: 3
1st-Class 50s scored: 31
1st-Class 100s scored: 7
One-Day 50s: 13
Place in batting averages: 107th av. 28.97 (1988 83rd av. 30.92)
1st-Class catches 1989: 20 (career 87)
Parents: Michael and Patricia
Wife and date of marriage: Rachel, 21 December 1986
Children: Hannah, 3 April 1988
Education: Alleyn's School, Stevenage
Qualifications: 6 O-levels
Jobs outside cricket: Sales rep for Hall's Brewery
Off-season 1989–90: Playing and coaching for Port Melbourne CC

Overseas tours: Gloucestershire to Barbados 1980, 1985, 1986 and 1988; Sri Lanka 1987

Overseas teams played for: Port Melbourne 1981–85, 1989–90

Cricketers particularly learnt from: Barry Dudleston

Cricketers particularly admired: Viv Richards, Ian Botham, Javed Miandad, Malcolm Marshall, Courtney Walsh

Other sports played: Rugby, golf, soccer

Other sports followed: Rugby, golf, Chelsea FC

Relaxations: Eating out, drinking socially, listening to music, reading newspapers, playing golf

Extras: Appointed captain of Gloucestershire for 1990

Opinions on cricket: 'I would like to see 16 four-day games, played on good surfaces, and less 40-over cricket – possibly two groups of nine (include Minor Counties) leading to semi-finals and finals. Also, I would like to see our Test selectors stick by players. How can a young player be picked for one Test, then discarded for the next one. Sixty or so players over five years is ridiculous.'

Best batting performance: 161 Gloucestershire v Glamorgan, Bristol 1987

Best bowling performance: 1-16 Gloucestershire v Yorkshire, Harrogate 1989

LAST SEASON: BATTING

	I.	N.O.	R.	H.S.	AV.
TEST					
1ST-CLASS	41	1	1159	130	28.97
INT					
RAL	16	4	419	81	34.91
NAT.W.	1	0	1	1	1.00
B & H	5	0	136	49	27.20

LAST SEASON: BOWLING

	O.	M.	R.	W.	AV.
TEST					
1ST-CLASS	6	2	16	1	16.00
INT					
RAL	0.2	0	4	0	–
NAT.W.					
B & H					

CAREER: BATTING

	I.	N.O.	R.	H.S.	AV.
TEST					
1ST-CLASS	240	14	6058	161	26.80
INT					
RAL	63	9	1131	81	20.94
NAT.W.	11	0	398	88	36.18
B & H	16	0	346	66	21.62

CAREER: BOWLING

	O.	M.	R.	W.	AV.
TEST					
1ST-CLASS	9	2	30	1	30.00
INT					
RAL	4.2	0	22	0	–
NAT.W.					
B & H					

159. When did England last defeat Australia at Lord's?

WYATT, J. G.　　　　　　　Somerset

Full Name: Julian George Wyatt
Role: Right-hand bat, off-spin and
right-arm medium bowler
Born: 19 June 1963, Paulton,
Somerset
Height: 5′ 10″ **Weight:** 12st
Nickname: Jules, Earp, Harold
County debut: 1983
1st-Class 50s scored: 12
1st-Class 100s scored: 3
One-Day 50s: 5
Place in batting averages: —
(1988 156th av. 23.12)
1st-Class catches 1989: 0 (career 27)
Parents: Christopher Hedley and
Dinah Ruby
Marital status: Single
Family links with cricket: 'Father
played a game of six-a-side two years
ago, and my brother once hit three boundaries in an over – two on the right
and one on the left!'
Education: Farrington Gurney Primary; Wells Cathedral School, Somerset
Qualifications: 5 O-levels, NCA Senior Coaching Certificate
Jobs outside cricket: Brandon Tool Hire 1980–83; van driver; shelf-stacker,
driver for handicapped school etc.
Off-season 1989–90: 'Playing football for Timsbury Athletic and frantically
seeking employment.'

LAST SEASON: BATTING

	I.	N.O.	R.	H.S.	AV.
TEST					
1ST-CLASS	4	0	46	23	11.50
INT					
RAL	6	0	93	40	15.50
NAT.W.	1	0	9	9	9.00
B & H					

LAST SEASON: BOWLING

	O.	M.	R.	W.	AV.
TEST					
1ST-CLASS					
INT					
RAL					
NAT.W.					
B & H					

CAREER: BATTING

	I.	N.O.	R.	H.S.	AV.
TEST					
1ST-CLASS	115	5	2789	145	25.35
INT					
RAL	30	2	565	89	20.17
NAT.W.	4	0	20	9	5.00
B & H	6	0	138	55	23.00

CAREER: BOWLING

	O.	M.	R.	W.	AV.
TEST					
1ST-CLASS	23	5	97	3	32.33
INT					
RAL					
NAT.W.					
B & H					

Overseas tours: Somerset to Barbados 1985

Overseas teams played for: Kew CC, Melbourne 1984–85; Manley CC, Sydney 1987–88; Kew 1988–89

Cricketers particularly admired: Brian Rose, Peter Denning, Colin Dredge, Trevor Gard, David Gower, Steve Waugh

Other sports played: Squash, football, golf

Other sports followed: Rugby, soccer, horse racing – most except snooker and darts

Relaxations: 'Socialising at Hunter's Rest, Clutton. Sport.'

Opinions on cricket: 'A simple game complicated by intelligent people who lack common sense.'

Best batting performance: 145 Somerset v Oxford University, Oxford 1985

Best bowling performance: 1-0 Somerset v Sussex, Hove 1984

160. When was the phrase 'The Ashes' first used to describe Test matches between England and Australia?

161. When did South Africa last tour England?

162. Which current county captain studied Russian at University, and played professional football?

163. Which cricket writer, still regularly writing, saw W. G. Grace play?

164. Who has the highest batting average in all Test cricket, and what is it?

ROLL OF HONOUR

BRITANNIC ASSURANCE COUNTY CHAMPIONSHIP
(1988 positions in brackets)

		P	W	L	D	Bt	Bl	Pts
1	Worcestershire (1)	22	12	3	7	44	83	319
2	Essex* (3)	22	13	2	7	59	71	313
3	Middlesex (7)	22	9	2	11	50	72	266
4	Lancashire (9)	22	8	5	9	57	65	250
5	Northamptonshire (12) ...	22	7	8	7	47	63	222
6	Hampshire (15)	22	6	8	8	55	65	216
7	Derbyshire (14)	22	6	6	10	45	75	216
8	Warwickshire* (6)	22	5	4	13	44	75	207
9	Gloucestershire (10)	22	6	11	5	38	70	204
10	Sussex (16)	22	4	4	14	60	68	192
11	Nottinghamshire* (5)	22	6	6	10	54	65	190
12	Surrey (4)	22	4	7	11	50	69	183
13	Leicestershire (7)	22	4	8	10	43	74	181
14	Somerset (11)	22	4	6	12	50	54	168
15	Kent (2)	22	3	8	11	53	53	154
16	Yorkshire (13)	22	3	9	10	41	60	149
17	Glamorgan (17)	22	3	6	13	38	59	145

* Warwickshire total includes 8 points for drawn game where scores were level. Essex and Nottinghamshire deducted 25 points for substandard pitch

---

165. Who was the oldest cricketer to play for Australia v England last season, and how old was he?

166. Who was the youngest cricketer to play for Australia v England last season, and how old was he?

167. What record is shared by C. B. Fry and Don Bradman?

168. Which England captain played 22 times for England (not always as a captain) spread over 22 years?

169. In which famous match was the new ball taken 12 times, and who bowled no less than 766 balls himself?

REFUGE ASSURANCE LEAGUE
(1988 positions in brackets)

	P	W	L	T	NR	Pts
1 Lancashire (3)	16	12	2	0	2	52
2 Worcestershire (1)	16	11	4	0	1	46
3 Essex (10)	16	11	4	0	1	46
4 Nottinghamshire (17)	16	9	6	0	1	38
5 Derbyshire (12)	16	9	6	0	1	38
6 Hampshire (9)	16	8	6	1	1	36
7 Surrey (5)	16	9	7	0	0	36
8 Northamptonshire (14)	16	8	6	0	2	36
9 Middlesex (4)	16	8	7	1	0	34
10 Somerset (12)	16	7	8	1	0	30
11 Yorkshire (8)	16	7	9	0	0	28
12 Kent (7)	16	7	9	0	0	28
13 Sussex (14)	16	6	8	1	1	28
14 Leicestershire (14)	16	5	10	0	1	22
15 Warwickshire (10)	16	5	10	0	1	22
16 Gloucestershire (2)	16	3	13	0	0	12
17 Glamorgan (5)	16	2	12	0	2	12

REFUGE ASSURANCE CUP
Winners: Essex
Runners-up: Nottinghamshire
Losing semi-finalists: Worcestershire and Lancashire

NATWEST TROPHY
Winners: Warwickshire
Runners-up: Middlesex
Losing semi-finalists: Worcestershire and Hampshire

BENSON & HEDGES CUP
Winners: Nottinghamshire
Runners-up: Essex
Losing semi-finalists: Somerset and Kent

UMPIRES

BALDERSTONE, J. C.

Full Name: John Christopher
Balderstone
Role: Right-hand bat, slow left-arm
bowler, slip fielder
Born: 16 November 1940,
Huddersfield, Yorkshire
Height: 6′ 2″ **Weight:** 12st 7lbs
Nickname: Baldy, Chris, Dad
Parents: Frank and Jenny
Counties: Yorkshire, Leicestershire
County debut: 1961 (Yorkshire),
1971 (Leicestershire)
County cap: 1973 (Leicestershire)
Testimonial: 1984 (£64,470 jointly
with Ken Higgs)
Test debut: 1976
No. of Tests: 2
1000 runs in a season: 11
1st-Class 50s scored: 102
1st-Class 100s scored: 32
1st-Class 5 w. in innings: 5
One-Day 50s: 32
One-Day 100s: 5
1st-Class catches: 210

Appointed to 1st-Class list: 1988
Wife and date of marriage: Madeline, April 1962
Children: Sally Victoria, 15 September 1970; Michael James, 3 January
1973
Education: Paddock County School, Huddersfield
Qualifications: Advanced cricket coach, soccer coach
Jobs outside cricket: Professional footballer with Huddersfield Town, Carlisle
United, Doncaster Rovers, Queen of the South, Enderby Town. Representative for a sports shop
Off-season 1989–90: Coaching cricket
Overseas tours: With Leicester to Zimbabwe 1981; to Oman 1984
Cricketers particularly learnt from: 'Everyone.'
Other sports played: Golf, professional football
Relaxations: Do-it-yourself, golf, reading and all sports

557

Extras: Played for Yorkshire 1961–70. Once played first-class cricket match and a league football match on the same day, 15 September 1975 (Leicestershire v Derbyshire at Chesterfield 11.30 am to 6.30 pm and Doncaster Rovers v Brentford at Doncaster 7.30 pm to 9.10 pm). Former Chairman of Cricketers' Association

Best batting performance: 181* Leicestershire v Gloucestershire, Leicester 1984

Best bowling performance: 6-25 Leicestershire v Hampshire, Southampton 1978

CAREER: BATTING

	I.	N.O.	R.	H.S.	AV.
TEST	4	0	39	35	9.75
1ST-CLASS	615	61	18995	181*	34.28
INT					
RAL	125	23	2673	96	26.20
NAT.W.	32	2	891	119*	29.70
B & H	57	12	2059	113*	45.76

CAREER: BOWLING

	O.	M.	R.	W.	AV.
TEST	16	0	80	1	80.00
1ST-CLASS	3187	957	8080	309	26.14
INT					
RAL	58.3	2	296	12	24.66
NAT.W.	48	12	176	11	16.00
B & H	30	4	103	5	20.60

BIRD, H. D.

Full Name: Harold Dennis Bird
Role: Right-hand opening bat
Born: 19 April 1933, Barnsley
Height: 5′ 10½″ **Weight:** 11st 6lbs
Nickname: Dickie
Parents: James Harold and Ethel
Counties: Yorkshire, Leicestershire
County debut: 1956 (Yorkshire), 1960 (Leicestershire)
County cap: 1960 (Leicestershire)
1000 runs in a season: 1
1st-Class 50s scored: 14
1st-Class 100s scored: 2
1st-Class catches: 20
Appointed to 1st-Class list: 1969
Appointed to Test panel: 1972
No. of Tests umpired: 43
No. of One-Day Internationals umpired: 77
Marital status: Bachelor
Education: Raley School, Barnsley
Jobs outside cricket: 'Cricket is my life.'

Off-season 1989–90: Umpiring in Sharjah, six international matches between West Indies, Pakistan, and India. After-dinner speaking

Cricketing superstitions or habits: Twitch of the shoulders. Wearing a distinctive white cap

Other sports followed: Football

Cricketers particularly learnt from: Johnny Wardle, Sir Gubby Allen

Cricketers particularly admired: Sir Garfield Sobers, Dennis Lillee, Viv Richards

Relaxations: 'Listening to Barbra Streisand and Diana Ross records.'

Opinions on cricket: 'The greatest game in the world. A game to be enjoyed by young and old. I have consistently advocated playing through all light unless the umpire is convinced there is a genuine physical danger to the batsman.'

Extras: Awarded MBE, June 1986. Only man to umpire in three World Cup Finals, 1975, 1979 and 1983. Voted Yorkshire Personality of the Year, 1977. Umpired Centenary Test Match, England v Australia, 1980. Umpired Queen's Silver Jubilee Test Match, England v Australia, Lord's 1977. Author of *Not Out* (1978), *That's Out* (1985), *From the Pavilion End* (1988). Member of the TCCB Cricket Committee

Best batting performance: 181* Yorkshire v Glamorgan, Bradford 1959

CAREER: BATTING

	I.	N.O.	R.	H.S.	AV.
TEST					
1ST-CLASS	170	10	3314	181*	20.71
INT					
RAL					
NAT.W.	2	0	9	7	4.50
B & H					

CAREER: BOWLING

	O.	M.	R.	W.	AV.
TEST					
1ST-CLASS	8	2	22	0	–
INT					
RAL					
NAT.W.					
B & H					

170. Which cricketer only played two seasons of county cricket, scored 1000 runs each season, played in eight Test matches, captained England in one of them, and still practises today as a dentist?

171. Who was the first black captain of the West Indies?

172. Who scored a century on his county cricket debut, and took a wicket with his first first-class ball?

BOND, J. D.

Full Name: John David Bond
Role: Right-hand bat
Born: 6 May 1932, Kersley, Lancashire
Nickname: Jackie
Counties: Lancashire, Nottinghamshire
County debut: 1955 (Lancashire), 1974 (Nottinghamshire)
County cap: 1961 (Lancashire)
Benefit: 1970 (£7,230)
1000 runs in a season: 2
1st-Class 50s scored: 54
1st-Class 100s scored: 14
1st-Class catches: 223
Appointed to 1st-Class list: 1988
Education: Bolton School
Extras: Lancashire, under his captaincy, won Gillette Cup 1970, 1971, 1972. Won John Player League, 1969, 1970. Scored 2125 first-class runs in 1962. Missed part of 1963 with a broken wrist. Was captain of Lancashire 1968–72. Cricket Manager of Lancashire from 1980–86
Best batting performance: 157 Lancashire v Hampshire, Old Trafford 1962

CAREER: BATTING

	I.	N.O.	R.	H.S.	AV.
TEST					
1ST-CLASS	548	80	12125	157	25.90
INT					
RAL	42	12	416	43	13.87
NAT.W.	17	4	181	35*	13.92
B & H	3	0	16	14	5.33

CAREER: BOWLING

	O.	M.	R.	W.	AV.
TEST					
1ST-CLASS	12.1	1	69	0	–
INT					
RAL					
NAT.W.					
B & H					

173. Which Australian who played in 35 Tests before and after the First World War was nicknamed 'The Governor-General'?

174. Who were the first English team to go to USSR to play cricket?

CONSTANT, D. J.

Full Name: David John Constant
Role: Left-hand bat, slow left-arm bowler
Born: 9 November 1941, Bradford-on-Avon, Wiltshire
Nickname: Connie
Counties: Kent 1961–63, Leicestershire 1965–68
County debut: 1961 (Kent), 1965 (Leicestershire)
1st-Class 50s scored: 6
1st-Class catches: 33
Appointed to 1st-Class list: 1969
Appointed to Test panel: 1971
No. of Tests umpired: 34
No. of One-day Internationals umpired: 27
Best batting performance: 80 Leicestershire v Gloucestershire, Bristol 1966

CAREER: BATTING

	I.	N.O.	R.	H.S.	AV.
TEST					
1ST-CLASS	93	14	1517	80	19.20
INT					
RAL					
NAT.W.	1	0	5	5	–
B & H					

CAREER: BOWLING

	O.	M.	R.	W.	AV.
TEST					
1ST-CLASS	12.3	3	36	1	–
INT					
RAL					
NAT.W.					
B & H					

175. What is the nickname of the Australian fast bowler Geoff Lawson?

176. How much did an umpire receive for standing in a Test match, in the Ashes series, 1989: £500, £1500, or £2000?

DUDLESTON, B.

Full Name: Barry Dudleston
Role: Right-hand bat, slow
left-arm bowler
Born: 16 July 1945, Bebington,
Cheshire
Height: 5′ 9″ **Weight:** 11st 8lbs
Nickname: Danny
Parents: Percy and Dorothy Vera
Counties: Leicestershire,
Gloucestershire
County debut: 1966 (Leicestershire),
1981 (Gloucestershire)
County cap: 1969 (Leicestershire)
Benefit: 1980 (£25,000)
1000 runs in a season: 8
1st-Class 100s scored: 31
1st-Class 200s scored: 1
1st-Class catches: 234
One-Day 50s: 21
One-Day 100s: 4

Appointed to 1st-Class list: 1984
Wife and date of marriage: Lindsey Vivien Stratford, 5 April 1980
Children: Sharon Louise, 29 October 1968
Education: Stockport School
Qualifications: O-levels. Junior Coaching Certificate. Shell marketing exams
Jobs outside cricket: Retail and commercial representative for Shell
Overseas tours: With Derrick Robins' XI to Rhodesia
Overseas teams played for: Rhodesia 1966–67 to 1979–80 in Currie Cup
competition
Cricketers particularly learnt from: Vinoo Mankad
Cricket records: Leicestershire CCC 1st wicket record of 390, 7th wicket
record of 206, with Jack Birkenshaw v Kent at Canterbury in 1969. Fastest to
1000 runs in Currie Cup ever for Rhodesia, 2nd fastest of all time in Currie
Cup. Highest score by overseas player on debut in South Africa, 142 v
Western Province
Relaxations: Bridge and philately, watching all sports, red wine
Extras: England Under-25. Has suffered badly from broken fingers. Broke
fingers on same hand three times in 1978. Made debut for Leicestershire in
1966, gaining county cap in 1969. Released by Leicestershire at end of 1980
season and made debut for Gloucestershire 1981
Opinions on cricket: 'Now we are playing on covered wickets I should like
to see a Championship programme of 16 four-day games, two one-day

matches and a day off per week, which would then be a balanced programme.'
Best batting performance: 202 Leicestershire v Derbyshire, Leicester 1979
Best bowling performance: 4-6 Leicestershire v Surrey, Leicester 1972

CAREER: BATTING

	I.	N.O.	R.	H.S.	AV.
TEST					
1ST-CLASS	501	47	14747	202	32.48
INT					
RAL	123	8	2490	152	24.41
NAT.W.	18	1	586	125	34.47
B & H	42	5	1171	90	31.65

CAREER: BOWLING

	O.	M.	R.	W.	AV.
TEST					
1ST-CLASS	406	87	1365	47	29.04
INT					
RAL	1	0	4	0	–
NAT.W.	3	0	14	0	–
B & H					

EELE, P. J.

Full Name: Peter James Eele
Role: Left-hand bat,
wicket-keeper
Born: 27 January 1935, Taunton
Height: 5′ 6″ **Weight:** 11st 8lbs
County: Somerset
Benefit: 1969
1st-Class 100s scored: 1
Appointed to 1st-Class list: 1981
Marital status: Single
Education: Taunton School
Qualifications: 2 A-levels,
10 O-levels
Jobs outside cricket: 'At various
times, bank official, accountant,
company administrator, organ
tuner's mate.'
Off-season 1989–90: 'Trying to lose
weight!'
Other sports played: 'Squash – geriatric. Golf – handicap, the clubs!'

CAREER: BATTING

	I.	N.O.	R.	H.S.	AV.
TEST					
1ST-CLASS	70	20	612	103*	12.24
INT					
RAL					
NAT.W.					
B & H					

CAREER: WICKET KEEPING

	C.	ST.			
TEST					
1ST-CLASS	87	19			
INT					
RAL					
NAT.W.					
B & H					

Relaxations: 'Classical music: an ardent supporter of the Bournemouth Symphony Orchestra. Crosswords.'

Opinions on cricket: 'When players complain about over-rate fines, they forget about the time wasted by bowlers bowling practice deliveries to mid-off and mid-on, and the length of time taken by fast bowlers glaring at batsmen, and strolling back to the end of their over-long run-ups.'

Best batting performance: 103* Somerset v Pakistan Eaglets, Taunton 1963

EVANS, D. G. L.

Full Name: David Gwillim Lloyd Evans

Role: Right-hand bat, wicket-keeper

Born: 27 July 1933, Lambeth

County: Glamorgan

County debut: 1956

County cap: 1959

Benefit: 1969 (£3,500)

Appointed to 1st-Class list: 1971

Appointed to Test panel: 1981

Extras: Evans was the first man both to have played and umpired in the Sunday League

Best batting performance: 46* Glamorgan v Oxford University, Oxford 1961

CAREER: BATTING

	I.	N.O.	R.	H.S.	AV.
TEST					
1ST-CLASS	364	91	2875	46*	10.53
INT					
RAL					
NAT.W.	2	0	9	8	4.50
B & H					

CAREER: WICKET KEEPING

	C.	ST.		
TEST				
1ST-CLASS	503	56		
INT				
RAL				
NAT.W.	4	–		
B & H				

177. Who first said 'Gower is a good captain'?

178. Who has bowled the most balls in Test cricket?

HAMPSHIRE, J. H.

Full Name: John Harry Hampshire
Role: Right-hand bat, leg-break bowler
Born: 10 February 1941, Thurnscoe
Height: 6′ **Weight:** 13st
Nickname: Hamp
Parents: Jack and Vera
Counties: Yorkshire, Derbyshire
County debut: 1961 (Yorkshire), 1982 (Derbyshire)
County cap: 1963 (Yorkshire), 1982 (Derbyshire)
Test debut: 1969
No. of Tests: 8
1000 runs in a season: 15
1st-Class 50s scored: 142
1st-Class 100s scored: 43
1st-Class catches: 445
1st-Class 5 w. in innings: 1
One-Day 50s: 39
One-Day 100s: 7
Appointed to 1st-Class list: 1985
Appointed to Test panel: 1989
No. of Tests umpired: 1
No. of One-Day Internationals umpired: 1
Education: Oakwood Technical High School, Rotherham
Wife and date of marriage: Judith Ann, 4 September 1964
Children: Ian Christopher, 6 January 1969; Paul Wesley, 12 February 1972
Family links with cricket: Father and brother Alan both played for Yorkshire
Jobs outside cricket: Coaching
Other sports played: Golf
Relaxations: Gardening, reading

CAREER: BATTING

	I.	N.O.	R.	H.S.	AV.
TEST	16	1	403	107	26.67
1ST-CLASS	908	111	27063	183*	33.96
INT	3	1	48	25*	24.00
RAL	172	20	4994	119	32.85
NAT.W.	33	5	930	110	33.21
B & H	45	6	1091	85*	27.97

CAREER: BOWLING

	O.	M.	R.	W.	AV.
TEST					
1ST-CLASS	16.6 402.5	1 85	1637	30	54.57
INT					
RAL	4	1	22	1	–
NAT.W.	2	0	4	0	–
B & H					

Extras: Scored 107 in his first Test Match v West Indies at Lord's
Best batting performance: 183* Yorkshire v Sussex 1971
Best bowling performance: 7-52 Yorkshire v Glamorgan 1963

HARRIS, J. H.

Full Name: John Henry Harris
Role: Left-hand bat, right-arm
fast-medium bowler, leg-spinner
googly bowler
Born: 13 February 1936, Taunton
Height: 5′ 11″ **Weight:** 14st
Nickname: Arry, Boater
Parents: Jack and Freda Harris,
Bill and Doris Rowlan
Counties: Somerset, Suffolk,
Devon
County debut: 1952 (at 16 years 99
days)
1st-Class catches: 6
Appointed to 1st-Class list: 1983
Wife and date of marriage: Morag
Elspeth Jane, 20 October 1984
Children: Karen, Mark, Andrew,
Tim
Family links with cricket:
Grandfather (Harry Fernie) was Head Groundsman at Somerset County
Ground, Taunton for twenty-five years
Education: Coopers Lane, Grove Park, London; Priory School, Taunton,
Somerset
Jobs outside cricket: Devon League Cricket inspector of grounds
Off-season 1989–90: Cricket and football coaching; groundsman for Exeter
Cathedral School, Exeter, Devon
Cricketers particularly learnt from: Arthur Wellard, Harry Parks, Johnnie
Lawrence
Cricketers particularly admired: Harold Gimblett
Other sports played: Golf
Other sports followed: Golf, squash
Relaxations: Gardening, Glen Miller music, TV, reading, 'plus a few beers
with the lads'
Extras: Played for Suffolk 1960–62 and Devon 1975. Qualified football and
basketball referee

Best batting performance: 41 Somerset v Worcestershire, Taunton 1957
Best bowling performance: 3-29 Somerset v Worcestershire, Bristol 1959

CAREER: BATTING

	I.	N.O.	R.	H.S.	AV.
TEST					
1ST-CLASS	18	4	154	41	11.00
INT					
RAL					
NAT.W.					
B & H					

CAREER: BOWLING

	O.	M.	R.	W.	AV.
TEST					
1ST-CLASS	217.2	42	619	19	32.57
INT					
RAL					
NAT.W.					
B & H					

HARRIS, M. J.

Full Name: Michael John Harris
Role: Right-hand bat,
wicket-keeper, leg-break bowler
Born: 25 May 1944, St Just-
in-Roseland, Cornwall
Height: 6′ 1″ **Weight:** 15st
Nickname: Pasty
Parents: Winnie and Dick
Counties: Middlesex,
Nottinghamshire
County debut: 1964 (Middlesex),
1969 (Nottinghamshire)
County cap: 1970 (Nottinghamshire)
Benefit: 1977
1000 runs in a season: 11
1st-Class 50s scored: 98
1st-Class 100s scored: 40
1st-Class 200s scored: 1
Wife and date of marriage: Danielle
Ruth, 10 September 1969
Children: Jodene, Elizabeth, Richard
Family links with cricket: Father and uncles on both sides played top village
cricket
Education: Gerrans C/P
Qualifications: MCC Advanced Coach, SRA Squash Coach
Jobs outside cricket: Squash club manager
Cricketing superstitions or habits: Left boot and pad go on first
Overseas tours: With Derrick Robins' XI to West Indies 1974; with Inter-
national Wanderers to South Africa and Rhodesia in 1974

Overseas teams played for: Eastern Province in 1971–72 Currie Cup Competition; Wellington in New Zealand Shell Shield Competition 1975–76
Appointed to 1st-Class list: On reserve list
Cricket records: Scored nine centuries in 1971 to equal county record. Shared in first wicket partnership record for Middlesex, 312 with W. E. Russell v Pakistan, Lord's 1967
Cricketers particularly learnt from: Eric Russell of Middlesex
Other sports played: Squash, golf, football
Extras: Made debut for Middlesex in 1964. Left staff after 1968 to join Nottinghamshire in 1969. Scored 2238 at an average of 50.86 in 1971. Scored two centuries in a match twice in 1971, 118 and 123 v Leicestershire at Leicester, and 107 and 131* v Essex at Chelmsford

CAREER: BATTING

	I.	N.O.	R.	H.S.	AV.
TEST					
1ST-CLASS	581	58	19196	201*	36.70
INT					
RAL	139	31	3303	104*	30.58
NAT.W.	25	1	579	101	24.13
B & H	34	7	925	101	34.26

CAREER: BOWLING

	O.	M.	R.	W.	AV.
TEST					
1ST-CLASS	1047.5	229	3459	79	43.78
INT					
RAL	6.4	1	41	3	13.67
NAT.W.					
B & H	9	0	46	1	–

HASSAN, S. B.

Full Name: Sheikh Basharat Hassan
Role: Right-hand bat, right-arm medium bowler, occasional wicket-keeper, fielded close to the wicket in bat-pad position
Born: 24 March 1944, Nairobi, Kenya
Height: 5' 11" **Weight:** 11st
Nickname: Basher, Scooby Doo
Parents: Haji Sarwar Hussain (deceased) and Sairan Sheikh
County: Nottinghamshire
County debut: 1966
County cap: 1970
Benefit: 1978
1000 runs in a season: 5
1st-Class 50s scored: 80
1st-Class 100s scored: 15
One-Day 50s scored: 36

One-Day 100s scored: 4
1st-Class catches: 308 + 1 stumping
Wife: Dorothy Ann
Children: Jamil, 22 October 1980; Sarah Jane, 30 June 1982
Family links with cricket: Father and brothers played
Education: City High School, Nairobi; Kenya Polytechnic
Qualifications: City and Guilds in Printing; Advanced Coaching Certificate
Jobs outside cricket: Sales representative for a printing firm
Cricketing superstitions or habits: 'Never take off my "necklace" which was given to me by my father.'
Overseas tours: Kenya 1967; West Indies 1974; Dubai 1982; Bermuda 1987
Overseas teams played for: Kenya 1960–66; East Africa 1961–66
Appointed to 1st-Class list: 1989
Cricketers particularly learnt from: M. J. K. Smith, M. Ali (Kenya), Sir Garfield Sobers, Tom Graveney
Cricketers particularly admired: Richard Hadlee, Viv Richards, Garfield Sobers
Other sports played: Hockey, golf, football
Other sports followed: Athletics, golf, football, hockey
Relaxations: 'TV, gardening, going for long walks with my pet dog (Sheik) and listening to music.'
Extras: Played first Test for Kenya at age of 15½, the youngest in the country. Made debut for East Africa Invitation XI v MCC 1963–64. Played for Kenya against touring sides. Scored a century with the aid of a runner v Kent at Canterbury in 1977. Best sprinter at Nottinghamshire. Short-listed for Kenyan Olympic team in 1960. Announced retirement in 1985 while fielding substitute for England in Trent Bridge Test v Australia
Best batting performance: 182* Nottinghamshire v Gloucestershire, Trent Bridge 1977
Best bowling performance: 3-33 Nottinghamshire v Lancashire, Old Trafford 1976

CAREER: BATTING

	I.	N.O.	R.	H.S.	AV.
TEST					
1ST-CLASS	549	54	14394	182*	29.07
INT					
RAL	196	21	5168	120*	29.53
NAT.W.	27	1	568	79	21.84
B & H	48	7	1070	99*	26.09

CAREER: BOWLING

	O.	M.	R.	W.	AV.
TEST					
1ST-CLASS	141.2	35	407	6	67.83
INT					
RAL	16.3	0	131	2	65.60
NAT.W.	7.1	2	20	3	6.66
B & H					

HOLDER, J. W.

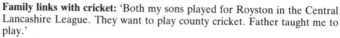

Full Name: John Wakefield Holder
Role: Right-arm fast bowler
Born: 19 March 1945, Barbados
Height: 6′ **Weight:** 13½st
Nickname: Benson, Hod
Parents: Charles and Carnetta
County: Hampshire
County debut: 1968
50 wickets in a season: 1
1st-Class 5 w. in innings: 5
1st-Class 10 w. in match: 1
1st-Class catches: 12
Appointed to 1st-Class list: 1983
Appointed to Test panel: 1989
No. of Tests umpired: 2
No. of One-Day Internationals umpired: 1
Wife: Glenda
Children: Christopher, 1968; Nigel, 1970

Family links with cricket: 'Both my sons played for Royston in the Central Lancashire League. They want to play county cricket. Father taught me to play.'
Education: St Giles Boys School; Combermere High School, Barbados
Qualifications: 3 O-levels. MCC Advanced Coach
Jobs outside cricket: Part-time cricket coach. Training as driving instructor
Off-season 1989–90: Selling life insurance
Overseas tours: Coached in Eastern Goldfields for Western Australian Cricket Association 1987–88; India 1989 as umpire in Nehru Cup; Pakistan 1989 as Test umpire
Cricketers particularly learnt from: Wes Hall, Everton Weekes
Cricketers particularly admired: Sir Garfield Sobers, Dennis Lillee, Richard Hadlee
Other sports followed: Manchester United FC, boxing
Relaxations: Watching documentaries about wildlife. Would like to become an accomplished after-dinner speaker
Extras: Holds best bowling performance ever for Rothmans International Cavaliers cricket matches. Playing for Hampshire Cavaliers, took 6-7 at Tichbourne Park, 1968. Between 1974 and 1982, played professional league cricket in Lancashire and Yorkshire. One first-class hat-trick, Hampshire v Kent 1972, 'but finished with 3 for 100!'
Opinions on cricket: 'There has been much argument about the need for a

neutral international panel of umpires for Test cricket. The emphasis should be on competence rather than neutrality. The captains of the Test-playing countries know who the best umpires are. If there is going to be a panel, the captains should get together officially and put forward to the ICC the names of whom they regard as the best umpires internationally. Had a fabulous five weeks in Pakistan, and was pleasantly surprised at the standard of hotels, organisation and great hospitality of the people. Would have no qualms about returning if asked.'

Best batting performance: 33 Hampshire v Sussex, Hove 1971
Best bowling performance: 6-49 and 7-79 (in same match) Hampshire v Gloucestershire, Gloucester 1972

CAREER: BATTING

	I.	N.O.	R.	H.S.	AV.
TEST					
1ST-CLASS	49	14	374	33	10.68
INT					
RAL	21	7	87	25	6.21
NAT.W.	2	0	4	3	2.00
B & H	3	1	23	14	11.50

CAREER: BOWLING

	O.	M.	R.	W.	AV.
TEST					
1ST-CLASS	1183	229	3415	139	24.56
INT					
RAL	237	14	984	38	25.89
NAT.W.	47	10	144	5	28.80
B & H	26	4	85	3	28.33

HOLDER, V. A.

Full Name: Vanburn Alonza Holder
Role: Right-hand bat, right arm fast medium bowler
Born: 8 October 1945, St Michael, Barbados
Height: 6′ 3″ **Weight:** 14½st
Nickname: Softy, Pacer, Vanny
Parents: James and Enid
County: Worcestershire
County debut: 1968
County cap: 1970
Test debut: 1969
No. of Tests: 40
Benefit: 1979 (£25,000)
1st-Class 50s scored: 4
1st-Class 100s scored: 1
1st-Class 5 w. in innings: 38
1st-Class 10 w. in match: 3
1st-Class catches: 98
Appointed to 1st-Class list: On reserve list
Wife and date of marriage: Christine

Children: James Vanburn, 2 September 1981
Education: St Leonard's Secondary Modern, Community High School
Cricketing superstitions or habits: 'Never look at the wicket before play.'
Overseas tours: With West Indies to England 1969, 1973, and 1976; India, Sri Lanka and Pakistan 1974–75; Australia 1975–76; India and Sri Lanka 1978–79 as vice-captain
Overseas teams played for: Barbados in Shell Shield Competition 1967–1978
Cricketers particularly learnt from: 'Sir Gary Sobers, because he played hard and attacking cricket, and always wanted to win.'
Cricketers particularly admired: Sir Gary Sobers, Wesley Hall
Other sports played: 'I used to play basketball in my schooldays, but I don't now.'
Other sports followed: Soccer, basketball
Relaxations: Music, doing crosswords, watching TV
Extras: Made debut for Barbados 1966–67 in Shell Shield Competition
Opinions on cricket: 'Cricket has suffered over the last ten years or so because so much money has come into the game. Players are forgetting how to play the game properly. Probably, the money that has come into the game has done a lot for cricketers but not for cricket. And too many players are earning money without having to work for it. They have it too easy.'
Best batting performance: 122 Barbados v Trinidad, Bridgetown 1973–74
Best bowling performance: 7-40 Worcestershire v Glamorgan, Cardiff 1974

CAREER: BATTING

	I.	N.O.	R.	H.S.	AV.
TEST	59	11	682	42	14.21
1ST-CLASS	295	70	2877	122	12.79
INT	6	1	64	30	12.80
RAL	61	15	323	35*	7.02
GILLETTE	14	5	79	25*	8.78
B & H	17	8	67	17*	7.44

CAREER: BOWLING

	O.	M.	R.	W.	AV.
TEST	166.6 1293	21 346	3629	109	33.27
1ST-CLASS	160.3 7499	27 1736	19556	838	23.34
INT	7.5 103.2	1 8	454	19	23.89
RAL	864.5	99	2970	176	16.88
GILLETTE	197.3	34	604	22	27.45
B & H	238.4	44	691	37	18.68

179. Which bowler has been hit for the most runs in Test cricket?

180. Who first scored 1000 runs and took 200 wickets in Tests?

181. Who was 'not out' more than any other Test player?

182. What do Medlycott, Pienaar, Geoff Miller, Angus Fraser and Franklyn Stephenson have in common?

JONES, A. A.

Full Name: Allan Arthur Jones
Role: Left-arm fast bowler
Born: 9 December 1947, Horley,
Surrey
Height: 6' 3½" **Weight:** 14st
Nickname: Jonah
Parents: Leslie and Hazel
Counties: Sussex, Somerset,
Middlesex, Glamorgan
County debut: 1966 (Sussex),
1970 (Somerset),
1976 (Middlesex),
1980 (Glamorgan)
County cap: 1972 (Somerset),
1976 (Middlesex)
50 wickets in a season: 4
1st-Class 5 w. in innings: 23
1st-Class 10 w. in match: 3
1st-Class catches: 50

Appointed to 1st-Class list: 1985
Wife and date of marriage: Marilyn, 1979
Children: Clare Michelle, 4 July 1979
Education: St John's College, Horsham
Qualifications: 5 O-levels, MCC 'A' coach, NCA staff coach
Off-season 1989–90: 'Doing as little as possible.'
Overseas teams played for: N. Transvaal 1971–72; Orange Free State 1976–77
Cricketers particularly learnt from: Brian Close, Mike Brearley, Tom Cartwright
Cricketers particularly admired: Brian Close, Barry Richards, John Snow
Other sports played: Golf
Other sports followed: Golf
Relaxations: Horse racing, cinema, reading
Opinions on cricket: 'It is about time to scrap one of the one-day competitions, ideally Sundays. Ban overseas players except for one-day cricket. Play either 16 four-day games, or go back to uncovered wickets – Tests as well – which used to work well before. Have the groundsmen paid by the TCCB to encourage better wickets. As for cricket correspondents, most of them should take a look at their own knowledge of the game, and be seen to be watching, rather than just copying the scorecards. Also it might be good if they stuck to writing about cricket, and not cricketers.'

573

Best batting performance: 33 Middlesex v Kent, Canterbury 1978
Best bowling performance: 9-51 Somerset v Sussex, Hove 1976

CAREER: BATTING

	I.	N.O.	R.	H.S.	AV.
TEST					
1ST-CLASS	216	68	799	33	5.40
INT					
RAL	56	27	90	18*	3.10
NAT.W.	9	6	13	5*	4.33
B & H	18	8	51	14	5.10

CAREER: BOWLING

	O.	M.	R.	W.	AV.
TEST					
1ST-CLASS	4994.1	997	15414	549	28.08
INT					
RAL	952.1	99	3995	187	21.36
NAT.W.	167	14	658	29	22.68
B & H	352.2	60	1115	65	17.15

JULIAN, R.

Full Name: Raymond Julian
Role: Right-hand bat, wicket-keeper
Born: 23 August 1936, Cosby, Leicestershire
Height: 5′ 11″
Weight: 11st 4lbs
Nickname: Julie
Parents: George Ernest and Doris
County: Leicestershire
County debut: 1953
County cap: 1961
1st-Class 50s scored: 2
Wife and date of marriage: Ruth Ann, 30 April 1958
Children: Peter, 1 February 1958; John, 13 October 1960; David, 15 October 1963; Paul, 22 September 1967
Family links with cricket: Father and two brothers all played local club cricket; two sons also play
Education: Wigston Secondary Modern School
Jobs outside cricket: Painter and decorator, cricket kit salesman
Off-season 1989–90: Working for Somerset CCC, painting
Overseas tours: MCC to West Africa, 1975, as wicket-keeper and umpire
Cricketers particularly learnt from: Keith Andrew and Bill Alley
Cricketers particularly admired: Gary Sobers, Keith Andrew, Willie Watson, Ray Illingworth, Richard Hadlee, Clive Rice
Other sports played: Ex-1st-Class football referee (local), linesman on

574

Southern League for four seasons, refereed one FA Cup match. Football goalkeeper
Relaxations: Gardening, sunbathing, theatre-going
Extras: Youngest player to make debut (age 15) for Leicestershire v Gloucestershire, Bristol 1953. Gave 8 lbw decisions on the trot, Glamorgan v Sussex, Cardiff 1986. Played for Army 1955–57. Three Benson & Hedges semi-finals, one Gillette Cup semi-final
Opinions on cricket: 'My contract does not allow me to comment, but I am in favour of four-day cricket, and a Saturday league of 55 overs.'
Best batting performance: 51 Leicestershire v Worcestershire, Worcester 1962

CAREER: BATTING

	I.	N.O.	R.	H.S.	AV.
TEST					
1ST-CLASS	288	23	2581	51	9.73
INT					
RAL					
NAT.W.	3	0	6	4	2.00
B & H					

CAREER: WICKET KEEPING

	C.	ST.		
TEST				
1ST-CLASS	381	40		
INT				
RAL				
NAT.W.	–	–		
B & H				

KITCHEN, M. J.

Full Name: Mervyn John Kitchen
Role: Left-hand bat, right-arm medium bowler
Born: 1 August 1940, Nailsea, Somerset
County: Somerset
County debut: 1960
County cap: 1966
Benefit: 1973 (£6000)
1000 runs in a season: 7
1st-Class 50s scored: 68
1st-Class 100s scored: 17
One-Day 50s: 22
One-Day 100s: 1
1st-Class catches: 157
Appointed to 1st-Class list: 1982
Education: Backwell Secondary Modern, Nailsea

Best batting performance: 189 Somerset v Pakistan, Taunton 1967

CAREER: BATTING

	I.	N.O.	R.	H.S.	AV.
TEST					
1ST-CLASS	612	32	15230	189	26.25
INT					
RAL	111	10	2069	82	20.48
NAT.W.	27	1	815	116	31.34
B & H	25	1	504	70	21.00

CAREER: BOWLING

	O.	M.	R.	W.	AV.
TEST					
1ST-CLASS	30.1	7	109	2	54.50
INT					
RAL	17.5	0	89	4	22.25
NAT.W.	3	2	8	1	–
B & H					

LEADBEATER, B.

Full Name: Barrie Leadbeater
Role: Right-hand opening bat, right-arm medium bowler, slip fielder
Born: 14 August 1943, Leeds
Height: 6′ **Weight:** 13st 2lbs
Nickname: Leady
Parents: Ronnie (deceased) and Nellie
County: Yorkshire
County debut: 1966
County cap: 1969
Benefit: 1980 (£33,846 shared with G. A. Cope)
1st-Class 50s scored: 27
1st-Class 100s scored: 1
One-Day 50s: 11
1st-Class catches: 82
Appointed to 1st-Class list: 1981
Wife and date of marriage:
Jacqueline, 18 September 1971
Children: Richard Barrie, 23 November 1972; Michael Spencer, 21 March 1976; Daniel Mark Ronnie, 19 June 1981
Family links with cricket: Father played works cricket
Education: Brownhill County Primary; Harehills Secondary Modern, Leeds
Qualifications: 2 O-levels (English and Maths). Between leaving school and joining Yorkshire CCC, had five years' training with Leeds & Holbeck Building Society
Jobs outside cricket: Coach, driver, working for Leeds & Holbeck Building Society
Off-season 1989–90: Driver for Supercook Group

Cricketing superstitions or habits: 'As a player always touched down behind my crease at the end of an over.'

Overseas tours: Duke of Norfolk's XI to West Indies 1970

Overseas teams played for: Johannesburg Municipals 1978–79

Cricketers particularly learnt from: Brian Close, Willie Watson, Arthur Mitchell, Maurice Leyland, Doug Padgett

Cricketers particularly admired: Colin Cowdrey, Clive Rice, Richard Hadlee, Gary Sobers, Michael Holding, Fred Trueman, Tony Nicholson, Mike Procter

Other sports played: Golf, table tennis, snooker

Other sports followed: Rugby union and rugby league, most other sports

Injuries 1989: 'Sore ears from all the appealing!'

Relaxations: Family, car maintenance, music, DIY, reading

Extras: Scored maiden century on two pitches, the original having been vandalised. Man of the Match in Gillette Cup Final, 1969

Opinions on cricket: 'Disappointed in players who cannot show self-control and maintain personal and professional standards on the field. I'm concerned at the level of honesty in the game at some levels.'

Best batting performance: 140* Yorkshire v Hampshire, Portsmouth 1976

CAREER: BATTING

	I.	N.O.	R.	H.S.	AV.
TEST					
1ST-CLASS	241	29	5373	140*	25.34
INT					
RAL	68	14	1423	86*	26.35
NAT.W.	9	0	155	76	17.22
B & H	21	5	601	90	37.56

CAREER: BOWLING

	O.	M.	R.	W.	AV.
TEST					
1ST-CLASS	5	1	5	1	5.00
INT					
RAL	8.5	0	38	2	19.00
NAT.W.					
B & H					

183. Only one England batsman has scored seven Test centuries against the West Indies. Who is he?

184. Only one West Indian batsman has scored 11 Test centuries against England. Who is he?

185. Who was England's first Test captain v West Indies, and when?

MEYER, B. J.

Full Name: Barrie John Meyer
Role: Right-hand bat, wicket-keeper
Born: 21 August 1932, Bournemouth
Height: 5' 10½" **Weight:** 12st 4lbs
Nickname: BJ
County: Gloucestershire
County debut: 1957
County cap: 1958
1st-Class 50s scored: 11
Appointed to 1st-Class list: 1973
Appointed to Test panel: 1978
No. of Tests umpired: 21
No. of One-Day Internationals umpired: 18
Wife and date of marriage: Gillian, 4 September 1965
Children: Stephen Barrie, Christopher John, Adrian Michael
Education: Boscombe Secondary, Bournemouth
Jobs outside cricket: Ex-salesman
Overseas tours: Gloucestershire to Bermuda 1960
Cricketers particularly learnt from: Andy Wilson of Gloucestershire
Cricketers particularly admired: Keith Andrew, Bob Taylor, Alan Knott, John Lever
Other sports played: Ex-professional footballer, golf (7 handicap)
Relaxations: Music, reading, TV
Best batting performance: 63 Gloucestershire v Indians, 1959; Gloucestershire v Oxford University, 1962; Gloucestershire v Sussex, 1964

CAREER: BATTING

	I.	N.O.	R.	H.S.	AV.
TEST					
1ST-CLASS	569	190	5367	63	14.16
INT					
RAL	16	3	65	15	5.00
NAT.W.	9	2	69	21	9.86
B & H					

CAREER: WICKET KEEPING

	C.	ST.		
TEST				
1ST-CLASS	708	117		
INT				
RAL	31	2		
NAT.W.	16	3		
B & H				

186. Who scored the most Test runs for England v Australia?

OSLEAR, D. O.

Full Name: Donald Osmund Oslear
Born: 3 March 1929, Cleethorpes
Height: 6′ **Weight:** 14st 2lbs
Parents: John Osmund and
Violet Maude
Appointed to 1st-Class list: 1975
Appointed to Test panel: 1980
No. of Tests umpired: 5
**No. of One-Day Internationals
umpired:** 9
Marital status: Divorced
Children: Sara Elizabeth,
25 February 1960
Family links with cricket: 'Father,
younger brother and myself all
played for Cleethorpes CC. Brother
still plays and captains 2nd XI, aged
54.'
Education: Elliston Street Secondary
School, Cleethorpes
Qualifications: Member of General Council ACU. Training Officer of ACU.
Member of TCCB Electronic Aids Committee
Jobs outside cricket: Fishing Industry in Grimsby. Lecturing to umpires
overseas
Off-season 1989–90: Lecturing to umpires, and coaching overseas at school
level
Cricketers particularly admired: Garth Le Roux, Ray Illingworth, Mike
Brearley, Keith Fletcher. 'I feel that David Hughes of Lancashire and Ian
Greig of Surrey have done a great deal for their counties over the past couple
of years.'
Other sports followed: Anything which England are engaged in
Relaxations: The study of cricket law and the changes in the laws over the
years. Reading cricket books
Extras: The only English umpire to have 'stood' in Test Matches, who has not
played county cricket. Played soccer for Grimsby and ice-hockey for Grimsby
and an England Select side. Life member of the Association of Cricket
Umpires. Training Officer of the ACU. Member of General Council of ACU.
'In 1988, I figured in two instances where the striker has been stumped off a
wide ball. In all my career, I have never seen it happen before.'

PALMER, K. E.

Full Name: Kenneth Ernest Palmer
Role: Right-hand bat, right-arm fast-medium bowler, all-rounder
Born: 22 April 1937, Winchester
Height: 5′ 10″ **Weight:** 13st
Nickname: Pedlar
Parents: Harry and Cecilia
County: Somerset
County debut: 1955
County cap: 1958
Test debut: 1965
No. of Tests: 1
1000 runs in a season: 1
50 wickets in a season: 6
1st-Class 50s scored: 27
1st-Class 100s scored: 2
1st-Class 5 w. in innings: 46
1st-Class 10 w. in match: 5
1st-Class catches: 156
Appointed to 1st-Class list: 1972
Appointed to Test panel: 1978
No. of Tests umpired: 17
No. of One-Day Internationals umpired: 8
Wife and date of marriage: Joy Valerie, 6 September 1962
Children: Gary, 1 November 1965
Family links with cricket: Son Gary professional cricketer with Somerset. Brother umpire on first-class list and also played for Somerset
Jobs outside cricket: Coached cricket for Somerset for some time
Other sports played: Squash
Relaxations: 'I enjoy watching my son play cricket on the rare occasions that I get the opportunity.'
Extras: Toured with Commonwealth side to Pakistan, 1962. Toured West Indies with Denis Compton's team January 1963. 'I had the opportunity to see him score 100 in great style with a straw hat on!' Umpired in two Benson & Hedges Finals and two NatWest Finals. Also twice on World Cup panel in England. Won Carling Single Wicket Competition in 1961. Did the 'double' in 1961: 114 wickets and 1036 runs. Batting with former Australia and Somerset cricketer (and former Test umpire) Bill Alley, holds 6th wicket partnership record for Somerset. Wife, Joy, is a PE teacher
Best batting performance: 125* Somerset v Northamptonshire, Northampton 1961

Best bowling performance: 9-57 Somerset v Nottinghamshire, Trent Bridge 1963

CAREER: BATTING

	I.	N.O.	R.	H.S.	AV.
TEST	1	0	10	10	–
1ST-CLASS	480	105	7751	125*	20.66
INT					
RAL	6	1	28	14	5.60
NAT.W.	13	4	109	35	12.11
B & H					

CAREER: BOWLING

	O.	M.	R.	W.	AV.
TEST	63	7	189	1	–
1ST-CLASS	7260.4	1767	18304	865	21.16
INT					
RAL	59	6	282	11	25.64
NAT.W.	163.3	35	451	23	19.60
B & H					

PALMER, R.

Full Name: Roy Palmer
Role: Right-hand bat, right-arm fast-medium bowler
Born: 12 July 1942, Devizes, Wiltshire
County: Somerset
County debut: 1965
50 wickets in a season: 1
1st-Class 50s scored: 1
1st-Class 5 w. in innings: 4
1st-Class catches: 25
Appointed to 1st-Class list: 1980
Family links with cricket: Brother Ken played for Somerset and is also a first-class umpire. Nephew, Gary, plays for Somerset
Education: Southbroom Secondary Modern
Best batting performance: 84 Somerset v Leicestershire, Taunton 1967
Best bowling performance: 6-45 Somerset v Middlesex, Lord's 1967

CAREER: BATTING

	I.	N.O.	R.	H.S.	AV.
TEST					
1ST-CLASS	110	32	1037	84	13.29
INT					
RAL	19	2	168	25	9.88
NAT.W.	9	2	30	11	4.28

CAREER: BOWLING

	O.	M.	R.	W.	AV.
TEST					
1ST-CLASS	1697.1	336	5439	172	31.62
INT					
RAL	220	14	963	37	26.03
NAT.W.	148.1	19	532	30	17.73

PLEWS, N. T.

Full Name: Nigel Trevor Plews
Born: 5 September 1934, Nottingham
Height: 6′ 6½″ **Weight:** 16st 12lbs
Appointed to 1st-Class list: 1982
Appointed to Test panel: 1989
No. of Tests umpired: 2
No. of One-Day Internationals umpired: 2
Wife and date of marriage: Margaret, 1956
Children: Elaine, 1961; Douglas, 1964
Education: Mundella Grammar School, Nottingham
Qualifications: School Certificate, Royal Society of Arts, Advanced Book-keeping
Jobs outside cricket: Nottingham City Police for 25 years as a Det. Sgt in Fraud Squad
Off-season 1989–90: Employed off season by international chartered accountants Spicer and Oppenheim in insolvency work, as each year since 1980
Other sports played: Table tennis, swimming
Other sports followed: Rugby Union
Relaxations: Hill walking, reading, travel
Extras: Did not play first-class cricket, but did play in local league and club cricket in Nottingham

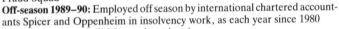

187. Who scored the most runs for Australia v England?

188. Who has taken the most wickets for England v Australia?

189. Who has taken the most wickets for Australia v England?

190. Which Test captain has taken the most wickets in one Test match?

191. Which English captain has taken most wickets in one Test match?

RHODES, H. J.

Full Name: Harold James Rhodes
Role: Right-hand bat, right-arm fast bowler
Born: 22 July 1936, Hadfield, Derbyshire
Height: 6′ 2″ **Weight:** 14st 7lbs
Nickname: Dusty
Parents: Bert and Vera
County: Derbyshire
County debut: 1953
County cap: 1958
Test debut: 1959
No. of Tests: 2
50 wickets in a season: 11
1st-Class 5 w. in innings: 42
1st-Class 10 w. in match: 4
1st-Class catches: 86
Appointed to 1st-Class list: On reserve list
Wife and date of marriage: Barbara, 17 September 1960
Children: Marcus, 31 May 1961; Julie, 26 September 1962; Simon, 9 March 1968; Jonathan, 24 August 1969
Family links with cricket: Father was first-class and Test umpire
Education: Vernon High School, Derby
Jobs outside cricket: Mortgage manager, Abbey Life Assurance Co.
Off-season 1989–90: Mortgage manager, full-time
Overseas tours: South Africa 1959 with Denis Compton's Commonwealth team; Round the World 1960, with R. Benaud's Commonwealth team; to West Indies with E. W. Swanton's Commonwealth team; Round the World 1967 with Mickey Stewart's Commonwealth team; MCC to Far East 1983
Cricketers particularly learnt from: Les Jackson, Cliff Gladwin
Cricketers particularly admired: Brian Statham, Richard Hadlee, Fred Trueman
Other sports played: Golf
Other sports followed: Rugby, soccer
Relaxations: Reading, gardening
Extras: Top of first-class bowling averages 1965 – 119 wickets, av. 11.09. Test career ruined by throwing controversy, cleared 1968 after eight years of deliberations. Autobiography published March 1987. Advanced coach and senior cricket coach at Lord's Indoor School
Opinions on cricket: 'Too much cricket played. Would like to see semi-professional system: this would give better security for players, and would

give an opportunity for *all* to participate. Uncovered wickets to bring back skills and provide more interesting games for spectators. Except for a few, cricket is a badly paid sport. If cricket was conducted as a business, as it should be, – after all it employs professional people – the selectors, managers, etc., would have been long gone. How long is it since we won a Test Match?'

Best batting performance: 48 Derbyshire v Middlesex, Chesterfield 1958

Best bowling performance: 7-38 Derbyshire v Warwickshire, Edgbaston 1965

CAREER: BATTING

	I.	N.O.	R.	H.S.	AV.
TEST	1	1	0	0*	–
1ST-CLASS	398	142	2427	48	9.48
INT					
RAL	11	5	23	6*	3.83
NAT.W.	10	6	84	26*	21.00
B & H	5	2	17	8*	5.66

CAREER: BOWLING

	O.	M.	R.	W.	AV.
TEST	74.5	10	244	9	27.11
1ST-CLASS	9128.4	2425	20901	1064	19.64
INT					
RAL	242.4	32	933	38	24.55
NAT.W.	173.4	41	435	22	19.77
B & H	98	18	302	11	27.45

SHEPHERD, D. R.

Full Name: David Robert Shepherd
Role: Right-hand bat, right-arm medium bowler
Born: 27 December 1940, Bideford, Devon
County: Gloucestershire
County debut: 1965
County cap: 1969
Benefit: 1978 (shared with J. Davey)
1000 runs in a season: 2
1st-Class 50s scored: 55
1st-Class 100s scored: 12
One-Day 50s: 18
One-Day 100s: 2
1st-Class catches: 95
Appointed to 1st-Class list: 1981
Appointed to Test panel: 1985
No. of Tests umpired: 9
No. of One-Day Internationals umpired: 28
Education: Barnstaple GS; St Luke College, Exeter
Extras: Superstitious enough to stand on one leg when the score is on a

'Nelson'. Only Gloucestershire player to score a hundred on first-class debut

Best batting performance: 153 Gloucestershire v Middlesex, Bristol 1968

CAREER: BATTING

	I.	N.O.	R.	H.S.	AV.
TEST					
1ST-CLASS	476	40	10672	153	24.47
INT					
RAL	118	9	2274	100	20.86
NAT.W.	24	3	457	72*	21.76
B & H	30	5	580	81	23.20

CAREER: BOWLING

	O.	M.	R.	W.	AV.
TEST					
1ST-CLASS	32.4	4	106	2	53.00
INT					
RAL	1	0	6	0	–
NAT.W.	0.2	0	4	0	–
B & H					

TAYLOR, K.

Full Name: Kenneth Taylor
Role: Right-hand opening bat, cover point fielder
Born: 21 August 1935
Height: 5′ 9½″ **Weight:** 13st
Nickname: K. Ty (Katy)
Parents: Harold and Amy
County: Yorkshire
County debut: 1953
County cap: 1957
Benefit: 1968 (£6301)
1000 runs in a season: 6
1st-Class 50s scored: 68
1st-Class 100s scored: 15
1st-Class 200s scored: 1
1st-Class 5 w. in innings: 1
Appointed to 1st-Class list: On reserve list
Wife and date of marriage: Avril, 26 March 1960
Children: Nicholas Simon, 2 June 1963; James Cameron, 5 June 1966
Family links with cricket: Son, Nicholas, was on playing staff with Surrey and Somerset, 1986
Education: Huddersfield School of Art; Slade College of Art; London University
Qualifications: National Diploma in Design, Slade certificate
Jobs outside cricket: Professional footballer with Huddersfield Town AFC 1953–68, England B and U-23 squads, art teacher, cricket coach

Off-season 1989–90: Teaching art, painting and drawing at Beeston Hall School; coaching

Overseas tours: Jim Swanton's Commonwealth side to India 1963–64; MCC to Bangladesh 1978–79

Overseas teams played for: Auckland, New Zealand 1963–64

Cricketers particularly learnt from: Sir Len Hutton

Cricketers particularly admired: Sir Len Hutton, Sir Gary Sobers

Other sports played: Golf, tennis

Other sports followed: 'Absolutely everything.'

Relaxations: Photography

Extras: Youngest player to play first-class cricket and First Division soccer: at age 17 played for Yorkshire v Northamptonshire at Headingley, 24 June 1953; at age 18 played for Huddersfield v Liverpool, 6 June 1954. His 160 runs is the highest score by a Yorkshire player in a county match against the Australian tourists this century, in 1964. Scored four goals in one game for Huddersfield v West Ham

Best batting performance: 203* Yorkshire v Warwickshire, Edgbaston 1961

Best bowling performance: 6-75 Yorkshire v Lancashire, Old Trafford 1961

CAREER: BATTING

	I.	N.O.	R.	H.S.	AV.
TEST	5	0	57	24	11.40
1ST-CLASS	519	36	12996	203*	26.90
INT					
RAL					
NAT.W.	10	0	134	30	13.40
B & H					

CAREER: BOWLING

	O.	M.	R.	W.	AV.
TEST	2	0	6	0	–
1ST-CLASS	1769.5	607	3757	131	28.67
INT					
RAL					
NAT.W.	61	12	168	11	15.27
B & H					

192. What do Kim Barnett, Phil Neale, Jeff Dujon, Franklyn Stephenson and Steve Waugh have in common?

193. What do Allan Border of Australia, John Jameson of England, and Clive Lloyd of West Indies all have in common?

194. Which Test cricketer was born in one country, played for a second, and was banned from playing in a third because he had played in a fourth?

THOMPSETT, D. S.

Full Name: Donald Stanley
Thompsett
Born: 8 April 1935, Piltdown,
Sussex
Height: 6' **Weight:** 13st
Appointed to 1st-Class list: On
reserve list since 1985
Parents: John and Dorothy
Wife and date of marriage: Valerie,
10 October 1957
Children: Glen, Clifford, Steven,
Debbie and Linzie
Family links with cricket: Sons Cliff
and Steve play club cricket for
Chippenham in Western League
Education: Secondary
Jobs outside cricket: Poultry farmer
Off-season 1989–90: Working on
farm

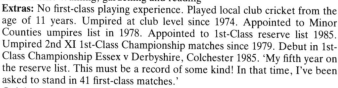

Other sports played: Bowls (indoor), football
Relaxations: Walking, gardening and reading
Extras: No first-class playing experience. Played local club cricket from the age of 11 years. Umpired at club level since 1974. Appointed to Minor Counties umpires list in 1978. Appointed to 1st-Class reserve list 1985. Umpired 2nd XI 1st-Class Championship matches since 1979. Debut in 1st-Class Championship Essex v Derbyshire, Colchester 1985. 'My fifth year on the reserve list. This must be a record of some kind! In that time, I've been asked to stand in 41 first-class matches.'
Opinions on cricket: 'Like many people I do feel that we have opened the floodgates for too many overseas players, therefore depriving us of some 25 or 30 places for youngsters coming into the game throughout the country.'

---

195. Which cricketer has the same figures on his Test debut as his brother had on his Test debut?

196. What was last season's Britannic Championship winner's prize money: £25,000, £37,000, or £75,000?

WHITE, R. A.

Full Name: Robert Arthur White
Role: Left-hand bat, off-break bowler, all-rounder
Born: 6 October 1936, Fulham
Height: 5′ 9½″ **Weight:** 12st 4lbs
Nickname: Knocker
Counties: Middlesex, Nottinghamshire
County debut: 1958 (Middlesex), 1966 (Nottinghamshire)
County cap: 1963 (Middlesex), 1966 (Nottinghamshire)
1000 runs in a season: 1
50 wickets in a season: 2
1st-Class 50s scored: 50
1st-Class 100s scored: 5
1st-Class 5 w. in innings: 28
1st-Class 10 w. in match: 4
1st-Class catches: 190
Appointed to 1st-Class list: 1982
Wife: Janice
Children: Robin, Vanessa
Family links with cricket: Father played club cricket
Education: Chiswick Grammar School
Qualifications: Matriculation
Jobs outside cricket: Self-employed sales agent
Off-season 1989–90: Selling fireworks
Cricketers particularly learnt from: 'I tried to learn from everyone I encountered.'
Cricketers particularly admired: 'Garfield Sobers more than anyone.'
Other sports played: 'Golf – very indifferently – three times a week.'
Other sports followed: Ice-hockey
Relaxations: Theatre-going
Extras: Independent coaching trips to South Africa, 1959, 1960, 1966, 1967,

CAREER: BATTING

	I.	N.O.	R.	H.S.	AV.
TEST					
1ST-CLASS	642	105	12452	116*	23.19
INT					
RAL	78	28	844	86*	16.88
NAT.W.	20	1	284	39	14.95
B & H	21	9	251	52*	20.92

CAREER: BOWLING

	O.	M.	R.	W.	AV.
TEST					
1ST-CLASS	7946	2219	21138	693	30.50
INT					
RAL	607	54	2448	103	23.76
NAT.W.	147	15	488	14	34.86
B & H	234.5	32	800	19	42.11

1968. Together with M. J. Smedley holds the Nottinghamshire 6th wicket record partnership of 204, v Surrey, at The Oval, 1966

Opinions on cricket: 'Too controversial to go into print.'

Best batting performance: 116* Nottinghamshire v Surrey, The Oval 1967

Best bowling performance: 7-41 Nottinghamshire v Derbyshire, Ilkeston 1971

WHITEHEAD, A. G. T.

Full Name: Alan Geoffrey Thomas Whitehead

Role: Left-hand bat, slow left-arm bowler

Born: 28 October 1940, Butleigh, Somerset

County: Somerset

County debut: 1957

1st-Class 5 w. in innings: 3

1st-Class catches: 20

Appointed to 1st-Class list: 1970

Appointed to Test panel: 1982

No. of Tests umpired: 4

Best batting performance: 15 Somerset v Hampshire, Southampton 1959

Best bowling performance: 6-74 Somerset v Sussex, Eastbourne 1959

CAREER: BATTING

	I.	N.O.	R.	H.S.	AV.
TEST					
1ST-CLASS	49	25	137	15	5.71
INT					
RAL					
NAT.W.					
B & H					

CAREER: BOWLING

	O.	M.	R.	W.	AV.
TEST					
1ST-CLASS	846.4	250	2306	67	34.42
INT					
RAL					
NAT.W.					
B & H					

197. The winner's prize money for last season's Refuge Assurance League, NatWest Trophy, and Benson & Hedges Cup was the same for each competition. Was it: £22,000, £37,000, or £55,000?

WIGHT, P. B.

Full Name: Peter Bernard Wight
Role: Right-hand bat, off-break
bowler, slip fielder
Born: 25 June 1930, Georgetown,
British Guiana
Height: 5′ 10″ **Weight:** 11st
Nickname: Flipper
Parents: Henry De Lisle and
Mary Matilda
County: Somerset
County debut: 1953
County cap: 1954
Benefit: 1963 (£5000)
1000 runs in a season: 10
1st-Class 50s scored: 207
1st-Class 100s scored: 26
1st-Class 200s scored: 2
1st-Class 5 w. in innings: 1
1st-Class catches: 204
Appointed to 1st-Class list: 1966
Wife and date of marriage: Joyce, 26 January 1957
Children: Paul Anthony, 22 August 1965, Anne-Marie, 14 October 1967
Family links with cricket: Brother Leslie played for West Indies and British
Guiana. Brothers Norman and Arnold played for British Guiana
Education: St Stanislaus College
Jobs outside cricket: Has own indoor cricket school. Has coached in East
Africa and New Zealand
Off-season 1989–90: Coaching cricket
Overseas teams played for: British Guiana; Canterbury CC, New Zealand
Overseas tours: British Guiana to Jamaica 1949
Cricketers particularly admired: Denis Compton, Alec Bedser, Gary
Sobers, Peter May, Ken Barrington, Tony Lock, Everton Weekes, Frank
Worrell
Other sports played: Football, hockey, squash, skittles
Other sports followed: Rugby, ice-hockey, snooker, – 'all ball games'

CAREER: BATTING

	I.	N.O.	R.	H.S.	AV.
TEST					
1ST-CLASS	590	53	17773	222*	33.10
INT					
RAL					
NAT.W.	6	0	56	38	9.33
B & H					

CAREER: BOWLING

	O.	M.	R.	W.	AV.
TEST					
1ST-CLASS	789.1	224	2262	68	33.26
INT					
RAL					
NAT.W.					
B & H					

Relaxations: Gardening, decorating
Best batting performance: 222* Somerset v Kent, Taunton 1959
Best bowling performance: 6-29 Somerset v Derbyshire, Chesterfield 1957

198. Who is the current President of MCC?

199. Who was the immediate past President of MCC?

200. For which English county did Australian Test cricketer Merv Hughes play?

201. Why was J. D. Robertson not out when he knocked over his stumps while batting at Lord's in July 1944?

NOW YOU KNOW WHO'S WHO, WHY NOT FIND OUT WHAT'S WHAT?

Talk to Refuge about Life Assurance,
Investments, Car Insurance, Mortgages,
Pensions or House and Home Insurance.

ANSWERS

1. Pakistan
2. West Indies
3. Graham Gooch
4. Allan Lamb
5. £10,250
6. Sir Learie Constantine
7. Middlesex
8. Clive Radley
9. True
10. Mark Nicholas
11. Mike Atherton
12. Robin Smith, at 61.44
13. Steve Waugh, at 126.50
14. Neil Foster, with 12 wickets at 35.8 runs
15. Terry Alderman, with 41 wickets at 17.38 runs
16. A. P. F. Chapman and F. R. Brown
17. L. M. Sawle
18. 28
19. M. C. Cowdrey: 27 times
20. J. B. Hobbs, 61,237; F. E. Woolley, 58,969; E. H. Hendren, 57,611
21. D. G. Bradman, 95.14; V. M. Merchant, 71.22; W. H. Ponsford, 65.18
22. G. Boycott: 56.83
23. AB, or Herbie (from Herbaceous Border)
24. Nottinghamshire beat Essex
25. Essex beat Nottinghamshire
26. They all played for MCC v France
27. New Zealand v England, Auckland 1954–55; 26
28. South Africa v England, Durban 1938–39; 10 days
29. Mushtaq Mohammad, for Pakistan v West Indies
1958–59; aged 15 years, 124 days
30. I. D. Craig, v South Africa 1952–53; 17 years, 239 days
31. J. Southerton, v Australia 1876–77; 49 years, 119 days
32. 1787
33. 316 not out, J. B. Hobbs, Surrey v Middlesex 1926
34. 175 yards from hit to pitch, Rev. W. Fellows in practice at Oxford in 1856
35. K. G. Suttle: 423 for Sussex, 1954–69
36. He was the only French-born member of the French team
37. J. G. Binks, 1955–1969
38. W. Rhodes, Yorkshire, 1898–1930
39. C. H. Lloyd, West Indies: 74 times
40. 499, Hanif Mohammad, Karachi v Bahawalpur 1958–59
41. 424: A. C. Maclaren, Lancashire v Somerset 1895
42. G. S. Chappell: 48 times
43. They all scored centuries on their first-class debuts
44. Zaheer Abbas: 8 times
45. P. B. H. May: 41 times
46. Worcestershire
47. Essex
48. Geoff Marsh
49. Jack Russell
50. Terry Alderman
51. Ian Healy
52. A. R. Butcher, Glamorgan
53. Jimmy Cook, Somerset and South Africa

54. The footballer whose innocent tackle on Denis Compton set off Compton's long-lingering knee trouble
55. *A La Recherche du Cricket Perdu* by Simon Barnes
56. Officer of the Order of Australia
57. Jack Russell
58. Lubo
59. Gunner
60. Kippy
61. C. Blyth: 17, Kent v Northamptonshire, Northampton 1907
62. J. C. Laker: 19, England v Australia, Manchester 1956
63. Only man ever to take four first-class wickets with consecutive balls, twice
64. J. S. Rao, Services v Northern Punjab 1963
65. D. V. P. Wright, Kent and England: 7
66. A. P. Freeman: 304, 1928
67. W. Rhodes, Yorkshire and England: 4187
68. True
69. Score a century and take a hat-trick in the same match, twice
70. J. P. Stephenson, Essex and England: 20
71. They have all played for Minor Counties
72. Cable and Wireless
73. Nasser Hussain
74. They both made their highest Test scores of 31 (Cook) and 59 (Small)
75. David Graveney of Gloucestershire
76. Mike Gatting
77. Australia and New Zealand
78. 1996
79. True
80. He hit his maiden first-class century
81. Jimmy Cook of Somerset and South Africa
82. They both used the same bat
83. Andy Goram of Scotland
84. Yorkshire, 20 July 1989
85. Both played cricket for South Africa and rugger for England
86. Bristol
87. F. R. Brown
88. Ted Dexter
89. Mike Denness
90. 10
91. 6
92. 4
93. Sir C. Aubrey Smith, England v South Africa, Port Elizabeth 1889
94. Colin Cowdrey: 114
95. Sunil Gavaskar, for India: 106
96. W. Rhodes aged 52, v West Indies 1929–30
97. H. Ironmonger, aged 50, v England 1932–33
98. 50, in 1899, v Australia at Nottingham
99. Lord Harris, and Sir Pelham Warner
100. Each scored a century in his first game as county captain
101. J. W. Lloyds of Gloucestershire
102. V. P. Terry of Hampshire
103. M. Roseberry of Middlesex
104. 1981–82 v England
105. T. B. Horan
106. J. E. Morris
107. G. Gooch
108. A. R. Butcher
109. K. Curran

110. R. Smith
111. R. Pienaar
112. G. Mendis
113. D. Gower
114. Mike Gatting
115. Kevin Curran and A. J. Wright
116. Allan Lamb
117. Tim Robinson
118. Jimmy Cook
119. Monte Lynch
120. A. P. Wells
121. D. A. Reeve
122. A. Hick
123. M. D. Moxon
124. O. Mortensen
125. D. R. Pringle
126. S. Watkin
127. C. A. Walsh
128. Malcolm Marshall
129. Richard Ellison
130. Wasim Akram
131. W. K. Benjamin
132. Angus Fraser
133. Nick Cook
134. M. Field-Buss
135. 91
136. G. D. Rose
137. 10
138. N. M. Kendrick
139. A. R. Clarke
140. T. A. Merrick
141. S. R. Lampitt
142. P. W. Jarvis
143. Vic Marks: 843.5
144. Steve Barwick: 745.2
145. Steve Watkin: 703
146. Jimmy Cook: 2173
147. J. E. Morris and P. D. Bowler
148. Alec Stewart: 1633
149. A. P. Wells: 1629
150. J. Southerton, aged 49, England v Australia, Melbourne 1876–77
151. 26, New Zealand v England, Auckland 1954–55
152. R. W. Marsh: 355
153. Bob Taylor of Derbyshire and England: 10, all caught, v India, Bombay 1979–80
154. Jonathan Griffiths of Wales
155. Dean
156. Robert Menzies of Australia
157. F. S. Trueman of Yorkshire and England
158. Mike Atherton of Cambridge, Lancashire and England
159. 1934
160. 1883
161. 1965
162. Phil Neale
163. E. W. Swanton
164. Sir Donald Bradman of Australia: 99.94
165. Trevor Hohns, 35
166. Steve Waugh, 23
167. Six first-class centuries in six successive innings
168. F. R. Brown
169. 'Timeless Test', England v South Africa, Durban March 1939; Hedley Verity of Yorkshire and England
170. Ken Cranston of Lancashire, 1947–48
171. George Headley, 1947–48
172. Freddie Stocks of Nottinghamshire
173. Charles Macartney
174. Gentlemen of Hampstead CC in July 1988
175. Henry
176. £1,500, plus £50 for every five Tests previously umpired

177. Shakespeare, *Henry V*, Act 4, Scene 7
178. Lance Gibbs: 27,115 balls
179. Ian Botham
180. Ray Lindwall of Australia
181. Bob Willis
182. They were all awarded their county caps in 1988
183. Sir L. Hutton
184. Sir G. Sobers
185. A. P. F. Chapman, 1928
186. Sir J. B. Hobbs: 3,636
187. Sir D. G. Bradman: 5,028
188. I. T. Botham
189. D. K. Lillee
190. Fazal Mahmood: 12-100, Pakistan v West Indies, Dacca 1958–59
191. A. E. R. Gilligan: 11-90, v South Africa, Edgbaston 1924
192. They were *Wisden*'s Cricketers of the Year in the 1989 volume
193. They have all been run out in both innings of a Test Match
194. Robin Jackman, India, England, West Indies, South Africa
195. Ian and Tony Greig: 4-53
196. £37,000
197. £22,000
198. Sir Denys Roberts
199. Field Marshal Lord Bramall
200. For Essex 2nd XI, and Essex 1st XI once, v New Zealand 1983
201. Because he did so while throwing himself flat on the ground to avoid a German bomb

INDEX OF PLAYERS
BY COUNTY

Shastri, R.
Smith, I.
Somaia, K.
Watkin, S. L.

GLOUCESTERSHIRE

Alleyne, M. W.
Athey, C. W. J.
Bainbridge, P.
Ball, M. C. J.
Butcher, I. P.
Curran, K. M.
Graveney, D. A.
Greene, V. S.
Hodgson, G. D.
Ibadulla, K. B.
Jarvis, K. B. S.
Lawrence, D. V.
Lloyds, J. W.
Pooley, M. W.
Pritchard, N. M. A.
Romaines, P. W.
Russell, R. C.
Stovold, A. W.
Tedstone, G. A.
Walsh, C. A.
Wright, A. J.

HAMPSHIRE

Andrew, S. J. W.
Aymes, A. N.
Bakker, P.-J.
Connor, C. A.
Gower, D. I.
James, K. D.

Jefferies, S. T.
Marshall, M. D.
Maru, R. J.
Middleton, T. C.
Nicholas, M. C. J.
Parks, R. J.
Scott, R. J.
Shine, K. J.
Smith, C. L.
Smith, R. A.
Terry, V. P.
Tremlett, T. M.
Turner, D. R.
Turner, I. J.
Udal, S. D.
Wood, J. R.

KENT

Alleyne, H. L.
Benson, M. R.
Cowdrey, C. S.
Cowdrey, G. R.
Davis, R. P.
Dobson, M. C.
Ealham, M. A.
Ellison, R. M.
Farbrace, P.
Fleming, M. V.
Harman, M. D.
Hinks, S. G.
Igglesden, A. P.
Kelleher, D. J. M.
Llong, N. J.
Longley, J. I.
Marsh, S. A.
Patel, M. M.
Penn, C.
Pienaar, R. F.
Taylor, N. R.

Ward, T. R.
Wells, V. J.
Wren, T. N.

LANCASHIRE

Allott, P. J. W.
Atherton, M. A.
Austin, I. D.
Defreitas, P. A. J.
Fairbrother, N. H.
Fitton, J. D.
Folley, I.
Fowler, G.
Hegg, W. K.
Hughes, D. P.
Jesty, T. E.
Lloyd, G. D.
Martin, P. J.
Mendis, G. D.
Patterson, B. P.
Simmons, J.
Speak, N. J.
Stanworth, J.
Wasim Akram
Watkinson, M.

LEICESTERSHIRE

Agnew, J. P.
Benjamin, W. K. M.
Benson, J. D. R.
Boon, T. J.
Briers, N. E.
Cobb, R. A.
Edmunds, R. H.
Ferris, G. J. F.
Gidley, M. I.

Hepworth, P. N.
Lewis, C. C.
Nixon, P. A.
Parsons, G. J.
Potter, L.
Such, P. M.
Taylor, L. B.
Tennant, L.
Whitaker, J. J.
Whitticase, P.
Willey, P.

MIDDLESEX

Boden, D. J. P.
Brown, K. R.
Butcher, R. O.
Carr, J. D.
Cowans, N. G.
Downton, P. R.
Ellcock, R. M.
Emburery, J. E.
Fraser, A. R. C.
Gatting, M. W.
Haynes, D. L.
Hughes, S. P.
Hutchinson, I. J. F.
Pooley, J. C.
Ramprakash, M. R.
Roseberry, M. A.
Sykes, J. F.
Tufnell, P. C. R.
Williams, N. F.

NORTHAMPTONSHIRE

Ambrose, C. E. L.
Bailey, R. J.

Brown, S. J.
Capel, D. J.
Cook, G.
Cook, N. G. B.
Davis, W. W.
Felton, N. A.
Fordham, A.
Govan, J. W.
Lamb, A. J.
Larkins, W.
Noon, W. M.
Penberthy, A. L.
Ripley, D.
Roberts, A. R.
Robinson, M. A.
Stanley, N. A.
Thomas, J. G.
Walker, A.
Wild, D. J.
Williams, R. G.

NOTTINGHAMSHIRE

Afford, J. A.
Broad, B. C.
Cairns, C. L.
Cooper, K. E.
Evans, K. P.
Field-Buss, M.
French, B. N.
Hemmings, E. E.
Johnson, P.
Martindale, D. J. R.
Mike, G. W.
Millns, D. J.
Newell, M.
Pick, R. A.
Pollard, P.
Randall, D. W.
Robinson, R. T.

Saxelby, K.
Saxelby, M.
Scott, C. W.
Stephenson, F. D.

SOMERSET

Atkinson, J. C. M.
Bartlett, R. J.
Burns, N. D.
Cleal, M. W.
Cook, S. J.
Foster, D. J.
Gard, T.
Harden, R. J.
Hardy, J. J. E.
Hayhurst, A. N.
Jones, A. N.
Mallender, N. A.
Marks, V. J.
Palmer, G. V.
Pringle, N. J.
Roebuck, P. M.
Rose, G. D.
Scriven, T. J. A.
Tavaré, C. J.
Trump, H. R. J.
Unwin, P. D.
Wyatt, J. G.

SURREY

Alikhan, R. K.
Arnold, G. G.
Atkins, P. D.
Bicknell, D. J.
Bicknell, M. P.

Boiling, J.
Bullen, C. K.
Clarke, S. T.
Clinton, G. S.
Feltham, M. A.
Greig, I. A.
Kendrick, N. M.
Lynch, M. A.
Medlycott, K. T.
Murphy, A. J.
Peters, N. H.
Robinson, J. D.
Sadiq, Z. A.
Sargeant, N. F.
Stewart, A. J.
Tazelaar, D.
Thorpe, G. P.
Ward, D. M.

SUSSEX

Babington, A. M.
Bunting, R. A.
Clarke, A. R.
Dodemaide, A. I. C.
Donelan, B. T. P.
Falkner, N. J.
Gould, I. J.
Green, A. M.
Greenfield, K.
Hansford, A. R.
Kimber, S. J. S.
Lenham, N. J.
Moores, P.
Parker, P. W. G.
Pigott, A. C. S.
Remy, C. C.
Salisbury, I. D. K.
Smith, D. M.
Speight, M. P.

Wells, A. P.
Wells, C. M.

WARWICKSHIRE

Asif Din, M.
Banks, D. A.
Benjamin, J. E.
Booth, P. A.
Donald, A. A.
Green, S. J.
Humpage, G. W.
Kallicharran, A. I.
Lloyd, T. A.
Merrick, T. A.
Moles, A. J.
Munton, T. A.
Pierson, A. R. K.
Piper, K. J.
Ratcliffe, J. D.
Reeve, D. A.
Small, G. C.
Smith, G.
Smith, N. M. K.
Smith, P. A.
Thorne, D. A.
Twose, R. G.

WORCESTERSHIRE

Bent, P.
Bevins, S. R.
Botham, I. T.
Curtis, T. S.
Dilley, G. R.
D'Oliveira, D. B.
Hick, G. A.

Illingworth, R. K.
Lampitt, S. R.
Leatherdale, D. A.
Lord, G. J.
McEwan, S. M.
Neale, P. A.
Newport, P. J.
O'Shaughnessy, S. J.
Pridgeon, A. P.
Radford, N. V.
Rhodes, S. J.
Tolley, C. M.
Weston, M. J.

YORKSHIRE

Bairstow, D. L.
Batty, J. D.

Blakey, R. J.
Byas, D.
Carrick, P.
Fletcher, S. D.
Gough, D.
Hartley, P. J.
Hartley, S. N.
Houseman, I. J.
Jarvis, P. W.
Kellett, S. A.
Love, J. D.
Metcalfe, A. A.
Moxon, M. D.
Nicholson, N. G.
Oldham, S.
Pickles, C. S.
Priestley, I. M.
Robinson, P. E.
Sharp, K.
Sidebottom, A.
Swallow, I. G.

NOTES/AUTOGRAPHS